# 2007 COMPENDIUM

## of Selected Publications

Volume I:

Committee Opinions
and Policy Statements

THE AMERICAN COLLEGE
OF OBSTETRICIANS
AND GYNECOLOGISTS

*Women's Health Care Physicians*

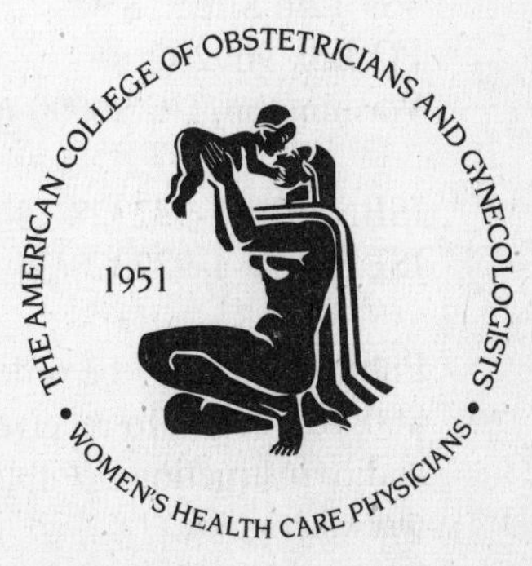

The following resources from ACOG also contain ACOG practice guidelines and should be considered adjuncts to the documents in the *2007 Compendium of Selected Publications*.

*Ethics in Obstetrics and Gynecology*, Second Edition
*Guidelines for Perinatal Care*, Fifth Edition
*Guidelines for Women's Health Care*, Second Edition
*Health Care for Adolescents*
*Special Issues in Women's Health*

These documents are available online to members at www.acog.org

The *2007 Compendium of Selected Publications* contains current clinical practice documents published by the American College of Obstetricians and Gynecologists (ACOG) as of December 31, 2006. The information in these documents should not be viewed as establishing standards or dictating rigid rules. The guidelines are general and intended to be adapted to many different situations, taking into account the needs and resources particular to the locality, the institution, or the type of practice. Variations and innovations that improve the quality of patient care are to be encouraged rather than restricted. The purpose of these guidelines will be well served if they provide a firm basis on which local norms may be built.



The American College of Obstetricians and Gynecologists
409 12th Street, SW
PO Box 96920
Washington, DC 20090-6920

ISBN: 978-1-932328-33-2 (Volume I)
ISBN: 978-1-932328-34-9 (Volume II)

12345/10987

Publications may be ordered through the ACOG Distribution Center by calling toll free 800-762-2264. To receive order forms via facsimile, call (732) 885-6364 and follow the audio instructions. Publications also may be ordered from the ACOG web site at www.acog.org.

# Contents VOLUME I

# Foreword

The *2007 Compendium of Selected Publications* is a compilation of selected ACOG clinical practice guidelines in effect and considered current as of December 31, 2006:

- Committee Opinions: Brief focused documents that address clinical issues of an urgent or emergent nature or nonclinical topics such as policy, economics, and social issues that relate to obstetrics and gynecology. They are consensus statements that may or may not be based on scientific evidence.
- Practice Bulletins: Evidence-based guidelines developed to indicate a preferred method of diagnosis and management of a condition. The evidence is graded, and peer-reviewed research determines the recommendations in the document.
- Policy Statements: Position papers on key issues approved by the Executive Board.
- Technology Assessments in Obstetrics and Gynecology: Documents that describe specific technologies and their application.

These series are developed by committees of experts and reviewed by leaders in the specialty and the College. Each document is reviewed periodically and either reaffirmed, replaced, or withdrawn to ensure its continued appropriateness to practice. The contribution of the many groups and individuals who participated in the process is gratefully acknowledged.

The 2007 Compendium is being published in two volumes to make the content more accessible and easy to use. Volume I is devoted to Committee Opinions, including Technology Assessments and Policy Statements, and Volume II contains Practice Bulletins. Each volume contains a full table of contents and a combined subject index of both volumes. The documents have been reorganized based on the committee responsible for them, and a complete list precedes each section. At the end is a list of current titles by series, with those published or withdrawn during the year indicated.

As the practice of medicine evolves, so do ACOG documents. As a part of the continuing process of review and revision, many documents initially published as a separate installment of a series evolve to become a part of a broader effort to educate and inform our Fellows. Books such as *Guidelines for Perinatal Care* or *Guidelines for Women's Health Care* carry equal weight as practice guidelines and should be considered adjuncts to the documents in the series. For ease of reference, the contents of these volumes are included in the appendix.

The Compendium is available in CD-ROM format as well as print. Copies may be purchased by calling 800-762-2264 ($59 for members, $99 for nonmembers).

Throughout the year, new documents will be published in ACOG's official journal, *Obstetrics & Gynecology*. Single copies can be obtained from the Resource Center (202-863-2518), and the series are available for sale as complete sets or subscriptions (call 800-762-2264 to order). These documents also are available to members on our web site: www.acog.org. To verify the status of documents, contact the Resource Center or check our web site.

We are making every effort to provide health professionals with current, quality information on the practice of obstetrics and gynecology. The *2007 Compendium of Selected Publications* represents still another way to disseminate material designed to promote women's health.

—Ralph W. Hale, MD, Executive Vice President

# The Scope of Practice of Obstetrics and Gynecology

Obstetrics and gynecology is a discipline dedicated to the broad, integrated medical and surgical care of women's health throughout their lifespan. The combined discipline of obstetrics and gynecology requires extensive study and understanding of reproductive physiology, including the physiologic, social, cultural, environmental and genetic factors that influence disease in women. This study and understanding of the reproductive physiology of women gives obstetricians and gynecologists a unique perspective in addressing gender-specific health care issues.

Preventive counseling and health education are essential and integral parts of the practice of obstetricians and gynecologists as they advance the individual and community-based health of women of all ages.

Obstetricians and gynecologists may choose a scope of practice ranging from primary ambulatory health care to concentration in a focused area of specialization.

Approved by the Executive Board
February 6, 2005

# Code *of* Professional Ethics

## of the American College of Obstetricians and Gynecologists

Obstetrician–gynecologists, as members of the medical profession, have ethical responsibilities not only to patients, but also to society, to other health professionals, and to themselves. The following ethical foundations for professional activities in the field of obstetrics and gynecology are the supporting structures for the Code of Conduct. The Code implements many of these foundations in the form of rules of ethical conduct. Certain documents of the American College of Obstetricians and Gynecologists, including Committee Opinions and *Ethics in Obstetrics and Gynecology*, also provide additional ethical rules. Selections relevant to specific points are set forth in the Code of Conduct, and those particular documents are incorporated into the Code by reference. Noncompliance with the Code, including referenced documents, may affect an individual's initial or continuing Fellowship in the American College of Obstetricians and Gynecologists. These documents may be revised or replaced periodically, and Fellows should be knowledgeable about current information.

### Ethical Foundations

I. The patient–physician relationship: The welfare of the patient *(beneficence)* is central to all considerations in the patient–physician relationship. Included in this relationship is the obligation of physicians to respect the rights of patients, colleagues, and other health professionals. The respect for the right of individual patients to make their own choices about their health care *(autonomy)* is fundamental. The principle of justice requires strict avoidance of discrimination on the basis of race, color, religion, national origin, or any other basis that would constitute illegal discrimination *(justice)*.

II. Physician conduct and practice: The obstetrician–gynecologist must deal honestly with patients and colleagues *(veracity)*. This includes not misrepresenting himself or herself through any form of communication in an untruthful, misleading, or deceptive manner. Furthermore, maintenance of medical competence through study, application, and enhancement of medical knowledge and skills is an obligation of practicing physicians. Any behavior that diminishes a physician's capability to practice, such as substance abuse, must be immediately addressed and rehabilitative services instituted. The physician should modify his or her practice until the diminished capacity has been restored to an acceptable standard to avoid harm to patients *(nonmaleficence)*. All physicians are obligated to respond to evidence of questionable conduct or unethical behavior by other physicians through appropriate procedures established by the relevant organization.

409 12th Street, SW
PO Box 96920
Washington, DC 20090-6920

III. Avoiding conflicts of interest: Potential conflicts of interest are inherent in the practice of medicine. Physicians are expected to recognize such situations and deal with them through public disclosure. Conflicts of interest should be resolved in accordance with the best interest of the patient, respecting a woman's autonomy to make health care decisions. The physician should be an advocate for the patient through public disclosure of conflicts of interest raised by health payer policies or hospital policies.

IV. Professional relations: The obstetrician–gynecologist should respect and cooperate with other physicians, nurses, and health care professionals.

V. Societal responsibilities: The obstetrician–gynecologist has a continuing responsibility to society as a whole and should support and participate in activities that enhance the community. As a member of society, the obstetrician–gynecologist should respect the laws of that society. As professionals and members of medical societies, physicians are required to uphold the dignity and honor of the profession.

## Code of Conduct

### I. Patient–Physician Relationship

1. The patient–physician relationship is the central focus of all ethical concerns, and the welfare of the patient must form the basis of all medical judgments.
2. The obstetrician–gynecologist should serve as the patient's advocate and exercise all reasonable means to ensure that the most appropriate care is provided to the patient.
3. The patient–physician relationship has an ethical basis and is built on confidentiality, trust, and honesty. If no patient–physician relationship exists, a physician may refuse to provide care, except in emergencies (1). Once the patient–physician relationship exists, the obstetrician–gynecologist must adhere to all applicable legal or contractual constraints in dissolving the patient–physician relationship.
4. Sexual misconduct on the part of the obstetrician–gynecologist is an abuse of professional power and a violation of patient trust. Sexual contact or a romantic relationship between a physician and a current patient is always unethical (2).
5. The obstetrician–gynecologist has an obligation to obtain the informed consent of each patient (3). In obtaining informed consent for any course of medical or surgical treatment, the obstetrician–gynecologist must present to the patient, or to the person legally responsible for the patient, pertinent medical facts and recommendations consistent with good medical practice. Such information should be presented in reasonably understandable terms and include alternative modes of treatment and the objectives, risks, benefits, possible complications, and anticipated results of such treatment.
6. It is unethical to prescribe, provide, or seek compensation for therapies that are of no benefit to the patient.
7. The obstetrician–gynecologist must respect the rights and privacy of patients, colleagues, and others and safeguard patient information and confidences within the limits of the law. If during the process of providing information for consent it is known that results of a particular test or other information must be given to governmental authorities or other third parties, that must be explained to the patient (4).
8. The obstetrician–gynecologist must not discriminate against patients based on race, color, national origin, religion, or any other basis that would constitute illegal discrimination.

### II. Physician Conduct and Practice

1. The obstetrician–gynecologist should recognize the boundaries of his or her particular competencies and expertise and must provide only those services and use only those techniques for which he or she is qualified by education, training, and experience.

2. The obstetrician–gynecologist should participate in continuing medical education activities to maintain current scientific and professional knowledge relevant to the medical services he or she renders. The obstetrician–gynecologist should provide medical care involving new therapies or techniques only after undertaking appropriate training and study.

3. In emerging areas of medical treatment where recognized medical guidelines do not exist, the obstetrician–gynecologist should exercise careful judgment and take appropriate precautions to protect patient welfare.

4. The obstetrician–gynecologist must not publicize or represent himself or herself in any untruthful, misleading, or deceptive manner to patients, colleagues, other health care professionals, or the public.

5. The obstetrician–gynecologist who has reason to believe that he or she is infected with the human immunodeficiency virus (HIV) or other serious infectious agents that might be communicated to patients should voluntarily be tested for the protection of his or her patients. In making decisions about patient-care activities, a physician infected with such an agent should adhere to the fundamental professional obligation to avoid harm to patients (5).

6. The obstetrician–gynecologist should not practice medicine while impaired by alcohol, drugs, or physical or mental disability. The obstetrician–gynecologist who experiences substance abuse problems or who is physically or emotionally impaired should seek appropriate assistance to address these problems and must limit his or her practice until the impairment no longer affects the quality of patient care.

## III. Conflicts of Interest

1. Potential conflicts of interest are inherent in the practice of medicine. Conflicts of interest should be resolved in accordance with the best interest of the patient, respecting a woman's autonomy to make health care decisions. If there is an actual or potential conflict of interest that could be reasonably construed to affect significantly the patient's care, the physician must disclose the conflict to the patient. The physician should seek consultation with colleagues or an institutional ethics committee to determine whether there is an actual or potential conflict of interest and how to address it.

2. Commercial promotions of medical products and services may generate bias unrelated to product merit, creating or appearing to create inappropriate undue influence. The obstetrician–gynecologist should be aware of this potential conflict of interest and offer medical advice that is as accurate, balanced, complete, and devoid of bias as possible (6, 7).

3. The obstetrician–gynecologist should prescribe drugs, devices, and other treatments solely on the basis of medical considerations and patient needs, regardless of any direct or indirect interests in or benefit from a pharmaceutical firm or other supplier.

4. When the obstetrician–gynecologist receives anything of substantial value, including royalties, from companies in the health care industry, such as a manufacturer of pharmaceuticals and medical devices, this fact should be disclosed to patients and colleagues when material.

5. Financial and administrative constraints may create disincentives to treatment otherwise recommended by the obstetrician–gynecologist. Any pertinent constraints should be disclosed to the patient.

## IV. Professional Relations

1. The obstetrician–gynecologist's relationships with other physicians, nurses, and health care professionals should reflect fairness, honesty, and integrity, sharing a mutual respect and concern for the patient.

2. The obstetrician–gynecologist should consult, refer, or cooperate with other physicians, health care professionals, and institutions to the extent necessary to serve the best interests of their patients.

## V. Societal Responsibilities

1. The obstetrician–gynecologist should support and participate in those health care programs, practices, and activities that contribute positively, in a meaningful and cost-effective way, to the welfare of individual patients, the health care system, or the public good.

2. The obstetrician–gynecologist should respect all laws, uphold the dignity and honor of the profession, and accept the profession's self-imposed discipline. The professional competence and conduct of obstetrician–gynecologists are best examined by professional associations, hospital peer-review committees, and state medical and licensing boards. These groups deserve the full participation and cooperation of the obstetrician–gynecologist.

3. The obstetrician–gynecologist should strive to address through the appropriate procedures the status of those physicians who demonstrate questionable competence, impairment, or unethical or illegal behavior. In addition, the obstetrician–gynecologist should cooperate with appropriate authorities to prevent the continuation of such behavior.

4. The obstetrician–gynecologist must not knowingly offer testimony that is false. The obstetrician–gynecologist must testify only on matters about which he or she has knowledge and experience. The obstetrician–gynecologist must not knowingly misrepresent his or her credentials.

5. The obstetrician–gynecologist testifying as an expert witness must have knowledge and experience about the range of the standard of care and the available scientific evidence for the condition in question during the relevant time and must respond accurately to questions about the range of the standard of care and the available scientific evidence.

6. Before offering testimony, the obstetrician–gynecologist must thoroughly review the medical facts of the case and all available relevant information.

7. The obstetrician–gynecologist serving as an expert witness must accept neither disproportionate compensation nor compensation that is contingent upon the outcome of the litigation (8).

## References


1. American College of Obstetricians and Gynecologists. Seeking and giving consultation. In: Ethics in obstetrics and gynecology. 2nd ed. Washington, DC: ACOG; 2004. p. 77–81.
2. American College of Obstetricians and Gynecologists. Sexual misconduct. In: Ethics in obstetrics and gynecology. 2nd ed. Washington, DC: ACOG; 2004. p. 101–3.
3. American College of Obstetricians and Gynecologists. Informed consent. In: Ethics in obstetrics and gynecology. 2nd ed. Washington, DC: ACOG; 2004. p. 9–17.
4. American College of Obstetricians and Gynecologists. Patient testing. In: Ethics in obstetrics and gynecology. 2nd ed. Washington, DC: ACOG; 2004. p. 26–8.
5. American College of Obstetricians and Gynecologists. Human immunodeficiency virus. In: Ethics in obstetrics and gynecology. 2nd ed. Washington, DC: ACOG; 2004. p. 29–33.
6. American College of Obstetricians and Gynecologists. Relationships with industry. In: Ethics in obstetrics and gynecology. 2nd ed. Washington, DC: ACOG; 2004. p. 107–10.
7. American College of Obstetricians and Gynecologists. Commercial enterprises in medical practice. In: Ethics in obstetrics and gynecology. 2nd ed. Washington, DC: ACOG; 2004. p. 83–5.
8. American College of Obstetricians and Gynecologists. Expert testimony. In: Ethics in obstetrics and gynecology. 2nd ed. Washington, DC: ACOG; 2004. p. 116–7.

# COMMITTEE OPINIONS

## COMMITTEE ON ADOLESCENT HEALTH CARE



*Published in 2006

# COMMITTEE OPINIONS

ACOG Committee Opinion

Committee on
Adolescent Health Care

Number 300, October 2004

The Committee wishes to thank S. Paige Hertweck, MD, for her assistance in the development of this opinion. This document reflects emerging clinical and scientific advances as of the date issued and is subject to change. The information should not be construed as dictating an exclusive course of treatment or procedure to be followed.



ISSN 1074-861X

**The American College of Obstetricians and Gynecologists**
409 12th Street, SW
PO Box 96920
Washington, DC 20090-6920

12345/87654

Cervical cancer screening in adolescents. ACOG Committee Opinion No. 300. American College of Obstetricians and Gynecologists. Obstet Gynecol 2004;104:885–9.

# Cervical Cancer Screening in Adolescents

*ABSTRACT: The American Cancer Society recently published a recommendation that cervical cancer screening should begin approximately 3 years after the onset of vaginal intercourse or no later than age 21 years. Once initiated, screening should occur annually for young women. The decision about the initiation of cervical cytology screening in an adolescent patient should be based on the clinician's assessment of risks, including 1) age of first sexual intercourse, 2) behaviors that may place the adolescent patient at greater risk for human papillomavirus infection, and 3) risk of noncompliance with follow-up visits. Patients and parents need to be provided with information about this new recommendation so they understand that there is still a need for preventive health care other than Pap testing. Additional research is needed to facilitate the provision of the best care for adolescent patients and avoid overtreatment of abnormal cervical cytology.*

## Background

The American Cancer Society (ACS) recommends that cervical cancer screening should begin approximately 3 years after the onset of vaginal intercourse or no later than age 21 years (1). Once initiated, screening should occur annually for adolescents (2). This recommendation is based on the consensus of a national panel of experts who reviewed evidence and concluded that there is little risk of missing an important cervical lesion within 3–5 years after initial exposure to human papillomavirus (HPV). Specific types of HPV (most notably HPV 16, 18, 31, and 45) are associated with nearly all cases of squamous cell cervical cancer (3, 4). The National Cancer Institute's Surveillance, Epidemiology, and End Results program indicates that there were no cases of cervical cancer in females younger than 20 years (5). The ACS further supports this recommendation by stating that screening less than 3 years after the onset of vaginal intercourse may result in overdiagnosis of cervical lesions, which often regress spontaneously, and that inappropriate intervention may cause more harm than good. The ACS recommendation states that it is critical for adolescents who may not need cervical cytology testing to receive gynecologic health care, including preventive measures such as sexually transmitted disease (STD) testing in sexually active patients.

## Initiation of Cervical Cancer Screening in Adolescents

Adolescent females have a higher prevalence of abnormal Pap test results (atypical squamous cells of undetermined significance or ASCUS* and above) when compared with adult females (6, 7). However, the severity of lesions tends to be lower in adolescents (7). High-grade squamous intraepithelial lesions (HSIL) still do occur in adolescents. The highest reported prevalence of abnormal Pap test results with evidence of HSIL in adolescents is 18% (6). The decision about the initiation of cervical cytology screening should be based on the clinician's assessment of risks, including 1) age of first sexual intercourse, 2) behaviors that may place the adolescent patient at greater risk for HPV infection, and 3) risk of noncompliance with follow-up visits. Obtaining a complete and accurate sexual history is, therefore, critical.

### *Assessing Age at First Sexual Intercourse*

According to the 2003 Youth Risk Behavior Surveillance Survey, 45% of female high-school students have had sexual intercourse; 62% of female 12th graders have had sexual intercourse (8). Age-specific data show the percentage of female adolescents who have had sexual intercourse increases steadily with age. Specifically, 24% of 15-year-old females, 38% of 16-year-old females, 51% of 17-year-old females, and 62% of 18-year-old females have had sexual intercourse (9). Therefore, most females are sexually active before reaching age 18 years. Non-Hispanic black females and Hispanic females begin sexual activity at younger ages than non-Hispanic white females (8, 9). One study found that only 51% of mothers of sexually active teenagers were aware of such activity (10).

One of the difficulties in caring for the adolescent gynecologic patient is that many adolescents, particularly those who begin sexual activity at a young age or experience abuse, are unlikely to acknowledge sexual activity without sensitive and direct questioning (see box "Sexual History Taking"). Therefore, they may not be screened appropriately. The sexual history should include questions about all types of sexual behavior, age at first vaginal intercourse, history of sexual abuse, number of sexual partners, and recent change in sexual partners because these factors have been linked to HPV infection (1, 11–13). An up-to-date history should be completed at each gynecologic visit with an adolescent.

### *Risk Factors for Human Papillomavirus Infection*

Some adolescents may be at increased risk of HPV infection (see box "Risk Factors for Human Papillomavirus"). Prevalence of HPV infection in sexually active young women ranges from 17% to 84%, with most studies reporting prevalence greater than 30% (14). Adolescent females may be more susceptible to HPV infection than adult females because of biologic or physical factors (ie, cervical biologic immaturity) (15–17). Those women who had first intercourse (voluntary or involuntary) at a young age, have a history of other STDs, or have had multiple sexual partners are also at higher risk of HPV infection or cervical intraepithelial neoplasia or both (1, 11–13). According to the 1995 National Survey of Family Growth, 46% of women aged 15–19 years who had sex in the past year had 2 or more partners during the year (18). Immune suppression is another risk factor for HPV infection (see box "Causes of Immunocompromised States"). Studies in women with HIV infection, who undergo dialysis, or who have had a kidney transplant, demonstrate that HPV detection is particularly common with immune suppression (19–22).

### *Difficulties in Follow-up for High-risk Adolescents*

High-risk adolescents often have difficulty obtaining affordable health care. They are, therefore, more likely to receive episodic care and have difficulty in returning for routine follow-up care. In the adolescent, noncompliance with follow-up appointments for abnormal Pap test results ranges from 25% to 66% (23–27).

## Abnormal Cervical Cytology and Its Overtreatment in Adolescents

The Pap test is a screening tool, not a diagnostic tool. Those patients with abnormal cytology should be counseled and monitored closely. It is important

*According to the Bethesda 2001 System for the description of cytologic abnormalities, the epithelial abnormality ASCUS has been replaced by "atypical squamous cells" (ASC) with the subcategories "atypical squamous cells of undetermined significance" (ASC-US) and "atypical squamous cells cannot exclude HSIL" (ASC-H).

**Sexual History Taking**

- Discuss confidentiality
  —Inform the patient that they have a private and privileged relationship with you and identify any restrictions on the confidential nature of that relationship. For instance, the physician should explain that if the patient discusses any risk of bodily harm to herself or others, confidentiality will be breached. The physician also should discuss any state or federal privacy laws that affect the confidential nature of the relationship. In addition, state laws may mandate the reporting of physical or sexual abuse of minors.
  —Inform the patient that if you feel you need to talk to the parent about something that the patient has said, you will discuss that fact and what you plan to say with the patient first.
- Start with nonthreatening topics first and gradually move to more sensitive issues. Have all discussions about sexuality while the adolescent is dressed.
- Introduce the subject of sexual activity by explaining that you ask all of your patients these questions and why this information is important. Discussions should be appropriate for the adolescents' developmental level and should identify risky behaviors.
- Consider using 1 of the following questions to initiate the discussion of the patient's sexual history:
  —Are you dating anyone?
  —Are you intimate with anyone?
  —Are you physically close with anyone?
- Move on to additional questions for clarification. The age of first vaginal intercourse, whether voluntary or involuntary, is critical for proper determination of Pap test recommendations.
- Questions need to leave room for coerced or nonconsensual sexual contact, including sexual violence, abuse, and incest.
  —Did you choose to have sex?
  —Has anyone forced you to have sex?
- Questions need to leave room for casual sex partners (who, for example, may not be perceived as "boyfriends").
- Don't assume heterosexual behavior. Establish the sex of partner or partners first. If the patient is heterosexual, consider the following questions:
  —Many girls are concerned about sex. Some girls have vaginal sex...that is, the boyfriend puts his penis in her vagina... is this something that your friends have done? Have you ever done this or thought about doing it?
  —Many girls your age have sex. They also have sex in many different ways. Some girls have vaginal sex, that is, the boyfriend puts his penis in their vagina. Has this ever happened for you?
- As you progress with the patient's sexual history, make sure you ask about oral and anal sex, and describe what you mean by this. Anal intercourse can occur among heterosexual adolescents. It may be used by some teenagers specifically to preserve virginity and protect against pregnancy, therefore deterring the use of barrier methods and increasing the risk for human immunodeficiency virus infection and other STDs.
- Questions need to be asked about the number of partners and STD and pregnancy prevention methods used to assess the patient's risks.
- While assuring confidentiality, the provider should encourage adolescents to discuss these issues with their parents. The provider can assist the adolescent in determining how and what to tell her parents about her sexual activity.
- Congratulate the patient for sharing the information with you as a demonstration of her ability to think about her sexual health and be responsible.

Modified from: Asking the Right Questions. STD/HIV Prevention Training Center of New England. Available at http://www.state.ma.us/dph/cdc/stdtcmai/section1.pdf. Retrieved June 14, 2004.

to avoid aggressive management of benign lesions because most cervical intraepithelial neoplasia lesions of grades 1 and 2 regress. There are no data pertaining to the overtreatment of abnormal cervical cytology. It is a concern because the surgical excision or destruction of cervical tissue in a nulliparous adolescent may be detrimental to future fertility and cervical competency. Therapy should not be a part of management in adolescents who have cervical intraepithelial neoplasia 1 (28). An acceptable option is follow-up without initial colposcopy using a protocol of repeat cytologic testing at 6- and 12-month intervals with a threshold of atypical squamous cells for referral for colposcopy, or of HPV DNA testing at 12 months with a referral for colposcopy if test results are positive for high-risk HPV DNA (29). Cervical intraepithelial neoplasia 2 represents a significant abnormality that typically requires therapy. It can be managed in adolescents with either ablative or excisional therapy or observation (28).

**Risk Factors for Human Papillomavirus**

- Multiple sexual partners
- Male partner with multiple sexual partners
- History of other sexually transmitted diseases
- Early age of first intercourse (including cases of sexual abuse)

**Causes of Immunocompromised States**

- Human immunodeficiency virus infection
- Organ transplant
- Cancer chemotherapy
- Chronic steroid use for chronic renal or bowel disease
- Conditions such as lupus

## Patient and Parent Education

The new ACS recommendation may be confusing to both adolescents and their parents. Many adolescent girls and their mothers are unaware of the difference between a Pap test and a pelvic examination for any other reason (30). Therefore, they could misinterpret this recommendation as stating that a gynecologic examination or other STD testing is not needed until 3 years after first vaginal intercourse or by age 21 years. In addition, there is concern that adolescents in need of counseling or screening regarding sexual activity may have used the previous recommendation for a Pap test at age 18 as a way to justify a visit to a gynecologist to their parents. Without this justification, it is possible that adolescents will receive less care. Patient and parent education is, therefore, critical. Education should include information about the need for preventive care exclusive of the need for cervical cancer screening and recommended timing for this care. It should be stressed that adolescents should visit an obstetrician–gynecologist before becoming sexually active. Data indicate that currently this is not the case. Most (79%) young women wait 1 month or more after their first intercourse to see a health care provider, with the median wait being 22 months after first intercourse (31). The American College of Obstetricians and Gynecologists recommends that the first visit to an obstetrician–gynecologist for health guidance, screening, and provision of preventive services should take place around ages 13–15 years. This visit is even more important in light of the new cervical cancer screening recommendations and is an ideal time to begin to provide education about preventive care needs, including the need for STD testing in sexually active adolescents. This visit often does not include a pelvic examination, especially with the onset of urine-based STD screening options. Thereafter, annual preventive health care visits to a gynecologist are strongly recommended (32).

## Need for Additional Research

There are limited data on the following issues pertaining to HPV infection in adolescents, and additional research in these areas is needed:

- There are limited data on the incidence of HSIL within 0–3 years after the first exposure to HPV. Based on currently available data, the average time between initial Pap test and HSIL detection is 20 months (7).
- There are limited data on the regression of low-grade squamous intraepithelial lesions and HSIL in adolescents (33). Confirmatory data are needed.
- Data on the progression of low-grade squamous intraepithelial lesions and HSIL in adolescents are lacking. Although not seen in the Surveillance, Epidemiology, and End Results program, international data show invasive carcinoma of the cervix occurs very rarely in adolescents (11).
- There are no data pertaining to the overtreatment of abnormal cervical cytology. Additional research is needed to determine the extent of this problem and appropriate ways to address it.
- Additional research is needed for better understanding of appropriate management of adolescents with cervical cytological abnormalities.

Obtaining additional data in these research areas will facilitate the provision of the best possible care for adolescent patients.

## References

1. Saslow D, Runowicz CD, Solomon D, Moscicki AB, Smith RA, Eyre HJ, Cohen C. American Cancer Society guidelines for the early detection of cervical neoplasia and cancer. American Cancer Society. CA Cancer J Clin 2002;52:342–62.
2. Cervical cytology screening. ACOG Practice Bulletin No. 45. American College of Obstetricians and Gynecologists. Obstet Gynecol 2003;102:417–27.
3. Bosch FX, Manos MM, Munoz N, Sherman M, Jansen AM, Peto J, et al. Prevalence of human papillomavirus in cervical cancer: a worldwide perspective. International

biological study on cervical cancer (IBSCC) Study Group. J Natl Cancer Inst 1995;87:796–802.

4. Walboomers JM, Jacobs MV, Manos MM, Bosch FX, Kummer JA, Shah KV, et al. Human papillomavirus is a necessary cause of invasive cervical cancer worldwide. J Pathol 1999;189:12–9.
5. Reis LA, Eisner MP, Kosary CL, Hankey BF, Miller BA, Clegg L, et al, editors. SEER cancer statistics review, 1975-2001. 2002. Available at: http://seer.cancer.gov/csr/1975_2001. Retrieved May 19, 2004.
6. Mount SL, Papillo JL. A study of 10,296 pediatric and adolescent Papanicolaou smear diagnoses in northern New England. Pediatrics 1999;103:539–45.
7. Simsir A, Brooks S, Cochran L, Bourquin P, Ioffe OB. Cervicovaginal smear abnormalities in sexually active adolescents. Implications for management. Acta Cytol 2002;46:271–6.
8. Grunbaum JA, Kann L, Kinchen S, Ross J, Hawkins J, Lowry R, et al. Youth risk behavior surveillance - United States, 2003. MMWR Surveill Summ 2004;53(2):1–96.
9. Abma JC, Sonenstein FL. Sexual activity and contraceptive practices among teenagers in the United States, 1988 and 1995. Vital Health Stat 23. 2001;(21):1–79.
10. Blum RW. Mothers' influence on teen sex: connections that promote postponing sexual intercourse. Center for Adolescent Health and Development, University of Minnesota. Minneapolis (MN): 2002. Available at: http://www.allaboutkids.unm.edu/presskit/MonographMS.pdf. Retrieved July 19, 2004.
11. La Vecchia C, Fransechi S, Decarli A, Fasoli M, Gentile A, Parazzini F, et al. Sexual factors, venereal disease, and the risk of intraepithelial and invasive cervical neoplasia. Cancer 1986;58:935–41.
12. Moscicki AB, Palefsky J, Gonzales J, Schoolnik GK. Human papillomavirus infection in sexually active adolescent females: prevalence and risk factors. Pediatr Res 1990;28:507–13.
13. Moscicki AB, Hills N, Shiboski S, Powell K, Jay N, Hanson E. Risks for incident human papillomavirus infection and low-grade intraepithelial lesion development in young females. JAMA 2001;285:2995–3002.
14. Prevention of genital human papillomavirus infection. Centers for Disease Control and Prevention. 2004. Available at: http://www.cdc.gov/std/HPV/2004HPV%20Report.pdf. Retrieved April 14, 2004.
15. Moscicki AB, Winkler B, Irwin CE Jr, Schachter J. Differences in biologic maturation, sexual behavior, and sexually transmitted disease between adolescents with and without cervical intraepithelial neoplasia. J Pediatr 1989;115:487–93.
16. Shew ML, Fortenberry JD, Miles P, Amortegui AJ. Interval between menarche and first sexual intercourse, related to the risk of human papillomavirus infection. J Pediatr 1994;125:661–6.
17. Moscicki AB, Burt VG, Kanowitz S, Darragh T, Shiboski S. The significance of squamous metaplasia in the development of low grade squamous intraepithelial lesions in young women. Cancer 1999;85:1139–44.
18. Finer LB, Darroch JE, Singh S. Sexual partnership patterns as a behavioral risk factor for sexually transmitted diseases. Fam Plann Perspect 1999;31;228–36.
19. Fairley CK, Chen S, Tabrizi SN, McNeil J, Becker G, Walker R, et al. Prevalence of HPV DNA in cervical specimens in women with renal transplants: a comparison with dialysis-dependent patients and patients with renal impairment. Nephrol Dial Transplant 1994;9:416–20.
20. Moscicki AB, Ellenberg JH, Vermund SH, Holland CA, Darragh T, Crowley-Nowick PA, et al. Prevalence of and risks for cervical human papillomavirus infection and squamous intraepithelial lesions in adolescent girls: impact of infection with human immunodeficiency virus. Arch Pediatr Adolesc Med 2000;154:127–34.
21. Jamieson DJ, Duerr A, Burk R, Klein RS, Paramsothy P, Schuman P, et al. Characterization of genital human papillomavirus infection in women who have or who are at risk of having HIV infection. Am J Obstet Gynecol 2002; 186:21–7.
22. Sun XW, Kuhn L, Ellerbrock TV, Chiasson MA, Bush TJ, Wright TC Jr. Human papillomavirus infection in women infected with the human immunodeficiency virus. N Eng J Med 1997;337:1343–9.
23. Cartwright PS, Reed G. No-show behavior in a county hospital colposcopy clinic. Am J Gynecol Health 1990; 4:181–7.
24. Michielutte R, Diseker RA, Young LD, May WJ. Noncompliance in screening follow-up among family planning clinic patients with cervical dysplasia. Prev Med 1985;14:248–58.
25. Lavin C, Goodman E, Perlman S, Kelly LS, Emans SJ. Follow-up of abnormal Papanicolaou smears in a hospital-based adolescent clinic. J Pediatr Adolesc Gynecol 1997; 10:141–5.
26. Massad LS, Anoina D. Colposcopic and cytologic findings among adolescents referred to two urban teaching hospitals. J Pediatr Adolesc Gynecol 1996;9:190–4.
27. Arora CD, Schmidt DS, Rader AE, Abdul-Karim F, Lazebnik R. Adolescents with ASCUS: are they a high risk group? Clin Pediatr (Phila) 2001;40:133–8.
28. Wright TC Jr, Cox JT, Massad LS, Carlson J, Twiggs LB, Wilkinson EJ. 2001 consensus guidelines for the management of women with cervical intraepithelial neoplasia. American Society for Colposcopy and Cervical Pathology. Am J Obstet Gynecol 2003;189:295–304.
29. Wright TC Jr, Cox JT, Massad LS, Twiggs LB, Wilkinson EJ. 2001 Consensus Guidelines for the management of women with cervical cytological abnormalities. ASCCP-Sponsored Consensus Conference. JAMA 2002;287: 2120–9.
30. Blake DR, Weber B, Fletcher KE. Adolescent and young adult women's misunderstanding of the term 'pap smear' [abstract]. J Adolesc Med 2003;32:145.
31. Finer LB, Zabin LS. Does the timing of the first family planning visit still matter? Fam Plann Perspect 1998;30: 30–3, 42.
32. American College of Obstetricians and Gynecologists. Health care for adolescents. Washington, DC: ACOG; 2003.
33. Moscicki AB, Hills N, Shiboski S. High rate of regression of low-grade squamous intra-epithelial lesions in adolescents [abstract]. Baltimore (MD): Pediatric Academic Society Annual Meeting; 2002.

ACOG

Committee on
Adolescent Health Care

# Committee Opinion

Number 301, October 2004

## Sexually Transmitted Diseases in Adolescents

*ABSTRACT: Sexually transmitted diseases are common among adolescents in the United States. Female adolescents face numerous obstacles to care and experience a disproportionate burden related to the sequelae of sexually transmitted diseases. These diseases are a primary cause of short and long-term morbidity in adolescents that can result in infertility, chronic pelvic pain, ectopic pregnancy, vertical transmission to newborns, malignancy, chronic illness, and even death. Clinicians treating female adolescents should be prepared to offer confidential and comprehensive counseling, screening, and treatment according to established guidelines. They should also work within their communities and at the state and national levels to assure access to medical care for all adolescents. Adolescence is a period during which life-long health behaviors are established. It is, therefore, a critical time for promoting responsible behaviors and reducing risks through health promotion and prevention strategies.*

The Committee wishes to thank Melisa Holmes, MD, Stephen Vermillion, MD, and David Soper, MD, for their assistance in the development of this opinion.
This document reflects emerging clinical and scientific advances as of the date issued and is subject to change. The information should not be construed as dictating an exclusive course of treatment or procedure to be followed.



ISSN 1074-861X

**The American College of Obstetricians and Gynecologists**
409 12th Street, SW
PO Box 96920
Washington, DC 20090-6920

12345/87654

Sexually transmitted diseases in adolescents. ACOG Committee Opinion No. 301. American College of Obstetricians and Gynecologists. Obstet Gynecol 2004;104:891–8.

### Epidemiology

Approximately 18.9 million new cases of sexually transmitted diseases (STDs) occurred in 2000, of which 9.1 million (48%) were among persons aged 15–24 years (1). Many STDs are found at disproportionately high rates in the female adolescent population, especially among high-risk populations such as homeless and runaway adolescents and adolescents in detention facilities (2–4). The Centers for Disease Control and Prevention (CDC) estimates that more than 1 in 10 sexually active female adolescents have chlamydial infection (5). In 2002, as in previous years, females aged 15–24 years had the highest rates of gonorrhea compared with females in all other age categories (2). Prevalence of human papillomavirus infection in sexually active young women ranges from 17% to 84%, with most studies reporting prevalence greater than 30% (6). The incidence of hepatitis B virus (HBV) per year has decreased from an average of 260,000 cases in the 1980s to approximately 78,000 cases in 2001. The greatest decrease has occurred among children and adolescents as a result of routine HBV vaccination. It is estimated that there are 1.25 million chronically infected Americans, of whom 20–30% acquired the HBV infection in childhood (7). It is estimated that at least one half of all new human immunodeficiency virus (HIV) infections in the United States are among individuals younger than 25 years (8). In 2000, the estimated direct medical costs of STDs acquired by individuals aged 15–24 years in the United States were $6.5 billion (in year 2000 dollars). Many of these costs are borne inordinately by female adolescents. For example, the average lifetime cost per case of chlamydial infection to female adolescents is $244 compared with a per-case cost of $20 to male adolescents (8).

## Risk Factors

Although many of the issues pertaining to high-risk sexual behavior and STDs are common to both adolescents and adults, they often are intensified among adolescents and contribute to their high prevalence rates of STDs. This is caused by developmental changes that affect adolescents physically, behaviorally, and emotionally, as well as access-related and financial barriers to health care.

Adolescents often engage in high-risk sexual behaviors as they respond to their physical and emotional changes and strive for peer approval. Depending on their developmental status, some adolescents may not possess the foresight to recognize and understand the potential consequences of their risky behaviors, such as the potential fatality related to the acquisition of HIV. This lack of foresight often is compounded by the use of alcohol or drugs or both.

The likelihood of adolescents engaging in sexual intercourse increases steadily with age. In 2003, 28% of girls in the ninth grade and 62% of girls in the 12th grade reported having sexual intercourse (9). Adolescents who have sexual intercourse at an early age are more likely to have multiple partners, more likely to have had nonvoluntary or unwanted sex, and less likely to use barrier protection (10). Although approximately two thirds of adolescents report having used condoms, only 45% report using condoms consistently (11). In addition, condom use among adolescents is greater in the early stages of the relationship and decreases significantly as the relationship progresses, leaving adolescents vulnerable to STDs (12). Although many adolescents may say that they have only 1 sexual partner, they change partners frequently. Specifically, 14.4% of high-school students already have had 4 or more sexual partners during their lifetime (9). Within 1 year, the majority of sexually active female adolescents will have sex with more than 1 sexual partner or with a partner who also has other sexual partners (13).

Use of alcohol and other substances that impair judgment can increase the likelihood of engaging in sexual intercourse without a condom, with multiple partners, or with high-risk partners. Adolescents with tattoos or body piercings may be at an increased risk for STDs, particularly HBV infection because of the nature of the piercing process and the vulnerability of open sores to infection.

Biologic factors also contribute to the female adolescent's greater risk for acquiring an STD compared with adult women. During puberty and the early postpubertal years, the cervix develops a prominent ectropion with a large area of exposed columnar epithelium undergoing active metaplasia. The columnar epithelium is the primary site of invasion by both chlamydial and gonococcal agents (14). Adolescents also may have "immature" local immunity and low levels of existing antibodies against certain infections (15).

## Barriers to Care

Confidentiality concerns limit the use of medical care by adolescents. Adolescents are more willing to communicate with and seek health care from physicians who assure confidentiality (16). A recent study of girls younger than18 years attending family planning clinics found that 47% of girls would no longer attend if their parents had to be notified that they were seeking prescription birth control pills or devices, and another 10% would delay or discontinue STD testing and treatment (17). A study of pediatric patients in North Carolina found that whereas 92% of sexually active adolescent patients (primarily female) would consent to STD testing if their parents would not find out, the proportion decreased to 38% if their parents might find out and to 35% if their parents definitely would find out that they were tested (18). Physicians are encouraged to establish office policies regarding confidential care for adolescents and clearly communicate these policies to adolescents and their parents. Although providing confidentiality to adult patients is relatively easy, parental consent and billing issues for the treatment of adolescents can make confidentiality for adolescents a much more complex task. All states have statutes allowing minors to receive services related to STD testing and treatment without parental consent or involvement. The laws may specify the age at which minors can begin to consent to such care (19, 20). Physicians providing care for an adolescent population should be familiar with current state statutes on the rights of minors to consent to health care services, as well as those laws that affect confidentiality. Providers should encourage and, when appropriate, facilitate communication between a minor and her parent(s) (21).

The subtle and asymptomatic nature of many STDs further inhibits adolescents from seeking medical attention or adhering to prescribed treatment regimens. Adolescents may not be able to distinguish whether aspects of their health are physically normal or abnormal. They may fear a physical examination, which they perceive as painful; may be embarrassed about a pelvic examination; or may be concerned about the discovery of sexual activity or sexual abuse that they are afraid to reveal. In addition, they may be reluctant to face a diagnosis of an STD because it may have implications regarding the fidelity of their partner and the stability of their relationship.

Clinician-related barriers to STD testing also exist and include concern over lack of confidentiality, clinician discomfort with discussion of sexual behavior with adolescents, and clinician belief that their patients are not sexually active or that the prevalence of certain STDs is low in their patient population. These barriers result in lower than recommended STD screening rates (22).

The costs associated with diagnosis and treatment of STDs also may be a significant barrier to care. Adolescents who have insurance coverage for these services through their parents may not want to use this insurance for fear of loss of confidentiality. Others may be uninsured. In both cases, referral to a publicly funded clinic may be appropriate. Transportation difficulties may further impede access to care.

## Screening and Prevention Recommendations

### *Nonpregnant Adolescent Patients*

The provision of health guidance, screening, and preventive health care services is an essential component of reproductive health care for adolescents that should begin between the ages 13 years and 15 years. The provision of additional services beyond guidance and screening should be based on the information obtained at the initial visit. If the patient has had sexual intercourse, testing for STDs is appropriate. A pelvic examination also may be appropriate (21). In addition, adolescents who have had sexual intercourse should have their initial Pap test approximately 3 years after first vaginal–penile coitus, but no later than age 21 years (21, 23). Because the potential for risky behaviors is significant during adolescence, the initial consultation visit should be followed by annual preventive health care visits (21).

Oral–genital contact is a common behavior among adolescents and, along with anal–genital contact, contributes to the transmission of STDs. One study indicated that 9% of high-school virgins engaged in heterosexual fellatio with ejaculation, 10% engaged in heterosexual cunnilingus, and 1% engaged in heterosexual anal intercourse. Condom use for fellatio was rare (24). Vulva-to-vulva sex also can transmit STDs. Generally, STDs, including HIV, are less common in lesbians than in heterosexual women, but they can be passed from woman to woman. Also, many women who identify themselves as lesbians may have or may have had sexual intercourse with men. Because all of these activities increase the risk of acquiring an STD, clinicians should not limit their patient interview to questions about heterosexual vaginal–penile intercourse. Clinicians also should ascertain if their adolescent patients are in new relationships because being in a new sexual partnership is an important predictor of incident STDs (25). In addition, sexually active adolescents should receive screening annually for the following conditions:

- Gonorrhea and chlamydia (21, 26)—Urine screening should be considered when adolescents are reluctant to have pelvic examinations or are seen where pelvic examinations are not feasible (21).
- Cervical neoplasia—This screening should start approximately 3 years after first vaginal–penile coitus, but no later than age 21 years (21, 23).

Adolescents who have any of the following characteristics or who have a history of these characteristics should be screened annually for HIV and syphilis:

- STDs
- Multiple sexual partners or high-risk sexual partner
- Exchange of sex for drugs or money
- Intravenous drug use
- Blood transfusion before 1985 (HIV only)
- Admittance to jail or other detention facility
- Live in areas with high prevalence of HIV and syphilis (21, 26)

Counseling of adolescents before HIV testing should include a risk assessment profile, explanation of testing procedures, implications of test results, informed consent for testing, and the development of risk reduction strategies. It also may be helpful for the adolescent to identify an adult who knows she is being tested and will provide support. This is particularly helpful in cases of a positive HIV test result. In addition to informing the patient of the results of the test, posttest counseling should include a review of the meaning of the results and reinforcement of prevention strategies. Adolescents with negative test results who are still considered at risk may benefit from additional counseling services. Adolescent patients with confirmed positive HIV test results should receive additional psychologic and social counseling (27).

Because the risk of STDs increases with exposure to multiple partners, adolescents who are sexually active need to understand this risk and should be encouraged to limit that exposure. Some experts recommend that female adolescent patients be seen every 6 months for STD screening regardless of the number of sexual partners (28). The CDC recommends that all female adolescents and women with chlamydial infections be rescreened 3 or 4 months after treatment is completed. It also strongly encourages providers to rescreen all women treated for chlamydial infection at their next office visit within the following 12 months, regardless of whether the patient believes that her partner(s) was treated (27).

All adolescents should receive annual health guidance regarding sexuality. Such guidance should include counseling about what constitutes responsible, consensual sexual behavior and that abstinence from sexual intercourse is the only definitive way to prevent pregnancy and STDs (21). Abstinence from all risky behaviors also should be encouraged. These risky behaviors should be defined because in a study of college students, 24% defined anal intercourse, 37% defined oral intercourse, and 47% defined oral–anal contact as "abstinent" behavior (29). All sexually active adolescents should be encouraged to use condoms consistently and correctly with all sexual partners no matter what other birth control method is used. Recent studies indicate a potential association between use of hormonal contraception (depotmedroxyprogesterone acetate or oral contraceptives) and increased acquisition of cervical chlamydial and gonoccocal infections (30). Counseling should stress the effectiveness of latex condoms in reducing the risk of pregnancy and the STDs most likely to cause serious morbidity and mortality (21). When used consistently and correctly, male latex condoms are effective in preventing the sexual transmission of HIV infection and can reduce the risk for other STDs (eg, gonorrhea, chlamydia, and trichomonas). However, because condoms do not cover all exposed areas, they are likely to be more effective in preventing infections transmitted by fluids from mucosal surfaces (eg, gonorrhea, chlamydia, trichomoniasis, and HIV) than in preventing those transmitted by skin-to-skin contact (eg, herpes simplex virus, human papillomavirus, syphilis, and chancroid) (27, 31). Polyurethane condoms should be promoted among those allergic to latex although data regarding the effectiveness of this type of condom at preventing STDs are sparse (32).

### *Pregnant Adolescent Patients*

Pregnant adolescents should be counseled about the effects of STDs on themselves and their fetuses. They should receive repetitive reinforcement that condoms should be used during pregnancy for STD prevention (33). They should be screened for syphilis, HBV, and gonorrhea early in pregnancy. It is important to note that pregnancy is not a contraindication to HBV or hepatitis B immune globulin vaccine administration (27, 34). The American College of Obstetricians and Gynecologists (ACOG) recommends HIV testing of all pregnant women, with patient notification, as a routine component of prenatal care. If the patient declines HIV testing, it should be documented in the patient's record. However, physicians need to be aware of and follow their own states' prenatal HIV screening guidelines (35, 36). Repeat testing for HIV in the third trimester can be considered for high-risk patients, including those who use illicit drugs, exchange sex for money or drugs, have a history of STDs, have multiple sexual partners during pregnancy, have HIV-infected or high-risk partners, or have signs or symptoms suggestive of acute HIV infection at any time during the pregnancy (27). Testing for other STDs should be offered on the basis of the patient's history and physical examination or in response to public health guidelines.

Screening for chlamydia is recommended during the third trimester for women younger than 25 years. Screening during the first trimester for chlamydia might enable prevention of its adverse effects during pregnancy; however, evidence for preventing these adverse effects during pregnancy is limited (27). Among high-risk patients, repeat testing for gonorrhea, syphilis, and HBV should occur in the third trimester (27, 34). Health care providers should inquire regularly about changes in sexual partners because diligent rescreening is especially important in the adolescent population.

***Adolescent Victims of Sexual Assault***

Identification of STDs after a sexual assault is important for the psychologic and medical treatment of the patient. Appropriately sensitive care should be offered because of the trauma the patient has experienced. It is helpful to have a trained counselor available during the examination or to provide a referral for counseling. Although the clinical management of adolescent patients who have experienced sexual assault is the same as that of the adult patients who have experienced sexual assault (37), legal reporting requirements will vary by state depending on the age of the victim and her relationship with the perpetrator. It is important for clinicians to know their local reporting requirements, which can be obtained from their state attorney general's office or medical board. Provision of emergency contraception should be considered if the sexual assault occurred within 72 hours before the examination.

## Specific Treatment Guidelines

Current treatment recommendations regarding antimicrobial therapy for specific STDs are available in the CDC 2002 Guidelines for Treatment of Sexually Transmitted Diseases (27). It is especially important when treating an adolescent for an STD to use on-site single-dose antibiotics whenever possible and to give presumptive treatment because of the difficulties in getting adolescents to return for treatment. This also is an opportunity to facilitate STD prevention by providing condoms to adolescents. Current recommendations on immunizations have been developed by ACOG (38, 39).

## Reporting and Partner Notification

Success in controlling STDs requires vigorous ongoing prevention efforts, accurate identification, administration of appropriate treatments, and timely reporting of partner notification and treatment. Providers should encourage their patients to make partners aware of potential STD risk and urge them to seek diagnosis and treatment (27). Many local or state health departments offer assistance in partner notification specifically for patients who have received the diagnosis of HIV, syphilis, gonorrhea, chlamydia, and HBV. Health departments protect the privacy of patients in partner notification services, and in some cases, this is preferable to direct communication between the patient and her partner. Identifying an STD in an adolescent who denies sexual activity or is hesitant to address partner notification may lead to the discovery of forced or coerced sex. In such cases, partner notification becomes secondary and providing appropriate support, evaluation, and legal reporting takes precedence.

In the United States, syphilis, gonorrhea, and acquired immunodeficiency syndrome (AIDS) are reportable diseases in every state. Human immunodeficiency virus infection and chancroid are reportable in many states. The requirements for reporting other STDs vary among states. Reporting may be provider initiated or laboratory based or both. All clinicians should be familiar with their local STD reporting requirements. Sexually transmitted disease and HIV test results are maintained in the strictest of confidence and, in most jurisdictions, are protected by statute from subpoena (27).

## Conclusion

The American College of Obstetricians and Gynecologists considers STDs in the adolescent population a significant public health concern in need of attention. As such, ACOG advocates for improved access to health care for this population. Clinicians can work within their communities and at the state and national levels to assure access to medical care for all adolescents, especially homeless and runaway adolescents and those in detention facilities. Most importantly, clinicians can help to address this problem when caring for adolescent patients. Specifically, when providing health care for adolescents who have not yet become sexually active, abstinence from all risky behaviors should be encouraged. For sexually active adolescents, it is crucial to promote safe sexual behaviors, provide contraceptive information, encourage condom use, perform recommended STD screenings, prescribe appropriate antimicrobial therapies for infections, follow requirements for reporting and partner notification, and ensure continued support and follow-up care.

## References


1. Weinstock H, Berman S, Cates W Jr. Sexually transmitted diseases among American youth: incidence and prevalence estimates, 2000. Perspect Sex Reprod Health 2004; 36:6–10.
2. Centers for Disease Control and Prevention. Sexually transmitted disease surveillance 2002. Atlanta (GA): CDC; 2003.
3. Widom R, Hammett TM. HIV/AIDS and STDs in juvenile facilities. Research in Brief. 1996. Available at: http://www.ncjrs.org/pdffiles/hivjuve.pdf. Retrieved June 24, 2004.
4. National Coalition for the Homeless. Homeless youth. NCH Fact Sheet II. 1999. Available at: http://www.nationalhomeless.org/youth.html. Retrieved June 24, 2004.
5. Centers for Disease Control and Prevention. Tracking the hidden epidemics: trends in STDs in the United States 2000. 2001. Available at: http://www.cdc.gov/nchstp/od/news/RevBrochure/pdftoc.htm. Retrieved June 24, 2004.
6. Centers for Disease Control and Prevention. Prevention of genital human papillomavirus infection: report to Congress. 2004. Available at: http://www.cdc.gov/std/HPV/2004HPV%20Report.pdf. Retrieved June 24, 2004.
7. Centers for Disease Control and Prevention. Hepatitis B fact sheet. 2003. Available at: http://www.cdc.gov/ncidod/diseases/hepatitis/b/bfact.pdf. Retrieved June 24, 2004.
8. Cates JR, Herndon NL, Schulz SL, Darroch JE. Our voices, our lives, our futures: youth and sexually transmitted diseases. 2004. Available at: http://www.jomc.unc/edu/youthandSTDs/ourvoicesreport.pdf. Retrieved June 24, 2004.
9. Grunbaum JA, Kann L, Kinchen S, Ross J, Hawkins J, Lowry R, et al. Youth risk behavior surveillance - United States, 2003. MMWR Surveill Summ 2004;53(2):1–96.
10. Moore KA, Driscoll A. Partners, predators, peers, protectors: males and teen pregnancy: new data analyses of the 1995 National Survey of Family Growth. In: Moore KA, Driscoll AK, Ooms T, editors. Not just for girls: the roles of boys and men in teen pregnancy prevention. Washington, DC: National Campaign to Prevent Teen Pregnancy; 1997. p. 5–10.
11. Sonenstein FL, Ku L, Lindberg LD, Turner CF, Pleck JH. Changes in sexual behavior and condom use among teenaged males: 1988 to 1995. Am J Public Health 1998; 88:956–9.
12 Ku L, Sonenstein FL, Pleck JH. The dynamics of young men's condom use during and across relationships. Fam Plann Perspect 1994;26:246–51.
13. Finer LB, Darroch JE, Singh S. Sexual partnership patterns as a behavioral risk factor for sexually transmitted diseases. Fam Plann Perspect 1999;31:228–36.
14. Cates W Jr. The epidemiology and control of sexually transmitted diseases in adolescents. Adolesc Med 1990; 1:409–28.
15. Holmes KK, Mardh PA, Sparling PF, Lemon SM, Stamm WE, Piot P, et al, editors. Sexually transmitted diseases. 3rd edition. New York (NY): McGraw-Hill; 1999.
16. Ford CA, Millstein SG, Halpern-Felsher BL, Irwin CE Jr. Influence of physician confidentiality assurances on adolescents' willingness to disclose information and seek future health care. A randomized controlled trial. JAMA 1997;278;1029–34.
17. Reddy DM, Fleming R, Swain C. Effect of mandatory parental notification on adolescent girls' use of sexual health care services. JAMA 2002;288:710–4.
18. Ford CA, Best D, Miller WC. The pediatric forum: confidentiality and adolescents' willingness to consent to sexually transmitted disease testing. Arch Pediatr Adolesc Med 2001;155:1072–3.
19. The Alan Guttmacher Institute. Minors' access to STD services. State Policies in Brief. 2004. Available at: http://www.guttmacher.org/statecenter/spibs/spib_MASS.pdf. Retrieved June 24, 2004.
20. Center for Adolescent Health & the Law. State minor consent laws: a summary. 2nd ed. Chapel Hill (NC): CAHL; 2003.
21. American College of Obstetricians and Gynecologists. Health care for adolescents. Washington DC: ACOG; 2003.
22. Huppert JS, Adams Hillard PJ. Sexually transmitted disease screening in teens. Curr Womens Health Rep 2003; 3:451–8.
23. American College of Obstetricians and Gynecologists. Committee Opinion No. 300. Cervical cancer screening in the adolescent female. Washington, DC: ACOG; 2004.
24. Schuster MA, Bell RM, Kanouse DE. The sexual practices of adolescent virgins: genital sexual activities of high school students who have never had vaginal intercourse. Am J Public Health 1996;86:1570–6.
25. Niccolai LM, Ethier KA, Kershaw TS, Lewis JB, Meade CS, Ickovics JR. New sex partner acquisition and sexually transmitted disease risk among adolescent females. J Adolesc Health 2004;34:216–23.
26. HIV prevention through early detection and treatment of other sexually transmitted diseases—United States. Recommendations of the Advisory Committee for HIV and STD prevention. MMWR Recomm Rep 1998;47(RR-12):1–24.
27. Sexually transmitted diseases treatment guidelines 2002. Centers for Disease Control and Prevention. MMWR Recomm Rep 2002;51(RR-6):1–78. Available at: http://www.cdc.gov/STD/treatment/rr5106.pdf. Retrieved July 7, 2004.
28. Burstein GR, Gaydos CA, Diener-West M, Howell MR, Zenilman JM, Quinn TC. Incident chlamydia trachomatis infections among inner-city adolescent females. JAMA 1998;280:521–6.
29. Horan PF, Phillips J, Hagan NE. The meaning of abstinence for college students. J HIV/AIDS Prev Educ Adolesc Child 1998;2(2):51–66.
30. Morrison CS, Bright P, Wong EL, Kwok C, Yacobson I, Gaydos CA, et al. Hormonal contraceptive use, cervical ectopy, and the acquisition of cervical infections. Sex Transm Dis 2004;31:561–7.
31. National Institute of Allergy and Infectious Diseases, National Institutes of Health. Workshop summary: scientific evidence on condom effectiveness for sexually transmitted disease (STD) prevention. 2001. Available at: http://www.niaid.nih.gov/dmid/stds/condomreport.pdf. Retrieved June 24, 2004.

32. Frezieres RG, Walsh TL, Nelson AL, Clark VA, Coulson AH. Evaluation of the efficacy of a polyurethane condom: results from a randomized, controlled clinical trial. Fam Plann Perspect 1999;31:81–7.
33. Niccolai LM, Ethier KA, Kershaw TS, Lewis JB, Ickovics JR. Pregnant adolescents at risk: sexual behaviors and sexually transmitted disease prevalence. Am J Obstet Gynecol 2003;188:63–70.
34. American Academy of Pediatrics, American College of Obstetricians and Gynecologists. Guidelines for perinatal care. 5th ed. Elk Grove Village (IL): AAP; Washington, DC: ACOG; 2002.
35. American Academy of Pediatrics, American College of Obstetricians and Gynecologists. Joint statement on human immunodeficiency virus screening. ACOG Policy Statement 75. Elk Grove Village (IL): AAP; Washington, DC: ACOG; 1999.
36. Revised guidelines for HIV counseling, testing, and referral and revised recommendations for HIV screening of pregnant women. Centers for Disease Control and Prevention. MMWR Recomm Rep 2001;50(RR-19): 1–86; quiz CE1-19a2-CE6-19a2.
37. American College of Obstetricians and Gynecologists. Sexual assault. ACOG Educational Bulletin 242. Washington, DC: ACOG; 1997.
38. Primary and preventive care: periodic assessments. ACOG Committee Opinion No. 292. American College of Obstetricians and Gynecologists. Obstet Gynecol 2003; 102:1117–24.
39. Immunization during pregnancy. ACOG Committee Opinion No. 282. American College of Obstetricians and Gynecologists. Obstet Gynecol 2003;101:207–12.

## Resources

### *Publications*

The American College of Obstetricians and Gynecologists Tool Kit for Teen Care offers a fact sheet on the topic of STDs that may be helpful for patients and providers alike. This fact sheet is available online at http://www.acog.org/goto/teens. For information on the entire kit, go to sales.acog.org or contact the Department of Adolescent Health Care at 202-863-2497. Other ACOG resources are listed as follows:

American College of Obstetricians and Gynecologists. Health Care for Adolescents. Washington, DC: ACOG; 2003.

Patient Education Pamphlets

- How to Prevent Sexually Transmitted Diseases (1999) (AP009) (SP009—Spanish)
- Genital Herpes (1999) (AP054)
- Gonorrhea, Chlamydia, and Syphilis (2000) (AP071)
- Hepatitis B Virus in Pregnancy (2000) (AP093)
- HIV Infection in Women (2000) (AP082)
- Human Papillomavirus Infection (2003) (AP073)
- Protecting Yourself Against Hepatitis B (1998) (AP125)

### *Web Sites*

We have provided web sites and contact information for the following organizations because they have information that may be of interest to our readers. The American College of Obstetricians and Gynecologists does not necessarily endorse the views expressed or the facts presented by these organizations or on these web sites. Furthermore, ACOG does not endorse any commercial products that may be advertised or available from these organizations or on these web sites.

Advocates for Youth
2000 M St NW, Ste 750
Washington, DC 20036
Telephone: 202-419-3420
Fax: 202-419-1448
www.advocatesforyouth.org
E-mail: questions@advocatesforyouth.org

Alan Guttmacher Institute
120 Wall Street, 21st Fl
New York, NY 10005
Telephone: 212-248-1111
Fax: 212-248-1951
www.guttmacher.org
E-mail: info@guttmacher.org

American Academy of Family Physicians
11400 Tomahawk Creek Parkway
Leawood, KS 66211-2672
Telephone: 800-274-2237 or 913-906-6000
www.aafp.org
E-mail: fp@aafp.org

American Academy of Pediatrics
141 Northwest Point Boulevard
Elk Grove Village, IL 60007-1098
Telephone: 847-434-4000
Fax: 847-434-8000
www.aap.org
E-mail: kidsdocs@aap.org

American Social Health Association
PO Box 13827
Research Triangle Park, NC 27709
Telephone: 919-361-8400
Fax: 919-361-8425
www.ashastd.org
E-mail: std-hivnet@ashastd.org

AWARE Foundation
1015 Chestnut Street, Suite 1225
Philadelphia, PA 19107-4302
Telephone: 215-955-9847
www.awarefoundation.org
E-mail: info@awarefoundation.org

Centers for Disease Control and Prevention
National Center for Chronic Disease Prevention
and Health Promotion
Division of Adolescent and School Health
www.cdc.gov/HealthyYouth/index.htm
E-mail: healthyyouth@cdc.gov

Centers for Disease Control and Prevention
Office of Women's Health
1600 Clifton Road, MS E-89
Atlanta, GA 30333
Telephone: 404-498-2300
Fax: 404-498-2370
www.cdc.gov/health/od/spotlight/nwhw/default.htm
E-mail: owh@cdc.gov

Johns Hopkins AIDS Service
www.hopkins-aids.edu

National Sexually Transmitted Disease Hotline
Telephone: 800-227-8922

National Women's Health Information Center
Telephone: 800-994-WOMAN
www.4woman.org

Planned Parenthood Federation of America, Inc.
434 W 33rd St.
New York, NY 10001
Telephone: 215-541-7800
Fax: 212-245-1845
www.plannedparenthood.org
E-mail: communications@ppfa.org

Sexuality Information and Education Council
of the United States
130 West 42nd Street, Suite 350
New York, NY 10036-7802
Telephone: 212-819-9770
Fax: 212-819-9776
www.siecus.org
E-mail: siecus@siecus.org

The Society of Obstetricians and Gynecologists of Canada
Sexuality and U
www.sexualityandu.ca

# ACOG Committee Opinion

Committee on Adolescent Health Care

Number 302, October 2004

# Guidelines for Adolescent Health Research

*ABSTRACT: The risks of exposure to violence, human immunodeficiency virus, and other sexually transmitted diseases; alcohol, tobacco, and prescribed and illicit drug use; and unintended pregnancy, among others, threaten the health and well-being of adolescents in the United States. Research is needed in these and other areas to improve adolescent health care and to aid in health policy decisions. Adolescents often are prevented from participating in such research because of inadequate understanding of their legal status and the ethical considerations regarding their participation in research. There is confusion about what constitutes appropriate levels of protection for studies involving adolescents as research subjects and uncertainty about the need for parental permission. This document is designed to clarify the informed consent and parental permission issues as they pertain to adolescent health research.*

## Background

A basic criterion for ethical research is the protection of the rights and welfare of people participating in research. The U.S. federal government has promulgated regulations that govern research involving human subjects when the research is supported, conducted, or otherwise subject to regulation by the federal government (1). These federal regulations on protection of human subjects in research, known as the Code of Federal Regulations: Title 45-Public Welfare; Part 46: Protection of Human Subjects (45 CFR Part 46), provide for a nationwide system of local Institutional Review Boards (IRBs). These IRBs must review and approve all federally funded research involving human subjects and are regulated by the Office for Human Research Protections in the Department of Health and Human Services. Most universities and research institutions apply these regulations to privately funded research as well. These regulations serve as guidelines for IRB review and approval. They require that risks to research participants are minimized and that they are reasonable relative to the anticipated benefits and the importance of the knowledge that may be expected to result from the research. The regulations also require that the selection of research participants is equitable and that informed consent is provided from each prospective research participant

The Committee wishes to thank Abigail English, JD; S. Paige Hertweck, MD; Susan Kornetsky, MPH; Audrey Rogers, PhD, MPH; and John Santelli, MD, MPH for their assistance in the development of this opinion. This document reflects emerging clinical and scientific advances as of the date issued and is subject to change. The information should not be construed as dictating an exclusive course of treatment or procedure to be followed.



ISSN 1074-861X

**The American College of Obstetricians and Gynecologists**
409 12th Street, SW
PO Box 96920
Washington, DC 20090-6920

12345/87654

Guidelines for adolescent health research. ACOG Committee Opinion No. 302. American College of Obstetricians and Gynecologists. Obstet Gynecol 2004;104:899–902.

or the participant's legally authorized representative. Informed consent is the ability to understand the risks and benefits of one's participation in a research activity and to authorize one's participation in this activity freely (2). General requirements for informed consent are described in 45 CFR Part 46, Section 116 (1). Finally, the regulations require that the research plan makes adequate provisions for ensuring the safety of research participants and that adequate provisions are made to protect the privacy of research participants and to maintain the confidentiality of data. Subpart D of 45 CFR Part 46 contains special protections for children who participate as subjects in research.

Research involving adolescents, especially regarding behaviors related to sexuality, often raises questions about how to obtain adequate informed consent and protection of the research participants' confidential receipt of health care services. The Society for Adolescent Medicine provided early leadership to address these concerns. In 1995, they led the development of consensus guidelines to promote the ethical conduct of health research involving adolescents as research participants (3). The society recently issued a revised position statement to support the guidelines (4); the Society for Adolescent medicine also established a code of research ethics to encourage, enhance, and promote ethical standards for the conduct of research in adolescent health (5).

When considering the legal complexities of adolescent health research, it is important to recognize that the age of majority in almost every state is 18 years, and all states recognize the concept of emancipated minors, who generally are allowed to consent for their own health care. In addition, every state has enacted some minor consent laws that allow minors to consent for their own health care, whether or not they are legally emancipated. Such laws may be based on the status of the minor or the services they are seeking. Minors who may consent for their own health care based on their status include those who are married, are members of the armed forces, live apart from their parents, and are parents of a child. In addition, all states allow adolescents who are minors to consent for some categories of health care such as sexually transmitted disease (STD) services (all states), drug and alcohol care (almost all states), contraceptive services and pregnancy related care (a majority of states), outpatient mental health counseling (about one half of states), or sexual assault care (a few states). Some states specify the age at which a minor can begin to consent (6). Researchers in adolescent health should be familiar with current state statutes regarding age of majority and emancipation, as well as with minor consent statutes. An up-to-date listing of these statutes can be found online at http://www.guttmacher.org/pubs/spib.html.

## Regulations

In the federal regulations governing research, children are defined in 45 CFR 46 Section 102(a) as "persons who have not attained the legal age for consent to treatments or procedures involved in the research, under the applicable law of the jurisdiction in which the research will be conducted"(1). This definition refers to laws, primarily state laws related to consent for treatment of minors, age of majority, and emancipation status.

Federal regulations governing human subject research require parental permission and child assent for subjects who meet the regulatory definition of "children," ie, those who are younger than the state-mandated age at which people may give legally effective informed consent for treatments or procedures involved in the research. Assent means a child has given affirmative agreement to participate in research. Mere failure to object should not, absent affirmative agreement, be construed as assent. Assent is required when, in the judgment of the IRB, the children are capable of providing it (1).The federal regulations deliberately use the terms "permission" and "assent" to differentiate this process from the usual informed consent process. An individual can provide consent only for himself or herself. Therefore, parents give only permission for their child to be involved in research, not consent. Assent recognizes the importance of the emerging capacity of children to give informed consent for themselves, as well as the ethical importance of obtaining their agreement to participate even if they are not legally authorized to give informed consent.

In 1977, the National Commission for the Protection of Human Subjects of Biomedical and Behavioral Research recommended that individual IRBs be allowed to determine that parental permission is not appropriate in certain research studies, including research involving assessment for or care related to contraception and drug abuse (7). According to the federal regulations (1), informed consent may be waived under 45 CFR Part 46 Section 116(d) and parental permission may be waived under 45 CFR Part 46 Section 408(c).

Four criteria set forth by 45 CFR Part 46 116(d) allow an IRB to waive the requirement to obtain the informed consent for adult research subjects or permission of a parent or guardian for research subjects who are children if: 1) the research involves no more than "minimal risk" (which means that the probability and magnitude of harm or discomfort anticipated in the research are not greater in and of themselves than those ordinarily encountered in daily life or during the performance of routine physical or psychologic examinations or tests [1]), 2) the waiver will not adversely affect the rights and welfare of the subjects, 3) the research could not practically be carried out without a waiver, and 4) whenever appropriate, the subjects will be provided with additional pertinent information after participation (1). This section is commonly used when waiving informed consent for research involving existing data such as medical records.

In addition, 45 CFR Part 46 Section 408(c) specifically allows for a waiver of parental permission under Subpart D, which addresses research with children. Section 408(c) of 45 CFR Part 46 states: "...if an IRB determines that a research protocol is designed for conditions or a subject population for which parental permission is not a reasonable requirement to protect subjects (eg, neglected or abused children), it may waive consent requirements provided an appropriate mechanism for protecting the children who will participate as research subjects is substituted and provided the waiver is not inconsistent with federal, state, or local law.... The choice of an appropriate mechanism would depend on the nature and purpose of the activities described in the protocol, the risk and anticipated benefit to the research subjects, and their age, maturity, status, and condition" (1). In discussing the waiver of parental permission, the National Commission cited as examples of when the requirement might not be a reasonable one: "...[r]esearch designed to identify factors related to the incidence or treatment of certain conditions in adolescents for which, in certain jurisdictions, they legally may receive treatment without parental consent; [and] research in which the subjects are 'mature minors' and the procedures involved entail essentially no more than minimal risk that such individuals might reasonably assume on their own..." (7).

Based on these criteria, either 45 CFR Part 46 Section 408(c) or 45 CFR Part 46 Section 116(d) may be used to waive parental permission in a variety of studies, including, for example, surveys of adolescents. It is important to note that if these surveys are conducted in a school setting, federal educational law governing certain research conducted in schools may apply. Health researchers working in schools are, therefore, advised to become knowledgeable about these laws.

Section 408(c) of 45 CFR Part 46 also may be used to waive parental permission for research areas including STDs, birth control usage, high-risk behaviors, HIV prevention, and situations in which obtaining parental consent may be dangerous to the child (abuse situations). Finally, in certain research studies, adolescent minors would not be considered children and parental permission would not be required. Such research includes certain clinical studies involving pregnancy, family planning, and treatment of STDs where the adolescent minor can legally consent to such services. Again, familiarity with current state statutes on the rights of minors to consent to health care services is essential.

Researchers conducting and IRBs reviewing research involving adolescents should be knowledgeable of the federal regulations and the ethical principles that underlie these regulations. They should understand when parental permission is required and when it may be waived. Personal beliefs and attitudes should not enter into this decision. The Society for Adolescent Medicine's *Guidelines for Adolescent Health Research* (4) provide a comprehensive approach to understanding these issues. Parental permission should not be a barrier to the inclusion of adolescents in studies that meet federal regulations and are designed to improve their health.

## Conclusions

1. Researchers developing study protocols and materials for submission for IRB review and approval and the IRBs themselves should be familiar with, and adhere to, current federal regulations, 45 CFR Part 46 (1), and federal and state laws that affect research (including laws regarding age of majority and emancipation, minor consent statutes, and federal educational law governing certain research conducted in schools).
2. Investigators will communicate better with IRB panels regarding the involvement of adolescent participants in research if they understand the purpose of human subject protection regulations

with respect to minors and review the guidelines provided by the Society for Adolescent Medicine (3–5).

3. Under the following circumstances it is reasonable to waive parental permission when adolescents are involved in studies: a) the waiver would not adversely affect the rights and welfare of the adolescent, b) the study poses no more than a minimal risk to adolescents, c) the study could not be practically carried out without a waiver, and d) requiring permission may not be reasonable to protect subjects. Parental permission is not a requirement for research involving the provision of health care for which adolescents do not legally need parental consent. It is important to review 45 CFR Part 46 for the necessary details.

## References

1. Protection of human subjects. 45 C.F.R §46 (2003). Available at http://www.access.gpo.gov/nara/cfr/cfr-tablesearch.html#page1. Retrieved July 8, 2004.
2. American College of Obstetricians and Gynecologists. Ethics in obstetrics and gynecology. 2nd ed. ACOG: Washington, DC; 2004.
3. Guidelines for adolescent health research. 1995. Society for Adolescent Medicine. J Adolesc Health 2003;33: 410–5.
4. Santelli JS, Smith Rogers A, Rosenfeld WD, DuRant RH, Dubler N, Morreale M, et al. Guidelines for adolescent health research: A position paper of the Society for Adolescent Medicine. J Adolesc Health 2003;33: 396–409.
5. Code of Research Ethics: position paper of the Society for Adolescent Medicine. J Adolesc Health 1999;24:277–82; discussion 283.
6. English A, Kenney KE. State minor consent laws: a summary. 2nd Ed. Chapel Hill (NC): Center for Adolescent Health & the Law; 2003.
7. The National Commission for the Protection of Human Subjects of Biomedical and Behavioral Research. Research involving children: report and recommendations. Bethesda (MD): U.S. Department of Health Education and Welfare; 1977.

ACOG Committee Opinion

ACOG Committee on Adolescent Health Care



The Committee wishes to thank Marc R. Laufer, MD; Joseph Sanfilippo, MD; and Jonathon Solnik, MD; for their assistance in the development of this document.



ISSN 1074-861X

**The American College of Obstetricians and Gynecologists**
409 12th Street, SW
PO Box 96920
Washington, DC 20090-6920

12345/98765

Endometriosis in adolescents. ACOG Committee Opinion No. 310. American College of Obstetricians and Gynecologists. Obstet Gynecol 2005;105:921–7.

Number 310, April 2005

# Endometriosis in Adolescents

*ABSTRACT: Historically thought of as a disease that affects adult women, endometriosis increasingly is being diagnosed in the adolescent population. This disorder, which was originally described more than a century ago, still represents a vague and perplexing entity that frequently results in chronic pelvic pain, adhesive disease, and infertility. The purpose of this Committee Opinion is to highlight the differences in adolescent and adult types of endometriosis. Early diagnosis and treatment during adolescence may decrease disease progression and prevent subsequent infertility.*

## Incidence

It has been difficult to establish accurate prevalence rates of endometriosis in adult and adolescent women. Documented rates in adolescent patients undergoing laparoscopy for chronic pelvic pain range from 19% to 73%. Goldstein et al (1) reported a 47% prevalence of endometriosis found at laparoscopy in a prospective study of adolescent females with pelvic pain. Other studies have shown that 25–38% of adolescents with chronic pelvic pain have endometriosis (2, 3). In addition, it has been shown that 50–70% of adolescents with pelvic pain not responding to combination hormone therapy (such as oral contraceptive pills [OCPs]) and nonsteroidal antiinflammatory drugs (NSAIDs) have endometriosis at the time of laparoscopy (4, 5).

Endometriosis also has been identified in premenarcheal girls who have started puberty and have some breast development (6, 7). The occurrence of endometriosis before menarche contributes to the argument that one etiology for endometriosis lies in the theory of embryonic müllerian rests or coelomic metaplasia as opposed to retrograde menses. Based on the occurrence of early endometriosis, some authors have argued that "thelarche be recognized as a developmental benchmark, after which endometriosis is included in the differential diagnosis of chronic pelvic pain" (6).

It is common for adult women who have endometriosis to bring in their adolescent daughters for evaluation and early diagnosis. Data from the Endometriosis Association indicate that 66% of adult women reported the onset of pelvic symptoms before age 20 years. Forty-seven percent of these women reported they had to see a doctor five times or more before receiving the diagnosis of endometriosis or referral. As the age of the onset of symptoms decreases, the number of doctors having to be seen to reach a diagnosis increases. Specifically, an average of 4.2 doctors were seen for patients whose symptoms began before age 15 years compared with an average of 2.64 doctors for patients whose symptoms began between the ages of 30 years and 34 years. There are, on average, 9.28 years from the onset of symptoms to the diagnosis (8). Endometriosis is believed to be a progressive disease because the prevalence and severity of the stage of the disease significantly increase with age (9, 10). With early diagnosis and treatment, it is hoped that disease progression and infertility can be limited, but this remains to be proved with prospective research.

## Presentation and Characteristics

The typical presentation of an adolescent with endometriosis may be different from that of an adult. One significant difference is that adolescents primarily seek medical attention because of pain rather than a concern for infertility. The most common symptom noted among published reviews is acquired or progressive dysmenorrhea, which was encountered in 64–94% of patients (4, 11). Other common symptoms included acyclic pain (36–91%), dyspareunia (14–25%), and gastrointestinal complaints (2–46%) (11). Adolescents found to have endometriosis most commonly present with both cyclic and acyclic pain (62.6%), as opposed to acyclic pain alone (28.1%), or cyclic pain alone (9.4%) (11).

In young women, pelvic pain associated with endometriosis often interferes with school attendance as well as physical and social activities. Prompt diagnosis and adequate therapy, therefore, may return normal psychosocial development and self-esteem, improve scholastic performance, and lead to a return to normal daily activities.

## Diagnosis

### *History and Physical Examination*

A thorough review of history and physical examination are necessary to assess a variety of differential diagnoses of pelvic pain such as appendicitis, pelvic inflammatory disease, müllerian anomalies or outflow obstruction, bowel disease, hernias, musculoskeletal disorders, and psychosocial complaints. Pelvic examination may be difficult, especially in patients who have not had vaginal intercourse.

When evaluating an adolescent for suspected endometriosis or dysmenorrhea, the clinician should aim to rule out a pelvic mass or a congenital anomaly of the reproductive tract. A bimanual examination may not be necessary to evaluate pelvic pain, especially in adolescents who are virgins. If a bimanual examination cannot be performed or is declined, a rectal–abdominal examination in the dorsal lithotomy position may be helpful to determine if a pelvic mass is present, and a cotton-tipped swab can be inserted into the vagina to evaluate for the presence of a transverse vaginal septum, vaginal agenesis, or agenesis of the lower vagina. If a bimanual examination is performed, the clinician should check for the existence of both diffuse and focal pelvic tenderness, and evaluate the pelvis for a displaced uterus or an adnexal mass. An ultrasound examination may be helpful in evaluating the pelvis of a young adolescent who declines a bimanual or rectal–abdominal examination.

### *Imaging Studies and Serum Markers*

Ultrasonography and magnetic resonance imaging are helpful in evaluating anatomical structures, but are not specific for diagnosing endometriosis. An adolescent will rarely have a pelvic mass from an endometrioma or uterosacral nodularity. CA 125, although very sensitive, is not specific and, thus, is not helpful in the diagnosis of adolescent endometriosis. No data exist regarding the use of CA 125 to monitor the clinical progression or regression of disease in adolescents with endometriosis.

### *Empiric Therapy*

If an adolescent younger than 18 years has persistent pain while taking combination hormone therapy and NSAIDs, endometriosis should be suspected and she should be offered a laparoscopic evaluation (discussion follows in section on "Surgical Diagnosis"). If, however, she is older than 18 years and had a negative assessment for an ovarian mass or tumor, she can be offered an empiric trial of gonadotropin-releasing hormone (GnRH) agonist therapy (12, 13). If the pain subsides with the use of GnRH agonist, then a diagnosis of endometriosis can be made. An empiric trial of GnRH agonist is not routinely offered to patients younger than 18 years because the effects of these medications on bone formation and long-term bone density have not been adequately studied. For patients younger than 18 years or who decline empiric therapy, diagnostic and therapeutic laparoscopy can be initiated. An algorithm for therapy is provided in Figure 1 (14).

### *Surgical Diagnosis*

After a comprehensive preoperative evaluation and trial of combination hormone therapy and NSAIDs to treat dysmenorrhea, laparoscopy should be recommended for diagnosing and treating presumed endometriosis in an adolescent. Laparoscopy can be safely performed in adolescents. At the time of surgical diagnosis, most adolescents have Stage I disease as classified by the American Society for Reproductive Medicine classification system (15). Goldstein et al commented that almost 60% of the

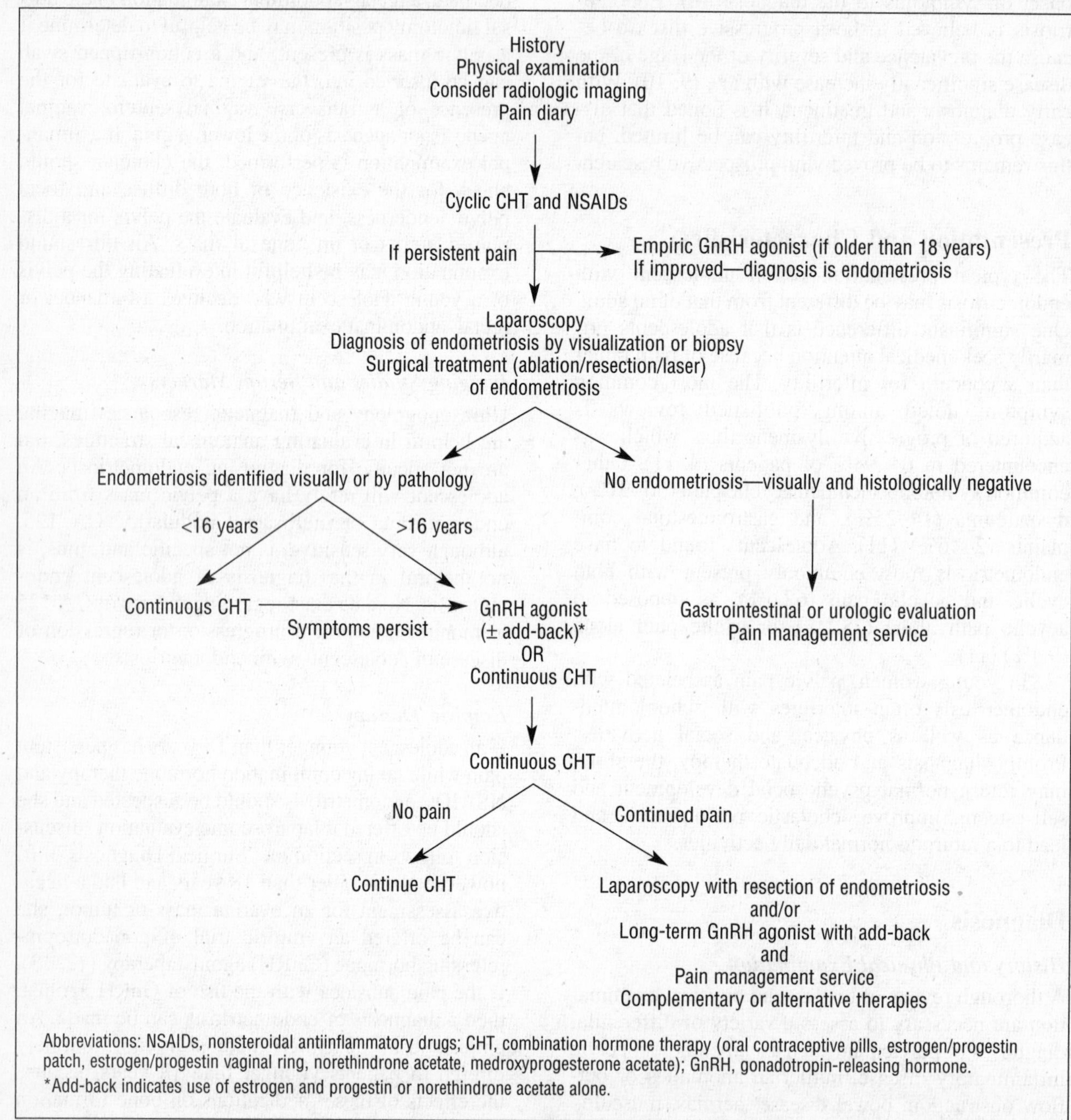


**Fig. 1.** Protocol for evaluation and treatment of adolescent pelvic pain and endometriosis. (Modified with permission from Bandera CA, Brown LR, Laufer MR. Adolescents and endometriosis. Clin Consult Obstet Gynecol 1995;7:206.)

patients in their cohort had Stage I disease (1), whereas 80% of the cases reported by other researchers had minimal to mild disease (4). Gynecologic surgeons who perform laparoscopy in adolescents with pelvic pain should be familiar with the typical lesions of endometriosis in adolescents, which tend to be red, clear, or white (15) as opposed to the powder-burn lesions seen commonly in adults who have endometriosis. The use of a liquid medium in the pelvis may facilitate the identification of clear lesions, which are very common in adolescents (11).

### *Müllerian Anomalies and Endometriosis*

The development of endometriosis in adolescent patients has been associated with müllerian anomalies with outflow tract obstruction. The published incidence of anomalies of the reproductive system and associated endometriosis has been reported to be as high as 40%, but most studies quote a rate of 5–6%. The clinical outcome in patients with outflow tract obstructions has been reported to differ from those without such obstruction because regression of disease usually has been observed once surgical correction of the anomaly has been accomplished (16).

## Treatment

The premise for treating the symptomatic adolescent is based on the concept that endometriosis has been shown to be a progressive disease without a known cure. A physician treating an adolescent with endometriosis should adopt a multidimensional approach and consider the use of the following components: surgery, hormonal manipulation, pain medications, mental health support, complementary and alternative therapies, and education.

Patients younger than 18 years with persistent pelvic pain while taking combination hormone therapy should routinely be offered a laparoscopic procedure for diagnosis and surgical management of endometriosis. The gynecologic surgeon must be familiar with the appearance of endometriosis in adolescents and should remove or destroy all visible lesions of endometriosis. Only procedures that preserve fertility options should be applied; oophorectomy or hysterectomy should not be offered to adolescents.

Long-term follow-up studies of treatments for adolescent endometriosis have not been performed. Current treatments for adolescents have been extrapolated and adapted from the literature of adult cases of endometriosis. The goal of therapy for adolescent endometriosis should be suppression of pain, suppression of disease progression, and preservation of fertility. Consequently, after surgery, all adolescents who have endometriosis should be treated with medical therapy until they have completed child bearing to suppress pain, progression of disease, and resulting potential infertility.

First-line treatment modalities should involve the use of NSAIDs and hormone therapy. Because red lesions have been shown to be active producers of prostaglandins, and adolescents with endometriosis typically report severe dysmenorrhea, NSAIDs may be used in conjunction with hormonal menstrual suppressive therapy to provide sufficient relief. Most pharmacologic agents bring about relief by inducing an anovulatory or a hypoestrogenic state or both. Continuous combination hormone therapy (OCPs, combination hormonal contraceptive patch, or vaginal ring) for menstrual suppression can be used to create a "pseudopregnancy" state, which was described more than 40 years ago (17). This method routinely has been promoted for adolescents who have endometriosis. Although this method may provide effective relief, the Cochrane Database Review 2003 provided data suggesting that further studies are needed to prove long-term benefits (18). Most clinicians advocate continuous use of combination hormone therapy to induce amenorrhea, but this modality can result in significant breakthrough bleeding. One randomized controlled trial compared a 28-day regimen with continuous combination oral contraceptives and found no increase in spotting days after 9 months of therapy, with fewer total bleeding days in the group taking continuous combination oral contraceptives (19). Thus, continuous use of combination hormone therapy is believed to be both safe and effective for adolescents with endometriosis-related pain and, thus, is the first-line hormone therapy for adolescents younger than 16 years with endometriosis. Gonadotropin-releasing hormone agonists are not offered as first-line therapy for adolescents in this age range.

Progestin-only protocols have been used for the treatment of adult endometriosis with mixed results. In a recent critical review, progestins were shown to be as effective as danazol or GnRH agonists (20). Common side effects include irregular bleeding and weight gain. Some studies suggest that these side effects are well tolerated (20), however in a data set of 3,751 women who have endometriosis, treatment with medroxyprogesterone acetate or depot medroxyprogesterone acetate was the least well tolerated and was the least effective in treating pain compared with combination OCPs, GnRH agonists, and pain medications (8). Furthermore, depot medroxyprogesterone acetate used for longer than 2 years has been shown to decrease bone density in adolescents (21, 22, 23). The U.S. Food and Drug Administration has warned against the long-term use of depot medroxyprogesterone acetate because of adverse affects on bone density (24).

Danazol, an androgenic and antiestrogenic agent, is extremely effective in treating symptomatic endometriosis in adults. Doses of 400–800 mg daily have been advocated for 6 months followed by continuous OCP use for maintenance suppression of the hypothalamic–pituitary ovarian axis. This choice of pharmacotherapy was more common in the 1980s, but the androgenic side effects have made this a poor option for adolescents.

Gonadotropin-releasing hormone agonists create a hypoestrogenic state by downregulating the hypothalamic–pituitary axis. Whereas these agents are greatly effective in the treatment of endometriosis-related pain in adolescents, their use alone (without add-back therapy described in the following paragraph) usually is limited to 6 months because of the resultant profound hypoestrogenic state and its subsequent effect on bone mineralization. This is a major issue for an adolescent who is accruing peak bone mineral density. Therefore, it has been suggested that this therapy not be offered as a first-line treatment for adolescents younger than 16 years (14). At 6 months, GnRH agonist induces a 5% loss in trabecular bone mineral density and a 2% loss in femoral neck bone mineral density in adult women. In a cross-sectional study, researchers collected bone mineral density test results of 265 females, aged 8–50 years (25). They determined that the majority of bone mass growth is achieved by age 20 years and that after the age 18 years, no significant differences in bone mass or bone mineral density were noted at most skeletal sites. This emphasizes that a drug-induced hypoestrogenic state could significantly affect peak bone mineralization that occurs during adolescence, particularly in females younger than 16 years.

Investigators have determined that to reduce the symptoms and bone loss related to a hypoestrogenic state, add-back therapy with norethindrone acetate (5 mg per day) or conjugated estrogens/medroxyprogesterone acetate (0.625/2.5 mg per day) can help preserve bone density (26, 27). Add-back therapy has been shown not to influence the primary therapeutic effect and resulted in less bone loss 12 months after cessation of therapy in adult women. There is some evidence in adults to suggest that immediate add-back therapy may result in even less bone loss (28). No data exist on the long-term effects of GnRH agonist use with add-back therapy in the adolescent population and, thus, it should be reserved for adolescents refractory to continuous combination hormone therapy (14, 29). Lifestyle modifications, such as adequate physical exercise and calcium and vitamin D intake, also are essential to maintaining proper bone health when taking GnRH agonists (with or without add-back therapy).

Aside from medical management, surgery also has proved to be an effective form of treatment for adult patients with pain (30). Surgery for the management of endometriosis-related pain is an important option for adolescents, but clearly, radical procedures (oophorectomy, bilateral oophorectomy, or hysterectomy) should be avoided in this age group, even in rare cases of severe endometriosis. A double-blinded randomized controlled trial compared laser vaporization of endometriosis and laser uterosacral nerve ablation with controls in 63 adult patients with proven endometriosis. At 6 months of follow-up, 63% of patients reported significant relief compared with 23% of controls (31). Patients with more advanced disease had better outcomes in pain management compared with those with minimal disease. At 1-year follow-up, 90% of those in the treatment arm who initially responded had continued pain relief (32). Among the symptomatic controls, an even distribution of patients was noted to have progression, regression, and maintenance of disease. Both new and recurrent disease was noted at second look. In a Cochrane review of these data, adult patients were almost 5 times more likely to benefit from surgical management of endometriosis compared with controls (33). One study demonstrated, in a prospective review of 643 patients with pain, or infertility, or both, that there was a significant relationship between pain and the depth of infiltration of the endometriosis implants (9). This study also confirmed that red implants were more common in younger patients and that the depth of invasion increased with age, suggesting that endometriosis is a progressive disease. The concept that endometriosis is a progressive disease supports the recommendation for long-term medical treatment for pain management of adolescent endometriosis and until a woman has completed childbearing. Long-term studies are needed to determine if medical treatment can inhibit the progression of endometriosis diagnosed in adolescents and preserve future fertility.

In addition to surgery and hormonal manipulation, complementary and alternative medicine has been used for the treatment of endometriosis. A multidisciplinary pain management service, including support groups and age-appropriate educational information, may be beneficial for an adolescent with chronic pelvic pain caused by endometriosis.

## Summary

Endometriosis can be a debilitating disease that affects adolescent girls and young women. Pediatricians, adolescent health care providers, and gynecologists should recognize that thelarche and the presence of endogenous estrogen can be considered a developmental milestone and benchmark for inclusion of adolescent endometriosis in the differential diagnosis of postpubertal girls and young women with chronic pelvic pain. Adolescent patients typically present with progressive and severe dysmenorrhea, but also may present with acylic pelvic pain. Standard therapy (combination hormone therapy and NSAIDs) for dysmenorrhea should be initiated, and if symptoms do not resolve after 3 months, further evaluation for endometriosis is indicated. Prompt evaluation and consideration of the adverse effects of endometriosis is, therefore, essential in this age group.

Findings of the physical examination of adolescents may vary from the adult population because uterosacral nodularity and endometriomas are found in more advanced disease and, thus, are uncommon in adolescents. A bimanual pelvic examination may not be necessary for further evaluation of pelvic pain and should not be a requirement before the diagnosis of endometriosis and initiation of therapy for adolescents. It is important to evaluate the vagina for a possible obstructive anomaly and the ovaries for a possible ovarian mass. This can be accomplished with an evaluation of the vagina with a cotton-tipped swab and an ultrasound examination of the pelvis.

Endometriosis in adolescents typically presents as early disease (Stage I) and clear, red, and white lesions are the most common. Treatment should focus on conservative measures with surgical and medical interventions. Only procedures that preserve fertility options should be applied. Long-term endometriosis treatment may be required for chronic pain relief. Because there is no cure for endometriosis, long-term treatment should continue until desired family size is reached or fertility no longer needs to be preserved. A multidisciplinary team approach to the adolescent who has endometriosis may be the most rewarding for the adolescent, her family, and the clinician.

## Resources

Endometriosis Association
(www.endometriosisassn.org)

The Center for Young Women's Health
(www.youngwomenshealth.org)

## References


1. Goldstein DP, De Cholnoky C, Emans SJ. Adolescent endometriosis. J Adolesc Health Care 1980;1:37–41.
2. Vercellini P, Fedele L, Arcaini L, Bianchi S, Rognoni MT, Candiani GB. Laparoscopy in the diagnosis of chronic pelvic pain in adolescent women. J Reprod Med 1989;34:827–30.
3. Kontoravdis A, Hassan E, Hassiakos D, Botsis D, Kontoravdis N, Creatsas G. Laparoscopic evaluation and management of chronic pelvic pain during adolescence. Clin Exp Obstet Gynecol 1999;26:76–7.
4. Reese KA, Reddy S, Rock JA. Endometriosis in an adolescent population: the Emory experience. J Pediatr Adolesc Gynecol 1996;9:125–8.
5. Laufer MR, Goitein L, Bush M, Cramer DW, Emans SJ. Prevalence of endometriosis in adolescent girls with chronic pelvic pain not responding to conventional therapy. J Pediatr Adolesc Gynecol 1997;10:199–202.
6. Batt RE, Mitwally MF. Endometriosis from thelarche to midteens: pathogenesis and prognosis, prevention and pedagogy. J Pediatr Adolesc Gynecol 2003;16:337–47.
7. Marsh EE, Laufer MR. Endometriosis in premenarcheal girls without an associated obstructive anomaly. Fertil Steril 2005;83:758–60.
8. Ballweg ML. Big picture of endometriosis helps provide guidance on approach to teens: comparative historical data show endo starting younger, is more severe. J Pediatr Adolesc Gynecol 2003;16(suppl):S21–6.
9. Koninckx PR, Meuleman C, Demeyere S, Lesaffre E, Comillie FJ. Suggestive evidence that pelvic endometriosis is a progressive disease, whereas deeply infiltrating endometriosis is associated with pelvic pain. Fertil Steril 1991;55:759–65.
10. D'Hooghe TM, Bambra CS, Raeymaekers BM, Koninckx PR. Serial laparoscopies over 30 months show that endometriosis in captive baboons (Papio anubis, Papio cynocephalus) is a progressive disease. Fertil Steril 1996;65:645–9.

11. Laufer MR. Identification of clear vesicular lesions of atypical endometriosis: a new technique. Fertil Steril 1997; 68:739–40.
12. Ling FW. Randomized controlled trial of depot leuprolide in patients with chronic pelvic pain and clinically suspected endometriosis. Pelvic Pain Study Group. Obstet Gynecol 1999;93:51–8.
13. American College of Obstetricians and Gynecologists. Medical management of endometriosis. ACOG Practice Bulletin 11. Washington, DC: ACOG; 1999.
14. Laufer MR, Sanfilippo J, Rose G. Adolescent endometriosis: diagnosis and treatment approaches. J Pediatr Adolesc Gynecol 2003;16(suppl):S3–11.
15. Revised American Society for Reproductive Medicine classification of endometriosis: 1996. Fertil Steril 1997; 67:817–21.
16. Sanfilippo JS, Wakim NG, Schikler KN, Yussman MA. Endometriosis in association with uterine anomaly. Am J Obstet Gynecol 1986;154:39–43.
17. Kistner RW. The treatment of endometriosis by inducing pseudopregnancy with ovarian hormones. Fertil Steril 1959;10:539–56.
18. Moore J, Kennedy S, Prentice A. Modern combined oral contraceptives for pain associated with endometriosis. *The Cochrane Database of Systematic Reviews* 1997, Issue 4. Art. No.: CD001019. DOI: 10.1002/14651858.CD001019.
19. Miller L, Hughes JP. Continuous combination oral contraceptive pills to eliminate withdrawal bleeding: a randomized trial. Obstet Gynecol 2003;101:653–61.
20. Vercellini P, Cortesi I, Crosignani PG. Progestins for symptomatic endometriosis: a critical analysis of the evidence. Fertil Steril 1997;68:393–401.
21. Cromer BA, Blair JM, Mahan JD, Zibners L, Naumovski Z. A prospective comparison of bone density in adolescent girls receiving depot-medroxyprogesterone acetate (Depo-Provera), levonorgestrel (Norplant), or oral contraceptives. J Pediatr 1996;129:671–6.
22. Berenson AB, Radecki CM, Grady JJ, Rickert VI, Thomas A. A prospective, controlled study of the effects of hormonal contraception on bone mineral density. Obstet Gynecol 2001;98:576–82.
23. Lara-Torre E, Edwards CP, Perlman S, Hertweck SP. Bone mineral density in adolescent females using depot medroxyprogesterone acetate. J Pediatr Adolesc Gynecol 2004;17:17–21.
24. Black box warning added concerning long-term use of depo-provera contraceptive injection. FDA talk paper. Rockville (MD): U.S. Food and Drug Administration; 2004. Available at: http://www.fda.gov/bbs/topics/ANSWERS/2004/ANS01325.html. Retrieved December 8, 2004.
25. Matkovic V, Jelic T, Wardlaw GM, Ilich JZ, Goel PK, Wright JK, et al. Timing of peak bone mass in Caucasian females and its implication for the prevention of osteoporosis: inference from a cross-sectional model. J Clin Invest 1994;93:799–808.
26. Barbieri RL. Hormone treatment of endometriosis: the estrogen threshold hypothesis. Am J Obstet Gynecol 1992;166:740–5.
27. Surrey ES, Hornstein MD. Prolonged GnRH agonist and add-back therapy for symptomatic endometriosis: long-term follow-up. Obstet Gynecol 2002;99:709–19.
28. Kiesel L, Schweppe KW, Sillem M, Siebzehnrubl E. Should add-back therapy for endometriosis be deferred for optimal results? Br J Obstet Gynaecol 1996;103(suppl 14):15–7.
29. Lubianca JN, Gordon CM, Laufer MR. "Add-back" therapy for endometriosis in adolescents. J Reprod Med 1998; 43:164–72.
30. Abbott J, Hawe J, Hunter D, Holmes M, Finn P, Garry R. Laparoscopic excision of endometriosis: a randomized, placebo-controlled trial. Fertil Steril 2004;82:878–84.
31. Sutton CJ, Ewen SP, Whitelaw N, Haines P. Prospective, randomized, double-blind, controlled trial of laser laparoscopy in the treatment of pelvic pain associated with minimal, mild and moderate endometriosis. Fertil Steril 1994;62:696–700.
32. Sutton CJ, Pooley AS, Ewen SP, Haines P. Follow-up report on a randomized controlled trial of laser laparoscopy in the treatment of pelvic pain associated with minimal to moderate endometriosis. Fertil Steril 1997;68: 1070–4.
33. Jacobson TZ, Barlow DH, Garry R, Koninckx PR. Laparoscopic surgery for pelvic pain associated with endometriosis. *The Cochrane Database of Systematic Reviews* 2001, Issue 4. Art. No.: CD001300. DOI: 10.1002/14651858.CD001300.

# ACOG Committee Opinion

Committee on Adolescent Health Care

Number 314, September 2005

# Meningococcal Vaccination for Adolescents

*ABSTRACT: Every year in the United States, approximately 1,400–2,800 individuals are infected with meningococcal disease. The Advisory Committee on Immunization Practices (ACIP) to the Centers for Disease Control and Prevention (CDC) released recommendations in early 2005 to reduce the incidence of meningococcal disease during adolescence and young adulthood. To achieve this goal, routine vaccination of preadolescents with meningococcal conjugate vaccine (MCV4) is now recommended. For adolescents who have not received MCV4, the CDC now recommends vaccination before entry into high school, at approximately 15 years of age. The American College of Obstetricians and Gynecologists supports these recommendations and encourages all health care providers caring for adolescent and young adult patients to provide meningococcal vaccination with MCV4 when appropriate. This includes vaccination of college freshmen who live in dormitories. Pregnant women may be vaccinated with meningococcal polysaccharide vaccine (MPSV4) as indicated. Health care providers also are encouraged to discuss meningococcal vaccination with patients whose children have reached preadolescence, adolescence, or young adulthood and to increase awareness of the signs and symptoms of meningococcal disease.*

## Background

Meningococcal disease is caused by bacteria (*Neisseria meningitidis*) that infect the bloodstream and the meninges, resulting in serious illness. Every year in the United States, approximately 1,400–2,800 individuals are infected with meningococcal disease. *Neisseria meningitidis* has become a leading cause of bacterial meningitis in the United States. Ten percent to 14% of individuals with meningococcal disease die, and 11–19% percent of those who survive have permanent disabilities, such as mental retardation, hearing loss, and loss of limbs (1). The disease often begins with generalized symptoms that can be mistaken for a common illness, such as the flu. Meningococcal disease is particularly dangerous because it progresses rapidly and can be fatal within hours (2). Therefore, it is important to prevent the disease, through use of meningococcal vaccination, for individuals at highest risk.

Two meningococcal vaccines are available in the United States, meningococcal polysaccharide vaccine (MPSV4) and meningococcal conjugate vac-

This information should not be construed as dictating an exclusive course of treatment or procedure to be followed.



ISSN 1074-861X

**The American College of Obstetricians and Gynecologists**
409 12th Street, SW
PO Box 96920
Washington, DC 20090-6920

12345/98765

Meningococcal vaccination for adolescents. ACOG Committee Opinion No. 314. American College of Obstetricians and Gynecologists. Obstet Gynecol 2005;106:667–9.

cine (MCV4). Studies indicate that both vaccines can prevent four types of meningococcal disease (serogroups A, C, Y, W-135). Of all cases of meningococcal disease among individuals 11 years and older, 75% are caused by serogroups C, Y, or W-135. Both vaccines protect approximately 90% of individuals vaccinated.

Meningococcal polysaccharide vaccine is a tetravalent meningococcal polysaccharide vaccine that has been available in the United States since the 1970s. Each dose consists of purified bacterial capsular polysaccharides (50 μg each) from serogroups A, C, Y, and W-135. Meningococcal polysaccharide vaccine is available in single-dose (0.5 mL) and 10-dose (5 mL) vials (1).

Meningococcal conjugate vaccine is a tetravalent meningococcal conjugate vaccine that was licensed for use in the United States in January 2005. A 0.5-mL single dose of vaccine contains 4 μg each of capsular polysaccharide from serogroups A, C, Y, and W-135 conjugated to 48 μg of diphtheria toxoid. Meningococcal conjugate vaccine is available only in single-dose vials and is expected to be more effective, longer lasting, and more capable of preventing transmission of the disease from person to person (1).

These vaccines have been shown to be highly effective at reducing meningococcal disease. However, they do not protect individuals against meningococcal disease caused by serogroup B of *N meningitidis*. This type of bacteria causes one third of all meningococcal cases. More than half of the cases among infants younger than 1 year are caused by serogroup B, for which no vaccine is available in the United States (1).

Studies of vaccination with MPSV4 during pregnancy have not documented adverse effects among either pregnant women or newborns. On the basis of these data, the Centers for Disease Control and Prevention (CDC) states that pregnancy should not preclude vaccination with MPSV4, if indicated. No data are available on the safety of MCV4 during pregnancy (1).

## Recommendations of the Advisory Committee on Immunization Practices to the Centers for Disease Control and Prevention

The Advisory Committee on Immunization Practices (ACIP) to the CDC released recommendations in early 2005 to reduce meningococcal disease during adolescence and young adulthood. Routine vaccination of preadolescents 11–12 years of age with MCV4 is now recommended. For adolescents who have not received MCV4, the CDC now recommends vaccination before entry into high school, at approximately 15 years of age. The goal is to implement, within 3 years, routine vaccination with MCV4 of all preadolescents beginning at 11 years of age. Other adolescents and young adults who want to decrease their risk for meningococcal disease also can be given the immunization. The recommendations state that MCV4 is preferred, but MPSV4 is acceptable (1).

Meningococcal vaccination also is recommended for other high-risk groups including (1):

- Anyone traveling to or living in a part of the world where meningococcal disease is endemic
- Anyone who is asplenic or has a damaged spleen
- Anyone who has terminal complement component deficiency (an immune system disorder)
- Anyone possibly exposed to meningitis during an outbreak
- Young men and women entering the military
- College freshmen living in dormitories

College freshmen who live in dormitories are at higher risk for meningococcal disease than other individuals of the same age because lifestyle factors common among freshman college students appear to be linked to the disease. These factors include: living in crowded housing, going to bars, smoking, and having irregular sleeping habits. Because of the feasibility constraints in targeting freshmen in dormitories, the CDC indicates that colleges may elect to target their vaccination campaigns to all matriculating freshmen. The risk for meningococcal disease among nonfreshmen college students is similar to that for the general population of similar age (18–24 years). However, the vaccines are safe and immunogenic and can be provided to nonfreshmen college students who want to reduce their risk for meningococcal disease (1).

## ACOG Recommendations

The American College of Obstetricians and Gynecologists supports the recommendations of the ACIP for routine vaccination of preadolescents against meningococcal disease. Several medical professional organizations, including the American Academy of Pediatrics, the Society for Adolescent Medicine, and the American Academy of Family Physicians also support the recommendations of the ACIP (3–5). The American College of Obstetricians and Gynecologists encourages all health care providers caring for adolescent and young adult patients to provide meningococcal vaccination with MCV4 when appropriate. Because of the lack of data regarding the safety of MCV4 during pregnancy, MPSV4 can be considered for adolescents and young adults who are pregnant and those having unprotected sex who may be at risk for unintended pregnancy. Health care providers are encouraged to discuss meningococcal vaccination with patients whose children have reached preadolescence, adolescence, or young adulthood. It is important to increase parents', adolescents', and young adults' awareness of the signs and symptoms of meningococcal disease even though they are frequently nonspecific. This can result in earlier medical care and improved clinical outcomes.

## References

1. Bilukha OO, Rosenstein N. Prevention and control of meningococcal disease. Recommendations of the Advisory Committee on Immunization Practices (ACIP). National Center for Infectious Diseases, Centers for Disease Control and Prevention (CDC). MMWR Recomm Rep 2005;54(RR-7):1-21. Available at: http://www.cdc.gov/mmwr/preview/mmwrhtml/rr5407a1.htm. Retrieved June 6, 2005.
2. Centers for Disease Control and Prevention. Meningococcal vaccines: what you need to know. Available at http://www.cdc.gov/nip/publications/vis/vis-mening.rtf. Retrieved May 18, 2005.
3. American Academy of Family Physicians. Meningococcal immunization. Available at: http://www.aafp.org/x34406.xml. Retrieved June 8, 2005.
4. Middleman AB, Rickert VI, Rosenthal SL. Meningococcal vaccine: position statement of the Society for Adolescent Medicine. J Adolesc Health 2005;37:262.
5. Prevention and control of meningococcal disease: recommendations for use of meningococcal vaccines in pediatric patients. Pediatrics 2005;116:496–505.

# ACOG Committee Opinion

Committee on Adolescent Health Care

Number 330, April 2006

## Evaluation and Management of Abnormal Cervical Cytology and Histology in the Adolescent

*ABSTRACT: The management of abnormal cervical cytology in adolescents differs from that for the adult population in many cases. Certain characteristics of adolescents may warrant special management considerations. It is important to avoid aggressive management of benign lesions in adolescents because most cervical intraepithelial neoplasia grades 1 and 2 regress. Surgical excision or destruction of cervical tissue in a nulliparous adolescent may be detrimental to future fertility and cervical competency. Care should be given to minimize destruction of normal cervical tissue whenever possible. A compliant, health-conscious adolescent may be adequately served with observation in many situations.*

This document reflects emerging clinical and scientific advances as of the date issued and is subject to change. The information should not be construed as dictating an exclusive course of treatment or procedure to be followed.

The College wishes to thank Richard Guido, MD, and Abigail English, JD, for their assistance in the development of this document.



ISSN 1074-861X

**The American College of Obstetricians and Gynecologists**
409 12th Street, SW
PO Box 96920
Washington, DC 20090-6920

12345/09876

Evaluation and management of abnormal cervical cytology and histology in the adolescent. ACOG Committee Opinion No. 330. American College of Obstetricians and Gynecologists. Obstet Gynecol 2006;107:963–8.

### Background

The past decade has seen a remarkable increase in the knowledge of the natural history of cervical dysplasia, the role of human papillomavirus (HPV) in cervical cancer, and the development of new technologies for cervical cancer screening, specifically HPV testing and liquid-based cytology. This new information prompted the American Cancer Society (ACS) to develop new guidelines pertaining to cervical cancer screening (1). Based on the natural history data and the rarity of cervical cancer in the population of women younger than 21 years, the ACS recommendations for initial Pap testing changed, and the new criteria have been endorsed by the American College of Obstetricians and Gynecologists (ACOG) (2). Adolescents should undergo their first Pap test approximately 3 years after the onset of vaginal intercourse or no later than age 21 years. The decision about the initiation of cervical cytology screening in an adolescent patient should be based on the clinician's assessment of risks, including 1) age of first sexual activity, 2) behaviors that may place the adolescent patient at greater risk for HPV infection, and 3) risk of noncompliance with follow-up visits. Obtaining a complete and accurate sexual history, therefore, is critical (3).

The new information also prompted ACOG to develop new guidelines on the management of abnormal cervical cytology and histology (4). Some of these guidelines are unique for adolescents. The objectives of this Committee Opinion are to 1) highlight when the management of abnormal cervical cytology in adolescents differs from that for the adult population and 2) identify characteristics of adolescents that may warrant special considerations. It is important to avoid aggressive management of benign lesions in adolescents because most cervical intraepithelial neoplasia (CIN) grades 1 and 2 regress. Surgical excision or destruction of cervical tissue in a nulliparous adolescent may be detrimental to future fertility and cervical competency. Care should be given to minimize destruction of normal cervical tissue whenever possible. A compliant, health-conscious adolescent may be adequately served with observation in many situations.

### *Natural History of Human Papillomavirus*

Most women infected with HPV are asymptomatic. The virus is detected by an abnormal Pap test result, HPV test result, or the presence of clinically evident genital warts, and most likely will resolve without treatment. In natural history studies of adolescents with newly acquired HPV infection, the average length of detectable HPV is 13 months. In most adolescent patients with an intact immune system, an HPV infection will resolve within 24 months (5). Further evidence that the HPV infection will resolve without treatment comes from the high rates of resolution of CIN 1 and CIN 2, 70% and 50% respectively (6–9).

### *Managing Abnormal Cervical Cytology in Adolescents*

The new guidelines provided by ACOG address the therapy of cytologic and histologic abnormalities. These guidelines are based on best evidence when possible and expert opinion when limited data are available. For some but not all of the abnormalities, the guidelines have specific recommendations for care of the adolescent population that may differ from recommendations for adults and are summarized in Table 1. The following recommendations are unique to the adolescent population and address the clinical situations that can be managed by cytologic follow-up, HPV testing, colposcopy, or a combination of these approaches. A positive HPV test result refers to the presence of high-risk HPV DNA as determined by Hybrid Capture II. Testing for low-risk HPV types has no role in cervical cancer prevention.

## Management Considerations

### *Atypical Squamous Cells of Undetermined Significance*

Atypical squamous cells of undetermined significance (ASC-US) is a cytologic abnormality that in many cases identifies a woman harboring HPV infection. In the adolescent population, the prevalence of HPV in ASC-US will be higher than its prevalence in the older population. The risk of invasive cancer in adolescents approaches zero, and the likelihood of HPV clearance is very high. The preferred method of triage for patients with ASC-US who have undergone liquid-based cytologic screening is testing for high-risk HPV and, for those with a positive test result, triage to colposcopy. The ACOG guidelines address the high rate of HPV clearance by allowing less expensive alternative care than immediate colposcopy for adolescents with ASC-US and a positive high-risk HPV test result. Adolescents with atypical squamous cells and high-risk HPV-positive results may be monitored with cytology twice at 6-month intervals or a single high-risk HPV test at 12 months. If repeat cytology test results are abnormal, or there is evidence of persistent HPV, colposcopy should be performed. These alternatives are equally sensitive for the detection of CIN 2, CIN 3, or cervical cancer; avoid the expense of colposcopy and biopsy; and allow for the clearance of CIN and HPV (10). Immediate colposcopy is an acceptable alternative for the management of the adolescent who tests positive for ASC-US and HPV. Adolescents with ASC-US who have an HPV test result negative for high-risk HPV DNA should have a Pap test in 12 months.

### *Low-Grade Squamous Intraepithelial Lesions or Atypical Squamous Cells: Cannot Exclude High-Grade Squamous Intraepithelial Lesions*

The Atypical Squamous Cells of Undetermined Significance/Low-Grade Squamous Intraepithelial Lesions Triage Study (ALTS) has demonstrated that the patients with the cytologic report of low-grade squamous intraepithelial lesions (LSIL) and ASC-US behave in a very similar manner with regard to the clearance of HPV and the risk for developing

**Table 1.** Summary of Treatment Recommendations for Cytologic and Histologic Abnormalities in Adolescent and Adult Patients

| Diagnosis | ACOG Recommendations for Adults | ACOG Alternative Recommendations for Adolescents |
|---|---|---|
| ASC-US with positive high-risk HPV | Immediate colposcopy | Repeat Pap test in 6 and 12 months or high-risk HPV test alone in 12 months |
| ASC-US with negative high-risk HPV | Repeat Pap test in 12 months | Repeat Pap test in 12 months |
| ASC-H | Colposcopy | Colposcopy |
| LSIL | Colposcopy | Repeat Pap test in 6 and 12 months or high-risk HPV test alone in 12 months |
| HSIL | Colposcopy | Colposcopy |
| AGC | Colposcopy, endocervical assessment, possible endometrial evaluation | Colposcopy, endocervical assessment, possible endometrial evaluation |
| Cancer | Colposcopy with endocervical assessment | Colposcopy with endocervical assessment |
| CIN 1 | Pap test at 6 and 12 months or high-risk HPV test at 12 months, colposocopy for any abnormality | Pap test at 6 and 12 months or high-risk HPV test at 12 months, colposocopy for any abnormality |
| CIN 2 | Ablative or excision therapy | Close follow-up at 4–6 month intervals (cytology or colposcopy)* |
| CIN 3 | Ablative or excision therapy | Ablative or excision therapy |

ACOG indicates American College of Obstetricians and Gynecologists; AGC, atypical glandular cells; ASC-H, atypical squamous cells: cannot rule out high-grade squamous intraepithelial lesions; ASC-US, atypical squamous cells of undetermined significance; CIN, cervical intraepithelial neoplasia; HPV, human papillomavirus; HSIL, high-grade squamous intraepithelial lesions; LSIL, low-grade squamous intraepithelial lesions.

*Close follow-up without therapy is not appropriate for patients with a history of proven noncompliance.

Cervical cytology screening. ACOG Practice Bulletin No. 45. American College of Obstetricians and Gynecologists. Obstet Gynecol 2003;102:417–27.

CIN 2, CIN 3, or cervical cancer. Because of the similarity in natural history of these two reports, the ACOG recommendations for treatment of LSIL are identical to those for ASC-US-positive HPV. Adolescents with an LSIL test result can be monitored by repeat cytology at 6-month intervals or by a high-risk HPV test in 12 months. These individuals should undergo colposcopy for any cytologic abnormality or the persistence of HPV infection at 1 year. Immediate colposcopy is an acceptable alternative for adolescents with LSIL (see Fig. 1).

No studies specifically address atypical squamous cells: cannot rule out high-grade squamous intraepithelial lesions (ASC-H) in adolescents. Because of a lack of specific evidence and the higher rate of CIN 2, CIN 3, and cervical cancer in individuals with ASC-H, the adolescent with ASC-H should undergo immediate colposcopic evaluation.

### *High-Grade Squamous Intraepithelial Lesions*

High-grade squamous intraepithelial lesions (HSIL) are a significant cytologic abnormality that requires colposcopic evaluation because of a much higher rate of histologically confirmed CIN 2, CIN 3, or cervical cancer. Colposcopy with endocervical assessment is the recommended treatment for adult and adolescent women with HSIL. In the adult population, ACOG guidelines include a "see and treat" alternative for individuals with HSIL using a loop electrosurgical excision procedure (LEEP). Although this is an acceptable alternative in the adult, it should be avoided in the adolescent population. A significant number of adolescents with HSIL will have CIN 2 on biopsy. Because of the high rate of resolution of CIN 2 in adolescents and the low rate of cervical cancer, adolescents with biopsy-confirmed CIN 2 with adequate colposcopy and normal histology test results on endocervical assessment may be monitored without intervention. The specific method of follow-up should be individualized by the health care professional. A reasonable approach to the follow-up could be either cytology or colposcopy at 4–6-month intervals.

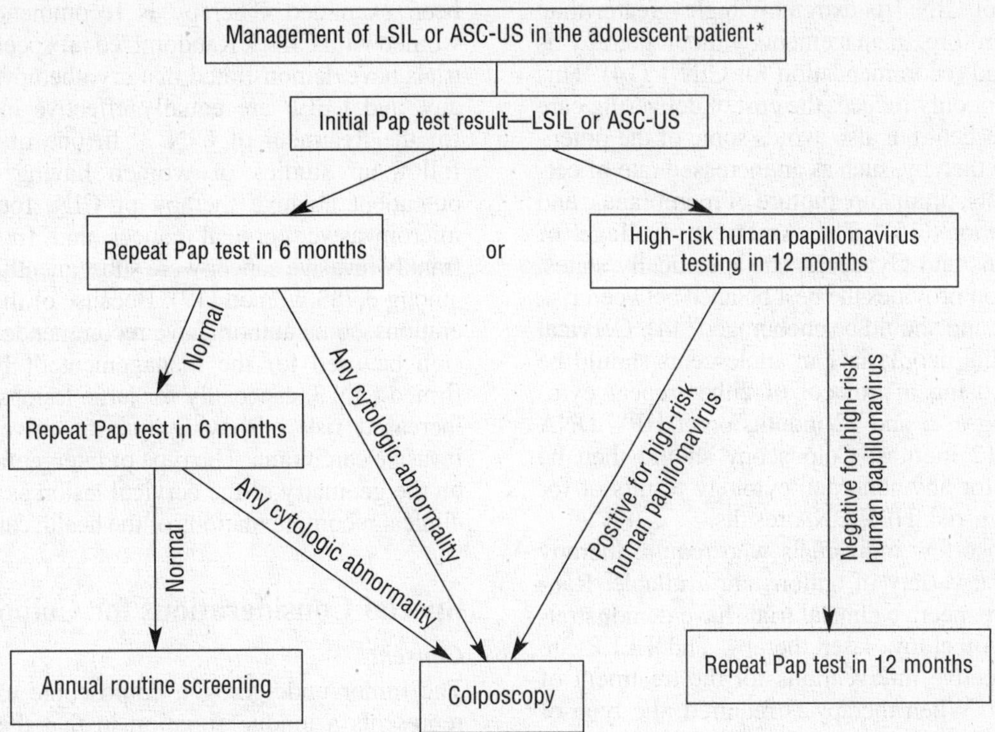


**Fig. 1.** Management of low-grade squamous intraepithelial lesions (LSIL) or atypical squamous cells of undetermined significance (ASC-US) in the adolescent patient.

### *Postcolposcopy Diagnosis of CIN 1 or Less in an Adolescent With HSIL Cytology*

Because interobserver variability is most pronounced in younger women (11), the risk of invasive cancer is extremely low, and the likelihood of spontaneous resolution of CIN 1 or CIN 2 is high, follow-up with colposcopy and cytology at 4–6 months may be undertaken (12), as long as the colposcopy is adequate and the endocervical assessment is negative. Excision is an acceptable alternative to colposcopic follow-up, but it is known to increase the risk of cervical stenosis and preterm labor.

### *Atypical Glandular Cells*

The Bethesda 2001 system for reporting cytologic abnormalities separates atypical glandular cells (AGC) into "not otherwise specified" (NOS) and "favor dysplasia." The cytology report further classifies the abnormalities based on the probable location of the cell of origin (endocervix, endometrium, or unknown). The prevalence of AGC cytology in the adolescent population is very low, and most of these abnormalities will arise from the squamous component of the cervix (13). Because of the rare nature of this diagnosis, a gynecologist with expertise in managing cervical dysplasia should manage cases of AGC cytology in the adolescent. The adolescent with AGC should undergo a colposcopy and endocervical sampling. Endometrial sampling would not be used in most adolescents unless they are morbidly obese, they have abnormal uterine bleeding or oligomenorrhea, or there is a suspicion of endometrial cancer.

### *Treatment of Dysplasia in Adolescents*

#### Cervical Intraepithelial Neoplasia 1

Depending on the time from HPV exposure to evaluation, the adolescent who is infected may have a normal cervix, a mildly abnormal cervix, or biopsy-confirmed CIN 1. Assuming that CIN 2 or greater has been ruled out by colposcopy, prospective studies of an adult population demonstrate that the risk of CIN 2 or greater developing over a 2-year period is 10% (10). In the adolescent population, the rate of resolution of CIN 1 is extremely high (greater than 85%). Therefore, management without therapy is the preferred recommendation for CIN 1 (14). This approach not only reduces the cost of delivering care to the adolescent but also avoids some of the potential risks of therapy, such as an increased rate of cervical stenosis, premature rupture of membranes, and preterm labor (15). The American College of Obstetricians and Gynecologists specifically states, "Observation provides the best balance between risk and benefit and should be encouraged" (4). Cervical intraepithelial neoplasia 1 in adolescents should be monitored using a protocol of either repeat cytologic testing at 6 and 12 months or of HPV DNA testing at 12 months. Colposcopy should then be performed for any abnormal cytology results or for positive high-risk HPV DNA results.

For those few individuals who require therapy for CIN 1, a variety of options are available. Randomized prospective clinical trials have demonstrated that cryotherapy, laser therapy, and LEEP are equally effective interventions for the treatment of CIN 1 (16). When therapy is required, the type of intervention is based on the geometry of the cervical lesion as well as the clinical recommendations of the clinician who is caring for the patient. Care should be taken to remove the least amount of cervical tissue that is necessary to eradicate the lesion.

#### Cervical Intraepithelial Neoplasia 2

Cervical intraepithelial neoplasia 2 is a significant abnormality that has classically required therapy. A variety of studies, including the ALTS trial, have demonstrated that this lesion may have a significant rate of resolution (up to 40%) in adults. This rate of resolution is suspected to be higher in adolescents. Based on these data and expert opinion, CIN 2 can be managed in adolescents with either observation or ablative or excision therapy. The adolescent patient who is monitored without therapy should be an individual deemed to be reliable regarding follow-up and have a good understanding of the nature of the abnormality and its risks. Follow-up can be individualized, with colposcopy or cytology every 4–6 months being a very conservative approach.

#### Cervical Intraepithelial Neoplasia 3

Cervical intraepithelial neoplasia 3 is a significant cervical abnormality. Despite the fact that cervical cancer is very rare in the adolescent population, the natural history of CIN 3 in this population has not been examined. Therapy is recommended for all women with CIN 3. Randomized prospective clinical trials have demonstrated that cryotherapy, laser therapy, and LEEP are equally effective interventions for the treatment of CIN 3. In one of the largest follow-up studies of women having undergone outpatient ablative therapy of CIN, four cases of microinvasive cervical cancer and five cases of frankly invasive cancer were subsequently diagnosed among 3,783 women (17). Because of these considerations, some authors have recommended that excision be used for the management of biopsy-confirmed CIN 3, especially for large lesions that are at increased risk of having microinvasive or occult invasive carcinoma. The type of intervention is based on the geometry of the cervical lesion as well as the clinical recommendations of the health care provider.

## Special Considerations for Colposcopy

### *Consent*

The minor undergoing a colposcopic examination represents a unique situation in that the abnormal Pap test result frequently is obtained during confidential screening for sexually transmitted diseases (STDs) or during counseling for contraception. Both interactions frequently occur without the knowledge of a parent or guardian.

Minors undergoing a colposcopic examination might find it helpful to have parental involvement for the procedure. However, colposcopic examinations are considered evaluation for STDs, and minors generally are allowed to consent for diagnosis of STDs (18). For that reason, parental consent, although preferred, should not be required. If parental consent is not obtained, consent for the examination should be obtained from the minor and indicated in the medical record.

The issues regarding parental consent for biopsy or therapy for cervical dysplasia are more complicated. The need for consent depends on whether the biopsy or therapy is considered part of STD evaluation and treatment and on the specifics of state law. Even if the minor legally can consent, the law may not ensure confidentiality. Some states allow minors to consent for STD care but give the health care provider discretion to disclose information to parents, particularly if it is necessary to protect the minor's health (18).

Biopsy and therapy for cervical dysplasia are more invasive than a colposcopic examination and carry a higher risk of complication. They also are likely to generate a bill, which can compromise confidentiality. These issues need to be considered when determining whether parental consent should be obtained, even if it is not legally required, before providing biopsy or therapy for a minor. Medical care providers throughout the United States provide such care without parental consent under the umbrella of the treatment of STDs. Any health care provider who delivers such care should be fully informed of their state laws and established local standards of care.

### *Screening for Sexually Transmitted Diseases*

The adolescent population represents an at-risk population for cervical infection, specifically chlamydia and gonorrhea. Little evidence exists to support the routine screening of the cervix for chlamydia and gonorrhea before performing a colposcopy. Screening for STDs should be based on the ACOG guidelines for screening adolescents who are sexually active (19, 20).

## References


1. Saslow D, Runowicz CD, Solomon D, Moscicki AB, Smith RA, Eyre HJ, et al. American Cancer Society guideline for the early detection of cervical neoplasia and cancer. American Cancer Society. CA Cancer J Clin 2002;52:342–62.
2. Cervical cytology screening. ACOG Practice Bulletin No. 45. American College of Obstetricians and Gynecologists. Obstet Gynecol 2003:102:417–27.
3. Cervical cancer screening in adolescents. ACOG Committee Opinion No. 300. American College of Obstetricians and Gynecologists. Obstet Gynecol 2004; 104:885–9.
4. Management of abnormal cervical cytology and histology. ACOG Practice Bulletin No. 66. American College of Obstetricians and Gynecologists. Obstet Gynecol 2005; 106:645–64.
5. Woodman CB, Collins S, Winter H, Bailey A, Ellis J, Prior P, et al. Natural history of cervical human papillomavirus infection in young women: a longitudinal cohort study. Lancet 2001;357:1831–6.
6. Results of a randomized trial on the management of cytology interpretations of atypical squamous cells of undetermined significance. ASCUS-LSIL Triage Study (ALTS) Group. Am J Obstet Gynecol 2003;188:1383–92.
7. A randomized trial on the management of low-grade squamous intraepithelial lesion cytology interpretations. ASCUS-LSIL Triage Study (ALTS) Group. Am J Obstet Gynecol 2003;188:1393–400.
8. Human papillomavirus testing for triage of women with cytologic evidence of low-grade squamous intraepithelial lesions: baseline data from a randomized trial. The Atypical Squamous Cells of Undetermined Significance/ Low-Grade Squamous Intraepithelial Lesions Triage Study (ALTS) Group. J Natl Cancer Inst 2000;92: 397–402.
9. Cox JT, Schiffman M, Solomon D. Prospective follow-up suggests similar risk of subsequent cervical intraepithelial neoplasia grade 2 or 3 among women with cervical intraepithelial neoplasia grade 1 or negative colposcopy and directed biopsy. ASCUS-LSIL Triage Study (ALTS) Group. Am J Obstet Gynecol 2003;188:1406–12.
10. Guido R, Schiffman M, Solomon D, Burke L. Postcolposcopy management strategies for women referred with low-grade squamous intraepithelial lesions of human papillomavirus DNA-positive atypical squamous cells of undetermined significance: a two-year prospective study. ASCUS-LSIL Triage Study (ALTS) Group. Am J Obstet Gynecol 2003;188:1401–5.
11. Kato I, Santamaria M, De Ruiz PA, Aristizabal N, Bosch FX, De Sanjose S, et al. Inter-observer variation in cytological and histological diagnoses of cervical neoplasia and its epidemiologic implication. J Clin Epidemiol 1995;48:1167–74.
12. Hellberg D, Nilsson S, Valentin J. Positive cervical smear with subsequent normal colposcopy and histology—frequency of CIN in a long-term follow-up. Gynecol Oncol 1994;53:148–51.
13. Raab SS. Can glandular lesions be diagnosed in pap smear cytology? Diagn Cytopathol 2000;23:127–33.
14. Moscicki AB, Shiboski S, Hills NK, Powell KJ, Jay N, Hanson EN, et al. Regression of low-grade squamous intra-epithelial lesions in young women. Lancet 2004; 364:1678–83.
15. Sadler L, Saftlas A, Wang W, Exeter M, Whittaker J, McCowan L. Treatment for cervical intraepithelial neoplasia and risk of preterm delivery. JAMA 2004;291: 2100–6.
16. Mitchell MF, Tortolero-Luna G, Cook E, Whittaker L, Rhodes-Morris H, Silva E. A randomized clinical trial of cryotherapy, laser vaporization, and loop electrosurgical excision for treatment of squamous intraepithelial lesions of the cervix. Obstet Gynecol 1998;92:737–44.
17. Pearson SE, Whittaker J, Ireland D, Monaghan JM. Invasive cancer of the cervix after laser treatment. Br J Obstet Gynaecol 1989;96:486–8.
18. English A, Kenney KE. State minor consent laws: a summary. 2nd ed. Chapel Hill (NC): Center for Adolescent Health & the Law; 2003.
19. Sexually transmitted diseases in adolescents. ACOG Committee Opinion No. 301. American College of Obstetricians and Gynecologists. Obstet Gynecol 2004; 104:891–8.
20. Harel Z, Riggs S. On the need to screen for Chlamydia and gonorrhea infections prior to colposcopy in adolescents. J Adolesc Health 1997;21:87–90.


## Resources


Guidelines on management of women with histological abnormalities. ASCCP Consensus Guidelines. American Society for Colposcopy and Cervical Pathology. Hagerstown (MD): ASCCP; 2003. Available at: http://www.asccp.org/consensus/histological.shtml. Retrieved November 18, 2005.

Guidelines on management of women with cytological abnormalities. ASCCP Consensus Guidelines. American Society for Colposcopy and Cervical Pathology. Hagerstown (MD): ASCCP; 2002. Available at: http://www.asccp.org/consensus/cytological.shtml. Retrieved November 18, 2005.

ACOG Committee Opinion

Committee on Adolescent Health

Number 335, May 2006

This document reflects emerging clinical and scientific advances as of the date issued and is subject to change. The information should not be construed as dictating an exclusive course of treatment or procedure to be followed.

The Committee wishes to thank LeighAnn Frattarelli, MD; Federico Mariona, MD; and Lesley Breech, MD; for their assistance in the development of this document.



ISSN 1074-861X

**The American College of Obstetricians and Gynecologists**
409 12th Street, SW
PO Box 96920
Washington, DC 20090-6920

12345/09876

The initial reproductive health visit. ACOG Committee Opinion No. 335. American College of Obstetricians and Gynecologists. Obstet Gynecol 2006;107:1215–9.

# The Initial Reproductive Health Visit

*ABSTRACT: The American College of Obstetricians and Gynecologists (ACOG) recommends that the first visit to the obstetrician–gynecologist take place between the ages of 13 and 15 years (1). This visit will provide health guidance, screening, and preventive health care services and provide an excellent opportunity for the obstetrician–gynecologist to start a physician–patient relationship. This visit generally does not include an internal pelvic examination.*

## Timing of the Initial Visit

The first visit to the obstetrician–gynecologist for screening and the provision of preventive health care services and guidance should take place between the ages of 13 and 15 years (1, 2). From a developmental standpoint, patients of this age may manifest characteristics of early, middle, or late adolescence. An attempt to determine the patient's developmental stage is helpful during the interview and evaluation because characteristics, such as body image, peer influence, and identity development vary by stage. The scope of the initial visit to the obstetrician–gynecologist will depend on the individual's need, medical history, and her physical and emotional development; however, this visit should not be viewed by the parent or guardian, primary health care provider, or obstetrician–gynecologist as the right time for the first internal pelvic examination, unless indicated.

If feasible, the obstetrician–gynecologist may attempt to concentrate adolescent office visits on a separate office day or time on the schedule. Many adolescents prefer after-school appointments. This will enhance the individual adolescent's understanding of the practitioner's interest in her specific concerns. Also, nonpregnant adolescents often are intimidated by a reception area full of obstetric patients. It also may be helpful to include age-appropriate and culturally inclusive reading materials and audiovisual aids in the reception area and examination rooms. Having one or two rooms where adolescents are seen and examined allows for the removal or de-emphasizing of materials and equipment that may make adolescents uncomfortable when they are being seen.

## Confidentiality

It is helpful to discuss issues of confidentiality with both the adolescent and her parent or guardian (3). Lack of confidentiality often is a barrier to the delivery of health care services, especially reproductive health care, for adolescents. To overcome this obstacle, obstetrician–gynecologists should initiate a discussion of this topic at the initial visit and advise the adolescent and her parent or guardian of relevant state and local statutes. The importance of open communication between the health care provider, patient, and parents or guardians should be emphasized. Parents or guardians and adolescents should be informed of any restrictions on the confidential nature of the physician–patient relationship. For example, the physician should explain that if the patient discloses any evidence or risk of bodily harm to herself or others, confidentiality will be breached (4). Furthermore, state laws mandate the reporting of physical or sexual abuse of minors. Physicians should be familiar with state and local statutes regarding the rights of minors to health care services and the federal and state laws that affect confidentiality. For a listing of state laws that is updated monthly, go to www.guttmacher.org/statecenter/spibs/index.html and consult with your state medical society.

## The Initial Visit

The primary goal of the initial reproductive health visit is to provide preventive health care services, including educational information and guidance, rather than problem-focused care. The visit also allows patients and parents or guardians the chance to visit the office, meet the physician or health care provider, alleviate fears, and develop trust. After greeting the adolescent and parent or guardian, a thorough explanation of the scope of the visit and confidentiality issues should be provided while the patient is dressed and an adult is present.

The scope of the visit will vary based on the needs of the individual and her parents or guardians. Discussions regarding such topics as adolescent development, normal menses, sexual orientation and gender identity, healthy eating habits, safety and injury prevention, and date rape prevention are important.

Conversations regarding normal pubertal development and menstruation can be reassuring both to parents or guardians and patients because frequently neither appreciates the parameters of normal. The use of visual materials, such as models, diagrams, and charts is strongly encouraged for teaching about anatomy and physiology of the reproductive tract. Because menarche and subsequent menses are physiologically and emotionally important milestones in an adolescent's development, it is beneficial to educate patients and their parents or guardians regarding expectations for both menarche, if it has not yet occurred, and normal menstrual variation. Adolescents who have been provided such information seem to experience less anxiety when bleeding occurs (5). Discussions regarding appropriate menstrual flow, menstrual hygiene, and duration and frequency of bleeding can help the adolescent assess what constitutes normal menstrual cycles or patterns of bleeding and avoid delays in evaluation of adolescents with patterns outside the normal range. Initiation of a menstrual diary during adolescence can help identify bleeding patterns that fall outside of established parameters so they may be evaluated and possible abnormalities detected. In addition, assessment for dysmenorrhea and discussion about treatment options is important so that patients do not experience significant morbidity from menstrual cramps.

Inclusion of topics, such as prevention of pregnancy and sexually transmitted diseases (STDs) is important for adolescent females because more than 85% of them will have had some form of sexual contact (vaginal, anal, oral, or same-sex) by age 19 years (6); nearly one third of all ninth graders report having had sexual intercourse, and more than 60% of all twelfth graders report having had sexual intercourse (7). Informing adolescents about the proper use of condoms, other contraceptive options, and the availability and proper use of emergency contraception is important.

Many adolescents will engage in unhealthy and risky behaviors, such as tobacco, alcohol, and other substance use, and these issues should be identified and addressed. Data from the 2003 Youth Risk Behavior Surveillance Report indicate that many adolescents will begin engaging in risk-taking behaviors by age 13 years. For example, 27.8% of adolescents report alcohol use before age 13 years (7). Screening for eating disorders and other weight issues, blood pressure problems, and mental health disturbances, such as anxiety, depression, and physical, sexual, and emotional abuse is important as is a review of immunization status and the provision of appropriate vaccinations. Screening for many of the previously mentioned issues can be facilitated by use of a questionnaire as an alternative to direct interviewing. (See ACOG resources for information on the ACOG Adolescent Visit Record and ACOG Adolescent Visit Questionnaire.) For more information on these topics, refer to the Primary and Preventive Health Care for Female Adolescents chapter of the American College of Obstetricians and Gynecologists' book, *Health Care for Adolescents.*

## Examination

An internal pelvic examination generally is unnecessary during the initial reproductive health visit; a general physical examination, including a visual breast examination and external genital examination, may be done because it allows assessment of secondary sexual development, reassurance, and education. A "teaching" external-only genital examination can provide an opportunity to familiarize adolescents with normal anatomy, assess adequacy of hygiene, and allow the health care provider an opportunity to visualize the perineum for any anomalies. If the patient has had sexual intercourse, screening for STDs is important. Urine-based STD screening is an efficient means for accomplishing such screening without a speculum examination. Because ACOG currently recommends that female adolescents have their first Pap test approximately 3 years after the onset of vaginal intercourse or no later than age 21 years, some adolescents may visit the gynecologist several times before a speculum or manual pelvic examination is indicated. The delay allows the development of a comfortable physician–patient relationship, in addition to adequate patient preparation (8).

An age-appropriate pelvic examination may be performed if issues or problems are discovered in the medical history (eg, pubertal aberrancy, abnormal bleeding, or abdominal or pelvic pain). If a speculum or bimanual examination is necessary, a thorough explanation and patient consent should always precede the procedure. It is helpful to provide the adolescent with written information regarding the first physical pelvic examination if it is to occur (see "Resources"). When choosing a speculum for the examination, the patient's age, developmental status, hymenal opening, and sexual experience should influence the decision. A Huffman speculum (1/2 in. × 4 in.) or a Pederson speculum (7/8 in. × 4 in.) usually is preferred in this population. If a Pap test will be performed, the reason for this test and the steps necessary to obtain the sample should be clearly explained. Many adolescents and their mothers are unaware of the difference between a Pap test and a pelvic examination for any other reason (9).

## Current Procedural Terminology Coding*

To decrease or avoid claim rejections, delays, and denials, the physician's office will be well served by developing a series of resources for accurate coding and billing to be used by health care providers and administrative personnel for the initial reproductive health visit. These resources should contain the "covered benefits" of the office's most frequently billed third-party payers. It also should include the copayment amounts for the different beneficiaries.

### *Preventive Medicine Services*

Code 99384 is used for the initial comprehensive preventive medicine evaluation and management of a new patient aged 12–17 years. It covers the history, examination, counseling/anticipatory guidance/risk factor reduction interventions, and the ordering of appropriate immunization(s) and laboratory or diagnostic procedures. It is important to note that laboratory services, radiologic services, immunizations, and other procedures and screening tests that are identified with their own code are separately reported.

Code 99394 is used for a preventive visit by an established patient, aged 12–17 years. Annual gynecologic visits may be included in this category. Different payers may vary in their definition of an annual gynecologic visit; however, a pelvic and breast examination and a Pap test are included in this nomenclature. It is important to note, however, that a Pap test will likely not be a part of many of the initial visits.

The previously mentioned services are reported for evaluation and management (E/M) services provided to asymptomatic patients and may be used only once a year. The length of time is not reported for these visits. It is important to remember that E/M guidelines do not apply to preventive services codes (see Table 1).

---

### *Individual Counseling in Preventive Medicine*

Code 99401 is used for preventive medicine counseling or risk factor reduction intervention(s) or both provided to an individual as a separate procedure that lasts approximately 15 minutes. This code cannot be used at the same time as the code for an E/M visit. As the time spent on counseling increases to 30 minutes, 45 minutes, and 60 minutes, the code changes to 99402, 99403, and 99404, respectively (see Table 2).

### *Preventive Services and a Problem-Oriented Visit*

When preventive and problem-oriented care are provided in the same visit, two separate codes are necessary:

1. The preventive medicine code
2. The code for added level of E/M service with modifier –25. Check payer for local use of modifiers.

It is important to note that some insurers may not accept preventive and problem-oriented codes during the same encounter. For more information, refer to the *ACOG Tool Kit for Teen Care*.

**Table 1.** Coding Preventive Medicine Visits*

| Description of Preventive Visit | E/M Code |
|---|---|
| New patient visit, age 12–17 years | 99384 |
| New patient visit, age 18–39 years | 99385 |
| Established patient visit, age 12–17 years | 99394 |
| Established patient visit, age 18–39 years | 99395 |

* Rules: Comprehensive history and comprehensive examination suitable for the age group are required. Counseling is preventive in nature. Sometimes during preventive medicine services, a significant, separately identifiable problem or symptom also is evaluated. In these cases, both a problem E/M service and a preventive medicine service may be reported. Modifier –25 is added to problem E/M service. Counseling is included in the comprehensive preventive medicine individual counseling service. The preventive counseling codes may be reported only at a separate encounter.

**Table 2.** Coding Individual Preventive Counseling or Risk Factor Reduction Intervention(s)

| Counseling Time | E/M Code |
|---|---|
| 15 minutes | 99401 |
| 30 minutes | 99402 |
| 45 minutes | 99403 |
| 60 minutes | 99404 |

## Conclusion

The initial visit provides an excellent venue for the obstetrician–gynecologist to start a physician–patient relationship, build trust, and counsel patients and parents or guardians regarding healthy behaviors while dispelling myths and fears. It also will assist an adolescent in establishing a "health home" and negotiating entry into the health care system when she has a specific health care need. Health care for the adolescent should include review of normal menstruation, diet and exercise, healthy sexual decision-making, the development of healthy, safe relationships, immunizations, and injury prevention. Preventive counseling also is beneficial for parents or guardians or other supportive adults and can include discussions regarding physical, sexual, and emotional development; signs and symptoms of common conditions affecting adolescents; and encouragement of lifelong healthy behaviors. The initial reproductive health visit does not include an internal pelvic examination unless indicated by the medical history.

## References


1. American College of Obstetricians and Gynecologists. Primary and preventive health care for female adolescents. In: Health Care for Adolescents. Washington, DC: ACOG; 2003. p. 1–24.
2. Sanfilippo JS, Davis A, Hertweck SP. Obstetrician-gynecologists can and should provide adolescent health care. ACOG Clin Rev 2003;8:1, 15–16.
3. American College of Obstetricians and Gynecologists. Confidentiality in adolescent health care. In: Health Care for Adolescents. Washington, DC: ACOG; 2003. p.25–35.
4. American Medical Association. Policy compendium on confidential health services for adolescents. Chicago (IL): AMA; 1993.
5. Frank D, Williams T. Attitudes about menstruation among fifth-, sixth-, and seventh-grade pre- and post-menarcheal girls. J Sch Nurs 1999;15:25–31.
6. Mosher WD, Chandra A, Jones J. Sexual behavior and selected health measures: men and women 15–44 years of age, United States, 2002. Adv Data 2005;362:1–55.
7. Grunbaum JA, Kann L, Kinchen S, Ross J, Hawkins J, Lowry R, et al. Youth risk behavior surveillance - United States, 2003 [published errata appear in MMWR Morb Mortal Wkly Rep 2004;53:536. MMWR Morb Mortal Wkly Rep 2005;54:608]. MMWR Surveill Summ 2004; 53:1–96.
8. Cervical cancer screening in adolescents. ACOG Committee Opinion No. 300. American College of Obstetricians and Gynecologists. Obstet Gynecol 2004;104:885–9.
9. Blake DR, Weber BM, Fletcher KE. Adolescent and young adult women's misunderstanding of the term Pap smear. Arch Pediatr Adolesc Med 2004;158:966–70.

## Resources

### *ACOG Resources*

American College of Obstetricians and Gynecologists. ACOG Adolescent Visit Record and ACOG Adolescent Visit Questionnaire. Washington, DC: ACOG; 2003.

American College of Obstetricians and Gynecologists. Birth control (Especially for teens). ACOG Patient Education Pamphlet AP112. Washington, DC: ACOG; 2005.

American College of Obstetricians and Gynecologists. Growing up (Especially for teens). ACOG Patient Education Pamphlet AP041. Washington, DC: ACOG; 1997.

Primary and preventive care: periodic assessments. ACOG Committee Opinion No. 292. Obstet Gynecol 2003;102:1117–24.

American College of Obstetricians and Gynecologists. Tool kit for teen care. Washington, DC: ACOG; 2003.

American College of Obstetricians and Gynecologists. You and your sexuality (Especially for teens). ACOG Patient Education Pamphlet AP042. Washington, DC: ACOG; 1996.

American College of Obstetricians and Gynecologists. Your first ob-gyn visit (Especially for teens). ACOG Patient Education Pamphlet AP150. Washington, DC: ACOG; 2001.

### *Other Resources*

The following lists are for information purposes only. Referral to these sources and web sites does not imply the endorsement of ACOG. These lists are not meant to be comprehensive. The exclusion of a source or web site does not reflect the quality of that source or web site. Please note that web sites are subject to change without notice.

American Academy of Family Physicians
11400 Tomahawk Creek Parkway
Leawood, KS 66211-2672
Tel: (913) 906-6000 or 800-274-2237
Web: http://www.aafp.org

American Academy of Pediatrics
141 Northwest Point Boulevard
Elk Grove Village, IL 60007-1098
Tel: (847) 434-4000
Fax: (847) 434-8000
Web: http://www.aap.org

American Medical Association
515 North State Street
Chicago, IL 60610
Tel: (312) 464-5000 or 800-621-8335
Web: http://www.ama-assn.org
and
http://www.ama-assn.org/ama/pub/category/3116.html
(for information on coding resources)

Society for Adolescent Medicine
1916 NW Copper Oaks Circle
Blue Springs, MO 64015
Tel: (816) 224-8010
Fax: (816) 224-8009
Web: http://www.adolescenthealth.org

The Society of Obstetricians and Gynecologists of Canada
780 Echo Drive
Ottawa ON
Canada K1S 5R7
Tel: (613) 730-4192; 800-561-2416
Fax: (613) 730-4314
Web: http://www.sexualityandu.ca

### *Resources for Your Patients and Their Parents or Guardians*

Center for Young Women's Health
333 Longwood Avenue, 5th floor
Boston, MA 02115
Tel: (617) 355-CYWH (2994)
Fax: (617) 730-0192
Web: http://www.youngwomenshealth.org

Go Ask Alice! (by Columbia University Health Education Program)
Lerner Hall
2920 Broadway, 7th Floor
MC 2608
New York, NY 10027
Tel: (212) 854-5453
Fax: (212) 854-8949
Web: http://www.goaskalice.columbia.edu

National Women's Health Information Center (by DHHS Office on Women's Health)
8270 Willow Oaks Corporate Drive
Fairfax, VA 22031
Tel: 800-994-WOMAN (9662)
Web: http://www.4woman.gov
and
www.4girls.gov

ACOG Committee Opinion

Committee on
Adolescent Health Care
and
The ACOG Working
Group on Immunization



The College wishes to thank Eduardo Lara-Torre, MD, Marc R. Laufer, MD, Abigail English, JD, Jennifer E. Dietrich, MD, MSc, Richard S. Guido, MD, John Santelli, MD, MPH, Stanley Gall, MD, and Barbara Moscicki, MD, for their assistance in the development of this document.



ISSN 1074-861X

**The American College of Obstetricians and Gynecologists**
409 12th Street, SW
PO Box 96920
Washington, DC 20090-6920

12345/09876

Human papillomavirus vaccination. ACOG Committee Opinion No. 344. American College of Obstetricians and Gynecologists. Obstet Gynecol 2006;108:699–705.

Number 344, September 2006

# Human Papillomavirus Vaccination

*ABSTRACT: The U.S. Food and Drug Administration recently approved a quadrivalent human papillomavirus (HPV) vaccine for females aged 9–26 years. The American College of Obstetricians and Gynecologists recommends the vaccination of females in this age group. The Advisory Committee on Immunization Practices has recommended that the vaccination routinely be given to girls when they are 11 or 12 years old. Although obstetrician–gynecologists are not likely to care for many girls in this initial vaccination target group, they are critical to the widespread use of the vaccine for females aged 13–26 years. The quadrivalent HPV vaccine is most effective if given before any exposure to HPV infection, but sexually active women can receive and benefit from the vaccination. Vaccination with the quadrivalent HPV vaccine is not recommended for pregnant women. It can be provided to women who are breastfeeding. The need for booster vaccination after 5 years has not been established. Health care providers are encouraged to discuss with their patients the benefits and limitations of the quadrivalent HPV vaccine and the need for continued routine cervical cytology screening.*

The relationship between infection with human papillomavirus (HPV) and both cervical cancer and genital warts has been recognized for many years (1). More than 100 genotypes of HPV have been discovered to date with approximately 30 found in the genital mucosa. However, only 15 have been shown to be associated with cervical cancer. Approximately 70% of cervical cancers result from infection with HPV genotypes 16 and 18, and 90% of cases of genital warts result from infection with HPV genotypes 6 and 11 (2).

The American Cancer Society estimates there will be 9,710 new cases of cervical cancer and 3,700 deaths from cervical cancer in the United States in 2006 (3). Cervical cancer is the second largest cause of female cancer mortality worldwide (4). Worldwide, an estimated 493,000 new cases occur each year and of these cases, 274,000 women die annually from cervical cancer (5). Eighty percent of these deaths occur where resources are the most limited (6). Although the implementation of cervical cytology screening programs and treatment of precancerous lesions has led to a decrease in cervical cancer deaths in the United States, there continues to be a significant population of women not receiving adequate screening. In 2003, only 67% of uninsured women aged 18–64 years obtained cervical cytology screening within the past 3 years compared with 86% of insured women in that age group (7).

The U.S. Food and Drug Administration (FDA) recently licensed the first vaccine shown to be effective at preventing infection with some genotypes of HPV. The prophylactic quadrivalent human papillomavirus L1 virus-like particle vaccine offers protection against cervical cancer, cervical dysplasias, vulvar or vaginal dysplasias, and genital warts associated with HPV genotypes 6, 11, 16, and 18. The FDA approval is for administration of this three-dose vaccine to females aged 9–26 years at intervals of 0, 2, and 6 months (see the box). The need for booster doses remains to be demonstrated (8). To date, protection has been shown to last at least 5 years (9).

A second, bivalent formulation of an HPV vaccine is in development. Results of initial studies of this vaccine indicate that it offers protection similar to the quadrivalent vaccine against HPV infections caused by genotypes 16 and 18 (10, 11).

Studies of the quadrivalent HPV vaccine have shown that in subjects naive to the vaccine genotypes who followed protocol, the vaccine was 100% effective in preventing cervical intraepithelial neoplasia (CIN) 2, CIN 3, and condylomatous vulvar disease related to the HPV genotypes covered by the vaccine (8). In contrast, for a woman with current or past HPV infection, there is no evidence of protection from disease caused by the HPV genotypes with which she was infected. There is, however, evidence of protection from disease caused by the remaining HPV vaccine genotypes (8, 12).

To be maximally effective against all HPV genotypes included in the quadrivalent vaccine, it should be given before any exposure to HPV infection. If the vaccine is given after the onset of sexual activity, patients may have already been infected with HPV and develop abnormal cervical cytology related to the HPV genotypes in the vaccine as well as to those genotypes not included in the vaccine.

## Recommendations

### *Vaccination of Girls, Adolescents, and Young Women*

The American College of Obstetricians and Gynecologists (ACOG) Committee on Adolescent Health Care and the ACOG Working Group on Immunization recommend the vaccination of females aged 9–26 years against HPV. The Advisory Committee on Immunization Practices has recommended the initial vaccination target of females aged 11 or 12 years (13). Although obstetrician–gynecol-

### Key Information Regarding Gardasil

**Dosage:**
The quadrivalent human papillomavirus (HPV) vaccine should be administered intramuscularly as three separate 0.5-mL doses according to the following schedule:

First dose: at elected date

Second dose: 2 months after the first dose

Third dose: 6 months after the first dose

**Storage:**
The quadrivalent vaccine should be refrigerated at 2–8°C (36–46°F). It should not be frozen and should be protected from light.

**Contraindications:**

- Hypersensitivity to the active substances or to any of the excipients of the quadrivalent vaccine. Individuals who develop symptoms indicative of hypersensitivity after receiving a dose of quadrivalent vaccine should not receive further doses of the product.

**Precautions:**

- As with any vaccine, vaccination may not result in protection in all vaccine recipients.
- The quadrivalent vaccine is not intended to be used for treatment of active genital warts; cervical cancer; cervical intraepithelial neoplasia, vulvar intraepithelial neoplasia, or vaginal intraepithelial neoplasia.
- The quadrivalent vaccine has not been shown to protect against disease due to nonvaccine HPV types.
- The vaccine is not recommended for use in pregnant women. The manufacturer maintains a pregnancy registry to monitor fetal outcomes of pregnant women exposed to the vaccine. Any exposure to it during pregnancy can be reported by calling 800-986-8999.

**Vaccine Adverse Event Reporting:**
To report an adverse event associated with administration of the quadrivalent vaccine, go to http://vaers.hhs.gov/.

**Advisory Committee on Immunization Practices Recommendations:**
For current recommendations by the Advisory Committee on Immunization Practices, go to http://www.cdc.gov/nip/ACIP/.

**CPT Code:**
The American Medical Association has established a Current Procedural Terminology* code of 90649 for quadrivalent HPV vaccination.

ogists are not likely to care for many girls in this initial vaccination target group, they are critical to the widespread use of the vaccine for females aged 13–26 years. The American College of Obstetricians and Gynecologists has recommended that the first adolescent reproductive health care visit take place between ages 13 years and 15 years (14). Adolescents and young women aged 16–26 years who are in the vaccination age groups visit obstetrician–gynecologists for primary care, contraceptive or other gynecologic needs, or pregnancy-related services. These visits are a strategic time to discuss HPV and the potential benefit of the HPV vaccine and to offer vaccination to those who have not already received it. During a health care visit with a girl or woman in the age range for vaccination, an assessment of the patient's HPV vaccine status should be conducted and documented in the patient record.

***Cervical Cytology Screening***

Current cervical cytology screening recommendations remain unchanged and should be followed regardless of vaccination status (1, 14–17). Cervical cancer screening should begin approximately 3 years after the onset of vaginal intercourse or no later than age 21 years (16). After the first screening, annual cervical cytology screening should be conducted for women younger than 30 years (17). It must be emphasized that the currently approved quadrivalent vaccine protects against acquisition of HPV genotypes that account for only 70% of HPV-related cervical cancer and only 90% of genital warts cases (2). The vaccine is a preventive tool and is not a substitute for cancer screening.

***Human Papillomavirus Testing***

Testing for HPV is currently not recommended before vaccination. Testing for HPV DNA would not identify past HPV infections, only current HPV infections. Serologic assays for HPV are unreliable and currently not commercially available. Requiring any type of screening test would raise the cost of vaccination programs dramatically and reduce the cost-effectiveness of vaccination.

***Vaccination of Sexually Active Women***

Sexually active women can receive the quadrivalent HPV vaccine. Women with previous abnormal cervical cytology or genital warts also can receive the quadrivalent HPV vaccine. These patients should be counseled that the vaccine may be less effective in women who have been exposed to HPV before vaccination than in women who were HPV naive at the time of vaccination (8, 12). Women with previoius HPV infection will benefit from protection against disease caused by the HPV vaccine genotypes with which they have not been infected. The need for annual cervical cytology screening should be emphasized.

***Vaccination of Women With Previous Cervical Intraepithelial Neoplasia***

There is concern that provision of the vaccination to women with previous CIN may create a false sense of protection, potentially deterring patients from continuing their regular screening and management. The quadrivalent vaccine can be given to patients with previous CIN, but practitioners need to emphasize that the benefits may be limited, and cervical cytology screening and corresponding management based on ACOG recommendations must continue.

***Vaccination Is Not Treatment***

The quadrivalent HPV vaccine is not intended to treat patients with cervical cytologic abnormalities or genital warts. Patients with these conditions should undergo the appropriate evaluation and treatment. It is important to note that many early cytologic abnormalities can be detected and managed conservatively given the significant rate of regression. This is especially true in adolescents and young women (15, 18).

***Vaccination of Pregnant and Lactating Women***

The quadrivalent HPV vaccine has been classified by the FDA as pregnancy category B. Although its use in pregnancy is not recommended, no teratogenic effects have been reported in animal studies. In clinical studies, the proportion of pregnancies with an adverse outcome were comparable in women who received the quadrivalent HPV vaccine and in women who received a placebo (8). The manufacturer's pregnancy registry should be contacted if pregnancy is detected during the vaccination schedule. Completion of the series should be delayed until pregnancy is completed. It is not known whether vaccine antigens or antibodies found in the quadrivalent vaccine are excreted in human milk (8). Lactating women can receive the quadrivalent HPV vaccine because inactivated vaccines such as this vaccine do not affect the safety of breastfeeding for mothers or infants (19).

***Vaccination of Immunosuppressed Patients***

The presence of immunosuppression, like that experienced in patients with HIV infection, is not a contraindication to the quadrivalent HPV vaccine. However, the immune response may be smaller in the immunocompromised patient than in immunocompetent patients (8).

***Vaccination of Women Older Than 26 Years and Males***

Research regarding vaccination of women older than 26 years and males is currently under way. Data available are insufficient to make recommendations for these populations.

***Other Methods for Prevention of HPV Infection***

Abstinence from sexual activity is the most effective way to avoid sexually transmitted diseases (STDs), including HPV infection. Limiting the number of sexual partners also may decrease one's risk for STDs, including HPV. Use of latex condoms is the only method currently available for sexually active individuals to reduce the likelihood of HPV acquisition and HPV-related cervical dysplasia (20, 21).

***Research Needs***

ACOG supports additional research to evaluate the need for booster vaccination, the effectiveness of vaccination in women older than 26 years, and the effectiveness of vaccination of males.

***Educational Efforts***

The quadrivalent HPV vaccine is a major breakthrough in efforts to prevent cervical cancer; obstetrician–gynecologists can play a critical role in its widespread use. It is important for clinicians to provide patient education about HPV-related disease and be prepared to respond to questions from patients regarding the HPV vaccine. Studies have shown that physician recommendation plays an important role in the acceptance of the vaccine by patients (22). Limitations of the currently approved quadrivalent vaccine also should be discussed, including that it provides coverage for only two of the 15 HPV genotypes associated with cancer and only two of the genotypes that cause genital warts. In addition, the health care provider can discuss with patients that despite the high prevalence of HPV infection, few infections result in cervical cancer.

As the HPV vaccines have been developed, market research has addressed the acceptability of HPV vaccination by parents, guardians, and patients. A study of 880 females aged 15–45 years demonstrated that more than 80% of mothers would support vaccinating their daughters. In most additional studies, a higher level of acceptability was associated with educating mothers and patients about the consequences of HPV disease and the potential for decreased rates of cervical cancer (23–25). Professional recommendations for HPV vaccination are essential in ensuring widespread acceptance and use of the vaccine. Requiring vaccination for child care, school, or college attendance and multicomponent interventions that include community education have been effective in improving the use of vaccination (26, 27).

***Consent for HPV Vaccination***

As for all immunizations, consent for HPV vaccination must be obtained from someone who is legally authorized to provide it. Generally, for children and adolescents who are minors, typically those younger than 18 years, the consent of a parent is required for medical care, including vaccinations. There are, however, numerous exceptions to this requirement (28). For example, individuals other than a parent are sometimes authorized to consent for a child or adolescent's care. These may include a legal guardian, a judge, or an individual who has been authorized either by a parent or by a court to consent for a minor's care. In addition, in certain situations, adolescents who are minors are legally allowed to consent to their own care. This is usually determined by state law and varies by state. Depending on the state, certain minors are allowed to consent for care because of their status; these may include minors who have reached a certain age or are pregnant, married, parents, living apart from their parents, or emancipated (28). In all states, minors are allowed to consent for diagnosis and treatment for STDs; however, many of the laws that authorize them to do so do not mention vaccinations (28).

Clinicians should be familiar with state and local statutes regarding the rights of minors to health care services and the federal and state laws that affect confidentiality. When necessary, they should seek appropriate legal advice. Careful analysis would be required to determine the circumstances in which an adolescent minor might be able to consent for her own HPV vaccination in a particular state. Often, state medical societies can be helpful in this capacity. A list of state medical society web sites is available at http://www.ama-assn.org/ama/pub/category/7630.html.

### *Advocacy Efforts*

In the United States, cervical cancer rates are highest for low income and uninsured women. Third party payers and government agencies are encouraged to assist in covering the costs of HPV vaccination to patients, even if they are underinsured or uninsured. Pharmaceutical company–sponsored patient assistance programs for vaccines should be implemented as well as the provision of the vaccine at significantly discounted rates to the Vaccines for Children (VFC) program. The VFC program provides free vaccines to children who are Medicaid-eligible, uninsured, Native American, or underinsured children who visit federally qualified or rural health centers. Health care providers are encouraged to become VFC providers. (For more information, go to http://www.cdc.gov/nip/vfc/.)

## References


1. Human papillomavirus. ACOG Practice Bulletin No. 61. American College of Obstetricians and Gynecologists. Obstet Gynecol 2005;105:905–18.
2. Bosch FX, Manos MM, Munoz N, Sherman M, Jansen AM, Peto J, et al. Prevalence of human papillomavirus in cervical cancer: a worldwide perspective. International biological study on cervical cancer (IBSCC) Study Group. J Natl Cancer Inst 1995;87:796–802.
3. American Cancer Society. Cancer facts and figures 2006. Atlanta (GA): ACS; 2006. Available at: http://www.cancer.org/downloads/STT/CAFF2006PWSecured.pdf. Retrieved June 29, 2006.
4. World Health Organization. State of the art new vaccines: research and development. Initiative for Vaccine Research. Geneva: WHO; 2003. Available at: http://www.who.int/vaccine_research/documents/en/stateofart_excler.pdf. Retrieved November 21, 2003.
5. International Agency for Research on Cancer. GLOBOCAN 2002 database. Lyon (FR): IARC; 2002.
6. Parkin DM, Pisani P, Ferlay J. Estimates of the worldwide incidence of eighteen major cancers in 1985. Int J Cancer 1993;54:594–606.
7. National Center for Health Statistics. Health, United States, 2005 with chartbook on trends in the health of Americans. Hyattsville (MD): NCHS; 2005.
8. Prescribing information for GARDASIL. Whitehouse Station (NJ): Merck & Co., Inc.; 2006. Available at: http://www.merck.com/product/usa/pi_circulars/g/gardasil/gardasil_pi.pdf. Retrieved June 26, 2006.
9. Centers for Disease Control and Prevention. HPV and HPV vaccine—information for healthcare providers. Available at: http://www.cdc.gov/std/HPV/STDFact-HPV-vaccine-hcp.htm#hpvvaccine. Retrieved July 7, 2006.
10. Harper DM, Franco EL, Wheeler C, Ferris DG, Jenkins D, Schuind A, et al. Efficacy of a bivalent L1 virus-like particle vaccine in prevention of infection with human papillomavirus types 16 and 18 in young women: a randomised controlled trial. GlaxoSmithKline HPV Vaccine Study Group. Lancet 2004;364:1757–65.
11. Harper DM, Franco EL, Wheeler CM, Moscicki AB, Romanowski B, Roteli-Martins CM, et al. Sustained efficacy up to 4.5 years of a bivalent L1 virus-like particle vaccine against human papillomavirus types 16 and 18: follow-up from a randomised control trial. Lancet 2006;367:1247–55.
12. Mao C, Koutsky LA, Ault KA, Wheeler CM, Brown DR, Wiley DJ, et al. Efficacy of human papillomavirus-16 vaccine to prevent cervical intraepithelial neoplasia: a randomized controlled trial [published erratum appears in Obstet Gynecol 2006;107:1425]. Obstet Gynecol 2006; 107:18–27.
13. Centers for Disease Control and Prevention. HPV vaccine [human papillomavirus (HPV) and the HPV vaccine]. Atlanta (GA): CDC. Available at: http://www.cdc.gov/nip/vaccine/hpv/. Retrieved July 26, 2006.
14. American College of Obstetricians and Gynecologists. Primary and preventive health care for female adolescents. In: Health care for adolescents. Washington, DC: ACOG; 2003. p. 1–24.
15. Evaluation and management of abnormal cervical cytology and histology in the adolescent. ACOG Committee Opinion No. 330. American College of Obstetricians and Gynecologists. Obstet Gynecol 2006:107:963–8.
16. Cervical cancer screening in adolescents. ACOG Committee Opinion No. 300. American College of Obstetricians and Gynecologists. Obstet Gynecol 2004; 104:885–9.
17. Cervical cytology screening. ACOG Practice Bulletin No. 45. American College of Obstetricians and Gynecologists. Obstet Gynecol 2003;102:417–27.
18. Moscicki AB, Shiboski S, Broering J, Powell K, Clayton L, Jay N, et al. The natural history of human papillomavirus infection as measured by repeated DNA testing in adolescent and young women. J Pediatr 1998;132: 277–84.
19. Atkinson WL, Pickering LK, Schwartz B, Weniger BG, Iskander JK, Watson JC. General recommendations on immunization. Recommendations of the Advisory Committee on Immunization Practices (ACIP) and the American Academy of Family Physicians (AAFP). Centers for Disease Control and Prevention. MMWR Recomm Rep 2002;51(RR-2):1–35.
20. Hogewoning CJ, Bleeker MC, van den Brule AJ, Voorhorst FJ, Snijders PJ, Berkhof J, et al. Condom use promotes regression of cervical intraepithelial neoplasia and clearance of human papillomavirus: a randomized clinical trial. Int J Cancer 2003;107:811–6.
21. Winer RL, Hughes JP, Feng Q, O'Reilly S, Kiviat NB, Holmes KK, et al. Condom use and the risk of genital human papillomavirus infection in young women. N Engl J Med 2006;354:2645–54.
22. Zimet GD, Mays RM, Winston Y, Kee R, Dickes J, Su L. Acceptability of human papillomavirus immunization. J Womens Health Gend Based Med 2000;9:47–50.

23. Lazcano-Ponce E, Rivera L, Arillo-Santillan E, Salmeron J, Hernandez-Avila M, Munoz N. Acceptability of a human papillomavirus (HPV) trial vaccine among mothers of adolescents in Cuernavaca, Mexico. Arch Med Res 2001;32:243–7.
24. Hoover DR, Carfioli B, Moench EA. Attitudes of adolescent/young adult women toward human papillomavirus vaccination and clinical trials. Health Care Women Int 2000;21:375–91.
25. Davis K, Dickman ED, Ferris D, Dias JK. Human papillomavirus vaccine acceptability among parents of 10- to 15-year-old adolescents. J Low Genit Tract Dis 2004; 8:188–94.
26. Centers for Disease Control and Prevention. The guide to community preventive services. Effectiveness of multicomponent interventions that include education to increase vaccination coverage. Atlanta (GA): CDC; 2003. Available at: http://www.thecommunityguide.org/vaccine/vpd-int-demand-multicomponent-ed.pdf. Retrieved July 11, 2006.
27. Centers for Disease Control and Prevention. The guide to community preventive services. Effectiveness of requiring vaccinations for child care, school, and college attendance to increase vaccination coverage. Atlanta (GA): CDC; 2003. Available at: http://www.thecommunityguide.org/vaccine/vpd-int-demand-require.pdf. Retrieved July 11, 2006.
28. English A, Kenney KE. State minor consent laws: a summary. 2nd ed. Chapel Hill (NC): Center for Adolescent Health & the Law; 2003.

## Resources

### *ACOG Resources*

American College of Obstetricians and Gynecologists. Cómo prevenir las enfermedades de transmisión sexual. ACOG Patient Education Pamphlet SP009. Washington, DC: ACOG; 2005.

American College of Obstetricians and Gynecologists. Genital HPV (human papillomavirus) in adolescents fact sheet. Washington, DC: ACOG; 2005.

American College of Obstetricians and Gynecologists. How to prevent sexually transmitted diseases. ACOG Patient Education Pamphlet AP009. Washington, DC: ACOG; 2005.

American College of Obstetricians and Gynecologists. Human papillomavirus infection. ACOG Patient Education Pamphlet AP073. Washington, DC: ACOG; 2003.

American College of Obstetricians and Gynecologists. Tool kit for teen care. Washington, DC: ACOG; 2003.

Cervical cancer screening in adolescents. ACOG Committee Opinion No. 300. American College of Obstetricians and Gyne-cologists. Obstet Gynecol 2004;104:885–9.

Cervical cytology screening. ACOG Practice Bulletin No. 45. American College of Obstetricians and Gynecologists. Obstet Gynecol 2003;102:417–27.

Human papillomavirus. ACOG Practice Bulletin No. 61. American College of Obstetricians and Gynecologists. Obstet Gynecol 2005;105:905–18.

Sexually transmitted diseases in adolescents. ACOG Committee Opinion No. 301. American College of Obstetricians and Gynecologists. Obstet Gynecol 2004;104:891–8.

### *Other Resources*

The following lists are for information purposes only. Referral to these sources and web sites does not imply the endorsement of ACOG. These lists are not meant to be comprehensive. The exclusion of a source or web site does not reflect the quality of that source or web site. Please note that web sites are subject to change without notice. Furthermore, ACOG does not endorse any commercial products that may be advertised or available from these organizations or on these web sites.

American Cancer Society
1599 Clifton Rd. NE
Atlanta, GA 30329
1-800-ACS-2345 (or 1-866-228-4327 for TTY)
http://www.cancer.org

The American Social Health Association
PO Box 13827
Research Triangle Park, NC 27709
(919) 361-8400
(919) 361-8488: National Herpes Hotline
http://www.ashastd.org
http://www.iwannaknow.org
http://www.ashastd.org/hpvccrc

American Society for Colposcopy and Cervical Pathology
20 West Washington St., Suite 1
Hagerstown, MD 21740
(301) 733-3640
1-800-787-7227
http://www.asccp.org

Center for Young Women's Health
Children's Hospital Boston
333 Longwood Ave., 5th Floor
Boston, MA 02115
(617) 355-2994
http://www.youngwomenshealth.org

Centers for Disease Control and Prevention
1600 Clifton Rd.
Atlanta, GA 30333
(404) 639-3311
1-800-311-3435
http://www.cdc.gov
http://www.cdc.gov/std/hpv/STDFact-HPV-vaccine.htm

Go Ask Alice!
Columbia University
7th Floor, Lerner Hall
2920 Broadway, Mail Code 2608
New York, NY 10027
(212) 854-5453
http://www.goaskalice.columbia.edu

Merck Inc.
Make the Connection
1-888-447-8266
http://www.maketheconnection.org

National Cervical Cancer Public Education Campaign
1-866-280-6605
http://www.cervicalcancercampaign.org

National Women's Health Resource Center
157 Broad St., Suite 315
Red Bank, NJ 07701
(732) 530-3425
1-877-986-9472
http://www.healthywomen.org

Planned Parenthood Federation of America
434 West 33rd St.
New York, NY 10001
1-800-230-7526
http://www.plannedparenthood.org
http://www.teenwire.org

Society for Adolescent Medicine
1916 Copper Oaks Circle
Blue Springs, MO 64015
(816) 224-8010
http://www.adolescenthealth.org
http://www.adolescenthealth.org/cme/program_hpv

Society of Obstetricians and Gynaecologists of Canada
780 Echo Drive
Ottawa, ON K1S 5R7
Canada
(613) 730-4192
1-800-561-2416
http://www.sogc.org
http://www.sexualityandu.ca

U.S. Food and Drug Administration
5600 Fishers Lane
Rockville, MD 20857-0001
1-888-INFO-FDA (1-888-463-6332)
http://www.fda.gov/cber/products/hpvmer060806.htm
http://www.fda.gov/womens/getthefacts/hpv.html

ACOG Committee Opinion

Committee on Adolescent Health Care

American Academy of Pediatrics

DEDICATED TO THE HEALTH OF ALL CHILDREN™

Committee on Adolescence

Number 349, November 2006

This document reflects emerging clinical and scientific advances as of the date issued and is subject to change. The information should not be construed as dictating an exclusive course of treatment or procedure to be followed.

The committees would like to thank Lesley Breech, MD; Angela Diaz, MD; S. Paige Hertwick, MD; Paula Adams Hillard, MD; and Marc Laufer, MD, for their assistance in the development of this document.



ISSN 1074-861X

**The American College of Obstetricians and Gynecologists**
409 12th Street, SW
PO Box 96920
Washington, DC 20090-6920

12345/09876

Menstruation in girls and adolescents: using the menstrual cycle as a vital sign. ACOG Committee Opinion No. 349. American Academy of Pediatrics; American College of Obstetricians and Gynecologists. Obstet Gynecol 2006;108:1323–8.

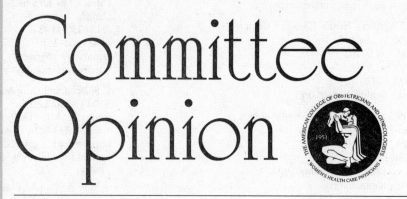

# Menstruation in Girls and Adolescents: Using the Menstrual Cycle as a Vital Sign

*ABSTRACT: Young patients and their parents often are unsure about what represents normal menstrual patterns, and clinicians also may be unsure about normal ranges for menstrual cycle length and amount and duration of flow through adolescence. It is important to be able to educate young patients and their parents regarding what to expect of a first period and about the range for normal cycle length of subsequent menses. It is equally important for clinicians to have an understanding of bleeding patterns in girls and adolescents, the ability to differentiate between normal and abnormal menstruation, and the skill to know how to evaluate young patients' conditions appropriately. Using the menstrual cycle as an additional vital sign adds a powerful tool to the assessment of normal development and the exclusion of serious pathologic conditions.*

Young patients and their parents frequently have difficulty assessing what constitutes normal menstrual cycles or patterns of bleeding. Girls may be unfamiliar with what is normal and may not inform their parents about menstrual irregularities or missed menses. Additionally, girls often are reluctant to discuss this very private topic with a parent, although they may confide in another trusted adult. Some girls will seek medical attention for cycle variations that actually fall within the normal range. Others are unaware that their bleeding patterns are abnormal and may be attributable to significant underlying medical issues with the potential for long-term health consequences.

Clinicians also may be unsure about normal ranges for menstrual cycle length and for amount and duration of flow through adolescence. Clinicians who are confident in their understanding of early menstrual bleeding patterns may convey information to their patients more frequently and with less prompting; girls who have been educated about menarche and early menstrual patterns will experience less anxiety when they occur (1). By including an evaluation of the menstrual cycle as an additional vital sign, clinicians reinforce its importance in assessing overall health status for both patients and parents. Just as abnormal blood pressure, heart rate, or respiratory rate may be key to the diagnosis of potentially serious health conditions, identification of abnormal menstrual patterns through adolescence may permit early identification of potential health concerns for adulthood.

## Normal Menstrual Cycles

### *Menarche*

From the early 1800s to the mid-1950s, menarche occurred at increasingly younger ages in the United States, but there has been no further decline in the past 40–50 years. This finding also has been seen in international studies of other developed urban populations (2). The U.S. National Health and Nutrition Examination Surveys have found no significant change in the median age at menarche over the past 30 years except among the non-Hispanic black population, which has a 5.5-month earlier age at menarche than it did 30 years ago (3). Age at menarche varies internationally and especially in less developed countries; in Haiti, for example, the mean age at menarche is 15.37 years (4, 5). This knowledge may be especially pertinent for practitioners with a large number of immigrant families in their patient population. Although onset of puberty and menarche typically occur at a later age in females from less well-developed nations, two large studies have confirmed that a higher gain in body mass index (BMI) during childhood is related to an earlier onset of puberty (6, 7). This earlier onset of puberty may result from attainment of a minimal requisite body mass at a younger age. Other possible explanations for the perceived trend in timing and progression of puberty are environmental factors, including socioeconomic conditions, nutrition, and access to preventive health care (8).

Despite variations worldwide and within the U.S. population, median age at menarche has remained relatively stable, between 12 and 13 years, across well-nourished populations in developed countries. The median age of females when they have their first period or menarche is 12.43 years (see the box) (3). Only 10% of females are menstruating at age 11.11 years; 90% are menstruating by age 13.75 years. The median age at which black females begin to menstruate is earlier (12.06 years) than the median age for Hispanic females (12.25 years) and non-Hispanic white females (12.55 years) (3). Although black girls start to mature earlier than non-Hispanic white and Hispanic girls, U.S. females complete secondary sexual development at approximately the same ages (9). Menarche typically occurs within 2–3 years after thelarche (breast budding), at Tanner stage IV breast development, and is rare before Tanner stage III development (10). Menarche correlates with age at onset of puberty and breast development. In girls with early onset of breast development, the interval to menarche is longer (3 years or more) than in girls with later onset (11–13). By age 15 years, 98% of females will have had menarche (3, 14). Traditionally, primary amenorrhea has been defined as no menarche by age 16 years; however, many diagnosable and treatable disorders can and should be detected earlier, using the statistically derived guideline of age 14–15 years (3, 14). Thus, an evaluation for primary amenorrhea should be considered for any adolescent who has not reached menarche by 15 years or has not done so within 3 years of thelarche. Accordingly, lack of breast development by age 13 years also should be evaluated (15).

**Normal Menstrual Cycles in Young Females**

| | |
|---|---|
| Menarche (median age): | 12.43 years |
| Mean cycle interval: | 32.2 days in first gynecologic year |
| Menstrual cycle interval: | typically 21–45 days |
| Menstrual flow length: | 7 days or less |
| Menstrual product use: | three to six pads or tampons per day |

### *Cycle Length and Ovulation*

Menstrual cycles often are irregular through adolescence, particularly the interval from the first to the second cycle. According to the World Health Organization's international and multicenter study of 3,073 girls, the median length of the first cycle after menarche was 34 days, with 38% of cycle lengths exceeding 40 days. Variability was wide: 10% of females had more than 60 days between their first and second menses, and 7% had a first-cycle length of 20 days (16). Most females bleed for 2–7 days during their first menses (17–19). Early menstrual life is characterized by anovulatory cycles (20, 21), but the frequency of ovulation is related to both time since menarche and age at menarche (21–23). Early menarche is associated with early onset of ovulatory cycles. When age at menarche is younger than 12 years, 50% of cycles are ovulatory in the first gynecologic year (year after menarche).

By contrast, it may take 8–12 years after menarche until females with later-onset menarche are fully ovulatory (23). Despite variability, most normal cycles range from 21 to 45 days, even in the first gynecologic year (16–18), although short cycles of fewer than 20 days and long cycles of more than 45 days may occur. Because long cycles most often occur in the first 3 years postmenarche, that overall trend is toward shorter and more regular cycles with increasing age. By the third year after menarche, 60–80% of menstrual cycles are 21–34 days long, as is typical of adults (16, 18, 24). An individual's normal cycle length is established around the sixth gynecologic year, at a chronologic age of approximately 19 or 20 years (16, 18).

Two large studies, one cataloging 275,947 cycles in 2,702 females and another reporting on 31,645 cycles in 656 females, support the observation that menstrual cycles in girls and adolescents typically range from 21 to approximately 45 days, even in the first gynecologic year (25, 26). In the first gynecologic year, the fifth percentile for cycle length is 23 days and the 95th percentile is 90 days. By the fourth gynecologic year, fewer females are having cycles that exceed 45 days, but anovulation is still significant for some, with the 95th percentile for cycle length at 50 days. By the seventh gynecologic year, cycles are shorter and less variable, with the fifth percentile for cycle length at 27 days and the 95th percentile at only 38 days. Thus, during the early years after menarche, cycles may be somewhat long because of anovulation, but 90% of cycles will be within the range of 21–45 days (16).

## Abnormal Menstrual Cycles

### *Prolonged Interval*

A number of medical conditions can cause irregular or missed menses. Although secondary amenorrhea has been defined as the absence of menses for 6 months, it is statistically uncommon for girls and adolescents to remain amenorrheic for more than 3 months or 90 days—the 95th percentile for cycle length. Thus, it is valuable to begin evaluation of secondary amenorrhea after the absence of menses for 90 days. Therefore, girls and adolescents with chaotically irregular cycles with more than 3 months between periods should be evaluated, not reassured that it is "normal" to have irregular periods in the first gynecologic years.

Irregular menses may be associated with many conditions, including pregnancy, endocrine disorders, and acquired medical conditions because all of these conditions are associated with derangement of hypothalamic–pituitary endocrine function (see the box). Commonly, polycystic ovary syndrome (PCOS) causes prolonged intervals between menstrual periods, especially in patients with signs of androgen excess. The pathogenesis of PCOS is unclear; many experts believe that PCOS results from primary functional intraovarian overproduction of androgen. Others believe that excessive luteinizing hormone secretion from the pituitary gland, which stimulates a secondary ovarian androgen excess, has a role in causing the disorder. Still others hypothesize that PCOS may be related to hyperinsulinism. Whatever its origins, PCOS accounts for 90% of hyperandrogenism among females and, by definition, is characterized by amenorrhea and oligomenorrhea. Before the diagnosis is confirmed, hyperprolactinemia, adrenal and ovarian tumors, and drug effects (such as those caused by danazol and several psychotropic medications) must be ruled out. Additionally, although uncommon in the general population, congenital adrenal hyperplasia should be ruled out by a negative 17α-hydroxyprogesterone test result (serum concentrations of less than 1,000 ng/dL) (27). Treatment of PCOS should target menstrual irregularities, hirsutism if present, obesity, or insulin resistance.

Menstrual irregularities can be caused by disturbance of the central gonadotropin-releasing hormone pulse generator as well as by significant weight loss, strenuous exercise, substantial changes in sleeping or eating habits, and severe stressors. Menstrual disturbances also occur with chronic diseases, such as

**Causes of Menstrual Irregularity**

- Pregnancy
- Endocrine causes
  - Poorly controlled diabetes mellitus
  - Polycystic ovary syndrome
  - Cushing's disease
  - Thyroid dysfunction
  - Premature ovarian failure
  - Late-onset congenital adrenal hyperplasia
- Acquired conditions
  - Stress-related hypothalamic dysfunction
  - Medications
  - Exercise-induced amenorrhea
  - Eating disorders (both anorexia and bulimia)
- Tumors
  - Ovarian tumors
  - Adrenal tumors
  - Prolactinomas

poorly controlled diabetes mellitus; with genetic and congenital conditions, such as Turner's syndrome; and with other forms of gonadal dysgenesis. The diagnosis of pregnancy always should be excluded, even if the history suggests the patient has not been sexually active.

## Excessive Menstrual Flow

A female's first period usually is reported to be of medium flow, and the need for menstrual hygiene products is not typically excessive. Although experts typically report that the mean blood loss per menstrual period is 30 mL per cycle and that chronic loss of more than 80 mL is associated with anemia, this has limited clinical utility because most females are unable to measure their blood loss. However, a recent study in adult women confirms that the perception of heavy menstrual flow is correlated with a higher objective volume of blood loss (28).

Attempts to measure menstrual blood loss on the basis of the number of pads or tampons used per day or the frequency of pad changes are subject to variables such as the individual's fastidiousness, her familiarity or comfort with menstrual hygiene products, and even variation among types and brands of pads or tampons (29). Most report changing a pad approximately three to six times a day, although external constraints such as school rules and limited time between classes may make menstrual hygiene more problematic for adolescents than for adults. Menstrual flow requiring changes of menstrual products every 1–2 hours is considered excessive, particularly when associated with flow that lasts more than 7 days at a time. This type of acute menorrhagia, although most often associated with anovulation, also has been associated with the diagnosis of hematologic problems, including von Willebrand's disease and other bleeding disorders, or other serious problems, including hepatic failure and malignancy (30–33).

The prevalence of von Willebrand's disease is 1% in the general population. Von Willebrand's disease is the most common medical disorder associated with menorrhagia at menarche (34). As many as one in six girls presenting to an emergency department with acute menorrhagia may have von Willebrand's disease (30). Therefore, hematologic disorders should be considered in patients presenting with menorrhagia—especially those presenting acutely at menarche. Hormonal treatment, in the form of estrogen therapy, may affect hematologic factors and mask the diagnosis. Blood collection to screen for hematologic disorders should be obtained before initiating treatment. Evaluating the patient may include referral to a hematologist or a specialized hemophilia treatment center for appropriate screening.

## Anticipatory Guidance

Because development of secondary sex characteristics begins at ages as young as 8 years, primary care clinicians should include pubertal development in their anticipatory guidance to children and parents from this age on. Clinicians should take an ongoing history and perform a complete annual examination, including the inspection of the external genitalia. It is important to educate children and parents about the usual progression of puberty. This includes the likelihood that a child's initial breast growth may be unilateral and slightly tender. Breast development will likely then become bilateral, but some asymmetry is normal. Young females and their parents should understand that the progression of puberty also includes the development of pubic hair, which will increase in amount over time and become thicker and curlier. Additionally, clinicians should convey that females will likely begin to menstruate approximately 2–2.5 years after breast development begins, keeping in mind that recent studies have suggested that the onset of both breast development and menarche may occur slightly earlier for black girls than for white girls (35). Young females should understand that menstruation is a normal part of development and should be instructed on use of feminine products and on what is considered normal menstrual flow. Ideally, both parents and clinicians can participate in this educational process.

## Evaluation

Once young females begin menstruating, evaluation of the menstrual cycle should be included with an assessment of other vital signs. By including this information with the other vital signs, clinicians emphasize the important role of menstrual patterns in reflecting overall health status. Clinicians should ask at every visit for the first date of the patient's last menstrual period. Clinicians should convey that the menstrual cycle is from the first day of a period to the first day of the next period and may vary in length.

Both the American Academy of Pediatrics and the American College of Obstetricians and Gynecologists recommend preventive health visits during adolescence to begin a dialogue and establish an environment where a patient can feel good about taking responsibility for her own reproductive health and feel confident that her concerns will be addressed in a confidential setting (36, 37). These visits are also an opportunity to provide guidance to young females and their parents on adolescent physical development based on data that define normal pubertal development, menarche, and menstrual cyclicity (38). Even during visits with adult patients who interact with adolescents or have children, education about appropriate expectations and normal patterns for the menstrual cycle may be helpful guidance in the decision to consider evaluation.

Asking the patient to begin to chart her menses may be beneficial, especially if the bleeding history is too vague or considered to be inaccurate. Although uncommon, abnormalities do occur. Confirming normal internal and external genital anatomy with a pelvic examination or ultrasonography can rule out significant abnormalities. Therefore, one might consider the menstrual cycle as a type of vital sign and an indicator of other possible medical problems. Using menarche or the menstrual cycle as a sensitive vital sign adds a powerful tool to the assessment of normal hormonal development and the exclusion of serious abnormalities, such as anorexia nervosa, inflammatory bowel disease, and many other chronic illnesses. Menstrual conditions that suggest the need for further evaluation are listed in the box.

Because menarche is such an important milestone in physical development, it is important to be able to educate young females and their parents regarding what to expect of a first period and about the range for normal cycle length of subsequent menses. Girls who have been educated about early menstrual patterns will experience less anxiety as development progresses (1). It is equally important for clinicians to have an understanding of bleeding patterns of young females, the ability to differentiate between normal and abnormal menstruation, and the skill to know how to evaluate the young female patient appropriately.

**Menstrual Conditions That May Require Evaluation**

Menstrual periods that:

- Have not started within 3 years of thelarche
- Have not started by 13 years of age with no signs of pubertal development
- Have not started by 14 years of age with signs of hirsutism
- Have not started by 14 years of age with a history or examination suggestive of excessive exercise or eating disorder
- Have not started by 14 years of age with concerns about genital outflow tract obstruction or anomaly
- Have not started by 15 years of age
- Are regular, occurring monthly, and then become markedly irregular
- Occur more frequently than every 21 days or less frequently than every 45 days
- Occur 90 days apart even for one cycle
- Last more than 7 days
- Require frequent pad or tampon changes (soaking more than one every 1–2 hours)

## References

1. Frank D, Williams T. Attitudes about menstruation among fifth-, sixth-, and seventh-grade pre- and post-menarcheal girls. J Sch Nurs 1999;15:25–31.
2. Wyshak G, Frisch RE. Evidence for a secular trend in age of menarche. N Engl J Med 1982;306:1033–5.
3. Chumlea WE, Schubert CM, Roche AF, Kulin HE, Lee PA, Himes JH, et al. Age at menarche and racial comparisons in US girls. Pediatrics 2003;111:110–3.
4. Thomas F, Renaud F, Benefice E, de Meeus T, Guegan JF. International variability of ages at menarche and menopause: patterns and main determinants. Hum Biol 2001; 73:271–90.
5. Barnes-Josiah D, Augustin A. Secular trend in the age at menarche in Haiti. Am J Hum Biol 1997;7:357–62.
6. He Q, Karlberg J. BMI in childhood and its association with height gain, timing of puberty and final height. Pediatr Res 2001;49:244–51.
7. Wang Y. Is obesity associated with early sexual maturation? A comparison of the association in American boys versus girls. Pediatrics 2002;110:903–10.
8. Apter D, Hermanson E. Update on female pubertal development. Curr Opin Obstet Gynecol 2002;14:475–81.
9. Sun SS, Schubert CM, Chumlea WC, Roche AF, Kulin HE, Lee PA, et al. National estimates of the timing of sexual maturation and racial differences among US children. Pediatrics 2002;110:911–9.
10. Marshall WA, Tanner JM. Variations in pattern of pubertal changes in girls. Arch Dis Child 1969;44:291–303.
11. Marti-Henneberg C, Vizmanos B. The duration of puberty in girls is related to the timing of its onset. J Pediatr 1997;131:618–21.
12. Llop-Vinolas D, Vizmanos B, Closa Monasterolo R, Escribano Subias J, Fernandez-Ballart JD, Marti-Henneberg C. Onset of puberty at eight years of age in girls determines a specific tempo of puberty but does not affect adult height. Acta Paediatr 2004;93:874–9.

13. Largo RH, Prader A. Pubertal development in Swiss girls. Helv Paediatr Acta 1983;38:229–43.
14. National Center for Health Statistics. Age at menarche: United States. Rockville (MD): NCHS; 1973. Available at: http://www.cdc.gov/nchs/data/series/sr_11/sr11_133.pdf. Retrieved June 26, 2006.
15. Reindollar RH, Byrd JR, McDonough PG. Delayed sexual development: a study of 252 patients. Am J Obstet Gynecol 1981;140:371–80.
16. World Health Organization multicenter study on menstrual and ovulatory patterns in adolescent girls. II. Longitudinal study of menstrual patterns in the early postmenarcheal period, duration of bleeding episodes and menstrual cycles. World Health Organization Task Force on Adolescent Reproductive Health. J Adolesc Health Care 1986;7:236–44.
17. Flug D, Largo RH, Prader A. Menstrual patterns in adolescent Swiss girls: a longitudinal study. Ann Hum Biol 1984;11:495–508.
18. Widholm O, Kantero RL. A statistical analysis of the menstrual patterns of 8,000 Finnish girls and their mothers. Acta Obstet Gynecol Scand Suppl 1971;14:(suppl 14):1–36.
19. Zacharias L, Rand WM, Wurtman RJ. A prospective study of sexual development and growth in American girls: the statistics of menarche. Obstet Gynecol Surv 1976;31:325–37.
20. Venturoli S, Porcu E, Fabbri R, Magrini O, Paradisi R, Pallotti G, et al. Postmenarchal evolution of endocrine pattern and ovarian aspects in adolescents with menstrual irregularities. Fertil Steril 1987;48:78–85.
21. Venturoli S, Porcu E, Fabbri R, Magrini O, Grammi L, Paradisi R, et al. Longitudinal evaluation of the different gonadotropin pulsatile patterns in anovulatory cycles of young girls. J Clin Endocrinol Metab 1992;74:836–41.
22. Apter D, Vihko R. Early menarche, a risk factor for breast cancer, indicates early onset of ovulatory cycles. J Clin Endocrinol Metab 1983;57:82–6.
23. Vihko R, Apter D. Endocrine characteristics of adolescent menstrual cycles: impact of early menarche. J Steroid Biochem 1984;20:231–6.
24. Hickey M, Balen A. Menstrual disorders in adolescence: investigation and management. Hum Reprod Update 2003;9:493–504.
25. Treloar AE, Boynton RE, Behn BG, Brown BW. Variation of the human menstrual cycle through reproductive life. Int J Fertil 1967;12:77–126.
26. Vollman RF. The menstrual cycle. Major Probl Obstet Gynecol 1977;7:1–193.
27. Cowan JT, Graham MG. Polycystic ovary syndrome: more than a reproductive disorder. Patient Care 2003;37:23–33.
28. Warner PE, Critchley HO, Lumsden MA, Campbell-Brown M, Douglas A, Murray GD. Menorrhagia I: measured blood loss, clinical features, and outcome in women with heavy periods: a survey with follow-up data. Am J Obstet Gynecol 2004;190:1216–23.
29. Grimes DA. Estimating vaginal blood loss. J Reprod Med 1979;22:190–2.
30. Claessens E, Cowell CA. Acute adolescent menorrhagia. Am J Obstet Gynecol 1981;139:277–80.
31. Bevan JA, Maloney KW, Hillery CA, Gill JC, Montgomery RR, Scott JP. Bleeding disorders: a common cause of menorrhagia in adolescents. J Pediatr 2001;138:856–61.
32. Ellis MH, Beyth Y. Abnormal vaginal bleeding in adolescence as the presenting symptom of a bleeding diathesis. J Pediatr Adolesc Gynecol 1999;12:127–31.
33. Duflos-Cohade C, Amandruz M, Thibaud E. Pubertal metrorrhagia. J Pediatr Adolesc Gynecol 1996;9:16–20.
34. Castaman G, Federici AB, Rodeghiero F, Mannucci PM. Von Willebrand's disease in the year 2003: towards complete identification of gene defects for correct diagnosis and treatment. Haematologica 2003;88:94–108.
35. Herman-Giddens ME, Slora EJ, Wasserman RC, Bourdony CJ, Bhapkar MV, Koch GG, et al. Secondary sexual characteristics and menses in young girls seen in office practice: a study from the Pediatric Research in Office Settings Network. Pediatrics 1997;99:505–12.
36. American Academy of Pediatrics. Guidelines for health supervision III. Elk Grove Village (IL): AAP; 2002.
37. American College of Obstetricians and Gynecologists. Health care for adolescents. Washington, DC: ACOG; 2003.
38. Adams Hillard PJ. Menstruation in young girls: a clinical perspective. Obstet Gynecol 2002;99:655–62.

ACOG Committee Opinion

Committee on Adolescent Health Care

THE AMERICAN COLLEGE OF OBSTETRICIANS AND GYNECOLOGISTS
1951
WOMEN'S HEALTH CARE PHYSICIANS

Number 350, November 2006

# Breast Concerns in the Adolescent

*ABSTRACT: Breast disease in the adolescent female encompasses an expansive array of topics. Benign disease overwhelmingly dominates the differential diagnosis and dictates a different protocol for care in the adolescent compared with the adult patient to avoid inappropriately high assessments of risk and unnecessary diagnostic procedures and surgery. There also are emerging issues pertaining to the care of the adolescent breast, such as breast augmentation, nipple piercing, and management of the adolescent patient with a family history of breast cancer.*

Breast disease in the adolescent female encompasses an expansive array of topics. Common presenting signs and symptoms in the adolescent patient are breast pain, nipple discharge, and the discovery of a mass (1, 2). Benign disease overwhelmingly dominates the differential diagnosis and dictates a different protocol for care in the adolescent compared with the adult patient. Family practitioners, pediatricians, nurse practitioners, and obstetrician–gynecologists most commonly encounter and manage adolescent patients with breast disease. Many of these adolescents are referred for evaluation to general surgeons and breast centers with little experience with or familiarity with the data for this population. Their adult frame of reference can lead to inappropriately high assessments of risk and unnecessary diagnostic procedures and surgery.

## Breast Development

As growth of the pubertal breast begins, it is often asymmetric. A unilateral breast lump just beneath the areola in an 8–10-year-old patient is invariably a developing breast bud. Biopsy in prepubertal girls or girls in early puberty is rarely indicated and should almost always be avoided because it can irreversibly damage the breast bud. It is estimated that approximately 25% of adolescent females have breast asymmetry that persists into adulthood (3). In addition to the most common cause of breast asymmetry, normal variation in breast size, the differential diagnosis includes unilateral hypoplasia or amastia, unilateral hypertrophy or large breast mass, and Poland's syndrome (congenital underdevelopment or absence of the chest muscle on one side of the body). Failure of bilateral development of the breasts can be caused by delayed puberty or rarely by bilateral hypoplasia or amastia. Careful assess-

This document reflects emerging clinical and scientific advances as of the date issued and is subject to change. The information should not be construed as dictating an exclusive course of treatment or procedure to be followed.

The Committee would like to thank Nichole Zidenberg, MD, and Patricia S. Simmons, MD, for their assistance in the development of this document.



ISSN 1074-861X

**The American College of Obstetricians and Gynecologists**
409 12th Street, SW
PO Box 96920
Washington, DC 20090-6920

12345/09876

Breast concerns in the adolescent. ACOG Committee Opinion No. 350. American College of Obstetricians and Gynecologists. Obstet Gynecol 2006;108:1329–36

ment of unilateral or bilateral breast hypoplasia is important before any surgical intervention is initiated.

## Common Adolescent Breast Concerns

### *Mastalgia*

Breast pain, or mastalgia, is a common symptom in the adolescent. Symptoms also may include mild swelling and palpable nodularity, consistent with fibrocystic changes, usually in the upper outer quadrant. The symptoms are typically cyclic and worse premenstrually. Supportive measures and reassurance are the best treatment. For adolescent patients who are smokers, smoking cessation should be encouraged because nicotine has been shown to increase breast pain. Some studies suggest that dietary modifications, such as eliminating coffee, tea, and caffeinated sodas, can reduce breast pain (4, 5). A well fitting bra, particularly a "sports bra" during exercise has been shown to reduce pain during movement. Analgesics such as naproxen sodium or ibuprofen alleviate the symptoms. Oral contraceptives also may be helpful with fibrocystic changes.

### *Nipple discharge*

Nipple discharge in the adolescent can be white, clear, red, yellow, green, or brown and is usually benign in nature. Nipple discharge often is secondary to local irritation or stimulation, pregnancy, or use of medications such as antipsychotics, oral contraceptives, or opiates. Ductal ectasia is a benign and common finding in the developing breast. It consists of dilation of the mammary ducts, periductal fibrosis and inflammation. The patient may present with nipple discharge that may be bloody or dark brown in nature, or a mass, or both. A bloody nipple discharge, when associated with a mass, can be seen in papilloma or papillomatosis and should be evaluated because of the malignant potential of these conditions. Ultrasonography is often used to assist in the diagnosis and to reassure the patient of her status. Except in papilloma or papillomatosis, observation is recommended. As in adults, hyperprolactinemia can cause galactorrhea in adolescents, thus the appropriate laboratory and imaging studies should be ordered in the evaluation process. Treatment is directed by the results of the history, physical examination, and laboratory studies. As indicated, use of the offending drugs is stopped, hypothyroidism is treated, and prolactin tumors are managed medically or surgically. Typically, the patient should be educated regarding behavioral changes to avoid nipple stimulation, and observation is recommended.

### *Breast Mass*

Of all breast masses diagnosed in adolescents, recent retrospective chart reviews demonstrate that approximately 67% are fibroadenomas, 15% are fibrocystic changes, and 3% are abscess or mastitis (see the box) (6). In one longitudinal study of adolescent females with a breast mass, follow-up over a 7–9 month period demonstrated that 77% of adolescents had lesions that either resolved or did not enlarge, and no malignancies were diagnosed (7).

**Breast Masses in the Adolescent Female**

**Benign**

- Fibroadenoma
- Fibrocystic changes or cysts
- Unilateral thelarche
- Hemangioma
- Intramammary lymph node
- Fat necrosis
- Abscess
- Mastitis
- Lipoma
- Hematoma
- Hamartoma
- Micromastia (juvenile hypertrophy)
- Galactocele
- Intraductal papilloma
- Juvenile papillomatosis
- Lymphangioma

**Malignant**

- Malignant cystosarcoma phyllodes
- Breast carcinoma
- Metastatic disease
- Lymphoma, neuroblastoma, sarcoma, rhabdomyosarcoma, acute leukemia

Data from Dehner LP, Hill DA, Deschryver K. Pathology of the breast in children, adolescents, and young adults. Semin Diagn Pathol 1999;16:235–47; Simmons PS. Diagnostic considerations in breast disorders of children and adolescents. Obstet Gynecol Clin North Am 1992; 19:91–102; and Laufer MR, Goldstein DP. The breast: examination and lesions. In: Emans SJ, Laufer MR, Goldstein DP, editors. Pediatric and adolescent gynecology. 5th ed. Philadelphia (PA): Lippincott Williams & Wilkins; 2005. p. 729–59.

***Breast Hypertrophy***

Idiopathic breast hypertrophy occurs in adolescents and adults. When noted in adolescents, it is referred to as "juvenile" or "virginal" breast hypertrophy. Juvenile breast hypertrophy involves the uncontrolled overgrowth of breast tissue that occurs in adolescents whose breasts develop normally during puberty, but then continue to grow. This rapid growth can be unilateral or bilateral and usually occurs shortly after thelarche.

For many adolescents, breast hypertrophy and persistent significant asymmetry can result in both psychologic and physical consequences. These adolescents often receive negative attention, experience difficulties with athletics, and have more socialization problems that may lead to poor self-esteem and isolation from family and peers (8). These consequences have resulted in the development of eating disorders in some adolescent females to compensate for their breast size (9).

Surgical correction by enlarging one breast with an implant, surgical reduction of the larger breast, or a bilateral reduction mammoplasty can improve the quality of life considerably. Studies have demonstrated that the improvement of self-esteem seems to be the most significant benefit of breast surgery (10, 11). Studies also have demonstrated that breast reduction in adolescents with large breasts relieves back, shoulder, and neck pain (10, 12).

Postoperatively, adolescent patients have the same short- and long-term potential complications as adult patients, including incisional separation, scarring, sensory loss, and infection. Long-term complications, such as the possible inability to breastfeed, also have been described in adults undergoing reduction mammoplasty; however, there are numerous surgical techniques, some of which preserve the ability to breastfeed (8). One study of adolescent patients who underwent reduction mammoplasty between the ages of 15 years and 17 years, found that these patients subsequently breastfed their infants with complication rates similar to those in the general population (13). Overall, the most commonly cited short-term complication is pain; the long-term complications cited are related to scarring (10, 12). The adolescent patient population reports satisfaction with reduction mammoplasty exceeding 75%, even when surveyed several years postoperatively (11, 12). In one study of adolescent patients who underwent bilateral breast reduction, 94% would recommend it to a teenaged friend with a similar condition (10).

There is no definitive guideline for when breast reduction should be suggested. An assessment of the adolescent's emotional, psychologic, and physical maturity is recommended to guide this decision. Breast development is variable, and several recommendations regarding the timing of surgery have been made, including postponing surgery until breast maturity is reached, waiting for 6 months with no change in bra size, or after the age of 18 years. Surgery can be considered earlier when severe symptoms are encountered (14). The incidence of breast regrowing after initial reduction during adolescence is not known, but it has been reported (15). A psychologic evaluation is a reasonable surgical prerequisite because the plastic surgeon needs to fully understand the motivation, maturity, and psychosocial and emotional attributes of the patient seeking this surgery. The plastic surgeon should be confident that the adolescent has realistic goals and fully understands the risks and benefits, including the limitations of breast surgery (14).

***Breast Augmentation***

Plastic surgery involving augmentation of adolescent breasts stimulates debate both socially and medically. Over the past several years, the number of cosmetic surgical procedures performed in patients aged 18 years or younger has increased substantially (16). Breast augmentations were less than 5% of the total number of cosmetic surgical procedures performed on this age group.

The number of adolescent females seeking breast augmentation for aesthetic purposes is considerable. This can be attributed to factors such as media influence and distorted perceptions of an ideal body type. In response to this trend, the American Society for Plastic Surgery has adopted guidelines for the appropriate selection of adolescents for aesthetic breast surgery (17). The guidelines acknowledge that the U.S. Food and Drug Administration considers the use of breast implants for aesthetic breast augmentation in patients younger than 18 years to be an off-label use. They state that adolescent candidates for purely aesthetic breast augmentation should be at least 18 years of age and recognize that aesthetic breast surgery in the adolescent female encompasses unique mental and physical components. The adolescent and her parent should be counseled regarding risks, activity restrictions, and recovery time for the procedure being considered.

It is important to understand that for some adolescents, breast augmentation leads to a successful outcome. A less mature adolescent may have unrealistic expectations and be disappointed by the outcome. For example, self-esteem issues may not be resolved. An assessment of an adolescent's emotional, psychologic, and physical maturity is, therefore, a reasonable surgical prerequisite. The adolescent and her parent should be counseled that breast implants are not typically associated with breastfeeding difficulties or an increased risk of breast cancer. The surgery may, however, make future mammographic screening more difficult.

***Nipple Piercing***

Nipple piercing has become increasingly popular and an emerging concern, particularly for the adolescent. There is a paucity of research in the area of nipple piercing, specifically addressing prevalence and complications. The most common health risks associated with piercing include infections, pain, bleeding, hematoma, cyst formation, allergic reaction, and keloid formation (18, 19). Nipple piercing has been associated with a transmission risk for hepatitis B and hepatitis C (20) and human immunodeficiency virus (HIV) (21). There also are a growing number of case reports of development of a breast abscess after nipple piercing. A recent review of the literature reports 10 cases of breast abscess after nipple piercing (22). The average time from piercing to diagnosis is 5 months because of a prolonged incubation and wound healing time for nipple piercing. The healing time after nipple piercing is 3–6 months, which is longer than piercing of some other sites (Table 1). In addition, patients may delay seeking treatment after nipple piercing. Major complications associated with an abscess after nipple piercing can include endocarditis, heart valve injury, cardiac prosthesis infection, metal foreign body reaction in breast tissue, or recurrent infections. Undue anxiety may be caused by an incorrect initial diagnosis of breast cancer in the pierced breast. Based on current data, clinical recommendations for patients with postpiercing infections should include antibiotic treatment and removal of the nipple ring; screening for hepatitis B, hepatitis C, and HIV; and glucose testing to exclude diabetes mellitus, with its risk of increased infection rate (22). Given the increasing popularity of piercing, clinicians should routinely screen adolescents for intent to undergo a piercing. For those who intend to undergo a piercing, education should be provided regarding safer piercing strategies. Clinicians also should encourage these individuals to become immunized against hepatitis B and tetanus before the piercing, if they are not already immune. Adolescents who have any of the following factors should be advised to avoid nipple piercing: alcohol or substance intoxication, metal allergies (especially to nickel), anticoagulant therapy, a history of chronic or acute infections, steroid therapy, diabetes, and heart valve defects or any other causes of immune suppression. For many adolescents seeking advice regarding nipple piercing, the Internet is often their primary and sole reference (see Resources). It is common for adolescents to present with piercing complications and quote or follow the advice provided on these Internet web sites. Information on many of the Internet web sites on nipple piercing conflict with expert medical opinion.

***Breast cancer***

Primary breast cancer occurs rarely in the adolescent patient. During the period 1998–2002, the incidence of breast cancer in patients younger than 20 years was 0 per 100,000. During the same period, the incidence of breast cancer in women younger than 24 years of age was 1.3 per 100,000 (23). Malignancies that occur in the adolescent breast are more likely metastatic from another primary malignancy (24). Although primary breast cancer is uncommon, risk

**Table 1.** Healing Time for Piercing by Body Part

| Pierced Body Part | Time It Takes to Heal |
|---|---|
| Nipple | 3–6 months |
| Ear lobe | 6–8 weeks |
| Ear cartilage | 4 months to 1 year |
| Eyebrow | 6–8 weeks |
| Nostril | 2–4 months |
| Nasal septum | 6–8 months |
| Nasal bridge | 8–10 weeks |
| Tongue | 4 weeks |
| Lip | 2–3 months |
| Navel | 4 months to 1 year |
| Female genitalia | 4–10 weeks |
| Male genitalia | 4 weeks to 6 months |

Center for Young Women's Health, Children's Hospital Boston. Body piercing: a guide for teens. Available at: http://www.youngwomenshealth.org/body-piercing.html. Retrieved June 13, 2006.  Modified and reprinted with permission.

factors for malignancy of the breast should be assessed. Clinical evidence demonstrates that radiation exposure, such as that seen with the treatment of childhood cancer, to the prepubertal and pubertal breast of females between the ages of 10 years and 30 years is associated with the greatest risk of radiation-induced breast cancer later in life (25).

## Clinical Management of a Breast Abnormality

Ultrasonography generally is the best imaging modality to study the adolescent breast (26, 27). Mammography is not indicated in adolescents because it offers poor image quality and is associated with both false-positive and false-negative results due to the dense nature of the fibroglandular tissues (28). Mammography also has been associated with unnecessary surgery and the increased risk of radiation-induced malignant changes (29–31). Although aspiration for relief of pain of cysts can be useful in the adolescent with a breast mass, fine needle aspiration for diagnostic purposes has not been well established in adolescents and should be discouraged.

Most breast masses diagnosed in adolescents are fibroadenomas. The majority of longitudinal studies on fibroadenomas demonstrate that most lesions decrease in size, and many even completely resolve and, therefore, should not be excised. Specifically, a large epidemiologic study of benign breast tumor cases showed a 13.9% incidence of fibroadenomas at registration, an increase in fibroadenoma after 5 years, and then a gradual decrease in fibroadenoma over 8 years (32). Over a 5-year period, one study examined 25 fibroadenomas and found that 52% became smaller, 16% remained the same size, and 32% became larger (33). Another study found an actuarial probability of disappearance of 46% of lesions at 5 years and 69% at 9 years. It was found that women 20 years and younger had a higher probability of resolution of a fibroadenoma than women older than 20 years. Size or multiplicity of lesions did not affect the probability of resolution (34). Given the low risk of malignancy, high likelihood of spontaneous resolution, and risks of deformity in the growing breast, conservative, nonsurgical management is most often appropriate. Excisional biopsy and surgery should be reserved for breast masses that are enlarging or associated with overlying skin changes, abscesses not responding to medical therapy, or suspicious masses presenting in an adolescent with a history of a previous malignancy.

## Family History of Breast Cancer

One area of growing interest to gynecologists is the management of the adolescent patient with a family history of breast cancer. It is important to be aware of the complexities of genetic testing, screening recommendations, and preventive health guidelines. Currently, a woman living in the United States has a 13.2% lifetime risk of developing breast cancer (35). A significant risk factor for the development of breast cancer is a family history of the disease. The risk in a patient with a first-degree relative affected by breast cancer increases twofold to threefold (36). The cumulative risk of breast cancer in women with *BRCA1* or *BRCA2* genes ranges from 3.2% at 30 years to 85% at 70 years of age (37). The daughter of a woman or man who is a *BRCA* carrier has a 50% chance of having inherited the gene mutation. Decisions regarding genetic testing in the adolescent are complex and should include consideration of the medical and psychologic implications of genetic testing for each individual patient and her family. Referral for genetic counseling by an appropriately qualified individual is advised for patients considering genetic testing. Current recommendations outlined by the Cancer Genetics Studies Consortium do not recommend radiographic surveillance for *BRCA1* carriers until 25–35 years of age (38). The National Cancer Institute's most recent summary (April 2005) concludes that bilateral prophylactic mastectomy is associated with a reduction in breast cancer by as much as 90% in adult women with an increased risk of breast cancer because of strong family history. However, because of the physical and psychologic effects of this surgery and its permanence, decisions on this matter are usually deferred until the individual is at least 35 years of age and has completed childbearing (39). Therefore, there is no urgency for testing the adolescent patient. The role of *BRCA1* and *BRCA2* testing in adolescents is an area of much needed research for both evidence-based management and ethical practice (1).

## Prevention of Breast Cancer

Effective and accurate counseling for adolescents and their parents regarding breast cancer prevention should be a routine component of preventive health services for adolescents. Smoking, alcohol consumption, and exposure to treatment with ionizing radiation during adolescence have all been associated with an increase in breast cancer in adulthood (40). It is prudent to advise adolescents to avoid these exposures. Additional preventive health guidance in all adolescents should include encouraging exercise in 12–24-year-old females because physical activity has been shown to reduce the risk of breast cancer significantly (41). There are no rigorous recent scientific data to support an association between abortions and breast cancer. One recent prospective study examined 44,000 women with breast cancer from 53 studies and 16 countries. This study demonstrated that pregnancies that end in therapeutic abortion do not increase a woman's risk of developing breast cancer later in life (42). Some parents and patients are opposed to oral contraceptive use because of a fear of associated breast cancer. The National Institute of Child Health evaluated the risk of breast cancer in more than 4,500 women who were current or past users of oral contraceptives. The study found no significant increased risk of breast cancer when oral contraceptive users were compared with controls (43).

A case–control study found that oral contraceptive use before age 30 years and oral contraceptive use for more than 5 years were associated with an increased risk of breast cancer for *BRCA1* carriers, but not in *BRCA2* carriers (44). A more recent cohort study focused on cases of breast cancer diagnosed before age 40 years and included a substantial number of *BRCA1* and *BRCA2* mutation carriers (45). Compared with nonuse of oral contraceptives, use of current low-dose oral contraceptive formulations did not increase the risk of breast cancer in carriers of *BRCA1* or *BRCA2* mutations. A positive family history of breast cancer, including *BRCA1* or *BRCA2* mutations, should not be regarded as contraindications to oral contraceptive use (46).

## Breast Self-Examination

Historically, experts have recommended teaching adolescents to perform breast self-examination for a variety of reasons, including cancer detection, teaching self-detection for future application, and contributing to greater understanding and comfort with their changing bodies. There are currently no data to support these rationales. More recently, experts observe that it might actually be ill advised to encourage breast self-examination in the adolescent because girls who identify a breast mass themselves may experience multiple physician visits, invasive testing, and perhaps unwarranted surgery. These extensive and expensive evaluations usually lead to benign findings and unnecessary angst (47). The American College of Obstetricians and Gynecologists states that, despite a lack of definitive data for or against breast self-examination, breast self-examination may be recommended beginning at age 19 years. Counseling regarding breast self-examination for those aged 13–18 years is not recommended (48). Some experts have recommended teaching breast self-examination to adolescent females whose mothers carry the *BRCA1* or *BRCA2* gene, beginning at age 18–21 years. Early breast self-examination has been recommended in those at high risk for breast cancer, such as those with a personal history of malignancy. Women with previous exposure to therapeutic chest radiation therapy are advised to begin breast self-examination 10 years after radiation therapy (1, 2, 49).

## Conclusion

- Breast disorders in the adolescent female can cause increased anxiety for the patient and her family and pose a clinical challenge for her health care provider.
- Malignancy is rare in the adolescent breast. A different emphasis for care in the adolescent compared with the adult patient is, therefore, recommended. Conservative, nonsurgical management is most often appropriate.
- To increase the likelihood of satisfactory outcomes from breast-reduction or augmentation surgery, the surgeon should assess the adolescent's emotional, psychologic, and physical maturity.
- Given the increasing popularity of piercing, including nipple piercing, clinicians should routinely screen adolescents for intent to undergo a piercing. Preventive counseling and relevant immunizations should be offered to adolescents interested in piercing. For patients with post-piercing infections, prompt treatment of infections and appropriate screening and testing is essential.
- Further investigation is needed to better counsel adolescent patients about genetic testing for breast cancer and the role of breast self-examination.

## Resources

### ACOG Resources

American College of Obstetricians and Gynecologists. Detecting and treating breast problems. ACOG Patient Education Pamphlet AP026. Washington, DC: ACOG; 2004.

American College of Obstetricians and Gynecologists. Fibrocystic breast changes. ACOG Patient Education Pamphlet AP138. Washington, DC: ACOG; 2000.

Role of the obstetrician–gynecologist in the screening and diagnosis of breast masses. ACOG Committee Opinion No. 334. American College of Obstetricians and Gynecologists. Obstet Gynecol 2006;107:1213–4.

### Other Resources

The following lists are for informational purposes only. Referral to these sources and web sites does not imply the endorsement of ACOG. These lists are not meant to be comprehensive. The exclusion of a source or web site does not reflect the quality of that source or web site. Please note that web sites are subject to change without notice.

Association of Professional Piercers
PO Box 1287
Lawrence, KS 66044
Web: www.safepiercing.org

### Resources for Your Patients

American Academy of Family Physicians
11400 Tomahawk Creek Parkway
Leawood, KS 66211-2672
Tel: (913) 906-6000
Web: www.aafp.org

American Academy of Pediatrics
NY Chapter 2
420 Lakeville Road, Suite 244
New Hyde Park, NY 11042
Web: www.ny2aap.org/tattoos.html

AWARE Foundation
1015 Chestnut Street
Philadelphia, PA 19107-4302
Tel: (215) 955-9847
Web: www.awarefoundation.org

Center for Young Women's Health
Children's Hospital Boston
333 Longwood Avenue, 5th floor
Boston, MA 02115
Tel: (617) 355-CYWH (2994)
Web: www.youngwomenshealth.org

Go Ask Alice! (by Columbia University Health Education Program)
Lerner Hall
2920 Broadway, 7th Floor
MC 2608
New York, NY 10027
Tel: (212) 854-5453
Web: www.goaskalice.columbia.edu

## References

1. Simmons PS. Breast disorders in adolescent females. Curr Opin Obstet Gynecol 2001;13:459–61.
2. Templeman C, Hertweck SP. Breast disorders in the pediatric and adolescent patient. Obstet Gynecol Clin North Am 2000;27:19–34.
3. Beach RK. Routine breast exams: a chance to reassure, guide, and protect. Contemp Pediatr 1987;4:70–100.
4. Minton JP, Foecking MK, Webster DJ, Matthews RH. Caffeine, cyclic nucleotides, and breast disease. Surgery 1979;86:105–9.
5. Abraham GE. Nutritional factors in the etiology of the premenstrual tension syndromes. J Reprod Med 1983; 28:446–64.
6. Laufer MR, Goldstein DP. The breast: examination and lesions. In: Emans SJ, Laufer MR, Goldstein DP, editors. Pediatric and adolescent gynecology. 5th ed. Philadelphia (PA): Lippincott Williams & Wilkins; 2005. p. 729–59.
7. Neinstein LS, Atkinson J, Diamant M. Prevalence and longitudinal study of breast masses in adolescents. J Adolesc Health 1993;14:277–81.
8. Corriveau S, Jacobs JS. Macromastia in adolescence. Clin Plast Surg 1990;17:151–60.
9. Losee JE, Serletti JM, Kreipe RE, Caldwell EH. Reduction mammoplasty in patients with bulimia nervosa. Ann Plast Surg 1997;39:443–6.
10. McMahan JD, Wolfe JA, Cromer BA, Ruberg RL. Lasting success in teenage reduction mammoplasty. Ann Plast Surg 1995;35:227–31.
11. McGrath MH, Mukerji S. Plastic surgery and the teenage patient. J Pediatr Adolesc Gynecol 2000;13:105–18.
12. Lee MC, Lehman JA Jr, Tantri MD, Parker MG, Wagner DS. Bilateral reduction mammoplasty in an adolescent population: adolescent bilateral reduction mammoplasty. J Craniofac Surg 2003;14:691–5.
13. Aillet S, Watier E, Chevrier S, Pailheret JP, Grall JY. Breast feeding after reduction mammaplasty performed during adolescence. Eur J Obstet Gynecol Reprod Biol 2002;101:79–82.
14. McGrath MH, Schooler WG. Elective plastic surgical procedures in adolescence. Adolesc Med Clin 2004;15: 487–502.
15. Mayl N, Vasconez LO, Jurkiewicz MJ. Treatment of macromastia in the actively enlarging breast. Plast Reconstr Surg 1974;54:6–12.
16. American Society of Plastic Surgeons. National Clearinghouse of Plastic Surgery Statistics. Procedural statistics trends 1992-2005. Available at: http://www.plasticsurgery.org/public_education/Statistical-Trends.cfm. Retrieved June 12, 2006.
17. American Society of Plastic Surgeons. Plastic surgery for teenagers. Available at: http://www.plasticsurgery.org/news_room/loader.cfm?url=/commonspot/security/getfile.cfm&PageID=14990. Retrieved June 12, 2006.
18. Mayers LB, Moriarty BW, Judelson DA, Rundell KW. Complications of body art. Consultant 2002;42:1744–52.
19. Braithwaite RL, Stephens T, Sterk C, Braithwaite K. Risks associated with tattooing and body piercing. J Public Health Policy 1999;20:459–70.
20. Conry-Cantilena C, VanRaden M, Gibble J, Melpolder J, Shakil AO, Viladomiu L, et al. Routes of infection,

viremia, and liver disease in blood donors found to have hepatitis C virus infection. N Engl J Med 1996;334: 1691–6.
21. Pugatch D, Mileno M, Rich JD. Possible transmission of human immunodeficiency virus type 1 from body piercing. Clin Infect Dis 1998;26:767–8.
22. Jacobs VR, Golombeck K, Jonat W, Kiechle M. Mastitis nonpeurperalis after nipple piercing: time to act. Int J Fertil Womens Med 2003;48:226–31.
23. Ries LA, Eisner MP, Kosary CL, Hankey BF, Miller BA, Clegg L, et al, editors. SEER cancer statistics review, 1975–2002. Bethesda (MD): National Cancer Institute; 2005. Available at: http://seer.cancer.gov/csr/1975_2002. Retrieved June 13, 2006.
24. Simmons PS, Wold LE. Surgically treated breast disease in adolescent females: a retrospective review of 185 cases. Adolesc Pediatr Gynecol 1989;2:95–8.
25. Goss PE, Sierra S. Current perspectives on radiation-induced breast cancer. J Clin Oncol 1998;16(1):338–47.
26. Boothroyd A, Carty H. Breast masses in childhood and adolescence. A presentation of 17 cases and a review of the literature. Pediatr Radiol 1994;24:81–4.
27. Adler DD. Ultrasound of benign breast conditions. Semin Ultrasound CT MR1989;10:106–18.
28. Hart BL, Steinbock RT, Mettle FA, Jr, Pathak DR, Bartow SA. Age and race related changes in mammographic parenchymal patterns. Cancer 1989;63:2537–9.
29. Feig SA. Radiation risk from mammography: is it clinically significant? AJR Am J Roentgenol 1984;143:469–75.
30. Eddy DM, Hasselblad V, McGivney W, Hendee W. The value of mammography screening in women under age 50 years. JAMA 1988;259:1512–9.
31. Brenner DJ, Sawant SG, Hande MP, Miller RC, Elliston CD, Fu Z, et al. Routine screening mammography: how important is the radiation-risk side of the benefit-risk equation? Int J Radiat Biol 2002;78:1065–7.
32. Arihiro K. Trends in benign breast tumors in Japanese women, 1973–1995: experience of Hiroshima Tumor Tissue Registry. Jpn J Cancer Res 2002;93:610–5.
33. Carty NJ, Carter C, Rubin C, Ravichandran D, Royle GT, Taylor I. Management of fibroadenoma of the breast. Ann R Coll Surg Engl 1995;77:127–30.
34. Cant PJ, Madden MV, Coleman MG, Dent DM. Non-operative management of breast masses diagnosed as fibroadenoma. Br J Surg 1995;82:792–4.
35. American Cancer Society. Breast cancer facts & figures 2005–2006. Atlanta (GA): ACS; 2005. Available at: http://www.cancer.org/downloads/STT/CAFF2005BrF.pdf. Retrieved June 12, 2006.
36. Ottman R, Pike MC, King MC, Henderson BE. Practical guide for estimating risk for familial breast cancer. Lancet 1983;2:556–8.
37. Ford E, Easton DF, Bishop DT, Narod SA, Goldgar DE. Risk of cancer in BRCA1-mutation carriers: Breast Cancer Linkage Consortium. Lancet 1994;343:692–5.
38. NIH consensus conference. Ovarian cancer. Screening, treatment, and follow-up. NIH Consensus Development Panel on Ovarian Cancer. JAMA 1995;273:491–7.
39. Seeber B, Driscoll DA. Hereditary breast and ovarian cancer syndrome: should we test adolescents? J Pediatr Adolesc Gynecol 2004;17:161–7.
40. Marcus PM, Newman B, Millikan RC, Moorman PG, Baird DD, Qaqish B. The associations of adolescent cigarette smoking, alcoholic beverage consumption, environmental tobacco smoke, and ionizing radiation with subsequent breast cancer risk (United States). Cancer Causes Control 2000;11:271–8.
41. Lagerros YT, Hseih SF, Hsieh CC. Physical activity in adolescence and young adulthood and breast cancer risk: a quantitative review. Eur J Cancer Prev 2004;13:5–12.
42. Beral V, Bull D, Dell R, Peto R, Reeves G. Breast cancer and abortion: collaborative reanalysis of data from 53 epidemiological studies, including 83,000 women with breast cancer from 16 countries. Collaborative Group on Hormonal Factors in Breast Cancer. Lancet 2004;363: 1007–16.
43. Marchbanks PA, McDonald JA, Wilson HG, Folger SG, Mandel MG, Daling JR, et al. Oral contraceptives and the risk of breast cancer. N Engl J Med 2002;346:2025–32.
44. Narod SA, Dube MP, Klijn J, Lubinski J, Lynch HT, Ghadirian P, et al. Oral contraceptives and the risk of breast cancer in BRCA1 and BRCA2 mutation carriers. J Natl Cancer Inst 2002;94:1773–9.
45. Milne RL, Knight JA, John EM, Dite GS, Balbuena R, Ziogas A, et al. Oral contraceptive use and risk of early-onset breast cancer in carriers and noncarriers of BRCA1 and BRCA2 mutations. Cancer Epidemiol Biomarkers Prev 2005;14:350–6.
46. Use of hormonal contraception in women with coexisting medical conditions. ACOG Practice Bulletin No. 73. American College of Obstetricians and Gynecologists. Obstet Gynecol 2006;107:1453–72.
47. Goldbloom RB. Self-examination by adolescents. Pediatrics 1985;76:126–8.
48. Primary and preventive care: periodic assessments. ACOG Committee Opinion No. 292. American College of Obstetricians and Gynecologists. Obstet Gynecol 2003; 102:117–24.
49. Burke W, Daly M, Garber J, Botkin J, Kahn MJ, Lynch P, et al. Recommendations for follow-up care of individuals with an inherited predisposition to cancer. II. BRCA1 and BRCA2. Cancer Genetics Studies Consortium. JAMA 1997;277:997–1003.

ACOG Committee Opinion

Committee on Adolescent Health Care

Number 351, November 2006

This information should not be construed as dictating an exclusive course of treatment or procedure to be followed.

The Committee wishes to thank Nichole Zidenberg, MD; Mary McKenna, PhD; and William H. Dietz, MD, PhD, for their assistance in the development of this document.



ISSN 1074-861X

**The American College of Obstetricians and Gynecologists**
409 12th Street, SW
PO Box 96920
Washington, DC 20090-6920

12345/09876

The overweight adolescent: prevention, treatment, and obstetric–gynecologic implications. ACOG Committee Opinion No. 351. American College of Obstetricians and Gynecologists. Obstet Gynecol 2006;108:1337–48.

# The Overweight Adolescent: Prevention, Treatment, and Obstetric–Gynecologic Implications

*ABSTRACT: The number of overweight adolescents has grown to epidemic proportions in the United States. Adolescent females who are overweight have significant health sequelae. The American College of Obstetricians and Gynecologists recommends that all adolescents be screened annually for overweight by determining weight and stature, calculating a body mass index for age percentile, and asking about body image and eating patterns. Health care providers should promote healthy eating and physical activity to adolescent patients and their parents during routine preventive health care visits. Adolescents with a body mass index greater than or equal to the 95th percentile for age should have an in-depth dietary and health assessment to determine psychosocial morbidity and risk for future cardiovascular disease. Obstetrician–gynecologists are strongly encouraged to provide this assessment. Additional research is needed to determine the most appropriate approach for the successful prevention and treatment of overweight adolescents. Until this research has been completed, it is best to extrapolate an approach from data and studies pertaining to children and adults, while remaining cognizant of the special needs that surround adolescent growth and development. Sound nutritional recommendations and regular physical activity are essential components of prevention and treatment plans.*

The number of overweight adolescents has grown to epidemic proportions in the United States. The overweight female adolescent faces unique challenges with her medical, psychologic, and reproductive health. Early intervention is paramount to prevent associated short- and long-term morbidities. The goal of this document is to review the most timely and pertinent information regarding the overweight adolescent, as well as to provide prevention and treatment strategies to guide the practitioner in providing gynecologic and obstetric care for such a patient.

## Definitions of Overweight and Obesity

The discussion of "overweight" or "obesity" in adolescents is complicated by the inconsistent use of definitions in clinical practice, research, and publications. These definitions have been applied to adults and adolescents. The term obesity is now used less frequently to avoid the associated negative connotations, especially for children and adolescents. Body mass index (BMI) is the most widely used tool for assessment of overweight and obesity. It is calculated using the following formula: weight in kilograms divided by height in meters squared (weight [kg] / height squared [$m^2$]). There are now teen BMI calculators available online. A link to one such calculator can be found at http://www.acog.org/goto/teens. This calculator determines the teen's BMI for age percentile. Alternatively, Figures 1 and 2 can be used. The Centers for Disease Control and Prevention (CDC) defines an adolescent as overweight if she has a BMI greater than or equal to the 95th percentile for age. For example, a girl aged 16 years whose height is 60 inches and weight is 155 pounds has a BMI of 30.3, as can be seen in Figure 1. By looking at Figure 2, it can be determined that this girl's BMI is above the 95th percentile; therefore, she is considered to be overweight. An adolescent whose BMI is equal to or greater than the 85th percentile for age, but less than the 95th percentile for age is considered by the CDC to be at risk for becoming overweight. Adult obesity is defined by the CDC as a BMI greater than or equal to 30 and the term *overweight* is used to describe a BMI greater than or equal to 25, but less than or equal to 29.9 (see Table 1) (1). (An adult BMI calculator is available at http://www.nhlbisupport.com/bmi/.) The American College of Obstetricians and Gynecologists (ACOG) uses the CDC definitions.

## Prevalence and Trends

According to National Health and Nutrition Examination Survey 2003–2004 data, 16% of females aged 12–19 years were considered overweight. Thirty-two percent of adolescent females were either overweight or at risk of becoming overweight (2). By comparison, only 6% of females aged 12–19 years were considered overweight in the NHANES study conducted in 1971–1974 (see Figure 3) (3). There are substantial racial differences in the prevalence of overweight for adolescents. Specifically, Latino, Mexican-American, Asian/Pacific Islander, and black populations were more likely to be overweight or at risk for overweight in adolescence than the white population (2, 4).

## Health Risks of Overweight Adolescents

Overweight status in the adolescent female population has been associated with lower educational achievement and income, even after controlling for intelligence and socioeconomic status at baseline (5). These effects persisted even if the adolescent lost weight and was no longer considered overweight (6). Overweight adolescents often experience significant low self-esteem and depression (7–9). Overweight white girls are more likely to develop a negative body image, and are at greater risk of developing eating disorders. Overweight adolescent females have reported experiences with intentional weight-related teasing, jokes, and derogatory name calling, as well as less intentional, potentially hurtful comments by peers, family members, employers, strangers, and health care providers. Overweight adolescents report that others often make negative assumptions about them, including that they are inactive or lazy, do not have feelings, and are unclean (10).

Among adults who were overweight during childhood, there is an increased relative risk of 1.5 of all-cause mortality and 2.0 of cardiovascular disease mortality (11). Adolescents who are at risk of becoming overweight or who are overweight have a significantly higher prevalence of moderate to severe asthma when compared with a peer group (12). Hypertension, sleep apnea, dyslipidemia, increased fasting insulin levels, and sudden death have been associated with being overweight (13–16). More recently, overweight adolescents have been shown to be at increased risk of type 2 diabetes (17). Furthermore, a variety of orthopedic complications occur in overweight adolescents, such as slipped capital femoral epiphysis and Blount's disease (a growth disorder of the shin bone that causes the lower leg to angle inward) (18). Finally, overweight adolescents face increased morbidity and mortality later in their reproductive lives.

## Obstetric and Gynecologic Implications for Overweight Adolescents

### *Irregular Menses*

Overweight adolescents often report amenorrhea, oligomenorrhea, or menometrorrhagia to their

| | Height | m | 1.24 | 1.27 | 1.3 | 1.32 | 1.35 | 1.37 | 1.4 | 1.42 | 1.45 | 1.47 | 1.5 | 1.52 | 1.55 | 1.57 | 1.6 | 1.63 | 1.65 | 1.68 | 1.7 | 1.73 | 1.75 | 1.78 | 1.8 | 1.83 | 1.85 | 1.88 | 1.9 | 1.93 |
|---|---|---|---|---|---|---|---|---|---|---|---|---|---|---|---|---|---|---|---|---|---|---|---|---|---|---|---|---|---|---|
| | | in | 49 | 50 | 51 | 52 | 53 | 54 | 55 | 56 | 57 | 58 | 59 | 60 | 61 | 62 | 63 | 64 | 65 | 66 | 67 | 68 | 69 | 70 | 71 | 72 | 73 | 74 | 75 | 76 |
| Weight | | | | | | | | | | | | | | | | | | | | | | | | | | | | | | |
| kg | lb | | | | | | | | | | | | | | | | | | | | | | | | | | | | | |
| 20 | 45 | | 13.2 | 12.7 | 12.2 | 11.7 | 11.3 | 10.8 | 10.5 | 10.1 | 9.7 | 9.4 | 9.1 | 8.8 | 8.5 | | | | | | | | | | | | | | | |
| 23 | 50 | | 14.6 | 14.1 | 13.5 | 13.0 | 12.5 | 12.1 | 11.6 | 11.2 | 10.8 | 10.4 | 10.1 | 9.8 | 9.4 | 9.1 | 8.9 | 8.6 | 8.3 | | | | | | | | | | | |
| 25 | 55 | | 16.1 | 15.5 | 14.9 | 14.3 | 13.8 | 13.3 | 12.8 | 12.3 | 11.9 | 11.5 | 11.1 | 10.7 | 10.4 | 10.1 | 9.7 | 9.4 | 9.2 | 8.9 | | | | | | | | | | |
| 27 | 60 | | 17.6 | 16.9 | 16.2 | 15.6 | 15.0 | 14.5 | 13.9 | 13.5 | 13.0 | 12.5 | 12.1 | 11.7 | 11.3 | 11.0 | 10.6 | 10.3 | 10.0 | 9.7 | 9.4 | 9.1 | | | | | | | | |
| 29 | 65 | | 19.0 | 18.3 | 17.6 | 16.9 | 16.3 | 15.7 | 15.1 | 14.6 | 14.1 | 13.6 | 13.1 | 12.7 | 12.3 | 11.9 | 11.5 | 11.2 | 10.8 | 10.5 | 10.2 | 9.9 | 9.6 | | | | | | | |
| 32 | 70 | | 20.5 | 19.7 | 18.9 | 18.2 | 17.5 | 16.9 | 16.3 | 15.7 | 15.1 | 14.6 | 14.1 | 13.7 | 13.2 | 12.8 | 12.4 | 12.0 | 11.6 | 11.3 | 11.0 | 10.6 | 10.3 | 10.0 | | | | | | |
| 34 | 75 | | 22.0 | 21.1 | 20.3 | 19.5 | 18.8 | 18.1 | 17.4 | 16.8 | 16.2 | 15.7 | 15.1 | 14.6 | 14.2 | 13.7 | 13.3 | 12.9 | 12.5 | 12.1 | 11.7 | 11.4 | 11.1 | 10.8 | 10.5 | | | | | |
| 36 | 80 | | 23.4 | 22.5 | 21.6 | 20.8 | 20.0 | 19.3 | 18.6 | 17.9 | 17.3 | 16.7 | 16.2 | 15.6 | 15.1 | 14.6 | 14.2 | 13.7 | 13.3 | 12.9 | 12.5 | 12.2 | 11.8 | 11.5 | 11.2 | 10.8 | | | | |
| 39 | 85 | | 24.9 | 23.9 | 23.0 | 22.1 | 21.3 | 20.5 | 19.8 | 19.1 | 18.4 | 17.8 | 17.2 | 16.6 | 16.1 | 15.5 | 15.1 | 14.6 | 14.1 | 13.7 | 13.3 | 12.9 | 12.6 | 12.2 | 11.9 | 11.5 | 11.2 | | | |
| 41 | 90 | | 26.4 | 25.3 | 24.3 | 23.4 | 22.5 | 21.7 | 20.9 | 20.2 | 19.5 | 18.8 | 18.2 | 17.6 | 17.0 | 16.5 | 15.9 | 15.4 | 15.0 | 14.5 | 14.1 | 13.7 | 13.3 | 12.9 | 12.6 | 12.2 | 11.9 | 11.6 | | |
| 43 | 95 | | 27.8 | 26.7 | 25.7 | 24.7 | 23.8 | 22.9 | 22.1 | 21.3 | 20.6 | 19.9 | 19.2 | 18.6 | 17.9 | 17.4 | 16.8 | 16.3 | 15.8 | 15.3 | 14.9 | 14.4 | 14.0 | 13.6 | 13.2 | 12.9 | 12.5 | 12.2 | | |
| 45 | 100 | | 29.3 | 28.1 | 27.0 | 26.0 | 25.0 | 24.1 | 23.2 | 22.4 | 21.6 | 20.9 | 20.2 | 19.5 | 18.9 | 18.3 | 17.7 | 17.2 | 16.6 | 16.1 | 15.7 | 15.2 | 14.8 | 14.3 | 13.9 | 13.6 | 13.2 | 12.8 | 12.5 | 12.2 |
| 48 | 105 | | 30.7 | 29.5 | 28.4 | 27.3 | 26.3 | 25.3 | 24.4 | 23.5 | 22.7 | 21.9 | 21.2 | 20.5 | 19.8 | 19.2 | 18.6 | 18.0 | 17.5 | 16.9 | 16.4 | 16.0 | 15.5 | 15.1 | 14.6 | 14.2 | 13.9 | 13.5 | 13.1 | 12.8 |
| 50 | 110 | | 32.2 | 30.9 | 29.7 | 28.6 | 27.5 | 26.5 | 25.6 | 24.7 | 23.8 | 23.0 | 22.2 | 21.5 | 20.8 | 20.1 | 19.5 | 18.9 | 18.3 | 17.8 | 17.2 | 16.7 | 16.2 | 15.8 | 15.3 | 14.9 | 14.5 | 14.1 | 13.7 | 13.4 |
| 52 | 115 | | 33.7 | 32.3 | 31.1 | 29.9 | 28.8 | 27.7 | 26.7 | 25.8 | 24.9 | 24.0 | 23.2 | 22.5 | 21.7 | 21.0 | 20.4 | 19.7 | 19.1 | 18.6 | 18.0 | 17.5 | 17.0 | 16.5 | 16.0 | 15.6 | 15.2 | 14.8 | 14.4 | 14.0 |
| 54 | 120 | | 35.1 | 33.7 | 32.4 | 31.2 | 30.0 | 28.9 | 27.9 | 26.9 | 26.0 | 25.1 | 24.2 | 23.4 | 22.7 | 21.9 | 21.3 | 20.6 | 20.0 | 19.4 | 18.8 | 18.2 | 17.7 | 17.2 | 16.7 | 16.3 | 15.8 | 15.4 | 15.0 | 14.6 |
| 57 | 125 | | 36.6 | 35.2 | 33.8 | 32.5 | 31.3 | 30.1 | 29.0 | 28.0 | 27.0 | 26.1 | 25.2 | 24.4 | 23.6 | 22.9 | 22.1 | 21.5 | 20.8 | 20.2 | 19.6 | 19.0 | 18.5 | 17.9 | 17.4 | 17.0 | 16.5 | 16.0 | 15.6 | 15.2 |
| 59 | 130 | | 38.1 | 36.6 | 35.1 | 33.8 | 32.5 | 31.3 | 30.2 | 29.1 | 28.1 | 27.2 | 26.3 | 25.4 | 24.6 | 23.8 | 23.0 | 22.3 | 21.6 | 21.0 | 20.4 | 19.8 | 19.2 | 18.7 | 18.1 | 17.6 | 17.1 | 16.7 | 16.2 | 15.8 |
| 61 | 135 | | 39.5 | 38.0 | 36.5 | 35.1 | 33.8 | 32.5 | 31.4 | 30.3 | 29.2 | 28.2 | 27.3 | 26.4 | 25.5 | 24.7 | 23.9 | 23.2 | 22.5 | 21.8 | 21.1 | 20.5 | 19.9 | 19.4 | 18.8 | 18.3 | 17.8 | 17.3 | 16.9 | 16.4 |
| 64 | 140 | | 41.0 | 39.4 | 37.8 | 36.4 | 35.0 | 33.8 | 32.5 | 31.4 | 30.3 | 29.3 | 28.3 | 27.3 | 26.4 | 25.6 | 24.8 | 24.0 | 23.3 | 22.6 | 21.9 | 21.3 | 20.7 | 20.1 | 19.5 | 19.0 | 18.5 | 18.0 | 17.5 | 17.0 |
| 66 | 145 | | 42.5 | 40.8 | 39.2 | 37.7 | 36.3 | 35.0 | 33.7 | 32.5 | 31.4 | 30.3 | 29.3 | 28.3 | 27.4 | 26.5 | 25.7 | 24.9 | 24.1 | 23.4 | 22.7 | 22.0 | 21.4 | 20.8 | 20.2 | 19.7 | 19.1 | 18.6 | 18.1 | 17.6 |
| 68 | 150 | | 43.9 | 42.2 | 40.5 | 39.0 | 37.5 | 36.2 | 34.9 | 33.6 | 32.5 | 31.3 | 30.3 | 29.3 | 28.3 | 27.4 | 26.6 | 25.7 | 25.0 | 24.2 | 23.5 | 22.8 | 22.1 | 21.5 | 20.9 | 20.3 | 19.8 | 19.3 | 18.7 | 18.3 |
| 70 | 155 | | 45.4 | 43.6 | 41.9 | 40.3 | 38.8 | 37.4 | 36.0 | 34.7 | 33.5 | 32.4 | 31.3 | 30.3 | 29.3 | 28.3 | 27.5 | 26.6 | 25.8 | 25.0 | 24.3 | 23.6 | 22.9 | 22.2 | 21.6 | 21.0 | 20.4 | 19.9 | 19.4 | 18.9 |
| 73 | 160 | | 46.8 | 45.0 | 43.2 | 41.6 | 40.0 | 38.6 | 37.2 | 35.9 | 34.6 | 33.4 | 32.3 | 31.2 | 30.2 | 29.3 | 28.3 | 27.5 | 26.6 | 25.8 | 25.1 | 24.3 | 23.6 | 23.0 | 22.3 | 21.7 | 21.1 | 20.5 | 20.0 | 19.5 |
| 75 | 165 | | 48.3 | 46.4 | 44.6 | 42.9 | 41.3 | 39.8 | 38.3 | 37.0 | 35.7 | 34.5 | 33.3 | 32.2 | 31.2 | 30.2 | 29.2 | 28.3 | 27.5 | 26.6 | 25.8 | 25.1 | 24.4 | 23.7 | 23.0 | 22.4 | 21.8 | 21.2 | 20.6 | 20.1 |
| 77 | 170 | | 49.8 | 47.8 | 45.9 | 44.2 | 42.5 | 41.0 | 39.5 | 38.1 | 36.8 | 35.5 | 34.3 | 33.2 | 32.1 | 31.1 | 30.1 | 29.2 | 28.3 | 27.4 | 26.6 | 25.8 | 25.1 | 24.4 | 23.7 | 23.1 | 22.4 | 21.8 | 21.2 | 20.7 |
| 79 | 175 | | | 49.2 | 47.3 | 45.5 | 43.8 | 42.2 | 40.7 | 39.2 | 37.9 | 36.6 | 35.3 | 34.2 | 33.1 | 32.0 | 31.0 | 30.0 | 29.1 | 28.2 | 27.4 | 26.6 | 25.8 | 25.1 | 24.4 | 23.7 | 23.1 | 22.5 | 21.9 | 21.3 |
| 82 | 180 | | | 50.6 | 48.7 | 46.8 | 45.0 | 43.4 | 41.8 | 40.4 | 38.9 | 37.6 | 36.4 | 35.2 | 34.0 | 32.9 | 31.9 | 30.9 | 30.0 | 29.0 | 28.2 | 27.4 | 26.6 | 25.8 | 25.1 | 24.4 | 23.7 | 23.1 | 22.5 | 21.9 |
| 84 | 185 | | | | 50.0 | 48.1 | 46.3 | 44.6 | 43.0 | 41.5 | 40.0 | 38.7 | 37.4 | 36.1 | 35.0 | 33.8 | 32.8 | 31.8 | 30.8 | 29.9 | 29.0 | 28.1 | 27.3 | 26.5 | 25.8 | 25.1 | 24.4 | 23.8 | 23.1 | 22.5 |
| 86 | 190 | | | | | 49.4 | 47.6 | 45.8 | 44.2 | 42.6 | 41.1 | 39.7 | 38.4 | 37.1 | 35.9 | 34.7 | 33.7 | 32.6 | 31.6 | 30.7 | 29.8 | 28.9 | 28.1 | 27.3 | 26.5 | 25.8 | 25.1 | 24.4 | 23.7 | 23.1 |
| 88 | 195 | | | | | 50.7 | 48.8 | 47.0 | 45.3 | 43.7 | 42.2 | 40.8 | 39.4 | 38.1 | 36.8 | 35.7 | 34.5 | 33.5 | 32.4 | 31.5 | 30.5 | 29.6 | 28.8 | 28.0 | 27.2 | 26.4 | 25.7 | 25.0 | 24.4 | 23.7 |
| 91 | 200 | | | | | | 50.1 | 48.2 | 46.5 | 44.8 | 43.3 | 41.8 | 40.4 | 39.1 | 37.8 | 36.6 | 35.4 | 34.3 | 33.3 | 32.3 | 31.3 | 30.4 | 29.5 | 28.7 | 27.9 | 27.1 | 26.4 | 25.7 | 25.0 | 24.3 |
| 93 | 205 | | | | | | | 49.4 | 47.6 | 46.0 | 44.4 | 42.8 | 41.4 | 40.0 | 38.7 | 37.5 | 36.3 | 35.2 | 34.1 | 33.1 | 32.1 | 31.2 | 30.3 | 29.4 | 28.6 | 27.8 | 27.0 | 26.3 | 25.6 | 25.0 |
| 95 | 210 | | | | | | | | 48.8 | 47.1 | 45.4 | 43.9 | 42.4 | 41.0 | 39.7 | 38.4 | 37.2 | 36.0 | 34.9 | 33.9 | 32.9 | 31.9 | 31.0 | 30.1 | 29.3 | 28.5 | 27.7 | 27.0 | 26.2 | 25.6 |
| 98 | 215 | | | | | | | | 50.0 | 48.2 | 46.5 | 44.9 | 43.4 | 42.0 | 40.6 | 39.3 | 38.1 | 36.9 | 35.8 | 34.7 | 33.7 | 32.7 | 31.7 | 30.8 | 30.0 | 29.2 | 28.4 | 27.6 | 26.9 | 26.2 |
| 100 | 220 | | | | | | | | | 49.3 | 47.6 | 46.0 | 44.4 | 43.0 | 41.6 | 40.2 | 39.0 | 37.8 | 36.6 | 35.5 | 34.5 | 33.4 | 32.5 | 31.6 | 30.7 | 29.8 | 29.0 | 28.2 | 27.5 | 26.8 |
| 102 | 225 | | | | | | | | | 50.4 | 48.7 | 47.0 | 45.4 | 43.9 | 42.5 | 41.1 | 39.9 | 38.6 | 37.4 | 36.3 | 35.2 | 34.2 | 33.2 | 32.3 | 31.4 | 30.5 | 29.7 | 28.9 | 28.1 | 27.4 |
| 104 | 230 | | | | | | | | | | 49.8 | 48.1 | 46.4 | 44.9 | 43.5 | 42.1 | 40.7 | 39.5 | 38.3 | 37.1 | 36.0 | 35.0 | 34.0 | 33.0 | 32.1 | 31.2 | 30.3 | 29.5 | 28.7 | 28.0 |
| 107 | 235 | | | | | | | | | | | 49.1 | 47.5 | 45.9 | 44.4 | 43.0 | 41.6 | 40.3 | 39.1 | 37.9 | 36.8 | 35.7 | 34.7 | 33.7 | 32.8 | 31.9 | 31.0 | 30.2 | 29.4 | 28.6 |
| 109 | 240 | | | | | | | | | | | 50.2 | 48.5 | 46.9 | 45.3 | 43.9 | 42.5 | 41.2 | 39.9 | 38.7 | 37.6 | 36.5 | 35.4 | 34.4 | 33.5 | 32.5 | 31.7 | 30.8 | 30.0 | 29.2 |
| 111 | 245 | | | | | | | | | | | | 49.5 | 47.8 | 46.3 | 44.8 | 43.4 | 42.0 | 40.8 | 39.5 | 38.4 | 37.2 | 36.2 | 35.2 | 34.2 | 33.2 | 32.3 | 31.5 | 30.6 | 29.8 |
| 113 | 250 | | | | | | | | | | | | 50.5 | 48.8 | 47.2 | 45.7 | 44.3 | 42.9 | 41.6 | 40.3 | 39.2 | 38.0 | 36.9 | 35.9 | 34.9 | 33.9 | 33.0 | 32.1 | 31.2 | 30.4 |
| 116 | 255 | | | | | | | | | | | | | 49.8 | 48.2 | 46.6 | 45.2 | 43.8 | 42.4 | 41.2 | 39.9 | 38.8 | 37.7 | 36.6 | 35.6 | 34.6 | 33.6 | 32.7 | 31.9 | 31.0 |
| 118 | 260 | | | | | | | | | | | | | | 49.1 | 47.5 | 46.1 | 44.6 | 43.3 | 42.0 | 40.7 | 39.5 | 38.4 | 37.3 | 36.3 | 35.3 | 34.3 | 33.4 | 32.5 | 31.6 |
| 120 | 265 | | | | | | | | | | | | | | 50.1 | 48.5 | 46.9 | 45.5 | 44.1 | 42.8 | 41.5 | 40.3 | 39.1 | 38.0 | 37.0 | 35.9 | 35.0 | 34.0 | 33.1 | 32.3 |
| 122 | 270 | | | | | | | | | | | | | | | 49.4 | 47.8 | 46.3 | 44.9 | 43.6 | 42.3 | 41.0 | 39.9 | 38.7 | 37.7 | 36.6 | 35.6 | 34.7 | 33.7 | 32.9 |
| 125 | 275 | | | | | | | | | | | | | | | | 48.7 | 47.2 | 45.8 | 44.4 | 43.1 | 41.8 | 40.6 | 39.5 | 38.4 | 37.3 | 36.3 | 35.3 | 34.4 | 33.5 |
| 127 | 280 | | | | | | | | | | | | | | | | 49.6 | 48.1 | 46.6 | 45.2 | 43.8 | 42.6 | 41.3 | 40.2 | 39.0 | 38.0 | 36.9 | 35.9 | 35.0 | 34.1 |
| 129 | 285 | | | | | | | | | | | | | | | | 50.5 | 48.9 | 47.4 | 46.0 | 44.6 | 43.3 | 42.1 | 40.9 | 39.7 | 38.6 | 37.6 | 36.6 | 35.6 | 34.7 |
| 132 | 290 | | | | | | | | | | | | | | | | | 49.8 | 48.3 | 46.8 | 45.4 | 44.1 | 42.8 | 41.6 | 40.4 | 39.3 | 38.3 | 37.2 | 36.2 | 35.3 |
| 134 | 295 | | | | | | | | | | | | | | | | | 50.6 | 49.1 | 47.6 | 46.2 | 44.8 | 43.6 | 42.3 | 41.1 | 40.0 | 38.9 | 37.9 | 36.9 | 35.9 |
| 136 | 300 | | | | | | | | | | | | | | | | | | 49.9 | 48.4 | 47.0 | 45.6 | 44.3 | 43.0 | 41.8 | 40.7 | 39.6 | 38.5 | 37.5 | 36.5 |

**Fig. 1.** Body mass index chart for children and adolescents. (For more information on body mass index for adolescents, visit the Centers for Disease Control and Prevention web site at www.cdc.gov/nccdphp/dnpa/bmi/childrens_BMI/about_childrens_BMI.htm.)

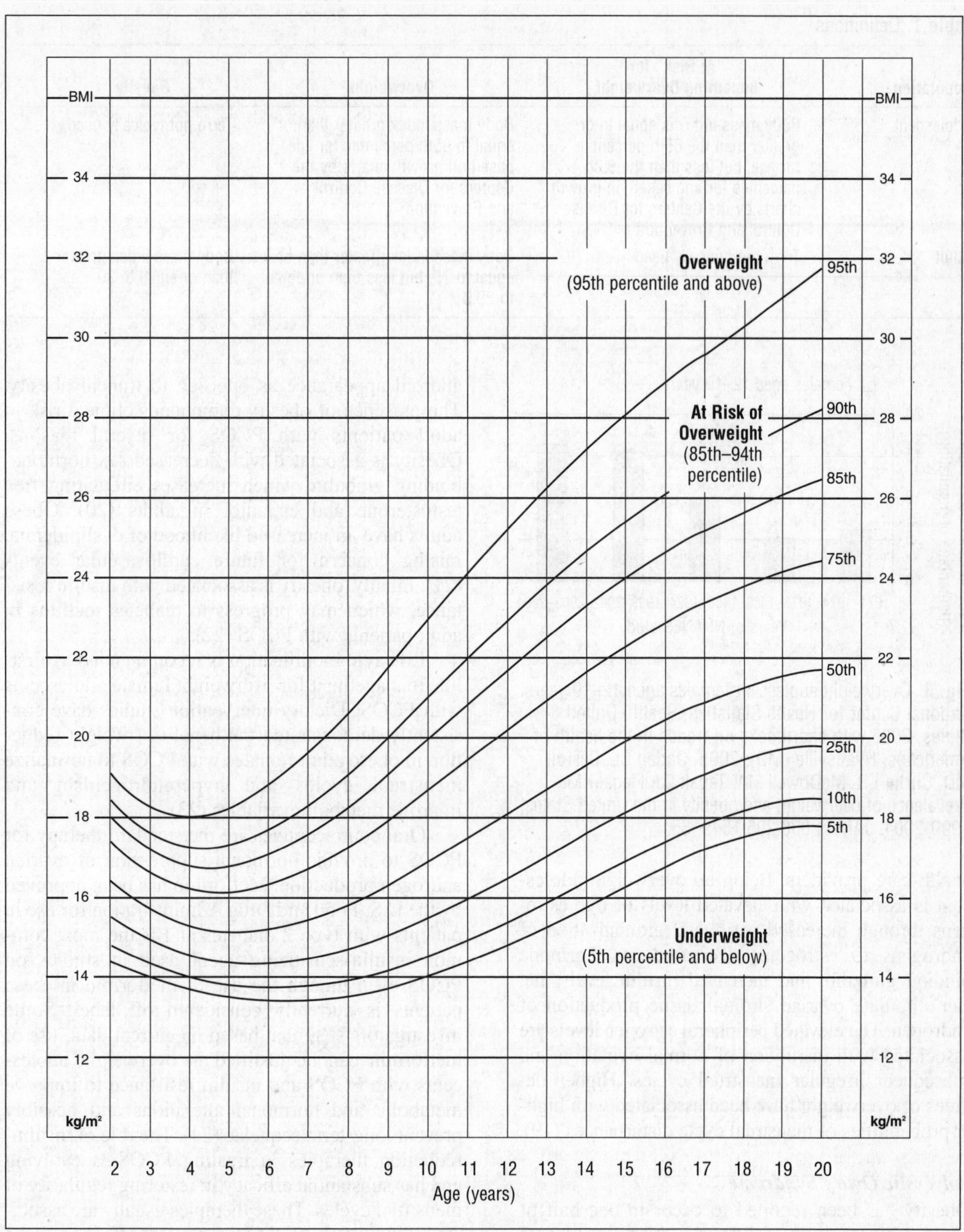


**Fig. 2.** Body mass index for age percentiles: Girls, aged 2–20 years. (Developed by the National Center for Health Statistics in collaboration with the National Center for Chronic Disease Prevention and Health Promotion [2000].)

**Table 1.** Definitions

| Population | "At Risk" for Becoming Overweight | Overweight | Obesity |
|---|---|---|---|
| Adolescent | Body mass index is equal to or greater than the 85th percentile for age, but less than the 95th percentile for age based on growth charts by the Centers for Disease Control and Prevention | Body mass index greater than or equal to 95th percentile for age based on growth charts by the Centers for Disease Control and Prevention | Term not typically used |
| Adult | Term not typically used | Body mass index greater than or equal to 25, but less than or equal to 29.9 | Body mass index greater than or equal to 30 |

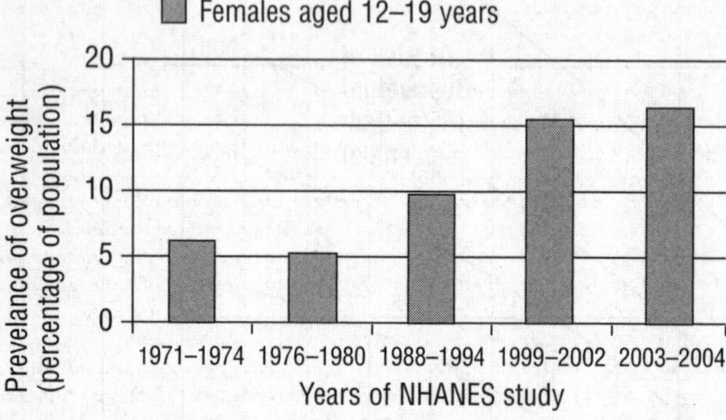


**Fig. 3.** Overweight adolescent females aged 12–19 years. National Center for Health Statistics. Health, United States, 2005 with chartbooks on trends in the health of Americans. Hyattsville (MD): 2005. Ogden CL, Carroll MD, Curtin LR, McDowell MA, Tabak CJ, Flegal KM. Prevalence of overweight and obesity in the United States, 1999-2004. JAMA 2006;295:1549–55.

health care providers. Being an overweight adolescent is associated with elevated levels of free estrogens through increased peripheral aromatization of androgens to estrogens, decreased sex hormone binding globulin, and increased insulin levels that can stimulate ovarian stromal tissue production of androgen. The elevated peripheral estrogen levels are associated with disruption of normal ovulation and subsequent irregular menstrual cycles. Higher degrees of overweight have been associated with higher probabilities of menstrual cycle disturbances (19).

### *Polycystic Ovary Syndrome*

Obesity has been reported to occur in one half of adult patients with polycystic ovary syndrome (PCOS). Obesity in adult patients with PCOS is characterized by an increased waist-to-hip ratio or android appearance as opposed to truncal obesity. The presence of obesity compounds clinical risk in adult patients with PCOS for several reasons. Obesity is associated with decreased sex hormone-binding globulin, which increases circulating free testosterone and estradiol in adults (20). Obese adults have an increased likelihood of dyslipidemia, raising concern for future cardiovascular events (21). Finally, obesity is associated with insulin resistance, which may progress to diabetes mellitus in adult patients with PCOS (22).

Lifestyle modification is recommended as first-line management for overweight female adolescents with PCOS. Dietary intervention studies have consistently demonstrated the benefit of weight reduction in obese adult females with PCOS to normalize menstrual cycles and hyperandrogenism and improve metabolic variables (23).

Oral contraceptives are the standard therapy for PCOS to provide hormonal suppression of ovarian androgen production. Metformin has been approved by the U.S. Food and Drug Administration for use in patients with type 2 diabetes and is the most common insulin-sensitizing agent used in studies on PCOS even though the use of metformin in these patients is currently considered off label. Some investigators state that based on current data, use of metformin can be justified in overweight adolescents with PCOS and insulin resistance to improve metabolic and hormonal alterations and possibly prevent long-term sequelae (24). The role of insulin-reduction therapies in treating PCOS is evolving and has substantial efficacy in restoring regularity of menstrual cycles. These therapies usually are associated with initial weight loss, are less effective in the treatment of hirsutism, and may cause gastrointestinal side effects (25).

### *Hormonal Contraception*

Recent studies suggest that women weighing more than 70.5 kg have an increased risk of unintended pregnancy while using combination oral contraceptives compared with women who have normal body mass (relative risk 1.6) (26, 27). Another study demonstrated that women with BMIs greater than 32.2 had a higher risk of accidental pregnancy while using combination oral contraceptives than did women who have normal body mass (27). Several mechanisms have been proposed to account for the elevated failure rates in obese adult women. It has been theorized that obese adult women metabolize steroids differently than lean women possibly because of a larger blood volume to transport steroid hormones and fat cells sequestering steroid hormones (28). In obese adult users of combination oral contraceptives, the risk of thromboembolism is increased (29). For overweight adolescents at risk of pregnancy, it is important to balance the risks and benefits of combination oral contraceptives, including the risks from pregnancy. Consideration should be given to progestin-only oral contraceptives and intrauterine methods when counseling overweight adolescents regarding contraceptive choices. Women who weigh more than 90 kg may have a disproportionately higher likelihood of contraceptive failure with the transdermal contraceptive patch (30).

Serum levonorgestrel levels are lower in obese adult women compared with nonobese adult women using a two-rod implant (not yet commercially available). Yet, effective contraception is thought to last 5 years regardless of weight (31). The effectiveness of the etonogestrel single-rod implant that has been recently approved by the U.S. Food and Drug Administration for use in overweight women has not been adequately studied. However, serum concentrations of the synthetic progestin etonogestrel are inversely related to body weight and decrease with time after insertion. It is, therefore, possible that with time this single-rod implant may be less effective in overweight women (32). No changes in efficacy have been shown with the vaginal ring regardless of patient weight. Although injectable contraception has not been demonstrated to decrease contraceptive efficacy based on weight, it has been associated with weight gain (see Table 2).

### *Intrauterine Device*

The effectiveness of the intrauterine device (IUD) in obese adult women is similar to that demonstrated in adults of average weight. Insertion of an IUD can be technically challenging in the obese adult woman and often requires the use of a larger speculum for adequate visualization of the cervix. Placing a condom with the tip removed over the speculum blades can aid in exposure. Ultrasonography also may be a useful tool both before and during IUD insertion (33). This information may be applied to the adolescent population until other data are available.

### *Pregnancy-Related Issues*

Maternal obesity (BMI greater than or equal to 30) is an important obstetric risk factor independent of maternal age (34). Nearly all complications of pregnancy, except intrauterine growth restriction, are more frequent in obese adult women (35). In a recent prospective Danish study, overweight and obese adult women had increased risks of diabetes, hypertension, preeclampsia, and cesarean delivery (36). Obesity is associated with a more than doubled risk of stillbirth (odds ratio, 2.8; 95% confidence interval [CI], 1.5–5.3) and neonatal death (odds ratio, 2.6; 95% CI, 1.2–5.8) compared with women of normal weight. Much of these data are based on adult women, but may be applied to the pregnant adolescent population until other data are available.

Most adolescent pregnancies (80%) are unintended (37). This precludes the physician from providing preconception counseling that would address diet and exercise. The goals of this counseling include avoiding specific pregnancy complications, such as macrosomia, operative deliveries, late fetal deaths, neural tube defects, gestational hypertension, and gestational diabetes. There is a significant increase in cesarean deliveries in primiparous adolescents with BMIs greater than or equal to 30 compared with those with BMIs less than or equal to 20 (38). Maternal weight also has an effect on the child. Regardless of maternal age, maternal obesity in the first trimester of pregnancy is associated with elevated risk of overweight in the child. Specifically, the relative risk of overweight in the child was 2.0 (95% CI, 1.7–2.3) at age 2 years, 2.3 (95% CI, 2.0–2.6) at age 3 years, and 2.3 (95% CI, 2.0–2.6) at age 4 years (39).

African-American adolescents who are overweight before their first pregnancy become more overweight; on average, 3.3 years following the index pregnancy. They also are at increased risk of retaining gestational weight gain (40). The association between ethnicity, overweight, and obstetric and

**Table 2.** The Effect of Weight on Birth Control Methods

| Birth Control Method | Average Associated Weight Gain | Does weight affect how well it prevents pregnancy? |
|---|---|---|
| Abstinence | None | No |
| Male condom | None | No |
| Female condom | None | No |
| Emergency contraception | None | No |
| Vaginal spermicide | None | No |
| Diaphragm | None | If gain or loss of 10 pounds or more occurs, it may need to be refitted |
| Cervical cap | None | If gain or loss of 10 pounds or more occurs, it may need to be refitted |
| Combination oral contraceptives | None | If weight is 176 pounds or more, it may not prevent pregnancy as well |
| Progestin-only oral contraceptives (mini pills) | None | If weight is 176 pounds or more, it may not prevent pregnancy as well |
| Contraceptive injection | 5 pounds in first year of use | No |
| Vaginal ring | None | No |
| Patch | None | If weight is 176 pounds or more, it may not prevent pregnancy as well |
| Copper T intrauterine device | None | No |
| Mirena intrauterine system | None | No |
| Sterilization | None | No |

Created by the SAFE Study: Computer-Aided Counseling to Prevent Teen Pregnancy/STDs, Principal Investigator: Melanie A. Gold, D.O., University of Pittsburgh School of Medicine, supported by NICHD grant #HD41058. Modified and reprinted with permission.

neonatal outcomes needs further exploration in the adolescent population.

Information regarding pregnancy termination also is scarce. In second trimester dilation and evacuation abortions, obesity has been linked with technical difficulty, longer operating times, and more blood loss (41, 42).

## Prevention

The American College of Obstetricians and Gynecologists recommends that all adolescents be screened annually for overweight by determining weight and stature, calculating a BMI for age, and asking about body image and eating patterns (43). The U.S. Preventive Services Task Force concluded that there is "insufficient evidence to recommend for or against routine screening for overweight in adolescents in primary care settings" (44). This is based on the lack of evidence that screening and therapeutic intervention improve health outcomes for overweight adolescents. Although ACOG recognizes the recent report and the limitations in the data, ACOG continues to support the screening of adolescents because screening and interventions may demonstrate benefit if used in combination with several modalities.

Although the research on prevention of overweight status in adolescents has resulted in few effective recommendations, some prevention strategies have been generated. Parents play a significant role. A surgeon general report highlights the probable protective benefit of breastfeeding in preventing overweight in children and adults (45). Health care providers should promote healthy eating and physical activity to adolescent patients and their parents during routine preventive health care visits (43, 45). Parents can help their children and adolescents to follow the Dietary Guidelines for Americans at home and at school. These guidelines include recommendations to decrease consumption of fat, saturated fat, sodium, and added sugars; increase consumption of fruit, vegetables, whole grains, and other foods that are rich in fiber; increase the consumption of milk or other foods or beverages that are good sources of calcium; and participate in at least 60 minutes of physical activity on most, preferably all, days of the week (45, 46). Adolescents can be encouraged to increase the amount of regular daily activity by making small lifestyle changes, such as climbing the stairs instead of taking an elevator. They also can be encouraged to choose an activity that can become a part of their everyday life, such as bicycling or walking. Leisure activities that are sedentary, such as television viewing and playing computer games, should be restricted to less than 2 hours per day. Parents also should be encouraged to model healthy eating habits and physical activity and should be informed that food should never be used as a tool for punishment or reward. Eating breakfast and regular meals is important to promoting and maintaining a healthy weight. A recent study funded by the National Institutes of Health monitored nearly 2,400 females aged 9–19 years for 10 years and found that those who regularly ate breakfast, particularly ones that included cereal, were slimmer than those who skipped the morning meal (47). Schools can support healthy behavior by using several means, including the provision of instruction, the enactment of physical activity and nutrition policies, and by ensuring that the school environment supports healthy eating and physical activity (48).

## Screening and Treatment

Adolescence can be a difficult time for assessing weight status because of pubertal changes and differences in individual patterns of growth. A dietary and health assessment should be conducted on adolescents with BMIs greater than or equal to the 85th percentile for age, but less than the 95th percentile for age to determine psychosocial morbidity and risk for future cardiovascular disease if:

- Their BMI has increased by two or more units during the previous 12 months
- They have a family history of premature heart disease, obesity, hypertension, or diabetes mellitus
- They express concern about their weight
- They have elevated blood pressure or serum cholesterol levels (43)

Adolescents with a BMI greater than or equal to the 95th percentile for age should have an in-depth dietary and health assessment to determine psychosocial morbidity and risk for future cardiovascular disease. Obstetrician–gynecologists are strongly encouraged to provide this assessment (43). Early referral to a nutritional specialist skilled in adolescent care may be warranted. The patient usually is acutely aware of her weight issue and has likely attempted many of her own weight loss strategies. These adolescents need clear and direct support, guidance, and encouragement. Also they need a better understanding of the widespread nature of the disease to feel less alone and isolated. Family involvement in the treatment plan is critical. Any proposed diet should be consistent with the Dietary Guidelines for Americans and allow for individualized caloric intake recommendations that support gradual, not rapid, weight loss.

It is important to note that weight loss is recommended only for adolescents in certain circumstances (46). For example, older overweight adolescents who have completed linear growth or those with comorbidities, may require weight loss (18, 49). More often, the goal is to slow the rate of weight gain while achieving normal growth and development. Discussion of portion sizes, snacking, and eating at restaurants and outside the home is helpful (46). (See box for examples of healthy snacks.) Wake Forest University has developed a web site (http://www1.wfubmc.edu/Nutrition/Count+Your+Calories/dtd.htm) that provides the nutritional and caloric information of several of the largest fast food chains in the United States. This web site may be useful to adolescent patients and their parents.

There are sufficient adult data indicating that physical activity contributes to weight loss, both

### Healthy Snacks

Providing some examples of healthy snacks may be useful when discussing the dietary needs of an overweight adolescent female. These examples may include:

- A bean burrito
- A cheese quesadilla with salsa and lettuce
- A yogurt and fruit smoothie with graham crackers
- A bowl of whole-grain cereal topped with sliced fruit and milk
- A small salad with sliced deli meat, tuna or beans
- Fruit, cheese, and whole-grain crackers

alone and when it is combined with dietary therapy. Efforts to achieve weight loss with physical activity alone generally produce moderate weight loss. Even so, increased physical activity is a useful adjunct to low-calorie diets in promoting weight reduction. Also, physical activity reduces obesity-associated comorbidities (1).

The amount of time an adolescent spends performing aerobic versus sedentary activities should be assessed. As stated previously, it is recommended that adolescents participate in at least 60 minutes of physical activity on most, preferably all, days of the week (46). Increased activity and decreased television viewing has been shown to reduce an adolescent's weight (50). In children, family-based programs that encompass diet, physical activity, reduction of sedentary behavior, and behavioral therapy have been shown to help children lose weight compared with no treatment. It is important to provide recommendations on diet and physical activity that are achievable given the patient's family environment. It also is important to evaluate the adolescent's psychologic well-being (18). Often, collaboration with a mental health professional is indicated.

There are limited data to document the efficacy of prescription medications or over-the-counter drugs for weight loss in adolescents. The role of surgical intervention for overweight adolescents has yet to be established, but some recent studies have suggested that surgical weight loss improves the early mortality experienced by these adolescents (51). Bariatric surgery currently is recommended for adolescents who have a BMI greater than 40 and have comorbid conditions. Those who may be candidates for bariatric surgery should be referred to a multidisciplinary weight management team with expertise in treating overweight adolescents (52). Long-term studies are needed to determine the risk and benefits of bariatric surgery in adolescents. Nationally, a new paradigm has been proposed with an emphasis on promoting a healthy lifestyle in overweight patients instead of focusing solely on weight loss. This idea of "health at any size" may encourage patients to focus on their overall health improvement, rather than only their weight status (53).

## Conclusion

Adolescent females who are overweight have significant health sequelae. There are limited evidence-based data for the successful prevention and treatment of overweight adolescents. Because additional research is needed, our best tool is to extrapolate an approach from data and studies pertaining to children and adults, while remaining cognizant of the special needs that surround adolescent growth and development. Sound nutritional recommendations and regular physical activity are essential components for overall good health because they convey myriad benefits for growth, brain and cognitive development, self-esteem, immunity, and disease prevention (54).

## References


1. National Heart, Lung, and Blood Institute (NHLBI), National Institute for Diabetes and Digestive and Kidney Diseases (NIDDK). Clinical guidelines on the identification, evaluation, and treatment of overweight and obesity in adults. The evidence report. NIH Publication No. 98-4083. Bethesda (MD): NIH; 1998. Available at: http://www.nhlbi.nih.gov/guidelines/obesity/ob_gdlns.pdf. Retrieved July 25, 2006.
2. Ogden CL, Carroll MD, Curtin LR, McDowell MA, Tabak CJ, Flegal KM. Prevalence of overweight and obesity in the United States, 1999-2004. JAMA 2006;295:1549–55.
3. National Center for Health Statistics. Health, United States, 2005 with chartbooks on trends in the health of Americans. Hyattsville (MD): NCHS; 2005.
4. Haas JS, Lee LB, Kaplan CP, Sonneborn D, Phillips KA, Liang S. The association of race, socioeconomic status, and health insurance status with the prevalence of overweight among children and adolescents. Am J Public Health 2003;93:2105–10.
5. Gortmaker SL, Must A, Perrin JM, Sobol AM, Dietz WH. Social and economic consequences of overweight in adolescence and young adulthood. N Engl J Med 1993; 329:1008–12.
6. Sargent JD, Blanchflower DG. Obesity and stature in adolescence and earnings in young adulthood. Analysis of a British birth cohort. Arch Pediatr Adolesc Med 1994; 148:681–7.
7. Erickson SJ, Robinson TN, Haydel F, Killen JD. Are overweight children unhappy? Body mass index, depressive symptoms, and overweight concerns in elementary school children. Arch Pediatr Adolesc Med 2000;154:931–5.
8. Strauss RS. Childhood obesity and self-esteem. Pediatrics 2000;105; e15.
9. Swallen KC, Reither EN, Haas SA, Meier AM. Overweight, obesity, and health-related quality of life among adolescents: the National Longitudinal Study of Adolescent Health. Pediatrics 2005;115:340–7.
10. American Obesity Association. Obesity in youth. AOA fact sheet. Available at: http://www.obesity.org/subs/fastfacts/obesity_youth.shtml. Retrieved April 3, 2006.
11. Must A, Strauss RS. Risks and consequences of childhood and adolescent obesity. Int J Obes Relat Metab Disord 1999;23(suppl 2):S2–11.
12. Rodriguez MA, Winkelby MA, Ahn D, Sundquist J, Kraemer HC. Identification of population subgroups of

children and adolescents with high asthma prevalence: findings from the Third National Health and Nutrition Examination Survey. Arch Pediatr Adolesc Med 2002; 156:269–75.

13. Reinehr T, Andler W, Demer C, Siegried W, Mayer H, Wabitsch M. Cardiovascular risk factors in overweight German children and adolescents: relation to gender, age and degree of overweight. Nutr Metab Cardiovasc Dis 2005;15;181–7.
14. Wing YK, Hui SH, Pak WM, Ho CK, Cheung A, Li AM, et al. A controlled study of sleep related disordered breathing in obese children. Arch Dis Child 2003;88: 1043–7.
15. Viner RM, Segal TY, Lichtarowicz-Krynska E, Hindmarsch P. Prevalence of the insulin resistance syndrome in obesity. Arch Dis Child 2005;90:10–4.
16. Bharati S, Lev M. Cardiac conduction system involvement in sudden death of obese young people. Am Heart J 1995;129:273–81.
17. Wabitsch M, Hauner H, Hertrampf M, Muche R, Hay B, Mayer H, et al. Type II diabetes mellitus and impaired glucose regulation in Caucasian children and adolescents with obesity living in Germany. Int J Obes Relat Metabl Disord 2004;28:307–13.
18. Daniels SR, Arnett DK, Eckel RH, Gidding SS, Hayman LL, Kumanyika S, et al. Overweight in children and adolescents: pathophysiology, consequences, prevention, and treatment. Circulation 2005;111:1999–2012.
19. Castillo-Martinez L, Lopez-Alvarenga JC, Villa AR, Gonzalez-Barranco J. Menstrual cycle length disorders in 18-40-y-old obese women. Nutrition 2003;19:317–20.
20. Chang RJ. A practical approach to the diagnosis of polycystic ovary syndrome. Am J Obstet Gynecol 2004; 191:713–7.
21. Guzick DS. Cardiovascular risk in women with polycystic ovarian syndrome. Semin Reprod Endocrinol 1996:14: 45–9.
22. Legro, RS, Kunselman AR, Dodson WC, Dunaif A. Prevalence and predictors of risk for type 2 diabetes mellitus and impaired glucose control in polycystic ovarian syndrome: a prospective, controlled study in 254 affected women. J Clin Endocrinol Metab 1999:84:165–9.
23. Norman R, Davies M, Lord J, Moran LJ. The role of lifestyle modification in polycystic ovarian syndrome. Trends Endocrinol Metab 2002;13:251–7.
24. Pelusi C, Pasquali R. Polycystic ovary syndrome in adolescents: pathophysiology and treatment implications. Treat Endocrinol 2003;2:215–30.
25. Ehrmann DA. Polycystic ovary syndrome. N Engl J Med 2005;352:1223–36.
26. Holt VL, Cushing-Haugen KL, Daling JR. Body weight and risk of oral contraceptive failure. Obstet Gynecol 2002;99:820–7.
27. Holt VL, Scholes D, Wicklund KG, Cushing-Haugen KL, Daling JR. Body mass index, weight, and oral contraceptive failure risk. Obstet Gynecol 2005;105:46–52.
28. Speerhas R. Drug metabolism in malnutrition and obesity: clinical concerns. Cleve Clin J Med 1995;62:73–5.
29. Nightingale AL, Lawrenson RA, Simpson EL, Williams TJ, MacRae KD, Farmer RD. The effects of age, body mass index, smoking and general health on the risk of venous thromboembolism in users of combined oral contraceptives. Eur J Contracept Rep Health Care 2000: 5:265–74.
30. Zieman M, Guillebaud J, Weisberg E, Shangold GA, Fisher AC, Creasy GW. Contraceptive efficacy and cycle control with the Ortho Evra/Evra transdermal system: the analysis of pooled data. Fertil Steril 2002;77(suppl): S13–8.
31. Sivin I, Wan L, Ranta S, Alvarez F, Brache V, Mishell DR Jr, et al. Levonorgestrel concentrations during 7 years of continuous use of Jadelle contraceptive implants. Contraception 2001;64:43–9.
32. Implanon [package insert]. Roseland (NJ): Organon: 2006. Available at: http://www.fda.gov/cder/foi/label/2006/021529lbl.pdf. Retrieved Sepember 20, 2006.
33. Grimes DA, Shields WC. Family planning for obese women: challenges and opportunities. Contraception 2005;72:1–4.
34. Kristensen J, Vestergaard M, Wisborg K, Kesmodel U, Secher NJ. Pre-pregnancy weight and the risk of stillbirth and neonatal death. BJOG 2005;112:403–8.
35. Andreasen KR, Andersen ML, Schantz AL. Obesity and pregnancy. Acta Obstet Gynecol Scand 2004;83:1022–9.
36. Rode L, Nilas L, Wojdemann K, Tabor A. Obesity-related complications in Danish single cephalic term pregnancies. Obstet Gynecol 2005;105:537–42.
37. National Campaign to Prevent Teen Pregnancy. Teen sexual activity, contraceptive use, pregnancy and childbearing: general facts and stats. Washington, DC: NCPTP; 2003. Available at: http://www.teenpregnancy.org/resources/reading/fact_sheets/genfacts.asp. Retrieved July 25, 2006.
38. Young TK, Woodmansee B. Factors that are associated with cesarean delivery in a large private practice: the importance of prepregnancy body mass index and weight gain. Am J Obstet Gynecol 2002;187:312–8; discussion 318–20.
39. Whitaker RC. Predicting preschooler obesity at birth: the role of maternal obesity in early pregnancy. Pediatrics 2004;114:e29–36.
40. Segel JS, McAnarney ER. Adolescent pregnancy and subsequent obesity in African-American girls. J Adolesc Health 1994;15:491–4.
41. Dark AC, Miller L, Kothenbeutel RL, Mandel L. Obesity and second-trimester abortion by dilation and evacuation. J Reprod Med 2002;47:226–30.
42. Marchiano DA, Thomas AG, Lapinski R, Balwan K, Patel J. Intraoperative blood and gestational age at pregnancy termination. Prim Care Update Ob Gyns 1998;5:204–5.
43. American College of Obstetricians and Gynecologists. Health care for adolescents. Washington, DC: ACOG; 2003.
44. Screening and interventions for overweight in children and adolescents: recommendation statement. US Preventive Services Task Force. Pediatrics 2005;116:205–9.
45. U.S. Department of Health and Human Services. The Surgeon General's call to action to prevent and decrease overweight and obesity. Rockville (MD): USDHHS; 2001. Available at: http://www.surgeongeneral.gov/topics/obesity/calltoaction/CalltoAction.pdf. Retrieved July 18, 2006.
46. U.S. Department of Agriculture, U.S. Department of Health and Human Services. Dietary guidelines for Americans, 2005. 6th ed. Washington, DC: United States Government Printing Office; 2005. Available at: http://

www.health.gov/dietaryguidelines/dga2005/document/pdf/DGA2005.pdf. Retrieved April 3, 2006.

47. Barton BA, Eldridge AL, Thompson D, Affenito SG, Striegel-Moore RH, Franko DL, et al. The relationship of breakfast and cereal consumption to nutrient intake and body mass index: the National Heart, Lung, and Blood Institute Growth and Health study. J Am Diet Assoc 2005;105:1383–9.
48. Wechsler H, McKenna ML, Lee SM, Dietz WH. The role of schools in preventing childhood obesity. State Educ Stand 2004;5:4–12.
49. Barlow SE, Dietz WH. Obesity evaluation and treatment: expert committee recommendations. The Maternal and Child Health Bureau, Health Resources and Services Administration and the Department of Health and Human Services. Pediatrics 1998;102:E29. Available at: http://www.pediatrics.org/cgi/content/full/102/3/e29. Retrieved July 25, 2006.
50. Austin SB, Field AE, Wiecha J, Peterson KE, Gortmaker SL. The impact of a school-based obesity prevention trial on disordered weight-control behaviors in early adolescent girls. Arch Pediatr Adolesc Med 2005;159:225–30.
51. Jain A. What works for obesity? A summary of the research behind obesity interventions. London: BMJ Publishing Group; 2004. Available at: http://www.unitedhealthfoundation.org/obesity.pdf. Retrieved April 11, 2006.
52. Inge T, Krebs NF, Garcia VF, Skelton JA, Guice KS, Strauss RS, et al. Bariatric surgery for severely overweight adolescents: concerns and recommendations. Pediatrics 2004;114:217–23.
53. O'Dea JA. Prevention of child obesity: 'first, do no harm'. Health Educ Res 2005;20:259–65.
54. Berg F, Buechner J, Parham E. Guidelines for childhood obesity prevention programs: promoting healthy weight in children. Weight Realities Division of the Society for Nutrition Education. J Nutr Educ Behav 2003;35:1–4.

# Resources

## *ACOG Resources*

American College of Obstetricians and Gynecologists. Eating disorders. In: Health care for adolescents. Washington, DC: ACOG; 2003. p.81–94.

American College of Obstetricians and Gynecologists. Eating disorders. ACOG Patient Education Pamphlet AP144. Washington, DC: ACOG; 2000.

American College of Obstetricians and Gynecologists. Healthy eating. ACOG Patient Education Pamphlet AP130. Washington, DC: ACOG; 2006.

Obesity in pregnancy. ACOG Committee Opinion No. 315. American College of Obstetricians and Gynecologists. Obstet Gynecol 2005;106:671–5.

American College of Obstetricians and Gynecologists. Primary and preventive health care for female adolescents. In: Health care for adolescents. Washington, DC: ACOG; 2003. p.1–24.

The role of the obstetrician–gynecologist in the assessment and management of obesity. ACOG Committee Opinion No. 319. American College of Obstetricians and Gynecologists. Obstet Gynecol 2005;106:895–9.

American College of Obstetricians and Gynecologists. Tool kit for teen care. Washington, DC: ACOG; 2003.

American College of Obstetricians and Gynecologists. Weight & adolescent females. Fact Sheets for Teens FS019. Washington, DC: ACOG; 2003.

American College of Obstetricians and Gynecologists. Weight control: eating right and keeping fit. ACOG Patient Education Pamphlet AP064. Washington, DC: ACOG; 2006.

## *Other Resources*

We have provided information on the following organizations and web sites because they have information that may be of interest to our readers. The American College of Obstetricians and Gynecologists does not necessarily endorse the views expressed or the facts presented by these organizations or on these web sites. Further, ACOG does not endorse any commercial products that may be advertised or available from these organizations or on these web sites.

American Academy of Family Physicians
11400 Tomahawk Creek Parkway
Leawood, KS 66211-2672
Telephone: 800-274-2237 or 913-906-6000
http://www.aafp.org

American Academy of Pediatrics
141 Northwest Point Boulevard
Elk Grove Village, IL 60007-1098
Telephone: 847-434-4000
http://www.aap.org/obesity

American Alliance for Health, Physical Education, Recreation, and Dance
1900 Association Drive
Reston, VA 20191-1598
Telephone: 800-213-7193 or 703-476-3400
http://www.aahperd.org

American College of Sports Medicine
401 West Michigan Street
Indianapolis, IN 46202-3233
Telephone: 317-637-9200
http://www.acsm.org

American Dietetic Association
120 South Riverside Plaza, Suite 2000
Chicago, IL 60606-6995
Telephone: 800-877-1600
http://www.eatright.org

American Heart Association
7272 Greenville Avenue
Dallas, TX 75231
Telephone: 800-242-8721
http://www.americanheart.org

American Obesity Association
1250 24th Street NW, Suite 300
Washington, DC 20037
Telephone: 202-776-7711
http://www.obesity.org

AWARE Foundation
1015 Chestnut Street, Suite 1225
Philadelphia, PA 19107-4302
Telephone: 215-955-9847
http://www.awarefoundation.org

Centers for Disease Control and Prevention
Division of Adolescent and School Health
Healthy Youth
PO Box 8817
Silver Spring, MD 20907
Telephone: 800-CDC-INFO (800-232-4636)
http://www.cdc.gov/nccdphp/dash

Centers for Disease Control and Prevention
National Center for Chronic Disease Prevention and Health Promotion
1600 Clifton Rd
Atlanta, GA 30333
Telephone: 404-639-3311 or 800-311-3435 or 800-232-4636
http://www.cdc.gov/nccdphp/dnpa/obesity
http://www.cdc.gov/nccdphp/dnpa/bmi/index.htm

Institute of Medicine
500 Fifth Street NW
Washington DC 20001
Telephone: 202-334-2352
http://www.iom.edu/

National Association for Health & Fitness
The Network of State and Governor's Councils
c/o Be Active New York State
65 Niagara Square, Room 607
Buffalo NY 14202
Telephone: 716-583-0521
http://www.physicalfitness.org

National Heart, Lung, and Blood Institute
PO Box 30105
Bethesda, MD 20824-0105
Telephone: 301-592-5873
http://www.nhlbi.nih.gov/index.htm

Society for Adolescent Medicine
1916 NW Copper Oaks Circle
Blue Springs, MO 64015
Telephone: 816-224-8010
http://www.adolescenthealth.org

U.S. Surgeon General
Office of Surgeon General
5600 Fishers Lane—Room 18-66
Rockville MD 20857
301-443-4000
http://www.surgeongeneral.gov/topics/obesity/calltoaction/fact_adolescents.htm

ACOG Committee Opinion

Committee on
Adolescent Health Care

Number 355, December 2006 (Replaces No. 274, July 2002)

This document reflects emerging clinical and scientific advances as of the date issued and is subject to change. The information should not be construed as dictating an exclusive course of treatment or procedure to be followed.

The Committee would like to thank Marc R. Laufer, MD, for his assistance in the development of this document.



ISSN 1074-861X

**The American College of Obstetricians and Gynecologists**
409 12th Street, SW
PO Box 96920
Washington, DC 20090-6920

12345/09876

Vaginal agenesis: diagnosis, management, and routine care. ACOG Committee Opinion No. 355. American College of Obstetricians and Gynecologists. Obstet Gynecol 2006;108:1605–9.

# Vaginal Agenesis: Diagnosis, Management, and Routine Care

*ABSTRACT: Vaginal agenesis occurs in 1 of every 4,000–10,000 females. The most common cause of vaginal agenesis is congenital absence of the uterus and vagina, which also is referred to as müllerian aplasia, müllerian agenesis, or Mayer–Rokitansky–Küster–Hauser syndrome. The condition usually can be successfully managed nonsurgically with the use of successive dilators if it is correctly diagnosed and the patient is sufficiently motivated. Besides correct diagnosis, effective management also includes evaluation for associated congenital renal or other anomalies and careful psychologic preparation of the patient before any treatment or intervention. If surgery is preferred, a number of approaches are available; the most common is the Abbe–McIndoe operation. Women who have a history of müllerian agenesis and have created a functional vagina require routine gynecologic care and can be considered in a similar category to that of women without a cervix and thus annual cytologic screening for cancer may be considered unnecessary in this population.*

Vaginal agenesis is an uncommon, but not rare, condition. Given an incidence ranging from 1 per 4,000 to 1 per 10,000 females (1), vaginal agenesis is a condition that general gynecologists will encounter once or twice during their professional careers. The most common cause of vaginal agenesis is congenital absence of the uterus and vagina, which also is referred to as müllerian aplasia, müllerian agenesis, or Mayer–Rokitansky–Küster–Hauser syndrome. The term müllerian aplasia will be used to describe this congenital reproductive anomaly throughout this document. Müllerian aplasia is caused by embryologic growth failure of the müllerian duct, with resultant anomalies in the müllerian structures. With absence of the vagina, there is variation on the presence or absence of the uterus. A single midline uterus can be present or uterine horns (with or without an endometrial cavity) can exist. The ovaries, given their separate embryologic source, are normal in structure and function.

To manage vaginal agenesis effectively, correct diagnosis of the underlying condition is important. Evaluation for associated congenital, renal, or other anomalies also is essential. Both diagnosis and evaluation usually can be completed without surgery. Patient counseling should be provided before any treatment or intervention. Nonsurgical creation of the neovagina should be the first-line approach.

## Differential Diagnosis

Patients with müllerian aplasia have a normal 46,XX karyotype, normal female phenotype, and normal ovarian hormonal and oocyte function. Puberty and development of secondary sexual characteristics progress normally except that menarche does not occur. Therefore, patients with müllerian aplasia typically present in adolescence with primary amenorrhea. The practitioner should remember that it is usually 2–3 years from the onset of breast development until the first period. If menarche has not occurred within 3 years of the onset of breast development, further evaluation is indicated. Müllerian aplasia is the second most common cause of primary amenorrhea, with gonadal dysgenesis being the most common cause (2).

On physical examination, patients with müllerian aplasia have normal breast development, normal secondary sexual body proportions, body hair, and hymenal tissue. A vagina is absent unless it has been created by sexual encounters. Differential diagnosis of vaginal agenesis includes congenital absence of the vagina (with or without uterine structures), androgen insensitivity (absence or alteration of androgen-receptor function), 17 α-hydroxylase deficiency, a low transverse vaginal septum, and imperforate hymen.

In cases of androgen insensitivity, the gonads are testes, producing normal androgens in karyotypic 46,XY individuals. The lack of androgen tissue receptors results in sparse or no pubic and axillary hair. Patients with androgen insensitivity typically have normal breast development because of peripheral conversion of circulating androgens to estrogens. They may have a small lower vagina, or a normal length vagina can occur; however, no uterus or cervix is present. In pubertal females, the differential diagnosis between androgen insensitivity and müllerian aplasia is easily made by assessing serum testosterone levels. A testosterone level in the pubertal male range confirms the diagnosis of androgen insensitivity.

In postpubertal patients, the presence of functioning ovarian tissue seen on pelvic ultrasound examinations may serve as a secondary confirmation of the diagnosis of müllerian aplasia, excluding the diagnosis of androgen insensitivity. Chromosomal studies, although more costly than a serum testosterone level assessment, provide the diagnostic tool to differentiate between müllerian aplasia in genetic females and disorders of testosterone synthesis in genetic males. Chromosomal analysis also is helpful in prepubertal children who do not yet have postpubertal sex steroid production.

In cases of 17 α-hydroxylase deficiency, 46XY individuals will have complete male pseudohermaphroditism with female external genitalia, a blind short vaginal pouch, no uterus or fallopian tubes, and intraabdominal testes. Affected males are usually raised as girls, with the underlying disorder being recognized when the patient is evaluated for lack of pubertal development (3, 4).

The differential diagnosis of vaginal agenesis also includes imperforate hymen and low transverse vaginal septum. Patients with these latter conditions will have a normal cervix and uterus, both of which may be palpable on rectal examination. In contrast to most patients with müllerian aplasia, the patient with an imperforate hymen will not have the typical fringe of hymenal tissue. The patient with a low transverse vaginal septum will have a normal hymen, like the patient with müllerian aplasia. Conventional ultrasonography, three-dimensional ultrasonography, and magnetic resonance imaging can be used to better define the müllerian structures and are helpful in definitively defining anatomy.

Correct diagnosis of the underlying condition affecting the genital anatomy is crucial before any surgical intervention. If the patient undergoes an operation because of an incorrect diagnosis (eg, an incorrect preoperative diagnosis of an imperforate hymen in cases of vaginal agenesis), it can be extremely difficult to correct the anomaly because of scar tissue.

## Evaluation of the Patient With Müllerian Aplasia

Most patients with müllerian aplasia have small rudimentary müllerian bulbs without any endometrial activity. In 2–7% of patients with müllerian aplasia, active endometrium is found in these uterine structures (1). These patients will present with cyclic or chronic abdominal pain. Magnetic resonance imaging has been suggested to assess the reproductive anatomy, although it is rarely needed in the initial evaluation unless ultrasound evaluation for the presence of functional endometrium in a müllerian structure is equivocal (5). Although laparoscopy is not necessary to diagnose müllerian aplasia, it may be useful in the evaluation of patients with cyclic abdominal pain to exclude the possibility of endometrial activity in müllerian structures (6). When obstructed hemi-uteri are identified (uterine horns with the presence of active endometrium without associated cervix and upper vagina), then removal of the unilateral or bilateral obstructed uterine structures should be performed. The removal of the obstructed uterine structures can be accomplished laparoscopically (7, 8).

Patients with müllerian aplasia often have concomitant congenital malformations, especially of the abdominal wall, urinary tract, and skeleton. Inguinal hernias occur at an increased incidence in patients with müllerian aplasia. Ultrasonography can be used to screen for the more common findings of renal agenesis or a pelvic kidney. This evaluation can be performed during the study of ovarian and müllerian structures. The implications of ureteral duplication in the case of later abdominal or pelvic surgery can be discussed, or intravenous pyelography can be used to exclude this possibility. Scoliosis is the most common skeletal abnormality associated with müllerian aplasia. It also should be noted that there is an increased, but small, rate of hearing impairment in patients with müllerian aplasia.

After the diagnosis of müllerian aplasia, the adolescent should be offered counseling to emphasize that a normal sex life will be possible after a neovagina has been created. Ultimately, however, infertility may be a more difficult aspect of this disorder for the patient to accept. Future fertility options should be addressed with adolescents and their parent(s) or guardian(s). Discussion of assisted reproductive techniques and use of a gestational carrier (surrogate) is appropriate. Specifically, it is important to explain that eggs can be harvested from patients with müllerian aplasia and used in assisted reproductive technology; daughters of women with Mayer–Rokitansky–Küster–Hauser syndrome conceived by assisted reproductive technology have been shown to have normal reproductive tracts (9). This information allows teens to understand their reproductive potential for becoming a biologic parent and may help them accept the diagnosis and its implications. Referral to a mental health professional is very worthwhile for some patients. The best predictor of good emotional outcome after diagnosis and vaginoplasty is a good relationship between the patient and her parents or guardians and the ability to share feelings with family and friends (7). Contact with a support group or young women with the same diagnosis may be helpful (6) (see Resources).

Patients should be given a brief, written medical summary of their condition, including a summary of concomitant malformations. This information may be useful if the patient requires urgent medical care or emergency surgery from a health care provider unfamiliar with müllerian aplasia.

## Nonsurgical Creation of a Neovagina

Timing for nonsurgical or surgical creation of a neovagina is elective; however, it is best planned when the patient is emotionally mature. Nonsurgical creation of the vagina is the appropriate first-line approach in most patients because it is the least morbid procedure. In a recently reported series of patients with müllerian aplasia, more than 90% were able to achieve anatomic and functional success by vaginal dilation (10).

Patients are asked to manually place successive dilators on the perineal dimple for 30 minutes to 2 hours per day. Another option of sitting on a bicycle seat stool provides the perineal pressure and allows the patient to participate in simultaneous productive activities, such as doing homework or practicing a musical instrument (11). Many young women find that sitting on the bicycle seat stool is too uncomfortable or awkward, thus they may have better success using dilators while reclining on a bed after a relaxing bath. Use of dilators in the management of vaginal agenesis is appropriate and successful in most patients. Mature, highly motivated patients who wish to avoid surgery and are aware that it will take several months to achieve their goal are likely to be successful (11, 12). Because the nonoperative approach is noninvasive and usually successful, it is strongly recommended as first-line therapy.

Clinicians often use "buddies," other patients with vaginal agenesis who have successfully dilated, as support to the young woman attempting dilation. Young married patients make excellent buddies. If fertility issues are a major concern to the patient or her family, it may be helpful to find a buddy who has used assisted reproductive techniques to become a mother.

## Surgical Creation of a Neovagina

Surgery becomes an option for patients who are unsuccessful with dilators or patients who prefer surgery after a thorough discussion with the patient and her parent(s) or guardian(s) of the risks and benefits of the procedure and the available nonsurgical alternatives. It should be stressed to the young woman that a surgical vaginoplasty is not a "quick fix" and that she will still need to use vaginal dilators postoperatively to maintain her surgically created vagina. The aim of surgery is the creation of a vaginal canal in the correct axis of adequate size and secretory capacity to allow intercourse to occur without the need for continued postoperative dilation. The timing of the surgery depends on the patient and the type or procedure planned. Surgeries often are performed in late adolescence (ages 17–21 years) when the patient is more mature and better able to adhere to postoperative dilation or instructions. Surgery usually is scheduled during summer vacation to allow for an adequate recovery time without missing school and to reduce questions from peers (6, 13).

A number of operations are appropriate for the correction of vaginal agenesis. The approach usually is based on the experience of the operating surgeon. Pediatric surgeons are more likely to use bowel segments for the creation of a neovagina; gynecologists are more likely to use a perineal approach. Whatever technique is chosen, the surgeon must be experienced with the procedure because the initial surgery is more likely to succeed than follow-up procedures. Reoperation in these cases increases the chance of operative injury to surrounding tissues and the possibility of a poor functional outcome. At present, there is no consensus in the literature regarding the best option for surgical correction (14).

The most common surgical procedure used by U.S. gynecologists to create a neovagina is the Abbe–McIndoe operation. This involves the dissection of a space between the rectum and bladder, placement of a mold covered with a split-thickness skin graft into the space, and the diligent use of vaginal dilation postoperatively. Postoperative dilation must be continued to prevent significant skin graft contracture. This surgery is inappropriate if the patient rejects the nonsurgical technique because she has concerns about or objections to dilation. If postoperative dilation is not done, the patient will have a nonfunctional vagina. The dilators are used long-term on a less frequent basis until the woman is having vaginal intercourse because at that time the penis will act as a dilator to maintain the length of the vagina.

Other procedures for the creation of the neovagina are the Vecchietti procedure and laparoscopic modifications of operations previously performed by laparotomy. The Vecchietti procedure involves the creation of a neovagina via dilation with a traction device attached to the abdomen, sutures placed subperitoneally via laparotomy, and a plastic "olive" placed on the vaginal dimple. In the laparoscopic modification, traction sutures are placed laparoscopically. The two techniques are comparable in terms of producing a functional neovagina (15). Davydov developed a three-stage operation involving dissection of the rectovesical space with abdominal mobilization of the peritoneum, with creation of the vaginal fornices and attachment of the peritoneum to the introitus. The newer adaptation involves dissection of the rectovaginal space, with mobilization of the peritoneum from below and laparoscopic assistance from above. This is followed by closure of the abdominal end of the neovagina with a laparoscopically placed pursestring suture (8, 16, 17).

## General Gynecologic Care

Women who have a history of müllerian agenesis and have created a functional vagina do require routine gynecologic care. Annual pelvic examinations should be performed to examine for vaginal stricture or stenosis. Women with müllerian agenesis should be aware that the neovagina has the same risk as a native vagina for sexually transmitted diseases and thus they should be appropriately screened. In addition, vaginal speculum examination and inspection should be performed to look for possible malignancies (in cases of skin graft or bowel vaginas), colitis or ulceration (in cases of bowel vaginas), or other problems. No data exists regarding the need or lack of need for routine Pap testing in women with a neovagina. It is reasonable to consider these women in the same category as women without a cervix because of hysterectomy for the treatment of benign disease. Thus, annual cytologic screening for cancer can be considered unnecessary, although no data are available to support or oppose this concept.

## Conclusion

The most important steps in the effective management of müllerian aplasia are correct diagnosis of the underlying condition; evaluation for associated congenital, renal, or other anomalies; and preparation of the patient before any treatment or intervention. If any of these are neglected, the success of the intervention will be compromised.

Laparoscopy is seldom required to make the diagnosis but may be appropriate in the patient presenting with pelvic pain. Nonsurgical creation of the neovagina should be the first-line approach. In cases in which surgical intervention is required, referrals to centers with expertise in this area should be considered. Few surgeons have extensive experience in construction of the neovagina, and the initial surgery has the greatest chance for success. In addition, experts at these centers may be more successful in promoting the nonsurgical approach, given their experience.

## References


1. Evans TN, Poland ML, Boving RL. Vaginal malformations. Am J Obstet Gynecol 1981;141:910–20.
2. Reindollar RH, Byrd JR, McDonough PG. Delayed sexual development: a study of 252 patients. Am J Obstet Gynecol 1981;140:371–80.
3. New MI. Male pseudohermaphroditism due to 17 alpha-hydroxylase deficiency. J Clin Invest 1970;49:1930–41.
4. Nieman LK, Kovacs WJ. Uncommon causes of congenital adrenal hyperplasia. In: Rose BD, editor. UpToDate. Waltham (MA); 2006.
5. Fedele L, Dorta M, Brioschi D, Giudici MN, Candiani GB. Magnetic resonance imaging in Mayer-Rokitansky-Kuster-Hauser syndrome. Obstet Gynecol 1990;76: 593–6.
6. Laufer MR, Goldstein DP, Hendren WH. Structural abnormalities of the female reproductive tract. In: Emans SJ, Laufer MR, Goldstein DP, editors. Pediatric and adolescent gynecology. 5th ed. Philadelphia (PA): Lippincott Williams & Wilkins; 2005. p. 334–416.
7. Poland ML, Evans TN. Psychologic aspects of vaginal agenesis. J Reprod Med 1985;30:340–4.
8. Adamyan LV. Laparoscopic management of vaginal aplasia with or without functional noncommunicating rudimentary uterus. In: Arregui ME, Fitzgibbons RJ Jr, Katkhouda N, McKernan JB, Reich H, editors. Principles of laparoscopic surgery: basic and advanced techniques. New York (NY): Springer–Verlag; 1995. p. 646–51.
9. Petrozza JC, Gray MR, Davis AJ, Reindollar RH. Congenital absence of the uterus and vagina is not commonly transmitted as a dominant genetic trait: outcomes of surrogate pregnancies. Fertil Steril 1997;67:387–9.
10. Roberts CP, Haber MJ, Rock JA. Vaginal creation for müllerian agenesis. Am J Obstet Gynecol 2001; 185:1349–52; discussion 1352–3.
11. Williams JK, Lake M, Ingram JM. The bicycle seat stool in the treatment of vaginal agenesis and stenosis. J Obstet Gynecol Neonatal Nurs 1985;14:147–50.
12. Rock JA, Breech LL. Surgery for anomalies of the Müllerian ducts. In: Rock JA, Jones HW 3rd, editors. Te Linde's operative gynecology. 9th ed. Philadelphia (PA): Lippincott Williams & Wilkins; 2003. p. 705–52.
13. Templeman CL, Lam AM, Hertweck SP. Surgical management of vaginal agenesis. Obstet Gynecol Surv 1999;54:583–91.
14. Laufer MR. Congenital absence of the vagina: in search of the perfect solution. When, and by what technique, should a vagina be created? Curr Opin Obstet Gynecol 2002;14:441–4.
15. Borruto F, Chasen ST, Chervenak FA, Fedele L. The Vecchietti procedure for surgical treatment of vaginal agenesis: comparison of laparoscopy and laparotomy. Int J Gynaecol Obstet 1999;64:153–8.
16. Davydov SN, Zhvitiashvili OD. Formation of vagina (colpopoiesis) from peritoneum of Douglas pouch. Acta Chir Plast 1974;16:35–41.
17. Adamyan LV. Therapeutic and endoscopic perspectives. In: Nichols DH, Clarke-Pearson DL, editors. Gynecologic, obstetric, and related surgery. 2nd ed. St. Louis (MO): Mosby; 2000. p. 1209–17.


## Resources

MRKH.org, Inc.
PO Box 301494
Jamaica Plain, MA 02130
Web: www.mrkh.org

The Center for Young Women's Health
Children's Hospital Boston
333 Longwood Avenue, 5th Floor
Boston, MA 02115
(617) 730-0192
Web:www.youngwomenshealth.org

A guide to vaginal agenesis in teens. Available at www.youngwomenshealth.org/vaginalagenesis.html

MRKH (Mayer Rokitansky Kuster Hauser Syndrome) and vaginal agenesis: a guide for parents and guardians. Available at www.youngwomenshealth.org/mrkh_parent.html

# COMMITTEE OPINIONS

## COMMITTEE ON CODING AND NOMENCLATURE

# COMMITTEE OPINIONS

# ACOG Committee Opinion

Committee on Coding and Nomenclature

Number 205, August 1998

## Tubal Ligation with Cesarean Delivery

Tubal ligation at the time of cesarean delivery requires significant additional physician work even though the technical work of the procedure is brief. Informed consent by the patient requires considerably more counseling by the physician regarding potential risks and benefits of this procedure than is necessary with alternative means of sterilization and contraception. Also, many states require completion of special informed consent documents in addition to the customary consent forms required by hospitals. These forms must be completed before scheduling the procedure.

Patients have the right to change their minds. Thus, it is important to reconfirm the patient's decision shortly before the operation.

Tubal ligation with cesarean delivery involves removal of a segment of fallopian tube, which is sent for histologic confirmation. With most cesarean deliveries, tissue is not evaluated by a pathologist. Accordingly, it is important for the surgeon to verify the pathology report, which adds an additional component to post-service work.

The risk of professional liability for operative complications is increased with this procedure. This risk is low, but real. Furthermore, sterilization failure occurs in about 1 in 100 cases even though the operation was performed properly. This failure also carries a liability risk.

Because tubal ligation is a discrete extra service, it should be coded accordingly: 59510 or 59618—routine obstetric care including antepartum care, cesarean delivery, and postpartum care—and 58611—ligation or transection of fallopian tube(s) done at the time of cesarean delivery or intra-abdominal surgery.


ISSN 1074-861X

**The American College of Obstetricians and Gynecologists**
409 12th Street, SW
PO Box 96920
Washington, DC 20090-6920

12345/21098

ACOG Committee Opinion

Committee on Coding and Nomenclature

Number 249, January 2001

# Coding Responsibility

Physicians are responsible for accurately coding the services they provide to their patients. Likewise, insurers are obligated to process all legitimate insurance claims for covered services accurately and in a timely manner. It is inappropriate for physicians to code or for insurers to process claims incorrectly in order to enhance or reduce reimbursement. When either party engages in such a practice intentionally and repetitively, it should be considered dishonest and may be subject to civil and criminal penalties.



ISSN 1074-861X

**The American College of Obstetricians and Gynecologists**
409 12th Street, SW
PO Box 96920
Washington, DC 20090-6920

12345/54321

# ACOG Committee Opinion

Committee on Coding and Nomenclature

Number 250, January 2001

## Inappropriate Reimbursement Practices by Third-Party Payers

The American College of Obstetricians and Gynecologists (ACOG) Committee on Coding and Nomenclature believes that physicians must code accurately the services they provide and the diagnoses that justify those services for purposes of appropriate payment. This requirement is consistent with the rules established by the American Medical Association (AMA) Current Procedural Terminology Editorial Panel and published as the *Current Procedural Terminology* (CPT) and with those established by the International Classification of Diseases, Ninth Revision, Clinical Modification (ICD-9-CM), which are published in the American Hospital Association's *ICD-9-CM Coding Clinic*. In fairness, payers should be equally obligated to pay physicians based on the CPT standards and accept for processing all ICD-9-CM codes recorded on the claim. Currently, no such obligation for payers exists.

### Inappropriate Billing Denials

Five frequently encountered billing situations account for most payers' inappropriate first-time total or partial denials of correctly coded services. Each of these situations can inappropriately deny payment to physicians for medically indicated and correctly coded services because of payers' payment policies.

1. *Inappropriately bundling correctly coded multiple surgical procedures—Current Procedural Terminology* clearly describes surgical procedures that may be performed to treat various conditions. Each CPT code describes a specific procedure that was valued under the Resource Based Relative Value Scale (RBRVS) on the basis of a description of the work it entails. Many patients, especially those with complex clinical situations, need more than one surgical procedure to be performed at an operative session. For instance, a patient may require a vaginal hysterectomy because of severe irregular bleeding, but also might require repair of a symptomatic cystocele and rectocele. Because no single CPT code describes this combination of procedures, the physician should apply multiple CPT codes with appropriate modifiers to the secondary procedures as mandated by



ISSN 1074-861X

**The American College of Obstetricians and Gynecologists**
409 12th Street, SW
PO Box 96920
Washington, DC 20090-6920

12345/54321

CPT rules. Furthermore, the physician should expect reimbursement for all of the provided services defined by the CPT codes.

Despite the accuracy of the above statement regarding reimbursement for multiple procedures, payers often cite the efforts of Medicare to reduce payments for inappropriately unbundled CPT codes by physicians as justification for denial of physician claims for appropriately coded services. Indeed, the Health Care Financing Administration has established the Correct Coding Initiative (CCI), a process for bundling together many services that should not be paid separately. The process continues to undergo refinement with input from the AMA and medical specialty societies.

Unfortunately, some commercial software products that do not adhere to either CPT or CCI guidelines are being used by third-party payers to identify CPT codes for services that will not be reimbursed when coded together. For example, some of these products incorrectly bundle anterior and posterior colporrhaphy with enterocele repair into the code for vaginal hysterectomy, presumably because all of these procedures are performed through a vaginal approach. The AMA Correct Coding and Policy Committee, with input from ACOG staff, has identified many instances of inappropriate denial of reimbursement with some of these commercial bundling products. Physicians should appeal such denials (see the box) and cite the content of this document in requesting appropriate payment for these services.

2. *Ignoring modifiers that explain qualifying circumstances*—Current Procedural Terminology modifiers provide a coding shorthand that helps explain situations for which either increased or reduced payment is justified. There is, at present, no insurance industry standard for recognizing modifiers.

The American College of Obstetricians and Gynecologists believes that third-party payers should follow existing CPT guidelines and coding options, including recognition of all CPT modifiers, to ensure that all circumstances concerning the service performed are recognized. Payers who ignore correctly applied CPT modifiers inappropriately underreimburse physicians for the services provided.

3. *Denying payment for diagnostic and therapeutic procedures performed on the same day of service*—In certain clinical situations, a diagnostic surgical procedure is performed to determine

**Seven Steps for Appealing Denied Claims**

Take these steps when appealing inappropriate reimbursement practices by third-party payers:

1. Keep in mind that this is a negotiation process that will succeed only if the insurer is convinced that a charge is fair for the patient and the physician. It is important to use accepted coding standards when attempting to show that an insurer's policy is wrong. Polite but direct communication is more likely to achieve desired results than confrontation.
2. Have your staff contact the claims department of the insurer and discuss the reason for denial with the claims processor. These discussions should be based on clinical facts that rely on the Current Procedural Terminology (CPT) code definition of the service and the standard of care implied by the CPT code as it was valued under the Medicare Resource Based Relative Value Scale (RBRVS) system. Document all communication with the insurer (date, person from office making the call, person spoken with, results).
3. If staff is unsuccessful, contact the medical director of the payer yourself. Maintain open lines of communication with the medical director to discuss inappropriate payment policies and accepted coding standards.
4. Involve the state medical society in disputes with insurers. Many state societies will become very involved when patterns of abuse emerge.
5. Contact the American College of Obstetricians and Gynecologists (ACOG) for assistance in dealing with inappropriately denied medically indicated services that are covered by the patient's insurance policy and clearly were correctly reported. Contact ACOG's Department of Health Economics by fax or mail after downloading a complaint form from ACOG's web site (www.acog.org), or call (202) 863-2447 for assistance.
6. Send a copy of any correspondence between the practice and the payer dealing with unresolved problems to the insurance commissioner or equivalent regulatory authority in your state.
7. Involve your patient when inappropriate billing problems cannot be resolved in other ways. Physicians are not responsible for the insurance plan selected by the patient. Many third-party payers will revise their payment policies when they receive a complaint from the patient or patient's employer or union.

whether a therapeutic surgical procedure is required. When this occurs, it often is appropriate for the two procedures to be done at one time rather than at two distinct times. For example, if a diagnostic laparoscopy for a suspected benign condition reveals cancer, the physician may decide to perform a laparotomy to remove the cancer at the same operative session. In such a situation, many payers deny payment for the diagnostic laparoscopy even though performance of both the diagnostic and therapeutic procedures at the same time is medically indicated and requires additional physician work above that of the therapeutic procedure alone. In accordance with CPT guidelines, both procedures should be coded and the physician should be paid for both when the procedures have been documented appropriately and coded correctly. In the example, proper coding for the diagnostic service in addition to a therapeutic procedure would at the present time require the use of modifier –59 to identify the diagnostic procedure as distinct. In addition, however, the diagnostic procedure must be justified with a specific ICD-9-CM diagnostic code, which may or may not be the same as the ICD-9-CM code for the therapeutic procedure.

The practice by payers of bundling diagnostic and therapeutic procedures to reduce physicians' payment is inappropriate. Physicians have a legal obligation to code correctly. Insurers are equally obligated not to alter coding by physicians that is in accordance with approved CPT guidelines.

4. *Precertifying consultations at a predetermined level*—Some payers require precertification of a consultation and typically authorize a predetermined level of service based on the diagnostic information provided by the physician who requested the consultation. By contrast, the CPT guidelines state that the correct level of consultation is determined by the extent of the history, physical examination, and complexity of the medical decision-making process for each patient. This definition of services was used by Medicare under RBRVS to assign the relative value for physician consultation. Each patient who requires a consultation does so with a medical history typically including co-morbidities that can dramatically alter the physician work required to provide this service. Often such co-morbidities will necessitate a more thorough history and physical examination and involve more complex medical decision making than required in their absence. For example, a request for a consultation to assess fetal well-being in an otherwise healthy patient who has had an uneventful pregnancy will not resemble a consultation for this same problem when the patient has preexisting complications of pregnancy, such as cardiac disease, uncontrolled diabetes mellitus, or a history of poor obstetric outcomes.

   Because it is not possible to determine prospectively the level of service that will be required to evaluate and recommend treatment based on the uniqueness of each patient's problems, payers should precertify for an unspecified level of consultation that is paid at the appropriate level once the service has been provided.

5. *Denying diagnostic tests or studies performed at the same encounter as a distinct evaluation and management service*—The CPT manual states:

> The actual performance and/or interpretation of diagnostic tests/studies ordered during a patient encounter are not included in the levels of [evaluation and management (E/M)] services. Physician performance of diagnostic tests/studies for which specific CPT codes are available may be reported separately, in addition to the appropriate E/M code.

With this statement, CPT has clarified that diagnostic tests and studies, including colposcopies, biopsies, diagnostic ultrasound examinations, and cystometrics, are ordered on the basis of clinical criteria for each patient and not as a routine service. This definition means that tests performed at the time of an outpatient or other E/M encounter are not to be paid as part of the E/M service, but rather are to be paid separately. The E/M codes in CPT were valued under the Medicare RBRVS fee schedule on the basis of the CPT guidelines; these values do not include any diagnostic tests or studies.

The payer may deny reimbursement of diagnostic tests or studies at the time of an E/M encounter because the payer's payment policies might have been formulated with a lack of understanding of CPT coding standards that separate physician work included with the E/M service from the diagnostic test or study. This lack of understanding may lead the payer to inappropriately include all services provided to the patient at the E/M encounter as part of that service. The payer also may deny payment because the physician failed to add a modifier –25 to the billed E/M code to bypass the payer's established coding edits to ensure appropriate payment for both services.

## Possible Remedies

The physician should ensure that his or her billing staff are knowledgeable about:

- What is normally included and what is excluded from the service being billed (This information is provided in the most current edition of ACOG's *OB-GYN Coding Manual: Components of Correct Procedural Coding.**)
- How to link each service billed with one or more specific ICD-9-CM diagnostic codes that specifically justifies the reason for the service (This information is available in the most current edition of ACOG's *ICD-9-CM: Diagnostic Coding in Obstetrics and Gynecology.**)
- The correct application of CPT modifiers, when indicated (This information may be found in the appendixes of the current AMA CPT manual and in the current edition of ACOG's *CPT Coding in Obstetrics and Gynecology.**)
- Billing rules established by individual payers

The billing office should communicate clearly the indication for performing all coded services on the same date of service by reporting the most specific ICD-9-CM diagnostic codes. In some encounters, the justification for all services rendered may be documented by a single ICD-9-CM code. When a patient has multiple complaints or problems, multiple ICD-9-CM codes should be used.

* These resources are available from the American College of Obstetricians and Gynecologists.

# COMMITTEE OPINIONS

## COMMITTEE ON ETHICS



*Published in 2006
†Issued since publication of *Ethics in Obstetrics and Gynecology*, Second Edition

# COMMITTEE OPINIONS

ACOG Committee Opinion

Committee on Ethics

Number 294, May 2004

# At-Risk Drinking and Illicit Drug Use: Ethical Issues in Obstetric and Gynecologic Practice

ABSTRACT: *Abuse of alcohol and drugs is a major health problem for American women across differences in socioeconomic status, race, ethnicity, and age, and it is costly to individuals and to society. Obstetrician–gynecologists have an ethical obligation to learn and use a protocol for universal screening questions, brief intervention, and referral to treatment in order to provide patients and their families with medical care that is state-of-the-art, comprehensive, and effective. In this Committee Opinion, the American College of Obstetricians and Gynecologists' Committee on Ethics proposes an ethical rationale for this protocol in both obstetric and gynecologic practice and provides guidelines for resolving common ethical dilemmas related to drug and alcohol use that arise in the clinical setting.*



ISSN 1074-861X

**The American College of Obstetricians and Gynecologists**
409 12th Street, SW
PO Box 96920
Washington, DC 20090-6920

12345/87654

At-risk drinking and illicit drug use: ethical issues in obstetric and gynecologic practice. ACOG Committee Opinion No. 294. American College of Obstetricians and Gynecologists. Obstet Gynecol 2004;103:1021–31.

Abuse of alcohol and drugs is a major health problem for American women across differences in socioeconomic status, race, ethnicity, and age, and it is costly to individuals and to society. Women who are heavy drinkers (5 or more drinks on 1 occasion on 5 or more days in the past 30 days) represent 5.3% of 18–24 year olds and 3.4% of women aged 25 years or older. Among them, more than 2.5 million U.S. women are estimated to be alcohol dependent (1). Heavy drinking carries a higher risk of cardiac and hepatic complications for women than men. The alcohol-associated mortality rate is 50–100 times higher, and there is an increased burden of mental and physical disability (2). Among pregnant women, 12% admit to drinking some alcohol during the previous month (1), which puts the fetus at risk for fetal alcohol syndrome (FAS), the leading cause of mental retardation in the United States (3). Maternal alcoholism is one of the leading preventable causes of fetal neurodevelopmental disorders (4). The total costs of alcohol misuse and abuse are estimated at more than $667 billion yearly, including $2.8 billion attributable to FAS alone (5). Illicit drug use has major physical and mental health consequences and is associated with increased rates of sexually transmitted infections in women, including hepatitis and human immunodeficiency virus (HIV), as well as depression, domestic violence, poverty, and significant prenatal and neonatal complications (6, 7). In 2001, 8.3% of nonpregnant women and 3.7% of pregnant women reported illicit drug use, but among pregnant women aged 15–17 years, the rate of use increased to 15% (1). Drug abuse costs are estimated at more than $144 billion yearly, including $503 million associated with health care costs for drug-exposed newborns (5).

As a result of intensive research in addiction over the past decade, evidence-based recommendations have been consolidated into a protocol for universal screening questions, brief intervention, and referral to treatment (8). The rate of abstinence from drugs of abuse after treatment (the treatment success rate) is now comparable to the level of medication compliance achieved in diabetes, hypertension, or other chronic illnesses (9). Brief physician advice has been shown unequivocally to be both powerful and feasible in a clinical office setting (8, 10, 11). The American Medical Association has endorsed universal screening (12), and health services researchers have determined that treatment saves $7 for every dollar spent (13). For these reasons, the American College of Obstetricians and Gynecologists (ACOG) recently collaborated with the Physician Leadership on National Drug Policy at Brown University to produce a slide–lecture presentation that addresses the identification and treatment of drug abuse (14). The presentation was distributed to obstetric–gynecologic clerkship and residency program directors and is available at www.acog.org.

Physicians have been slow to implement universal screening, and rates of detection and referral to treatment among nonpregnant women remain very low (15). Studies using simulated patients have demonstrated that women are less likely than men to be screened or referred (16, 17). Physicians lack accurate knowledge about physiology (ie, the equivalency of 1.5 oz of distilled spirits, 12 oz of beer or wine cooler, and 5 oz of wine), risk factors, and sex differences in problem presentation and treatment response (18). These knowledge gaps are compounded by state laws designed to criminalize drug use during pregnancy, by women's fears that they might lose custody of their children, and by the social stigma experienced by women who abuse alcohol or use illicit drugs (19, 20). In one study, for example, the physicians surveyed defined "light drinking" as an average of 1.2 drinks per day, an amount that exceeds the National Institute on Alcohol Abuse and Alcoholism (NIAAA) guidelines for at-risk drinking for women (21). Furthermore, communicating about difficult issues takes time, requires skills, and is poorly reimbursed by procedure-oriented insurance coverage. Physicians are concerned about the consequences of legally mandated reporting, they lack familiarity with treatment resources, and they do not have the extensive time required to make an appropriate referral (9). These are all problems that must be solved in order to provide medically appropriate and ethically necessary care to women who engage in at-risk drinking or use illicit drugs.

Substance abuse presents complex ethical issues and challenges. This Committee Opinion proposes an ethical rationale for universal screening questions, brief intervention, and referral to treatment in both obstetric and gynecologic practice and provides guidelines for resolving common ethical dilemmas that arise in the clinical setting.

## The Ethical Rationale for Universal Screening Questions, Brief Intervention, and Referral to Treatment

Support for universal screening questions, brief intervention, and referral to treatment is derived from 4 basic principles of ethics. These principles are 1) beneficence, 2) nonmaleficence, 3) justice, and 4) respect for autonomy.

### *Beneficence*

Therapeutic intent, or beneficence, is the foundation of medical knowledge, training, and practice. Experts at the NIAAA and the National Institute on Drug Abuse (NIDA) confirm that addiction is not primarily a moral weakness, as it has been viewed in the past, but a "brain disease" that should be included in a review of systems just like any other biologic disease process (22). A medical diagnosis of addiction requires medical intervention in the same manner that a diagnosis of diabetes requires nutritional counseling or therapeutic agents or both. Positive behavior change arises from the trust implicit in the physician–patient relationship, the respect that patients have for physicians' knowledge, and the ability of physicians to help patients see the links between substance use behaviors and real physical consequences. Brief physician advice has been shown to be as effective as conventional treatment for substance abuse and can produce dramatic reductions in drinking and drug use, improved health status, and decreased costs to society (8, 11, 13, 15, 23–25). The Center for Substance Abuse Prevention has now implemented more than 147 projects for pregnant and postpartum women and their children (26), and there are several different successful models for prevention and treatment for women and their families: AR-Cares (27), Choices (28), SafePort (29), Early Start (30), and the Mom/Kid Trial (31).

Given this capacity for dramatic improvement in health status, physicians have an obligation to be therapeutic—in this case to learn the techniques of screening and brief intervention—and to inform themselves as they would if a new test or therapy were developed for any other recognized disease entity. The practice of universal screening questions, brief intervention, and referral to treatment falls well within the purview of the obstetrician–gynecologist's role as a provider of primary care to women and has potential for major impact on recognized obstetric and gynecologic outcomes. Furthermore, if the topic is raised respectfully, the physician–patient relationship may be substantially enhanced, even if no substantive changes in lifestyle are achieved immediately. Therapy is called "patient care" because both physicians and patients recognize and value the commitment of the medical profession to engage in a nurturing relationship in the course of providing carefully selected therapeutic modalities. Nurturance of healthy behaviors through universal screening questions, brief intervention, and referral to treatment is, thus, part of the traditional healing role and an appropriate focus for the obstetrician–gynecologist's role as a primary care provider.

### *Nonmaleficence*

The obligation to do no harm, or nonmaleficence, also applies to universal screening questions, brief intervention, and referral to treatment. Medical care can be compromised if physicians are unaware of a patient's alcohol or drug abuse and, thus, miss related diagnoses or medication interactions with alcohol or illegal substances. If the problem is not identified, major health risks, such as HIV exposure and depression, also may be missed. These are examples of harms that may occur as a result of omission (nondetection of a serious problem). Furthermore, patients may be harmed when substance abuse is treated by a physician as a moral rather than medical issue (32). Women who abuse alcohol or use illicit drugs are more likely than men to be stigmatized and labeled as hopeless (33). In particular, physicians should avoid using humiliation as a tool to force change because such behavior is ethically inappropriate, engenders resistance, and may act as a barrier to successful treatment and recovery.

### *Justice*

The ethical principle of justice governs access to care and fair distribution of resources. Elimination of health disparities and promotion of quality care for all are at the top of the list of goals for *Healthy People 2010*, the nation's health agenda. Injustice may result from a variety of sources.

Physicians may fail to apply principles of universal screening. When women are less likely to be screened or referred for treatment, their burden of disability is increased and health status decreased. The principle of justice requires that screening questions related to alcohol and drug use should be asked equally of men and women and regardless of race or economic status. It also requires that women be screened with tests such as TWEAK, T-ACE, or the NIAAA quantity and frequency questions that are more accurate in detecting women's patterns of substance abuse, which differ from those of men (34) (see box on next page). Women, for example, are more likely to be hidden drinkers and frequently underreport alcohol use, especially during pregnancy. Tests to detect the problem in women must include questions about tolerance, which are not included in the most commonly employed screen, CAGE, which has a sensitivity of only 75% compared with 87% for TWEAK (35).

Pregnant women are more likely to be screened than nonpregnant women. Although the vulnerability of the fetus is an important concern, the lives of nonpregnant women also have compelling value, and there is much evidence to suggest that women who abuse alcohol or use illicit drugs have coexisting or preexisting conditions (ie, mental health disorders, domestic violence, stress, childhood sexual abuse, poverty, and lack of resources) that put them in a vulnerable status (6, 36, 37). Universal application of screening questions, brief intervention, and referral to treatment eliminates these disparities related to justice.

Additionally, failure to diagnose and treat substance abuse with the same evidence-based approach applied to other chronic illnesses reduces patients'

## Substance Abuse Screening

**T-ACE**

T **T**olerance: How many drinks does it take to make you feel high? *More than 2 drinks is a positive response—score 2 points.*

A Have people **A**nnoyed you by criticizing your drinking? *If "Yes"—score 1 point.*

C Have you ever felt you ought to **C**ut down on your drinking? *If "Yes"—score 1 point.*

E **E**ye opener: Have you ever had a drink first thing in the morning to steady your nerves or get rid of a hangover? *If "Yes"—score 1 point.*

A total score of 2 or more points indicates a positive screen for pregnancy risk drinking.

Reprinted from The American Journal of Obstetrics & Gynecology, Vol 160, Sokol RJ, Martier SS, Ager JW, The T-ACE questions: practical prenatal detection of risk drinking, 863–8; discussion 868–70, Copyright 1989, with permission from Elsevier.

**TWEAK**

T **T**olerance: How many drinks can you hold? *If 5 or more drinks, score 2 points.*

W Have close friends or relatives **W**orried or complained about your drinking in the past year? *If "Yes" 2 points.*

E **E**ye Opener: Do you sometimes take a drink in the morning when you get up? *If "Yes" 1 point.*

A **A**mnesia: Has a friend or family member ever told you about things you said or did while you were drinking that you could not remember? *If "Yes" 1 point.*

K(C) Do you sometimes feel the need to **C**ut down on your drinking? *If "Yes" 1 point.*

The TWEAK is used to screen for pregnant at-risk drinking, defined here as the consumption of 1 oz or more of alcohol per day while pregnant. A total score of 2 points or more indicates a positive screen for pregnancy risk drinking.

Adapted from Chan AW, Pristach EA, Welte JW, Russell M. Use of the TWEAK test in screening for alcoholism/heavy drinking in three populations. Alcohol Clin Exp Res 1993;17:1188–92.

**NIAAA Questionnaire**

Do you drink? Do you use drugs?

On average, how many days per week do you drink alcohol (beer, wine, liquor)?

On a typical day when you drink, how many drinks do you have?

Positive score: >14 drinks per week for men and >7 drinks per week for women

What is the maximum number of drinks you had on any given occasion during the past month?

Positive score: >4 for men and >3 for women

National Institute on Alcohol Abuse and Alcoholism. Helping patients with alcohol problems: a health practitioner's guide. Bethesda (MD): NIAAA; 2003. Available at: http://www.niaaa.nih.gov/publications/Practitioner/PractitionersGuideFINAL.pdf. Retrieved January 7, 2004.

access to health services and resources. Justice requires that physicians counsel patients presenting with drug or alcohol problems and refer them to an appropriate treatment resource when available. No physician would withhold hypertension therapy because the medication compliance rate is only 60%. Physicians who detect the serious medical condition of addiction are equally obligated to intervene.

### *Respect for Autonomy*

On the one hand, no person has a right to use illegal drugs, and a pregnant woman has a moral obligation to avoid use of both illicit drugs and alcohol in order to safeguard the welfare of her fetus. On the other hand, effective intervention with respect to substance abuse by a pregnant or a nonpregnant woman requires that a climate of respect and trust exist within the physician–patient relationship. Patients who begin to disclose behaviors that are stigmatized by society may be harmed if they feel that their trust is met with disrespect. Criticism and shaming statements actually increase resistance and impede change. Effective interventions, as summarized in the NIAAA Treatment Improvement Protocol (TIP) number 35, are designed to increase motivation to change by respecting autonomy, supporting self-efficacy, and offering hope and resources (8).

Effective intervention also requires that universal screening questions, brief intervention, and referral to treatment be conducted with full protection of confidentiality. Patients who fear that acknowledging substance abuse may lead to disclosure to others will be inhibited from honest reporting to their physicians (38). A difficult dilemma is created by state laws that require physicians to report the nonmedical use of controlled substances by a pregnant woman or that require toxicology tests after delivery when there is evidence of possible use of a controlled substance (eg, Minnesota statutes 626.5561 and 626.5562). Although such laws have the goals of referring the pregnant woman for assessment and chemical dependency treatment if indicated and of protecting fetuses and newborns from harm, these laws may unwittingly result in pregnant women not seeking prenatal care or concealing drug use from their obstetricians. Although it is always appropriate for a physician to negotiate with a patient about her willingness to accept a medical recommendation, respect for autonomy includes respect for refusal to be screened.

## Special Responsibilities to Pregnant Patients

Federal warnings about the need to abstain from alcohol use in pregnancy were first issued in 1984. The American College of Obstetricians and Gynecologists recommended screening early in pregnancy in its 1977 *Standards for Ambulatory Obstetric Care*, and a pamphlet was issued in 1982 entitled "Alcohol and Your Unborn Baby." Screening during pregnancy was subsequently supported in a variety of documents and is recommended in a joint publication issued by ACOG and the American Academy of Pediatrics (39). Although obstetricians report screening 97% of pregnant women for alcohol use, only 25% used any of the standard screening tools, and only 20% of those surveyed knew that abstinence is the only known way to avoid all 4 adverse pregnancy outcomes (spontaneous abortion, nervous system impairment, birth defects, and FAS). This is a particularly significant gap in knowledge because there is no level of alcohol use, even the most minimal drinking, that has been determined to be absolutely safe. More than one half of the respondents (63%) reported that they lacked adequate information about referral resources (40). Screening rates for illicit drugs are lower than for alcohol (89%, according to unpublished ACOG survey data).

Ethical issues related to beneficence and nonmaleficence and the ethics of care (41) are similar for pregnant and nonpregnant women and for women who do and do not have children. In each of these cases, universal screening questions, brief intervention, and referral to treatment enables physicians to collaborate with patients to improve their own health, reduce the likelihood of preterm birth and neonatal complications in both current and future pregnancies, and improve the parenting capacity of the family unit.

As noted previously, autonomy issues are particularly challenging in pregnancy. In a survey of obstetricians, pediatricians, and family practice physicians, more than one half of the respondents believed that pregnant women have a legal as well as moral responsibility to ensure that they have healthy newborns (42). Although 61% were concerned that fear of criminal charges would be a barrier to receiving prenatal care, more than one half supported a statute that would permit removal of children from any woman who abused alcohol or drugs (42). This position is particularly troubling because these physicians did not state that there needed to be evidence of physical or emotional neglect (adverse effects on basic needs and safety) for children to be so removed. Both ethical and legal perspectives require that the best interests of the child be served, which requires both protecting children and assisting their mothers to be healthy so as to provide an optimal situation for growth and development.

Physicians' concerns about mothers who abuse alcohol or drugs undoubtedly reflect a desire to protect children. However, recommended screening and referral protocols may be perceived as punitive measures when they are connected with legally mandated testing, or reporting, or both. Such measures endanger the relationship of trust between physician and patient, place the obstetrician in an adversarial relationship with the patient, and possibly conflict with the therapeutic obligation. If pregnant women become reluctant to seek medical care because they fear being reported for alcohol or illegal drug use, these strategies will actually increase the risks to the woman and the fetus rather than reduce the consequences of substance abuse. Furthermore, threats and incarceration have been proved to be ineffective in reducing the incidence of alcohol or drug abuse, and removing children from the home may only subject them to worse risks in the foster care system (43). Treatment is both more effective and less expensive than restrictive policies (44), and it results in a mean net saving of $4,644 in medical expenses per mother/infant pair (45). Moreover, women who have custody of their children complete treatment at a higher rate than those who do not. Putting women in jail, where drugs may be available but treatment is not, jeopardizes the health of pregnant women and that of their existing and future children (46).

Referral to treatment, especially if combined with training in parenting skills, is the clinically appropriate professional action, both medically and ethically (31). Criminal charges against pregnant women on grounds of child abuse have been struck down in almost all cases because courts have upheld the right to privacy, which includes the right to decide whether to have a child, the right to bodily integrity, and the right to "be let alone" (47), and have found that states could better protect fetal health through "education and making available medical care and drug treatment centers for women" (48). The United States Supreme Court recognized the importance of privacy to the physician–patient relationship when it ruled in 2001 to prohibit a public hospital from performing nonconsensual drug tests on pregnant women without a warrant and providing police with positive results (49). Despite a decade of efforts and the 1992 passage of a federal Alcohol Drug Abuse and Mental Health Administration Reorganization Act explicitly prohibiting pregnancy discrimination, few treatment programs focus on the needs of pregnant women. In the absence of appropriate and adequate drug treatment services for pregnant women, criminal charges on grounds of child abuse are unjust in that they indict the woman for failing to seek treatment that actually may not be available to her.

Justice issues also are problematic in that punitive measures are not applied evenly across sex, race, and socioeconomic status. Although several types of legal sanctions against pregnant women who abuse alcohol or drugs are being tested in the courts, there has been no attempt to impose similar sanctions for paternal drug use (50), despite the significant involvement of male partners in pregnant women's substance abuse (51). In a landmark study among pregnant women anonymously tested for drug use, drug prevalence was similar between African-American women and white women, but African-American women were 10 times more likely than white women to be reported as a result of positive screens (52). Similar patterns of injustice have been noted for the types of drugs sanctioned by the legal system. For example, mandatory incarceration and more severe penalties are applied to crack cocaine, which is primarily used by African Americans, than to powder cocaine or heroin, which is primarily used by whites. In the case of *Ferguson v. City of Charleston*, 40 of 41 pregnant women arrested in the immediate postpartum period as a result of cocaine-positive drug screens were African American. When similarly drawn drug screens were positive for methamphetamine or heroin, which were more commonly used by white patients, physicians were more likely to refer to social services rather than to the courts (49).

Some physicians are reluctant to record information related to alcohol or drug abuse in medical records because of competing obligations. On the one hand, the physician may be concerned about nonmaleficence. Because medical records may not be safe from inappropriate disclosure despite federal and state privacy protections, the patient may experience real harms—such as job loss unrelated to workplace performance issues, eviction from public housing, or termination of insurance—if a diagnosis of dependency is recorded in the medical record. Although legal redress for harms that result from inappropriate transfer of information may be possible, it may not be feasible for a woman in straitened circumstances. On the other hand, the principle of beneficence often requires disclosure of information needed by the medical team to provide appropriate medical care. Without this disclosure, a physician treating the patient for a problem unrelated to pregnancy or an emergency room physician seeing the patient for the first time may miss a major complication related to substance abuse. Concerns about protection of confidentiality and nonmaleficence can be addressed most appropriately by including only medically necessary, accurate information in the medical record and informing the patient about the purpose of any disclosure.

## Responsibilities to Neonates

The use of illicit drugs and alcohol during pregnancy has demonstrated adverse effects on the neonate, and these children are subsequently at risk for altered neurodevelopmental outcome and poor health status (53). Detection and treatment are essential precursors of appropriate therapeutic intervention in the immediate setting. Early recognition of parental substance abuse also may lead to interventions designed to decrease associated risks to a child's physical and psychologic health and safety (26–31). Doing so may obviate the necessity for placement in an already overburdened foster care system (54). Underrecognition of prenatal alcohol and drug effects is common, however (55). A toxicology screen and scoring for craniofacial features suggestive of FAS should be performed by the neonate's physician whenever clinically indicated. According to the American Academy of Pediatrics' statement on neonatal drug withdrawal (56), maternal characteristics that suggest a need for biochemical screening of the neonate include no prenatal care, previous unexplained fetal demise, precipitous labor, abruptio placentae, hypertensive episodes, severe mood swings, cerebrovascular accidents, myocardial infarction, and repeated spontaneous abortions. Infant characteristics that may be associated with maternal drug use include preterm birth, unexplained intrauterine growth restriction, neurobehavioral abnormalities, congenital abnormalities, atypical vascular incidents, myocardial infarction, and necrotizing enterocolitis in otherwise healthy term infants. The legal implications of testing and the need for maternal consent vary from state to state; therefore, physicians should be aware of local laws that may influence regional practice.

Biophysical testing, however, has major limitations (57–59). Both urine and meconium screens have a high rate of false-negative results because of factors related to the timing and amount of the last maternal drug use (for urine) and the failure to detect drug metabolites (for meconium). Hair is associated with a substantial false-positive rate because of passive exposure to minute quantities of illicit substances in the environment. Physicians and nurses often fail to recognize the physical manifestations of FAS (60). Maternal self-report of use or consent to testing, elicited using nonjudgmental, supportive interview techniques within a physician–patient relationship of trust, can thus provide the best information for guiding neonatal treatment and the best prognosis for family intervention. Maternal substance abuse does not by itself guarantee child neglect or prove inadequate parenting capacity (61, 62). Parenting skills programs, assistance with employment and housing issues, and access to substance abuse treatment have been shown to be successful support mechanisms for families of affected neonates, and these elements should be part of a comprehensive approach to substance abuse problems. If there is evidence to suggest the likelihood of neglect or abuse, referral to children's protective services may be indicated (63). A children's protective services referral should never be undertaken as a punitive measure, but with the aim of evaluating circumstances, protecting the child, and providing services to maintain or reunify the family unit if at all possible.

## Special Issues for Girls and Adolescent Women

Use of alcohol and illicit drugs among youth is prevalent, and studies that included both male and female youth indicate that age of first use is decreasing. Youth who begin drinking at age 14 years are at least 3 times more likely to experience dependence (using criteria from the *Diagnostic and Statistical Manual of Mental Disorders*, 4th Edition) than those who delay drinking to age 21 years (64). Early onset of drinking increases the likelihood of alcohol-related unintentional injuries (65), motor vehicle crash involvement after drinking (66), unprotected intercourse (67), and getting into fights after drinking, even after controlling for frequency of heavy drinking, alcohol dependence, and other factors related to age of onset (68). A study among a large community sample of lifetime drinkers showed that those who reported first drinking at the ages of 11–14 years experienced a rapid progression to alcohol-related harm, and 16% developed dependence by age 24 years (69). Among youth aged 18–25 years surveyed in 2001, 22.8% drove under the influence of alcohol (1). The use of alcohol and illicit substances by youth and the impact of parental alcohol and substance use on children have adverse health outcomes (70, 71). Prevention (universal screening questions, brief intervention, and referral to treatment) has thus been described by leaders in obstetrics and gynecology and by pediatricians as a moral obligation (72). In 1993, the American Academy of Pediatrics developed substance abuse guidelines for clinical practice. These guidelines have now been refined and developed into competencies that provide practical direction for clinicians engaged in educating, supporting, and treating patients and families affected by substance abuse (73).

Confidentiality is as essential to the physician–patient relationship with children as it is with adults. Many state laws protect the confidentiality of minors with regard to substance abuse detection and treatment (73). Autonomy issues are of particular importance in the detection and treatment of substance abuse for adolescents, who are at a developmental stage in which it is a normative task to test new identities and engage in risk-taking in the process (74). The ACOG Committee on Adolescent Health Care lists the following key points concerning informed consent, parental permission, and assent (75):

- Concern about confidentiality is a major obstacle to the delivery of health care to adolescents. Physicians should address confidentiality issues with the adolescent patient to build a trusting relationship with her and to facilitate a candid discussion regarding her health and health behaviors.
- Physicians also should discuss confidentiality issues with the parent(s) or guardian(s) of the adolescent patient. Physicians should encourage their involvement in the patient's health and health care decisions and, when appropriate, facilitate communication between the two.
- The right of a "mature minor" to obtain selected medical care has been established in most states.

In a document about testing for drugs of abuse in children and adolescents, the American Academy of Pediatrics states that the goal of care is a therapeutic, rather than adversarial relationship with the child and, therefore, makes the following recommendations (76):

- Screening or testing under any circumstances is improper if clinicians cannot be reasonably certain that the laboratory results are valid and that patient confidentiality is ensured.
- Diagnostic testing for the purpose of drug abuse treatment is within the ethical tradition of health care, and in the competent patient, it should be conducted noncovertly, confidentially, and with informed consent in the same context as for other medical conditions.
- Parental permission is not sufficient for involuntary testing of the adolescent with decisional capacity.
- Suspicion that an adolescent is using a psychoactive drug does not justify involuntary testing, and testing adolescents requires their consent unless 1) the patient lacks decision-making capacity or 2) there are strong medical indications or legal requirements to do so.
- Minors should not be immune from the criminal justice system, but physicians should not initiate or participate in a criminal investigation, except when required by law, as in the case of court-ordered drug testing or child abuse reporting.

## Guidance for Physicians

The health care system as it is currently constituted creates barriers to the practice of universal screening questions, brief intervention, and referral to treatment for alcohol and drug abuse. Because of a lack of medical school curricular content about addiction, physicians often are unfamiliar with screening procedures. Many institutions do not have appropriate protocols in place for intervention and referral. Time constraints, mandatory reporting laws, and lack of treatment resources may impede both screening and referral, and some of these problems may be beyond the ability of the individual physician to modify. Nevertheless, in fulfillment of the therapeutic obligation, physicians must make a substantial effort to:

- Learn established techniques for rapid, effective screening, intervention, and referral, and practice universal screening questions, brief intervention, and referral to treatment in order to provide benefit and do no harm. Where possible, create a team approach to deal with barriers of time limitations, using the skills of social workers, nurses, and peer educators for universal screening questions, brief intervention, and referral to treatment. Use external resources (ie, hospital social worker, health department, addiction specialist) to develop a list of treatment resources.
- Treat the patient with a substance abuse problem with dignity and respect in order to form a therapeutic alliance.
- Protect confidentiality and the integrity of the physician–patient relationship wherever possible within the requirements of legal obligations, and communicate honestly and directly with patients about what information can and cannot be protected. In states where there are laws requiring disclosure, inform patients in advance about specific items for which disclosure is mandated.
- Recognize that the most effective safeguard for children is treatment for family members who have a substance abuse problem.
- Balance competing obligations carefully, consulting with other physicians or an ethicist if troubling situations arise.
- Participate, whenever possible, in the policy process at institutional, state, and national levels as an advocate for the health care needs of patients.
- Consider whether elements of personal beliefs and values may be resulting in biases in medical practice. Be aware that some physicians minimize the universality and impact of alcohol or

prescription drug abuse to protect against evaluating their own alcohol or substance abuse problems. A physician who has questions about his or her own use should seek help.

## Conclusion

Substance abuse is a common medical condition that can have devastating physical and emotional consequences for women and their children. The traditional role of healer, the contemporary role of medical expert, and the newer role of primary care physician all require obstetrician–gynecologists to develop an evidence-supported knowledge base about methods for detection and treatment of substance abuse. The close working relationship between the physician and the patient that is both a goal of care and a means to improved health outcomes offers tremendous potential to influence patients' lifestyles positively. Despite this relationship, physicians seldom practice universal screening because of a lack of appreciation of prevalence, misunderstandings about treatment success rates, unfamiliarity with treatment resources, and inadequate knowledge about sex differences in presentation and the course of the disease. However, common barriers to universal screening questions, brief intervention, and referral to treatment can and should be addressed. Physicians have an ethical obligation to learn and use techniques for universal screening questions, brief intervention, and referral to treatment in order to provide patients and their families with medical care that is state-of-the-art, comprehensive, and effective.

## References


1. Substance Abuse and Mental Health Services Administration. Results from the 2001 National Household Survey on Drug Abuse: volume I. Summary of national findings. Rockville (MD): SAMHSA; 2002.
2. Smith WB, Weisner C. Women and alcohol problems: a critical analysis of the literature and unanswered questions. Alcohol Clin Exp Res 2000;24:1320–1.
3. National Institute on Alcohol Abuse and Alcoholism. Fetal alcohol exposure and the brain. Alcohol Alert 2000; 50:1–6.
4. American Academy of Pediatrics. Committee on Substance Abuse and Committee on Children with Disabilities. Fetal alcohol syndrome and alcohol-related neurodevelopmental disorders. Pediatrics 2000;106:358–61.
5. Office of National Drug Control Policy. The economic costs of drug abuse in the United States, 1992–1998. Washington, DC: Executive Office of the President; 2001. Publication No. NCJ-190636.
6. Amaro H, Fried LE, Cabral H, Zuckerman B. Violence during pregnancy and substance abuse. Am J Public Health 1990;80:575–9.
7. Hutchins E, DiPietro J. Psychosocial risk factors associated with cocaine use during pregnancy: a case-control study. Obstet Gynecol 1997;90:142–7.
8. Substance Abuse and Mental Health Services Administration. Enhancing motivation for change in substance abuse. Treatment Improvement Protocol (TIP) series; 35. Rockville (MD): SAMHSA; 1999.
9. McLellan AT, Lewis DC, O'Brien CP, Kleber HD. Drug dependence, a chronic medical illness: implications for treatment, insurance, and outcomes evaluation. JAMA 2000;284:1689–95.
10. Bien TH, Miller WR, Tonigan JS. Brief interventions for alcohol problems: a review. Addiction 1993;88:315–35.
11. Fleming MF, Mundt MP, French MT, Manwell LB, Stauffacher EA, Barry KL. Benefit-cost analysis of brief physician advice with problem drinkers in primary care settings. Med Care 2000;38:7–18.
12. Blum LN, Nielsen NH, Riggs JA. Alcoholism and alcohol abuse among women: report of the Council on Scientific Affairs. American Medical Association. J Womens Health 1998;7:861–71.
13. Hubbard RL, French MT. New perspectives on the benefit-cost and cost-effectiveness of drug abuse treatment. NIDA Res Monogr 1991;113:94–113.
14. Chez RA, Andres RL, Chazotte C, Ling FW. Illicit drug use and dependence in women: a slide lecture presentation. Washington, DC: American College of Obstetricians and Gynecologists; 2002. Available at: http://www.acog.org/from_home/departments/underserved/DependenceinWomen.ppt. Retrieved October 27, 2003.
15. Fleming MF, Barry KL. The effectiveness of alcoholism screening in an ambulatory care setting. J Stud Alcohol 1991;52:33–6.
16. Wilson L, Kahan M, Liu E, Brewster JM, Sobell MB, Sobell LC. Physician behavior towards male and female problem drinkers: a controlled study using simulated patients. J Addict Dis 2002;21:87–99.
17. Volk RJ, Steinbauer JR, Cantor SB. Patient factors influencing variation in the use of preventive interventions for alcohol abuse by primary care physicians. J Stud Alcohol 1996;57:203–9.
18. Gearhart JG, Beebe DK, Milhorn HT, Meeks GR. Alcoholism in women. Am Fam Physician 1991;44: 907–13.
19. Gomberg ES. Women and alcohol: use and abuse. J Nerv Ment Dis 1993;181:211–9.
20. Marcenko MO, Spense M. Social and psychological correlates of substance abuse among pregnant women. Soc Work Res 1995;19:103–9.
21. Abel EL, Kruger ML, Friedl J. How do physicians define "light," "moderate" and "heavy" drinking? Alcohol Clin Exp Res 1998;22:979–84.
22. National Institute on Drug Abuse. Mind over matter: the brain's response to drugs. Rockville (MD): NIDA; 1997. Available at: http://www.drugabuse.gov/MOM/MOMindex.html. Retrieved October 27, 2003.

23. Chang G, Goetz MA, Wilkins-Haug L, Berman S. A brief intervention for prenatal alcohol use: an in-depth look. J Subst Abuse Treat 2000;18:365–9.
24. Bernstein E, Bernstein J, Levenson S. Project ASSERT: an ED-based intervention to increase access to primary care, preventive services, and the substance abuse treatment system. Ann Emerg Med 1997;30:181–9.
25. Manwell LB, Fleming MF, Mundt MP, Stauffacher EA, Barry KL. Treatment of problem alcohol use in women of childbearing age: results of a brief intervention trial. Alcohol Clin Exp Res 2000;24:1517–24.
26. Rosensweig MA. Reflections on the Center for Substance Abuse Prevention's pregnant and postpartum women and their infants program. Womens Health Issues 1998; 8:206–7.
27. Whiteside-Mansell L, Crone CC, Conners NA. The development and evaluation of an alcohol and drug prevention and treatment program for women and children: The AR-CARES program. J Subst Abuse Treat 1999;16:265–75.
28. Ingersoll K, Floyd L, Sobell M, Velasquez MM. Reducing the risk of alcohol-exposed pregnancies: a study of a motivational intervention in community settings. Project CHOICES Intervention Research Group. Pediatrics 2003;111:1131–5.
29. Metsch LR, Wolfe HP, Fewell R, McCoy CB, Elwood WN, Wohler-Torres B, et al. Treating substance-using women and their children in public housing: preliminary evaluation findings. Child Welfare 2001;80:199–200.
30. Armstrong MA, Gonzales Osejo V, Lieberman L, Carpenter DM, Pantoja PM, Escobar GJ. Perinatal substance abuse intervention in obstetric clinics decreases adverse neonatal outcomes. J Perinatol 2003;23:3–9.
31. Peterson L, Gable S, Saldana L. Treatment of maternal addiction to prevent child abuse and neglect. Addict Behav 1996;21:789–801.
32. Boyd CJ, Guthrie B. Women, their significant others, and crack cocaine. Am J Addict 1996;5:156–66.
33. Ehrmin JT. Unresolved feelings of guilt and shame in the maternal role with substance-dependent African American women. J Nurs Scholarsh 2001;33:47–52.
34. Chang G, Wilkins-Haug L, Berman S, Goetz MA, Behr H, Hiley A. Alcohol use and pregnancy: improving identification. Obstet Gynecol 1998;91:892–8.
35. Cherpitel CJ. Screening in alcohol problems in the emergency department. Ann Emerg Med 1995;26:158–66.
36. Berenson AB, Weimann CM, Wilkinson GS, Jones WA, Anderson GD. Perinatal morbidity associated with violence experienced by pregnant women. Am J Obstet Gynecol 1994;170:1760–6; discussion 1766–9.
37. Sheehan TJ. Stress and low birth weight: a structural modeling approach using real life stressors. Soc Sci Med 1998;47:1503–12.
38. Poland ML, Dombrowski MP, Ager JW, Sokol RJ. Punishing pregnant drug users: enhancing the flight from care. Drug Alcohol Depend 1993;31:199–203.
39. American Academy of Pediatrics, American College of Obstetricians and Gynecologists. Guidelines for perinatal care. 5th ed. Elk Grove Village (IL): AAP; Washington, DC: ACOG; 2003.
40. Diekman ST, Floyd RL, Decoufle P, Schulkin J, Ebrahim SH, Sokol R. A survey of obstetrician–gynecologists on their patients' alcohol use during pregnancy. Obstet Gynecol 2000;95:756–63.
41. American College of Obstetricians and Gynecologists. Ethical decision making in obstetrics and gynecology. In: Ethics in obstetrics and gynecology. 2nd ed. Washington, DC: ACOG; 2004. p. 3–8.
42. Abel EL, Kruger M. Physician attitudes concerning legal coercion of pregnant alcohol and drug abusers. Am J Obstet Gynecol 2002;186:768–72.
43. Drug exposed infants: recommendations. Center for the Future of Children. Future Child 1991;1:8–9.
44. Rydell CP, Everingham SS. Controlling cocaine: supply versus demand programs. Santa Monica (CA): RAND; 1994.
45. Svikis DS, Golden AS, Huggins GR, Pickens RW, McCaul ME, Velez ML, et al. Cost-effectiveness of treatment for drug-abusing pregnant women. Drug Alcohol Depend 1997;45:105–13.
46. Paltrow LM. Punishing women for their behavior during pregnancy: an approach that undermines the health of women and children. In: Wetherington CL, Roman AB, editors. Drug addiction research and the health of women. Bethesda (MD): National Institute on Drug Abuse; 1998. p. 467–501. Available at: http://www.nida.nih.gov/PDF/DARHW/467-502_Paltrow.pdf. Retrieved January 22, 2004.
47. OLMSTEAD v U.S., 277 U.S. 438 (1928).
48. Gostin LO. The rights of pregnant women: the Supreme Court and drug testing. Hastings Cent Rep 2001;31:8–9.
49. Ferguson v. City of Charleston, 532 U.S. 67 (2001).
50. Nelson LJ, Marshall MF. Ethical and legal analyses of three coercive policies aimed at substance abuse by pregnant women (#030790). Robert Wood Johnson Foundation, 1998.
51. Frank DA, Brown J, Johnson S, Cabral H. Forgotten fathers: an exploratory study of mothers' report of drug and alcohol problems among fathers of urban newborns. Neurotoxicol Teratol 2002;24:339–47.
52. Chasnoff IJ, Landress HJ, Barrett ME. The prevalence of illicit-drug or alcohol use during pregnancy and discrepancies in mandatory reporting in Pinellas County, Florida. N Engl J Med 1990;322:1202–6.
53. Wagner CL, Katikaneni LD, Cox TH, Ryan RM. The impact of prenatal drug exposure on the neonate. Obstet Gynecol Clin North Am 1998;25:169–94.
54. United States General Accounting Office. Foster care: health needs of many young children are unknown and unmet. Washington, DC: General Accounting Office; 1995.
55. Stoler JM, Holmes LB. Under-recognition of prenatal alcohol effects in infants of known alcohol abusing women. J Pediatr 1999;135:430–6.
56. Neonatal drug withdrawal. American Academy of Pediatrics Committee on Drugs [published erratum appears in Pediatrics 1998;102:660]. Pediatrics 1998; 101:1079–88.
57. Lester BM, ElSohly M, Wright LL, Smeriglio VL, Verter J, Bauer CR, et al. The Maternal Lifestyle Study: drug use by meconium toxicology and maternal self-report. Pediatrics 2001;107:309–17.
58. Millard DD. Toxicology testing in neonates. Is it ethical and what does it mean? Clin Perinatol 1996;23:491–507.

59. Ostrea EM Jr, Knapp DK, Tannenbaum L, Ostrea AR, Romero A, Salari V, et al. Estimates of illicit drug use during pregnancy by maternal interview, hair analysis and meconium analysis. J Pediatr 2001;138:344–8.
60. Lyons Jones K. Early recognition of prenatal alcohol effects: a pediatrician's responsibility. J Pediatr 1999; 135:405–6.
61. Davis SK. Comprehensive interventions for affecting the parenting effectiveness of chemically dependent women. J Obstet Gynecol Neonatal Nurs 1997;26:604–10.
62. Smith BD, Test MF. The risk of subsequent maltreatment allegations in families with substance-exposed infants. Child Abuse Negl 2002;26:97–114.
63. MacMahon JR. Perinatal substance abuse: the impact of reporting infants to child protective services. Pediatrics 1997;100:E1.
64. Grant BF. The impact of a family history of alcoholism on the relationship between the age of onset of alcohol use and DSM-IV alcohol dependence. Results from the National Longitudinal Alcohol Epidemiologic Survey. Alcohol Health Res World 1998;22:144–8.
65. Hingson RW, Heeren T, Jamanka A, Howland J. Age of drinking onset and unintentional injury involvement after drinking. JAMA 2000;284:1527–33.
66. Hingson R, Heeren T, Zakocs R, Winter M, Wechsler H. Age of first intoxication, heavy drinking, driving after drinking and risk of unintentional injury among U.S. college students. J Stud Alcohol 2003;64:23–31.
67. Hingson R, Heeren T, Winter MR, Wechsler H. Early age of first drunkenness as a factor in college students' unplanned and unprotected sex attributable to drinking. Pediatrics 2003;111:34–41.
68. Substance Abuse and Mental Health Services Administration. The relationship between mental health and substance abuse among adolescents. Rockville (MD): SAMHSA; 1999. Available at http://www.samhsa.gov/oas/NHSDA/A-9/TOC.htm. Retrieved January 22, 2004.
69. DeWit DJ, Adlaf EM, Offord DR, Ogborne AC. Age at first alcohol use: a risk factor for the development of alcohol disorders. Am J Psychiatry 2000;157:745–50.
70. American Academy of Pediatrics: Committee on Substance Abuse. Alcohol use and abuse: a pediatric concern. Pediatrics 2001;108:185–9.
71. Fishman M, Bruner A, Adger H Jr. Substance abuse among children and adolescents. Pediatr Rev 1997;18: 394–403.
72. Chasnoff IJ. Silent violence: is prevention a moral obligation? Pediatrics 1999;102:145–8.
73. Adger H Jr, MacDonald DI, Wenger S. Core competencies for involvement of health care providers in the care of children and adolescents in families affected by substance abuse. Pediatrics 1999;103:1083–4.
74. Donovan JE, Jessor R, Costa FM. Adolescent problem drinking: stability of psychosocial and behavioral correlates across a generation. J Stud Alcohol 1999;60:352–61.
75. American College of Obstetricians and Gynecologists. Health care for adolescents. Washington, DC: ACOG; 2003.
76. Testing for drugs of abuse in children and adolescents. American Academy of Pediatrics Committee on Substance Abuse. Pediatrics 1996;98:305–7.

# ACOG Committee Opinion

Committee on Ethics

Number 297, August 2004

# Nonmedical Use of Obstetric Ultrasonography

*ABSTRACT: The American College of Obstetricians and Gynecologists (ACOG) has endorsed the "Prudent Use" statement from the American Institute of Ultrasound in Medicine (AIUM) discouraging the use of obstetric ultrasonography for nonmedical purposes (eg, solely to create keepsake photographs or videos). The ACOG Committee on Ethics provides reasons in addition to those offered by AIUM for discouraging this practice.*

The American College of Obstetricians and Gynecologists (ACOG) has endorsed the following statement from the American Institute of Ultrasound in Medicine (AIUM) discouraging the use of obstetric ultrasonography for nonmedical purposes (eg, solely to create keepsake photographs or videos) (1):

> The AIUM advocates the responsible use of diagnostic ultrasound. The AIUM strongly discourages the non-medical use of ultrasound for psychosocial or entertainment purposes. The use of either two-dimensional (2D) or three-dimensional (3D) ultrasound to only view the fetus, obtain a picture of the fetus or determine the fetal gender without a medical indication is inappropriate and contrary to responsible medical practice. Although there are no confirmed biological effects on patients caused by exposures from present diagnostic ultrasound instruments, the possibility exists that such biological effects may be identified in the future. Thus ultrasound should be used in a prudent manner to provide medical benefit to the patient.

In addition to the concerns noted by AIUM, the ACOG Committee on Ethics believes that nonmedical use of ultrasonography should be discouraged for the following reasons:

- Nonmedical ultrasonography may falsely reassure women. Even though centers that perform nonmedical ultrasonography and create keepsake photographs and videos of the fetus may offer disclaimers about the limitations of their product, customers may interpret an aesthetically pleasing image or entertaining video as evidence of fetal health and appropriate development. Ultrasonography performed for psychosocial or entertainment purposes may be limited by the extent and duration of the examination, the training of those acquiring the images, and the quality control in place at the ultrasound facility. Women may incorrectly believe that the limited scan is, in fact, diagnostic.



ISSN 1074-861X

**The American College of Obstetricians and Gynecologists**
409 12th Street, SW
PO Box 96920
Washington, DC 20090-6920

12345/87654

Nonmedical use of obstetric ultrasonography. ACOG Committee Opinion No. 297. American College of Obstetricians and Gynecologists. Obstet Gynecol 2004;104:423–4.

- Abnormalities may be detected in settings that are not prepared to discuss and provide follow-up for concerning findings. Without the ready availability of appropriate prenatal health care professionals, customers at sites for nonmedical ultrasonography may be left without necessary support, information, and follow-up for concerning findings. For example, customers may interpret a minor finding (eg, an echogenic intracardiac focus) as a major abnormality, resulting in unnecessary anxiety and concern. Conversely, in the event of concerning findings (eg, oligohydramnios), women may not receive appropriate follow-up. Obstetric ultrasonography is most appropriately obtained as part of an integrated system for delivering prenatal care.

## Reference

1. American Institute of Ultrasound in Medicine. Prudent use. AIUM Official Statements. Laurel (MD): AIUM; 1999. Available at http://www.aium.org/provider/statements/_statementSelected.asp?statement=2. Retrieved May 19, 2004.

ACOG Committee Opinion

Committee on Ethics

Number 321, November 2005

# Maternal Decision Making, Ethics, and the Law

*ABSTRACT: Recent legal actions and policies aimed at protecting the fetus as an entity separate from the woman have challenged the rights of pregnant women to make decisions about medical interventions and have criminalized maternal behavior that is believed to be associated with fetal harm or adverse perinatal outcomes. This opinion summarizes recent, notable legal cases; reviews the underlying, established ethical principles relevant to the highlighted issues; and considers six objections to punitive and coercive legal approaches to maternal decision making. These approaches 1) fail to recognize that pregnant women are entitled to informed consent and bodily integrity, 2) fail to recognize that medical knowledge and predictions of outcomes in obstetrics have limitations, 3) treat addiction and psychiatric illness as if they were moral failings, 4) threaten to dissuade women from prenatal care, 5) unjustly single out the most vulnerable women, and 6) create the potential for criminalization of otherwise legal maternal behavior. Efforts to use the legal system to protect the fetus by constraining pregnant women's decision making or punishing them erode a woman's basic rights to privacy and bodily integrity and are not justified. Physicians and policy makers should promote the health of women and their fetuses through advocacy of healthy behavior; referral for substance abuse treatment and mental health services when indicated; and development of safe, available, and efficacious services for women and families.*

Ethical issues that arise in the care of pregnant women are challenging to physicians, politicians, lawyers, and ethicists alike. One of the fundamental goals of medicine and society is to optimize the outcome of pregnancy. Recently, some apparent attempts to foster this goal have been characterized by legal action and policies aimed at specifically protecting the fetus as an entity separate from the woman. These actions and policies have challenged the rights of pregnant women to make decisions about medical interventions and have criminalized maternal behavior that is believed to be associated with fetal harm or adverse perinatal outcomes.

Practitioners who care for pregnant women face particularly difficult dilemmas when their patients reject medical recommendations, use illegal



ISSN 1074-861X

**The American College of Obstetricians and Gynecologists**
409 12th Street, SW
PO Box 96920
Washington, DC 20090-6920

12345/98765

Maternal decision making, ethics, and the law. ACOG Committee Opinion No. 321. American College of Obstetricians and Gynecologists. Obstet Gynecol 2005;106:1127–37.

drugs, or engage in a range of other behaviors that have the potential to cause fetal harm. In such situations, physicians, hospital representatives, and others have at times resorted to legal actions to impose their views about what these pregnant patients ought to do or to effect particular interventions or outcomes. Appellate courts have held, however, that a pregnant woman's decisions regarding medical treatment should take precedence regardless of the presumed fetal consequences of those decisions. In one notable 1990 decision, a District of Columbia appellate court vacated a lower court's decision to compel cesarean delivery in a critically ill woman at 26 weeks of gestation against her wishes, stating in its opinion that "in virtually all cases the question of what is to be done is to be decided by the patient—the pregnant woman—on behalf of herself and the fetus" (1). Furthermore, the court stated that it could think of no "extremely rare and truly exceptional" case in which the state might have an interest sufficiently compelling to override a pregnant patient's wishes (2). Amid often vigorous debate, most ethicists also agree that a pregnant woman's informed refusal of medical intervention ought to prevail as long as she has the ability to make medical decisions (3, 4).

Recent legislation, criminal prosecutions, and legal cases much discussed in both courtrooms and newsrooms have challenged these precedents, raising the question of whether there are circumstances in which a woman who has become pregnant may have her rights to bodily integrity and informed consent overridden to protect her fetus. In Utah, a woman who had used cocaine was charged with homicide for refusing cesarean delivery of a fetus that was ultimately stillborn. In Pennsylvania, physicians obtained a court order for cesarean delivery in a patient with suspected fetal macrosomia. Across the country, pregnant women have been arrested and prosecuted for being pregnant and using drugs or alcohol. These cases and the publicity they have engendered suggest that it is time to revisit the ethical issues involved.

The ethics of caring for pregnant women and an approach to decision making in the context of the maternal–fetal relationship have been discussed in previous statements by the American College of Obstetricians and Gynecologists (ACOG) Committee on Ethics. After briefly reiterating those discussions, this opinion will summarize recent, notable cases; review the underlying, established ethical principles relevant to the highlighted issues; consider objections to punitive and coercive legal approaches to maternal decision making; and summarize recommendations for attending to future ethical matters that may arise.

## Recent Cases

In March 2004, a 28-year-old woman was charged with first-degree murder for refusing to undergo an immediate cesarean delivery because of concerns about fetal well-being and later giving birth to a girl who tested positive for cocaine and a stillborn boy. According to press reports, the woman was mentally ill and intermittently homeless and had been brought to Utah by a Florida adoption agency to give birth to the infants and give them up. She ultimately pled guilty to two counts of child endangerment.

In January 2004, a woman who previously had given birth vaginally to six infants, some of whom weighed close to 12 pounds, refused a cesarean delivery that was recommended because of presumed macrosomia. A Pennsylvania hospital obtained a court order to perform the cesarean delivery and gain custody of the fetus before and after delivery, but the woman and her husband fled to another hospital, where she reportedly had an uncomplicated vaginal delivery of a healthy 11-pound infant.

In September 2003, a 22-year-old woman was prosecuted after her son tested positive for alcohol when he was born in Glens Falls, New York. A few days after the birth, the woman was arrested and charged with two counts of child endangerment for "knowingly feeding her blood," containing alcohol, to her fetus via the umbilical cord. Several months later, her lawyers successfully appealed her conviction.

In May 1999, a 22-year-old woman who was homeless regularly used cocaine while pregnant and gave birth to a stillborn infant in South Carolina. She became the first woman in the United States to be tried and convicted of homicide by child abuse based on her behavior during pregnancy and was given a 12-year prison sentence. The conviction was upheld in the South Carolina Supreme Court, and the U.S. Supreme Court recently refused to hear her appeal. At a postconviction relief hearing, expert testimony supported arguments that the woman had had inadequate representation, but the court held that there was no ineffective assistance of counsel and that she is not entitled to a new trial. This decision is being appealed.

## Ethical Considerations

### *Framing Ethics in Perinatal Medicine*

It is likely that the interventions described in the preceding cases were motivated by a shared concept—that a fetus can and should be treated as separable and legally, philosophically, and practically independent from the pregnant woman within whom it resides. This common method of framing ethical issues in perinatal medicine is not surprising given a number of developments in the past several decades. First, since the 1970s, the development of techniques for imaging, testing, and treating fetuses has led to the widespread endorsement of the notion that fetuses are independent patients, treatable apart from the pregnant women upon whom their existence depends (5). Similarly, some bioethical models now assert that physicians have moral obligations to fetal "patients" that are separate from their obligations to pregnant women (6). Finally, a number of civil laws, discussed later in this section, aim to create fetal rights separate from a pregnant woman's rights.

Although frameworks that treat the woman and fetus as separable and independent are meant to simplify and clarify complex issues that arise in obstetrics, many writers have noted that such frameworks tend to distort, rather than illuminate, ethical and policy debates (7). In particular, these approaches have been criticized for their tendency to emphasize the divergent rather than shared interests of the pregnant woman and fetus. This emphasis results in a view of the maternal–fetal relationship as paradigmatically adversarial, when in fact in the vast majority of cases, the interests of the pregnant woman and fetus actually converge.

In addition, these approaches tend to ignore the moral relevance of relationships, including the physically and emotionally intimate relationship between the woman and her fetus, as well as the relationships of the pregnant woman within her broader social and cultural networks. The cultural and policy context, for example, suggests a predominantly child-centered approach to maternal and child health, which has influenced current perspectives on the fetus. The prototype for the federal Maternal and Child Health Bureau dates back to 1912, when the first organization was called into existence by reformers such as Florence Kelley, who stated that "the U.S. should have a bureau to look after the child crop," and Julia Lathrop, who said that "the final purpose of the Bureau is to serve all children, to try to work out standards of care and protection which shall give to every child his fair chance in the world." The current home page of the Maternal and Child Health Bureau web site cites as its "vision" an equally child-centered goal (8).

At times, in the current clinical and policy contexts, when the woman and fetus are treated as separate individuals, the woman and her medical interests, health needs, and rights as moral agent, patient, and research subject fade from view. Consider, first, women's medical interests as patients. Researchers performing "fetal surgery"—novel interventions to correct fetal anatomic abnormalities—have been criticized recently not only for their tendency to exaggerate claims of success with regard to fetal and neonatal health, but also for their failure to assess the impact of surgery on pregnant women, who also undertake the risks of the major surgical procedures (9). As a result, several centers performing these techniques now use the term "maternal–fetal surgery" to explicitly recognize the fact that a woman's bodily integrity and health are at stake whenever interventions directed at her fetus are performed. Furthermore, a study sponsored by the National Institute of Child Health and Human Development comparing maternal–fetal surgery with postnatal repair of myelomeningocele (the Management of Myelomeningocele Study) is now assessing maternal as well as fetal outcomes, including measurement of reproductive and health outcomes, depression testing, and economic and family health outcomes in women who participate in the clinical trial.

Similarly, new civil laws that aim to treat the fetus as separate and independent have been criticized for their failure both to address the health needs of the woman within whose body the fetus resides and to recognize the converging interests of the woman and fetus. In November 2002, a revision of the state child health insurance program (sCHIP) that expanded coverage to "individual(s) under the age of 19 including the period from conception until birth" was signed into law. The program does not cover pregnant women older than 18 years except when medical interventions could directly affect the well-being of their fetuses. For example, under sCHIP, intrapartum anesthesia is covered, according to the U.S. Department of Health and Human Services, only because "if a woman's pain during a labor and delivery is not reduced or properly relieved, adverse and sometimes disastrous effects can occur for the unborn child" (10).

Furthermore, for beneficiaries of sCHIP, many significant women's health issues, even those that are precipitated by pregnancy (eg, molar gestation, postpartum depression, or traumatic injury from intimate partner violence not impacting the fetus), are not covered as a part of routine antenatal care (11). This approach has been criticized not only for its failure to address the health needs of women, but also for its failure to achieve the narrow goal of improving child health because it ignores the fact that maternal and neonatal interests converge. For instance, postpartum depression is associated with adverse effects in infants, including impaired maternal–infant interaction, delayed cognitive and emotional development, increased anxiety, and decreased self-esteem (12, 13). Thus, the law ignores the fact that a critical component of ensuring the health of newborns is the provision of comprehensive care for their mothers.

Likewise, in April 2004, the Unborn Victims of Violence Act was signed into law, creating a separate federal offense if, during the commission of certain federal crimes, an individual causes the death of, or bodily injury to, a fetus at any stage of pregnancy. The law, however, does not categorize the death of or injury to a pregnant woman as a separate federal offense, or create sentence enhancement for those who assault or murder a woman while pregnant. The statute's sponsors explicitly rejected proposals that had virtually identical criminal penalties but recognized the pregnant woman as the victim, despite the fact that murder is responsible for more pregnancy-associated deaths in the United States than any other cause, including hemorrhage and thromboembolic events (14, 15).

Beyond its impact on maternal and child health, a failure to recognize the interconnectedness of the pregnant woman and fetus has important ethical and legal implications. Because an intervention on a fetus must be performed through the body of a pregnant woman, an assertion of fetal rights must be reconciled with the ethical and legal obligations toward pregnant women *as women*, persons in their own right. Discussions about rights of the unborn often have failed to address these obligations. Regardless of what is believed about fetal personhood, claims about fetal rights require an assessment of the rights of pregnant women, whose personhood within the legal and moral community is indisputable.

Furthermore, many writers have noted a moral injury that arises from abstracting the fetus from the pregnant woman, in its failing to recognize the pregnant woman herself as a patient, person, and rights-bearer. This approach disregards a fundamental moral principle that persons never be treated solely as means to an end, but as ends in themselves. Within the rhetoric of conflict and fetal rights, the pregnant woman has at times been reduced to a vessel—even a "fortress" holding the fetus "prisoner" (16). As George Annas aptly described, "Before birth, we can obtain access to the fetus only through its mother, and in the absence of her informed consent, can do so only by treating her as a fetal container, a nonperson without rights to bodily integrity" (3).

Some writers have argued that at the heart of the distorting influence of the "two-patient" model of the maternal–fetal dyad is the fact that, according to traditional theories that undergird medical ethics, the very notion of a person or a patient is someone who is physically separate from others. Pregnancy, however, is marked by a "particular and particularly thoroughgoing kind of intertwinement" (17). Thus, the pregnant woman and fetus fit awkwardly at best into what the term "patient" is understood to mean. They are neither physically separate, as persons are understood to be, nor indistinguishably fused. A framework that instead defines the professional ethical obligations with a deep sensitivity to relationships of interdependency may help to avoid the distorting influence of the two-patient model as traditionally understood (18). Although this opinion does not specifically articulate a novel comprehensive conceptual model for perinatal ethics, in the discussion that follows, the Committee on Ethics takes as morally central the essential connection between the pregnant woman and fetus.

***Ethics Committee Opinions and the Maternal–Fetal Relationship***

In the context of a framework that recognizes the interconnectedness of the pregnant woman and fetus and emphasizes their shared interests, certain opinions previously published by the ACOG Committee on Ethics are particularly relevant. These include:

- "Informed Consent" (19)
- "Patient Choice in the Maternal–Fetal Relationship" (20)
- "At-Risk Drinking and Illicit Drug Use: Ethical Issues in Obstetric and Gynecologic Practice" (21)

One fundamental ethical obligation of health care professionals is to respect patients' autonomous decision making and to adhere to the requirement for informed consent for medical intervention. In January 2004, the Committee on Ethics published a revised edition of "Informed Consent" in which the following points are defended:

- "Requiring informed consent is an expression of respect for the patient as a person; it particularly respects a patient's moral right to bodily integrity, to self-determination regarding sexuality and reproductive capacities, and to the support of the patient's freedom within caring relationships."
- "The ethical requirement for informed consent need not conflict with physicians' overall ethical obligation to a principle of beneficence; that is, every effort should be made to incorporate a commitment to informed consent within a commitment to provide medical benefit to patients and thus respect them as whole and embodied persons."

Pregnancy does not obviate or limit the requirement to obtain informed consent. Intervention on behalf of the fetus must be undertaken through the body and within the context of the life of the pregnant woman, and therefore her consent for medical treatment is required, regardless of the treatment indication. However, pregnancy presents a special set of issues. The issues associated with informed refusal of care by pregnant women are addressed in the January 2004 opinion "Patient Choice in the Maternal–Fetal Relationship" (20). This opinion states that in cases of maternal refusal of treatment for the sake of the fetus, "court-ordered intervention against the wishes of a pregnant woman is rarely if ever acceptable." The document presents a review of general ethical considerations applicable to pregnant women who do not follow the advice of their physicians or do not seem to make decisions in the best interest of their fetuses. Although the possibility of a justifiable court-ordered intervention is not completely ruled out, the document presents several recommendations that strongly discourage coercive measures:

- "The obstetrician's response to a patient's unwillingness to cooperate with medical advice . . . should be to convey clearly the reasons for the recommendations to the pregnant woman, examine the barriers to change along with her, and encourage the development of health-promoting behavior."
- "[Even if] a woman's autonomous decision [seems] not to promote beneficence-based obligations (of the woman or the physician) to the fetus, . . . the obstetrician must respect the patient's autonomy, continue to care for the pregnant woman, and not intervene against the patient's wishes, regardless of the consequences."
- "The obstetrician must keep in mind that medical knowledge has limitations and medical judgment is fallible" and should therefore take great care "to present a balanced evaluation of expected outcomes for both [the woman and the fetus]."
- "Obstetricians should consider the social and cultural context in which these decisions are made and question whether their ethical judgments reinforce gender, class, or racial inequality."

In addition to revisiting questions of how practitioners should address refusal of treatment in the clinic and delivery room, the four cases outlined previously illustrate punitive and coercive policies aimed at pregnant women who engage in behaviors that may adversely affect fetal well-being. The 2004 opinion "At-Risk Drinking and Illicit Drug Use: Ethical Issues in Obstetric and Gynecologic Practice" (21) specifically addresses addiction and the prosecution of women who use drugs and alcohol during pregnancy and recommends strongly against punitive policies:

- "Addiction is not primarily a moral weakness, as it has been viewed in the past, but a 'brain disease' that should be included in a review of systems just like any other biologic disease process."
- "Recommended screening . . . connected with legally mandated testing or reporting . . . endanger[s] the relationship of trust between physician and patient, place[s] the obstetrician in an adversarial relationship with the patient, and possibly conflict[s] with the therapeutic obligation."
- Punitive policies "are unjust in that they indict the woman for failing to seek treatment that actually may not be available to her" and in that they "are not applied evenly across sex, race, and socioeconomic status."

- Physicians must make a substantial effort to "treat the patient with a substance abuse problem with dignity and respect in order to form a therapeutic alliance."

Finally, recent legal decisions affirm that physicians have neither an obligation nor a right to perform prenatal testing for alcohol or drug use without a pregnant woman's consent (22, 23). This includes consent to testing of the woman that could lead to any form of reporting, both to legal authorities for purposes of criminal prosecution and to civil child welfare authorities.

***Against Coercive and Punitive Legal Approaches to the Maternal–Fetal Relationship***

This section addresses specifically the ethical issues associated with the cases outlined previously and delineates six reasons why restricting patients' liberty and punishing pregnant women for their actions during pregnancy that may affect their fetuses is neither wise nor justifiable. Each raises important objections to punishing pregnant women for actions during pregnancy; together they provide an overwhelming rationale for avoiding such approaches.

1. *Coercive and punitive legal approaches to pregnant women who refuse medical advice fail to recognize that all competent adults are entitled to informed consent and bodily integrity.*

A fundamental tenet of contemporary medical ethics is the requirement for informed consent, including the right of competent adults to refuse medical intervention. The Committee on Ethics affirms that informed consent for medical treatment is an ethical requirement and is an expression of respect for the patient as a person with a moral right to bodily integrity (19).

The crucial difference between pregnant and nonpregnant individuals, though, is that a fetus is involved whose health interests could arguably be served by overriding the pregnant woman's wishes. However, in the United States, even in the case of two completely separate individuals, constitutional law and common law have historically recognized the rights of all adults, pregnant or not, to informed consent and bodily integrity, *regardless of the impact of that person's decision on others*. For instance, in 1978, a man suffering from aplastic anemia sought a court order to force his cousin, who was the only compatible donor available, to submit to bone marrow harvest. The court declined, explaining in its opinion:

> For our law to compel the Defendant to submit to an intrusion of his body would change every concept and principle upon which our society is founded. To do so would defeat the sanctity of the individual and would impose a rule which would know no limits. . . . For a society that respects the rights of one individual, to sink its teeth into the jugular vein or neck of its members and suck from it sustenance for another member, is revolting to our hard-wrought concepts of jurisprudence. Forcible extraction of living body tissues causes revulsion to the judicial mind. Such would raise the specter of the swastika and the Inquisition, reminiscent of the horrors this portends. (24)

Justice requires that a pregnant woman, like any other individual, retain the basic right to refuse medical intervention, even if the intervention is in the best interest of her fetus. This principle was challenged unsuccessfully in June 1987 with the case of a 27-year-old woman who was at 25 weeks of gestation when she became critically ill with cancer. Against the wishes of the woman, her family, and her physicians, the hospital obtained a court order for a cesarean delivery, claiming independent rights of the fetus. Both mother and infant died shortly after the cesarean delivery was performed. Three years later, the District of Columbia Court of Appeals vacated the court-ordered cesarean delivery and held that the woman had the right to make health care decisions for herself and her fetus, arguing that the lower court had "erred in subordinating her right to bodily integrity in favor of the state's interest in potential life" (1).

2. *Court-ordered interventions in cases of informed refusal, as well as punishment of pregnant women for their behavior that may put a fetus at risk, neglect the fact that medical knowledge and predictions of outcomes in obstetrics have limitations.*

Beyond its importance as a means to protect the right of individuals to bodily integrity, the doctrine of informed consent recognizes the right of individuals to weigh risks and benefits for themselves. Women almost always are best situated to understand the importance of risks and benefits in the context of their own values, circumstances, and concerns. Furthermore, medical judgment in obstetrics itself has limitations in its ability to predict outcomes. In this document, the Committee on Ethics has argued that overriding a woman's autonomous choice, whatever its potential consequences, is neither ethically nor legally justified, given her fundamental rights to bodily integrity. Even those who challenge these fundamental rights in favor of protecting the fetus, however, must recognize and communicate that medical judgments in obstetrics are fallible (25). And fallibility—present to various degrees in all medical encounters—is sufficiently high in obstetric decision making to warrant wariness in imposing legal coercion. Levels of certainty underlying medical recommendations to pregnant women are unlikely to be adequate to justify legal coercion and the tremendous impact on the lives and civil liberties of pregnant women that such intervention would entail (26). Some have argued that court-ordered intervention might plausibly be justified only when certainty is especially robust and the stakes are especially high. However, in many cases of court-ordered obstetric intervention, the latter criterion has been met but not the former. Furthermore, evidence-based medicine has revealed limitations in the ability to concretely describe the relationship of maternal behavior to perinatal outcome. Criminalizing women in the face of such scientific and clinical uncertainty is morally dubious. Not only do these approaches fail to take into account the standards of evidence-based medical practice, but they are also unjust, and their application is likely to be informed by bias and opinion rather than objective assessment of risk.

Consider, first, the limitations of medical judgment in predicting birth outcomes based on mode of childbirth. A study of court-ordered obstetric interventions suggested that in almost one third of cases in which court orders were sought, the medical judgment was incorrect in retrospect (27). One clear example of the challenges of predicting outcome is in the management of risk associated with shoulder dystocia in the setting of fetal macrosomia—which is, and should be, of great concern for all practitioners. When making recommendations to patients, however, practitioners have an ethical obligation to recognize and communicate that accurate diagnosis of macrosomia is imprecise (20). Furthermore, although macrosomia increases the risk of shoulder dystocia, it is certainly not absolutely predictive; in fact, most cases of shoulder dystocia occur unpredictably among infants of normal birthweight. Given this uncertainty, ACOG makes recommendations about when cesarean delivery may be considered, not about when it is absolutely indicated. Because of the inability to determine with certainty when a situation is harmful to the fetus or pregnant woman and the inability to guarantee that the pregnant woman will not be harmed by the medical intervention, great care should be exercised to present a balanced evaluation of expected outcomes for both parties (20). The decision about weighing risks and benefits in the setting of uncertainty should remain the pregnant woman's to make in the setting of supportive, informative medical care.

Medical judgment also has limitations in that the relationship of maternal behavior to pregnancy outcome is poorly understood and may be exaggerated in realms often mistaken to be of moral rather than medical concern, such as drug use. For instance, recent child development research has not found the effects of prenatal cocaine exposure that earlier uncontrolled studies reported (28). It is now understood that poverty and its concomitants—poor nutrition and inadequate health care—can account for many of the effects popularly attributed to cocaine. Before these data emerged, the criminal justice approach to drug addiction during pregnancy was fueled to a great degree by what is now understood to be the distorting image of the "crack baby." Such an image served as a "convenient symbol for an aggressive war on drug users [that] makes it easier to advocate a simplistic punitive response than to address the complex causes of drug use" (29). The findings questioning the impact of cocaine on perinatal outcome are among many considerations that bring sharply into question any possible justification for a criminal justice approach, rather than a public health approach, to drug use during pregnancy. Given the incomplete understanding of factors underlying perinatal outcomes in general and the contribution of individual behavioral and socioeconomic factors in particular, to identify homeless and addicted women as personally, morally, and legally culpable for perinatal outcomes is inaccurate, misleading, and unjust.

*3. Coercive and punitive policies treat medical problems such as addiction and psychiatric illness as if they were moral failings.*

Regardless of the strength of the link between an individual's behaviors and pregnancy outcome, punitive policies directed at women who use drugs are not justified, because these policies are, in effect, punishing women for having a medical problem. Although once considered a sign of moral weakness, addiction is now, according to evidence-based medicine, considered a disease—a compulsive disorder requiring medical attention (30). Pregnancy should not change how clinicians understand the medical nature of addictive behavior. In fact, studies overwhelmingly show that pregnant drug users are very concerned about the consequences of their drug use for their fetuses and are particularly eager to obtain treatment once they find out they are pregnant (31, 32). Despite evidence-based medical recommendations that support treatment approaches to drug use and addiction (21), appropriate treatment is particularly difficult to obtain for pregnant and parenting women and the incarcerated (29). Thus, a disease process exacerbated by social circumstance—not personal, legal, or moral culpability—is at the heart of substance abuse and pregnancy. Punitive policies unfairly make pregnant women scapegoats for medical problems whose cause is often beyond their control.

In most states, governmental responses to pregnant women who use drugs have upheld medical characterizations of addiction. Consistent with longstanding U.S. Supreme Court decisions recognizing that addiction is an illness and that criminalizing it violates the Constitution's Eighth Amendment prohibitions against cruel and unusual punishment, no state has adopted a law that specifically creates unique criminal penalties for pregnant women who use drugs (33). However, in South Carolina, using drugs or being addicted to drugs was *effectively* criminalized when the state supreme court interpreted the word "child" in the state's criminal child endangerment statute to include viable fetuses, making the child endangerment statute applicable to pregnant women whose actions risk harm to a viable fetus (23). In all states, women retain their Fourth Amendment freedom from unreasonable searches, so that pregnant women may not be subject to nonconsensual drug testing for the purpose of criminal prosecution.

Partly on the basis of the understanding of addiction as a compulsive disorder requiring medical attention, medical professionals, U.S. state laws, and the vast majority of courts do not support unique criminal penalties for pregnant women who use drugs.

*4. Coercive and punitive policies are potentially counterproductive in that they are likely to discourage prenatal care and successful treatment, adversely affect infant mortality rates, and undermine the physician–patient relationship.*

Even if the aforementioned ethical concerns could be addressed, punitive policies would not be justifiable on utilitarian grounds, because they would likely result in more harm than good for maternal and child health, broadly construed. Various studies have suggested that attempts to criminalize pregnant women's behavior discourage women from seeking prenatal care (34, 35). Furthermore, an increased infant mortality rate was observed in South Carolina in the years following the *Whitner v State* decision (36), in which the state supreme court concluded that *anything* a pregnant woman does that might endanger a viable fetus (including, but not limited to, drug use) could result in either charges of child abuse and a jail sentence of up to 10 years or homicide and a 20-year sentence if a stillbirth coincides with a positive drug test (23). As documented previously (21), threats and incarceration have been ineffective in reducing the incidence of alcohol and drug abuse among pregnant women, and removing children from the home of an addicted mother may subject them to worse risks in the foster care system. In fact, women who have custody of their children complete substance abuse treatment at a higher rate (37–39).

These data suggest that punishment of pregnant women might not result in women receiving the desired message about the dangers of prenatal substance abuse; such measures might instead send an unintended message about the dangers of prenatal care. Ultimately, fear surrounding prenatal care would likely undermine, rather than enhance, maternal and child health. Likewise, court-ordered interventions and other coercive measures may result in fear about whether one's wishes in the delivery room will be respected and ultimately could discourage pregnant patients from seeking care. Encouraging prenatal care and treatment in a supportive environment will advance maternal and child health most effectively.

*5. Coercive and punitive policies directed toward pregnant women unjustly single out the most vulnerable women.*

Evidence suggests that punitive and coercive policies not only are ethically problematic in and of themselves, but also unfairly burden the most vulnerable women. In cases of court-ordered cesarean deliveries, for instance, the vast majority of court orders have been obtained against poor women of color (27, 40).

Similarly, decisions about detection and management of substance abuse in pregnancy are fraught with bias, unfairly burdening the most vulnerable despite the fact that addiction occurs consistently across race and socioeconomic status (41). In the landmark case of *Ferguson v City of Charleston*, which involved selective screening and arrest of pregnant women who tested positive for drugs, 29 of 30 women arrested were African American. Studies suggest that affluent women are less likely to be tested for use of illicit drugs than poor women of color, perhaps because of stereotyped but demonstrably inaccurate assumptions about drug use. One study found that despite similar rates of substance abuse across racial and socioeconomic status, African–American women were 10 times more likely than white women to be reported to public health authorities for substance abuse during pregnancy (42). These data suggest that, as implemented, many punitive policies centered on maternal behaviors, including substance use, are deeply unjust in that they reinforce social and racial inequality.

*6. Coercive and punitive policies create the potential for criminalization of many types of otherwise legal maternal behavior.*

In addition to raising concerns about race and socioeconomic status, punitive and coercive policies may have even broader implications for justice for women. Because many maternal behaviors are associated with adverse pregnancy outcome, these policies could result in a society in which simply being a woman of reproductive potential could put an individual at risk for criminal prosecution. For instance, poorly controlled diabetes is associated with numerous congenital malformations and an excessive rate of fetal death. Periconceptional folic acid deficiency is associated with an increased risk of neural tube defects. Obesity has been associated in recent studies with adverse pregnancy outcomes, including preeclampsia, shoulder dystocia, and antepartum stillbirth (43, 44). Prenatal exposure to certain medications that may be essential to maintaining a pregnant woman's health status is associated with congenital abnormalities. If states were to consistently adopt policies of punishing women whose behavior (ranging from substance abuse to poor nutrition to informed decisions about prescription drugs) has the potential to lead to adverse perinatal outcomes, at what point would they draw the line? Punitive policies, therefore, threaten the privacy and autonomy not only of all pregnant women, but also of all women of reproductive potential.

## Recommendations

In light of these six considerations, the Committee on Ethics strongly opposes the criminal prosecution of pregnant women whose activities may appear to cause harm to their fetuses. Efforts to use the legal system specifically to protect the fetus by constraining women's decision making or punishing them for their behavior erode a woman's basic rights to privacy and bodily integrity and are neither legally nor morally justified. The ACOG Committee on Ethics therefore makes the following recommendations:

- In caring for pregnant women, practitioners should recognize that in the majority of cases, the interests of the pregnant woman and her fetus converge rather than diverge. Promoting pregnant women's health through advocacy of healthy behavior, referral for substance abuse treatment and mental health services when necessary, and maintenance of a good physician–patient relationship is always in the best interest of both the woman and her fetus.
- Pregnant women's autonomous decisions should be respected. Concerns about the impact of maternal decisions on fetal well-being should be discussed in the context of medical evidence and understood within the context of each woman's broad social network, cultural beliefs, and values. In the absence of extraordinary circumstances, circumstances that, in fact, the Committee on Ethics cannot currently imagine, judicial authority should not be used to implement treatment regimens aimed at protecting the fetus, for such actions violate the pregnant woman's autonomy.
- Pregnant women should not be punished for adverse perinatal outcomes. The relationship between maternal behavior and perinatal outcome is not fully understood, and punitive approaches threaten to dissuade pregnant women from seeking health care and ultimately undermine the health of pregnant women and their fetuses.
- Policy makers, legislators, and physicians should work together to find constructive and evidence-based ways to address the needs of women with alcohol and other substance abuse problems. This should include the development of safe, available, and efficacious services for women and families.

## References


1. In re A.C., 573 A.2d 1235 (D.C. 1990).
2. Annas GJ. Foreclosing the use of force: A.C. reversed. Hastings Cent Rep 1990;20(4):27–9.
3. Annas GJ. Protecting the liberty of pregnant patients [editorial]. N Engl J Med 1987;316:1213–4.
4. Rhoden NK. The judge in the delivery room: the emergence of court-ordered cesareans. Calif Law Rev 1986; 74:1951–2030.
5. Bianchi DW, Crombleholme TM, D'Alton ME. Fetology: diagnosis and management of the fetal patient. New York (NY): McGraw-Hill; 2000.
6. McCullough LB, Chervenak FA. Ethics in obstetrics and gynecology. New York (NY): Oxford University Press; 1994.
7. Harris LH. Rethinking maternal-fetal conflict: gender and equality in perinatal ethics. Obstet Gynecol 2000;96: 786–91.
8. Maternal and Child Health Bureau. Mission statement. Rockville (MD): MCHB; 2005. Available at: http://www.mchb.hrsa.gov/about/default.htm. Retrieved June 17, 2005.
9. Lyerly AD, Gates EA, Cefalo RC, Sugarman J. Toward the ethical evaluation and use of maternal-fetal surgery. Obstet Gynecol 2001;98:689–97.
10. State Children's Health Insurance Program; eligibility for prenatal care and other health services for unborn children. Final rule. Centers for Medicare & Medicaid Services (CMS), HHS. Fed Regist 2002;67:61955–74.
11. Steinbock B. Health care coverage for not-yet-born children. Hastings Cent Rep 2003;33(1):49.
12. Murray L, Cooper P. Effects of postnatal depression on infant development. Arch Dis Child 1997;77:99–101.
13. Murray L, Fiori-Cowley A, Hooper R, Cooper P. The impact of postnatal depression and associated adversity on early mother-infant interactions and later infant outcome. Child Dev 1996;67:2512–26.
14. Horon IL, Cheng D. Enhanced surveillance for pregnancy-associated mortality—Maryland, 1993–1998. JAMA 2001;285:1455–9.
15. Frye V. Examining homicide's contribution to pregnancy-associated deaths [editorial]. JAMA 2001;285:1510–1.
16. Phelan JP. The maternal abdominal wall: a fortress against fetal health care? South Calif Law Rev 1991;65:461–90.
17. Little MO. Abortion, intimacy, and the duty to gestate. Ethical Theory Moral Pract 1999;2:295–312.
18. Mattingly SS. The maternal-fetal dyad. Exploring the two-patient obstetric model. Hastings Cent Rep 1992;22: 13–8.
19. Informed consent. In: American College of Obstetricians and Gynecologists. Ethics in obstetrics and gynecology. 2nd ed. Washington, DC: ACOG; 2004. p. 9–17.
20. Patient choice in the maternal–fetal relationship. In: American College of Obstetricians and Gynecologists. Ethics in obstetrics and gynecology. 2nd ed. Washington, DC: ACOG; 2004. p. 34–6.
21. At-risk drinking and illicit drug use: ethical issues in obstetric and gynecologic practice. ACOG Committee Opinion No. 294. American College of Obstetricians and Gynecologists. Obstet Gynecol 2004;103:1021–31.
22. Ferguson v. City of Charleston, 532 U.S. 67 (2001).
23. Whitner v. State, 328 S.C. 1, 492 S.E.2n 777 (1997).
24. McFall v. Shimp, 10 Pa. D. & C.3d (C.P. 1978).
25. Rhoden NK. Informed consent in obstetrics: some special problems. West N Engl Law Rev 1987;9:67–88.
26. Nelson LJ, Milliken N. Compelled medical treatment of pregnant women. Life, liberty, and law in conflict. JAMA 1988;259:1060–6.
27. Kolder VE, Gallagher J, Parsons MT. Court-ordered obstetrical interventions. N Engl J Med 1987;316:1192–6.
28. Frank DA, Augustyn M, Knight WG, Pell T, Zuckerman B. Growth, development, and behavior in early childhood following prenatal cocaine exposure: a systematic review. JAMA 2001;285:1613–25.
29. Chavkin W. Cocaine and pregnancy—time to look at the evidence [editorial]. JAMA 2001;285:1626–8.
30. Marwick C. Physician leadership on National Drug Policy finds that addiction treatment works. JAMA 1998;279: 1149–50.
31. Murphy S, Rosenbaum M. Pregnant women on drugs: combating stereotypes and stigma. New Brunswick (NJ): Rutgers University Press; 1999.
32. Kearney MH, Murphy S, Rosenbaum M. Mothering on crack cocaine: a grounded theory analysis. Soc Sci Med 1994;38:351–61.
33. Harris LH, Paltrow L. MSJAMA. The status of pregnant women and fetuses in US criminal law. JAMA 2003; 289:1697–9.
34. Poland ML, Dombrowski MP, Ager JW, Sokol RJ. Punishing pregnant drug users: enhancing the flight from care. Drug Alcohol Depend 1993;31:199–203.
35. United States. General Accounting Office. Drug exposed infants: a generation at risk: report to the chairman, Committee on Finance, U.S. Senate. Washington, DC: U.S. General Accounting Office; 1990.
36. The Annie E. Casey Foundation. 2004 kids count data book: moving youth from risk to opportunity. Baltimore (MD): AECF; 2004. Available at: http://www.aecf.org/publications/data/kc2004_e.pdf. Retrieved June 17, 2005.
37. Haller DL, Knisely JS, Elswick RK Jr, Dawson KS, Schnoll SH. Perinatal substance abusers: factors influencing treatment retention. J Subst Abuse Treat 1997;14: 513–9.
38. Hohman MM, Shillington AM, Baxter HG. A comparison of pregnant women presenting for alcohol and other drug treatment by CPS status. Child Abuse Negl 2003;27: 303–17.
39. Kissin WB, Svikis DS, Morgan GD, Haug NA. Characterizing pregnant drug-dependent women in treatment and their children. J Subst Abuse Treat 2001;21: 27–34.
40. Nelson LJ, Marshall MF. Ethical and legal analyses of three coercive policies aimed at substance abuse by pregnant women. Charleston (SC): Medical University of South Carolina, Program in Bioethics; 1998.
41. Mathias R. NIDA survey provides first national data on drug use during pregnancy. NIDA Notes 1995;10(1). Available

at: http://www.nida.nih.gov/NIDA_Notes/NNVol10N1/NIDASurvey.html. Retrieved June 17, 2005.
42. Chasnoff IJ, Landress HJ, Barrett ME. The prevalence of illicit-drug or alcohol use during pregnancy and discrepancies in mandatory reporting in Pinellas County, Florida. N Engl J Med 1990;322:1202–6.
43. Cedergren MI. Maternal morbid obesity and the risk of adverse pregnancy outcome. Obstet Gynecol 2004;103: 219–24.
44. Cnattingius S, Bergstrom R, Lipworth L, Kramer MS. Prepregnancy weight and the risk of adverse pregnancy outcomes. N Engl J Med 1998;338:147–52.

ACOG Committee Opinion

Committee on Ethics

Number 341, July 2006

# Ethical Ways for Physicians to Market a Practice

*ABSTRACT: It is ethical for physicians to market their practices through any form of public communication provided that the communication is truthful and not misleading or deceptive. Communications should not convey discriminatory attitudes involving race, ethnicity, gender, or sexual orientation. All paid advertising must be clearly identified as such. Producing fair and accurate advertising of medical practices and services can be challenging. It often is difficult to include detailed information because of cost and size restrictions or the limitations of the media form that has been selected. If the specific advertising form does not lend itself to clear and accurate description, an alternative media format should be selected. Finally, any advertising that seeks to denigrate the competence of other individual professionals or group practices is always considered unethical.*



ISSN 1074-861X

**The American College of Obstetricians and Gynecologists**
409 12th Street, SW
PO Box 96920
Washington, DC 20090-6920

12345/09876

Ethical ways for physicians to market a practice. ACOG Committee Opinion No. 341. American College of Obstetricians and Gynecologists. Obstet Gynecol 2006;108:239–42.

Traditionally, physicians and medical societies have raised concerns that advertising commercializes the practice of medicine and does not respect the dignity of the profession. Physicians have been expected to generate referrals from other physicians and from satisfied patients by providing good care to their patients. In the past, some state and national professional medical societies prohibited advertising in their code of ethics. In 1982, the Supreme Court ruled in favor of the Federal Trade Commission (FTC) in its claim that the American Medical Association was in restraint of trade because the American Medical Association's Code of Ethics prohibited advertising (1). The FTC argued that all businesses and professionals have the right to inform the public of the services they provide and that all consumers have the right to make informed choices based on truthful advertising. The purpose of this Committee Opinion is to provide objective criteria to help members of the American College of Obstetricians and Gynecologists determine whether or not a certain advertisement or method of marketing is ethical. In considering appropriate marketing practices, physicians should evaluate not only their own actions but also those undertaken on their behalf by hospitals or other health care centers that may be marketing their services.

It is ethical for physicians to market their practices through any form of public communication provided that the communication is truthful and not misleading or deceptive in any way. In addition, communications should not convey discriminatory attitudes involving race, ethnicity, gender, or sexual orientation.

## Appropriate Forms of Communication

According to the FTC guidelines, physicians must be allowed to make their services known through advertising to assist the public in obtaining medical services. A physician or practice should not be restricted from using any form of public media to market medical services, such as newspapers, magazines, telephone directories, radio, web pages, computer billboards, television, and direct mail. All of these media formats have the potential for both effective, ethical communication as well as misrepresentation, depending on their form and content. Advertising in any format may be ethical but still reflect poorly on the profession and undermine the public impressions of the profession. For example, use of a large billboard or television "infomercials" to advertise services is not unethical, but still might be considered by many to be unprofessional. Physicians should consider not just the intent of the advertisement but also its impact.

A paid advertisement promoting the activities of a physician or practice must be clearly identified as advertising. It is not ethical to compensate the communication media in any way for publicity in a news item. If a television infomercial is used to inform the public of services available, it should be very clear at all times that this is paid advertising and not part of a news program.

Care should be taken to choose information appropriate to the form of communication. The complexity of medical terms and treatments may not always lend itself to the restrictions of a particular advertisement design or media format. For example, the brevity of television and radio advertisements may require omitting so much information that the advertisement becomes misleading.

The location in which an advertisement is placed also may contribute to deception. For example, some readers may assume that a physician who advertises his or her practice under the subheading "Infertility" in the telephone directory has received extensive subspecialty training in that area and regularly treats patients with these problems. Advertisers should be careful not to imply subspecialty training when none exists.

Actively approaching specific individuals, in person or by phone, with the purpose of attracting them as patients usually is not considered ethical because the risk of undue pressure from the solicitor is too great. Common expectations for a physician–patient relationship may make the prospective patient feel obligated to respond affirmatively to the encounter. Although many physicians view such active approaches as always being unprofessional, they may be ethical in rare circumstances if extraordinary care is taken to avoid undue pressure. For example, it may be appropriate to pass out cards to potential clients at a community health fair.

## Appropriate Content of Advertisements

Advertisements must be truthful and not deceptive or misleading. Specifically, this means that all information must be accurate and must not create false or unjustified expectations. The omission of information should not render the advertisement misleading. Images and graphics can be as deceptive or misleading as text. Finally, the physician or clinic must be able to substantiate all claims made in the advertisement. Advertisements may include nondeceptive information, such as address, phone numbers, web site address, office hours, languages spoken, board certification, contracted insurance plans, publications by physicians, teaching positions, hospital affiliations, and methods of payment accepted.

Terms such as "top," "world-famous," "world-class," or even "pioneer," usually are misleading and designed to attract vulnerable patients. Statements that rank the competence of physicians or the quality of medical services usually are not factually supportable. If attributions of this type are used, the advertisement must describe how these rankings were established. The testimonial of one or two satisfied patients may mislead the public into believing that all patients, even those with dissimilar histories, have similar outcomes. The designation "Top Doctor" as voted by magazine readers, other doctors, or specific groups may be used in promotional material since the term is a factual statement of the results of a survey. However, advertisements must state if such a designation involved payment by the physician. Furthermore, any advertising that seeks to denigrate the competence of other individual professionals or group practices always is considered unethical.

Care must be taken in advertising procedures that are experimental or have never been proved to result in the desired outcome. It is deceptive to give the public the impression that experimental or unstudied procedures are of proven value or accepted practice.

Claims that a physician or group of physicians have a unique skill or offer a unique test or treatment often may be deceptive and rarely should be used. If a physician has carefully verified that he or she is the only practitioner to offer a certain treatment in a particular geographic area, then this information may be dispersed. If the uniqueness results from a restrictive commercial agreement, this fact needs to be disclosed in the advertisement.

Specific outcomes should rarely be advertised because the definition of a success rate, the selection of eligible patients for consideration in calculating rates, and the predictive value of rates are all important in accurately assessing outcomes. Whereas these should be discussed with an individual patient in the context of her care, they cannot be interpreted accurately by someone viewing an advertisement and may be very confusing or misleading to the patient trying to determine where to seek care. For example, a fertility clinic's "success rate" for assisted reproductive technologies is dependent on the patient's age, the clinic's patient selection and exclusion policies, and the clinic's criteria for cycle cancellation. "Success" may be stated in many ways, each of which results in a different rate: as clinical pregnancies, singleton pregnancies, or live births per started cycle, per egg retrieval, or per embryo transfer. Comparing hospitals by cesarean delivery rate is similarly difficult because rates vary with the characteristics of a patient population or the presence of a neonatal intensive care unit or both. Furthermore, a new program or site should not present the success rates of the parent site as its own because its new facilities are as yet untested. When advertisements do involve success rates or other outcomes, all claims must be supported by valid, reproducible data, must clearly state the method used to calculate outcomes, and must not lead patients or the public to believe that outcomes are better than they are.

Fee structures and costs may be advertised, as long as information is complete and titles for special programs do not mislead or encourage inaccurate assumptions. For example, promises of a "money-back guarantee" are frequently misleading because usually they refund only a portion of the patient's money if the desired outcome does not occur. "Shared-risk" plans usually do not share risk between the patient and the clinic, but among a group of patients. "Do one, get one free" treatments may involve extraordinary requirements and expenses for the initial treatment and may not truly save the patient any money. A "free initial consultation" should not contain any hidden costs or routinely involve recommendations for expensive tests or treatments. Any advertisements involving such financial plans should contain enough information so that the prospective patients are neither misled nor unduly induced to seek services at that clinic.

Producing fair and accurate advertising of medical practices and services can be challenging, even with the best intentions. It often is difficult to include detailed information because of cost and size restrictions or the limitations of the media form that has been selected. If the specific advertising form does not lend itself to clear and accurate description, an alternative media format should be selected.

## Concerns About Discrimination

Discriminatory attitudes about race, ethnicity, gender, or sexual orientation in advertisements are not acceptable. A line item stating that a provider speaks Spanish or Cantonese accurately states the services provided and would not be considered discriminatory. Similarly, a factual statement that the providers in a certain clinic are all women is ethical. However, wording that suggests that health care provided solely by women is superior to health care for women by men would be considered discriminatory and unethical in the absence of evidence supporting that claim. If the intent of stating the facts is to imply a value judgment rather than to offer supportable or useful information about access, then even a statement of fact may be unethical.

## Vulnerable Groups

Certain individuals and groups of individuals may be more easily misled by some claims made in advertisements. Special care should be taken when designing a marketing plan that targets these groups. Perimenopausal and postmenopausal women, fearful of cancer, may embrace "natural" therapies, even when these therapies have not been evaluated adequately for efficacy or risk. Patients with advanced cancer may be more likely to pursue unapproved procedures or pharmaceuticals. Patients with infertility or recurrent pregnancy losses, desperate to have a child, often are willing to pursue expensive new treatments that are completely unproved.

## Summary

Advertising by physicians or groups of physicians is unethical when it contains material that is false, unsubstantiated, deceptive, or misleading. Even if the advertisement follows the guidelines covered in this statement, the individual professional should be the one who chooses a marketing plan he or she believes respects the dignity of the profession.

## Reference

1. American Medical Assoc. v. FTC, 455 U.S. 676 (1982).

## Bibliography

American College of Obstetricians and Gynecologists. Code of professional ethics of the American College of Obstetricians and Gynecologists. Washington, DC: ACOG; 2004.

Guidelines for advertising by ART programs. Practice Committee, Society for Assisted Reproductive Technology; American Society for Reproductive Medicine. Fertil Steril 2004;82:527–8.

# ACOG Committee Opinion

Committee on Ethics

Number 347, November 2006

# Using Preimplantation Embryos for Research*

*ABSTRACT: Human embryonic stem cell research promises an increased understanding of the molecular process underlying cell differentiation. Transplantation of embryonic stem cells or their derivatives may, in the future, offer therapies for human diseases. In this Committee Opinion, the American College of Obstetricians and Gynecologists (ACOG) Committee on Ethics presents an ethical framework for examining issues surrounding research using preimplantation embryos and proposes ethical guidelines for such research. The Committee acknowledges the diversity of opinions among ACOG members and affirms that no physician who finds embryo research morally objectionable should be required or expected to participate in such research. The Committee supports embryo research within 14 days after evidence of fertilization but limits it according to ethical guidelines. The Committee recommends that cryopreserved embryos be the preferred source for research but believes that the promise of somatic cell nuclear transfer is such that research in this area is justified. The Committee opposes reproductive cloning. Intended parents for whom embryos are created should give informed consent for the disposition of any excess embryos. The donors of gametes or somatic cells used in the creation of such tissue should give consent for donation of embryos for research. Abandoned embryos should not be accepted for research. Potential research projects should be described to potential donors as much as possible. Donation of embryos for stem cell research requires specific consent. The Committee believes that compensation for egg donors for research is acceptable, consistent with American Society for Reproductive Medicine guidelines.*

The human **embryo**† has long attracted the interest of researchers. Initially, scientists studying embryos hoped to better understand human pregnancy and embryonic development. Later, with the emergence of assisted reproductive technologies such as in vitro fertilization (IVF), embryo research focused on optimizing pregnancy rates and outcomes. Most recently, research has targeted the **stem cells** derived from embryos because stem cell

*Update of "Preembryo Research" in *Ethics in Obstetrics and Gynecology*, Second Edition, 2004

†Terms defined in the glossary appear in bold type.



ISSN 1074-861X

**The American College of Obstetricians and Gynecologists**
409 12th Street, SW
PO Box 96920
Washington, DC 20090-6920

12345/09876

Using preimplantation embryos for research. ACOG Committee Opinion No. 347. American College of Obstetricians and Gynecologists. Obstet Gynecol 2006;108:1305–17.

research promises an increased understanding of the molecular process underlying cell differentiation (the process of acquiring characteristics of specific tissues and organs). Transplantation of **embryonic stem cells** or their derivatives may, in the future, offer therapies for human diseases. These possibilities, coupled with the demonstration in 1998 that stem cells could be isolated from either the **inner cell mass** of **blastocysts** or fetal germ cell tissue, have sparked public debate on the ethical foundation of stem cell work specifically and embryo research in general. The urgency of these questions makes it timely both to review the moral issues raised by human embryo research and to consider appropriate guidelines for the ethical conduct of these endeavors.

The Committee on Ethics acknowledges the diversity of opinions regarding these topics among members of the American College of Obstetricians and Gynecologists (ACOG), a diversity mirroring that in society at large. These diverse positions range from complete rejection of all human embryo research to approval of the deliberate creation of human embryos for research. Even among those who accept embryo research on ethical grounds, there is disagreement about the conditions under which it may ethically be conducted.

The purpose of this Committee Opinion is to present a relevant ethical framework within which to view contemporary embryo research and to propose ethical guidelines for such research. The opinion focuses specifically on issues relating to research using **preimplantation embryos**. The Committee recognizes that the science of this field, especially the science of stem cell research and therapy, is changing rapidly and anticipates that future changes will require revisiting past issues and either modifying previous guidelines or creating new ones in order to address formerly unimagined possibilities.

## Historical Perspective: Policies and Regulation

Oversight and regulation of research involving human reproduction, especially that involving fertilized eggs and embryos, have a long and contentious history linked both to the politics of abortion and to the introduction of IVF into clinical practice (Fig. 1). Certainly, clinical progress with assisted reproductive technologies requires research, yet performing such research raises important questions about how the needed tissues should be obtained and treated.

Several events and issues, including the U.S. Supreme Court's decision on abortion in *Roe v. Wade* and revelations of abuses in human subjects research, led Congress in 1974 to establish the National Commission for the Protection of Human Subjects. On the basis of guidelines proposed by the National Commission in 1975, the then Department of Health, Education, and Welfare issued regulations for federal funding of research involving human fetuses. These regulations defined the fetus as the product of conception from the time of **implantation** on (1). The regulations also recommended the appointment of an ethical advisory board to examine unresolved questions. The Ethics Advisory Board (EAB) was appointed in 1978, shortly before the first birth from IVF, with a mandate to review both IVF research and research using embryos resulting from IVF.

In its 1979 report, the EAB stated, "The human embryo is entitled to profound respect; but this respect does not necessarily encompass the full legal and moral rights attributed to persons" (2). The EAB statement supported the ethical acceptability of research to study and develop the safety and efficacy of IVF and embryo transfer techniques used for the treatment of infertility. The EAB also accepted the use of **gametes** of informed, married, and consenting donors in such research, provided that developing embryos were not sustained longer than 14 days in vitro, a limit chosen in part because the **primitive streak** is formed at this juncture. In its statement, the EAB did not distinguish between "excess" embryos from IVF therapy and embryos "created solely for research." In fact, the EAB implied that research may require the creation of embryos that, because of concerns for safety, would never be intended for transfer.

Because of public and political opposition to embryo research, however, EAB guidelines were never implemented, and the board's charter was allowed to expire in 1980, effectively imposing a moratorium on federal funding of IVF and embryo research because existing legislation required the oversight of an ethical advisory board as a prerequisite. Thus, any embryo research conducted in the United States at that time had to use private or university funding and often was undertaken in the context of infertility treatment. Recognizing the ethical and regulatory challenges associated with the conduct of research outside of federal oversight, the Ethics Committee of the American Fertility Society

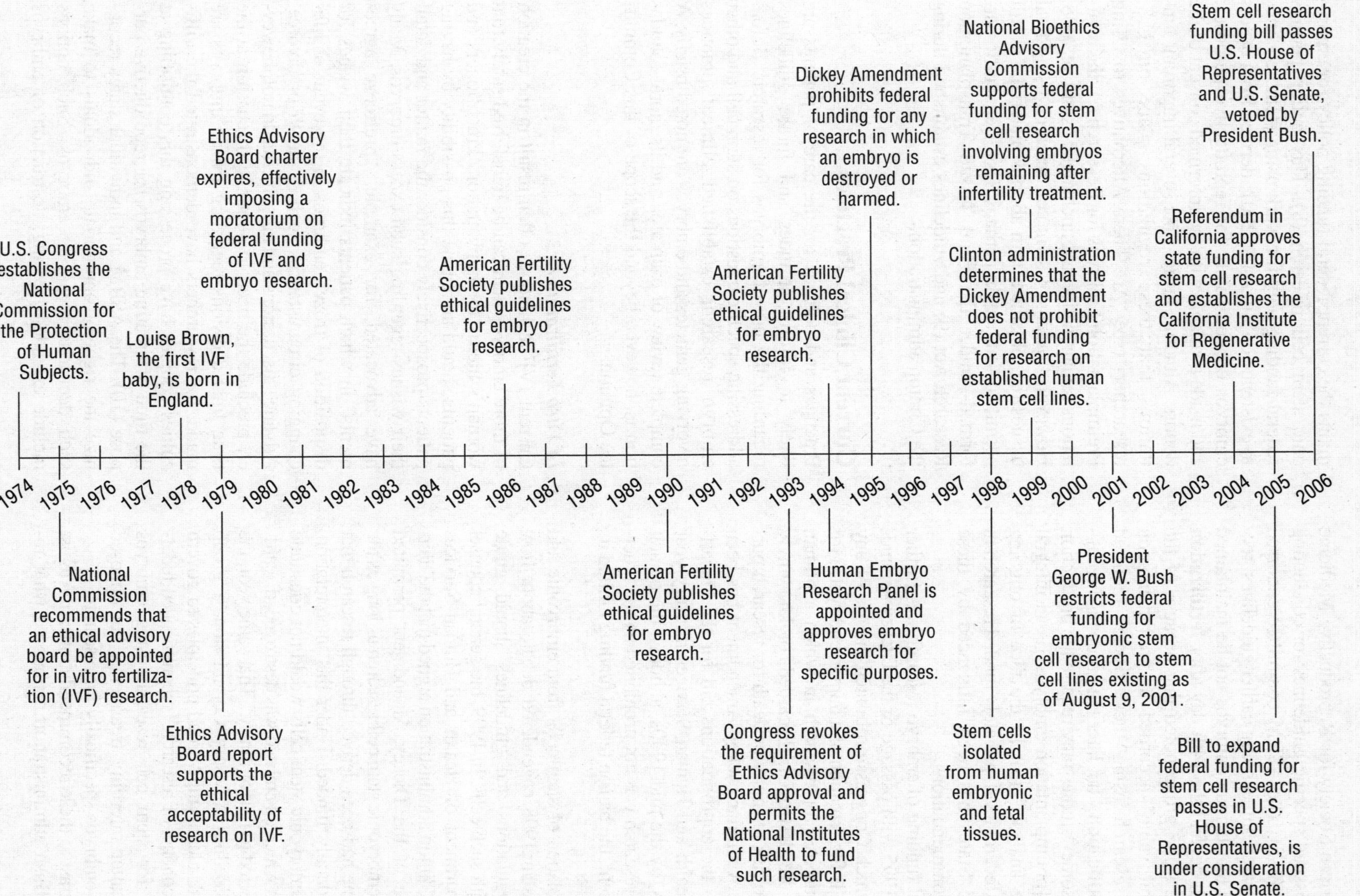

U.S. Congress establishes the National Commission for the Protection of Human Subjects.
National Commission recommends that an ethical advisory board be appointed for in vitro fertilization (IVF) research.
Louise Brown, the first IVF baby, is born in England.
Ethics Advisory Board report supports the ethical acceptability of research on IVF.
Ethics Advisory Board charter expires, effectively imposing a moratorium on federal funding of IVF and embryo research.
American Fertility Society publishes ethical guidelines for embryo research.
American Fertility Society publishes ethical guidelines for embryo research.
Congress revokes the requirement of Ethics Advisory Board approval and permits the National Institutes of Health to fund such research.
American Fertility Society publishes ethical guidelines for embryo research.
Human Embryo Research Panel is appointed and approves embryo research for specific purposes.
Dickey Amendment prohibits federal funding for any research in which an embryo is destroyed or harmed.
Stem cells isolated from human embryonic and fetal tissues.
National Bioethics Advisory Commission supports federal funding for stem cell research involving embryos remaining after infertility treatment.
Clinton administration determines that the Dickey Amendment does not prohibit federal funding for research on established human stem cell lines.
President George W. Bush restricts federal funding for embryonic stem cell research to stem cell lines existing as of August 9, 2001.
Referendum in California approves state funding for stem cell research and establishes the California Institute for Regenerative Medicine.
Bill to expand federal funding for stem cell research passes in U.S. House of Representatives, is under consideration in U.S. Senate.
Stem cell research funding bill passes U.S. House of Representatives and U.S. Senate, vetoed by President Bush.
1974
1975
1976
1977
1978
1979
1980
1981
1982
1983
1984
1985
1986
1987
1988
1989
1990
1991
1992
1993
1994
1995
1996
1997
1998
1999
2000
2001
2002
2003
2004
2005
2006


**Fig. 1.** Embryo research timeline. The American Fertility Society became the American Society for Reproductive Medicine in 1995.

(now American Society for Reproductive Medicine [ASRM]) issued specific guidelines for conducting such work (3–5). The ASRM committee endorsed embryo research but, echoing earlier guidelines, recommended that human embryos not be maintained for research beyond the 14th day after **fertilization** (3, 4). The same group noted that because of the "high moral value" accorded to preimplantation embryos, research using these tissues required "strong justification," but later the group also recognized that some "studies may require the production of human [preimplantation embryos] as an integral part of the analysis" (5). In the face of ongoing debate at a federal level, privately funded research in the United States has been influenced by these ASRM recommendations.

Federal funding of embryo research was further limited in 1995 with passage of the Dickey Amendment, in which Congress prohibited the use of any federal funds for "creation of a human embryo(s) for research purposes or research in which a human embryo(s) are destroyed, discarded, or knowingly subjected to risk of injury or death for research purposes" (6). A similar Dickey Amendment has been attached to the appropriations bill for the Department of Health and Human Services in every year since. Thus, by the mid-1990s, although the pursuit of embryo research was not prohibited by the federal government, the ban on federal funding limited its conduct.

The isolation of stem cells from embryonic and fetal tissues in 1998 engendered debate about how existing regulations and guidelines should guide research with such cells. In 1999, the general counsel of the Department of Health and Human Services during the Clinton administration argued that the literal language of the Dickey Amendment permitted funding of embryonic stem cell research as long as the stem cell line had been derived through research that was not federally funded. Under this interpretation, the use of embryonic stem cells would not constitute research "in which an embryo was destroyed, discarded, or subjected to risk of injury." That same year, the National Bioethics Advisory Commission, a group charged with identifying "broad principles to govern the ethical conduct of research," recommended federal support for stem cell research using embryos remaining after infertility treatments, but opposed creation of embryos specifically for research (7).

In contrast to these recommendations, in August 2001, the Bush administration announced what remains the current federal funding policy for embryonic stem cell research (8). This policy permits federal funding only for work using stem cell lines in existence on August 9, 2001; derived from excess embryos created solely for reproductive purposes; and made available with the informed consent of the donors. Although critics note several important limitations that these regulations place on U.S. researchers (see "Are There Alternatives to Using Preimplantation Embryos for Research?"), the regulations remain active and unchanged as of late 2006. However, funding of stem cell research using fetal tissues (eg, obtained from abortus materials) is still permitted—although perhaps less frequently performed—under the Fetal Tissue Transplantation Research Act (9) and guidelines established during the Clinton administration.

## Current Clinical Practices

Practices and policies for the care of patients are likely to inform attitudes and future guidelines regarding the use of embryos for research. Before addressing specific questions on stem cell and other embryo research, established clinical practices involving gametes and embryos are noted briefly. A complete review of each area and its moral foundation is, however, beyond the scope of this Committee Opinion.

### *In Vitro Fertilization*

Current IVF techniques often result in the creation of more embryos than can be transferred safely to a woman's uterus for implantation. Practitioners and patients should anticipate this possibility by having patients prospectively consider the matter and detail their wishes regarding such excess embryos. Many have advocated, for example, "prefreeze agreements" in which patients indicate their wishes for disposition of frozen embryos in the event of life-changing circumstances such as death or divorce. Advance discussions and agreements do not, however, preclude the need to continue discussion at the time final decisions regarding frozen embryos are made, for researchers have demonstrated the difficulties couples have processing this counseling at the time of creating embryos for reproductive purpose (10). The ASRM and individual states recognize the right of appropriate individuals to make such decisions regarding embryos. Such options include extended freezing, destruction of embryos either by failing to transfer or freeze or later thawing without transfer, and donation for attempted implantation by another individual or couple. The ACOG Committee on Ethics recognizes all of these options as reasonable and appropriate and in so doing accepts that it is the individual or couple who created the embryos, either with their own or donor gametes, who are entitled to make these decisions. This current Committee Opinion outlines ethical considerations related to the option of using preimplantation embryos for research.

### *Gamete Donation*

Both egg and sperm may be donated either anonymously or by directed donation to specific individuals or couples. Donated gametes are widely used for infertility treatment, and sperm and egg obtained in excess of what is needed for such treatments have, with appropriate consent, later been used for research. Gametes also have been donated for research purposes only, separate from any plans for infertility treatment and therapy, and the Committee on Ethics supports such donation. In the past, research using gametes has included studies designed to optimize IVF techniques and work examining gamete cryopreservation. The donation of **oocytes** for research purposes is controversial, however, and has raised what ASRM terms "special concern" (5) because of the risk, pain, and side effects involved in the process of egg donation and because of concerns about possible exploitation of donors.

## Embryo Research: Ethical Questions

### *What Is the Moral Status of the Embryo?*

In debates about the ethics of embryo research, the central ethical question historically has focused on the embryo's "moral status" and whether the embryo is deserving of the same rights and protections as a child or adult person. This Committee Opinion is based on the view that although the preimplantation embryo merits respect, its moral status is not equivalent to that of a human being. Scientific information alone will never resolve questions about the embryo's moral status. However, several distinguishing features of preimplantation embryos inform the evaluation of the moral status of the embryo and, hence, the ethical arguments concerning embryo research. Figure 2 outlines the development of pregnancy from gamete to fetus, a path that highlights the distinguishing characteristics of preimplantation embryos:

1. *Early embryonic cells are undifferentiated.* Until the blastocyst stage, each cell is **totipotent**, having the capacity to differentiate into any of the cell or tissue types of the fetus or to form placental and other extra-embryonic tissues. Each of the cells of the inner cell mass of the blastocyst is **pluripotent**, with the capacity to become any of the cell or tissue types of the fetus, but at this stage, these cells form a collection of undifferentiated cells rather than a unified organism.
2. *Embryos at early stages lack individuation.* This is evidenced by research demonstrating that, up to at least the 8-cell stage, one or more **blastomeres** can be removed from the embryo (eg, as for preimplantation genetic diagnosis [PGD]) and the remaining blastomeres can still produce a complete human being. Also, from the initial stages of cell division until the formation of the primitive streak, the embryo is capable of dividing into more than one entity (ie, twinning). Only after this period has differentiation of embryonic cells advanced to the point that separation can no longer result in two or more individuals (11–13).
3. *The formation of the primitive streak at day 14 marks the beginning of the differentiation of cells into the various tissues and organs of the human body.* Before the appearance of the primitive streak, the cells of the embryo are undifferentiated and pluripotent. Recognizing this biologic landmark, many, now including the ACOG Committee on Ethics, have recommended limiting embryo research to the first 14 days after fertilization.
4. *If the preimplantation embryo is left or maintained outside the uterus, it cannot develop into a human being.* Continuing potential for life exists if, but only if, the embryo is transferred to the uterus for implantation (this potential will have important implications for the conduct of research and therapy involving embryos). If never implanted, development ceases. In the United Kingdom, regulations focus on implantation as a key to distinguishing moral status of in vitro and cloned embryos from that of an in vivo pregnancy (14). In the United States, federal regulations on fetal research apply from the time of implantation on (1).

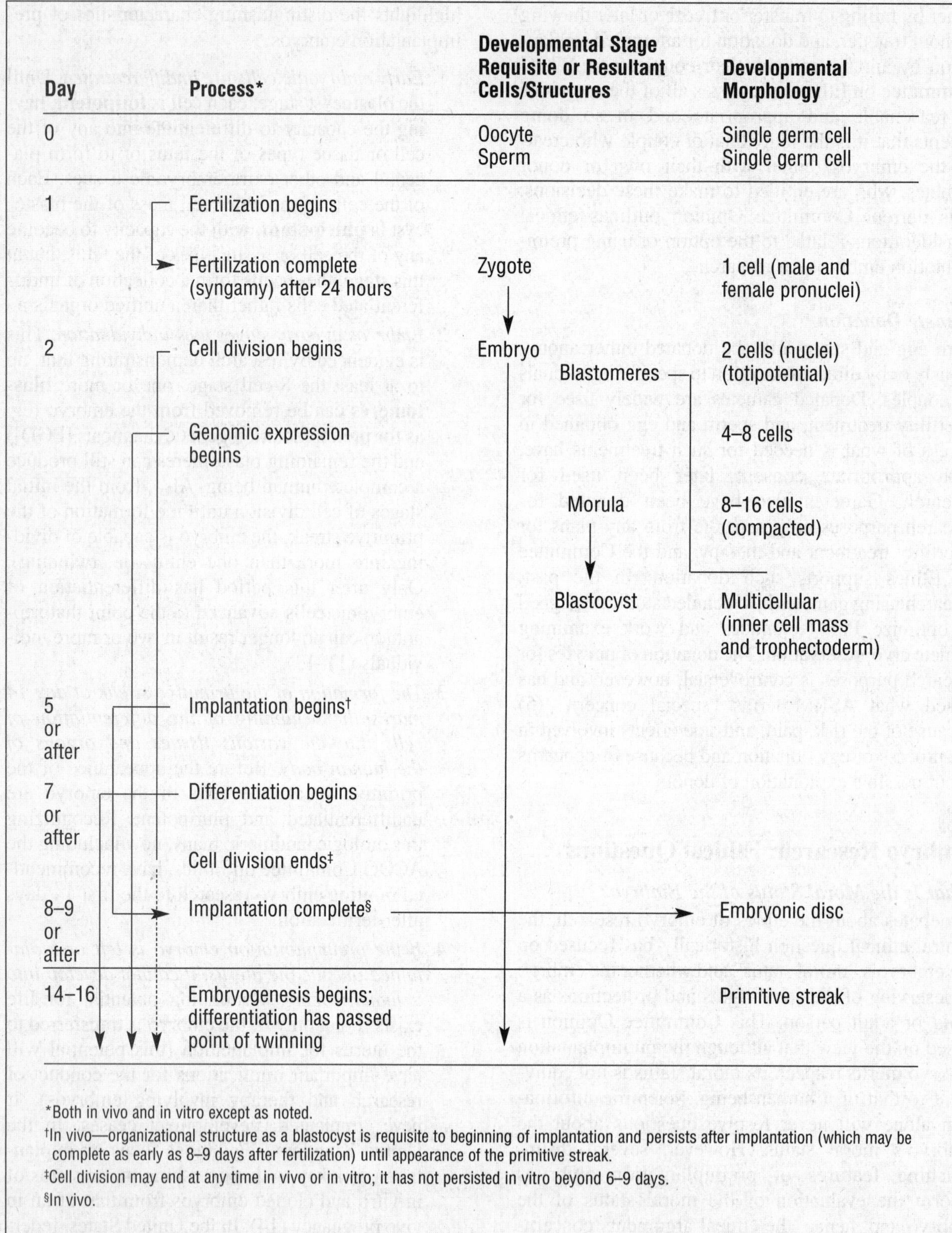

Day
Process*
Developmental Stage Requisite or Resultant Cells/Structures
Developmental Morphology
0
Oocyte
Sperm
Single germ cell
Single germ cell
1
Fertilization begins
Fertilization complete (syngamy) after 24 hours
Zygote
1 cell (male and female pronuclei)
2
Cell division begins
Embryo
Blastomeres
2 cells (nuclei) (totipotential)
Genomic expression begins
4–8 cells
Morula
8–16 cells (compacted)
Blastocyst
Multicellular (inner cell mass and trophectoderm)
5 or after
Implantation begins†
7 or after
Differentiation begins
Cell division ends‡
8–9 or after
Implantation complete§
Embryonic disc
14–16
Embryogenesis begins; differentiation has passed point of twinning
Primitive streak
*Both in vivo and in vitro except as noted.
†In vivo—organizational structure as a blastocyst is requisite to beginning of implantation and persists after implantation (which may be complete as early as 8–9 days after fertilization) until appearance of the primitive streak.
‡Cell division may end at any time in vivo or in vitro; it has not persisted in vitro beyond 6–9 days.
§In vivo.


**Fig. 2.** Early in vivo and in vitro human development process.

### *Why Pursue Embryo Research?*

Most contemporary discussions about embryo research center entirely on the question of the embryo's intrinsic moral status—whether or not the embryo meets specific criteria for moral personhood. Based on the understanding of the degree to which an embryo does or does not meet such criteria, these discussions have taken a stand about the permissibility of options for embryo disposition. Bioethicist Patricia King has noted that human embryo research policy should do more than reflect mere abstract assertions about the moral status of human embryos. Rather, the moral underpinnings of human embryo research should be derived from a range of values, including the facilitation of human procreation, the advancement of applied scientific knowledge, the reduction of human suffering, and the protection of vulnerable persons from coercion and exploitation (15).

There can be no compelling argument for embryo research without the promise of benefit. Potential benefits of embryo research include an improved understanding of fertilization, implantation, and early pregnancy biology and, with this understanding, possibly fewer undesired outcomes, such as miscarriage. For infertile couples, embryo research offers the possibility of more effective therapies: research efforts helped optimize conditions for intracytoplasmic sperm injection, embryo culture, and cryopreservation, for example. For others at risk for heritable genetic disease who feel pregnancy termination is undesirable or inappropriate, embryo research has led to the possibility of early, accurate genetic diagnosis: PGD provides diagnostic results at a point before implantation, so pregnancy termination can be avoided. In addition to these benefits of embryo research in general, stem cell research promises additional potential benefits, for such work may lead both to a better understanding of the processes leading to tissue differentiation and function and to possible therapies by creating lines that can replace diseased or nonfunctioning tissues. Those who donate gametes or embryos for research are offered the rewards of potentially extending scientific knowledge and, apart from any current or future hope of improving their own health, the opportunity to help others with this knowledge. Indeed, in considering the fate of excess embryos for which destruction is planned, some have argued that donation for research accords the embryo more respect than destruction alone (16, 17).

### *Are There Alternatives to Using Preimplantation Embryos for Research?*

As with all human research, research on embryos and embryonic stem cells should be engaged in only when alternative means of developing knowledge are inadequate. Whenever possible, animal models or cell and tissue culture systems should be used to advance the understanding of human biology. However, direct extrapolation of results from in vitro animal embryo studies to humans can be misleading. Unfertilized oocytes also do not offer the same opportunities for investigating growth processes that embryos do.

Some have argued that obtaining or using embryonic stem cells is unnecessary because stem cells have been or can be isolated from umbilical cord blood or adult tissues, such as brain and skin. Yet such adult stem cells, in contrast to embryonic stem cells, have already progressed along the path of differentiation and lack the plasticity of embryonic stem cells. It is unlikely that once differentiated, these cells can be induced to form the range of tissues that can, by contrast, be produced by less-differentiated embryonic stem cells (18, 19).

Umbilical cord blood stem cells have been shown in some studies to transdifferentiate to a limited extent into nonhematopoietic cells, including those of the brain, heart, liver, pancreas, bone, and cartilage, in experimental culture and animal systems (20, 21). Some have speculated that, on the basis of these observations, cord blood might serve as a source of cells to facilitate tissue repair and regeneration in the distant future. Research is needed to clarify the role, if any, of cord blood in this field of regenerative medicine.

For those with ethical objections, recent activity in stem cell research has led to a vigorous search for alternative sources of stem cells that might obviate the need to use or destroy fresh or frozen embryos (22). Suggested techniques include 1) extraction of cells from embryos already dead, 2) nonharmful biopsy of a single blastomere from a living embryo, 3) extraction of cells from artificially created nonembryonic but embryolike cellular systems (engineered to lack the essential elements of embryogenesis but still capable of some cell division and growth), and 4) dedifferentiation of somatic cells back to pluripotency. The Committee on Ethics recognizes that such techniques, if ultimately proved to be productive, would avoid some but not all of the arguments and objections that have been raised to embryo and stem cell research. The Committee believes, however, that until such hypothetical alternatives become realities for human tissues, their possibility should not stand as a barrier to pursuing available methods of demonstrated efficacy. Indeed, technical barriers to these proposed alternatives are not trivial, and the possibility of reprogramming adult stem cells to achieve the same potential as embryonic stem cells has been termed by experts as "exceedingly rare" (23). It also is not clear that all these suggestions are free from ethical concerns or objections (eg, distinguishing when an embryo is "dead").

In considering embryonic stem cell research, it is also important to indicate why progress requires isolation of lines different from those already established. Federal regulations prohibit funding for investigations of the many new embryonic stem cell lines created since August 2001, some of which have been used by both international and U.S. researchers to advance the field. Yet, advocates of stem cell research note that in contrast to several of these newer lines, all lines on the National Institutes of Health (NIH) registry were cultured in contact with mouse cells and bovine serum, which limits potential therapeutic applications. Furthermore, the U.S. federal guidelines prohibit federal funding of **somatic cell nuclear transfer** techniques (also known as SCNT techniques) and research, which may offer unique opportunities for human therapy by creating cells tailored to an individual's genotype and thus, in theory, requiring less need for immunosuppression if therapeutics can one day be created from such individualized cell lines.

***Are There Arguments Against Embryo Research?***

Balanced against any potential benefits of embryo research are known and potential risks. Embryo research usually will involve destruction of embryos and, as a result, most human embryo research will not benefit the embryo that is used—enhancing neither its developmental potential nor its chance of survival. It is this potential harm that has led national ethics advisory committees and commissions to evaluate the moral status of the embryo and has sharply separated the two sides of the embryo research and stem cell debate. Yet, as detailed previously, this document views destruction of in vitro embryos as different from destruction of a human being.

Short of destruction, the manipulation of embryos that are intended for transfer to the uterus (as with embryo biopsy for PGD) raises concern for potential manipulation-related damage in ongoing pregnancies. Some embryo research can be validated scientifically and be beneficial clinically only if there is a subsequent transfer of the embryo to a woman's uterus in an attempt to achieve pregnancy, yet until such transfer is accomplished, it remains unknown whether research interventions will enhance or reduce the prospects for healthy life.

Women and couples who either participate in research or donate gametes or embryos for research also may be at risk. If a couple decides to donate "excess" embryos for research, such as stem cell extraction, they may be at risk for psychologic harms such as uncertainty, stress, and anxiety. These potential hazards are not exclusively related to the option of donation of embryos for research purposes and may accompany all decisions regarding the disposition of frozen embryos. When research requires hormonal stimulation and retrieval of oocytes separate from plans for pregnancy (ie, tissues obtained or created for research alone), the oocyte donor faces risks similar to those involved in oocyte donation for reproductive purposes. It is essential to ensure that a woman's or couple's choice is free of coercion and possible exploitation and that the woman or couple gives informed consent.

Recognizing such risks, some have expressed concern regarding the potential to exploit women as oocyte donors. In part to answer such concerns, some guidelines such as those proposed by the National Academy of Sciences recommend no compensation for oocyte donation for research other than for out-of-pocket expenses (24). Such restrictions, however, seem inappropriate to the ACOG Committee on Ethics and are inconsistent with policy and practice concerning compensation both to oocyte donors for reproductive purposes and women participating in other types of research protocols. Compensation for oocyte donation for reproductive purposes is supported by ASRM (25) and is customary in the United States, and there is no strong argument for distinguishing this practice from donation in the research context. The risks to the woman and the need to protect against potential abuses are similar in the two situations. Payment to an oocyte donor should be understood to be compensation for the woman's time, effort, risk, and discomfort and not as payment for the eggs that may be recovered. The level of compensation should be consistent with ASRM guidelines intended to preclude payment levels that might be construed as exerting undue influence on the donor (25). In providing advice to those seeking oocyte donors, ASRM guidelines also highlight the importance of protecting vulnerable populations and providing compensation commensurate with the time and effort involved.

***Who Should Give Permission for Embryos to Be Used for Research?***

Individuals will differ in their beliefs about morality of and appropriate limits for embryo research. This is true for individuals or couples creating embryos as part of infertility treatment and later making decisions regarding frozen embryos, as well as for gamete donors, who may in some cases be different from the individuals for whom the embryos were created (26, 27). In considering the question of who should give consent for research using preimplantation embryos, it is important to recognize that such research may occur long after gametes have been donated and embryos created, and in addition, the details of future research questions and protocols are unlikely to be known at the time of donation. In many cases, of course, those supplying the egg and sperm will be the same as those for whom the embryo is created, and these circumstances present the easiest conditions for obtaining appropriate, informed consent for research. In such cases, couples may indicate at the time the embryos are frozen that they would be willing to consider future donation for research, but specific permission needs to be obtained at the later time when custody is transferred to the research team. If details of the research protocol are known at the time embryos are frozen, couples should be so informed. Alternatively, some couples will be willing to donate unused embryos to an appropriate party (eg, those operating the laboratory or storage facility) for use in future research projects as yet unformulated at the time of donation. If such work includes projects in stem cell research, this should be specifically discussed and the details of stem cell research (eg, creation of immortal cell lines) described insofar as they are known at the time of donation. If both members of the couple have not previously given consent at the time custody is transferred, embryos should not be used for research.

If gamete donors are different from those for whom embryos were created, research should proceed only if gamete donors have been made aware of the option of embryo research and have given their consent to such research. Given the emotions and discussion surrounding stem cell research, potential research projects should be described as much as possible. However, gamete donors need to recognize that the details of future research projects are unlikely to be available at the time of gamete donation, and therefore donors need to be comfortable consenting to research that is described only in general terms (28). Abandoned embryos, as defined by the ASRM Ethics Committee (29, 30), should not be accepted for research.

When embryo research is conducted in anticipation of transfer (for example, PGD research), the intended parents and, if different, the gamete donors must be provided with adequate information regarding the nature of the research, the risks to the embryo, and the chances for a successful pregnancy resulting in the birth of a healthy child, and they must provide their informed consent (31). If research is to be done on an embryo that is to be transferred eventually to a third party (a gestational carrier's uterus), this individual also should give informed consent for the research.

Finally, choices should be made in circumstances free of financial or other coercion. Full information should, therefore, include assurance that consent to donation of embryos for research is not a condition for receiving services and that fee scales are not contingent on consent to research. Moreover, donors of embryos should understand that they will receive no compensation for their donation of excess embryos. The consent process also should cover any possible identifiers that will be maintained with the tissue to link it back to the donors, access to current and future health information from donors, willingness of donors to be contacted in the future, ownership, patent rights, and commercial uses of stem cell lines that may be developed from the embryo. All providing consent also should understand that they may withdraw their consent up to the time that the donated tissues actually are used in research.

In the scenarios of adults donating gametes for the creation of embryos solely for research and adults donating somatic cells for somatic cell nuclear transfer, special considerations must be taken into account. The information provided to donors for embryonic stem cell research must acknowledge that the process of obtaining the embryonic stem cell line from the inner cell mass of the blastocyst will result in the destruction of the embryo and also should indicate that the derived stem cell lines may be propagated indefinitely. The consent process also should cover the same elements as consent obtained when unused embryos are donated for research. A woman wishing to donate oocytes for research must be informed of possible risks to her in the process of controlled ovarian hyperstimulation and retrieving oocytes, and egg donor programs should set up medical and psychologic screening procedures in order to safeguard potential donors.

### *May Embryos Be Created for Research?*

Many cryopreserved embryos exist in the United States. When such embryos are appropriate to the questions under investigation and appropriate consent can be obtained, the ACOG Committee on Ethics recommends that these embryos be the preferred resource for research. Not all frozen embryos are available or appropriate for research, however, and frozen embryos may not meet all criteria necessary for some therapeutic applications (32). Investigations of specific genetic defects, for example, may require specific tissues not available in already frozen embryos, and any future therapies using stem cells (eg, somatic cell nuclear transfer) by design may require that embryos and the derived embryonic stem cells have a genetic profile identical to the intended recipient. The Committee on Ethics believes that the promise of somatic cell nuclear transfer as a technique to create important and unique stem cell lines is such that research in this area is justified, a finding consistent with the practices of the United Kingdom's Human Fertilisation and Embryology Authority (33). Furthermore, the Committee on Ethics can imagine a future day when the creation of tissues via somatic cell nuclear transfer to be used in the isolation of human stem cell lines for therapeutic purposes will be possible and needed; if so, the Committee on Ethics would consider this process to be ethically appropriate.

Although there are no physical differences between "excess" embryos from an IVF therapy and "created-for-research" embryos, the moral distinction that many make seems to rest on the intent of the creation of the embryo, whether for procreation or research, and the special respect given to human embryos. An embryo originally created for procreation may be seen to be created for its own sake, as an "end in itself," whereas an embryo created for research may appear to be a "mere means" to the ends of others. For some, the respect given to the human embryo differentiates the embryo from mere human tissues or cells and necessitates greater obligation to justify valid scientific inquiry. Others judge that the potential benefits of research for societal health outweigh any limitations conferred by the respect due to human embryos, whether they are "excess" embryos or "created for research."

There is a precedent for creation of embryos for research purposes. The early work in human IVF by Edwards and colleagues consisted of fertilizing human oocytes for research in order to study the normality of the **zygotes** thus created before transfer to a woman was even considered (34). In 1994, the NIH Human Embryo Research Panel approved the creation of IVF embryos for research when the very nature of the research itself required the fertilization of oocytes and when a research project deemed to be exceptionally important required a particular type of embryo for its validity. Currently, there is little need for the creation of embryos by fertilization for research purposes, but in the future the supply of available tissues, research questions, or therapeutic paradigms may change. If a compelling need arises, the question of creating embryos by fertilization for use in research will need to be addressed carefully.

### *Does Experimental or Other Use of Stem Cells Lend Support to Reproductive Cloning?*

In the processes involved, associated risks, and intended outcomes, work involving stem cells and cloning for biomedical research with the intent of developing future therapies (eg, somatic cell nuclear transfer) may clearly be distinguished from reproductive cloning. The former areas of research and practice involve the isolation and manipulation of cells from embryos that are not allowed to progress past the 14-day stage and are not transferred to the uterus. Because reproductive cloning is designed to produce a human being, it raises a distinct set of issues and concerns, and these are not the focus of this Committee Opinion. The support expressed in this Committee Opinion for embryo research and cloning for research purposes does not imply endorsement of reproductive cloning, which the Committee on Ethics opposes.

## Guidelines

The Committee on Ethics takes the position that human embryo research can be justified under certain conditions. This position is based on an interpretation of the moral status of the embryo as a living entity with a human genetic code, deserving of some form of respect in itself and not solely for its usefulness in research. But this position also recognizes the value of the embryo as relative, in the sense that it does not require the degree of protection and absolute respect that is accorded human persons. In other words, the embryo is human—not simply like other human tissue (for it is genetically unique and has human potential)—but it also is not a human person.

Risks of harm to the embryo in research can be justified, but not without limits. Embryos, for example, should not be subjected to trivial or poorly designed research programs; if the embryos are designated for transfer to a woman's uterus, the goals of successful pregnancy should be given priority; and the real and symbolic values of the embryo should not be negated or trivialized. The Committee on Ethics recommends the following guidelines for clinical and laboratory research involving human embryos.

1. Research will be conducted only by scientifically qualified individuals and in settings that include appropriate and adequate resources and protections. The design of the research and each of its procedures should be clearly formulated in a research protocol that is submitted to a specially appointed independent committee for evaluation, guidance, and approval.
2. The question to be explored must be scientifically valid; must take into account scientific work to date, including animal studies; and cannot be answered through research on animal embryos or on unfertilized gametes.
3. The information sought should offer potential scientific and clinical benefit in areas such as embryonic development, human reproduction, chromosomal and genetic conditions, or, for embryonic stem cell lines, potential disease therapies.
4. The research will be conducted using embryos at the earliest possible developmental stage of the embryo, not to exceed 14 days after evidence of fertilization in any case.
5. Any embryo that has undergone research will be transferred to a uterus only if the original research was undertaken to prepare the embryo for selection or placement or to improve its chances for implantation and only if specific consent for transfer is obtained.
6. Intended parents for whom embryos are created (embryo donors) should be provided with the opportunity to provide informed consent as to the disposition of any excess embryos, whether for eventual destruction, donation for attempted implantation by another individual or couple, or scientific research. This presupposes an explicit policy on the part of the researchers and their sponsoring institutions that facilitates communication of options and provides for informed donor choice. If gamete donors differ from the embryo donors, then embryos may be donated for research only if the gamete donors also have given explicit consent for donation for research.
7. Those donating "excess" frozen embryos for embryonic stem cell research must be adequately informed of the goals, anticipated benefits, and potential hazards of the particular research. Each potential donor is informed that she or he is at liberty to decline participation in the research and, until such a point when the tissues are used or cell lines created, to withdraw consent for research.
8. Other information must be included in informed consent for donation of embryos for stem cell research:
    - Acknowledgment that removal of the inner cell mass will destroy the embryo
    - Statement that stem cell lines may continue indefinitely and be shared with other researchers
    - Discussion of potential ownership, patent, and commercial uses of stem cell lines that may be developed from the embryo
    - Information regarding whether any identifiers will be preserved in the stem cell lines derived
9. For research or therapy involving somatic cell nuclear transfer, oocyte donors and somatic cell donors must give informed consent for use of their eggs or somatic cells. In the rare circumstances in which IVF embryos are created for research, the gamete donors should provide informed consent for fertilization for research purposes. In both cases, informed consent should include points in guideline 8 and clearly describe the researchers' intention to deliberately create a human embryo for research.
10. Special care must be taken to ensure that potential donors of oocytes for research understand

the procedure and its risks. To safeguard donors as much as possible, medical and psychologic screening should be required. Although compensation for egg donors for research is acceptable, as it is for donors for infertility treatment, such compensation should be understood to be compensation for the woman's time, effort, risk, and discomfort and not as payment for the eggs that may be recovered. The level of compensation should be consistent with ASRM guidelines to minimize the possibility of exploitation of egg donors.

11. Techniques and research designed to clone human beings raise a different set of ethical concerns. The Committee on Ethics opposes reproductive cloning.

## Conclusion

The Committee on Ethics has offered a position that supports embryo research but limits it according to ethical guidelines. This position advocates treatment of the embryo with respect but not the same level of respect that is given to human persons. It is a position that will not be acceptable to those who believe that full rights should be extended to early-stage embryos. In arriving at its position, the Committee on Ethics considered scientific and clinical information relevant to ethical analysis, although it recognizes that such consideration necessarily involves both scientific and ethical interpretation of what cannot be simply incontrovertible "facts."

The Committee on Ethics once again acknowledges that no single position can encompass the variety of opinions within the membership of ACOG, and it affirms that no physician should be required or expected to participate in embryo research if he or she finds it morally objectionable. Nonetheless, it is important to public discourse and to the practice of responsible medicine that physicians become aware of the medical and ethical issues involved in the complex areas of embryo research. To advance this discourse, it is helpful for physicians to reflect on and share the basis of their own views and to recognize and explore the ethical perspectives of their patients and colleagues.

## References


1. Definitions. 45 CFR § 46.202 (2005).
2. U.S. Department of Health, Education, and Welfare. HEW support of research involving human in vitro fertilization and embryo transfer. Washington, DC: U.S. Government Printing Office; 1979.
3. Ethical considerations of the new reproductive technologies. Ethics Committee of the American Fertility Society. Fertil Steril 1986;46(suppl 1):1S–94S.
4. Ethical considerations of the new reproductive technologies. Ethics Committee of The American Fertility Society. Fertil Steril 1990;53(suppl 2):1S–104S.
5. Ethical considerations of assisted reproductive technologies. Ethics Committee of the American Fertility Society. Fertil Steril 1994;62(suppl 1):1S–125S.
6. The Balanced Budget Downpayment Act, I, Pub. L. No 104–99, §128, 110 Stat. 34 (1996).
7. National Bioethics Advisory Commission. Ethical issues in human stem cell research. Rockville (MD): NBAC; 1999.
8. Radio address by the President to the nation. Available at: http://www.whitehouse.gov/news/releases/2001/08/print/20010811-1.html. Retrieved March 9, 2006.
9. 42 U.S.C. § 289g-1 (2002).
10. Lyerly AD, Steinhauser K, Namey E, Tulsky JA, Cook-Deegan R, Sugarman J, et al. Factors that affect infertility patients' decisions about frozen embryos. Fertil Steril 2006;85:1623–30.
11. McCormick RA. Who or what is the preembryo? Kennedy Inst Ethics J 1991;1:1–15.
12. Grobstein C. Becoming an individual. In: Science and the unborn. New York (NY): Basic Books; 1988. p. 21–39.
13. Ford NM. When did I begin? Conception of the human individual in history, philosophy, and science. New York (NY): Cambridge University Press; 1988.
14. Report from the Select Committee on Stem Cell Research. House of Lords HL 2002;83(i). Available at: http://www.publications.parliament.uk/pa/ld200102/ldselect/ldstem/83/8301.htm. Retrieved June 28, 2006.
15. King PA. Embryo research: the challenge for public policy. J Med Philos 1997;22:441–55.
16. Kukla H. Embryonic stem cell research: an ethical justification. Georgetown Law J 2002;90:503–43.
17. Green RM. Benefiting from 'evil': an incipient problem in human stem cell research. Bioethics 2002;16:544–56.
18. Wilcox AJ, Weinberg CR, O'Connor JF, Baird DD, Schlatterer JP, Canfield RE, et al. Incidence of early loss of pregnancy. N Engl J Med 1988;319:189–94.
19. Weissman IL. Stem cells—scientific, medical, and political issues. N Engl J Med 2002;346:1576–9.
20. Porada GA, Porada C, Zanjani ED. The fetal sheep: a unique model system for assessing the full differentiative potential of human stem cells. Yonsei Med J 2004;45: 7–14.
21. Kogler G, Sensken S, Airey JA, Trapp T, Muschen M, Feldhahn N, et al. A new human somatic stem cell from placental cord blood with intrinsic pluripotent differentiation potential. J Exp Med 2004;200:123–35.
22. The President's Council on Bioethics. Alternative sources of human pluripotent stem cells. A white paper of the President's Council on Bioethics. Washington, DC: The President's Council on Bioethics; 2005. Available at: http://www.bioethics.gov/reports/white_paper/alternative_sources_white_paper.pdf. Retrieved June 28, 2006.

23. Wagers AJ, Weissman IL. Plasticity of adult stem cells. Cell 2004;116:639–48.
24. National Research Council; Institute of Medicine. Recruiting donors and banking hES cells. In: Guidelines for human embryonic stem cell research. Washington, DC: The Institute; 2005. p. 81–96.
25. Financial incentives for oocyte donors. The Ethics Committee of the American Society for Reproductive Medicine. Fertil Steril 2000;74:216–20.
26. Kalfoglou AL, Geller G. A follow-up study with oocyte donors exploring their experiences, knowledge, and attitudes about the use of their oocytes and the outcome of the donation. Fertil Steril 2000;74:660–7.
27. Klock SC, Sheinin S, Kazer RR. The disposition of unused frozen embryos. N Engl J Med 2001;345:69–70.
28. Lo B, Chou V, Cedars MI, Gates E, Taylor RN, Wagner RM, et al. Informed consent in human oocyte, embryo, and embryonic stem cell research. Fertil Steril 2004;82: 559–63.
29. Donating spare embryos for embryonic stem-cell research. Ethics Committee of the American Society for Reproductive Medicine. Fertil Steril 2004;82(suppl 1): S224–7.
30. Ethics Committee of the American Society for Reproductive Medicine. Disposition of abandoned embryos. Fertil Steril 2004;82(suppl 1):S253.
31. Wolf SM, Kahn JP. Bioethics matures: the field faces the future. Hastings Cent Rep 2005;35(4):22–4.
32. Hoffman DI, Zellman GL, Fair CC, Mayer JF, Zeitz JG, Gibbons WE, et al. Cryopreserved embryos in the United States and their availability for research. Society for Assisted Reproduction Technology (SART) and RAND. Fertil Steril 2003;79:1063–9.
33. Human Fertilisation & Embryology Authority. HFEA grants the first therapeutic cloning licence for research. Press release. London: HFEA; 2004. Available at: http://www.hfea.gov.uk/PressOffice/Archive/109223388. Retrieved June 28, 2006.
34. Edwards RG, Steptoe PC. A matter of life: the story of a medical breakthrough. London: Hutchinson; 1980.

## Glossary

***Blastocyst:** A preimplantation embryo of approximately 150 cells. The blastocyst consists of a sphere made up of an outer layer of cells (the trophectoderm), a fluid-filled cavity (the blastocoel), and a cluster of cells on the interior (the inner cell mass).

**Blastomere:** The cells derived from the first and subsequent cell divisions of the zygote.

***Embryo:** In humans, the developing organism from the time of fertilization until the end of the eighth week of gestation, when it becomes known as a fetus. Other ACOG guidelines address research involving postimplantation embryos and fetuses (ie, research during pregnancy). (American College of Obstetricians and Gynecologists. Research involving women. In: Ethics in obstetrics and gynecology. 2nd ed. Washington, DC: ACOG; 2004. p. 86–91.)

***Embryonic stem cells:** Primitive (undifferentiated) cells from the embryo that have the potential to become a wide variety of specialized cell types.

**Fertilization:** The process whereby male and female gametes unite.

**Gametes:** Mature reproductive cells, usually having half the adult chromosome number (ie, sperm or ovum).

**Implantation:** Attachment of the blastocyst to the endometrial lining of the uterus and subsequent embedding in the endometrium. Implantation begins approximately 5–7 days after fertilization and may be complete as early as 8–9 days after fertilization.

***Inner cell mass:** The cluster of cells inside the blastocyst. These cells give rise to the embryonic disk of the later embryo and, ultimately, the fetus.

**Oocyte:** An immature female reproductive cell, one that has not completed the maturing process to form an ovum (gamete).

**Pluripotent:** Able to differentiate into multiple cell and tissue types.

**Preimplantation embryo:** In humans, the developing organism from the time of fertilization until implantation in the uterus or other tissue (eg, ectopic pregnancy).

**Primitive streak:** The initial band of cells from which many tissue systems, including the neural system of the embryo, begin to develop, located at the caudal end of the embryonic disc. The primitive streak is present approximately 15 days after fertilization and marks the axis along which the spinal cord develops.

**Somatic cell nuclear transfer:** The transfer of a cell nucleus from a somatic cell into an egg from which the nucleus has been removed.

**Stem cells:** Undifferentiated multipotent precursor cells that are capable of perpetuating themselves indefinitely and of differentiating into specialized types of cells.

**Totipotent:** Able to differentiate into every cell and tissue type; the capacity of a cell or group of cells to produce all of the products of conception: the extra-embryonic membrane and tissue, the embryo, and, subsequently, the fetus.

**Zygote:** The single cell formed by the union of the male and female haploid gametes at syngamy.

*Definitions marked with an asterisk are adapted from the National Institutes of Health glossary, available at: http://stemcells.nih.gov.

# ACOG Committee Opinion

Committee on Ethics

Number 352, December 2006

# Innovative Practice: Ethical Guidelines

*ABSTRACT: Innovations in medical practice are critical to the advancement of medicine. Good clinicians constantly adapt and modify their clinical approaches in ways they believe will benefit patients. Innovative practice frequently is approached very differently from formal research, which is governed by distinct ethical and regulatory frameworks. Although opinions differ on the distinction between research and innovative practice, the production of generalizable knowledge is one defining characteristic of research. Physicians considering innovative practice must disclose to patients the purpose, benefits, and risks of the proposed treatment, including risks not quantified but plausible. They should attempt an innovative procedure only when familiar with and skilled in its basic components. A clinician should share results, positive or negative, with colleagues and, when feasible, teach successful techniques and procedures to other physicians. Practitioners should be wary of adopting innovative procedures or diagnostic tests on the basis of promotions and marketing when the value of the procedures or tests has not been proved. A practitioner should move an innovative practice into formal research if the innovation represents a significant departure from standard practice, if the innovation carries unknown or potentially significant risks, or if the practitioner's goal is to use data from the innovation to produce generalizable knowledge. If there is any question whether innovative practices should be formalized as research, clinicians should seek advice from the relevant institutional review board.*

## Overview

In 21st-century medicine, the pace at which innovations are introduced into clinical practice continues to increase. Many innovations differ considerably from previous practices and may or may not have been subjected to formal research protocols. In this context, the boundary between innovative practice and medical research becomes blurred, making it difficult for physicians to distinguish between them and to recognize the ethical issues that are involved.

When innovative practices are introduced, they may become widely accepted based on anecdotal reports of success. As a result, formal research



ISSN 1074-861X

**The American College of Obstetricians and Gynecologists**
409 12th Street, SW
PO Box 96920
Washington, DC 20090-6920

12345/09876

Innovative practice: ethical guidelines. ACOG Committee Opinion No. 352. American College of Obstetricians and Gynecologists. Obstet Gynecol 2006;108:1589–95.

may never be done that might show 1) that the innovative practice carries higher risk than other treatments or 2) that it is no more effective than standard treatment. An inappropriate introduction of an innovative practice, circumventing the formal study of the new technique, leaves patients and practitioners without the necessary data for appropriately assessing an innovation's risks and benefits, as well as its long-term effects on health.

In this Committee Opinion, the Committee on Ethics will review efforts to distinguish innovative practice from research, identify ethical concerns raised by innovative practice, and note current obstacles to the conduct of formal research. Recommendations will focus on two questions: 1) When does the clinician have an obligation to subject an innovative practice to formal research? 2) In situations where innovative practice is not regulated as research, what special ethical obligations might the clinician have—to patients, to the community of medical professionals, and to society at large?

## Distinguishing Innovative Practice From Research

In clinical practice, physicians aim to benefit their patients by providing the best possible procedures and treatments. The desire to improve currently available practices has given an important impetus to the development of new medical knowledge. The notion of what is best or most appropriate evolves with time, ongoing research, and changing individual and societal values. Good clinicians constantly adapt and modify their clinical approaches in ways they believe will benefit patients. The introduction of such innovative interventions is guided primarily by the judgment of the individual physician, although professional organizations often advise and monitor.

Formal research, however, is highly regulated in the United States. Research protocols involving human participants must be described in detail and submitted to an institutional review board (IRB) for approval. Federal regulations mandate that IRBs approve research protocols in order to ensure adequate disclosure to potential participants, informed consent from participants, appropriate risk–benefit ratio, protection of participants' privacy, and freedom of participants to withdraw from the study at any time.

Innovative practice has elements in common with research including, for example, the desire to learn and to improve treatment. Yet, innovation in practice frequently is approached very differently from formal research, which is governed by distinct ethical and regulatory frameworks. The federal research regulations as expressed in the "Common Rule" draw a sharp distinction between research, which is regulated, and innovation, which is not, stressing the production of generalizable knowledge—knowledge that can be applied beyond the particular individuals studied—as the defining characteristic of research (1). However, the distinction is somewhat artificial and is not always clearly delineated.

An innovative practice may later become the subject of a formal research protocol, with the results of this research then applied to guide evidence-based practice. In some cases, however, innovative practice that appears to be safe and effective may become accepted practice, even if it has never been subjected to formal research and an evidence base has never been developed to support efficacy and safety. When this happens, patients and practitioners are left without the data they need to make adequately informed decisions.

## Background: History and Evolution of Terminology

It often is difficult to draw a clear line between innovative practice and research. The history of research regulation illuminates the effort to clarify the distinction.

The National Commission for the Protection of Human Subjects, established by federal statute in 1975, developed the *Belmont Report* in 1978 to identify the basic ethical principles governing human research (2). In defining *research,* the National Commission first distinguished it from "the practice of accepted therapy." However, examples proposed to the National Commission led it to recognize that much practice is *experimental* (a term the American College of Obstetricians and Gynecologists' Committee on Ethics interprets as congruent with the term *innovative*), even though it is not formalized as research. Should all such experimental practice be treated as research and governed by the ethical and regulatory guidelines for research? The National Commission decided against taking this position and adopted a narrower definition of research, concluding that research occurs when the clinician or investigator intends the work to result in generalizable knowledge (2).

According to the National Commission, "'Research' designates an activity designed to test a hypothesis, permit conclusions to be drawn, and thereby to contribute to generalizable knowledge" rather than being "designed solely to enhance the well-being of an individual patient or client" (2). The fact that activities designed to enhance patient well-being may depart significantly from standard or accepted practice does not of itself make them research. However, the National Commission strongly urged that "radically new procedures" be tested by formal research at an early stage and that medical practice committees insist that new techniques and treatments be submitted to formal hypothesis testing. The National Commission did not, however, define "radically new," leaving its definition to the judgment of practitioners.

Federal research regulations in effect since 1981 incorporate these concepts to a limited degree, defining *research* as follows: "Research means a systematic investigation, including research development, testing and evaluation, designed to develop or contribute to generalizable knowledge" (3). The preamble to the regulations as finalized in 1981 explicitly states that the definition is restricted to "generalizable knowledge" because the regulations were not intended to encompass "innovative therapy" (4).

In March 2003, the Lasker Foundation, a charitable trust established to promote advances in medicine, sponsored the invitational "Lasker Forum on Ethical Challenges in Biomedical Research and Practice." The forum focused on the intersection of research and practice and questioned the artificial separation between "what is called research and therefore requires more regulatory oversight, and what is called 'care' and requires little or none" (5). The report on the Lasker Forum proposed that clinical innovation involving a significant departure from standard of care imposes particular moral duties on the practitioner. In the view expressed at the forum, a practitioner who attempts through innovation to benefit an individual patient also is morally obligated to facilitate the development of knowledge useful to other physicians and patients, thus suggesting an obligation to conduct research on the innovative practice.

The Lasker Forum report proposed criteria for identifying the ethical threshold that mandates moving from innovative practice to formal research. In this view, the most important criterion is the degree of departure from standard practice, followed by the potential for harm to the patient from the innovative practice. Other criteria proposed for consideration are the goal of the clinician investigator, the availability of organizational structures supportive of research, and the presence of commercial interests or conflict of interest (5). These considerations will be discussed more fully after examination of specific ethical concerns related to the introduction of innovative practices.

## Ethical Concerns Regarding Innovative Practice

A variety of problems may arise when innovative practices are inappropriately introduced apart from formal research protocols. These problems often have ethical implications related to patient safety, patient autonomy, and the patient's right to effective therapy:

- Premature adoption of innovative practices without adequate supporting evidence may promote wide acceptance of therapies that are ineffective. Examples of procedures that have been proved ineffective include:
  —Bed rest or home uterine activity monitoring for prevention of prematurity (6, 7)
  —Bone marrow transplant for breast cancer (8)
  —Diethylstilbestrol or paternal antigen sensitization for the prevention of recurrent miscarriage

  From an ethical perspective, recommending procedures that are not effective for the intended purpose is misleading to patients, incurs increased unnecessary costs both financial and personal, and violates the patient's autonomy-based right to consent to therapy after accurate disclosure. In addition, an unproven innovative treatment may carry additional risks or morbidity in comparison with standard treatment, as in the case of bone marrow transplant for breast cancer.

- Premature adoption of innovative practices without formal scientific testing may compromise the ability to determine effectiveness, weigh risk against benefit, compare the practice with other procedures, or develop alternative approaches. When results of an innovative practice are publicized without adequate testing, it may become increasingly difficult to recruit participants for a clinical trial, particularly one that involves randomization. Such may have been the case when techniques for maternal–fetal surgery, electronic fetal monitoring, and laparoscopic hysterectomy were first introduced as innovative and only later systematically studied.

When innovative practices are widely adopted without formal research testing, an incremental risk over standard practice may not be recognized, and relative effectiveness, safety, and risk–benefit ratio may never be determined. Such a situation may make it difficult or impossible for physicians to know if they are fulfilling their obligation to provide safe and efficacious treatment to patients (9).

- Long-term safety concerns may result when innovative practices are widely adopted as standard practice without adequate scientific testing. Examples in which careful, continued study after a technique's introduction demonstrated small but potentially important risks include:
  —Limb reductions associated with early chorionic villus sampling (10, 11)
  —Sex chromosome abnormalities associated with intracytoplasmic sperm injection used in assisted reproductive technology (ART) (12, 13)

Although innovations in obstetrics and ART offer important benefits to prospective parents, they also may carry long-term risks that are not recognized unless formal research is carried out. Because of their eagerness to become parents, infertile couples may be willing to overlook risks involved in the use of ART. It is the responsibility of practitioners to carry out the studies that are needed to ensure that patients are offered effective and safe procedures. Appropriately, many ART centers and practitioners have participated in the ongoing registries and collaborations needed for this research.

## Research Barriers to Be Overcome

Medicine cannot advance without innovation. Recent examples of highly valuable innovations include new efficient laparoscopic components that may improve visualization and new laparoscopic procedures, such as laparoscopic retroperitoneal lymph node dissection, that may speed or otherwise facilitate closed surgical procedures. This could reduce the need for open procedures that may be associated with longer or more complicated postoperative recovery. At times, it may be appropriate to introduce an innovative technique apart from a formal research protocol. However, both the National Commission for the Protection of Human Subjects and the National Bioethics Advisory Commission stipulate that innovations in clinical practice should be studied under a research protocol as soon as it is appropriate to study them systematically (2, 14).

A number of barriers to the conduct of formal research exist, with some of them specific to particular subspecialties:

1. *Lack of supportive structures.* In many clinical situations, the structures to facilitate research, such as administrative support and an IRB, may be lacking. Even if a particular innovation is ripe for formalization as research, research may be difficult to accomplish without the necessary supportive structures. Bureaucratic obstacles may be cited as an excuse for not conducting research; however, such obstacles do not provide valid reasons for failure to conduct appropriate research under ethical guidelines. Rather, clinicians ought to advocate changes in policy and collaborative efforts that will provide necessary support for research.
2. *Absence of financial reimbursement.* In addition to the lack of supportive structures, financial pressures may inhibit the pursuit of appropriate research. Insurance coverage may be available for treatment that is described as innovative therapy, but not for formal research. This reimbursement situation played a role in the promotion of the untested procedure of bone marrow transplant for breast cancer, for example (15).
3. *Lack of oversight for surgical innovation and research.* The absence of regulations that specifically govern surgical innovation and research has frequently been noted. Proposals have been suggested to ensure oversight of surgical innovation when formal research is not planned, for example, submission of a written plan to the department head for referral to an ad hoc committee. This committee would provide peer review of "medical and scientific plausibility, the adequacy of patient safeguards, and the legitimacy of [the] clinical rationale" (16).
4. *Prohibition of federal funding for ART and embryo research.* Because of the statutory pro-

hibition of federal funding for in vitro fertilization and early embryo research, most research on ART is privately funded and is conducted within the practice of clinical infertility treatment. Hence, it may be difficult to obtain funding for some types of research on ART, particularly basic research.

## Clinical Decisions on Moving From Innovation to Research

The field of medicine could neither progress nor be practiced without innovative therapy. Given the importance of formal research for evidence-based medicine, however, the medical community must determine when an innovative practice should be subjected to formal research. If there is any question whether an innovation should be formalized as research, it is advisable that the protocol be submitted to an IRB for review. From an ethical standpoint, the following considerations offer guidance and criteria to the clinician for a decision to move from innovation to formal research (5):

- *The degree of departure from standard practice.* As recommended by the Lasker Forum, if innovation constitutes a significant departure from standard practice, the innovative procedure should quickly be subjected to a formal research protocol. Significant departure from standard practice occurs, for example, in most maternal–fetal surgery and many new ART techniques. However, minor modifications, such as a change in a step during surgery, a different kind of suture, or a new instrument similar to an old one, clearly do not require formalization as research.
- *The potential for harm to the patient.* When an innovation carries risks that are unknown or that may be significant in proportion to expected benefits, its safety should be assessed through a formal research protocol with the oversight of an IRB, one of whose primary purposes is to protect the welfare of participants. In addition, formal research is essential in order to identify long-term risks that may affect the safety of large numbers of patients in the future.
- *The intent of the physician.* The original intent in an innovation may be solely the welfare of the individual patient. If the physician intends, however, to eventually use results of a trial of the innovation to produce generalizable knowledge, the trial should be formalized in a research protocol. Valid generalizable knowledge ordinarily requires randomized clinical trials rather than reliance on case series and unplanned observations (17).

## Special Ethical Requirements for Innovative Practice

### *Duties to Patients*

When patients become participants in a formal research project, they become protected by the federal regulations for research involving human participants. Even when a particular project does not strictly fall under federal regulations because it does not involve federal funding or oversight by the U.S. Food and Drug Administration, most institutions still comply with federal standards. Also, reputable journals require compliance with ethical guidelines as a condition for publication. Access to results of clinical trials, even trials with negative outcomes, is protected by the clinical trials registration process (18–20). Many journals now require evidence that trials were previously registered before accepting reports for consideration for publication.

The same protections do not hold for a patient who is offered innovative therapy. Although the intent of such innovation is to provide the most beneficial treatment possible for the patient, the patient may not realize that a therapy is new or experimental. The practitioner has the obligation to disclose information that would be material to the patient's decision, and in many cases, a patient would want to know that a proposed therapy is innovative. As with all therapies, the practitioner has the obligation to disclose the purpose, benefits, and risks of the proposed innovative treatment, including not quantified but plausible risks. In addition, the practitioner has a particular obligation to protect the patient from potential harms that are not proportionate to expected benefits, a role that the IRB assumes with respect to formal research protocols. To minimize risk, physicians also need to consider their own knowledge and skill levels and should attempt an innovative procedure only when familiar with and skilled in its basic components.

Patient protection requires transparent communication. In the words of the Lasker Forum report, "Where innovation is clearly present, the requirements for disclosure are likely to become more pressing" (5). It may be important to the patient to know how often this procedure has been done, what this particular physician's experience with the procedure is, and what is known and unknown about possible adverse events and long-term sequelae. Care should be taken that a patient is not unduly influenced to consent to an innovative procedure solely out of deference to her physician. When the advantages and disadvantages of a truly new approach are explained to the patient, the assistance of an experienced third-party communicator, such as a patient representative or social worker, may be helpful (5). Particular care is needed when discussing proposed treatments with vulnerable or possibly desperate patients because they may be eager to pursue innovative but unproven procedures or treatments.

### *Duties to the Profession and to Society*

Innovative practice, unlike research, is not directed specifically toward the production of generalized knowledge. Yet, it is expected that innovation would lead to the improvement of practice in general, not just the practice of an individual physician. This expectation imposes two duties on the physician: 1) to structure the process of innovation so as to learn from it, even if it is not as successful as hoped, and 2) to share what is learned with the medical community as a whole and, where appropriate, with society. A clinician should share results, positive or negative, with colleagues and, when feasible, cooperate in teaching successful techniques and procedures to other physicians.

Current focus on clinical trials, especially randomized clinical trials, suggests that they ordinarily provide the best opportunity for unbiased learning within the practice of medicine. Consequently, innovative practice should move toward clinical trials whenever possible in order to provide evidence-based knowledge to the medical community for the welfare of patients.

Practitioners need to be careful not to adopt innovative procedures or diagnostic tests on the basis of promotional and marketing campaigns when the value of such procedures and tests has not yet been proved. For example, serum-based screening tests for ovarian cancer have been promoted even though more research is needed to determine whether they are effective (21, 22). Similar cautions apply to off-label and unproven uses of pharmaceuticals that may be suggested to physicians. In all cases, physicians should rely on documented evidence to guide clinical practice.

## Summary

The introduction of innovative practices and techniques is essential to medical progress. Ordinarily, however, innovations should be subjected to systematic formal research as soon as feasible:

- In the absence of formal research, innovative practices may become widely accepted without adequate data for assessing risks and benefits.
- Without an adequate evidence base, practitioners cannot determine whether an innovative technique is the most safe and effective method for treating a patient.
- Without adequate data on the risks and benefits of new treatments, patients are unable to provide a true informed consent.

A practitioner should move an innovative practice into formal research when one of these criteria is satisfied:

- The innovation represents a significant departure from standard practice.
- The innovation carries risks that are unknown or that may be significant in proportion to expected benefits.
- The introduction of the innovation is expected to result in generalizable knowledge, which depends on results of formal clinical trials.

## References

1. Protection of human subjects. 45 CFR § 46 (2005).
2. National Commission for the Protection of Human Subjects. Belmont report: ethical principles and guidelines for the protection of human subjects of research. Fed Regist 1979;44:23192–7.
3. Definitions. 45 CFR § 46.102 (2005).
4. Final regulations amending basic HHS policy for the protection of human research subjects. U.S. Department of Health and Human Services. Fed Regist 1981;46: 8366–91.
5. Lasker Foundation. The Lasker Forum on Ethical Challenges in Biomedical Research and Practice, May 14–16, 2003. New York (NY): Lasker Foundation; 2003. Available at: http://www.laskerfoundation.org/ethics/ethics_report.html. Retrieved June 28, 2006.
6. Sosa C, Althabe F, Belizán J, Bergel E. Bed rest in singleton pregnancies for preventing preterm birth. Cochrane Database of Systematic Reviews 2004, Issue 1. Art. No.: CD003581. DOI: 10.1002/14651858.CD003581.pub2.

7. Assessment of risk factors for preterm birth. ACOG Practice Bulletin No. 31. American College of Obstetricians and Gynecologists. Obstet Gynecol 2001;98:709–16.
8. Farquhar C, Marjoribanks J, Basser R, Lethaby A. High dose chemotherapy and autologous bone marrow or stem cell transplantation versus conventional chemotherapy for women with early poor prognosis breast cancer. Cochrane Database of Systematic Reviews 2005, Issue 3. Art. No.: CD003139. DOI: 10.1002/14651858.CD003139.pub2.
9. Mayer M. When clinical trials are compromised: a perspective from a patient advocate. PLoS Med 2005; 2(11):e358. Available at: http://medicine.plosjournals.org/archive/1549-1676/2/11/pdf/10.1371_journal.pmed.0020358-L.pdf. Retrieved June 28, 2006.
10. World Health Organization Regional Office for Europe (WHO/EURO). Risk evaluation of chorionic villus sampling (CVS): report on a meeting. Copenhagen: WHO/EURO; 1992. (WHO/EURO document EUR/ICP/MCH 123).
11. Kuliev AM, Modell B, Jackson L, Simpson JL, Brambati B, Froster U, et al. Risk evaluation of CVS. Prenat Diagn 1993;13:197–209.
12. Rimm AA, Katayama AC, Diaz M, Katayama KP. A meta-analysis of controlled studies comparing major malformation rates in IVF and ICSI infants with naturally conceived children. J Assisted Reprod Genet 2004;21:437–43.
13. Perinatal risks associated with assisted reproductive technology. ACOG Committee Opinion No. 324. American College of Obstetricians and Gynecologists. Obstet Gynecol 2005;106:1143–6.
14. National Bioethics Advisory Commission. Ethical and policy issues in research involving human participants: report and recommendations of the National Bioethics Advisory Commission. Bethesda (MD): NBAC; 2001.
15. Mello MM, Brennan TA. The controversy over high-dose chemotherapy with autologous bone marrow transplant for breast cancer. Health Aff (Millwood) 2001;20:101–17.
16. Jones JW, McCullough LB, Richman BW. The ethics of innovative surgical approaches for well-established procedures. J Vasc Surg 2004;40:199–201.
17. Horton R. Surgical research or comic opera: questions, but few answers [letter]. Lancet 1996;347:984–5.
18. DeAngelis C, Drazen JM, Frizelle FA, Haug C, Horton R, Kotzin S, et al. Clinical trial registration: a statement from the International Committee of Medical Journal Editors. International Committee of Medical Journal Editors [editorial]. Lancet 2004;364:911–2.
19. Mayor S. Drug companies agree to make clinical trial results public [news]. BMJ 2005;330:109.
20. DeAngelis C, Drazen JM, Frizelle FA, Haug C, Hoey J, Horton R, et al. Is this clinical trial fully registered? A statement from the International Committee of Medical Journal Editors. Ann Intern Med 2005;143:146–8.
21. American College of Obstetricians and Gynecologists, Committee on Gynecologic Practice. Position regarding OvaCheck™, February 25, 2005.
22. Petricoin EF, Ardekani AM, Hitt BA, Levine PJ, Fusaro VA, Steinberg SM, et al. Use of proteomic patterns in serum to identify ovarian cancer. Lancet 2002;359:572–7.

# COMMITTEE OPINIONS

## COMMITTEE ON GENETICS



*Published in 2006
■ Technology Assessment

# COMMITTEE OPINIONS

# ACOG Committee Opinion

Committee on Obstetric Practice

Committee on Genetics

Number 183, April 1997

## Routine Storage of Umbilical Cord Blood for Potential Future Transplantation

Reconstitution of the bone marrow can be a life-saving procedure in the treatment of hematologic disease (eg, Fanconi anemia) or advanced malignancy. The necessary hematopoietic stem and progenitor cells are usually obtained from allogeneic or autologous bone marrow. If autologous marrow is not an option, then a human leukocyte antigen (HLA)-identical sibling is the donor most likely to result in successful engraftment and minimization of the risk of graft-versus-host (GVH) disease. Most people do not have an HLA-identical sibling available, and they must look outside of their families. There is a national registry of potential bone marrow donors, but finding an identical match and convincing that individual to undergo the unpleasant donation procedure is not always easy. Many individuals who could potentially benefit from transplantation die while awaiting donors.

A recently recognized potential source for hematopoietic stem and progenitor cells is human fetal cord blood. Early results from more than 200 transplants of human cord stem cells, primarily to treat childhood malignancies, seem very encouraging for several reasons. There appears to be a relatively high success rate for the procedure even in the face of HLA mismatches at one or more loci. There also appears to be a somewhat lower risk for GVH disease than that which is true for traditional bone marrow transplantation. These encouraging preliminary reports have generated considerable enthusiasm because the 4 million births per year in the United States would appear to provide a large reservoir of genetically diverse, potentially transplantable specimens. Large volumes of cord blood are now being "wasted" as "discarded human material" that could theoretically be easily collected, typed, screened for infections, and banked cryogenically for transplantation.

The use of this technology raises a number of scientific, legal, and ethical issues that need to be addressed:

- Should cord blood specimens be collected and banked centrally for allogeneic transplantation in a system analogous to the way that we now handle blood, or would parents be well-advised to bank their own child's cord blood at birth for potential future autologous use should it ever be necessary?


ISSN 1074-861X

**The American College of Obstetricians and Gynecologists**
409 12th Street, SW
PO Box 96920
Washington, DC 20090-6920

12345/10987

- What is the probability that any individual will ever need his or her own cord blood for transplantation? If that need does arise 18 years later, what is the probability that a specimen stored for 18 years will still be viable?
- Most transplants to date have been done in babies and young children. More cells are needed to reconstitute the bone marrow of persons of larger size. What percentage of cord blood specimens will have adequate numbers of cells to reconstitute the bone marrow of adults?
- Are cord blood stem and progenitor cells more efficient at reconstituting marrow than are cells obtained from adult marrow? Would fewer cells on a per-kilogram body weight basis be as effective?
- Could the number of stem and progenitor cells in a specimen of cord blood be expanded in vitro to provide enough cells for a reliable reconstitution of the bone marrow of persons of adult size?
- If the apparently lower incidence of GVH disease compared with adult marrow sources is real, it may represent reduced immunocompetence of cord stem and progenitor cells. This may be disadvantageous in treating patients with cancer. It may also permit a higher incidence of second primary cancers in transplant survivors.
- As many as 38% of cord blood specimens may be contaminated with maternal cells. What effect will this contamination with adult cells that are (presumably) immunocompetent have upon graft success rate?
- In the future, there may be other medical approaches to manage these diseases.
- Should this technology continue to show promise, and the decision is made to establish cord blood banks, should cord blood continue to be regarded as "discarded human material?"
- Could cord blood be collected routinely at deliveries without consent?
- All specimens would need to be tested for infectious and selected genetic diseases before use. Should parents be informed if their child's specimen tests positive for an infection (eg, human immunodeficiency virus) or genetic disease?
- If nonpaternity is discovered in the course of testing, should that be disclosed to the mother, father, or child?
- Physicians should resist the pressures of marketing, and they should evaluate thoroughly the potential benefits and risks—emotional as well as physical—of all new medical interventions.

Privately owned for-profit companies have been established to bank cord blood samples for potential future use by those individuals or their family members. There is a significant cost associated with the initial specimen processing (approximately $1,500) and an annual storage fee (approximately $100). Given the low probability of needing a stem cell transplant (which has been estimated at between 1 in 1,000 and 1 in 200,000 by age 18) and the other uncertainties regarding success rates with increasing body mass and time in storage, is this a "good" investment? In view of the apparent success rate, despite HLA mismatch, will there be an advantage to receiving one's own banked cells, or could one do just as well with someone else's cord blood? Once banked, to whom do the cells there belong? Do they belong to the parents who paid the fees or the child from whom they came? Do the parents have the right to give them away or sell them, or should they be held for the person from whom they came until he or she reaches the age of majority? If the cells are to be used for someone other than the person from whom they came, must both parents agree or is consent from one adequate? What happens if the parents disagree?

There are clearly many questions about this technology that remain to be answered. Some are relatively simple, such as the success rate of the procedure for various diseases and at various body weights. These simply await a larger number of cases. Some will be more difficult, such as the viability of cells in long-term storage; these questions will take time to answer. The most difficult will be the moral, ethical, and social questions, which need extensive public discussion and may never all be resolved to everyone's satisfaction. Until there is a fuller understanding of all of these issues, we must proceed with considerable circumspection. Parents should not be sold this service without a realistic assessment of their likely return on their investment. Commercial cord blood banks should not represent the service they sell as "doing everything possible" to ensure the health of children. Parents and grandparents should not be made to feel guilty if they are not eager or able to invest these considerable sums in such a highly speculative venture.

## Bibliography

Broxmeyer HE. Questions to be answered regarding umbilical cord blood hematopoietic stem and progenitor cells and their use in transplantation. Transfusion 1995;35:694-702

Kurtzberg J, Laughlin M, Graham ML, Smith C, Olson JF, Halperin EC, et al. Placental blood as a source of hematopoietic stem cells for transplantation into unrelated recipients. N Engl J Med 1996;335:157-166

Laporte JP, Gorin NC, Rubinstein P, Lesage S, Portnoi MF, Barbu V, et al. Cord-blood transplantation from an unrelated donor in an adult with chronic myelogenous leukemia. N Engl J Med 1996;335:167-170

Marshall E. Clinical promise, ethical quandary. Science 1996;271:586-588

Rubinstein P, Rosenfield RE, Adamson JW, Stevens CE. Stored placental blood for unrelated bone marrow reconstitution. Blood 1993;81:1679-1690

Scaradavou A, Carrier C, Mollen N, Stevens C, Rubenstein P. Detection of maternal DNA in placental/umbilical cord blood by locus-specific amplification of the noninherited maternal HLA gene. Blood 1996;88:1494-1500

Silberstein LE, Jefferies LC. Placental-blood banking—a new frontier in transfusion medicine. N Engl J Med 1996;335:199-201

Wagner JE, Rosenthal J, Sweetman R, Shu XO, Davies SM, Ramsay NK, et al. Successful transplantation of HLA-matched and HLA-mismatched umbilical cord blood from unrelated donors: analysis of engraftment and acute graft-versus-host disease. Blood 1996:88:795-802

# ACOG Committee Opinion

Committee on Genetics

Number 189, October 1997

# Advanced Paternal Age:

## Risks to the Fetus

Advanced maternal age increases the risk of having a liveborn infant with autosomal trisomies 21, 18, or 13, or with the sex chromosome aneuploidies 47,XXY or 47,XXX. Genetic counseling traditionally has been offered when a woman will be 35 years of age or older as of her estimated delivery date. With increased paternal age, however, there does not appear to be an increased risk of chromosomal anomalies in offspring. Insufficient evidence exists to provide a specific cutoff level for assessing risk in association with paternal age.

Although advancing paternal age does affect pregnancy outcome, effects on genetic disease are less completely understood. There is general agreement that advancing paternal age predisposes the fetus to mutations in autosomal dominant diseases such as neurofibromatosis, achondroplasia, Apert syndrome, and Marfan syndrome. The increased risk rises exponentially, rather than linearly, with increasing paternal age. Increasing paternal age may be associated with spontaneous germline mutations in X-linked genes that are transmitted through carrier daughters to affected grandsons. This phenomenon has been called the "grandfather effect" and may occur with several X-linked disorders, including hemophilia A and Duchenne muscular dystrophy.

Although paternal age affects autosomal dominant diseases, the exact risk for any specific disorder is small. Most of the autosomal dominant diseases affect only 1 in 5,000–10,000 individuals, so even a doubling of risk constitutes a very low overall risk. It is the collective risk of autosomal dominant diseases that constitutes the increased risk, not the risk of a particular disorder.

Currently, it is not possible to screen prenatally for all autosomal dominant and X-linked diseases in the presence of advanced paternal age. Fetal ultrasonography may detect some autosomal dominant disorders, but this technique cannot be relied upon as a screening modality. Chromosomal analysis cannot be used to detect these disorders. Only genetic counseling on an individual basis is recommended for couples to address their specific concerns if advancing paternal age is an issue.


ISSN 1074-861X

**The American College of Obstetricians and Gynecologists**
409 12th Street, SW
PO Box 96920
Washington, DC 20090-6920

12345/43210

## Bibliography

American College of Medical Genetics. Statement on guidance for genetic counseling in advanced paternal age. Bethesda, Maryland: ACMG, 1996

Ashton GC. Mismatches in genetic markers in a large family study. Am J Hum Genet 1980;32:601–613

de Michelena MI, Burstein E, Lama JR, Vasquez JC. Paternal age as a risk factor for Down syndrome. Am J Med Genet 1993;45:679–682

Friedman JM. Genetic disease in the offspring of older fathers. Obstet Gynecol 1981;57:745–749

Hook EB. A search for a paternal-age effect upon cases of 47, +21 in which the extra chromosome is of paternal origin. Am J Hum Genet 1984;36:413–421

McIntosh GC, Olshan AF, Baird PA. Paternal age and the risk of birth defects in offspring. Epidemiology 1995;6:282–288

Olshan AF, Anath CV, Savitz DA. Intrauterine growth retardation as an endpoint in mutation epidemiology: an evaluation based on paternal age. Mutat Res 1995;344:89–94

Olshan AF, Schnitzer PG, Baird PA. Paternal age and the risk of congenital heart defects. Teratology 1994;50:80–84

Risch N, Reich EW, Wishnick MM, McCarthy JG. Spontaneous mutation and parental age in humans. Am J Hum Genet 1987;41:218–248

ACOG Committee Opinion

Committee on Genetics

Number 212, November 1998

# Screening for Canavan Disease

Canavan disease is a severe progressive genetic disorder of the central nervous system. The clinical features of Canavan disease usually appear after the first few months of life and include developmental delay, macrocephaly, hypotonia, and poor head control. As the disease progresses, seizures, optic atrophy, gastrointestinal reflux, and deterioration of swallowing develop. Most children with Canavan disease die in the first decade of life. Presently, there is no cure or effective therapy for Canavan disease.

Canavan disease is caused by a deficiency of the enzyme aspartoacylase, which leads to increased excretion of its substrate, N-acetylaspartic acid (NAA). A diagnosis of Canavan disease is established by determining an increased level of urinary NAA by organic acid analysis. These abnormally high levels of NAA lead to demyelination and spongy degeneration of the brain, which cause the neurologic features of Canavan disease.

As in Tay–Sachs disease, Canavan disease is inherited as an autosomal recessive condition and is more prevalent among individuals of Eastern European Jewish (Ashkenazi) background. It is estimated that the carrier frequency in the Ashkenazi Jewish population is approximately 1 per 40. Thus, the risk for an affected offspring in this population approximates 1 in 6,400 births. Unlike Tay–Sachs disease, however, there do not appear to be other high-risk ethnic populations, although Canavan disease has been reported in individuals of non-Ashkenazi Jewish background.

Molecular studies have revealed two specific mutations in the aspar-toacylase gene on chromosome 17. These account for approximately 97% of the mutations causing Canavan disease in the Ashkenazi Jewish population. One is a mutation in codon 285 of the aspartoacylase gene, and the other is a mutation in codon 231. Screening of Ashkenazi Jewish individuals can be performed by analyzing for these two mutations. In non-Jewish persons, the mutations may be different and more diverse. The most common mutation is in codon 305, which has been noted in approximately 36% of the 70 identified alleles from unrelated non-Jewish individuals.

Carrier screening for Canavan disease requires molecular diagnostic methods. Simple enzymatic assays, as commonly used in Tay–Sachs screening, cannot be used for Canavan disease because the activity of the deficient enzyme, aspartoacylase, is not detectable in blood. Testing for the three most common Canavan disease mutations will identify about 97% of Ashkenazi Jewish carriers and 40–50% of non-Jewish carriers.


ISSN 1074-861X

The American College of Obstetricians and Gynecologists
409 12th Street, SW
PO Box 96920
Washington, DC 20090-6920

12345/21098

When both parents are carriers of identifiable Canavan disease mutations, prenatal diagnosis by chorionic villus sampling (CVS) or amniocentesis can be accomplished using DNA analysis. In couples where one or both members have unknown mutations, biochemical analysis of NAA levels in the amniotic fluid can be used reliably. Elevated NAA levels can be used to detect an affected fetus. The analysis should be done in a laboratory that has personnel who have expertise in performing this test. Enzyme analysis of aspartoacylase in cultured fetal cells from CVS or amniocentesis is not reliable.

Based on the preceding information, the Committee on Genetics makes the following recommendations:

1. Ideally, molecular carrier screening for Canavan disease should be offered preconceptionally if both members of the couple are of Ashkenazi Jewish genetic background. This screening could be combined with screening for Tay–Sachs disease because both disorders are more common in this group. Many specialized laboratories already offer screening for both diseases. Those with a family history consistent with Canavan disease also should be offered screening, which should be voluntary; informed consent and assurance of confidentiality are required. If potential carriers have not been screened preconceptionally, screening may be offered during early pregnancy.
2. If only one partner is of high risk (of Ashkenazi Jewish descent or with a family history consistent with Canavan disease), this partner should be screened first. Ideally, this should be performed preconceptionally. If it is determined that the high-risk partner is a carrier, the other partner should be offered screening. The couple, however, must be informed of the limitations of testing. If the woman is already pregnant, it may be necessary to screen both partners simultaneously so that results are obtained in a timely fashion and to ensure that all options are available for the couple.
3. If it is determined by DNA-based analysis that both partners are carriers of Canavan disease, prenatal diagnosis should be offered either by CVS or amniocentesis, using DNA-based testing of the fetal cells.

## Bibliography

American College of Medical Genetics Board of Directors. Position statement on carrier testing for Canavan disease. Bethesda, Maryland: January 10, 1998

American College of Obstetricians and Gynecologists. Screening for Tay–Sachs disease. ACOG Committee Opinion 162. Washington, DC: ACOG, 1995

Bennett MJ, Gibson KM, Sherwood WG, Divry P, Rolland MO, Elpeleg ON, et al. Reliable prenatal diagnosis of Canavan disease (aspartoacylase deficiency): comparison of enzymatic and metabolite analysis. J Inherit Metab Dis 1993;16:831–836

Kaul R, Gao GP, Matalon M, Aloya M, Su Q, Jin M, et al. Identification and expression of eight novel mutations among non-Jewish patients with Canavan disease. Am J Hum Genet 1996;59:95–102

Kronn D, Oddoux C, Philips J, Ostrer H. Prevalence of Canavan disease heterozygotes in the New York metropolitan Ashkenazi Jewish population. Am J Hum Genet 1995;57:1250–1252

Matalon R. Canavan disease: diagnosis and molecular analysis. Genetic Testing 1997;1:21–25

Matalon R, Michals K, Kaul R. Canavan disease: from spongy degeneration to molecular analysis. J Pediatr 1995;127:511–517

# ACOG Committee Opinion

Committee on Genetics

Number 230, January 2000

## Maternal Phenylketonuria

Phenylketonuria (PKU) is an autosomal recessive disorder of phenylalanine metabolism that, if untreated, can cause severe mental retardation. Phenylketonuria is caused by a deficiency of the enzyme phenylalanine hydroxylase. Children of women with PKU will carry at least one abnormal gene, which is inherited from their homozygous affected mother. Even though the fetus is unlikely to be affected, approximately 1 in 120 children will inherit an abnormal phenylalanine hydroxylase gene from both parents and also have PKU. The remainder of children are carriers and should receive genetic counseling in the future. Phenylalanine crosses the placenta by an active transport process that results in a fetal-to-maternal plasma phenylalanine ratio of 1.5. This results in higher levels of phenylalanine in fetal blood than would be expected based on maternal blood levels.

Routine screening for PKU in newborns and early dietary therapy with a phenylalanine-restricted diet have markedly reduced mental retardation in affected individuals. As a result of these advances in the detection and treatment of PKU, there are large numbers of young adults with PKU who received early dietary treatment for this disorder and have IQs in the normal or near-normal range. The failure of young women with PKU to adhere to dietary restrictions has led to a new public health challenge. The heterozygous fetus is metabolically normal. However, these metabolically normal fetuses of women with PKU who are on an unrestricted diet may develop microcephaly, low birth weight, heart defects, and mental retardation due to maternal hyperphenylalaninemia. Children of women with PKU on unrestricted diets are at a 92% risk for mental retardation, a 73% risk for microcephaly, and a 12% risk for congenital heart defects (1).

In the United States, approximately 3,000 women of reproductive age are affected with PKU. Evidence indicates that women with PKU will benefit from remaining on a phenylalanine-free diet throughout their lives. Many of these women are not currently on phenylalanine-restricted diets, which require the consumption of phenylalanine-free products and supplements that many women find unpalatable. Unless these women are identified and placed on an appropriate diet before and during pregnancy, they are at risk for having children affected with PKU. It has been suggested that dietary control should be implemented at least 3 months prior to conception to help prevent fetal structural defects, including cardiac defects (2). If phenylalanine levels are normalized by 8 weeks of gestation, there is evidence to suggest a reduction in intrauterine growth restriction (3).



ISSN 1074-861X

**The American College of Obstetricians and Gynecologists**
409 12th Street, SW
PO Box 96920
Washington, DC 20090-6920

12345/43210

## Conclusions and Recommendations

1. All women with PKU should be strongly encouraged to receive family planning and preconceptional counseling.
2. Women with PKU should begin dietary phenylalanine restriction prior to conception (4).
3. Ideally, pregnant women with PKU should be managed in consultation with practitioners from experienced PKU centers.

## References

1. Lenke RR, Levy HL. Maternal phenylketonuria and hyperphenylalaninemia. An international survey of the outcome of untreated and treated pregnancies. N Engl J Med 1980; 303:1202–1208
2. Waisbren SE, Hamilton BD, St. James PJ, Shiloh S, Levy HL. Psychosocial factors in maternal phenylketonuria: women's adherence to medical recommendations. Am J Public Health 1995;85:1636–1641
3. Koch R, Friedman E, Azen C, Hanley W, Levy H, Matalon R, et al. The international collaborative study of maternal phenylketonuria status report 1998. MRDD Res Rev 1999;5:117–121
4. Levy HL, Waisbren SE, Lobbregt D, Allred E, Schuler A, Trefz FK, et al. Maternal mild hyperphenylalaninaemia: an international survey of offspring outcome. Lancet 1994; 344: 1589–1594

## Bibliography

Koch R, Levy HL, Matalon R, Rouse B, Haney WB, Trefz F, et al. The international collaborative study of maternal phenylketonuria: status report 1994. Acta Paediatr Suppl 1994;407: 111–119

Levy HL, Waisbren SE. Effects of untreated maternal phenylketonuria and hyperphenylalaninemia on the fetus. N Engl J Med 1983;309:1269–1274

Lipson A, Beuhler B, Bartley J, Walsh D, Yu J, O'Halloran M, et al. Maternal hyperphenylalaninemia fetal effects. J Pediatr 1984;104:216–220

Luke B, Keith LG. The challenge of maternal phenylketonuria screening and treatment. J Reprod Med 1990;35:667–673

MacCready RA. Admissions of phenylketonuric patients to residential institutions before and after screening programs of the newborn infant. J Pediatr 1974;85:383–385

Platt LD, Koch R, Azen C, Hanley WB, Levy HL, Matalon R, et al. Maternal phenylketonuria collaborative study, obstetric aspects and outcome: the first 6 years. Am J Obstet Gynecol 1992;166:1150–1162

ACOG Committee Opinion

Committee on Genetics

Number 257, May 2001 *(Replaces No. 178, November 1996)*

# Genetic Evaluation of Stillbirths and Neonatal Deaths

In the burgeoning field of genetics, a complete evaluation of stillbirths and neonatal deaths yields more information than in the past. Autopsy findings supplemented by genetic studies may provide important information (1). This information may explain the cause of death, direct further investigation of the family, and be particularly valuable in counseling parents about recurrence risks in future pregnancies.

## Parental Consent

It is important to obtain parental consent; however, grief stricken parents may be reticent to consent to autopsy examination. They may view it as a violation of the sanctity of the dead body or as serving the physician's interests or curiosity. Even though bereaved parents may not want the information initially, care providers should strongly emphasize that results of the evaluation may be useful to the patient and her family in planning future pregnancies. If still reluctant to consent to a full autopsy, the family should be informed of the value of less invasive methods of evaluation, including photographs, X-rays, and sampling of tissues, such as blood or skin. These methods may help to identify a syndrome or chromosomal abnormality even without full autopsy data. Congenital anomalies are a significant cause of fetal death; 15–20% of stillbirths have a major malformation. Approximately 8% of stillbirths have chromosomal abnormalities and about 20% have dysmorphic features or skeletal abnormalities (2, 3). Malformations often are present in patterns that permit classification into a particular syndrome. Syndrome identification may delineate etiologic and pathogenetic factors that could have predictive significance for recurrence risk and the risk of other associated anomalies (4). Also, it is important to note that in addition to genetic causes, some fetal and neonatal deaths are caused by obstetric or medical complications for which preventive measures may be available.

This document reflects emerging clinical and scientific advances as of the date issued and is subject to change. The information should not be construed as dictating an exclusive course of treatment or procedure to be followed



ISSN 1074-861X

**The American College of Obstetricians and Gynecologists**
409 12th Street, SW
PO Box 96920
Washington, DC 20090-6920

12345/54321

## Management

After a stillbirth or neonatal death, proper management includes a careful perinatal and family history, a physical examination of the fetus or infant (with documentation by description and photography, if possible), and indicated laboratory studies (see box). To ascertain the etiology and provide appropriate counseling to the family, clinical–pathologic correlation is best accomplished by a team comprising obstetricians, pediatricians, neonatologists, pathologists, and geneticists.

## History

When stillbirth or neonatal death occurs, the obstetric history including exposures (eg, medications, viral infections), and family history, including a three-generation pedigree if possible, should be reviewed. Any pertinent information in the maternal or paternal pedigree should be documented and investigated further. Relevant original medical records and documentation should be obtained whenever possible. The gestational age by last menstrual period, maternal examinations, laboratory data, and ultrasonograms should be recorded for correlation with the physical examination of the neonate. Possible nongenetic causes also should be considered.

## Examination of the Stillbirth

The general examination of the stillborn infant should be done promptly, noting any dysmorphic features and obtaining body measurements, including crown–rump, crown–heel, and foot lengths, as well as weight (5–8). Foot length is especially useful before 23 weeks of gestation. These measurements help estimate gestational age and evaluate intrauterine growth. Further documentation by frontal and profile photographs, with close-ups of specific abnormalities, is valuable for subsequent review and consultations. Even if parents have declined an autopsy, a description of any obvious abnormalities of the stillbirth should be included in the medical record.

X-rays, examination of the placenta, and autopsy should be considered. This is especially true when dysmorphic features, inconsistent growth measurements, anomalies, hydrops, or growth restriction is present. Whole body X-ray with anterior–posterior and lateral views may reveal an unrecognized skeletal abnormality or further define a grossly apparent deformity. If possible, the infant should be positioned with extremities extended and the epiphyses viewed.

When a full autopsy is performed, it should follow the guidelines for perinatal autopsy published by the College of American Pathologists (www.cap.org) or other standard references (9, 10). The pathologist should be aware of the clinical history and suspected genetic diagnoses so that samples for cytogenetic, metabolic, and molecular studies may be taken.

**Management of Stillbirth or Fetal Death***

- Obtain informed consent from parents for autopsy
- Obtain perinatal and family history
- Perform physical examination of fetus and describe findings
- Photograph fetus
- Perform whole body X-rays of fetus
- Perform autopsy of fetus
- Perform gross and microscopic examination of placenta
- Perform cytogenetic studies
- Perform biochemical, molecular genetic, or infectious disease studies as indicated

*If these services are not available at your hospital, consider sending to a regional hospital center or contact your state board of pathology.

## Examination of the Placenta

Gross and microscopic examination of the placenta, membranes, and umbilical cord may corroborate autopsy findings or explain apparent fetal deformity. Gross evaluation of the umbilical cord and blood vessels, membranes for amniotic bands and other anomalies, and placenta for size and condition should be performed. Histologic study of placental samples also should be performed (11, 12).

## Laboratory Studies

Samples of amniotic fluid, umbilical cord blood, or amnion may be obtained for chromosomal and any other relevant studies. Analysis of bile, vitreous humor, urine, and fetal tissue may be helpful if umbilical cord blood is unobtainable (13, 14). Guidelines for the procurement of samples for chromosomal and genetic studies are outlined in the box on the following page.

Chromosomal analysis of amniotic fluid or chorionic villi ideally should be offered as soon as a fetal death is recognized. Although this information can be obtained at the time of delivery, the likelihood of obtaining a karyotype is decreased if there is a long interval between fetal death and delivery. This is

**Guidelines for the Procurement of Samples for Chromosomal and Genetic Studies**

- Obtain consent to take skin, eye, body fluids, and other tissue samples (separate from autopsy consent).
- For cytogenetic and molecular genetic studies, the following samples are acceptable:
  —Umbilical cord blood (3 mL)
  —Skin with attached dermis (1 $cm^2$)
  —Fascia from thigh, inguinal region, or Achilles tendon (1 cm) especially when maceration of the skin is present; and
  —Kidney, skeletal, muscle, liver, lung, and gonads, if indicated.
- Samples should be obtained using sterile techniques as soon as possible.
- Umbilical cord blood should be placed into sterile tube with heparin.
- Tissue samples should be placed in appropriate sterile medium obtained from cytogenetic laboratory or in normal saline if medium is not available. Do not use fixative solutions (eg, formaldehyde).
- Samples should be kept at room temperature.
- Freeze a 1 cm tissue sample.

especially true when dysmorphic features, inconsistent growth measurements, anomalies, hydrops, or growth restriction are present, or when a parent carries a balanced chromosomal rearrangement (eg, translocation or inversion) or has a mosaic karyotype. Based on the history, examination of the fetus, radiographic studies, and autopsy findings, specific molecular or biochemical tests may be indicated. For example, fluorescence in situ hybridization studies used to identify a deletion of chromosome 22q11.2 should be considered when a conotruncal cardiac defect (eg, interrupted aortic arch, truncus arteriosus) is detected (15).

## Counseling

The results of the autopsy, placental examination, laboratory tests, and cytogenetic studies should be communicated to the involved clinicians and to the family of the deceased infant in a timely manner. Further, the family should be counseled promptly after a consensus is reached. Counseling before the evaluation is complete or before different opinions of the various caregivers have been resolved may increase feelings of guilt or anger in parents who have experienced a perinatal death. When there is an abnormal child or a genetic defect, these feelings often are magnified. Specific testing of the parents may be offered. The results of the tests are important even when no specific diagnosis is identified (16). A list of diagnoses excluded may be useful in counseling the parents. Whether or not there is a specific diagnosis, compassionate counseling of the parents and sensitivity to their needs are required.

## References


1. Saller DN Jr, Lesser KB, Harrel U, Rogers BB, Oyer CE. The clinical utility of the perinatal autopsy. JAMA 1995; 273:663–665
2. Pauli RM, Reiser CA. Wisconsin Stillbirth Service Program: II. Analysis of diagnoses and diagnostic categories in the first 1,000 referrals. Am J Med Genet 1994; 50:135–153
3. Pauli RM, Reiser CA, Lebovitz RM, Kirkpatrick SJ. Wisconsin Stillbirth Service Program: I. Establishment and assessment of a community-based program for etiologic investigation of intrauterine deaths. Am J Med Genet 1994;50:116–134
4. Leppig KA, Werler MM, Cann CI, Cook CA, Holmes LB. Predictive value of minor anomalies. I. Association with major malformations. J Pediatr 1987;110:531–537
5. Reed GB, Claireaux AE, Cockburn F, eds. Diseases of the fetus and newborn: pathology, imaging, genetics, and management. 2nd ed. London: Chapman and Hall Medical, 1995
6. Stocker JT, Dehner LP. Pediatric pathology. Philadelphia: Lippincott, 1992
7. Naeye RL. Disorders of the placenta, fetus, and neonate: diagnosis and clinical significance. St Louis: Mosby-Year Book, Inc, 1992
8. Shepard TH, Shi M, Fellingham GW, Fujinaga M, FitzSimmons JM, Fantel AG, et al. Organ weight standards for human fetuses. Pediatr Pathol 1988;8:513–524
9. Valdes-Dapena MA, Huff DS. Perinatal autopsy manual. Collingdale, Pennsylvania: Diane Publishing, 1993
10. Bove KE. Practice guidelines for autopsy pathology: the perinatal and pediatric autopsy. Autopsy Committee of the College of American Pathologists. Arch Pathol Lab Med 1997;121:368–376
11. Benirschke K, Kaufman P. Pathology of the human placenta. 4th ed. New York: Springer-Verlag, 2000
12. Genest DR. Estimating the time of death in stillborn fetuses: II. Histologic evaluation of the placenta; a study of 71 stillborns. Obstet Gynecol 1992;80:585–592
13. Emery JL, Howat AJ, Variend S, Vawter GF. Investigation of inborn errors of metabolism in unexpected infant deaths. Lancet 1988;2:29–31
14. Rashed MS, Ozand PT, Bennett MJ, Barnard JJ, Govindaraju DR, Rinaldo P. Inborn errors of metabolism diagnosed in sudden death cases by acylcarnitine analysis of postmortem bile. Clin Chem 1995;41:1109–1114
15. Goldmuntz E, Clark BJ, Mitchell LE, Jawad AF, Reed L, McDonald-McGinn D, et al. Frequency of 22q11 deletions in patients with conotruncal defects. J Am Coll Cardiol 1998;32:492–498
16. Rushton DI. Prognostic role of the perinatal postmortem. Br J Hosp Med 1994;52:450–454

# ACOG Committee Opinion

Committee on Genetics

Number 287, October 2003

# Newborn Screening

*ABSTRACT: Newborn screening programs have enormous public health benefits and have been effective in identifying newborns who can benefit from early treatment. Because of advances in genetics and technology, newborn screening programs are capable of testing for more than 30 disorders, including infections, genetic diseases, and inherited and metabolic disorders. Many important issues surround the debate on universal screening, including financial resources, level of screening, continuity of care, and informed consent. To date, policy on newborn screening has been fragmented; however, efforts are underway to ensure uniformity and equity for all newborns. Obstetrician–gynecologists can continue to work to improve the health of their patients by informing expectant families of the newborn screening process.*

Newborn screening is a public health issue that has moved into the spotlight because of advances in genetic medicine. Although newborn screening tests are designed to detect infants with specific metabolic disorders who would benefit from early diagnosis and treatment, they also may identify couples who are carriers of disorders. Because of advances in genetics and technology, newborn screening programs are capable of testing for more than 30 disorders, including infections, genetic diseases, and inherited and metabolic disorders. Yet, many program and policy issues that surround state-based newborn screening programs remain controversial. Because newborn screening programs vary by state, obstetricians need to be aware of the status of newborn screening in their states and should be prepared to address questions or refer their patients to appropriate sources for additional information.

Dr. Robert Guthrie pioneered newborn screening in the early 1960s. His efforts were aimed at preventing mental retardation by screening for phenylketonuria (PKU) and instituting dietary changes for affected newborns. The blood specimen for the Guthrie test is collected on a piece of filter paper that soaks up a few drops of blood from a newborn's heel after it has been stuck with a lancet. The ideal period for specimen collection is 2–5 days after birth. However, most infants are tested at 24–48 hours of life just before they are discharged from the hospital. For many conditions, the test should be performed after the newborn has been fed but before blood transfusions are given. Specimens are sent to a laboratory to be analyzed by a bacterial inhibition assay, electrophoresis, high-pressure liquid chromatography, or newer technologies, such as tandem mass spectrometry. The hospital of birth, the

This document reflects emerging clinical and scientific advances as of the date issued and is subject to change. The information should not be construed as dictating an exclusive course of treatment or procedure to be followed.



ISSN 1074-861X

**The American College of Obstetricians and Gynecologists**
409 12th Street, SW
PO Box 96920
Washington, DC 20090-6920

12345/76543

Newborn screening. ACOG Committee Opinion No. 287. American College of Obstetricians and Gynecologists. Obstet Gynecol 2003;102:887–9.

pediatrician, or both are notified of any positive test results.

Newborn screening programs are designed for maximal sensitivity and specificity; the false-negative rate must be kept at an absolute minimum so that no cases will be missed. However, this results in significant false-positive rates. Therefore, confirmatory testing is essential. A false-positive test result can cause parental anxiety. Counseling by the obstetric provider can be of great value. Prenatal education about newborn screening not only provides parents with an understanding of the reasons for obtaining their newborn's blood specimen, but also informs them that an initial positive test result does not necessarily mean that their child will be affected.

Newborn screening is mandated by state statute or regulation and does not require written parental consent in most states; Maryland and Wyoming require written consent. Many states allow parents to refuse testing based on religious or personal grounds. Hospitals and newborn nurseries usually provide written materials to parents immediately postpartum to inform them of the newborn screening their children will undergo. Many patients will turn to their obstetricians for additional information regarding newborn testing and may ask why their newborns have a bandage on their heels.

Newborn screening programs have expanded in some states to include testing for congenital hypothyroidism, hemoglobinopathies, galactosemia, biotinidase deficiency, congenital adrenal hyperplasia, maple syrup urine disease, medium chain acyl-CoA dehydrogenase deficiency, human immunodeficiency virus (HIV), and toxoplasmosis. Currently, debate continues about which tests should be part of the newborn screening panel. There is no constitutional or federal mandate for newborn screening. Therefore, laws and policies regarding newborn screening are individually determined by each state. Each state program must have a system in place to notify the pediatrician, the parents, or both of the need for follow-up and treatment at a center equipped to care for an infant who receives a positive test result for a metabolic, hematologic, endocrine, infectious, or other congenital disorder.

Phenylketonuria and congenital hypothyroidism are the only tests that are performed in all 50 states and the District of Columbia. Forty-nine states screen for galactosemia, and all states screen at least selected populations for hemoglobinopathies, such as sickle cell disease. Some states screen for infectious diseases, such as HIV and toxoplasmosis, and inherited disorders, such as cystic fibrosis. All states have started to perform newborn hearing screening to identify infants with congenital moderate to profound hearing loss using noninvasive techniques called evoked otoacoustic emissions and auditory brainstem response. The current panel of tests in each state can be viewed at http://genes-r-us.uthscsa.edu/resources/newborn/screenstatus.htm.

The fee charged by state programs for each infant screened is variable and in 2002 ranged from $10 to $60. Some states use public funds for their newborn screening programs and do not bill individuals for newborn screening tests. Commercial laboratories have started to offer additional newborn screening tests to the public. Patients who are considering the expanded newborn screen should discuss the testing with their pediatrician and obtain a kit from the laboratories offering this service before delivery. It is important for parents to recognize that most of these additional disorders are relatively infrequent and many cannot be treated. However, they can occur in families without a positive family history, and early diagnosis and treatment for some of these disorders may prevent serious complications.

A state's financial resources often determine the level of newborn screening (eg, how many conditions for which they can test). The state must consider not only the cost of the test itself but also their financial capacity to provide subspecialty follow-up, services, and treatment. Many state public health agencies report inadequate financial resources to expand programs. This has led to inequity in access to care for newborns across state lines. In response to calls for a universal newborn screening program, the American Academy of Pediatrics (AAP) convened a national Task Force on Newborn Screening in May 1999, cosponsored by the Maternal and Child Health Bureau of the Health Resources and Services Administration. The American Academy of Pediatrics called for participation by both federal and state governments. It recommends that the federal government, acting through its established health care agencies, such as the Health Resources and Services Administration, the National Institutes of Health, and the Centers for Disease Control and Prevention, develop guidelines, standards, and policies for newborn screening and take a leadership role in bringing this information to states. The AAP report *Serving the Family from Birth to the Medical Home* "highlights the need for a more uniform national policy for the selection of newborn screening tests." According to *The Importance of Newborn Screening*, the March of Dimes also has advocated for newborn screening that is "universally available and… uniform quality." The March of Dimes has issued guidelines for a minimum core panel of 10 screening tests that should be included on each state's newborn screening panel. The core panel includes tests for PKU, congenital hypothyroidism, congenital adrenal hyperplasia, biotinidase deficiency, maple syrup urine disease, galactosemia, medium chain acyl-CoA dehydrogenase deficiency, homocystinuria, sickle cell anemia, and hearing loss.

## Emerging Technology

Tandem mass spectrometry recently has been added to the methods of newborn screening. This technology enables the testing of a single blood spot for many metabolites, including amino acids, organic acids, and fatty acids. Tandem mass spectrometry allows rapid testing for multiple diseases with high sensitivity and specificity without adding much to the cost of newborn screening. However, for some of these diseases, there are no effective treatments at this time. In addition, adding more diseases to screening panels will increase the need for follow-up services.

It is now feasible to store the blood spots obtained for newborn screening. However, this raises many ethical issues about personal privacy. The medical, ethics, and legal communities as well as the public and legislative representatives continue to grapple with this issue of privacy, including employment and insurance eligibility based on genetic information.

## Conclusion

Newborn screening programs have enormous public health benefits and have been effective in identifying newborns who can benefit from early treatment. In addition, many couples have been made aware of their carrier status because of diagnoses in their newborns. There are many important issues surrounding the debate on universal screening, including financial resources, level of screening, continuity of care, and informed consent. To date, policy on newborn screening has been fragmented, but efforts are underway to ensure uniformity and equity for all newborns. Obstetrician–gynecologists can continue to work to improve the health of their patients by informing expectant families of the newborn screening process.

## Bibliography

Hiller EH, Landenburger G, Natowicz MR. Public participation in medical policy-making and the status of consumer autonomy: the example of newborn-screening programs in the United States. Am J Public Health 1997;87:1280–8.

Howse JL, Katz M. The importance of newborn screening. Pediatrics 2000;106:595.

Kwon C, Farrell PM. The magnitude and challenge of false-positive newborn screening test results. Arch Pediatr Adolesc Med 2000;154:714–8.

Larsson A, Therrell B. Newborn screening: the role of the obstetrician. Clin Obstet Gynecol 2002;45:697–710; discussion 730–2.

National Newborn Screening and Genetics Resource Center. National Newborn Screening Report—2000. Austin (TX): NNSGRC; 2003.

Piper MA, Lindenmayer JM, Lengerich EJ, Pass KA, Brown WG, Crowder WB, et al. The role of state public health agencies in genetics and disease prevention: results of a national survey. Public Health Rep 2001;116:22–31.

Serving the family from birth to the medical home. Newborn screening: a blueprint for the future—a call for a national agenda on state newborn screening programs. Pediatrics 2000;106: 389–422.

Tandem mass spectrometry in newborn screening. American College of Medical Genetics/American Society of Human Genetics Test and Technology Transfer Committee Working Group. Genet Med 2000;2:267–9.

ACOG Committee Opinion

Committee on Obstetric Practice

Committee on Genetics

Number 296, July 2004 (Replaces No. 223, October 1999)

# First-Trimester Screening for Fetal Aneuploidy

*ABSTRACT: First-trimester screening for chromosomal abnormalities offers potential advantages over second-trimester screening. Studies in the 1990s demonstrated an association between chromosomal abnormalities and the ultrasonographic finding of abnormally increased nuchal translucency (an echo-free area at the back of the fetal neck) between 10 and 14 weeks of gestation. First-trimester screening using nuchal translucency, free β-hCG, and pregnancy-associated plasma protein-A has comparable detection rates and positive screening rates for Down syndrome as second-trimester screening using 4 serum markers (alpha-fetoprotein, β-hCG, unconjugated estriol, and inhibin-A). Although first-trimester screening for Down syndrome and trisomy 18 is an option, it should be offered only if certain criteria can be met.*

Maternal serum testing in the second trimester of pregnancy (15–20 weeks of gestation) is commonly offered to screen for Down syndrome (trisomy 21), trisomy 18, neural tube defects, and other fetal malformations. This approach detects approximately 60–75% of fetuses with Down syndrome at a screen positive rate of 5% in women younger than 35 years at the time of delivery and detects 85–95% of cases with a screen positive rate of 25% in women older than 35 years at the time of delivery (1). The detection rate for trisomy 18 is approximately 70% when a patient-specific risk of more than 1 in 100 is employed based on maternal age and serum analyte levels (2). First-trimester screening for chromosomal abnormalities offers potential advantages over second-trimester screening. When the results are negative, first-trimester screening may reduce maternal anxiety at an earlier gestational age. When the results are positive, such screening allows the patient to take advantage of first-trimester prenatal diagnosis by chorionic villus sampling or second-trimester amniocentesis (at 15 weeks of gestation or later). If the fetus is found to be affected earlier in the pregnancy, it provides women greater privacy if they elect to terminate the pregnancy. Earlier pregnancy termination is associated with reduced maternal morbidity.

## Nuchal Translucency

Studies in the 1990s demonstrated an association between chromosomal abnormalities and the ultrasonographic finding of abnormally increased

This document reflects emerging clinical and scientific advances as of the date issued and is subject to change. The information should not be construed as dictating an exclusive course of treatment or procedure to be followed.



ISSN 1074-861X

**The American College of Obstetricians and Gynecologists**

409 12th Street, SW
PO Box 96920
Washington, DC 20090-6920

12345/87654

First-trimester screening for fetal aneuploidy. ACOG Committee Opinion No. 296. American College of Obstetricians and Gynecologists. Obstet Gynecol 2004;104:215–17.

nuchal translucency (an echo-free area at the back of the fetal neck) between 10 and 14 weeks of gestation (3–5). Early data on nuchal translucency screening showed widely discordant efficacy caused by differences in the study populations, gestational age at screening, the ways in which nuchal translucency measurements were used with serum analytes, ultrasonographic techniques, and the level of training. When measuring nuchal translucency, the fetus should be in the sagittal view as for a crown–rump measurement and care should be taken to distinguish nuchal skin from the amnionic membrane. Interobserver and intraobserver variation in nuchal translucency measurements have been noted. The ability to measure nuchal translucency reliably is dependent on the operator, ultrasound equipment, proper magnification and contrast, fetal position, correct placement of the calipers, and maternal body habitus (6). Ultrasonographer training and ongoing quality assurance are essential if nuchal translucency is used as a screening method (6, 7).

Nuchal translucency increases with gestational age and, hence, a single cutoff value should not be defined as abnormal (3, 4, 8, 9). Like serum screening, nuchal translucency measurements may be reported in multiples of the median, which will be used to modify the patient's age-related risk for Down syndrome. Because small differences in nuchal translucency measurement can have a large impact on the Down syndrome risk prediction, proper quality assurance requires that either center- or ultrasonographer-specific medians need to be monitored closely (10). Nuchal translucency measurement, in the absence of serum screening has a low specificity; therefore, it is not recommended as a screening test for aneuploidy in singleton pregnancies (10).

Increased nuchal translucency also has been associated with other chromosomal abnormalities (eg, trisomy 13; 45,X; and triploidy) and congenital anomalies, in particular, cardiac defects, and some genetic disorders (3, 5, 11). The prevalence of major cardiac defects increases with increasing nuchal translucency thickness (11). Regardless of gestational age, in fetuses with increased nuchal translucency measurement and normal chromosomes, specialized ultrasound examination with detailed assessment of the heart or fetal echocardiography or both are recommended.

## Nuchal Translucency With Maternal Serum Screening Markers

Studies have shown that measurement of 2 serum analytes, pregnancy-associated plasma protein-A and free β-hCG, can be used to screen for Down syndrome in the first trimester (7, 12, 13). Pregnancy-associated plasma protein-A tends to be decreased and free β-hCG tends to be increased in Down syndrome. The detection rate with first-trimester biochemical screening is similar to second-trimester screening, approximately 60% with a positive screening rate of 5% (7, 12, 13). A multicenter study of 8,514 patients with singleton pregnancies in the United States demonstrates that combining first-trimester maternal serum screening markers with nuchal translucency measurement is a good alternative to second-trimester serum screening (14). The detection rate for Down syndrome was 78.7% (95% confidence interval [CI], 66.3–88.1) at a cutoff rate of 1:270 with a positive screening rate of 5%. The detection rate for trisomy 18 in women younger than 35 years at the time of delivery was 90.9% (95% CI, 58.7–99.8) at a positive screening rate of 2%.

First-trimester screening using nuchal translucency, free β-hCG, and pregnancy-associated plasma protein-A has comparable detection rates and positive screening rates for Down syndrome as second-trimester screening using 4 serum markers (alpha-fetoprotein, β-HCG, unconjugated estriol, and inhibin-A). The recently completed Serum Urine and Ultrasound Screening Study trial in the United Kingdom suggests that integrated screening (eg, combined first- and second-trimester screening) is the most sensitive and cost-effective test (15). Results from a large multicenter trial in the United States designed to compare the sensitivity of first-trimester screening using nuchal translucency and serum markers with second-trimester serum screening in the same population should be available in the near future. This study also will evaluate the utility of sequential and integrated screening of patients in the first and second trimesters (16).

Although first-trimester screening for Down syndrome and trisomy 18 is an option, it should be offered only if the following criteria can be met:

1. Appropriate ultrasound training and ongoing quality monitoring programs are in place.

2. Sufficient information and resources are available to provide comprehensive counseling to women regarding the different screening options and limitations of these tests.
3. Access to an appropriate diagnostic test is available when screening test results are positive.

## References


1. Haddow JE, Palomaki GE, Knight GJ, Williams J, Pulkkinen A, Canick JA, et al. Prenatal screening for Down's syndrome with use of maternal serum markers. N Engl J Med 1992;327:588–93.
2. Benn PA, Leo MV, Rodis JF, Beazoglou T, Collins R, Horne D. Maternal serum screening for fetal trisomy 18: a comparison of fixed cutoff and patient-specific risk protocols. Obstet Gynecol 1999;93:707–11.
3. Nicolaides KH, Azar G, Byrne D, Mansur C, Marks K. Fetal nuchal translucency: ultrasound screening for chromosomal defects in first trimester of pregnancy. BMJ 1992;304:867–9.
4. Nicolaides KH, Brizot ML, Snijders RJ. Fetal nuchal translucency: ultrasound screening for fetal trisomy in the first trimester of pregnancy. Br J Obstet Gynaecol 1994;101:782–6.
5. Taipale P, Hiilesmaa V, Salonen R, Ylostalo P. Increased nuchal translucency as a marker for fetal chromosomal defects. N Engl J Med 1997;337:1654–8.
6. Snijders RJ, Thom EA, Zachary JM, Platt LD, Greene N, Jackson LG, et al. First trimester trisomy screening: nuchal translucency measurement training and quality assurance to correct and unify technique. Ultrasound Obstet Gynecol 2002;19:353–9.
7. Haddow JE, Palomaki GE, Knight GJ, Williams J, Miller WA, Johnson A. Screening of maternal serum for fetal Down's syndrome in the first trimester. N Engl J Med 1998;338:955–61.
8. Pajkrt E, de Graaf IM, Mol BW, van Lith JM, Bleker OP, Bilardo CM. Weekly nuchal translucency measurements in normal fetuses. Obstet Gynecol 1998;91:208–11.
9. Schuchter K, Wald N, Hackshaw AK, Hafner E, Liebhart E. The distribution of nuchal translucency at 10-13 weeks of pregnancy. Prenat Diagn 1998;18:281–6.
10. Malone FD, D'Alton ME. First-trimester sonographic screening for Down syndrome. Society for Maternal-Fetal Medicine. Obstet Gynecol 2003;102:1066–79.
11. Hyett J, Perdu M, Sharland G, Snijders R, Nicolaides KH. Using fetal nuchal translucency to screen for major congenital cardiac defects at 10-14 weeks of gestation: population based cohort study. BMJ 1999;318: 81–5.
12. Wald NJ, Kennard A, Hackshaw AK. First trimester serum screening for Down's syndrome [published erratum appears in Prenat Diagn 1996;16:387]. Prenat Diagn 1995;15:1227–40.
13. Krantz DA, Larsen JW, Buchanan PD, Macri JN. First-trimester Down syndrome screening: free beta-human chorionic gonadotropin and pregnancy-associated plasma protein A. Am J Obstet Gynecol 1996;174:612–6.
14. Wapner R, Thom E, Simpson JL, Pergament E, Silver R, Filkins K, et al. First-trimester screening for trisomies 21 and 18. Trimester Maternal Serum Biochemistry and Fetal Nuchal Translucency Screening (BUN) Study Group. N Eng J Med 2003;349:1405–13.
15. Wald NJ, Rodeck C, Hackshaw AK, Walters J, Chitty L, Mackinson AM. First and second trimester antenatal screening for Down's syndrome: the results of the Serum, Urine, and Ultrasound Screening Study (SURUSS). Health Technol Assess 2003;7(11):1–77.
16. Malone FD, Berkowitz RL, Canick JA, D'Alton ME. First-trimester screening for aneuploidy: research or standard of care? Am J Obstet Gynecol 2000;182:490–6.

ACOG Committee Opinion

Committee on Genetics

Number 298, August 2004

This document reflects emerging clinical and scientific advances as of the date issued and is subject to change. The information should not be construed as dictating an exclusive course of treatment or procedure to be followed.



ISSN 1074-861X

**The American College of Obstetricians and Gynecologists**
409 12th Street, SW
PO Box 96920
Washington, DC 20090-6920

12345/87654

Prenatal and preconceptional carrier screening for genetic diseases in individuals of Eastern European Jewish descent. ACOG Committee Opinion No. 298. American College of Obstetricians and Gynecologists. Obstet Gynecol 2004;104:425–8.

# Prenatal and Preconceptional Carrier Screening for Genetic Diseases in Individuals of Eastern European Jewish Descent

*ABSTRACT: Certain autosomal recessive disease conditions are more prevalent in individuals of Eastern European Jewish (Ashkenazi) descent. Previously, the American College of Obstetricians and Gynecologists recommended that individuals of Eastern European Jewish ancestry be offered carrier screening for Tay–Sachs disease, Canavan disease, and cystic fibrosis as part of routine obstetric care. Based on the criteria used to justify offering carrier screening for Tay–Sachs disease, Canavan disease, and cystic fibrosis, the American College of Obstetricians and Gynecologists' Committee on Genetics recommends that couples of Ashkenazi Jewish ancestry also should be offered carrier screening for familial dysautonomia. Individuals of Ashkenazi Jewish descent may inquire about the availability of carrier screening for other disorders. Carrier screening is available for mucolipidosis IV, Niemann-Pick disease type A, Fanconi anemia group C, Bloom syndrome, and Gaucher's disease.*

Carrier screening for specific genetic conditions often is determined by an individual's ancestry. Certain autosomal recessive disease conditions are more prevalent in individuals of Eastern European Jewish (Ashkenazi) descent. Most individuals of Jewish ancestry in North America are descended from Ashkenazi Jewish communities and, thus, are at increased risk for having offspring with one of these conditions. Many of these disorders are lethal in childhood or associated with significant morbidity.

Tay–Sachs disease (TSD) was one of the first disorders amenable to carrier screening. As a result of carrier screening programs established in the 1970s, the incidence of TSD in the North American Ashkenazi Jewish population has decreased by more than 90%. Carrier screening also is recommended for individuals of French Canadian and Cajun descent. Initially, carrier screening was based on the measurement of hexosaminidase A levels (the enzyme deficient in TSD) in serum or leukocytes. As the genes for TSD and other diseases more prevalent in Ashkenazi Jews were identified, DNA carrier tests have been developed. Because each of these disorders is caused by a small number of common mutations, the carrier tests are very sensitive (94–99% detection rates). Previously, the American College of Obstetricians and Gynecologists (ACOG) recommended that individuals of Eastern European Jewish ancestry be offered carrier screening for TSD, Canavan disease, and cystic fibrosis as part of routine obstetric care. Because of recent advances in genetics, additional carrier tests are now available (Table 1).

In 2001, the gene for familial dysautonomia was identified. At least 2 mutations in the familial dysautonomia gene, *IKBKAP*, have been identified in patients with familial dysautonomia of Ashkenazi Jewish descent. One of the mutations ($IVS20^{+6T \rightarrow C}$) is found in more than 99% of patients with familial dysautonomia. It occurs almost exclusively in individuals of Ashkenazi Jewish descent; the carrier rate (1 in 32) is similar to TSD and cystic fibrosis. Familial dysautonomia, a disorder of the sensory and autonomic nervous system, is associated with significant morbidity. Clinical features include abnormal suck and feeding difficulties, episodic vomiting, abnormal sweating, pain and temperature insensitivity, labile blood pressure levels, absent tearing, and scoliosis. Treatment is available, which can improve the length and quality of life, but there currently is no cure. Based on the criteria used to justify offering carrier screening for TSD, Canavan disease, and cystic fibrosis, the ACOG Committee on Genetics recommends that couples of Ashkenazi Jewish ancestry also should be offered carrier screening for familial dysautonomia.

Carrier screening tests are available for several diseases that are less common (carrier rates 1 in 89 to 1 in 127), including Fanconi anemia group C, Niemann-Pick disease type A, Bloom syndrome, and mucolipidosis IV. These conditions are associated with significant neurologic or medical problems and very limited treatment options (see box). Carrier screening also is available for Gaucher's disease, the most common disorder in Eastern European Jews. Although Gaucher's disease affects 1 in 900 individuals, the age of onset (from a few months to 90 years) and severity are variable (see box). Gaucher's disease can be very mild, and treatment is available.

All of these tests have a high sensitivity in the Jewish population. The prevalence of these disorders in non-Jewish populations, except for TSD and cystic fibrosis, is unknown. The sensitivity of these carrier tests in non-Jewish populations has not been established. The mutations may be different and more diverse. Consequently, when only 1 partner is Jewish, it is difficult to assess the risk of having an affected offspring. Therefore, carrier screening of the non-Jewish partner is of limited value.

Based on these recent developments, the ACOG Committee on Genetics makes the following 7 recommendations:

1. The family history of individuals considering pregnancy, or who are already pregnant, should determine whether either member of the couple is of Eastern European (Ashkenazi) Jewish ancestry or has a relative with 1 or more of the genetic conditions listed in Table 1.

**Table 1.** Recessive Genetic Diseases Frequent Among Individuals of Eastern European Jewish Descent Amenable to Carrier Screening

| Disorder | Disease Incidence | Carrier Frequency* | Detection rate* |
|---|---|---|---|
| Tay–Sachs disease | 1/3,000 | 1/30 | 98% by Hex-A test, 94% by DNA-based test |
| Canavan disease | 1/6,400 | 1/40 | 98% |
| Cystic fibrosis | 1/2,500–3,000 | 1/29 | 97% |
| Familial dysautonomia | 1/3,600 | 1/32 | 99% |
| Fanconi anemia group C | 1/32,000 | 1/89 | 99% |
| Niemann-Pick disease type A | 1/32,000 | 1/90 | 95% |
| Mucolipidosis IV | 1/62,500 | 1/127 | 95% |
| Bloom syndrome | 1/40,000 | 1/100 | 95–97% |
| Gaucher's disease | 1/900 | 1/15 | 95% |

*Non-Jewish carrier frequency and detection rates are unknown except for Tay–Sachs disease. Carrier frequency for Tay–Sachs disease is 1 in 30 if French Canadian or Cajun ancestry and 1 in 300 for others with a 98% carrier detection rate by Hex-A test.

Modified from March of Dimes. Genetic screening pocket facts. White Plains (NY): MOD; 2001.

2. Carrier screening for TSD, Canavan disease, cystic fibrosis, and familial dysautonomia should be offered to Ashkenazi Jewish individuals before conception or during early pregnancy so that a couple has an opportunity to consider prenatal diagnostic testing options. If the woman is already pregnant, it may be necessary to screen both partners simultaneously so that the results are obtained in a timely fashion to ensure that prenatal diagnostic testing is an option.
3. Individuals of Ashkenazi Jewish descent may inquire about the availability of carrier screening for other disorders. Carrier screening is available for mucolipidosis IV, Niemann-Pick disease type A, Fanconi anemia group C, Bloom syndrome, and Gaucher's disease. Patient education materials can be made available so that interested patients can make an informed decision about having additional screening tests (see box). Some patients may benefit from genetic counseling.
4. When only 1 partner is of Ashkenazi Jewish descent, that individual should be screened first. If it is determined that this individual is a carrier, the other partner should be offered screening. However, the couple should be informed that the carrier frequency and the detection rate in non-Jewish individuals is unknown for all of these disorders, except for TSD and cystic fibrosis. Therefore, it is difficult to accurately predict the couple's risk of having a child with the disorder.
5. Individuals with a positive family history of 1 of these disorders should be offered carrier screen-

### Clinical Features of Autosomal Recessive Genetic Diseases Frequent Among Individuals of Eastern European Jewish Descent

**Bloom syndrome** is a genetic condition associated with increased chromosome breakage, a predisposition to infections and malignancies, prenatal and postnatal growth deficiency, skin findings (such as facial telangiectasias, abnormal pigmentation), and in some cases learning difficulties and mental retardation. The mean age of death is 27 years and usually is related to cancer. No effective treatment currently is available.

**Canavan disease** is a disorder of the central nervous system characterized by developmental delay, hypotonia, large head, seizures, blindness, and gastrointestinal reflux. Most children die within the first several years of life. Canavan disease is caused by a deficiency of the aspartoacylase enzyme. No treatment currently is available.

**Familial dysautonomia** is a neurologic disorder characterized by abnormal suck and feeding difficulties, episodic vomiting, abnormal sweating, pain and temperature insensitivity, labile blood pressure levels, absent tearing, and scoliosis. There currently is no cure for familial dysautonomia, but some treatments are available that can improve the length and quality of a patient's life.

**Fanconi anemia group C** usually presents with severe anemia that progresses to pancytopenia, developmental delay, and failure to thrive. Congenital anomalies are not uncommon, including limb, cardiac, and genital–urinary defects. Microcephaly and mental retardation may be present. Children are at increased risk for leukemia. Some children have been successfully treated with bone marrow transplantation. Life expectancy is 8–12 years.

**Gaucher's disease** is a genetic disorder that mainly affects the spleen, liver, and bones; it occasionally affects the lungs, kidneys, and brain. It may develop at any age. Some individuals are chronically ill, some are moderately affected, and others are so mildly affected that they may not know that they have Gaucher's disease. The most common symptom is chronic fatigue caused by anemia. Patients may experience easy bruising, nosebleeds, bleeding gums, and prolonged and heavy bleeding with their menses and after childbirth. Other symptoms include an enlarged liver and spleen, osteoporosis, and bone and joint pain. Gaucher's disease is caused by the deficiency of the β-glucosidase enzyme. Treatment is available through enzyme therapy, which results in a vastly improved quality of life.

**Mucolipidosis IV** is a neurodegenerative lysosomal storage disorder characterized by growth and psychomotor retardation, corneal clouding, progressive retinal degeneration, and strabismus. Most affected infants never speak, walk, or develop beyond the level of a 1–2 year old. Life expectancy may be normal, and there currently is no effective treatment.

**Niemann-Pick disease type A** is a lysosomal storage disorder typically diagnosed in infancy and marked by a rapid neurodegenerative course similar to Tay–Sachs disease. Affected children die by age 3–5 years. Niemann-Pick disease type A is caused by a deficiency of the sphingomyelinase enzyme. There currently is no treatment.

**Tay–Sachs disease (TSD)** is a severe, progressive disorder of the central nervous system leading to death within the first few years of life. Infants with TSD appear normal at birth but by age 5–6 months develop poor muscle tone, delayed development, loss of developmental milestones, and mental retardation. Children with TSD lose their eyesight at age 12–18 months. This condition usually is fatal by age 6 years. Tay–Sachs disease is caused by a deficiency of the hexosaminidase A enzyme. No effective treatment currently is available.

ing for the specific disorder and may benefit from genetic counseling.

6. When both partners are carriers of 1 of these disorders, they should be referred for genetic counseling and offered prenatal diagnosis. Carrier couples should be informed of the disease manifestations, range of severity, and available treatment options. Prenatal diagnosis by DNA-based testing can be performed on cells obtained by chorionic villus sampling or amniocentesis.
7. When an individual is found to be a carrier, his or her relatives are at risk for carrying the same mutation. The patient should be encouraged to inform his or her relatives of the risk and the availability of carrier screening. The provider does not need to contact these relatives because there is no provider–patient relationship with the relatives, and confidentiality must be maintained.

Carrier screening is voluntary. Informed consent and assurance of confidentiality are required. For all of these disorders, a negative screening test result for 1 or both partners significantly reduces the possibility of an affected offspring. However, it does not exclude it because the test sensitivity is less than 100% so not all carriers can be identified.

The number and choice of genetic tests available to patients is likely to increase as a result of the Human Genome Project and advances in technology. For some patients, it can be difficult to decide whether to have a specific test. There are many factors patients may consider, including the prevalence of the disease, the carrier risk, the disease severity and treatment options, cost, and reproductive choices. Counseling by a genetic counselor, geneticist, or physician with expertise in these diseases may assist patients in making an informed decision about carrier testing.

## Bibliography

American College of Obstetricians and Gynecologists. Screening for Canavan disease. ACOG Committee Opinion 212. Washington, DC: ACOG, 1998.

American College of Obstetricians and Gynecologists. Screening for Tay–Sachs disease. ACOG Committee Opinion 162. Washington, DC: ACOG, 1995.

Dong J, Edelmann L, Bajwa AM, Kornreich R, Desnick RJ. Familial dysautonomia: detection of the IKBKAP IVS20 (+6T→C) and R696P mutations and frequencies among Ashkenazi Jews. Am J Med Genet 2002;110:253–7.

Eng CM, Desnick RJ. Experiences in molecular-based prenatal screening for Ashkenazi Jewish genetic diseases. Adv Genet 2001;44:275–96.

Zlotogora J, Bach G, Munnich A. Molecular basis of mendelian disorders among Jews. Mol Genet Metab 2000; 69:169–80.

# ACOG Committee Opinion

Committee on Genetics

Number 318, October 2005 (Replaces No. 162, November 1995)

## Screening for Tay–Sachs Disease

This document reflects emerging clinical and scientific advances as of the date issued and is subject to change. The information should not be construed as dictating an exclusive course of treatment or procedure to be followed.



ISSN 1074-861X

**The American College of Obstetricians and Gynecologists**
409 12th Street, SW
PO Box 96920
Washington, DC 20090-6920

12345/98765

Screening for Tay–Sachs disease. ACOG Committee Opinion No. 318. American College of Obstetricians and Gynecologists. Obstet Gynecol 2005;106:893–4.

*ABSTRACT: Tay–Sachs disease (TSD) is a severe progressive neurologic disease that causes death in early childhood. Carrier screening should be offered before pregnancy to individuals and couples at high risk, including those of Ashkenazi Jewish, French–Canadian, or Cajun descent and those with a family history consistent with TSD. If both partners are determined to be carriers of TSD, genetic counseling and prenatal diagnosis should be offered.*

Tay–Sachs disease (TSD) is a lysosomal storage disease in which $GM_2$ gangliosides accumulate throughout the body. The accumulation of these gangliosides in the central nervous system results in a severe progressive neurologic disease that causes death in early childhood.

The TSD carrier rate in Jewish individuals of Eastern European descent (Ashkenazi) is approximately 1 in 30; the carrier rate for non-Jewish individuals is estimated to be 1 in 300. It has been determined that individuals of French–Canadian and Cajun descent also have a greater carrier frequency than the general population.

The enzyme hexosaminidase occurs in two principal forms, Hexosaminidase A and Hexosaminidase B. Hexosaminidase A is composed of one α subunit and one β subunit, whereas Hexosaminidase B is composed of two β subunits. Tay–Sachs disease is caused by a deficiency of Hexosaminidase A, whereas Sandhoff disease is caused by a deficiency of both Hexosaminidase A and Hexosaminidase B. Both of these diseases are transmitted in an autosomal recessive fashion. Laboratories report Hexosaminidase A levels as a percentage of total hexosaminidase activity. Hexosaminidase A is almost completely absent in patients with classical TSD. The percentage of Hexosaminidase A activity in carriers usually is less than 55% of total activity, whereas Hexosaminidase A activity in noncarriers generally is more than 60% of total activity. Tay–Sachs disease can be diagnosed prenatally by measuring hexosaminidase activity in samples obtained by amniocentesis or by chorionic villus sampling.

Carrier screening can be performed by molecular analysis, biochemical analysis, or both. Molecular analyses of the α subunit gene for TSD have been reported in both Jewish and non-Jewish populations. Molecular analysis of three mutations will detect 94% of carriers in the Ashkenazi Jewish population, compared with biochemical analysis, which will detect 98% of carriers.

Different mutations have been found in other ethnic groups. Biochemical analysis should be used in low-risk populations because molecular analysis detects less than 50% of carriers in these populations.

Test results of biochemical carrier screening using serum are inaccurate when performed in women who are pregnant or taking oral contraceptives. If the serum test is used for pregnant women, many of them will be misclassified as carriers. If biochemical testing is to be done in women who are pregnant or taking oral contraceptives, leukocyte testing must be used. If both partners are determined to be carriers of TSD, genetic counseling and prenatal diagnosis should be offered.

When the serum test result is inconclusive, biochemical analysis should be performed on leukocytes from peripheral blood. DNA analysis may be helpful for those individuals whose leukocyte test results are inconclusive and those individuals whose test results are positive to rule out a rare pseudodeficiency condition.

Pseudodeficiency refers to a state in which asymptomatic individuals have a low amount of Hexosaminidase A activity when tested with conventional artificial substrate. However, these normal individuals without Hexosaminidase A are able to catalyze the breakdown of natural substrate $GM_2$ ganglioside. Pseudodeficiency mutations comprise approximately one third of the mutations identified in non-Jewish individuals. Because some of these individuals are compound heterozygotes for a Tay–Sachs mutation and a pseudodeficiency allele, the delineation of their precise genotype for reproductive purposes usually requires further biochemical assessment complemented with DNA analysis.

Based on the preceding information, the Committee on Genetics makes the following recommendations:

1. Screening for TSD should be offered before pregnancy if both members of a couple are of Ashkenazi Jewish, French–Canadian, or Cajun descent. Those with a family history consistent with TSD also should be offered screening.
2. When one member of a couple is at high risk (ie, of Ashkenazi Jewish, French–Canadian, or Cajun descent or has a family history consistent with TSD) but the other partner is not, the high-risk partner should be offered screening. This is particularly important if there is uncertainty about ancestry or if there is a family history consistent with TSD. If the high-risk partner is determined to be a carrier, the other partner also should be offered screening. If the woman is already pregnant, it may be necessary to offer screening to both partners simultaneously to ensure that results are obtained promptly and that all options are available to the couple.
3. Biochemical analysis should be used for individuals in low-risk populations.
4. If TSD biochemical screening is performed in women who are pregnant or taking oral contraceptives, leukocyte testing must be used.
5. Ambiguous screening test results or positive screening test results in individuals should be confirmed by biochemical and DNA analysis for the most common mutations. This will detect patients who carry genes associated with mild disease or pseudodeficiency states. Referral to a specialist in genetics may be helpful in these cases.
6. If both partners are determined to be carriers of TSD, genetic counseling and prenatal diagnosis should be offered.

## Bibliography

Prenatal and preconceptional carrier screening for genetic diseases in individuals of Eastern European Jewish descent. ACOG Committee Opinion 298. American College of Obstetricians and Gynecologists. Obstet Gynecol 2004;104: 425–8.

Kaback M, Lim-Steele J, Dabholkar D, Brown D, Levy N, Zeiger K. Tay-Sachs disease—carrier screening, prenatal diagnosis, and the molecular era. An international perspective, 1970 to 1993. The International TSD Data Collection Network. JAMA 1993;270:2307–15.

Mules EH, Hayflick S, Dowling CE, Kelly TE, Akerman BR, Gravel RA, et al. Molecular basis of hexosaminidase A deficiency and pseudodeficiency in the Berks County Pennsylvania Dutch. Hum Mutat 1992;1:298–302.

Prence EM, Natowicz MR, Zalewski I. Unusual thermolability properties of leukocyte beta-hexosaminidase: implications in screening for carriers of Tay-Sachs disease. Clin Chem 1993;39:1811–4.

Triggs-Raine BL, Feigenbaum AS, Natowicz M, Skomorowski MA, Schuster SM, Clarke JT, et al. Screening for carriers of Tay-Sachs disease among Ashkenazi Jews. A comparison of DNA-based and enzyme-based tests. N Engl J Med 1990; 323:6–12.

# ACOG Committee Opinion

Committee on Obstetric Practice

Committee on Gynecologic Practice

Committee on Genetics

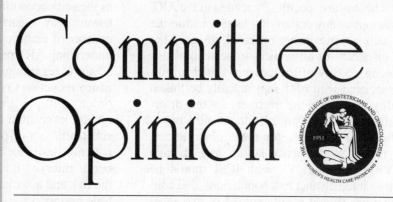

Number 324, November 2005

# Perinatal Risks Associated With Assisted Reproductive Technology

*ABSTRACT: Over the past two decades, the use of assisted reproductive technology (ART) has increased dramatically worldwide and has made pregnancy possible for many infertile couples. A growing body of evidence suggests an association between pregnancies resulting from ART and perinatal morbidity (possibly independent of multiple births), although the absolute risk to children conceived through ART is low. Prospective studies are needed to further define the risk of ART to offspring. The single most important health effect of ART for the offspring remains iatrogenic multiple fetal pregnancy. The American College of Obstetricians and Gynecologists supports the effort toward lowering the risk of multiple gestation with ART.*

Over the past two decades, the use of assisted reproductive technology (ART) has increased dramatically worldwide and has made pregnancy possible for many infertile couples. The American Society for Reproductive Medicine defines ART as treatments and procedures involving the handling of human oocytes and sperm, or embryos, with the intent of establishing a pregnancy (1). By this definition, ART includes in vitro fertilization (IVF) with or without intracytoplasmic sperm injection (ICSI), but it excludes techniques such as artificial insemination and superovulation drug therapy.

Several studies have been conducted to describe and compare the obstetric outcome of pregnancies resulting from ART with those of pregnancies conceived without treatment. Some retrospective and prospective follow-up studies suggest that pregnancies achieved by ART are associated with an increased risk of prematurity, low birth weight, and neonatal encephalopathy and a higher perinatal mortality rate, even after adjusting for age, parity, and multiple gestation (2, 3). Even in studies limited to singleton ART pregnancies, the prematurity rate is twice as high, and the proportion of infants with low birth weight is three times as high as that of the general population (4, 5). A meta-analysis of 15 studies comprising 12,283 singleton infants conceived by IVF and 1.9 million spontaneously conceived singleton infants showed significantly higher odds of perinatal mortality (odds ratio [OR], 2.2), preterm delivery (OR, 2.0), low birth weight (OR, 1.8), very low birth weight (OR, 2.7), and small for gestational age status (OR, 1.6) in IVF pregnancies, after adjusting for maternal age and parity (6).

This document reflects emerging clinical and scientific advances as of the date issued and is subject to change. The information should not be construed as dictating an exclusive course of treatment or procedure to be followed.



ISSN 1074-861X

**The American College of Obstetricians and Gynecologists**
409 12th Street, SW
PO Box 96920
Washington, DC 20090-6920

12345/98765

Perinatal risks associated with assisted reproductive technology. ACOG Committee Opinion No. 324. American College of Obstetricians and Gynecologists. Obstet Gynecol 2005; 106:1143–6.

It is difficult to determine the degree to which these associations are specifically related to the ART procedures versus any underlying factors within the couple, such as coexisting maternal disease, the cause of infertility, or differences in behavioral risk (eg, smoking). Many of the adverse obstetric outcomes associated with ART may actually be linked to infertility rather than the treatment for this disorder. Continued research is needed to examine possible confounding variables for these observations. Patients undergoing superovulation drug therapy alone, IVF alone, and IVF with ICSI should be examined as three distinct risk populations, and control populations should ideally consist of two separate groups—normal fertile couples and infertile couples who conceive without treatment.

Assisted reproductive technology has been associated with a 30-fold increase in multiple pregnancies compared with the rate of spontaneous twin pregnancies (1% in the general white population). The obstetric and neonatal risks associated with multiple gestation include preeclampsia, gestational diabetes, preterm delivery, and operative delivery. Multifetal births account for 17% of all preterm births (before 37 weeks of gestation), 23% of early preterm births (before 32 weeks of gestation), 24% of low-birth-weight infants (<2,500 g), and 26% of very-low-birth-weight infants (<1,500 g) (7–10). In a large population-based cohort study in the United States from 1996 to 1999, the proportion of multiple births attributable to ovulation induction or ART was 33% (11), although the rate of high-order multiple gestations from ART decreased significantly between 1998 and 2001 (12). Methods to limit high-order multiple pregnancies include monitoring hormone levels and follicle number during superovulation and limiting transfer to fewer embryos in IVF cycles (12–14). Transferring two embryos can limit the occurrence of triplets in younger candidates who have a good prognosis without significantly decreasing the overall pregnancy rate (15, 16). The American Society for Reproductive Medicine and the Society for Assisted Reproductive Technology have developed updated recommendations on the number of embryos per transfer to reduce the risk of multiple gestation (1). The multiple gestation risk of ART, unlike that of superovulation, can be effectively managed by limiting the number of embryos transferred. When considering how to minimize multiple gestation, ART can be viewed as the safer and more favorable approach compared with superovulation.

Informing couples of the obstetric risks as well as the socioeconomic consequences of multiple gestations may modify their decisions regarding the number of embryos to be transferred (17). Patients undergoing ART procedures should be counseled in advance regarding the option of multifetal pregnancy reduction to decrease perinatal risks if a high-order multiple pregnancy occurs. Because the intense motivation for a successful outcome and the substantial out-of-pocket cost of ART may increase patients' desire for the transfer of an excessive number of embryos, it is critical that couples be aware of the risk and associated morbidity of high-order multiple gestation.

Most retrospective and prospective follow-up studies of children born as a result of ART have provided evidence for congenital malformation rates similar to those reported in the general population (18–20). In contrast, an Australian study of 4,916 women found that the risk of one or more major birth defects in infants conceived with ART was twice the expected rate (8.6% for ICSI and 9.0% for IVF, compared with 4.2% in the general population) (21). As with other studies, the control group was not ideal because it did not include couples with infertility who conceived without ART. Prospective studies are needed to further define the risk of ART to offspring.

Male factor infertility is now recognized as an inherited disorder for some infertile couples. In vitro fertilization offers the opportunity to achieve pregnancy while increasing the couple's awareness of possible inherited disorders in their offspring. Genetic conditions can predispose to abnormal sperm characteristics that may be passed to male children. In addition, azoospermia is associated with congenital bilateral absence or atrophy of the vas deferens in men with gene mutations associated with cystic fibrosis. Congenital bilateral absence or atrophy of the vas deferens accounts for approximately 2% of all cases of male infertility (22, 23). Therefore, all patients with congenital bilateral absence or atrophy of the vas deferens and their partners considering IVF by sperm extraction procedure with ICSI should be offered genetic counseling to discuss testing for cystic fibrosis.

Approximately 10–15% of azoospermic and severely oligospermic (<5 million/mL) males have microdeletions of their Y chromosome that can be passed on to their male offspring (24, 25). There is speculation that a deletion could potentially expand in successive generations; however, the reproductive and nonreproductive health implications of this possibility are unknown (26). Some studies have suggested a 1% increased risk for fetal sex chromosome abnormalities following ICSI conception (27–29), but others have yielded conflicting results (30). Subfertile men, with a higher proportion of aneuploid sperm, may have an increased risk of transmitting chromosomal abnormalities to their children (31). These men should be aware of the possible reproductive consequences in their male offspring and the options for prenatal diagnosis.

There is some concern that the micromanipulation of the early embryonic environment in IVF may result in imprinting errors. Genomic imprinting is an epigenetic phenomenon in which one of the two alleles of a subset of genes is expressed differentially according to its parental origin. Imprinting is established early in gametogenesis and maintained in embryogenesis. Recent case series have reported an overrepresentation of two syndromes associated with abnormal imprinting in IVF offspring—Beckwith–Wiedemann syndrome and Angelman's syndrome (32, 33). Both of these conditions may be associated with severe learning disabilities, mental retardation, and congenital malformations. Because these conditions are so rare (1 in 100,000–1 in 300,000), large prospective studies of offspring conceived with ART would be necessary to confirm an increased risk (34). Currently, the risk of imprinting disorders with offspring conceived with ART is largely theoretical but warrants further investigation.

A growing body of evidence suggests an association between ART pregnancies and perinatal morbidity (possibly independent of multiple births), although the absolute risk to children conceived with IVF is low. There is observational evidence linking ART and chromosomal abnormalities following ICSI in severe male factor cases, and concerns have been raised about a possible relationship to genomic imprinting modifications. Given the large sample sizes required to firmly answer these questions, particularly for rare genetic disorders, no causal relationship can be established at this time. It is still unclear to what extent these associations are related to the underlying cause(s) of infertility versus the treatment. It would be prudent to acknowledge these possibilities and to counsel patients accordingly. The single most important health effect of ART for the offspring remains iatrogenic multiple fetal pregnancy. The American College of Obstetricians and Gynecologists supports the effort toward lowering the risk of multiple gestation with ART.

## References


1. Guidelines on the number of embryos transferred. Practice Committee of the Society for Assisted Reproductive Technology and the American Society for Reproductive Medicine. Fertil Steril 2004;82 Suppl 1:S1–2.
2. Badawi N, Kurinczuk JJ, Keogh JM, Alessandri LM, O'Sullivan F, Burton PR, et al. Antepartum risk factors for newborn encephalopathy: the Western Australian case-control study. BMJ 1998;317:1549–53.
3. Ozturk O, Bhattacharya S, Templeton A. Avoiding multiple pregnancies in ART: evaluation and implementation of new strategies. Hum Reprod 2001;16:1319–21.
4. Cetin I, Cozzi V, Antonazzo P. Fetal development after assisted reproduction—a review. Placenta 2003;24 Suppl B:S104–13.
5. Schieve LA, Ferre C, Peterson HB, Macaluso M, Reynolds MA, Wright VC. Perinatal outcome among singleton infants conceived through assisted reproductive technology in the United States. Obstet Gynecol 2004; 103:1144–53.
6. Jackson RA, Gibson KA, Wu YW, Croughan MS. Perinatal outcomes in singletons following in vitro fertilization: a meta-analysis. Obstet Gynecol 2004;103: 551–63.
7. Donovan EF, Ehrenkranz RA, Shankaran S, Stevenson DK, Wright LL, Younes N, et al. Outcomes of very low birth weight twins cared for in the National Institute of Child Health and Human Development Neonatal Research Network's intensive care units. Am J Obstet Gynecol 1998;179:742–9.
8. Martin JA, Hamilton BE, Sutton PD, Ventura SJ, Menacker F, Munson ML. Births: final data for 2002. Natl Vital Stat Rep 2003;52:1–113.
9. Powers WF, Kiely JL. The risks confronting twins: a national perspective. Am J Obstet Gynecol 1994;170: 456–61.
10. Stevenson DK, Wright LL, Lemons JA, Oh W, Korones SB, Papile LA, et al. Very low birth weight outcomes of the National Institute of Child Health and Human Development Neonatal Research Network, January 1993 through December 1994. Am J Obstet Gynecol 1998; 179:1632–9.
11. Lynch A, McDuffie R, Murphy J, Faber K, Leff M, Orleans M. Assisted reproductive interventions and multiple birth. Obstet Gynecol 2001;97:195–200.
12. Jain T, Missmer SA, Hornstein MD. Trends in embryo-transfer practice and in outcomes of the use of assisted reproductive technology in the United States. N Engl J Med 2004;350:1639–45.
13. Gleicher N, Oleske DM, Tur-Kaspa I, Vidali A, Karande V. Reducing the risk of high-order multiple pregnancy after ovarian stimulation with gonadotropins. N Engl J Med 2000;343:2–7.
14. Licciardi F, Berkeley AS, Krey L, Grifo J, Noyes N. A two- versus three-embryo transfer: the oocyte donation model. Fertil Steril 2001;75:510–3.

15. Staessen C, Janssenswillen C, Van den Abbeel E, Devroey P, Van Steirteghem AC. Avoidance of triplet pregnancies by elective transfer of two good quality embryos. Hum Reprod 1993;8:1650–3.
16. Templeton A, Morris JK. Reducing the risk of multiple births by transfer of two embryos after in vitro fertilization. N Engl J Med 1998;339:573–7.
17. Grobman WA, Milad MP, Stout J, Klock SC. Patient perceptions of multiple gestations: an assessment of knowledge and risk aversion. Am J Obstet Gynecol 2001;185: 920–4.
18. Bergh T, Ericson A, Hillensjo T, Nygren KG, Wennerholm UB. Deliveries and children born after in-vitro fertilisation in Sweden 1982–95: a retrospective cohort study. Lancet 1999;354:1579–85.
19. Ericson A, Kallen B. Congenital malformations in infants born after IVF: a population-based study. Hum Reprod 2001;16:504–9.
20. Wennerholm UB, Bergh C, Hamberger L, Lundin K, Nilsson L, Wikland M. Incidence of congenital malformations in children born after ICSI. Hum Reprod 2000;15:944–8.
21. Hansen M, Kurinczuk JJ, Bower C, Webb S. The risk of major birth defects after intracytoplasmic sperm injection and in vitro fertilization. N Engl J Med 2002;346:725–30.
22. Chillon M, Casals T, Mercier B, Bassas L, Lissens W, Silber S, et al. Mutations in the cystic fibrosis gene in patients with congenital absence of the vas deferens. N Engl J Med 1995;332:1475–80.
23. Dork T, Dworniczak B, Aulehla-Scholz C, Wieczorek D, Bohm I, Mayerova A, et al. Distinct spectrum of CFTR gene mutations in congenital absence of vas deferens. Hum Genet 1997;100:365–77.
24. Dohle GR, Halley DJ, Van Hemel JO, van den Ouwel AM, Pieters MH, Weber RF, et al. Genetic risk factors in infertile men with severe oligozoospermia and azoospermia. Hum Reprod 2002;17:13–6.
25. Feng HL. Molecular biology of male infertility. Arch Androl 2003;49:19–27.
26. Tournaye H. ICSI: a technique too far? Int J Androl 2003; 26:63–9.
27. Bonduelle M, Aytoz A, Van Assche E, Devroey P, Liebaers I, Van Steirteghem A. Incidence of chromosomal aberrations in children born after assisted reproduction through intracytoplasmic sperm injection. Hum Reprod 1998;13:781–2.
28. Bonduelle M, Ponjaert I, Van Steirteghem A, Derde MP, Devroey P, Liebaers I. Developmental outcome at 2 years of age for children born after ICSI compared with children born after IVF. Hum Reprod 2003;18:342–50.
29. In't Veld P, Brandenburg H, Verhoeff A, Dhont M, Los F. Sex chromosomal abnormalities and intracytoplasmic sperm injection. Lancet 1995;346:773.
30. Loft A, Petersen K, Erb K, Mikkelsen AL, Grinsted J, Hald F, et al. A Danish national cohort of 730 infants born after intracytoplasmic sperm injection (ICSI) 1994–1997. Hum Reprod 1999;14:2143–8.
31. Calogero AE, Burrello N, De Palma A, Barone N, D'Agata R, Vicari E. Sperm aneuploidy in infertile men. Reprod Biomed Online 2003;6:310–7.
32. Cox GF, Burger J, Lip V, Mau UA, Sperling K, Wu BL, et al. Intracytoplasmic sperm injection may increase the risk of imprinting defects. Am J Hum Genet 2002;71: 162–4.
33. DeBaun MR, Niemitz EL, Feinberg AP. Association of in vitro fertilization with Beckwith–Wiedemann syndrome and epigenetic alterations of L1T1 and H19. Am J Hum Genet 2003;72:156–60.
34. Niemitz EL, Feinberg AP. Epigenetics and assisted reproductive technology: a call for investigation. Am J Hum Genet 2004;74:599–609.

ACOG

Committee on Genetics

# Committee Opinion

Number 325, December 2005

This document reflects emerging clinical and scientific advances as of the date issued and is subject to change. The information should not be construed as dictating an exclusive course of treatment or procedure to be followed.



ISSN 1074-861X

**The American College of Obstetricians and Gynecologists**
409 12th Street, SW
PO Box 96920
Washington, DC 20090-6920

12345/98765

Update on carrier screening for cystic fibrosis. ACOG Committee Opinion No. 325. American College of Obstetricians and Gynecologists. Obstet Gynecol 2005;106:1465–8.

## Update on Carrier Screening for Cystic Fibrosis

*ABSTRACT: In 2001, the American College of Obstetricians and Gynecologists and the American College of Medical Genetics introduced guidelines for prenatal and preconception carrier screening for cystic fibrosis. The American College of Obstetricians and Gynecologists has updated current guidelines for cystic fibrosis screening practices among obstetrician–gynecologists.*

Prenatal and preconception carrier screening for cystic fibrosis was introduced into routine obstetric practice in 2001. *Preconception and Prenatal Carrier Screening for Cystic Fibrosis: Clinical and Laboratory Guidelines* (1), developed by the American College of Obstetricians and Gynecologists (ACOG) and the American College of Medical Genetics (ACMG), was sent to all ACOG members in practice. According to a survey of ACOG members 2 years later, most obstetricians are offering cystic fibrosis carrier screening to their pregnant patients (2). As recommended in the guidelines, most obstetricians ask their patients if there is a family history of cystic fibrosis and provide the pregnant patients with information on cystic fibrosis. In contrast, significantly fewer obstetrician–gynecologists offer nonpregnant patients cystic fibrosis carrier screening unless a patient requests the information or has a family history. After cystic fibrosis carrier screening was implemented, the ACMG convened a work group to review the prevalence of mutations in the general population and to evaluate the cystic fibrosis carrier screening program in the United States. The purpose of this document is to provide an update on cystic fibrosis carrier screening.

The goal of cystic fibrosis carrier screening is to identify couples at risk for having a child with classic cystic fibrosis. The ACOG/ACMG guidelines recommended that cystic fibrosis carrier screening be offered to Caucasian couples (including Ashkenazi Jews) who are planning a pregnancy or seeking prenatal care and be made available to all patients. This recommendation took into account differences in cystic fibrosis prevalence and test sensitivity. Cystic fibrosis is more common (ie, has higher carrier rate) in Caucasians (including Ashkenazi Jews) than in other populations, and the screening test detects a higher percentage of carriers in this population than in other populations (Table 1). In practice, two thirds of obstetricians offer cystic fibrosis carrier screening to all pregnant patients rather than using the selective criteria. Because it is becoming increasingly difficult to assign a single ethnicity, it is reasonable to offer cystic fibrosis carrier screening to all pregnant patients, provided that women are aware of their carrier risk and of the test limitations. The sensitivity of the screening test and the carrier risk vary among different ethnic groups. The results often are reported with a table of the residual carrier risk for each ethnic group, and it is the physician's responsibility to interpret the results based on the patient's ethnicity. A negative carrier screening test result can reduce but not eliminate the risk of being a cystic fibrosis carrier.

Generally, it is more cost-effective and practical to perform initial carrier screening for the patient. If the patient is a cystic fibrosis carrier then her partner should be tested. Concurrent screening of the patient and her partner is preferred if there are time constraints for decisions regarding prenatal diagnostic testing or termination of the affected pregnancy. If a woman is a carrier of a cystic fibrosis mutation and her partner is unavailable for testing, genetic counseling to review the risk of having an affected child and prenatal testing options and limitations in this situation may be helpful.

Preconception carrier screening allows carrier couples to consider the fullest range of reproductive options. A significant proportion of obstetrician–gynecologists are not offering screening to their nonpregnant patients unless there is a family history or the patient specifically requests screening. Knowledge of the risk for having an affected child may influence a carrier couple's decision to conceive, to use donor gametes, and to consider preimplantation or prenatal genetic testing.

The initial guidelines recommended that laboratories screen a panel of 25 pan-ethnic mutations that were present in at least 0.1% of patients with cystic fibrosis. Based on a review of the first 2 years of laboratory data from screening the general population, the ACMG Cystic Fibrosis Carrier Screening Work Group recommended that two mutations (I148T and 1078delT) be removed from the panel because they do not cause classic cystic fibrosis or occur less frequently than 0.1%. The work group did not recommend additions to the panel at this time because they would not substantially increase the test sensitivity but acknowledged that some laboratories may choose to add mutations to the standard panel to increase the sensitivity of testing for specific ethnic groups.

Cystic fibrosis screening may identify a 5T/7T/9T variant, located in a noncoding region of the gene for cystic fibrosis, the cystic fibrosis transmembrane regulator (CFTR) gene. During the first 2 years of carrier testing, some laboratories reported this variant indiscriminately, resulting in some confusion in the interpretation of test results. Testing for the variant as a reflex test is appropriate only when the R117H mutation is detected. Classic cystic fibrosis occurs when 5T is on the same chromosome with R117H and there is a CFTR mutation of the other chromosome. Other combinations of the 5T variant with a CFTR mutation on the opposite chromosome are not known to have a clinical significance in females. Males with this genotype are at increased risk for congenital bilateral absence of the vas deferens and atypical cystic fibrosis. Couples with the R117H mutation will benefit from genetic counseling.

Complete analysis of the CFTR gene by DNA sequencing is not appropriate for routine carrier screening. This type of testing generally is reserved for patients with cystic fibrosis, a family history of

**Table 1**. Cystic Fibrosis Detection and Carrier Rates Before and After Testing

| Racial or Ethnic Group | Detection Rate | Carrier Rate Before Testing | Carrier Risk After Negative Test Result |
|---|---|---|---|
| Ashkenazi Jewish | 94% | 1/24 | Approximately 1/400 |
| Non-Hispanic Caucasian | 88% | 1/25 | Approximately 1/208 |
| Hispanic American | 72% | 1/46 | Approximately 1/164 |
| African American | 65% | 1/65 | Approximately 1/186 |
| Asian American | 49% | 1/94 | Approximately 1/184 |

cystic fibrosis, infertile males with congenital bilateral absence of the vas deferens, or a positive newborn screening test result when mutation testing using an expanded panel of mutations has a negative result.

The decision to have cystic fibrosis carrier screening should be by informed choice. Patients should receive information about cystic fibrosis and its inheritance pattern. Educational brochures are available from ACOG (sales.acog.org) and a brief description is included in this document. It is important for patients and their partners to recognize the sensitivity and limitations of testing as well as their reproductive options. Molecular testing does not identify all carriers. The ability to identify carriers differs based on ethnic origin, ranging from less than 50% in Asian Americans to up to 94% in the Ashkenazi Jewish population (Table 1). Therefore, a negative carrier screening test result will reduce but not eliminate the risk of being a cystic fibrosis carrier. When both parents are carriers of CFTR mutations that cause the disease, prenatal diagnosis by chorionic villus sampling or amniocentesis can be accomplished using DNA analysis.

Based on the preceding information, the Committee on Genetics provides the following recommendations:

1. Information about cystic fibrosis screening should be made available to all couples. It is reasonable to offer cystic fibrosis carrier screening to all couples regardless of race or ethnicity as an alternative to selective screening.
2. Cystic fibrosis carrier screening should be offered before conception or early in pregnancy when both partners are of Caucasian, European, or Ashkenazi Jewish ethnicity. Patients may elect to use either sequential or concurrent carrier screening; the latter option may be preferred if there are time constraints for decisions regarding prenatal diagnostic testing or termination of the affected pregnancy.
3. For individuals with a family history of cystic fibrosis, medical records indicating the CFTR mutation in the affected family member should be obtained whenever possible. If the mutation has not been identified, screening with an expanded panel of mutations or, in some cases, complete analysis of the CFTR gene by sequencing may be indicated. Genetic counseling in this situation usually is beneficial.
4. Individuals who have a reproductive partner with cystic fibrosis or congenital bilateral absence of the vas deferens may benefit from screening with an expanded panel of mutations or, in some cases, a complete analysis of the CFTR gene by sequencing.
5. When both partners are cystic fibrosis carriers, genetic counseling is recommended to review prenatal testing and reproductive options. Prenatal diagnosis by chorionic villus sampling or amniocentesis, using DNA-based testing of the fetal cells, should be offered. If the partner is unavailable for testing, genetic counseling may be helpful.
6. Cystic fibrosis carrier screening may identify individuals with two cystic fibrosis mutations who have not previously received a diagnosis of cystic fibrosis. These individuals may have a milder form of cystic fibrosis and should be referred to a specialist in cystic fibrosis for further evaluation. Genetic counseling also is beneficial.

## Information on Cystic Fibrosis to Share With Your Patients

Cystic fibrosis is a progressive, multisystem disease that primarily affects the pulmonary, pancreatic, gastrointestinal, biliary, and reproductive systems. Individuals with cystic fibrosis typically present with cough, wheezing, failure to thrive, loose stools, abdominal pain, and, in males, infertility secondary to congenital bilateral absence of the vas deferens. Treatment involves pancreatic enzymes, proper nutrition, and respiratory therapy with aggressive treatment of infection. The current median survival is approximately 30 years, and the cause of death usually is respiratory failure. Approximately 15% of individuals with cystic fibrosis are pancreatic sufficient and have a milder disease course and a median survival of 56 years.

Cystic fibrosis is an autosomal recessive genetic condition. Therefore, when a patient and her partner are both carriers of a mutation in the cystic fibrosis gene, they have a one-in-four chance of having a child with cystic fibrosis. More than 1,300 mutations have been identified in the gene for cystic fibrosis, but screening for 23 common mutations is available and can reduce a couple's risk for having a child with cystic fibrosis. The risk of being a carrier depends on an individual's ethnicity and family history.

## References


1. American College of Obstetricians and Gynecologists, American College of Medical Genetics. Preconception and prenatal carrier screening for cystic fibrosis: clinical and laboratory guidelines. Washington, DC: ACOG; Bethesda (MD): ACMG; 2001.
2. Morgan MA, Driscoll DA, Mennuti MT, Schulkin J. Practice patterns of obstetrician–gynecologists regarding preconception and prenatal screening for cystic fibrosis. Genet Med 2004;6:450–5.


## Bibliography


Cystic fibrosis mutation database. Available at: http://www.genet. sickkids.on.ca/cftr/. Retrieved March 18, 2005.

Grosse SD, Boyle CA, Botkin JR, Comeau AM, Kharrazi M, Rosenfeld M, et al. Newborn screening for cystic fibrosis: evaluation of benefits and risks and recommendations for state newborn screening programs. MMWR Recomm Rep 2004; 53(RR-13):1–36.

Morgan MA, Driscoll DA, Zinberg S, Schulkin J, Mennuti MT. Impact of self-reported familiarity with guidelines for cystic fibrosis carrier screening. Obstet Gynecol 2005;105:1355–61.

Muller F, Simon-Bouy B, Girodon E, Monnier N, Malinge MC, Serre JL. Predicting the risk of cystic fibrosis with abnormal ultrasound signs of fetal bowel: results of a French molecular collaborative study based on 641 prospective cases. French Collaborative Group. Am J Med Genet 2002;110:109–15.

Watson MS, Cutting GR, Desnick RJ, Driscoll DA, Klinger K, Mennuti M, et al. Cystic fibrosis population carrier screening: 2004 revision of American College of Medical Genetics mutation panel [published errata appear in Genet Med 2004;6:548; Genet Med 2005;7:286]. Genet Med 2004;6:387–91.

# ACOG Committee Opinion

Committee on Genetics

Number 338, June 2006 (Replaces No. 161, October 1995)

# Screening for Fragile X Syndrome



ISSN 1074-861X

**The American College of Obstetricians and Gynecologists**
409 12th Street, SW
PO Box 96920
Washington, DC 20090-6920

12345/09876

Screening for fragile X syndrome. ACOG Committee Opinion No. 338. American College of Obstetricians and Gynecologists. Obstet Gynecol 2006;107:1483–5.

*ABSTRACT: Fragile X syndrome is the most common inherited form of mental retardation, affecting approximately 1 in 4,000 males and 1 in 8,000 females. DNA-based molecular analysis is the preferred method of diagnosis for fragile X syndrome and its premutations. Prenatal testing for fragile X syndrome should be offered to known carriers of the premutation or mutation. Testing for fragile X syndrome should be considered for any child with developmental delay of uncertain etiology, autism, or autistic behavior or for any individual with mental retardation of uncertain etiology. Women with ovarian failure or an elevated follicle-stimulating hormone level before 40 years of age without a known cause should be screened to determine whether they have the fragile X premutation.*

Fragile X syndrome is the most common inherited form of mental retardation, affecting approximately 1 in 4,000 males and 1 in 8,000 females from a variety of ethnic backgrounds. Mental retardation ranges from borderline to severe, although most patients have moderate degrees of mental retardation. Other associated phenotypic abnormalities include autistic behaviors, macroorchidism in adult males, characteristic narrow face with a large jaw, and speech and language problems. The abnormal facial features are subtle and become more noticeable with age, making phenotypic diagnosis difficult, especially in the newborn. Affected females may have a more subtle phenotype and it is sometimes hard to establish the diagnosis.

Fragile X syndrome is transmitted in a classic X-linked recessive fashion. However, the molecular genetics of the syndrome are complex. The disorder is caused by expansion of a repeated trinucleotide segment of DNA (cytosine–guanine–guanine) that leads to altered transcription of the fragile X mental retardation 1 *(FMR1)* gene. The number of repeats varies among individuals and has been classified into four groups depending on repeat size: unaffected, intermediate, premutation, and full mutation (see Table 1). A person with 61–200 repeats usually is phenotypically normal and is said to have a premutation. When more than 200 repeats are present, an individual has a full mutation that results in the full expression of fragile X syndrome in males and variable expression in females secondary to X inactivation. This condition occurs because the large number of repeats causes the *FMR1* gene to become methylated and inactivated in these patients. The number of repeats and the status of gene methylation are

**Table 1.** Mutation in the Fragile X Mental Retardation 1 Gene

| Status of Individual | Number of Triplet Repeats (Cytosine–Guanine–Guanine) |
|---|---|
| Unaffected | Less than 40 |
| Intermediate (also called "grey zone") | 41–60 |
| Premutation | 61–200 |
| Full mutation | More than 200 |

determined by use of DNA-based molecular tests (eg, Southern blot analysis and polymerase chain reaction). Chorionic villus sampling (CVS), although reliable for determinating the number of triplet repeats, may not be reliable for diagnosis because of gestational age differences in ultimate methylation patterns in the trophoblast and may not adequately determine the methylation status of the *FMR1* gene. DNA methylation is a process that controls tissue specific gene expression. Methylation "turns off" the regulatory region of a gene, thereby preventing DNA transcription. Rarely, the size of the triplet repeat and the methylation status do not correlate, making prediction of the clinical phenotype difficult.

Transmission of a disease-producing mutation to a fetus depends on the sex of the parent and the number of cytosine–guanine–guanine repeats present in the parental gene. Parents at risk for transmission of the disease are those who have the premutation or the full DNA mutation. When a female carries the premutation and the length of the repeat exceeds 90, premutation genes are much more likely to expand and result in the birth of an affected child. Women with an intermediate number of triplet repeats (41–60) rarely transmit a full mutation to their offspring, although there may be some continued expansion through the generations. Genetic counseling for intermediate results may be useful. Males may transmit the unexpanded premutation gene to their children, but expansion to a full mutation is extremely rare in the offspring of a male having the premutation gene. Typically, the children of a male premutation carrier receive the premutation unchanged; in children of female carriers, however, the premutation may expand during meiosis. Empirically determined risks are available for the purposes of genetic counseling.

Males and, to a lesser extent, females carrying a premutation are at increased risk for a late-onset neurodegenerative disorder characterized by tremor and ataxia. However, additional research is needed to define the relative risk. In addition, women carrying a premutation are at increased risk (20–30%) for premature ovarian failure. If a woman has ovarian failure or an elevated follicle-stimulating hormone level before the age 40 years without a known cause, fragile X carrier screening should be considered to determine whether she has a premutation. Recent studies also have demonstrated an increased frequency of autism or autisticlike behavior in children with a premutation.

The Committee on Genetics recommendations regarding testing for fragile X syndrome are listed as follows:

1. DNA-based molecular analysis (eg, Southern blot analysis and polymerase chain reaction) is the preferred method of diagnosis for fragile X syndrome and its premutations. In rare cases where there is discordancy between the triplet repeat number and the methylation status, the patient should be referred to a genetic specialist.
2. Patients with a family history of mental retardation or a history of fragile X mental retardation should receive genetic counseling and should be offered genetic testing to assess their risk for having an affected child.
3. Prenatal testing for fragile X syndrome by amniocentesis or CVS should be offered to known carriers of the fragile X premutation or mutation. Although it is reliable for determining the number of triplet repeats, CVS may not adequately determine the methylation status of the *FMR1* gene.
4. Testing for fragile X syndrome should be considered in any child with developmental delay of uncertain etiology, autism, or autisticlike behavior or any individual with mental retardation of uncertain etiology.
5. If a woman has ovarian failure or an elevated follicle-stimulating hormone level before the age 40 years without a known cause, fragile X carrier screening should be considered to determine whether she has a premutation.

## Bibliography

Warren ST, Sherman SL. The fragile x syndrome. In: Scriver CR, Beaudet AL, Sly WS, Valle D, editors. The metabolic and molecular bases of inherited disease. 8th ed. New York (NY): McGraw-Hill; 2001. p. 1257–89.

Hagerman RJ, Hagerman PJ, editors. Fragile X syndrome: diagnosis, treatment, and research. 3rd ed. Baltimore (MD): Johns Hopkins University Press; 2002.

Hagerman PJ, Hagerman RJ. The fragile-X premutation: a maturing perspective [published erratum appears in Am J Hum genet 2004;75:352]. Am J Hum Genet 2004;74:805–16.

Sherman S, Pletcher BA, Driscoll DA. Fragile X syndrome: diagnostic and carrier testing. Genet Med 2005;78:584–7.

ACOG
TECHNOLOGY ASSESSMENT
IN OBSTETRICS AND GYNECOLOGY

NUMBER 1, JULY 2002

# Genetics and Molecular Diagnostic Testing

This Technology Assessment was developed by the ACOG Committee on Genetics with the assistance of Deborah A. Driscoll, MD, FACOG; Katherine D. Wenstrom, MD, FACOG, and John Williams III, MD, FACOG. This document reflects emerging clinical and scientific advances as of the date issued and is subject to change. The information should not be construed as dictating an exclusive course of treatment or procedure to be followed. Variations in practice may be warranted based on the needs of the individual patient, resources, and limitations unique to the institution or type of practice.

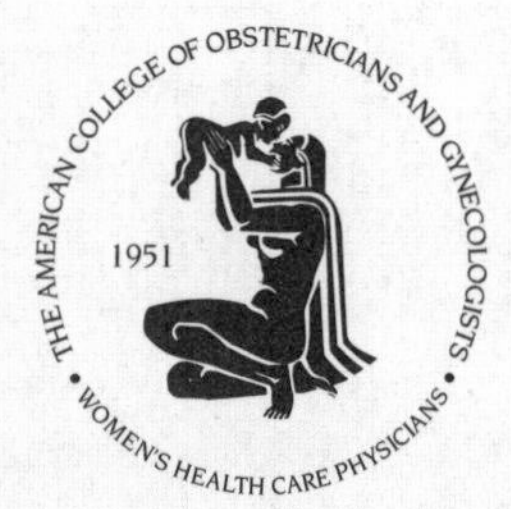


THE AMERICAN COLLEGE
OF OBSTETRICIANS
AND GYNECOLOGISTS
WOMEN'S HEALTH CARE PHYSICIANS

Knowledge of human genetics has increased dramatically in the past few decades. The genetic basis of disease and the response to therapy is rapidly being elucidated and may soon become a part of routine medical practice. A draft of the human genome was published in 2001 (1). This project produced a detailed map of the genes, markers, and other landmarks along each chromosome. It is hoped that these maps will facilitate the development of genetic screening and diagnostic tests, as well as novel therapies, technologies, and strategies for prevention. Obstetricians and gynecologists, who deal with inheritance and the genetic transmission of traits and disease on a daily basis, will be called on to incorporate genetics and recent developments in genetic testing into their medical practice. This document reviews the basics of genetic transmission and genetic technologies in current use. (See the "Glossary" for definitions of terms for genetics and molecular diagnostic testing.)

## ORGANIZATION OF THE GENOME

There are 2 meters of DNA, including approximately 30,000 genes, in each human nucleus. The DNA is wrapped very compactly around basic proteins called histones to form nucleosomes, which are then organized into solenoid structures and looped around a nonhistone protein scaffold to form chromatin. As the cell enters prophase, the chromatin begins to condense until it assumes the familiar structure of metaphase chromosomes. Each chromosome is composed of densely packed nontranscribed DNA near the centromeres, called heterochromatin, and less densely packed transcribed DNA called euchromatin.

Seventy-five percent of the genome is unique, single copy DNA, and the remainder consists of various classes of repetitive DNA. Surprisingly, virtually all of the repetitive DNA and a large portion of the single copy DNA have no apparent or recognized function. Less than 10% of the genome encodes genes. The single copy DNA contains all of the genes necessary to make and sustain the organism, while the repetitive DNA contains unique markers that identify each individual and can be used to study genetic variation between individuals.

## Genes

A gene is a unique series of four purine and pyrimidine bases that ultimately specifies an amino acid sequence for a polypeptide chain of a protein. The basic gene contains one or more exons, which are DNA sequences that will be transcribed into messenger RNA (mRNA), and introns (or intervening sequences), which are noncoding or nontranscribed regions that separate exons (Fig. 1). The regions upstream and downstream to the exons are called the 5′ untranslated region and the 3′ untranslated region, respectively. These regions are transcribed, but not translated (as the name implies), and they are important in gene regulation.

The processes of transcription and translation are more complex than previously recognized. The transcription of DNA to mRNA requires transcription factors. Enhancers and silencer DNA sequences located upstream or downstream of a gene can increase and decrease transcriptional activity of the gene, respectively. Transcription is initiated when the enzyme RNA polymerase II binds to the promoter, a DNA sequence upstream of a gene. RNA polymerase moves along a single strand of DNA and forms a complementary strand of mRNA. Once the mRNA is formed, a cap or chemically modified guanine nucleotide is added to the 5′ end to prevent the mRNA from being degraded, and a chain of 100–200 adenine bases (poly-A tail) is added to the 3′ end. Before the mRNA leaves the nucleus, the introns are excised by a process called gene splicing. The mature mRNA then moves to the ribosomes for translation. The protein product usually is created in a precursor form, and undergoes cleavage into a smaller active protein or combines with other polypeptides to form a larger functional protein. The protein may be further modified in the Golgi apparatus of the cell by glycosylation. Some genes contain more than one promoter in different parts of the gene or have alternative splice sites, which allows the same gene to encode different protein products.

Gene expression also is controlled by methylation of the regulatory region, which prevents gene transcription and effectively turns the gene off.

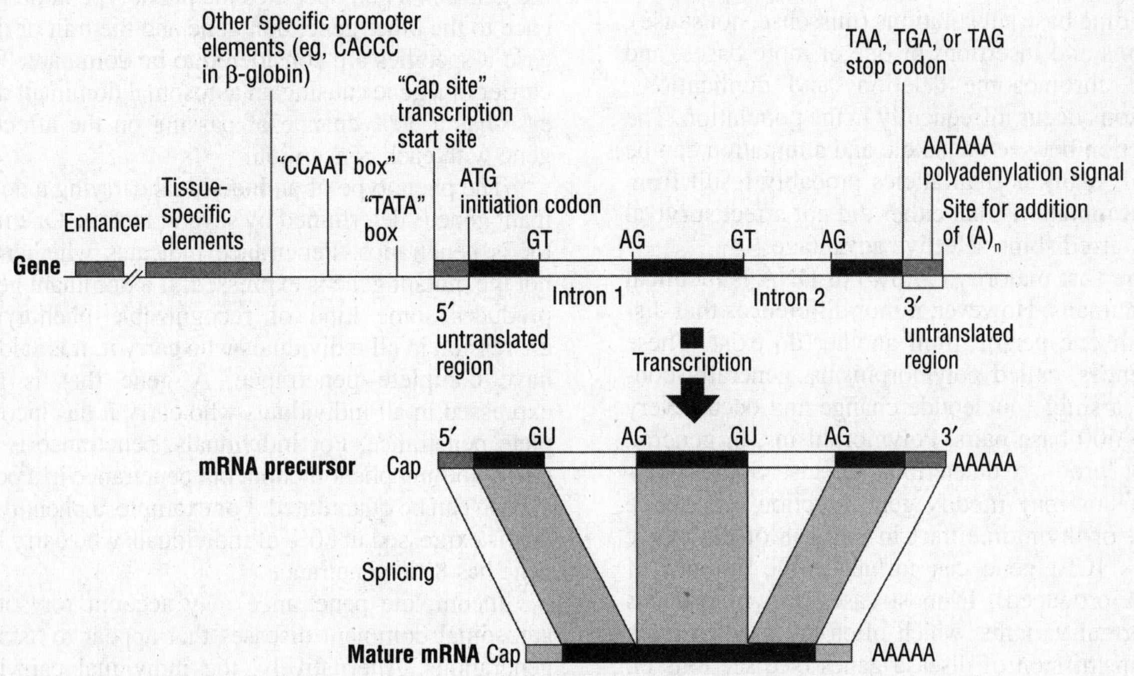


**Fig. 1.** Structure of a typical gene. In this example, the gene has three exons (solid dark regions) and two introns (white regions), a 5′ untranslated region and 3′ untranslated region. The intron splice donor site (GT) and the splice acceptor site (AG) identify where introns are removed in mRNA production. The upstream region (5′) contains an enhancer, tissue specific elements, and promoter elements, such as the CCAAT box and TATA box, which regulate expression. Typical locations for the translation initiation site (ATG), translation stop codons (TAA, TAG, TGA), and the polyadenylation signal (AATAAA) are shown. (Gelehrter TD, Ginsburg D, Collins FS. Principles of medical genetics. 2nd ed. Baltimore: Williams and Wilkins, 1997)

Methylation serves the important function of controlling tissue-specific gene activation. The expression of genes that are not essential for each specific tissue type is prevented by methylation, while necessary genes remain active. For example, the globin genes are methylated in all nonerythroid tissues but are not methylated in reticulocytes, ensuring that only red blood cells produce hemoglobin. Methylation also allows the temporal control of gene expression. Parental alleles may demonstrate different patterns of methylation that are not tissue specific (see section on "Imprinting").

Many genes exist in several alternate forms called alleles. These are normal variants within the population. For example, there are several normal alleles for the genes that determine blood type and Rh status. In contrast, a mutation is an alteration in the DNA sequence that results in a change in protein structure or function, which may have adverse effects. Mutations can occur in the germline (eg, gametes) and can be transmitted from one generation to the next, or can occur only in the somatic cells and can be associated with cancer. There are many types of mutations, such as single purine or pyrimidine base substitutions (missense, nonsense), deletions and insertions of one or more bases, and visible chromosome deletions and duplications. Mutations occur infrequently in the population. The distinction between an allele and a mutation can be blurred; many normal alleles probably result from ancient mutations that either did not affect survival or conferred some selective advantage.

The vast majority (99.8%) of DNA is identical in all humans. However, minor differences that distinguish one person from another do exist. These differences, called polymorphisms, generally consist of a single nucleotide change and occur every 200 to 500 base pairs. Polymorphisms, in general, do not produce deleterious effects. Some polymorphisms may modify gene function (eg, splice variant or thymidine tract in intron 8 of the cystic fibrosis [CF] gene can influence the amount of mRNA produced). In most cases, polymorphisms are normal variants, which often are used to track the transmission of disease genes (see sections on "Restriction Fragment Length Polymorphism Analysis" and "Linkage Analysis").

When newly discovered genes are analyzed, it can be difficult to distinguish a normal allele from a polymorphism or a mutation. For example, more than 100 variations of the *BRCA1* gene, one of the major genes associated with familial breast and ovarian cancers, have been identified. It is not currently known whether all of these variations are actually mutations associated with disease, or if some could be polymorphisms or allelic variants. The ability to distinguish alleles from mutations is essential for molecular diagnosis and screening programs.

## Single Gene (Mendelian) Disorders

A mendelian trait or disease is determined by a single gene. Diseases caused solely by abnormalities in a single gene are relatively rare. The phenotype of many single gene disorders is influenced by modifying genes, or by the independent actions of a combination of additional genes, often with environmental influences.

### Autosomal Dominant

All genes come in pairs; one copy of the gene is present on each of a pair of chromosomes. The influence of each gene in determining the phenotype is described as either dominant or recessive. If one of the genes in a pair specifies the phenotype in preference to the other gene, that gene and the trait or disease it specifies are considered to be dominant. The carrier of a gene causing an autosomal dominant disease has a 50% chance of passing on the affected gene with each conception.

The phenotype of an individual carrying a dominant gene is determined by several factors. One factor is penetrance. Penetrance indicates whether or not the mutant gene is expressed. If a dominant gene produces some kind of recognizable phenotypic expression in all individuals who carry it, it is said to have complete penetrance. A gene that is not expressed in all individuals who carry it has incomplete penetrance. For individuals, penetrance is an all-or-nothing phenomenon, but penetrance in a population can be quantitated. For example, a phenotype that is expressed in 80% of individuals who carry the gene has 80% penetrance.

Incomplete penetrance may account for some autosomal dominant diseases that appear to "skip" generations. Alternatively, the individual carrying the dominant gene may have very mild phenotypic abnormalities that have been overlooked, the disease may have a late onset, the gene carrier is either too young or died before the gene's effects were manifest, or phenotypic expression of the dominant gene could require the presence of a second mutated gene or certain epigenetic phenomena. An example of such a disease is retinoblastoma.

The degree to which a penetrant gene is expressed (the range of phenotypic features) is called expressivity. If all individuals carrying the affected gene do not have identical phenotypes, the gene has variable expressivity. Such a gene can produce a range of phenotypic features from mild to severe. An example of a disease with variable expressivity is neurofibromatosis.

### Autosomal Recessive

Autosomal recessive traits or diseases occur only when both copies of the gene in question are the same. Individuals who have only one abnormal gene (heterozygotes or carriers) may have some phenotypic alteration recognized at the biochemical or cellular level, but only individuals who have two copies of the affected gene (homozygotes) have the disease. Many enzyme deficiency diseases are autosomal recessive. The enzyme level in the carrier of an abnormal recessive gene will be approximately 50% of normal, but because enzymes are made in great excess, this reduction usually is not enough to cause disease. However, the reduced enzyme level can be used for genetic screening purposes. For example, to identify carriers of Tay–Sachs disease, hexosaminidase A levels are measured. Carriers of recessive conditions that do not produce any physical or quantitative biochemical change in the heterozygote can be identified only by molecular methods (eg, Canavan disease).

The carrier of a gene causing an autosomal recessive disease usually is recognized after the birth of an affected child, after the diagnosis of an affected family member, or as the result of a genetic screening program. A couple whose child has an autosomal recessive disease has a 25% recurrence risk with each conception. The likelihood that a normal sibling of an affected child is a carrier of the gene is 2 out of 3 (one fourth of all offspring will be homozygous normal, two fourths will be heterozygote carriers, and one fourth will be homozygous abnormal; thus, 3 of 4 children will be phenotypically normal and 2 of these 3 will be carriers). Carrier children will not have affected children unless their partners are gene carriers or are affected. Because genes leading to rare autosomal recessive conditions have a low prevalence in the general population, the chance that the partner will be a gene carrier is low unless the couple is related (consanguineous). When individuals inherit two different mutated alleles that result in abnormal phenotypes, they are called compound heterozygotes. For example, an individual who inherits a ΔF508 and W1282X mutation in the CF gene has CF without expressing two identical alleles.

### Co-Dominant

If the genes in a gene pair are different from each other, but both are expressed in the phenotype, they are considered to be co-dominant. For example, the genes responsible for the hemoglobinopathies are co-dominant. The individual with one hemoglobin gene directing the production of sickle hemoglobin, and the other directing the production of hemoglobin C, will produce both S and C hemoglobins. Likewise, the genes that determine blood type are co-dominant, because an individual is capable of expressing both A and B red cell antigens simultaneously.

### X-Linked

X-linked diseases usually are recessive, and primarily affect men because men have only one copy of the X chromosome. Examples of X-linked recessive disorders are color blindness, hemophilia A (classical hemophilia or factor VIII deficiency), and Duchenne muscular dystrophy. Women carrying an X-linked recessive gene generally are unaffected unless unfavorable lyonization (the inactivation of one X chromosome in every cell) results in the X chromosome carrying the abnormal gene being active in the majority of cells.

When a woman carries a gene causing an X-linked recessive condition, there is a 50% chance of passing on the gene with each conception; each of her sons has a 50% chance of being affected and each of her daughters has a 50% chance of being a carrier. When a man has an X-linked disease, all of his sons will be unaffected (because they receive the Y chromosome from their father) and all of his daughters will be carriers (because they receive the affected X chromosome from their father). X-linked dominant disorders have been described, and affect females predominantly because they tend to be lethal in male offspring. An example of this is X-linked hypophosphatemia.

## Duplication and Deletion Syndromes

A deletion refers to a region of a chromosome that is missing, while a duplication is the presence of an extra copy of a region of a chromosome. The carrier of a deletion is effectively monosomic for the genes in the missing segment, while the carrier of a duplication is trisomic for the duplicated genes. Deletions and duplications usually are described by their location (eg, duplication 4p) or by the two chromosomal break points defining the missing or extra segment (4p15.2→16.1). If the deletion is a common one, it may be defined by an eponym (eg, del 1q32-q41 also is called Van der Woude's syndrome). Terminal deletions and duplications are caused simply by chromosome breakage with loss or gain of the terminal chromosome segment. Interstitial deletions and duplications occur during prophase of meiosis when homologous chromosomes align and cross-overs occur. If the chromosomes are misaligned during this process, the unaligned loop containing the mismatched segment could be deleted. Alternatively, misalignment could lead to unequal crossing over, so that one chromosome has a deletion and the other a duplication. A similar problem with meiosis can produce deletions and duplications in the offspring of individuals who are carriers of chromosome inversions. Deletions and duplications also occur as a result of malsegregation during meiosis in carriers of balanced translocations.

When a deletion or duplication is identified in a fetus or child, the parents should be tested to see if it arose de novo in their offspring or if either parent is a carrier or has a translocation. Deletions and duplications may be identified by routine or high resolution cytogenetic analysis. Microdeletions and duplications, which are too small to be detected by traditional cytogenetic techniques, can now be recognized with molecular techniques, such as fluorescence in situ hybridization (FISH) (see section on "Fluorescence In Situ Hybridization").

Chromosome deletions and duplications can result in a constellation of phenotypic abnormalities with widely varying pathophysiology or pathogenesis because the genes that are in close proximity to one another on a chromosome may have completely unrelated functions and control independent traits. Deletion syndromes usually cause more serious phenotypic and functional abnormalities than duplication syndromes. Monosomy generally has more severe consequences than trisomy.

Syndromes caused by a microdeletion involving genes physically located together in a chromosome segment are called contiguous gene deletion syndromes, and their study has yielded a great deal of information about gene location and function. Although deletions can occur in any area of any chromosome, some deletions occur more frequently than would be expected by chance alone. Several common chromosome deletion syndromes have been recognized, such as DiGeorge syndrome, which most often results from a microdeletion of the long arm of chromosome 22 (del 22q11.2). Affected individuals typically have conotruncal cardiac defects; thymus and parathyroid gland hypoplasia or aplasia; atypical facies, including short palpebral fissures, micrognathia with a short philtrum, and ear anomalies; and learning and speech difficulties. Deletions of the terminal portions of the short arms of chromosomes 4 (4 p- or Wolf-Hirschhorn syndrome) and 5 (5 p- or cri du chat syndrome) also occur more frequently than would be expected by chance alone.

## NONMENDELIAN PATTERNS OF INHERITANCE

### Hereditary Unstable DNA

Mendel's first law states that genes are passed unchanged from parent to progeny. Barring the occurrence of new mutations, this law still applies to many genes or traits. However, it is now known that certain genes are inherently unstable, and their size and, consequently, their function may be altered as they are transmitted from parent to child. These genes generally contain a region of triplet repeats, such as $(CGG)_n$. The number of triplet repeats in gametes can increase as meiosis is completed prior to fertilization. If the number of triplet repeats reaches a critical level, the gene containing the triplets becomes methylated and is turned off, resulting in phenotypic abnormalities. Some triplet regions expand only during female meiosis, while others can expand when transmitted by either parent. Some triplet regions have been passed from parent to child for many generations without expansion, for unknown reasons.

An example of a genetic disease caused by such triplet repeats is fragile X syndrome. Fragile X syndrome is the most common form of all familial mental retardation, accounting for 4–8% of all individuals with mental retardation in all ethnic and racial groups. Affected individuals have mild to severe mental retardation, autistic behavior, attention deficit hyperactivity disorder, speech and language problems, a narrow face with a large jaw, long prominent ears, and macro-orchidism (in postpubertal males). Some children also have seizures. The incidence of the full fragile X syndrome generally is quoted as 1 per 1,500 males and 1 per 2,500 females.

Until recently, fragile X syndrome was diagnosed using a cytogenetic technique. Cells were cultured in a folate deficient medium, which resulted in fragile sites identified cytogenetically as nonstaining gaps or constrictions on the long arm of the X chromosome (Xq27-28). This technique was unreliable for carrier testing, and less than half the cells from affected males manifested the fragile site. Fortunately, the fragile X gene can now be directly examined using molecular techniques (see section on "Trinucleotide Repeat Analysis").

The fragile X mutation is now known to be a region of unstable DNA in the X chromosome. The region is best described as a series of CGG (cytosine–guanine–guanine) repeats at Xq27. The number of repeats and the degree of methylation determines whether or not an individual is affected. Individuals carrying 2–49 repeats are phenotypically normal. Individuals carrying 50–199 repeats are phenotypically normal but have a premutation, which can expand as it is passed on to their offspring, who would then be affected. Those with more than 200 repeats have the full mutation and, if methylation occurs, usually are affected. However, not all individuals carrying the full mutation are mentally retarded. Phenotypic variability results from lyonization (in females) and mosaicism for the size of the expansion, the degree of methylation, or both during mitosis in the zygote. Therefore, the phenotype cannot be predicted by analysis of either the parental gene or fetal cells.

The number of repeats usually remains stable when the gene is transmitted by a male. However, when the gene passes through female meiosis, it can expand. The risk of expansion generally correlates with the number of repeats in the premutation. Premutations with 100 or more repeats expand on transmission 100% of the time. The risk of expansion of mutations with 50–99 repeats increases proportionally with expansion size. If a female carries a premutation, which then increases in size as she transmits it to her offspring, it is possible for her to have a child with fragile X syndrome even though she is unaffected and has no family history of mental retardation.

The number of CGG repeats and the methylation status of the gene can be determined using restriction endonuclease digestion and Southern blot analysis (see section on "Trinucleotide Repeat Analysis"). It is now apparent that triplet repeat expansion is responsible for a number of primarily neurologic diseases, such as myotonic dystrophy, Huntington's chorea, and Friedreich's ataxia. The expansion of triplet repeats is an important mechanism of genetic disease, and is likely to play an important part in diseases for which preconceptional counseling and prenatal diagnosis may be considered.

## Imprinting

Another tenet of mendelian genetics is that gene function is not influenced by the sex of the parent transmitting the gene. In contrast to this rule, it is now apparent that the function of certain genes is altered by the sex of the parent from whom they were inherited, by a process known as "imprinting." Imprinting is a mechanism for epigenetic control of gene expression; that is, it changes the phenotype without permanently altering the genotype. An imprinted gene is inherited in an inactivated (transcriptionally silent) state, as the result of methylation of the promoter region. The extent of the imprinting, and thus the degree of inactivation, is determined by the sex of the transmitting parent.

When a gene is inherited in an imprinted or inactivated state, gene function is necessarily directed entirely by the active co-gene inherited from the other parent. It appears that imprinting exerts an effect in part by controlling the dosage of specific genes. Certain important genes appear to be monoallelic; that is, under normal circumstances only one member of the gene pair is functional (as opposed to most of the genes in the genome, which are biallelic). Only a fraction of human genes are imprinted. With imprinted genes, however, normal development occurs only when both a paternally derived and a maternally derived copy of the gene is present.

Imprinting was first recognized in association with genetic disease. Two very distinct genetic diseases with dissimilar phenotypes were discovered to be associated with the same chromosomal deletion, at 15q11-13. One of the diseases is Prader-Willi syndrome, which is characterized by obesity; hyperphagia; short stature; small hands, feet, and external genitalia; and mild mental retardation. The other disorder is Angelman's syndrome, which includes normal stature and weight, severe mental retardation, absent speech, seizure disorder, ataxia and jerky arm movements, and paroxysms of inappropriate laughter. Cytogenetic analysis has confirmed that both diseases are associated with the same deletion. If the maternally derived chromosome 15 is deleted, the result is Angelman's syndrome; if the paternally derived chromosome 15 is deleted, the result is Prader-Willi syndrome. Furthermore, a deletion is not required to produce the phenotype. If an individual has two normal intact copies of chromosome 15, but both came from the man (see section on "Uniparental Disomy"), the phenotype is consistent with Angelman's syndrome, because the maternal contribution is missing. Likewise, two complete copies of chromosome 15 of maternal origin produces Prader-Willi syndrome. Studies of the methylation patterns in individuals with the 15q11-13 deletion have shown that differential methylation (imprinting) is responsible for these observed phenotypic differences.

Several clinical examples from obstetrics illustrate the developmental importance of imprinting. Complete hydatidiform mole, which has an exclusively paternally derived diploid chromosome complement, is characterized by the abundant growth of placental tissue, but no fetal structures. Conversely, ovarian teratoma, which has a maternally derived diploid chromosome complement, is characterized by the growth of various fetal tissues, but no placental structures. Triploidy, characterized by a conceptus with three complete haploid chromosome complements (69 chromosomes), has two distinct phenotypes. If the extra haploid chromosome complement comes from the man, the embryo will be lost early in gestation and the placenta will be large and cystic, and severe early onset preeclampsia is likely to develop; if the extra chromosome complement comes from the woman, the fetus will be anomalous and the placenta will be extremely small. These observations confirm that both the paternally derived and maternally derived imprinted genes must be present for normal fetal development to occur.

## Uniparental Disomy

Uniparental disomy is a situation in which both members of one pair of chromosomes are inherited from one parent. Every gene on each of the chromosomes in question will have come from one parent. This usually occurs as the result of "correction" of a trisomic zygote by loss of a chromosome. When a conceptus with three copies of a chromosome loses one chromosome and retains the two chromosomes transmitted by the other parent, this results in heterodisomy (inheritance of two different homologous chromosomes from one parent). Less frequently, "rescue" of a monosomic conceptus with only one chromosome from one parent may occur by duplication of the chromosome during mitosis producing a cell with two copies of the same chromosome or uniparental isodisomy. For some chromosomes, uniparental disomy can result in functional or developmental fetal abnormalities, particularly if imprinting of the genes on that chromosome exists. Recent studies have demonstrated clinically significant uniparental disomy for chromosomes 6, 7, 11, 14, and 15. Uniparental disomy has no effect on the majority of chromosomes.

## Mitochondrial Inheritance

Every human cell contains hundreds of mitochondria. Because each mitochondrian contains its own genome and associated replication systems, each behaves as a virtually autonomous organism. The human oocyte contains approximately 100,000 mitochondria in the cytoplasm and mitochondrial DNAs. In contrast, a sperm contains only 100 mitochondria, which are selectively eliminated during fertilization. Therefore, mitochondria are inherited exclusively from the woman. Because mitochondria contain genetic information, mitochondrial inheritance allows the transmission of genes directly from the woman to her offspring without the possibility of recombination.

If a mutation occurs in the mitochondrial DNA, it may segregate into a daughter cell during cell division and thus be propagated. Over time, the percentage of mutant mitochondrial DNAs in different cell lines can drift towards either normal or pure mutant. If an oocyte containing largely mutant mitochondrial DNAs is fertilized, the offspring might have a mitochondrial disease. Several mitochondrial genetic diseases have been described. These include myoclonic epilepsy with ragged red fibers (MERRF), Leber's hereditary optic neuropathy, Kearns–Sayre syndrome, Leigh syndrome (ataxia, hypotonia, spasticity, and optic abnormalities), and pigmentary retinopathy.

## Germline Mosaicism

Some cytogenetically normal individuals have mosaicism (the presence of two or more populations of cells with different characteristics within one tissue or organ) confined to their gonads. Gonadal or germline mosaicism can arise as the result of a mitotic error occurring in the zygote; if the error occurs in cells destined to become the gonad, a portion of the germ cells may be abnormal. Because spermatogonia and oogonia continue to divide throughout fetal development, gonadal mosaicism also could occur as the result of a meiotic error in the dividing germ cells of the embryo. Germline mosaicism may explain the occurrence of a "new" (not previously occurring in a family) autosomal dominant mutation causing a disease, such as achondroplasia or osteogenesis imperfecta, or a new X-linked disease, such as Duchenne muscular dystrophy. It also explains the recurrence of such diseases in more than one offspring in a previously unaffected family. Because of the potential for germline mosaicism, the recurrence risk after the birth of a child with a disease caused by a new mutation is approximately 6%.

## Multifactorial and Polygenic Inheritance

Polygenic traits are determined by the combined effects of many genes; multifactorial traits are determined by multiple genes and environmental factors. It is now believed that the majority of inherited traits are multifactorial or polygenic. Traits determined by single genes and transmitted by strict mendelian inheritance, without the contribution of modifier genes, are probably relatively rare. Birth defects caused by multifactorial or polygenic inheritance are recognized by their tendency to recur in families, but not according to a mendelian inheritance pattern. Other characteristics that distinguish multifactorial traits from those with other inheritance patterns are listed in the box. When counseling couples regarding their offspring's risk of a familial multifactorial trait, it is important to consider the affected relative's degree of relatedness to the fetus, not the parents. The empiric recurrence risk for first-degree relatives (the fetus's parents or siblings) usually is quoted as 2–3%, but the risk declines exponentially with successively more distant relationships. Multifactorial traits generally fall into one of the three following categories: 1) continuously variable, 2) threshold, or 3) complex disorders.

Continuously variable traits have a normal distribution in the general population. By convention, abnormality is defined as a trait or measurement greater than two standard deviations above or below the population mean. These are typically measurable or quantitative traits like height or head size, and are believed to result from the individually small effects of many genes combined with environmental factors. Such traits tend to be less extreme in the offspring of affected individuals, because of the statistical principle of regression to the mean.

**Multifactorial Inheritance**

1. The disorder is familial, but there is no apparent pattern of inheritance.
2. The risk to first-degree relatives is the square root of the population risk.
3. The risk is sharply lower for second-degree relatives.
4. The recurrence risk is higher if more than one family member is affected.
5. The risk is higher if the defect is more severe (ie, the recurrence risk for bilateral cleft lip is higher than for unilateral cleft lip).
6. If the defect is more common in one sex, the recurrence risk is higher if the affected individual is of the less commonly affected sex.

Threshold traits do not appear until a certain threshold of liability is exceeded. Factors creating liability to the malformation are assumed to be continuously distributed in the population; only individuals who are at the extreme of this distribution exceed the threshold and have the trait or defect. The phenotypic abnormality is thus an all or none phenomenon. Individuals in high-risk families have enough abnormal genes or environmental influences that their liability is close to the threshold; for unknown reasons, some factor or factors increases the liability for certain family members still further and the threshold is crossed, resulting in the defect. Cleft lip and palate and pyloric stenosis are examples of threshold traits.

Certain threshold traits have a predilection for one gender, indicating that males and females have a different liability threshold. When a family includes an affected member who is the less frequently affected sex, this indicates that even more abnormal genes or environmental influences are present, and the affected individual (and possibly the family) has a more extreme position in the normal distribution of predisposing factors. The affected person's first-degree relatives (eg, their siblings) have a higher liability for that particular trait. For example, pyloric stenosis is more common in males. If a girl is born with pyloric stenosis, this indicates that she or her parents have even more abnormal genes or predisposing factors than usually are necessary to produce pyloric stenosis. After the birth of a girl with pyloric stenosis, the recurrence risk for her siblings or for her future children will be higher than expected; male siblings or offspring will have the highest liability because they are the most susceptible sex and they will inherit more than the usual number of predisposing genes.

The recurrence risk for threshold traits also is higher if the defect is severe, again indicating the presence of more abnormal genes or influences. For example, the recurrence risk after the birth of a child with bilateral cleft lip and palate is 8%, compared with only 4% after unilateral cleft lip without cleft palate.

Complex disorders of adult life are traits in which many genes determine an individual's susceptibility to environmental factors, with disease resulting from the most unfavorable combination of both. This category includes common diseases, such as heart disease and hypertension. These disorders usually are familial and behave as threshold traits but with a very strong environmental influence. The genetic mechanisms of many common adult diseases have not yet been elucidated, although several associated genes have been identified. In some cases, the identity of the associated gene provides a clue to the pathogenesis of the disease; in others, the related gene may simply be used as a disease marker. Premature cardiovascular diseases, for example, are associated with the gene for apolipoprotein E, a gene that likely influences the pathology of the disease. In contrast, the association of type 1 diabetes with HLA-DR3/4 is less clear.

## Molecular Diagnostic Testing

Advances in our understanding of the molecular basis of inherited disorders have led to the development of DNA-based tests, which may be used for the confirmation of a diagnosis, prenatal diagnosis, and carrier testing. Molecular diagnostic testing is now widely available for a number of single gene disorders, such as Tay–Sachs disease, Canavan disease, sickle cell disease, CF, muscular dystrophies, and fragile X syndrome. Molecular-cytogenetic testing has been developed for the detection of chromosomal abnormalities, including aneuploidy and submicroscopic deletions and duplications.

DNA can be obtained from many sources, including blood lymphocytes, skin, hair, cheek cells, and paraffin tissue blocks. Most diagnostic laboratories prefer either blood samples or buccal swabs for DNA testing. Cultured amniocytes, chorionic villi, and fetal blood are used for prenatal DNA testing of the fetus.

## Mutation Detection

Once a gene has been cloned and mutations have been identified, direct testing for the mutation is possible. This is the most accurate diagnostic method. Direct mutation tests usually are performed by commercial and hospital-based laboratories for common mutations, which are well characterized and account for the majority of cases. In some cases, the mutations are unique to a specific ethnicity. For example, two specific mutations in the aspartoacylase gene account for 97% of the mutations that cause Canavan disease in the Ashkenazi Jewish population. For some genetic disorders, the mutations are unique or specific to an individual family; therefore, mutation testing may not be routinely provided by a commercial laboratory. In these cases, there may be only one or two academic or hospital laboratories in the country that offer the testing. (This information is provided by GeneTests, a genetic testing resource web site at www.genetests.org.) In general, initial screening of a gene for mutations usually takes place in research laboratories under approved protocols and is not practical for diagnostic testing. Once a mutation has been identified, it may be possible to offer diagnostic or carrier testing to individuals at risk.

There are a variety of methods available for detecting mutations. The methodology usually is determined by the nature of the specific mutation. Allele specific oligonucleotide hybridization and restriction fragment length polymorphisms analysis frequently are used to detect point mutations. Southern blot analysis and polymerase chain reaction (PCR) often are used to detect gene deletions associated with disorders such as Duchenne muscular dystrophy and spinal muscular atrophy. A combination of PCR and Southern blot analysis are used to determine the number of trinucleotide repeats for disorders such as fragile X syndrome and myotonic dystrophy.

### Southern Blot Analysis

Southern blot analysis provides a basis for studying genetic disorders at the DNA level. This procedure, named after its inventor E. M. Southern, separates DNA fragments according to size and allows the identification of specific DNA fragments using radiolabeled DNA probes.

The steps to prepare a Southern blot are shown in Figure 2. First, DNA is extracted from nucleated cells (leukocytes, trophoblasts, or amniocytes) or tissue, and digested into small pieces with a restriction enzyme. Then, the DNA is loaded into an agarose gel, an electric current is applied, and DNA fragments migrate down the gel according to size (smaller fragments move faster). The DNA contained within the agarose gel is still double stranded and must be denatured by alkali treatment into single-stranded pieces and then transferred to a nitrocellulose or nylon membrane. The membrane contains many thousands of fixed DNA fragments. Specific DNA fragments can be detected using a DNA probe labeled with a radionuclide, such as $^{32}P$, although nonradioactive substances such as biotin–avidin may be used. The probes may be complementary DNA (cDNA), genomic DNA (exons, introns, or regulatory regions), or short pieces of single-stranded DNA called oligonucleotides, which usually range in size from 20 to 50 base pairs. The DNA probe will hybridize only with DNA fragments on the blot that are complementary. To visualize the DNA fragment, the blot is exposed to X-ray film at

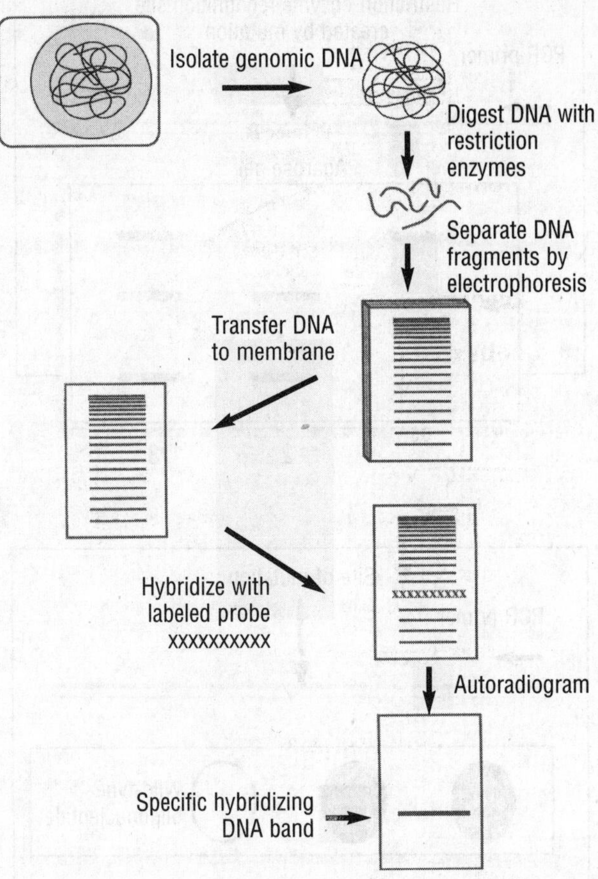


**Fig. 2.** Southern blot analysis. (Jameson JL. Principles of molecular medicine. Totowa, NJ: Humana Press, 1998:16)

-70°C, a process called autoradiography. The film is developed, and the presence or absence of DNA bands or fragments can be determined.

## Polymerase Chain Reaction

The development of the PCR has greatly simplified DNA analysis and shortened laboratory time. Polymerase chain reaction allows the exponential amplification of the targeted gene or DNA sequence. Only minute quantities of DNA, typically 0.1–1 μg, are necessary for PCR. DNA can be amplified from a single cell. One important prerequisite of PCR, which is not required for Southern blot analysis, is that the sequence of the gene, or at least the borders of the region of DNA to be amplified, must be known.

The PCR procedure has three steps (Fig. 3). First, DNA is denatured by heating to render it single stranded. Second, the PCR primers (primer A and B), which are short pieces of DNA (oligonucleotides) 20–30 base pairs in length exactly complementary to the ends of each piece of the double-stranded DNA to be amplified, anneal to their complementary regions of the DNA. Third, synthesis of the complementary strand of DNA occurs in the presence of the enzyme Taq polymerase and nucleotides triphosphates (dATP, dCTP, dGTP, and dTTP). The reaction cycle of denaturation, annealing, and extension is repeated 25–30 times to produce millions of copies of DNA.

Typically, fragments several kilobases (kb) in size can be amplified, but sequences up to 10 kb have been successfully amplified. The exact cycling parameters and conditions for PCR must be determined empirically for each set of primers. Polymerase chain reaction is very sensitive; therefore, extreme care must be taken to avoid amplification of contaminant DNA from aerosolized secretions or sloughed skin cells. These precautions are particularly important when DNA from a single cell is being amplified.

## Restriction Fragment Length Polymorphism Analysis

Restriction fragment length polymorphism analysis can be used when a mutation either creates or destroys a restriction endonuclease site. To detect the mutation, DNA around the site of the mutation is amplified by the PCR, incubated with the appropriate restriction enzyme, and analyzed by agarose gel electrophoresis. When a mutation creates a new restriction site, two DNA fragments will be detected if the mutation is present (Fig. 4A). An individual without the mutation will demonstrate a single fragment. This method frequently is used for the prenatal genetic diagnosis of sickle cell disease. Sickle cell disease is caused by a single base pair substitution (adenine to thymidine) in codon 6 of the β-subunit of hemoglobin, which results in the loss of the MstII restriction site. Individuals with sickle cell disease are homozygous for this mutation.

## Allele Specific Oligonucleotide Hybridization (Dot Blot)

Allele specific oligonucleotide hybridization (dot blot) frequently is used to detect point mutations. A segment of DNA surrounding the mutation is amplified by PCR and then an aliquot is spotted onto a filter membrane. The membrane is hybridized with an oligonucleotide probe specific for the normal sequence and one specific for the mutation. A positive hybridization signal is detected only when the sequence of the PCR product on the membrane is

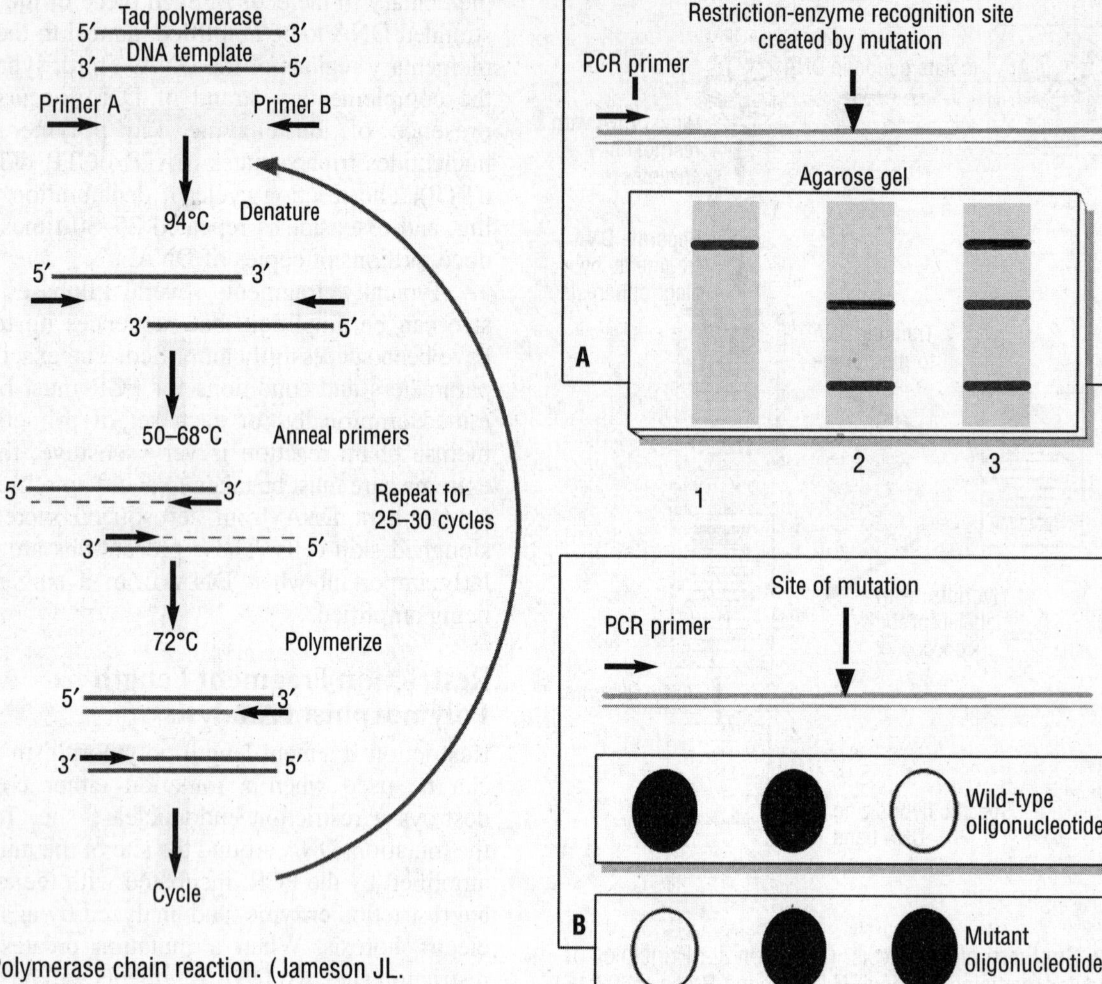


**Fig. 3.** Polymerase chain reaction. (Jameson JL. Principles of molecular medicine. Totowa, NJ: Humana Press, 1998:15)

**Fig. 4.** Mutation detection. **(A)** Restriction fragment length polymorphism (RFLP) analysis. The region of DNA surrounding the mutation is amplified by specific PCR primers, digested with a restriction enzyme, and analyzed by agarose-gel electrophoresis. In this example, the mutation creates a new restriction site. Individuals homozygous for the mutation have two DNA fragments (Lane 2) while an individual with two normal copies has one single fragment (Lane 1). A heterozygous individual has one normal uncut fragment and two cut fragments (Lane 3). **(B)** Allele specific oligonucleotide (ASO) hybridization. The amplified DNA from an individual homozygous for the mutation only hybridizes to the mutant oligonucleotide (MUT) whereas a heterozygous individual (HET) hybridizes to both the normal (wild-type) and the mutant. A normal individual will only hybridize to the normal oligonucleotide (WT). (Korf B. Molecular diagnosis. N Engl J Med 1995;332: 1500. Copyright © 1995 Massachusetts Medical Society. All rights reserved.)

complementary to the sequence of the oligonucleotide. For example, testing an individual who is heterozygous for the mutant allele will reveal a positive hybridization signal with both the normal sequence and the mutant oligonucleotide probe. DNA from individuals homozygous for the mutation will only hybridize to the mutant oligonucleotide (Fig. 4B). This technique is used for the detection of point mutations for many single gene disorders, including CF, Tay–Sachs disease, Gaucher's disease, Canavan disease, and sickle cell disease.

## Deletion Analysis

Intragenic deletions can be detected by PCR or Southern blot analysis or both. Polymerase chain reaction can be used to determine the absence or presence of exons within a gene. A sample of DNA is amplified by PCR and then the PCR products are analyzed by gel electrophoresis, stained with ethidium bromide to detect the absence or presence of DNA fragments (Fig. 5). The absence of a DNA fragment indicates the presence of a deletion. This method is used routinely for diagnostic and prenatal testing for Duchenne muscular dystrophy, an X-linked disorder. Approximately 60% of patients with Duchenne muscular dystrophy have intragenic deletions in the dystrophin gene and the majority of these can be detected by PCR. Most laboratories use a multiplex strategy to examine multiple exons in one PCR. However, PCR is not useful to determine carrier status in the mothers of affected males. This requires Southern blot analysis with cDNA probes from the dystrophin gene and scanning densitometry to assess gene dosage. Testing of females at risk to be carriers based on their family history is less reliable when an affected relative is not available for DNA testing. Dosage analysis also can be used to test male patients with Duchenne muscular dystrophy with a negative result by multiplex PCR to detect duplications within the dystrophin gene, which occur in approximately 6% of patients with Duchenne muscular dystrophy.

## Linkage Analysis

When the location of a gene is known but the gene has not yet been characterized, or when the mutations have not been identified, linkage analysis may be performed to predict the likelihood that a relative or fetus has inherited a disease-causing gene within an at-risk family. Linkage analysis requires that 1) at least two generations of family members, including affected individuals, are available and willing to be tested, and 2) highly polymorphic markers such as restriction fragment length polymorphisms, or short tandem repeat polymorphisms close to or within the gene are available. These polymorphic markers result from normal genetic variation and are not disease causing but may be used to track the inheritance of genetic diseases within families. The closer a marker is to a gene, the higher the likelihood that the marker and gene are transmitted or inherited together (linkage). The accuracy of linkage analysis depends on the correct diagnosis, the informativeness of the markers within the family, and the distance between the marker and the disease-causing gene. Markers closest to or within a gene are less likely to undergo recombination and will provide the

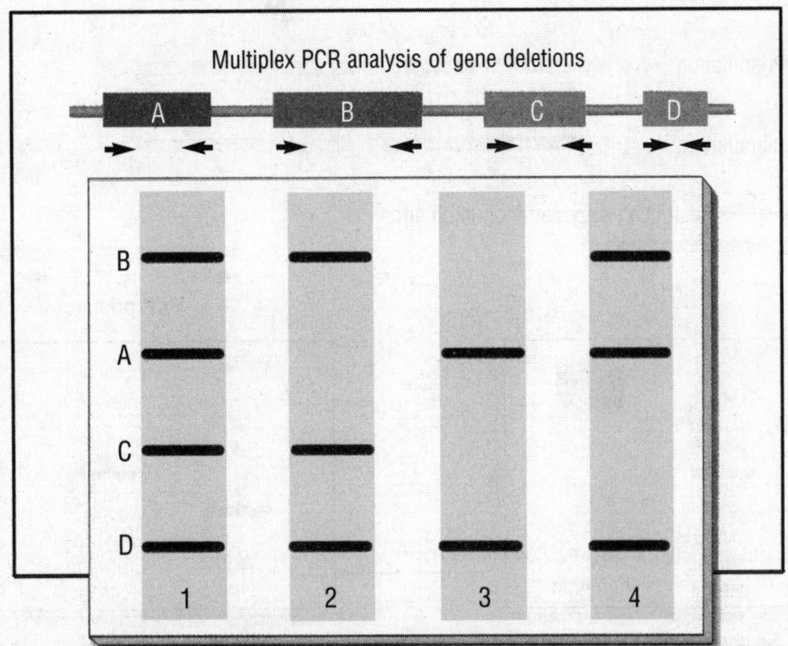

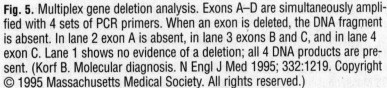

**Fig. 5.** Multiplex gene deletion analysis. Exons A–D are simultaneously amplified with 4 sets of PCR primers. When an exon is deleted, the DNA fragment is absent. In lane 2 exon A is absent, in lane 3 exons B and C, and in lane 4 exon C. Lane 1 shows no evidence of a deletion; all 4 DNA products are present. (Korf B. Molecular diagnosis. N Engl J Med 1995; 332:1219. Copyright © 1995 Massachusetts Medical Society. All rights reserved.)

most accurate prediction. Although linkage analysis is less accurate than direct mutation detection, under the specified circumstances it may provide families with helpful information.

## Trinucleotide Repeat Analysis

The detection of trinucleotide repeat expansions, associated with diseases such as fragile X syndrome, myotonic dystrophy, and Huntington's disease, often requires a combination of PCR and Southern blot analysis (Fig. 6). The size of normal alleles, premutation alleles, and, in some cases, full mutations can be determined by using PCR. However, full mutations associated with a large expansion (eg, >200 repeats in fragile X syndrome) may need to be detected using Southern blot analysis. It also is used to assess the methylation status in fragile X patients and pregnancies with the full mutation. The repeat region not only expands to more than 200 repeats but also becomes hypermethylated in affected individuals. DNA is digested with restriction enzymes including a methylation-sensitive enzyme such as BsshII, gel electrophoresed, and hybridized with a DNA probe from the repeat region of the fragile X gene (FMR-1).

## Fluorescence In Situ Hybridization

Fluorescence in situ hybridization (FISH) is performed on either metaphase chromosome preparations from cultured lymphocytes, amniocytes, or villi, or interphase nuclei from blood, tissue, chorionic villi, or amniotic fluid. After the chromosomes or nuclei are fixed on a microscope slide, they are hybridized with a fluorochrome-labeled DNA probe specific for a particular region of a chromosome. The probe will hybridize to complementary DNA sequences that can be visualized using a fluorescence microscope. Fluorescence in situ hybridization is used as an adjunct to routine cytogenetic analysis for the detection of submicroscopic chromosome

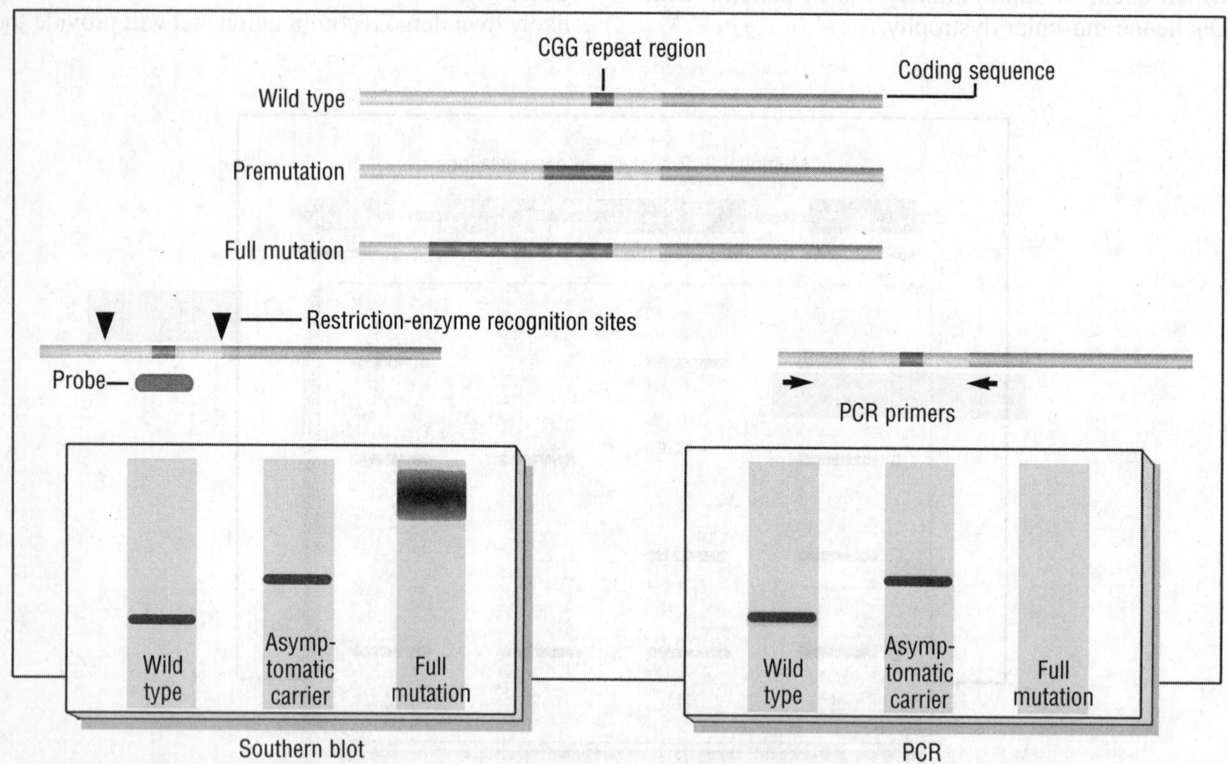


**Fig. 6.** Trinucleotide repeat analysis by PCR and Southern blot. A region of DNA containing the CGG repeat is amplified and the product is analyzed on an agarose gel. The DNA fragment from a carrier with a premutation is larger because of the expanded number of repeats. Sometimes the expansion is so large that the DNA fails to amplify and the number of repeats cannot be detected using PCR. In this case, a Southern blot is performed (left panel) and the DNA from an individual with a full mutation appears as a much larger band. (Korf B. Molecular diagnosis. N Engl J Med 1995;332: 1501. )

deletions and duplications. These deletions and duplications often are several 1,000 base pairs but are too small to be detected by conventional cytogenetics. DNA probes have been developed for the common deletion and duplication syndromes (Table 1). It also may be used to identify or confirm the presence of a subtle chromosomal rearrangement (eg, translocation) or characterize a marker chromosome. Fluorescence in situ hybridization of interphase nuclei is used prenatally for the rapid detection of common aneuploidies, such as trisomy 21. However, this is generally reserved for cases where confirmation of a chromosomal abnormality may influence a couple's reproductive options or obstetric management.

**Table 1.** Microdeletion Syndromes

| Syndrome | Chromosome Deletion |
|---|---|
| Aniridia/Wilm's tumor | 11p13 |
| Angelman's | 15q11-13 |
| DiGeorge/velocardiofacial | 22q11.2 |
| Langer-Giedion | 8q24 |
| Miller-Dieker | 17p13.3 |
| Prader-Willi | 15q11-13 |
| Smith-Magenis | 17p11.2 |
| Williams | 7q11.23 |

## Comparative Genomic Hybridization

Comparative genomic hybridization is a relatively new DNA-based cytogenetic technique to identify subtle chromosome deletions and duplications that have not been detected using traditional cytogenetic methods. To accomplish this, DNA from a patient is labeled with a green fluorochrome and normal control DNA is labeled with a red fluorochrome, which can be visualized with a fluorescence microscope. The DNA is hybridized to normal metaphase chromosomes. Wherever a chromosome region is duplicated, the metaphase chromosome will hybridize with the excess green-labeled DNA and appear green. Conversely, deletions will appear red. Clinically, comparative genomic hybridization is primarily used to detect cytogenetic changes in tumors but, it also has been used to identify subtle unbalanced translocations, the origin of marker or supernumerary chromosomes, and intrachromosomal duplications.

## Microarray Technology

DNA chip technology is a high throughput method used primarily to study gene expression. Miniature arrays of cDNA clones are spotted onto a glass slide and hybridized with labeled cDNA prepared from the tissue of interest. If a gene is strongly expressed in the tissue, the hybridization signal will be intense. This technique can analyze the gene expression of thousands of genes at one time. In the future, oligonucleotide arrays also may be used to search for gene mutations and polymorphisms. Chips containing gene specific oligonucleotides matching normal and single nucleotides substitution sequences are hybridized with fluorescent-labeled DNA. Improvements in chip technology will enable whole genome expression screening as well as improved mutation detection in the future.

## Indications for Molecular Testing

A variety of molecular diagnostic tests are available to determine whether an individual or fetus has inherited a disease-causing gene mutation. In general, testing is offered to individuals or couples identified as being at risk for a genetic disorder based on their family history, medical history, or ethnicity. Determination of an individual's carrier status for a genetic disorder provides a more accurate estimate of their risk of having an affected offspring and allows an individual or couple to consider prenatal testing options. This information also may assist couples with their reproductive decisions. Furthermore, it can identify other family members or relatives at risk for the disorder or at risk for being a carrier.

Molecular testing also may be used in clinical and prenatal situations to confirm a diagnosis. For example, screening for CF mutations may determine whether an infertile male with congenital bilateral absence of the vas deferens is a CF carrier. Prenatal molecular testing for some genetic disorders may be offered when a congenital anomaly is identified antenatally. For example, FISH for the 22q11.2 deletion may establish a cause when a conotruncal cardiac defect is detected by ultrasonography. Establishing an etiology enables clinicians to provide couples with accurate genetic risk assessments, prognostic information, and recommendations for obstetric and neonatal management.

Prior to diagnostic and carrier testing for genetic disorders, patients should be informed of the natural history of the disorder and current therapy, the inheritance and their risk of inheriting or transmitting the gene, benefits and limitations of testing, and the implications of negative and positive results. Preconceptional and prenatal testing also should include a discussion of reproductive options including prenatal testing, adoption, donor programs, and termination of pregnancy. Written informed consent should be obtained from all individuals undergoing genetic screening. Patients should understand that molecular testing is voluntary and that every effort will be made to ensure confidentiality of their medical records and test results.

## Accuracy and Limitations of Molecular Testing

Direct detection of a point mutation, deletion, or duplication is the most accurate test. However, the accuracy of molecular diagnosis also is dependent on an accurate diagnosis. If an affected relative is not available to identify the presence of a mutation or if medical records are not available to confirm the diagnosis, this may decrease the accuracy of testing for a specific mutation and for the suspected genetic disorder.

One of the limitations of molecular diagnostic testing is test sensitivity. There are a number of factors that determine the ability to detect mutations. Many genetic disorders result from a variety of genetic alterations. For example, more than 800 mutations have been reported in patients with CF. The mutation detection rates for many genetic disorders, including neurofibromatosis, CF, and hemophilia, are less than 100%. Therefore, the absence of a mutation does not exclude the possibility that an individual may be a carrier. Furthermore, there may be ethnic differences in the detection rates; 97% of CF mutations have been identified in the Ashkenazi Jewish population while only 30% in Asian Americans. The incidence and carrier risk for some genetic disorders also is dependent on ethnicity and has led to the current recommendations for carrier screening for specific genetic disorders. Differences in test sensitivity and the prevalence of mutations must be considered for each individual genetic disorder and discussed with the patient prior to testing. Disease prevalence and test sensitivity should be taken into account in future recommendations for molecular-based carrier testing.

Another limitation to molecular testing is genetic heterogeneity. In some cases, there may be more than one gene or chromosomal locus responsible for a genetic disorder. For example, at least two genes have been identified that cause tuberous sclerosis, an autosomal dominant disorder. Conversely, mutations in a single gene can cause different phenotypes. For example, mutations in fibroblast growth factor receptor 3 (FGFR3) are associated with several types of skeletal disorders, including achondroplasia, hypochondroplasia, thanatophoric dysplasia, and with craniosynostosis (eg, Crouzon's disease, coronal synostosis).

In some diseases, the identification of a genetic mutation cannot precisely predict the phenotype because of reduced penetrance or phenotypic variability or both. For example, 85% of women with a *BRCA1* mutation develop breast cancer during their lifetime; therefore, the finding of a *BRCA1* mutation indicates a strong predisposition to breast cancer but it does not indicate which women with the mutation will develop a malignancy. Some genetic disorders are highly variable even within families with the same mutation. Therefore, it may only be possible to provide patients with a description of the natural history of the disorder and an estimate of the frequency of specific features in patients with similar mutations. The lack of genotype phenotype correlation for some genetic disorders, such as CF, also can limit the ability to accurately predict the course of the disease. Therefore, when molecular testing indicates that a patient or fetus has inherited a mutation, it is helpful to consult a geneticist or someone with expertise in the specific disorder to provide current information regarding the prognosis, as well as, the limitations and accuracy of testing.

## Applications in Obstetrics and Gynecology

Genetics is taking an increasingly prominent role in the practice of obstetrics and gynecology. Gene identification, characterization of disease-causing mutations, and advances in genetic technology have led to an increased number of available genetic tests, which may be used for the diagnosis of genetic disorders, carrier detection, and prenatal or preimplantation genetic diagnosis. Testing for a specific genetic disorder most often occurs in an obstetric setting based on either the family history or the couple's ethnicity. Genetic counseling should be offered to couples at risk so they can review the nature of the disorder, the inheritance pattern, their specific risk for being a carrier and for having a child with the disorder, the current availability of prenatal and postnatal testing as well the accuracy and limitations of testing, and their reproductive options. Most molecular genetic testing for disorders, such as Duchenne muscular dystrophy, fragile X syndrome, neurofibromatosis, and hemophilia, is performed when a couple is at high risk based on their family history. Initially, testing is performed to determine whether the parent is a carrier. If the parent is a carrier, prenatal testing by amniocentesis or chorionic villus sampling is possible. Some couples may consider preimplantation genetic diagnosis. Single gene disorders and chromosomal abnormalities, such as deletions and translocations, may be identified in an embryo conceived through in vitro fertilization by testing a single blastomere. Genetic testing for disorders prevalent in specific ethnic populations such as CF for Caucasians and Tay–Sachs and Canavan disease for individuals of Eastern European Jewish ancestry, is used to determine if an individual is a carrier. Prenatal molecular diagnostic testing is available for couples who are both carriers of sickle cell disease and thalassemia determined by hemoglobin electrophoresis. The genetic testing options in pregnancy are rapidly growing with the completion of the human genome project; however, a thorough family history is essential to identify a couple at risk.

Genetic testing during pregnancy may establish a diagnosis that may influence obstetric management. For example, PCR of amniotic fluid is used to determine the Rh status of the fetus to determine if the fetus is at risk for hemolytic disease of the newborn when the woman is Rh sensitized and the man is a heterozygous carrier of antigen D. The fetus at risk will need close surveillance during the pregnancy. A specific molecular diagnostic test may be considered when the finding of a fetal malformation by ultrasonography raises the suspicion of a genetic disorder. For example, mutation testing for CF in a fetus with echogenic bowel, fibroblast growth factor receptor 2 (FGFR2) for suspected Apert's syndrome (craniosynostosis), and 22q11.2 deletion testing when a conotruncal cardiac defect is detected. Identification of an etiology provides the physician and couple with a better understanding of the prognosis that influences not only the obstetric and neonatal care of the infant but also a couple's reproductive decisions. Furthermore, it establishes an accurate assessment of the recurrence risk for this family and their relatives.

Some of the genes responsible for the inherited forms of some types of cancer (such as breast, ovarian, and colon) have been identified. Risk assessment for relatives in these families may include genetic testing in addition to evaluating other risk factors, such as family history. In some families, breast and ovarian cancer is attributed to an inherited genetic mutation, *BRCA1* or *BRCA2*. The genes responsible for hereditary nonpolyposis colorectal cancer, juvenile polyposis, and familial adenomatosis polyposis, have been identified. It is likely that other genes that contribute to cancer will be identified in the future, which may be useful for cancer risk assessment and management.

Genetic screening and testing should be considered a component of an infertility evaluation. Preconceptional genetic screening and counseling can identify couples at risk for having offspring with a genetic disorder and provide them with information that enables them to make informed decisions regarding their reproductive options. Genetic causes of severe oligospermia and azoospermia include balanced translocations, Klinefelter's syndrome (47,XXY), and Y chromosome abnormalities and microdeletions. Cytogenetic studies and PCR-based Y chromosome deletion testing should be considered. Approximately two thirds of males with congenital bilateral absence of the vas deferens have at least one CF mutation. Men with congenital bilateral absence of the vas deferens should be offered CF carrier testing. Partners of carriers and individuals with CF should be tested to assess their risk for having a child with CF. This information may be useful for an infertile couple considering their reproductive options, such as testicular aspiration and biopsy with intracytoplasmic sperm injection, preimplantation genetic diagnosis with in vitro fertilization, donor gamete, adoption, and prenatal testing.

## Summary

Human genetics and molecular testing is playing an increasingly important role in obstetric and gynecologic practice. It is essential that obstetricians and gynecologists are aware of the advances in our understanding of genetic disease and the fundamental principles of molecular testing and genetic screening as genetics is integrated into routine medical practice. In the future, elucidation of the genetic basis for reproductive disorders, common diseases, and cancer with improved high throughput technology for genetic testing will expand testing opportunities and influence treatment options and prevention strategies.

## REFERENCE

1. The human genome. Science 2001;291:1145–1434

## RESOURCES

Bell J. The new genetics in clinical practice. BMJ 1998;316: 618–620

Blackwood MA, Weber BL. BRCA1 and BRCA2: from molecular genetics to clinical medicine. J Clin Oncol 1998;16: 1969–1977

Brown PO, Botstein D. Exploring the new world of the genome with DNA microassays. Nat Genet 1999;21(suppl):33–37

Caskey CT. Medical genetics. JAMA 1997;277:1869–1870

Collins FS. Genetics: an explosion of knowledge is transforming clinical practice. Geriatrics 1999;54:41–47;quiz 48

Cooper DN, Schmidtke J. Diagnosis of human genetic disease using recombinant DNA. 4th ed. Hum Genet 1993;92:211–236

Davis JG. Predictive genetic tests: problems and pitfalls. Ann N Y Acad Sci 1997;833:42–46

Jameson JL. Principles of molecular medicine. Totowa, New Jersey: Humana Press, 1998

Korf B. Molecular diagnosis (1). N Engl J Med 1995;332: 1218–1220

Korf B. Molecular diagnosis (2). N Engl J Med 1995;332: 1499–1502

Makowski DR. The Human Genome Project and the clinician. J Fla Med Assoc 1996;83:307–314

Mark HF, Jenkins R, Miller WA. Current applications of molecular cytogenetic technologies. Ann Clin Lab Sci 1997;27: 47–56

Pyeritz RE. Family history and genetic risk factors: forward to the future. JAMA 1997;278:1284–1285

## SOURCES OF ONLINE INFORMATION

Tutorial in Genetics (HHMI)
www.hhmi.org/GeneticTrail/

Online Mendelian Inheritance in Man
www3.ncbi.nlm.nih.gov/Omim/

MEDLINE
www.ncbi.nlm.nih.gov/PubMed/

GeneTests
www.genetests.org

Genome Database
www.gob.org

Biochemical testing information
biochemgen.ucsd.edu/wbgtests/dz.tst.htm

Alliance of Genetic Support Groups
medhlp.netusa.net/www/agsg.htm

National Human Genome Research
www.nhgri.nih.gov

Centers for Disease Control and Prevention
www.cdc.gov/genetics

Gene Clinics
www.geneclinics.org

## GLOSSARY

**Allele:** One of two or more alternate forms of a gene.

**Allele specific oligonucleotides:** Synthetic oligonucleotide designed to hybridize to a specific sequence, and under the right conditions, to fail to hybridize to a related sequence. Allele specific oligonucleotides also are used as PCR primers in several methods similarly designed to distinguish between closely related alleles.

**Autosomal Dominant:** An allele located on an autosome (nonsex chromosome) that expresses itself phenotypically in the presence of the same or a different allele (ie, in a homozygous or heterozygous condition).

**Autosomal Recessive:** An allele located on an autosome that does not express itself phenotypically in the presence of a dominant allele (ie, in a heterozygous condition). It is only phenotypically expressed in a homozygous condition.

**Chimera:** An organism with tissues composed of two or more genetically distinct cell types.

**Chromatin:** An intranuclear and intrachromosomal complex made up of DNA, and histone and nonhistone proteins.

**Co-Dominant:** Alleles that are different from each other, but both are expressed in the phenotype.

**Codon:** A section of DNA (three nucleotide pairs in length) that codes for a single amino acid.

**Comparative Genomic Hybridization:** A cytogenetic method based on a combination of fluorescence microscopy and digital image analysis. Differentially labeled test DNA and normal reference DNA are hybridized simultaneously to normal chromosome spreads. Hybridization is detected with two different fluorochromes. Deletions, duplications, or amplifications are seen as changes in the ratio of the intensities of the two fluorochromes along the target chromosomes.

**Complementary DNA (cDNA) Probe:** A DNA sequence that is exactly complementary to mRNA, lacking introns and regulatory regions.

**Contiguous Gene Deletion Syndrome:** A syndrome caused by a deletion involving genes that are physically located together in a chromosome segment.

**Constitutive Heterochromatin:** Condensed genetically inactive chromatin located in the same regions of both homologous chromosomes.

**DNA:** A double-helical structure composed of two coils of nucleotide chains connected by nitrogen bases.

**DNA Hybridization:** A process whereby labeled nucleic acid molecules (oligonucleotide probe) bind to a DNA sequence on a target (Southern blot, metaphase chromosomes, or interphase nuclei) that is complementary to its own.

**DNA Methylation:** A process for control of tissue specific gene expression. Methylation "turns off" the regulatory region of a gene, thereby preventing DNA transcription.

**Epigenetic:** Non–DNA/RNA related process that affects genotype and phenotype (ie, methalization).

**Exon:** A region of a gene made up of DNA sequences that will be transcribed into mRNA.

**Expressivity:** The degree to which a genotype is expressed in the phenotype (range of phenotypic features).

**Fluorescence in situ Hybridization (FISH):** A procedure for detecting specific nucleic acid sequences in morphologically preserved chromosomes, cells, and tissue sections using fluorescent labeled oligonucleotide probes.

**Gene:** A unit of heredity responsible for the inheritance of a specific trait that occupies a fixed chromosomal site and corresponds to a sequence of nucleotides along a DNA molecule.

**Genome:** The entire complement of genetic material in a chromosome set.

**Genomic Imprinting:** The existence of parent-of-origin differences in the expression of certain genes.

**Germline Mosaicism:** Mosaicism that is confined to the gonad.

**Hereditary Unstable DNA (Triplet Repeat Expansion):** Gene containing a region of triplet codon repeats such as $(CGC)_n$. The number of triplet repeats can increase during meiosis. If the expansion of repeats reaches a critical number, the gene becomes methylated and is turned off, resulting in phenotypic abnormalities.

**Heterochromatin:** Chromatin that remains condensed throughout interphase. It contains DNA that is genetically inactive and replicates late in the S phase of the cell cycle. There are two types of heterochromatin: constitutive and facultative.

**Hybridization (Dot Blot):** A semiquantitative technique for evaluating the relative abundance of nucleic acid sequences in a mixture or the extent of similarity between homologous sequences.

**Imprinting:** The imposition of a stable behavior pattern in a young animal by exposure, during a particular period in its development, to one of a restricted set of stimuli.

**Intron:** A region of a gene, made up of noncoding DNA sequences that lies between exons.

**Karyotype:** The chromosome constitution of an individual.

**Linkage:** The association of genes on the same chromosome.

**Methylation:** (see DNA Methylation)

**Mitochondrial Inheritance:** Mitochondria are inherited exclusively from women. Because they contain DNA, mitochondrial inheritance allows transmission of genes directly from the woman to her offspring.

**Mosaicism:** The presence of two or more populations of cells with different characteristics within one tissue or organ.

**Multifactorial Inheritance:** Inheritance of traits that are determined by a combination of genetic and environmental factors.

**Mutation:** An alteration of DNA sequencing in a gene that results in a heritable change in protein structure or function that frequently has adverse effects.

**Deletion:** A mutation that is generated by removal of a sequence of DNA, with the regions on either side being joined together.

**Expansion** (see Hereditary Unstable DNA)

**Frame-shift:** A mutation caused by deletions or insertions that are not a multiple of three base pairs. Results in a change in the reading frame in which triplet codons are translated into protein.

**Insertion:** A mutation caused by the presence of an additional sequence of nucleotide pairs in DNA.

**Inversion:** A mutation involving the removal of a DNA sequence, its rotation through 180 degrees, and its reinsertion in the same location.

**Missense:** A mutation that alters a codon so that it encodes a different amino acid.

**Northern Blot:** A technique for transferring RNA from an electrophoresis gel to a nitrocellulose filter on which it can be hybridized to a complementary DNA (cDNA) probe.

**Nucleotide:** A component of a DNA or RNA molecule composed of a nitrogenous base, one deoxyribose or ribose sugar, and one phosphate group. In DNA, adenine specifically joins to thymine and guanine joins to cytosine. In RNA, uracil replaces thymine.

**Oligonucleotide Primer:** A short sequence of nucleotides that is necessary to hybridize to a DNA or RNA strand using the enzymes DNA polymerase or reverse transcriptase.

**Penetrance:** The ability of a mutant gene to be expressed in an individual who carries the gene.

**Phenotype:** Observable physical characteristics of an organism resulting from the expression of the genotype and its interaction with the environment.

**Polygenic Inheritance:** Inheritance of traits that are determined by the combined effects of many genes.

**Polymerase Chain Reaction (PCR):** A method for enzymatically amplifying a short sequence of DNA through repeated cycles of denaturation, binding with an oligonucleotide primer and extension of the primers by a DNA polymerase.

**Polymorphisms:** Minor differences that distinguish one individual from another.

**Recombinant DNA:** A new DNA sequence formed by the combination of two nonhomologous DNA molecules.

**Restriction Endonuclease:** An enzyme that recognizes and cleaves a specific DNA sequence (usually 4–10 nucleotide bases long).

**Restriction Fragment Length Polymorphism:** A polymorphic difference in DNA sequence between individuals that can be recognized by restriction endonucleases.

**Southern Blot:** A technique used to detect specific DNA sequences by separating restriction enzyme digested DNA fragments on an electrophoresis gel, transferring (blotting) these fragments from the gel onto a membrane or nitrocellulose filter, followed by hybridization with a labeled probe to a specific DNA sequence.

**Spectral Karyotype:** A molecular cytogenetic method in which all of the chromosomes in a metaphase spread are visualized in different colors (multicolor FISH).

**Uniparental Disomy:** Inheritance of two copies of part or all of a chromosome from one parent and no copy from the other parent.

**Uniparental Heterodisomy:** Inheritance of two homologous chromosomes from one parent.

**Uniparental Isodisomy:** Inheritance of two identical chromosomes from one parent.

**Threshold Traits:** Traits that are not manifested until a certain threshold of liability is exceeded.

**Transcription:** The process of RNA synthesis from a DNA template that is directed by RNA polymerase.

**Triplet Repeat Expansion** (see Hereditary Unstable DNA)

**Trinucleotide Repeat Analysis (Repeats):** Unstable DNA sequences found in several human genes. Normally the triplets are repeated in tandem 5–50 times. When the number rises above the normal range, mutant disease syndromes appear.

**X-inactivation:** A process by which one of the X chromosomes in each somatic cell of females is rendered inactive. This results in a balance in gene expression between the X chromosomal and autosomal genes, which is necessary because males have only one X chromosome.

**X-linked:** An allele for a trait or disorder that is located on the X chromosome, and may be either dominant or recessive.

**Western Blot:** A technique, conceptually related to the Southern and Northern blot that is used to detect specific proteins.



**The American College of Obstetricians and Gynecologists**
**409 12th Street, SW**
**PO Box 96920**
**Washington, DC 20090-6920**

12345/65432

Genetics and molecular diagnostic testing. ACOG Technology Assessment in Obstetrics and Gynecology No. 1. American College of Obstetricians and Gynecologists. Obstet Gynecol 2002;100:193–211

# COMMITTEE OPINIONS

## COMMITTEE ON GYNECOLOGIC PRACTICE



*Published in 2006

# COMMITTEE OPINIONS

## COMMITTEE ON GYNECOLOGIC PRACTICE *(Continued)*



* Published in 2006

■ Technology Assessment

ACOG Committee Opinion

Committee on Gynecologic Practice

Committee on Obstetric Practice

Number 240, August 2000 *(Replaces No. 145, November 1994)*

# Statement on Surgical Assistants

Competent surgical assistants should be available for all major obstetric and gynecologic operations. In many cases, the complexity of the surgery or the patient's condition will require the assistance of one or more physicians to provide safe, quality care. Often, the complexity of a given surgical procedure cannot be determined prospectively. Procedures including, but not limited to, operative laparoscopy, major abdominal and vaginal surgery, and cesarean delivery may warrant the assistance of another physician to optimize safe surgical care.

The primary surgeon's judgment and prerogative in determining the number and qualifications of surgical assistants should not be overruled by public or private third-party payers. Surgical assistants should be appropriately compensated.

This document reflects emerging clinical and scientific advances as of the date issued and is subject to change. The information should not be construed as dictating an exclusive course of treatment or procedure to be followed.



ISSN 1074-861X

**The American College of Obstetricians and Gynecologists**
409 12th Street, SW
PO Box 96920
Washington, DC 20090-6920

12345/43210

ACOG Committee Opinion

Committee on Gynecologic Practice

Number 243, November 2000

# Performance and Interpretation of Imaging Studies by Obstetrician–Gynecologists



ISSN 1074-861X

**The American College of Obstetricians and Gynecologists**
409 12th Street, SW
PO Box 96920
Washington, DC 20090-6920

12345/43210

Obstetrician–gynecologists are experienced in diagnostic imaging methods and receive privileges to perform and interpret imaging studies on the basis of their training, experience, and demonstrated current competence. Obstetrician–gynecologists can perform the immediate and timely interpretation of imaging studies, correlate these studies with clinical findings, counsel the patient, and assume the responsibility for determining the treatment of the patient.

## Education and Training

By virtue of their education and experience, obstetrician–gynecologists are qualified to perform the imaging studies that are a necessary and integral part of obstetric–gynecologic care. Training in diagnostic imaging is a part of obstetric–gynecologic residencies, and questions related to this field are a part of the certifying examinations of the American Board of Obstetrics and Gynecology. For example, the performance and interpretation of ultrasound images are required components of obstetric and gynecologic residency training and are monitored by the Residency Review Committee for Obstetrics and Gynecology. In addition to interpreting images in descriptive terms, obstetrician–gynecologists add functional, anatomical, and clinical assessments, resulting in patient-specific information. It is the obstetric–gynecologic interpretation of the images, in concert with the history and physical examination, that determines the course of treatment and carries with it the responsibility for patient care. A written report, signed by the interpreting physician, should be considered an integral part of the performance and interpretation of an imaging study.

## Timeliness

For optimal patient care, imaging studies should be performed and interpreted in a timely manner. Many obstetric–gynecologic imaging procedures are performed when the patient is in the obstetrician–gynecologist's office or in the labor and delivery suite so that judgments can be made, without delay, at the time of clinical decision making.

Appropriate management of certain obstetric–gynecologic emergencies, such as suspected ectopic pregnancy, requires timely performance and interpretation of imaging studies. In many cases, the obstetrician–gynecologist is the most appropriate physician to provide these services.

## Conclusion

The responsibility for obstetric–gynecologic patient care rests with the treating obstetrician–gynecologist and may include the immediate performance and interpretation of diagnostic imaging studies. Obstetrician–gynecologists are qualified to perform and interpret obstetric–gynecologic imaging studies. The American College of Obstetricians and Gynecologists believes that obstetrician–gynecologists are entitled to adequate compensation for the cost and work involved in providing these services. Any policy that prohibits obstetrician–gynecologists from performing and interpreting imaging studies of which they are competent interferes with the patient's access to optimal care. Such a policy is likely to ultimately increase the cost of providing such services and substantially increases the risk of less than optimal outcomes in those patients requiring timely management of obstetric–gynecologic emergencies.

# ACOG Committee Opinion

Committee on Gynecologic Practice

Number 253, March 2001

(*Replaces Statement of Policy on Liposuction, January 1988)*

## Nongynecologic Procedures

Cosmetic procedures (such as laser hair removal, body piercing, tattoo removal, and liposuction) are not considered gynecologic procedures and, therefore, generally are not taught in approved obstetric and gynecologic residencies. Because these are not considered gynecologic procedures, it is inappropriate for the College to establish guidelines for training. As with other surgical procedures, credentialing for cosmetic procedures should be based on education, training, experience, and demonstrated competence.



ISSN 1074-861X

**The American College of Obstetricians and Gynecologists**
409 12th Street, SW
PO Box 96920
Washington, DC 20090-6920

12345/54321

# ACOG Committee Opinion

Committee on Gynecologic Practice

Number 272, May 2002

This document reflects emerging clinical and scientific advances as of the date issued and is subject to change. The information should not be construed as dictating an exclusive course of treatment or procedure to be followed.



ISSN 1074-861X

**The American College of Obstetricians and Gynecologists**
409 12th Street, SW
PO Box 96920
Washington, DC 20090-6920

12345/65432

Follow-up of abnormal screening mammography. ACOG Committee Opinion No. 272. American College of Obstetricians and Gynecologists. Obstet Gynecol 2002;99:869

## Follow-up of Abnormal Screening Mammography

*ABSTRACT: Screening mammography facilitates the early diagnosis of breast carcinoma in women. Timely follow-up can optimize the diagnosis and treatment of women with abnormal screening test results. When test results reveal that additional studies are needed, no barriers should prohibit testing during the screening mammography visit.*

Screening mammography facilitates the early diagnosis of breast carcinoma in women. Timely follow-up of an abnormal screening mammogram can optimize the diagnosis and treatment of women with abnormal screening test results and may decrease patient anxiety, travel costs, and time off work. Timely follow-up is ethically encouraged and is consistent with the role of physicians as patient advocates.

When interpretation of a screening mammogram indicates that additional diagnostic studies are needed, there should be no barriers imposed by the patient's health insurance policy or other regulations that would prevent the performance of further diagnostic tests during the visit for screening mammography.

# ACOG Committee Opinion

Committee on Gynecologic Practice

Number 278, November 2002

This document reflects emerging clinical and scientific advances as of the date issued and is subject to change. The information should not be construed as dictating an exclusive course of treatment or procedure to be followed.



ISSN 1074-861X

**The American College of Obstetricians and Gynecologists**
409 12th Street, SW
PO Box 96920
Washington, DC 20090-6920

12345/65432

Avoiding inappropriate clinical decisions based on false-positive human chorionic gonadotropin test results. ACOG Committee Opinion No. 278. American College of Obstetricians and Gynecologists. Obstet Gynecol 2002;100:1057-9.

## Avoiding Inappropriate Clinical Decisions Based on False-Positive Human Chorionic Gonadotropin Test Results

*ABSTRACT: Clinically significant false-positive human chorionic gonadotropin (hCG) test results are rare. However, some individuals have circulating factors in their serum (eg, heterophilic antibodies or nonactive forms of hCG) that interact with the hCG antibody and cause unusual or unexpected test results. False-positive and false-negative test results can occur with any specimen, and caution should be exercised when clinical findings and laboratory results are discordant. Methods to rule out the presence of interfering substances include using a urine test, rerunning the assay with serial dilutions of serum, preabsorbing serum, and using another assay. Physicians must decide whether the risks of waiting for confirmation of results outweigh the risks of failing to take immediate medical action. Patients should be notified if they are at risk for recurrent false-positive hCG test results, and this information should be included in the patient's medical record.*

Clinical management of many gynecologic conditions has improved dramatically over recent decades through the development of very sensitive and highly specific assays for hormones, particularly human chorionic gonadotropin (hCG). These assays have revolutionized the management of ectopic pregnancy and gestational trophoblastic disease, which now have a substantially lower mortality rate as a result of the ability to quantitate circulating (serum) and urinary hCG.

With the technologic improvements, hCG assays are now capable of detecting the presence of a pregnancy before a missed menstrual period. It is vital to remember that, despite technical advances, the ability of laboratory measurements to guide the clinician appropriately in every circumstance is limited (1–3). The purpose of this Committee Opinion is to offer recommendations to better manage situations in which hCG assays may provide false-positive results.

Some individuals have circulating factors in their serum that interact with the hCG antibody. The most common are heterophilic antibodies. These are human antibodies directed against animal-derived antigens used in immunoassays (1, 4–9). Individuals who have worked as animal laboratory technicians or in veterinary facilities or who were reared on farms are more likely to develop heterophilic antibodies. Immunoassays of all kinds use animal antibodies. People with heterophilic antibodies might have unusual results in a number of different kinds of assays. However, because the animal antibodies are used in different amounts and with other reagents in each assay system, a person with heterophilic antibodies will not always have an unusual or unexpected result. Results can differ depending on the particular assay used.

Clinically significant false-positive results are rare. One report noted that 5 of 162 women studied had evidence of assay interference sufficient to provide misleading results (10). If results are misleading, they usually are seen with values below 1,000 mIU/mL. To rule out the presence of heterophilic antibodies or other interfering substances, several methods can be used:

- A urine test (either quantitative or qualitative) for hCG can be performed. Because heterophilic antibodies are not present in urine, if the urine test result is negative and the serum test result is persistently positive, interference in the serum immunoassay is confirmed if the serum value is ≥ 50 mIU/mL (3).
- The assay can be rerun with serial dilutions of the serum. Because heterophilic antibodies are directed to reagents in the immunoassay and not hCG, their interaction with the hCG curve will not be linear. Lack of linearity confirms assay interference.
- Some laboratories can preabsorb serum to remove heterophilic antibodies before performing the assay. If the result becomes negative after removal of the heterophilic antibody, interference can be confirmed (11).

There are other ways in which the amount of "true" hCG can be measured differently or even incorrectly by immunoassays. The size of the hCG molecule circulating in the blood of individuals may vary as a result of differences in the protein and carbohydrate structure of hCG. This type of variation is called *microheterogeneity* of hCG, and it sometimes can account for differences in measurements reported by different assays. Additionally, some individuals may produce aberrant forms of hCG that are not biologically active—or are other hormones entirely—that will cross-react with the hCG assays. Still others may partly break down circulating hCG into nonbiologically active forms that react differently with the various assay systems. In these circumstances, substances other than native, biologically active hCG may be recognized by the assay system. Repeating the hCG measurement in a different assay system can best detect this problem.

Wide variations between repeat runs of the same assay could result from serum factors interfering with the assay. Serial dilution of the specimen will be helpful in documenting nonlinearity and confirming the presence of interference.

Finally, inherent assay factors can result in false-positive hCG results. Repeat testing using a different assay system may confirm that the result was falsely positive if the result is now negative.

Patients with evidence of hCG assay interference should be notified that they are at risk for recurrent false-positive hCG assay results. These patients should be instructed to inform all future health care practitioners of this problem, and the information should be included in the patient's medical record.

In summary, modern assay methods have almost eliminated laboratory error. However, false-positive and false-negative test results can occur with any specimen. Caution should be exercised whenever clinical findings and laboratory results are discordant. Although false-positive serum hCG results are rare, if unrecognized, they may lead to unwarranted clinical interventions for conditions such as persistent trophoblastic disease. The physician must judge whether the risks of waiting for confirmation of results outweigh the risks of failing to take immediate action.

## References


1. Cole LA, Kardana A. Discordant results in human chorionic gonadotropin assays. Clin Chem 1992;38:263–70.
2. Cole LA, Rinne KM, Shahabi S, Omrani A. False-positive hCG assay results leading to unnecessary surgery and chemotherapy and needless occurrences of diabetes and coma. Clin Chem 1999;45:313–4.
3. Rotmensch S, Cole LA. False diagnosis and needless therapy of presumed malignant disease in women with false-positive human chorionic gonadotropin concentrations. Lancet 2000;355:712–5.
4. Boscato LM, Stuart MC. Incidence and specificity of interference in two-site immunoassays. Clin Chem 1986; 32:1491–5.
5. Boscato LM, Stuart MC. Heterophilic antibodies: a problem for all immunoassays. Clin Chem 1988;34:27–33.

6. Check JH, Nowroozi K, Chase JS, Lauer C, Elkins B, Wu CH. False-positive human chorionic gonadotropin levels caused by a heterophile antibody with the immunoradiometric assay. Am J Obstet Gynecol 1988;158:99–100.
7. Weber TH, Kapyaho KI, Tanner P. Endogenous interference in immunoassays in clinical chemistry. A review. Scand J Clin Lab Invest Suppl 1990;201:77–82.
8. Berglund L, Holmberg NG. Heterophilic antibodies against rabbit serum causing falsely elevated gonadotropin levels. Acta Obstet Gynecol Scand 1989;68:377–8.
9. King IR, Doody MC. False-positive hCG by enzyme immunoassay resulting in repeated chemotherapy. Obstet Gynecol 1995;86:682–3.
10. Rzasa PJ, Caride VJ, Prokop EK. Discordant inter-kit results in the radioimmunoassay for choriogonadotropin in serum. Clin Chem 1984;30:1240–3.
11. Cole LA. Phantom hCG and phantom choriocarcinoma. Gynecol Oncol 1998;71:325–9.

# ACOG Committee Opinion

Committee on
Gynecologic Practice

Society of
Gynecologic
Oncologists

Number 280, December 2002

This document reflects emerging clinical and scientific advances as of the date issued and is subject to change. The information should not be construed as dictating an exclusive course of treatment or procedure to be followed.

The Committee and Society wish to thank William T. Creasman, MD, FACOG, for his assistance in the development of this opinion.



ISSN 1074-861X

**The American College of Obstetricians and Gynecologists**
409 12th Street, SW
PO Box 96920
Washington, DC 20090-6920

12345/65432

The role of the generalist obstetrician–gynecologist in the early detection of ovarian cancer. ACOG Committee Opinion No. 280. American College of Obstetricians and Gynecologists. Obstet Gynecol 2002;100:1413–16.

## The Role of the Generalist Obstetrician–Gynecologist in the Early Detection of Ovarian Cancer

*ABSTRACT: The purpose of this Committee Opinion is to define the role of the generalist obstetrician–gynecologist in the early detection of ovarian cancer. Currently, it appears that the best way to detect early ovarian cancer is for both the patient and her clinician to have a high index of suspicion of the diagnosis in the symptomatic woman. In evaluating symptoms, physicians should perform a physical examination, including a pelvic examination. In premenopausal women with symptoms, a CA 125 measurement has not been shown to be useful in most circumstances. In postmenopausal women with a pelvic mass, a CA 125 measurement may be helpful in predicting a higher likelihood of a malignant tumor than a benign tumor, which may be useful in making consultation or referral decisions or both. A woman with a suspicious or persistent complex adnexal mass requires surgical evaluation by a physician trained to appropriately stage and debulk ovarian cancer. Data suggest that currently available screening tests do not appear to be beneficial for screening low-risk, asymptomatic women. An annual gynecologic examination with an annual pelvic examination is recommended for preventive health care.*

Although ovarian cancer is the second most common female reproductive cancer, preceded by cancer of the uterine corpus, more women die from ovarian cancer than from cervical and uterine cancer combined. In the United States, it is estimated that ovarian cancer will be diagnosed in 23,300 women, and 13,900 women will die from this malignancy in 2002. The principal reason for these poor outcomes is the advanced stage of disease at diagnosis in 70–75% of cases and an overall 5-year survival of only 20–30%. However, women with a diagnosis of stage I disease achieve a 90–95% probability of cure. The purpose of this Committee Opinion is to define the role of the generalist obstetrician–gynecologist in the early detection of ovarian cancer.

The poor prognosis of ovarian cancer often is attributed to the fact that it is a "silent" cancer, with symptoms appearing only late in the disease process. This is a misconception, in that studies have shown that women with ovarian cancers are symptomatic often several months before the diagnosis, even with early-stage disease. In a survey of 1,725 women with ovarian cancer, 70% recalled having symptoms for 3 months or longer before the diagnosis, and

35% recalled having symptoms for at least 6 months (1). About three fourths of these women had abdominal symptoms and half had pain or constitutional symptoms. Overall, only 5% were asymptomatic, including only 11% of those with stage I and stage II disease. Pelvic examinations and tests to evaluate symptoms in these women were done more frequently by obstetrician–gynecologists than by other primary care physicians, resulting in earlier disease diagnosis.

Currently, it appears that the best way to detect early ovarian cancer is for both the patient and her clinician to have a high index of suspicion of the diagnosis in the symptomatic woman. This requires education of both as to the symptoms commonly associated with ovarian cancer. Persistent symptoms such as an increase in abdominal size, abdominal bloating, fatigue, abdominal pain, indigestion, inability to eat normally, urinary frequency, pelvic pain, constipation, back pain, urinary incontinence of recent onset, or unexplained weight loss should be evaluated with ovarian cancer being included in the differential diagnosis. Because ovarian cancer occurs most frequently in the postmenopausal woman (median age, approximately 60 years), these symptoms should not be ignored in these women. Unfortunately, many women and clinicians are quick to attribute such symptoms to menopause, aging, dietary changes, stress, or functional bowel problems. As a result, delays of weeks or months often occur before medical advice is sought or diagnostic studies are performed.

In evaluating these symptoms, physicians should perform a physical examination, including a pelvic examination. Imaging studies (including vaginal ultrasonography) may be helpful before making the diagnosis of irritable bowel syndrome, depression, stress, or other diagnoses. In premenopausal women with symptoms, a CA 125 measurement has not been shown to be useful in most circumstances because elevated levels of CA 125 are associated with a variety of common benign conditions, including uterine leiomyomata, pelvic inflammatory disease, endometriosis, adenomyosis, pregnancy, and even menstruation. In postmenopausal women with a pelvic mass, a CA 125 measurement may be helpful in predicting a higher likelihood of a malignant tumor than a benign tumor, which may be useful in making consultation or referral decisions or both; however, a normal CA 125 measurement alone does not rule out ovarian cancer because up to 50% of early-stage cancers and 20–25% of advanced cancers are associated with normal values. The longer the delay in evaluating symptoms or suspicious findings by either the patient or the clinician, the more likely advanced disease will be found.

Diagnostic criteria based on physical examination and imaging techniques that should be used to consider referral to or consultation with a gynecologic oncologist are as follows:

- Postmenopausal women who have a pelvic mass that is suspicious for a malignant ovarian neoplasm, as suggested by at least one of the following indicators: elevated CA 125 level; ascites; a nodular or fixed pelvic mass; evidence of abdominal or distant metastasis; a family history of one or more first-degree relatives with ovarian or breast cancer
- Premenopausal women who have a pelvic mass that is suspicious for a malignant ovarian neoplasm, as suggested by at least one of the following indicators: very elevated CA 125 level (eg, >200 U/mL); ascites; evidence of abdominal or distant metastasis; a family history of one or more first-degree relatives with ovarian or breast cancer

A woman with a suspicious or persistent complex adnexal mass requires surgical evaluation. In these circumstances, a physician trained to appropriately stage and debulk ovarian cancer, such as a gynecologic oncologist, should perform the operation. This should be done in a hospital facility that has the necessary support and consultative services (eg, pathology) to optimize the patient's outcome. When a malignant ovarian tumor is discovered and the appropriate operation cannot be properly performed, a gynecologic oncologist should be consulted.

Of particular concern is the observation that many women with early-stage disease do not undergo appropriate surgical staging. Patients whose comprehensive surgical staging confirms early-stage disease have a much better prognosis than those patients who were thought to have early-stage disease but did not undergo comprehensive surgical staging, presumably because occult disease was missed. In the absence of clinically apparent malignant disease, intraoperative pathology consultation should be obtained if cancer remains a concern. If an apparent early-stage malignancy is present, comprehensive surgical staging should be performed, preferably during the same operation. At the time of surgery for a pelvic mass, samples for peritoneal cytology should be obtained when the abdomen is entered. The mass should be removed intact through an incision that permits thorough staging and surgical management of the primary tumor and possible sites of metastasis. After the liver, spleen, and all peritoneal surfaces, including both hemidiaphragms, are inspected and palpated, a bilateral pelvic and paraaortic lymphadenectomy is performed along with an omentectomy, peritoneal biopsies, removal of the uterus and adnexa, and biopsies or removal of any suspicious lesions. When the cancer appears to be confined to one ovary, especially if it is low grade, it may be appropriate to modify the staging procedure by leaving the uterus and the uninvolved ovary in place for younger women who wish to preserve their fertility.

Unfortunately, there is no screening test for ovarian cancer that has proved effective in screening low-risk asymptomatic women. Measurement of CA 125 levels and completion of pelvic ultrasonography (both abdominal and transvaginal) have been the two tests most thoroughly evaluated. One group of researchers evaluated 22,000 women with CA 125 screening, followed by pelvic ultrasonography if an elevated tumor marker was present (2, 3). More than 98% of women had normal CA 125 values. Of the remaining group, 41 (0.1%) had both increased CA 125 values and abnormal ultrasonograms and underwent surgical assessment. Only 11 women (0.05% of women screened) had ovarian cancer, which was stage III in 7 women. The false-positive rate among those undergoing surgery was 73%. Another group of researchers evaluated 14,469 asymptomatic women with transvaginal ultrasonography, performing 57,214 scans over a period of several years (4). During the period of evaluation, only 11 of 180 women who had surgery for abnormal adnexal masses (6% of operations and 0.07% of women screened) had primary epithelial ovarian cancers, 6 of whom had cancers beyond stage I. Unfortunately, 4 additional women developed primary epithelial ovarian cancers (stage II and stage III) within 12 months of a normal scan. In a mass screening study of 51,500 women conducted over several years using transvaginal ultrasonography, 324 women were identified with abnormalities requiring surgery (5). Only 17 of these women (5% of operations and 0.03% of women screened) were found to have primary epithelial ovarian cancers.

Data suggest that currently available tests do not appear to be beneficial for screening low-risk, asymptomatic women because their sensitivity, specificity, positive predictive value, and negative predictive value have all been modest at best. Because of the low incidence of disease, reported to be approximately one case per 2,500 women per year, it has been estimated that a test with even 100% sensitivity and 99% specificity would have a positive predictive value of only 4.8%, meaning 20 of 21 women undergoing surgery would not have primary ovarian cancer. Unfortunately, no test available approaches this level of sensitivity or specificity.

Hereditary ovarian cancer is estimated to represent only 5–10% of all ovarian cancers. Based on current data, a woman with a germline mutation of *BRCA1* or *BRCA2* has a lifetime risk of 15–45% of developing ovarian cancer. There are no data demonstrating that screening improves early detection of ovarian cancer in this population. These women should be offered genetic counseling to address issues that relate to their high risk of breast and ovarian cancer and the potential impact of these genetic mutations on their offspring. Even if this group were screened for ovarian cancer on a regular basis, more than 90% of all potential ovarian cancer patients would remain unscreened.

Despite varying recommendations regarding the frequency of cervical cytology screening, the Committee on Gynecologic Practice and the Society of Gynecologic Oncologists still believe that an annual gynecologic examination with an annual pelvic examination is recommended for preventive health care. Although newer tumor markers and proteomics are undergoing investigation and appear promising for screening, it is unclear whether they will help identify high-risk women or facilitate the early diagnosis of more women with ovarian cancer. Currently, there are no techniques that have proved to be effective in the routine screening of asymptomatic low-risk women for ovarian cancer.

## References


1. Goff BA, Mandel L, Muntz HG, Melancon CH. Ovarian carcinoma diagnosis. Cancer 2000;89:2068–75.
2. Jacobs IJ, Skates SJ, MacDonald N, Menon U, Rosenthal AN, Davies AP, et al. Screening for ovarian cancer: a pilot randomized controlled trial. Lancet 1999;353:1207–10.
3. Jacobs I, Davies AP, Bridges J, Stabile I, Fay T, Lower A, et al. Prevalence screening for ovarian cancer in postmenopausal women by CA 125 measurement and ultrasonography. BMJ 1993;306:1030–4.
4. van Nagell JR Jr, DePriest PD, Reedy MB, Gallion HH, Ueland FR, Pavlik EJ, et al. The efficacy of transvaginal sonographic screening in asymptomatic women at risk for ovarian cancer. Gynecol Oncol 2000;77:350–6.
5. Sato S, Yokoyama Y, Sakamoto T, Futagami M, Saito Y. Usefulness of mass screening for ovarian carcinoma using transvaginal ultrasonography. Cancer 2000;89:582–8.

# ACOG Committee Opinion

Committee on Gynecologic Practice

Number 285, August 2003

# Induced Abortion and Breast Cancer Risk



ISSN 1074-861X

**The American College of Obstetricians and Gynecologists**
409 12th Street, SW
PO Box 96920
Washington, DC 20090-6920

12345/76543

Induced abortion and breast cancer risk. ACOG Committee Opinion No. 285. American College of Obstetricians and Gynecologists. Obstet Gynecol 2003;102:433–5.

*ABSTRACT: The purpose of this Committee Opinion is to provide a review of recent studies regarding the potential relationship between induced abortion and subsequent breast cancer and to discuss methodologic challenges in this field of study. The American College of Obstetricians and Gynecologists' Committee on Gynecologic Practice concludes that early studies of the relationship between prior induced abortion and breast cancer risk have been inconsistent and are difficult to interpret because of methodologic considerations. More rigorous recent studies argue against a causal relationship between induced abortion and a subsequent increase in breast cancer risk.*

In 1995, the American College of Obstetricians and Gynecologists' Committee on Gynecologic Practice concluded that the available evidence was insufficient to support claims that induced abortion has an effect on the later development of breast cancer. It further noted that the available studies were inconsistent and that many of the available case–control studies had methodologic problems. The purpose of this Committee Opinion is to provide a review of more recent studies regarding the potential relationship between induced abortion and subsequent breast cancer and to discuss methodologic challenges in this field of study.

Three systematic reviews of the available studies on the relationship between prior induced abortion and breast cancer risk were performed in 1996 and 1997 (1–3). In the first review, one cohort and 18 case–control studies were identified, and it was concluded that any relationship between induced abortion and breast cancer risk is likely to be small or nonexistent (1). In the second review, 21 studies were reviewed, and it was concluded that induced abortion was associated with an increased risk of breast cancer (odds ratio [OR], 1.3; 95% confidence interval [CI], 1.2–1.4) (2). In the third review, 28 studies of induced abortion and breast cancer risk were examined, and the authors concluded that findings across studies were inconsistent and that definitive conclusions regarding the relationship of induced abortion and breast cancer risk were not possible at that point (3). The authors also concluded that breast cancer risk did not appear to be associated with an increasing number of induced abortions.

Two of the three systematic reviews noted two key methodologic considerations in studying any potential relationship between induced abortion and breast cancer (1, 3). The first consideration is that pregnancy may well have a dual effect on breast cancer risk, increasing the short-term risk of breast cancer while providing long-term protection against breast cancer (4–6). This dual effect of parity on breast cancer risk creates a complexity in interpreting available data. For any independent effect of induced abortion on breast cancer risk to be confirmed, investigators would have to demonstrate that terminating a pregnancy creates a larger increase in short-term breast cancer risk than continuing pregnancy to term or that terminating a pregnancy reduced the long-term protection against breast cancer seen with pregnancies continued to term. A second key methodologic consideration in interpreting the evidence for any relationship between abortion and breast cancer risk is the sensitive nature of abortion, which could affect the accuracy in retrospective studies of self-reports of having had an abortion; nearly all studies on this issue have been retrospective.

Cohort studies are less susceptible to bias in data collection than case–control (retrospective) studies. Two cohort studies have been conducted to assess the relationship between induced abortion and breast cancer risk. The first study, from Sweden, found a significantly reduced breast cancer risk after induced abortion (relative risk [RR], 0.8; 95% CI, 0.58–0.99) (7). The second study, from Denmark, found no effect on breast cancer risk (RR, 1; 95% CI, 0.94–1.06) (8). The Swedish study addressed the RR of parous women separate from that of nulliparous women and found that the risk was significantly reduced in the parous group (RR, 0.58; 95% CI, 0.38–0.84) but not in the nulliparous group (RR, 1.09; 95% CI, 0.71–1.56). The Danish study is particularly noteworthy because it used a population-based cohort that linked data from the National Registry of Induced Abortions, which included information on the number and dates of induced abortions, with all new cases of breast cancer identified through the Danish Cancer Registry.

A Dutch case–control study has indicated the potential importance of reporting bias in many of the available case–control studies and the importance of reporting risks of induced abortion separately among parous women and nulliparous women (9). Among parous women in that study, a history of induced abortion was associated with an increased risk of breast cancer (RR, 1.9; 95% CI, 1.1–3.2). By contrast, among nulliparous women, there was no association between induced abortion and breast cancer risk (RR, 0.9; 95% CI, 0.4–2.3). The authors of the Dutch study concluded that the increased risk among parous women was attributable to reporting bias caused by large differences in the willingness to report having had an abortion in two regions of the country. The population of the one region with an increased risk (RR, 14.6; 95% CI, 1.8–120) was largely composed of members of a religion that officially discourages abortion. The other region had no significant increase in risk (RR, 1.3; 95% CI, 0.7–2.6). Women without breast cancer in the former region may have been less likely than those with breast cancer to acknowledge having had a prior abortion. The authors also documented an underreporting of duration of oral contraceptive use among women in the former region.

The most recent studies, including those completed in China (10), the United Kingdom (11), and the United States (12, 13), argue against a causal link between induced abortion and breast cancer risk. The first of the two U.S. studies evaluated women in western Washington State and concluded that there was no association between prior induced abortion and breast cancer risk (RR, 0.9; 95% CI, 0.7–1.2) (12). The second study used a record linkage methodology in Iowa and likewise found no effect of induced abortion on breast cancer risk (RR, 1.1; 95% CI, 0.8–1.6) (13).

The National Cancer Institute recently convened the Early Reproductive Events and Breast Cancer Workshop to evaluate the current strength of evidence of epidemiologic, clinical, and animal studies addressing the association between reproductive events and the risk of breast cancer (14). The workshop participants concluded that induced abortion is not associated with an increase in breast cancer risk.

The Committee on Gynecologic Practice concludes that early studies of the relationship between prior induced abortion and breast cancer risk have been inconsistent and are difficult to interpret because of methodologic considerations. More rigorous recent studies argue against a causal relationship between induced abortion and a subsequent increase in breast cancer risk.

## References


1. Michels KB, Willett WC. Does induced or spontaneous abortion affect the risk of breast cancer? Epidemiology 1996;7:521–8.
2. Brind J, Chinchilli VM, Severs WB, Summy-Long J. Induced abortion as an independent risk factor for breast cancer: a comprehensive review and meta-analysis. J Epidemiol Community Health 1996;50:481–96.
3. Wingo PA, Newsome K, Marks JS, Calle EE, Parker SL. The risk of breast cancer following spontaneous or induced abortion. Cancer Causes Control 1997;8:93–108.
4. Lambe M, Hsieh C, Trichopoulos D, Ekbom A, Pavia M, Adami HO. Transient increase in the risk of breast cancer after giving birth. N Engl J Med 1994;331:5–9.
5. Bruzzi R, Negri E, La Vecchia C, Decarli A, Palli D, Parazzine F, et al. Short term increase in risk of breast cancer after full term pregnancy. BMJ 1988;297:1096–8.
6. Cummings P, Stanford JL, Daling JR, Weiss NS, McKnight B. Risk of breast cancer in relation to the interval since last full term pregnancy. BMJ 1994;308:1672–4.
7. Harris BM, Eklund G, Meirik O, Rutqvist LE, Wiklund K. Risk of cancer of the breast after legal abortion during first trimester: a Swedish register study. BMJ 1989;299: 1430–2.
8. Melbye M, Wohlfahrt J, Olsen JH, Frisch M, Westergaard T, Helweg-Larsen K, et al. Induced abortion and the risk of breast cancer. N Engl J Med 1997;336:81–5.
9. Rookus MA, van Leeuwen FE. Induced abortion and risk for breast cancer: reporting (recall) bias in a Dutch case-control study. J Natl Cancer Inst 1996;88:1759–64.
10. Sanderson M, Shu XO, Jin F, Dai Q, Wen W, Hua Y, et al. Abortion history and breast cancer risk: results from the Shanghai Breast Cancer Study. Int J Cancer 2001;92: 899–905.
11. Goldacre MJ, Kurina LM, Seagroatt V, Yeates D. Abortion and breast cancer: a case-control record linkage study. J Epidemiol Community Health 2001;55:336–7.
12. Tang MT, Weiss NS, Malone KE. Induced abortion in relation to breast cancer among parous women: a birth certificate registry study. Epidemiology 2000;11:177–80.
13. Lazovich D, Thompson JA, Mink PJ, Sellers TA, Anderson KE. Induced abortion and breast cancer risk. Epidemiology 2000;11:76–80.
14. Summary report: Early Reproductive Events and Breast Cancer Workshop. Bethesda (MD): National Cancer Institute; 2003. Available at http://www.nci.nih.gov/cancerinfo/ere-workshop-report. Retrieved March 28, 2003.

# ACOG Committee Opinion

Committee on Gynecologic Practice

Committee on Obstetric Practice

Committee on Professional Liability

Number 288, October 2003

## Professional Liability and Gynecology-Only Practice

*ABSTRACT: Some Fellows of the American College of Obstetricians and Gynecologists limit the scope of their practices solely to gynecology. The College considers early pregnancy complications (often up to 12–14 weeks of gestation) to be within the definition of gynecology. Liability insurance should cover the role of gynecologists in the management of early pregnancy-related conditions.*

Some Fellows of the American College of Obstetricians and Gynecologists limit the scope of their practices to gynecology and do not request professional liability coverage for obstetrics. The College considers early pregnancy complications (often up to 12–14 weeks of gestation) to be within the definition of gynecology. Management of conditions such as ectopic pregnancy and spontaneous and elective abortion, including early and mid-trimester abortion, often are included in such a practice. Liability insurance should cover this role of gynecologists in the management of such early pregnancy-related conditions.



ISSN 1074-861X

**The American College of Obstetricians and Gynecologists**
409 12th Street, SW
PO Box 96920
Washington, DC 20090-6920

12345/76543

Professional liability and gynecology-only practice. ACOG Committee Opinion No. 288. American College of Obstetricians and Gynecologists. Obstet Gynecol 2003;102:891.

ACOG

Committee on Gynecologic Practice

# Committee Opinion

Number 293, February 2004

This document reflects emerging clinical and scientific advances as of the date issued and is subject to change. The information should not be construed as dictating an exclusive course of treatment or procedure to be followed.



ISSN 1074-861X

**The American College of Obstetricians and Gynecologists**

409 12th Street, SW
PO Box 96920
Washington, DC 20090-6920

12345/87654

Uterine artery embolization. ACOG Committee Opinion No. 293. American College of Obstetricians and Gynecologists. Obstet Gynecol 2004;103:403–4

# Uterine Artery Embolization

*ABSTRACT: Uterine artery embolization for the treatment of symptomatic uterine leiomyomata has become increasingly popular. Based on current evidence, it appears that uterine artery embolization, when performed by experienced physicians, provides good short-term relief of bulk-related symptoms and a reduction in menstrual flow. Complication rates associated with the procedure are low, but in rare cases can include hysterectomy and death. There is insufficient evidence to ensure its safety in women desiring to retain their fertility, and pregnancy-related outcomes remain understudied. The American College of Obstetricians and Gynecologists' Committee on Gynecologic Practice considers the procedure investigational or relatively contraindicated in women wishing to retain fertility. The use of uterine artery embolization in postmenopausal women is rarely, if ever, indicated. The Committee strongly recommends that women who wish to undergo uterine artery embolization have a thorough evaluation with an obstetrician–gynecologist to help facilitate optimal collaboration with interventional radiologists and to ensure the appropriateness of this therapy, taking into account the reproductive wishes of the patient. It is also recommended that all patients considering uterine artery embolization be adequately informed about potential complications.*

Uterine artery embolization for the treatment of symptomatic uterine leiomyomata has become increasingly popular. The concept of selective arterial embolization was originally used in obstetrics and gynecology in 1979 to treat postpartum hemorrhage (1). It subsequently was used as an alternative to surgical removal of uterine leiomyomata in 1995 (2). This procedure typically is performed by inserting a catheter into the common femoral artery to access the uterine arteries. The uterine arteries are then embolized using polyvinyl alcohol particles or tris-acryl gelatin microspheres. Supplemental metal coils also may be used to assist with vascular occlusion.

To date, most data regarding patient satisfaction, leiomyomata and uterine size reduction, fertility, and complications are derived from case reports and case series. In general, these reports have shown a short-term reduction in leiomyomata and uterine size, as well as a short-term clinical improvement in bulk-related symptoms and reduction in menstrual bleeding. Recently, a large multicenter series reporting on 538 women and a nonrandomized controlled study have been published, which confirm these short-term findings (3, 4). In the latter study, though limited in sample size (n=51), patient satisfaction was followed for up to 5 years and was found to be comparable to myomectomy.

Complications from uterine artery embolization have likewise become more apparent as case reports have been published and as results from larger case series have become available. Reported complications include infection, abscess, sepsis, hysterectomy, permanent amenorrhea, labial necrosis, focal bladder necrosis, vesicouterine fistula, uterine wall defects, groin hematoma, pulmonary emboli, and, rarely, death. In addition, embolization of an undiagnosed leiomyosarcoma has been reported. In a large series of 400 patients undergoing uterine artery embolization, the following complication rates were reported: febrile morbidity, 2%; hemorrhage, 0.75%; performance of unintended procedure, 2.5%; life-threatening events, 0.5%; and readmission within 14 days of procedure, 3.5%. Overall, the complication rate, using these clinical indicators for perioperative morbidity, was 5% (5). The loss of ovarian function has been reported to be as high as 14% with uterine artery embolization (6). Embolic microspheres have been documented histologically in the ovarian arterial vasculature in patients undergoing the procedure (7). Although transient postoperative pain occurs in most cases, persistent postoperative pain leads to hysterectomy in less than 1% of cases (8).

Approximately 50 cases of pregnancy have been reported in patients who have undergone elective uterine artery embolization. Of the resulting births, 58% were delivered by cesarean birth, 28% were preterm births, and 13% of patients experienced postpartum hemorrhage (9). Further data are needed to draw conclusions regarding the safety of uterine artery embolization in patients desiring to become pregnant.

Based on current evidence, it appears that uterine artery embolization, when performed by experienced physicians, provides good short-term relief of bulk-related symptoms as well as a reduction of menstrual flow. Complication rates associated with the procedure are low, but in rare cases can include hysterectomy and death. There is insufficient evidence in the current literature to ensure safety in women desiring to retain their fertility. Furthermore, pregnancy-related outcomes remain understudied. Therefore, the procedure should be considered investigational or relatively contraindicated in women wishing to retain fertility. The use of uterine artery embolization in postmenopausal women is rarely, if ever, indicated.

It is strongly recommended that women who wish to undergo uterine artery embolization have a thorough evaluation with an obstetrician–gynecologist to help facilitate optimal collaboration with interventional radiologists and to ensure the appropriateness of this therapy, taking into account the reproductive wishes of the patient. It also is recommended that all patients considering uterine artery embolization be adequately informed about potential complications.

## References

1. Heaston DK, Mineau DE, Brown BJ, Miller FJ Jr. Transcatheter arterial embolization for control of persistent massive puerperal hemorrhage after bilateral surgical hypogastric artery ligation. AJR Am J Roentgenol 1979;133:152–4.
2. Ravina JH, Herbreteau D, Ciraru-Vigneron N, Bouret JM, Houdart E, Aymard A, et al. Arterial embolisation to treat uterine myomata. Lancet 1995;346:671–2.
3. Pron G, Bennett J, Common A, Wall J, Asch M, Sniderman K, et al. The Ontario Uterine Fibroid Embolization Trial. Part 2. Uterine fibroid reduction and symptom relief after uterine artery embolization for fibroids. Fertil Steril 2003;79:120–7.
4. Broder MS, Goodwin S, Chen G, Tang LJ, Costantino MM, Nguyen MH, et al. Comparison of long-term outcomes of myomectomy and uterine artery embolization. Obstet Gynecol 2002;100:864–8.
5. Spies JB, Spector A, Roth AR, Baker CM, Mauro L, Murphy-Skrynarz K. Complications after uterine artery embolization of leiomyomas. Obstet Gynecol 2002;100: 873–80.
6. Chrisman HB, Saker MB, Ryu RK, Nemcek AA Jr, Gerbie MV, Milad MP, et al. The impact of uterine fibroid embolization on resumption of menses and ovarian function. J Vasc Interv Radiol 2000;11:699–703.
7. Payne JF, Robboy SJ, Haney AF. Embolic microspheres within ovarian arterial vasculature after uterine artery embolization. Obstet Gynecol 2002;100:883–6.
8. Pron G, Mocarski E, Cohen M, Colgan T, Bennett J, Common A, et al. Hysterectomy for complications after uterine artery embolization for leiomyoma: results from a Canadian multicenter clinical trial. J Am Assoc Gynecol Laparosc 2003;10:99–106.
9. Goldberg J, Pereira L, Berghella V. Pregnancy after uterine artery embolization. Obstet Gynecol 2002;100: 869–72.

ACOG

ACOG Committee on Gynecologic Practice



ISSN 1074-861X

**The American College of Obstetricians and Gynecologists**
409 12th Street, SW
PO Box 96920
Washington, DC 20090-6920

12345/98765

Appropriate use of laparoscopically assisted vaginal hysterectomy. ACOG Committee Opinion No. 311. American College of Obstetricians and Gynecologists. Obstet Gynecol 2005;105:929–30.

# Committee Opinion

Number 311, April 2005

# Appropriate Use of Laparoscopically Assisted Vaginal Hysterectomy

*ABSTRACT: The technique used for hysterectomy should be dictated by the indication for the surgery, patient characteristics, and patient preference. Most patients requiring hysterectomy should be offered the vaginal approach when technically feasible and medically appropriate. If specific additional procedures that can be completed laparoscopically are anticipated before surgery, laparoscopically assisted vaginal hysterectomy may be an appropriate alternative to abdominal hysterectomy. The benefits of laparoscopically assisted vaginal hysterectomy must be weighed against the potentially increased risk and expense of two distinct operative procedures, laparoscopy and vaginal hysterectomy.*

The technique used for hysterectomy should be dictated by the indication for the surgery, patient characteristics, and patient preference. Most patients requiring hysterectomy should be offered the vaginal approach when technically feasible and medically appropriate because morbidity appears to be lower with the vaginal approach than with any other method (1–4). Laparoscopically assisted vaginal hysterectomy (LAVH), with or without bilateral salpingo-oophorectomy, usually offers no advantage when a conventional vaginal hysterectomy and bilateral salpingo-oophorectomy can otherwise be performed.

Prospective randomized trials demonstrate that LAVH is associated with faster recovery, less postoperative pain, and similar complication rates when compared with abdominal hysterectomy (1, 5–7). Specific additional procedures that can be completed laparoscopically to facilitate the performance of vaginal hysterectomy include:

- Lysis of adhesions
- Treatment of endometriosis
- Management of uterine leiomyomata that complicate the performance of vaginal hysterectomy
- Ligation of infundibulopelvic ligaments to facilitate difficult ovary removal
- Evaluation of the pelvic and abdominal cavity before hysterectomy

If these procedures are anticipated before surgery, LAVH may be an appropriate alternative to abdominal hysterectomy (8). The laparoscopic approach introduces the potential for additional complications when compared with vaginal hysterectomy. These complications include trocar injuries to vessels and viscera, bowel and omental herniation through large trocar sites, and urinary and bowel injuries (7, 9). The benefits of LAVH must be weighed against the potentially increased risk and expense of two distinct operative procedures, laparoscopy and vaginal hysterectomy, each with its own risks.

## References


1. Garry R, Fountain J, Mason S, Hawe J, Napp V, Abbott J, et al. The eVALuate study: two parallel randomised trials, one comparing laparoscopic with abdominal hysterectomy, the other comparing laparoscopic with vaginal hysterectomy [published erratum appears in BMJ 2004; 328:494]. BMJ 2004;328:129.
2. Harkki P, Kurki T, Sjoberg J, Titinen A. Safety aspects of laparoscopic hysterectomy. Acta Obstet Gynecol Scand 2001;80:383–91.
3. Schwartz RO. Complications of laparoscopic hysterectomy. Obstet Gynecol 1993;81:1022–4.
4. Summitt RL Jr, Stovall TG, Lipscomb GH, Ling FW. Randomized comparison of laparoscopy-assisted vaginal hysterectomy with standard vaginal hysterectomy in an outpatient setting. Obstet Gynecol 1992;80:895–901.
5. Summitt RL Jr, Stovall TG, Steege JF, Lipscomb GH. A multicenter randomized comparison of laparoscopically-assisted vaginal hysterectomy and abdominal hysterectomy in abdominal hysterectomy candidates. Obstet Gynecol 1998;92:321–6.
6. Olsson JH, Ellstrom M, Hahlin A. A randomised prospective trial comparing laparoscopic and abdominal hysterectomy. Br J Obstet Gynaecol 1996;103:345–50.
7. Falcone T, Paraiso MF, Mascha E. Prospective randomized clinical trial of laparoscopically assisted vaginal hysterectomy versus total abdominal hysterectomy. Am J Obstet Gynecol 1999;180:955–62.
8. Society of Pelvic Reconstructive Surgeons. Guideline for determining the route and method of hysterectomy for benign conditions. Atlanta (GA): SPRS;2004.
9. Meikle SF, Nugent EW, Orleans M. Complications and recovery from laparoscopy-assisted vaginal hysterectomy compared with abdominal and vaginal hysterectomy. Obstet Gynecol 1997;89:304–11.

ACOG Committee Opinion

Committee on Gynecologic Practice

This document reflects emerging clinical and scientific advances as of the date issued and is subject to change. The information should not be construed as dictating an exclusive course of treatment or procedure to be followed.

The Committee wishes to thank the ACOG Preconception Care Work Group co-chairs, Michele G. Curtis, MD, and Paula J. Adams Hillard, MD, and members, Hani K. Atrash, MD, MPH; Alfred Brann Jr, MD; Siobhan M. Dolan, MD, MPH; Ann Lang Dunlop, MD; Ann Weathersby, CNM, MSN; and Gerald Zelinger, MD, for their assistance in the development of this opinion.



ISSN 1074-861X

**The American College of Obstetricians and Gynecologists**
409 12th Street, SW
PO Box 96920
Washington, DC 20090-6920

12345/98765

The importance of preconception care in the continuum of women's health care. ACOG Committee Opinion No. 313. American College of Obstetricians and Gynecologists. Obstet Gynecol 2005;106:665–6

Number 313, September 2005

# The Importance of Preconception Care in the Continuum of Women's Health Care

*ABSTRACT: The goal of preconception care is to reduce the risk of adverse health effects for the woman, fetus, or neonate by optimizing the woman's health and knowledge before planning and conceiving a pregnancy. Because reproductive capacity spans almost four decades for most women, optimizing women's health before and between pregnancies is an ongoing process that requires access to and the full participation of all segments of the health care system.*

Although most pregnancies result in good maternal and fetal outcomes, some pregnancies may result in adverse health effects for the woman, fetus, or neonate. Although some of these outcomes cannot be prevented, optimizing a woman's health and knowledge before planning and conceiving a pregnancy—also referred to as preconception care or prepregnancy care—may eliminate or reduce the risk. For example, initiation of folic acid supplementation at least 1 month before pregnancy reduces the incidence of neural tube defects such as spina bifida and anencephaly (1–3). Similarly, adequate glucose control in a woman with diabetes before conception and throughout pregnancy can decrease maternal morbidity, spontaneous abortion, fetal malformation, fetal macrosomia, intrauterine fetal death, and neonatal morbidity (4).

Nearly half of all pregnancies in the United States are unintended (5). Therefore, the challenge of preconception care lies not only in addressing pregnancy planning for women who seek medical care and consultation specifically in anticipation of a planned pregnancy but also in educating and screening all reproductively capable women on an ongoing basis to identify potential maternal and fetal risks and hazards to pregnancy before and between pregnancies.

This Committee Opinion reinforces the importance of preconception care, provides resources for the woman's health care clinician, and proposes that every reproductively capable woman create a reproductive health plan. The specific clinical content of preconception care is outlined elsewhere (6–8).

Several national and international medical organizations and advocacy groups have focused on the optimization of health before conception, resulting in the development of clinical recommendations and educational materials (see Resources). Core preconception care considerations addressed by all include the following factors:

- Undiagnosed, untreated, or poorly controlled medical conditions
- Immunization history
- Medication and radiation exposure in early pregnancy
- Nutritional issues
- Family history and genetic risk
- Tobacco and substance use and other high-risk behaviors
- Occupational and environmental exposures
- Social issues
- Mental health issues

As medical care rapidly advances, the list of issues to consider when planning a pregnancy continues to grow.

Clinicians should encourage women to formulate a reproductive health plan and should discuss it in a nondirective way at each visit. Such a plan would address the individual's or couple's desire for a child or children (or desire not to have children); the optimal number, spacing, and timing of children in the family; and age-related changes in fertility. Because many women's plans change over time, creating a reproductive health plan requires an ongoing conscientious assessment of the desirability of a future pregnancy, determination of steps that need to be taken either to prevent or to plan for and optimize a pregnancy, and evaluation of current health status and other issues relevant to the health of a pregnancy.

A question such as "Are you considering pregnancy, or could you possibly become pregnant?" can initiate several preconception care interventions, including those listed as follows:

- A dialogue regarding the patient's readiness for pregnancy
- An evaluation of her overall health and opportunities for improving her health
- Education about the significant impact that social, environmental, occupational, behavioral, and genetic factors have in pregnancy
- Identification of women at high risk for an adverse pregnancy outcome

If pregnancy is not desired, current contraceptive use and options should be discussed to assist the patient in identifying the most appropriate and effective method for her.

Preconception and interpregnancy care are components of a larger health care goal—optimizing the health of every woman (9). Because reproductive capacity spans almost four decades for most women, optimizing women's health before and between pregnancies is an ongoing process that requires access to and the full participation of all segments of the health care system.

## References

1. Czeizel AE, Dudas I. Prevention of the first occurrence of neural-tube defects by periconceptional vitamin supplementation. N Engl J Med 1992;327:1832–5.
2. Prevention of neural tube defects: results of the Medical Research Council Vitamin Study. MRC Vitamin Study Research Group. Lancet 1991;338:131–7.
3. Botto LD, Moore CA, Khoury MJ, Erickson JD. Neural-tube defects. N Engl J Med 1999;341:1509–19.
4. Pregestational diabetes mellitus. ACOG Practice Bulletin No. 60. American College of Obstetricians and Gynecologists. Obstet Gynecol 2005;105:675–85.
5. Henshaw SK. Unintended pregnancy in the United States. Fam Plann Perspect 1998;30:24–9, 46.
6. American Academy of Pediatrics, American College of Obstetricians and Gynecologists. Guidelines for perinatal care. 5th ed. Elk Grove Village (IL): AAP; Washington, DC: ACOG; 2002.
7. American College of Obstetricians and Gynecologists. Guidelines for women's health care. 2nd ed. Washington, DC: ACOG; 2002.
8. American College of Obstetricians and Gynecologists, American College of Medical Genetics. Preconception and prenatal carrier screening for cystic fibrosis. Clinical and laboratory guidelines. Washington, DC: ACOG; 2001.
9. American College of Obstetricians and Gynecologists. Access to women's health care. ACOG Statement of Policy. Washington, DC: ACOG; 2003.

## Resources

American College of Obstetricians and Gynecologists
www.acog.org

American Academy of Family Physicians
www.aafp.org

American Academy of Pediatrics
www.aap.org

American College of Nurse-Midwives
www.acnm.org

American Society for Reproductive Medicine
www.asrm.org

Association of Women's Health, Obstetric and Neonatal Nurses
www.awhonn.org

Centers for Disease Control and Prevention National Center on Birth Defects and Developmental Disabilities
www.cdc.gov/ncbddd

March of Dimes
www.marchofdimes.com

# ACOG Committee Opinion

Committee on Gynecologic Practice

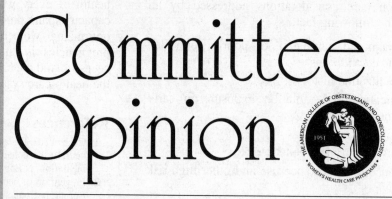

Number 319, October 2005

# The Role of the Obstetrician–Gynecologist in the Assessment and Management of Obesity



ISSN 1074-861X

**The American College of Obstetricians and Gynecologists**
409 12th Street, SW
PO Box 96920
Washington, DC 20090-6920

12345/98765

The role of the obstetrician–gynecologist in the assessment and management of obesity. ACOG Committee Opinion No. 319. American College of Obstetricians and Gynecologists. Obstet Gynecol 2005;106:895–9.

*ABSTRACT: Approximately one third of all women in the United States are obese. Obstetrician–gynecologists should evaluate all women for obesity by calculating a body mass index (BMI) measurement and should offer appropriate interventions or referrals to promote a healthy weight and lifestyle.*

The purpose of this Committee Opinion is to address the role of the obstetrician–gynecologist in the assessment and management of obesity in nonpregnant adult women. Definitions of overweight and obesity will be reviewed, the importance of calculating the body mass index (BMI) will be outlined, and resources for counseling and referral will be provided. The impact of obesity on pregnancy and the assessment of overweight and obesity in adolescents are addressed elsewhere (1, 2).

## Background

Obesity, defined as a BMI of 30 or greater, is the fastest-growing health problem in the United States, and its prevalence has increased sharply over the past 20 years (3). Approximately one third of all U.S. women are obese (3). Obesity is more prevalent in lower-income and minority women; 49% of African–American women and 38% of Mexican–American women are obese, compared with 31% of white women (3). Obesity has been associated with increased morbidity, including type 2 diabetes, hypertension, infertility, heart disease, gallbladder disease, osteoarthritis, and a variety of cancers, including breast, uterine, and colon cancers (4–7). Endometrial cancer is the most common gynecologic malignancy, and obese women are almost five times more likely than nonobese women (BMI 20–22.9) to develop endometrial cancer (8). Obesity and overweight are associated with an increased risk for heart disease, the leading cause of death of American women (4, 5, 9). An estimated 112,000 individuals die annually of obesity-associated causes (10).

## Assessment

The patient's medical, social, and family history should be reviewed for weight-related conditions. To determine if the patient is overweight or obese, the BMI should be calculated. If the patient's BMI is 30 or greater, the severity of obesity (Class I, II, or III) should be noted (Table 1).

Central adiposity, defined as a waist circumference greater than 35 inches (>88 cm) in women, may further identify women at risk for obesity-related morbidity (11). Waist circumference is measured at the end of a normal expiration of breath by placing a measuring tape around the abdomen at the level of the iliac crest.

**Table 1.** Body Mass Index Calculation, Chart, and Categories

The Body Mass Index (BMI) is an indirect measure of body fat and is used to determine obesity. The BMI is calculated as weight in kilograms (kg) divided by the square of height in meters ($m^2$).

$$\text{BMI} = \frac{\text{weight (kg)}}{\text{height squared (m}^2\text{)}}$$

Using a BMI chart is an easy and rapid way of identifying the BMI for all adult patients.

Body Mass Index Table

| | Normal | | | | | | Overweight | | | | | Obese | | | | | | | | | | Extreme Obesity | | | | | | | | | | | | | | |
|---|---|---|---|---|---|---|---|---|---|---|---|---|---|---|---|---|---|---|---|---|---|---|---|---|---|---|---|---|---|---|---|---|---|---|---|---|
| **BMI** | **19** | **20** | **21** | **22** | **23** | **24** | **25** | **26** | **27** | **28** | **29** | **30** | **31** | **32** | **33** | **34** | **35** | **36** | **37** | **38** | **39** | **40** | **41** | **42** | **43** | **44** | **45** | **46** | **47** | **48** | **49** | **50** | **51** | **52** | **53** | **54** |
| **Height (inches)** | **Body Weight (pounds)** | | | | | | | | | | | | | | | | | | | | | | | | | | | | | | | | | | | |
| 58 | 91 | 96 | 100 | 105 | 110 | 115 | 119 | 124 | 129 | 134 | 138 | 143 | 148 | 153 | 158 | 162 | 167 | 172 | 177 | 181 | 186 | 191 | 196 | 201 | 205 | 210 | 215 | 220 | 224 | 229 | 234 | 239 | 244 | 248 | 253 | 258 |
| 59 | 94 | 99 | 104 | 109 | 114 | 119 | 124 | 128 | 133 | 138 | 143 | 148 | 153 | 158 | 163 | 168 | 173 | 178 | 183 | 188 | 193 | 198 | 203 | 208 | 212 | 217 | 222 | 227 | 232 | 237 | 242 | 247 | 252 | 257 | 262 | 267 |
| 60 | 97 | 102 | 107 | 112 | 118 | 123 | 128 | 133 | 138 | 143 | 148 | 153 | 158 | 163 | 168 | 174 | 179 | 184 | 189 | 194 | 199 | 204 | 209 | 215 | 220 | 225 | 230 | 235 | 240 | 245 | 250 | 255 | 261 | 266 | 271 | 276 |
| 61 | 100 | 106 | 111 | 116 | 122 | 127 | 132 | 137 | 143 | 148 | 153 | 158 | 164 | 169 | 174 | 180 | 185 | 190 | 195 | 201 | 206 | 211 | 217 | 222 | 227 | 232 | 238 | 243 | 248 | 254 | 259 | 264 | 269 | 275 | 280 | 285 |
| 62 | 104 | 109 | 115 | 120 | 126 | 131 | 136 | 142 | 147 | 153 | 158 | 164 | 169 | 175 | 180 | 186 | 191 | 196 | 202 | 207 | 213 | 218 | 224 | 229 | 235 | 240 | 246 | 251 | 256 | 262 | 267 | 273 | 278 | 284 | 289 | 295 |
| 63 | 107 | 113 | 118 | 124 | 130 | 135 | 141 | 146 | 152 | 158 | 163 | 169 | 175 | 180 | 186 | 191 | 197 | 203 | 208 | 214 | 220 | 225 | 231 | 237 | 242 | 248 | 254 | 259 | 265 | 270 | 278 | 282 | 287 | 293 | 299 | 304 |
| 64 | 110 | 116 | 122 | 128 | 134 | 140 | 145 | 151 | 157 | 163 | 169 | 174 | 180 | 186 | 192 | 197 | 204 | 209 | 215 | 221 | 227 | 232 | 238 | 244 | 250 | 256 | 262 | 267 | 273 | 279 | 285 | 291 | 296 | 302 | 308 | 314 |
| 65 | 114 | 120 | 126 | 132 | 138 | 144 | 150 | 156 | 162 | 168 | 174 | 180 | 186 | 192 | 198 | 204 | 210 | 216 | 222 | 228 | 234 | 240 | 246 | 252 | 258 | 264 | 270 | 276 | 282 | 288 | 294 | 300 | 306 | 312 | 318 | 324 |
| 66 | 118 | 124 | 130 | 136 | 142 | 148 | 155 | 161 | 167 | 173 | 179 | 186 | 192 | 198 | 204 | 210 | 216 | 223 | 229 | 235 | 241 | 247 | 253 | 260 | 266 | 272 | 278 | 284 | 291 | 297 | 303 | 309 | 315 | 322 | 328 | 334 |
| 67 | 121 | 127 | 134 | 140 | 146 | 153 | 159 | 166 | 172 | 178 | 185 | 191 | 198 | 204 | 211 | 217 | 223 | 230 | 236 | 242 | 249 | 255 | 261 | 268 | 274 | 280 | 287 | 293 | 299 | 306 | 312 | 319 | 325 | 331 | 338 | 344 |
| 68 | 125 | 131 | 138 | 144 | 151 | 158 | 164 | 171 | 177 | 184 | 190 | 197 | 203 | 210 | 216 | 223 | 230 | 236 | 243 | 249 | 256 | 262 | 269 | 276 | 282 | 289 | 295 | 302 | 308 | 315 | 322 | 328 | 335 | 341 | 348 | 354 |
| 69 | 128 | 135 | 142 | 149 | 155 | 162 | 169 | 176 | 182 | 189 | 196 | 203 | 209 | 216 | 223 | 230 | 236 | 243 | 250 | 257 | 263 | 270 | 277 | 284 | 291 | 297 | 304 | 311 | 318 | 324 | 331 | 338 | 345 | 351 | 358 | 365 |
| 70 | 132 | 139 | 146 | 153 | 160 | 167 | 174 | 181 | 188 | 195 | 202 | 209 | 216 | 222 | 229 | 236 | 243 | 250 | 257 | 264 | 271 | 278 | 285 | 292 | 299 | 306 | 313 | 320 | 327 | 334 | 341 | 348 | 355 | 362 | 369 | 376 |
| 71 | 136 | 143 | 150 | 157 | 165 | 172 | 179 | 186 | 193 | 200 | 208 | 215 | 222 | 229 | 236 | 243 | 250 | 257 | 265 | 272 | 279 | 286 | 293 | 301 | 308 | 315 | 322 | 329 | 338 | 343 | 351 | 358 | 365 | 372 | 379 | 386 |
| 72 | 140 | 147 | 154 | 162 | 169 | 177 | 184 | 191 | 199 | 206 | 213 | 221 | 228 | 235 | 242 | 250 | 258 | 265 | 272 | 279 | 287 | 294 | 302 | 309 | 316 | 324 | 331 | 338 | 346 | 353 | 361 | 368 | 375 | 383 | 390 | 397 |
| 73 | 144 | 151 | 159 | 166 | 174 | 182 | 189 | 197 | 204 | 212 | 219 | 227 | 235 | 242 | 250 | 257 | 265 | 272 | 280 | 288 | 295 | 302 | 310 | 318 | 325 | 333 | 340 | 348 | 355 | 363 | 371 | 378 | 386 | 393 | 401 | 408 |
| 74 | 148 | 155 | 163 | 171 | 179 | 186 | 194 | 202 | 210 | 218 | 225 | 233 | 241 | 249 | 256 | 264 | 272 | 280 | 287 | 295 | 303 | 311 | 319 | 326 | 334 | 342 | 350 | 358 | 365 | 373 | 381 | 389 | 396 | 404 | 412 | 420 |
| 75 | 152 | 160 | 168 | 176 | 184 | 192 | 200 | 208 | 216 | 224 | 232 | 240 | 248 | 256 | 264 | 272 | 279 | 287 | 295 | 303 | 311 | 319 | 327 | 335 | 343 | 351 | 359 | 367 | 375 | 383 | 391 | 399 | 407 | 415 | 423 | 431 |
| 76 | 156 | 164 | 172 | 180 | 189 | 197 | 205 | 213 | 221 | 230 | 238 | 246 | 254 | 263 | 271 | 279 | 287 | 295 | 304 | 312 | 320 | 328 | 336 | 344 | 353 | 361 | 369 | 377 | 385 | 394 | 402 | 410 | 418 | 426 | 435 | 443 |

| Weight category | BMI |
|---|---|
| Underweight | <18.5 |
| Normal weight | 18.5–24.9 |
| Overweight | 25–29.9 |
| Obesity (Class I) | 30–34.9 |
| Obesity (Class II) | 35–39.9 |
| Extreme Obesity (Class III) | ≥40 |

The practical guide: identification, evaluation, and treatment of overweight and obesity in adults. National Heart, Lung, and Blood Institute and North American Association for the Study of Obesity. Bethesda (MD): National Institutes of Health; 2000.

Blood pressure measurements, fasting lipid panels, and fasting blood glucose measurements may be appropriate for identifying comorbidities. However, no single laboratory test or diagnostic evaluation is indicated for all patients with obesity, and the tests and evaluations performed should be based on the patient's symptoms and risk factors and the clinician's index of suspicion for specific comorbidities (12).

## Management

Weight management is a challenge for patients and their physicians. For many women, achieving and maintaining a healthy weight is a difficult and lifelong process. Improved health through weight loss and appropriate increased physical activity should be the goal. Counseling to support improvements in diet and physical activity are considered first-line interventions, although pharmacotherapy and surgery may be appropriate for some women (Table 2). The U.S. Preventive Services Task Force found the most successful nonsurgical approaches to be intensive, weight-focused counseling (more than one session per month) or multicomponent, intensive interventions that combine nutrition and exercise counseling with supportive, skill-building behavioral interventions (13). If available, referral for further evaluation and treatment should be considered whenever the resources of the clinician are insufficient to meet the patient's current needs, for women with a BMI of 40 or greater, and for women with a BMI of 35 or greater with comorbidities or who have failed appropriate prior intervention(s).

Reinforcing the importance of weight loss and exercise and assessing the patient's readiness to make behavioral changes should be the initial approach. The clinician should inform the patient in a sensitive manner that her weight is a health concern and assist her in developing a weight loss and exercise plan. Asking the patient if she is concerned about her weight and has ever tried to lose weight will help the clinician determine if she is interested in weight management. Applying the stages of change model, as adapted for overweight and obesity, may help determine patient motivation and interest in weight loss (Table 3). Educational handouts for the patient to read at home can be discussed at a follow-up visit. Setting an initial goal of losing 5–10% of total body weight over a 6-month period is realistic and achievable and can decrease the severity of obesity-associated risk factors (14). Contact information for community resources, support groups, and weight loss programs may be provided (see Patient Resources). Evaluation by a nutritionist may be of benefit, in addition to follow-up visits with a clinician to monitor progress and provide support. Patients can be informed that some insurance carriers may provide coverage for weight loss interventions.

Orlistat and sibutramine hydrochloride monohydrate have been approved by the U.S. Food and Drug Administration for patients with a BMI of 30 or greater and for those with a BMI of 27 or greater and other risk factors (eg, hypertension, diabetes, or dyslipidemia) when used in combination with lifestyle changes (see Table 2). These agents are the two most studied pharmacologic treatments for obesity, although efficacy and safety beyond 12 months have not been investigated in randomized, controlled trials (15, 16). Orlistat is a gastrointestinal lipase inhibitor that limits fat absorption. Side

**Table 2.** Guide to Selecting Treatment

| | Body Mass Index Category | | | | |
|---|---|---|---|---|---|
| **Treatment** | **25–26.9** | **27–29.9** | **30–34.9** | **35–39.9** | **≥40** |
| Diet, physical activity, and behavior therapy | With comorbidities | With comorbidities | + | + | + |
| Pharmacotherapy | | With comorbidities | + | + | + |
| Surgery | | | With comorbidities | With comorbidities | With comorbidities |

The + represents the use of indicated treatment regardless of comorbidities.

The practical guide: identification, evaluation, and treatment of overweight and obesity in adults. National Heart, Lung, and Blood Institute and North American Association for the Study of Obesity. Bethesda (MD): National Institutes of Health; 2000.

**Table 3.** Stages of Change Model to Assess Readiness for Weight Loss

| Stage | Characteristic | Patient Verbal Cue | Appropriate Intervention | Sample Dialogue |
|---|---|---|---|---|
| Precontemplation | Unaware of problem, no interest in change | "I'm not really interested in weight loss. It's not a problem." | Provide information about health risks and benefits of weight loss | "Would you like to read some information about the health aspects of obesity?" |
| Contemplation | Aware of problem, beginning to think of changing | "I know I need to lose weight, but with all that's going on in my life right now, I'm not sure I can." | Help resolve ambivalence; discuss barriers | "Let's look at the benefits of weight loss, as well as what you may need to change." |
| Preparation | Realizes benefits of making changes and thinking about how to change | "I have to lose weight, and I'm planning to do that." | Teach behavior modification; provide education | "Let's take a closer look at how you can reduce some of the calories you eat and how to increase your activity during the day." |
| Action | Actively taking steps toward change | "I'm doing my best. This is harder than I thought." | Provide support and guidance, with a focus on the long term | "It's terrific that you're working so hard. What problems have you had so far? How have you solved them?" |
| Maintenance | Initial treatment goals reached | "I've learned a lot through this process." | Relapse control | "What situations continue to tempt you to overeat? What can be helpful for the next time you face such a situation?" |

Assessment and management of adult obesity: a primer for physicians, assessing readiness and making treatment decisions. American Medical Association and the Robert Wood Johnson Foundation, Copyright 2003.

effects are common and include fecal urgency, flatulence, and oily rectal discharge. A recent literature review found six trials that demonstrated significant weight loss (2.8–4.5 kg in 6–12.5 months) by patients who took orlistat (120 mg, taken 3 times daily before meals) compared with patients who took a placebo (17). In three trials reporting response rates, 14–38% of patients treated with orlistat lost 10% of their body weight. This degree of weight loss was 9–19% more common in patients who received orlistat than patients who received a placebo (17). Sibutramine is a dopamine, norepinephrine, and serotonin reuptake inhibitor for which the method of action for weight loss is unknown. Side effects include increases in blood pressure and heart rate. Six clinical trials of sibutramine (10–20 mg daily) versus placebo have shown at 6–12 months of treatment that patients taking sibutramine have a weight loss of 2.8–7.8 kg more than patients taking a placebo (17). Loss of 10% of body weight occurred in 6–34% of patients who took sibutramine; this degree of weight loss was 5–27% more common in patients who took sibutramine than in patients who received a placebo (17). Unfortunately, discontinuation of pharmacotherapy may lead to rapid weight regain.

In some patients with severe obesity (BMI > 40) or patients with a BMI of 35 or greater with comorbid conditions, surgical intervention may be an option if nonsurgical methods of weight loss have failed (4). Surgical options can promote substantial, long-term weight loss (17). These patients should be evaluated by a comprehensive bariatric treatment team.

## Conclusion

Obstetrician–gynecologists should evaluate all women for obesity by calculating BMI. Clinicians should offer patients appropriate interventions or referrals to promote a healthy weight and lifestyle.

## References

1. Obesity in pregnancy. ACOG Committee Opinion 315. American College of Obstetricians and Gynecologists. Obstet Gynecol 2005;106:671–5.
2. American College of Obstetricians and Gynecologists. Health care for adolescents. Washington, DC: ACOG; 2003.
3. Hedley AA, Ogden CL, Johnson CL, Carroll MD, Curtin LR, Flegal KM. Prevalence of overweight and obesity among U.S. children, adolescents, and adults, 1999–2002. JAMA 2004;291:2847–50.
4. Clinical guidelines on the identification, evaluation, and treatment of overweight and obesity in adults—the evidence report. National Institutes of Health [published erratum appears in Obes Res 1998;6:464]. Obes Res 1998;6 Suppl 2:51S–209S.
5. Office of the Surgeon General. The Surgeon General's call to action to prevent and decrease overweight and obesity 2001. Rockville (MD): U.S. Department of Health and Human Services, Public Health Service, Office of the Surgeon General; 2001.
6. World Health Organization. Obesity: preventing and managing the global epidemic. WHO Technical Report Series 894. Geneva, Switzerland: World Health Organization; 2000.
7. Azziz R. Reproductive endocrinologic alterations in female asymptomatic obesity. Fertil Steril 1989;52:703–25.
8. Schouten LJ, Goldbohm RA, van den Brandt PA. Anthropometry, physical activity, and endometrial cancer risk: results from the Netherlands Cohort Study. J Natl Cancer Inst 2004;96:1635–8.
9. Mosca L, Appel LJ, Benjamin EJ, Berra K, Chandra-Strobos N, Fabunmi RP, et al. Evidence-based guidelines for cardiovascular disease prevention in women. American Heart Association. Circulation 2004;109:672–93.
10. Flegal KM, Graubard BI, Williamson DF, Gail MH. Excess deaths associated with underweight, overweight, and obesity. JAMA 2005;293:1861–7.
11. Janssen I, Katzmarzyk PT, Ross R. Body mass index, waist circumference, and health risk: evidence in support of current National Institutes of Health guidelines. Arch Intern Med 2002;162:2074–9.
12. Kushner RF, Weinsier RL. Evaluation of the obese patient. Practical considerations. Med Clin North Am 2000;84:387–99, vi.
13. Screening for obesity in adults: recommendations and rationale. U.S. Preventive Services Task Force. Ann Intern Med 2003;139:930–2.
14. Goldstein DJ. Beneficial health effects of modest weight loss. Int J Obes Relat Metab Disord 1992;16:397–415.
15. Li Z, Maglione M, Tu W, Mojica W, Arterburn D, Shugarman LR, et al. Meta-analysis: pharmacologic treatment of obesity. Ann Intern Med 2005;142:532–46.
16. Snow V, Barry P, Fitterman N, Qaseem A, Weiss K. Pharmacologic and surgical management of obesity in primary care: a clinical practice guideline from the American College of Physicians. Clinical Efficacy Assessment Subcommittee of the American College of Physicians. Ann Intern Med 2005;142:525–31.
17. McTigue KM, Harris R, Hemphill B, Lux L, Sutton S, Bunton AJ, et al. Screening and interventions for obesity in adults: summary of the evidence for the U.S. Preventive Services Task Force. Ann Intern Med 2003;139:933–49.

## Physician Resources

American Medical Association—Roadmaps for Clinical Practice series: Assessment and management of adult obesity
www.ama-assn.org/ama/pub/category/10931.html

American Society for Bariatric Surgery
www.asbs.org

ACOG Clinical Updates in Women's Health Care—Weight control: assessment and management
www.clinicalupdates.org

National Heart, Lung, and Blood Institute—Clinical guidelines on the identification, evaluation, and treatment of overweight and obesity in adults
www.nhlbi.nih.gov/guidelines/obesity/ob_home.htm

The Surgeon General's call to action to prevent and decrease overweight and obesity
www.surgeongeneral.gov/topics/obesity

U.S. Preventive Services Task Force—Screening for obesity in adults
www.ahrq.gov/clinic/uspstf/uspsobes.htm

## Patient Resources

American Obesity Association
www.obesity.org

American Society of Bariatric Physicians
www.asbp.org

MedlinePlus: Weight Loss and Dieting
www.nlm.nih.gov/medlineplus/weightlossanddieting.html

National Heart, Lung, and Blood Institute Obesity Education Initiative
www.nhlbi.nih.gov/about/oei/index.htm

Overeaters Anonymous
www.overeatersanonymous.org

TOPS—Take Off Pounds Sensibly
www.tops.org

Weight-control Information Network
www.win.niddk.nih.gov

ACOG Committee Opinion

Committee on Gynecologic Practice

Number 322, November 2005

# Compounded Bioidentical Hormones

*ABSTRACT: Compounded bioidentical hormones are plant-derived hormones that are prepared, mixed, assembled, packaged, or labeled as a drug by a pharmacist and can be custom made for a patient according to a physician's specifications. Most compounded products have not undergone rigorous clinical testing for safety or efficacy, and issues regarding purity, potency, and quality are a concern. Compounded hormone products have the same safety issues as those associated with hormone therapy agents that are approved by the U.S. Food and Drug Administration and may have additional risks intrinsic to compounding. There is no scientific evidence to support claims of increased efficacy or safety for individualized estrogen or progesterone regimens.*

Compounded drugs are agents that are prepared, mixed, assembled, packaged, or labeled as a drug by a pharmacist. Unlike drugs that are approved by the U.S. Food and Drug Administration (FDA) to be manufactured and sold in standardized dosages, compounded medications often are custom made for a patient according to a physician's specifications. One category of compounded products is referred to as "bioidentical hormones"; however, there is confusion over what this term implies. *Bioidentical hormones* are plant-derived hormones that are biochemically similar or identical to those produced by the ovary or body.

The steroid hormones most commonly compounded include dehydroepiandrosterone, pregnenolone, testosterone, progesterone, estrone, estradiol, and estriol (1). Bioidentical hormones made by a compounding pharmacist from a health care provider's prescription are available in various routes of administration, including oral, sublingual, and percutaneous or as implants, injectables, and suppositories. Examples of compounded hormones include Biest and Triest preparations. The name Biest (biestrogen) commonly refers to an estrogen preparation based on a ratio of 20% estradiol and 80% estriol on a milligram-per-milligram basis. A similar preparation, Triest (triestrogen), usually contains a ratio of 10% estradiol, 10% estrone, and 80% estriol. It is important to note that these ratios are not based on each agent's estrogenic potency but on the milligram quantity of the different agents added together (2). Purchases of compounded hormones are not typically reimbursed by insurance companies.

This document reflects emerging clinical and scientific advances as of the date issued and is subject to change. The information should not be construed as dictating an exclusive course of treatment or procedure to be followed.



**The American College of Obstetricians and Gynecologists**
409 12th Street, SW
PO Box 96920
Washington, DC 20090-6920

12345/98765

Compounded bioidentical hormones. ACOG Committee Opinion No. 322. American College of Obstetricians and Gynecologists. Obstet Gynecol 2005; 106:1139–40.

Most compounded products have not undergone any rigorous clinical testing for either safety or efficacy, and issues of quality assurance regarding the purity, potency, and quality of compounded products are a concern. From June 2001 to December 2001, the FDA analyzed 29 product samples from 12 compounding pharmacies (3). The types of products varied, but examples include oral, injectable, pellet implants, and inhalation compounds such as hormonal products, steroids, and antibiotics. Although none of the compounded products failed identity testing, 10 of the 29 products (34%) failed one or more standard quality tests performed. Nine of the 10 failing products failed assay or potency tests, with all products failing potency testing demonstrating subpotent results; that is, the products analyzed contained less of the active ingredient than expected. In comparison with these results, the analytical testing failure rate for drug therapies approved by the FDA is less than 2%.

Although many advocates and compounders of bioidentical hormones recommend the use of salivary hormone level testing as a means of offering individualized therapy, hormone therapy does not belong to a class of drugs with an indication for individualized dosing. Individualized dosing is indicated when a narrow therapeutic window exists for a drug or a drug class. Such drugs include those with nonlinear pharmacokinetics, those that are renally eliminated as the active drug, some that are not metabolized during first pass through the liver, and those with clearly defined therapeutic and toxic concentrations based on large population pharmacokinetic studies of serum concentrations. Steroid hormones such as estrogen and progesterone do not meet these criteria and, thus, do not require individualized dosing.

There is no evidence that hormonal levels in saliva are biologically meaningful. Whereas saliva is an ultrafiltrate of the blood and in theory should be amenable to testing for "free" (unbound) concentrations of hormones, this has not proved to be the case (4). The problem with salivary testing and monitoring of free hormone levels is twofold: 1) there is no biologically meaningful relationship between salivary sex steroidal hormone concentrations and free serum hormone concentrations and 2) there is large within-patient variability in salivary hormone concentrations (5–9). Salivary hormone levels vary depending on diet, time of day of testing, the specific hormone being tested, and other variables (6, 7, 10–12).

Currently, the FDA requires manufacturers of products approved by the FDA that contain estrogen and progestogen to use class labeling (the black box warning) reflective of the findings of the Women's Health Initiative. However, because compounded products are not approved by the FDA and have no official labeling (ie, a package insert), they are exempt from including the contraindications and warnings required by the FDA in class labeling for hormone therapy. Given the lack of well-designed and well-conducted clinical trials of these alternative therapies, compounded hormone products should be considered to have the same safety issues as those associated with hormone therapy agents that are approved by the FDA. They also may have additional risks intrinsic to compounding. There is no scientific evidence to support claims of increased efficacy or safety for individualized estrogen or progesterone regimens.

## References


1. Drisko JA. Natural isomolecular hormone replacement: an evidence-based medicine approach. Int J Pharmaceut Compounding 2000;4:414–20.
2. Boothby LA, Doering PL, Kipersztok S. Bioidentical hormone therapy: a review. Menopause 2004;11:356–67.
3. Food and Drug Administration, Center for Drug Evaluation and Research. Report: limited FDA survey of compounded drug products. Available at: http://www.fda.gov/cder/pharmcomp/survey.htm. Retrieved June 15, 2005.
4. Marder MZ, Joshi U, Mandel ID. Estrogen concentration in human parotid and submaxillary saliva. J Dent Res 1979;58:2370.
5. Hardiman P, Thomas M, Osgood V, Vlassopoulou V, Ginsburg J. Are estrogen assays essential for monitoring gonadotropin stimulant therapy? Gynecol Endocrinol 1990;4;261–9.
6. Klee GG, Heser DW. Techniques to measure testosterone in the elderly. Mayo Clin Proc 2000;75 Suppl:S19–25.
7. Lewis JG, McGill H, Patton VM, Elder PA. Caution on the use of saliva measurements to monitor absorption of progesterone form transdermal creams in postmenopausal women. Maturitas 2002;41:1–6.
8. Meulenberg PM, Ross HA, Swinkels LM, Benraad TJ. The effect of oral contraceptives on plasma-free and salivary cortisol and cortisone. Clin Chim Acta 1987;165: 379–85.
9. Wren BG, McFarland K, Edwards L, O'Shea P, Sufi S, Gross B, et al. Effect of sequential transdermal progesterone cream on endometrium, bleeding pattern, and plasma progesterone and salivary progesterone levels in postmenopausal women. Climacteric 2000;3:155–60.
10. Bolaji II, Tallon DF, O'Dwyer E, Fottrell PF. Assessment of bioavailability of oral micronized progesterone using a salivary progesterone enzymeimmunoassay. Gynecol Endocrinol 1993;7:101–10.
11. Raff H, Raff JL, Duthie EH, Wilson CR, Sasse EA, Rudman I, et al. Elevated salivary cortisol in the evening in healthy elderly men and women: correlation with bone mineral density. J Gerentol A Biol Sci Med Sci 1999; 54:M479–83.
12. Zava DT, Dollbaum CM, Blen M. Estrogen and progestin bioactivity of foods, herbs, and spices. Proc Soc Exp Biol Med 1998;217:369–78.

# ACOG Committee Opinion

Committee on Gynecologic Practice

Number 323, November 2005 (Replaces No. 164, December 1995)

## Elective Coincidental Appendectomy



**The American College of Obstetricians and Gynecologists**
409 12th Street, SW
PO Box 96920
Washington, DC 20090-6920

12345/98765

Elective coincidental appendectomy. ACOG Committee Opinion No. 323. American College of Obstetricians and Gynecologists. Obstet Gynecol 2005;106:1141–2.

*ABSTRACT: Because of a lack of evidence from randomized trials, it remains unclear whether the benefits of routine elective coincidental appendectomy outweigh the cost and risk of morbidity associated with this prophylactic procedure. Because the risk–benefit analysis varies according to patient age and history, the decision to perform an elective coincidental appendectomy at the time of an unrelated gynecologic surgical procedure should be based on individual clinical scenarios and patient characteristics and preferences.*

Elective coincidental appendectomy is defined as the removal of the appendix at the time of another surgical procedure unrelated to appreciable appendiceal pathology. Cases in which appendectomy may be indicated on the basis of appendiceal pathology are not addressed in this document.

The possible benefits of performing elective coincidental appendectomy include preventing a future emergency appendectomy and excluding appendicitis in patients with complicated differential diagnoses, such as those who have chronic pelvic pain or endometriosis. Other groups that may benefit from elective coincidental appendectomy include women in whom pelvic or abdominal radiation or chemotherapy is anticipated, women undergoing extensive pelvic or abdominal surgery in which major adhesions are anticipated postoperatively, and patients in whom making the diagnosis of appendicitis may be difficult because of diminished ability to perceive or communicate symptoms (eg, the developmentally disabled).

Most studies suggest that there is little, if any, increased morbidity associated with elective coincidental appendectomy at the time of gynecologic surgery, whether performed during an open surgical procedure (1–3) or during laparoscopy (4, 5). However, most of these studies are affected by methodological limitations such as retrospective design, small sample size, and lack of an appropriate control group. One large retrospective study using discharge data from all general hospitals in Ontario during a 10-year period highlights some of the challenges of addressing this issue with data from nonrandomized studies (6). This study compared in-hospital fatality rates, complication rates, and lengths of hospital stay between patients undergoing open primary cholecystectomy with and without incidental appendectomy. Initial results indicated a paradoxical reduction in morbidity and mortality after cholecystectomy when incidental appendectomy was performed. This most likely was because healthier, lower-risk patients are more likely to undergo an elective coincidental appendectomy. However, once multivariate adjustments were made to address these differences in patient characteristics, differences in complication rates were reduced or eliminated. Furthermore, when the study excluded high-risk subgroups, a consistently significant increase in complication rates among low-risk patients who underwent incidental appendectomy was found. These findings suggest that unmeasured or uncontrolled confounding or both make the interpretation of most nonrandomized studies of this topic difficult, but there is probably a small increased risk of nonfatal complications associated with elective coincidental appendectomy.

Given this presumed small but increased risk of complications, the primary debate surrounding elective coincidental appendectomy is whether the additional cost and morbidity incurred at the time of this prophylactic procedure outweigh the cost and risk of morbidity from developing appendicitis in the future. Because the estimated lifetime risk of appendicitis among women is less than 7% (7), a number of elective appendectomies will be required to prevent one case of acute appendicitis. Depending on hospital costs and physician reimbursement rates, the cost-effectiveness of this procedure will vary according to the clinical setting.

Although the incidence of acute appendicitis is greatest between the ages of 10 and 19 years and decreases with age (7), the risks associated with acute appendicitis increase with age. Therefore, the risk–benefit analysis changes according to patient age. A study involving open coincidental appendectomies in otherwise healthy women undergoing gynecologic procedures concluded that the greatest benefit was in patients younger than 35 years (8). The study also concluded that patients between 35 years and 50 years of age might benefit from elective coincidental appendectomy based on specific clinical circumstances. The data, however, did not support elective coincidental appendectomy for patients older than 50 years.

The benefit of elective coincidental appendectomy remains controversial and is still open to debate. It appears, from limited data, that women 35 years of age and younger benefit most from elective coincidental appendectomy. The decision to perform elective coincidental appendectomy at the time of gynecologic procedures should be based on individual clinical scenarios after a discussion of risks and benefits with the patient. In light of the low risk of morbidity based on current limited data, a patient's concern about developing future appendicitis may be considered. If there is a reasonable probability that the benefits outweigh the risks, based on age or history, elective coincidental appendectomy during a primary gynecologic procedure may be appropriate. Because there are clinical situations in which the benefits of an elective coincidental appendectomy may outweigh the risks, insurance companies should be encouraged to pay for this procedure in select cases.

## Reference

1. Salom EM, Schey D, Penalver M, Gomez-Marin O, Lambrou N, Almeida Z, et al. The safety of incidental appendectomy at the time of abdominal hysterectomy. Am J Obstet Gynecol 2003;189:1563–7; discussion 1567–8.
2. Tranmer BI, Graham AM, Sterns EE. Incidental appendectomy?—Yes. Can J Surg 1981;24:191–2.
3. Voitk AJ, Lowry JB. Is incidental appendectomy a safe practice? Can J Surg 1988;31:448–51.
4. Chiarugi M, Buccianti P, Decanini L, Balestri R, Lorenzetti L, Franceschi M, et al. "What you see is not what you get." A plea to remove a 'normal' appendix during diagnostic laparoscopy. Acta Chir Belg 2001;101: 243–5.
5. Nezhat C, Nezhat F. Incidental appendectomy during videolaseroscopy. Am J Obstet Gynecol 1991;165: 559–64.
6. Wen SW, Hernandez R, Naylor CD. Pitfalls in nonrandomized outcomes studies. The case of incidental appendectomy with open cholecystectomy. JAMA 1995;274: 1687–91.
7. Addiss DG, Shaffer N, Fowler BS, Tauxe RV. The epidemiology of appendicitis and appendectomy in the United States. Am J Epidemiol 1990;132:910–25.
8. Snyder TE, Selanders JR. Incidental appendectomy—yes or no? A retrospective case study and review of the literature. Infect Dis Obstet Gynecol 1998;6:30–7.

ACOG Committee Opinion

Committee on Gynecologic Practice

Number 332, May 2006 (Replaces No. 203, July 1998)

This document reflects emerging clinical and scientific advances as of the date issued and is subject to change. The information should not be construed as dictating an exclusive course of treatment or procedure to be followed.



ISSN 1074-861X

**The American College of Obstetricians and Gynecologists**
409 12th Street, SW
PO Box 96920
Washington, DC 20090-6920

12345/09876

Hepatitis B and hepatitis C virus infections in obstetrician–gynecologists. ACOG Committee Opinion No. 332. American College of Obstetricians and Gynecologists. Obstet Gynecol 2006;107:1207–8.

# Hepatitis B and Hepatitis C Virus Infections in Obstetrician–Gynecologists

*ABSTRACT: Hepatitis B and hepatitis C may be transmitted from patients to health care workers and from health care workers to patients. To reduce the risk, all obstetrician–gynecologists who provide clinical care should receive hepatitis B virus vaccine. Obstetrician–gynecologists who are hepatitis B surface antigen positive and e antigen positive should not perform exposure-prone procedures until they have sought counsel from an expert review panel. Because the risk of hepatitis C virus transmission is lower than that of hepatitis B virus transmission, routine testing of health care workers is not recommended, and hepatitis C virus-positive health care workers are not required to restrict professional activities.*

In health care settings, bloodborne pathogens, such as hepatitis B virus (HBV) and hepatitis C virus (HCV) may be transmitted from infected patients to health care workers as well as from infected health care workers to patients. To prevent transmission of bloodborne pathogens, such as hepatitis in the health care setting, it is critical that health care workers adhere to standard precautions, follow fundamental infection control principles, and use appropriate procedural techniques.

All obstetrician–gynecologists who provide clinical care should receive HBV vaccine. Postvaccination testing for the hepatitis B surface antigen (HBsAg) antibody (anti-HBs) 1–2 months after completing the vaccine series is recommended by the Centers for Disease Control and Prevention (1). Individuals who do not respond to the primary vaccine series (anti-HBs titers of less than 10 mIU/mL) should complete a second three-dose series or be evaluated to determine if they are HBsAg positive. Revaccinated persons should be retested at the completion of the second vaccine series (2).

Obstetrician–gynecologists who are HBsAg positive also should know their hepatitis B e antigen status, which indicates the presence of high viral concentrations. Because high viral load concentrations have been associated with an increased risk of transmission, obstetrician–gynecologists who are e antigen positive should not perform exposure-prone procedures until they have sought counsel from an expert review panel and have been advised under what circumstances, if any, they may continue to perform these procedures (3). The Centers for Disease Control and Prevention recommends that the expert review panel be a locally convened panel of experts representing a variety of perspectives and may include the following: 1) the obstetrician–gynecologist's personal physician, 2) an infectious disease specialist with expertise in hepatitis transmission, 3) a health care professional with expertise in the procedures performed by the obstetrician–gynecologist, 4) state or local public health official(s), and 5) a hospital epidemiologist or other member of the infection-control committee of the hospital. Exposure-prone procedures refer to certain procedures that have been implicated in hepatitis transmission despite adherence to the principles of standard precautions. Examples of exposure-prone procedures in obstetrics and gynecology that have been implicated in hepatitis transmission include deep pelvic surgery, particularly when sharp instruments are guided by the surgeon's fingers, and simultaneous presence of the surgeon's fingers and a needle or sharp instrument or object in a poorly visualized or highly confined anatomic site (4, 5).

Referral to a specialist may be necessary in cases involving persons who do not respond serologically after completing a second series of HBV vaccination and practicing obstetrician–gynecologists who are HBsAg positive but are e antigen negative. However, specific evidence-based guidance is lacking in these areas.

Although there is currently no immunization available to prevent infection with HCV, the risk of acquiring HCV infection appears lower than the risk of acquiring HBV (an average of 1.8% after a percutaneous exposure to an HCV-positive source patient compared with 20–60% for an HBV-positive source patient who is e antigen positive) (2). Routine HCV testing is not recommended for health care workers, and there are currently no recommendations in the United States to restrict the professional activities of health care workers with HCV infection (6). After an occupational exposure, such as a needle stick, the exposed health care worker, as well as the source patient, should be tested for the antibody to HCV. Postexposure prophylaxis is not effective and not recommended. However, early antiviral therapy may be effective in reducing the risk of progression to chronic HCV infection (7).

## References


1. Immunization of health-care workers: recommendations of the Advisory Committee on Immunization Practices (ACIP) and the Hospital Infection Control Practices Advisory Committee (HICPAC). MMWR Recomm Rep 1997;46(RR-18):1–42.
2. Updated U.S. Public Health Service Guidelines for the Management of Occupational Exposures to HBV, HCV, and HIV and Recommendations for Postexposure Prophylaxis. U.S. Public Health Service. MMWR Recomm Rep 2001;50(RR-11):1–52.
3. Recommendations for preventing transmission of human immunodeficiency virus and hepatitis B virus to patients during exposure-prone invasive procedures. MMWR Recomm Rep 1991;40(RR-8):1–9.
4. Welch, J, Webster M, Tilzey AJ, Noah ND, Banatvala JE. Hepatitis B infections after gynaecological surgery. Lancet 1989;1:205–7.
5. Carl M, Blakey DL, Francis DP, Maynard JE. Interruption of hepatitis B transmission by modification of a gynaecologist's surgical technique. Lancet 1982;1:731–3.
6. Recommendations for prevention and control of hepatitis C virus (HCV) infection and HCV-related chronic disease. Centers for Disease Control and Prevention. MMWR Recomm Rep 1998;47(RR-19):1–39.
7. Recommendations for follow-up of health-care workers after occupational exposure to hepatitis C virus. Centers for Disease Control and Prevention. MMWR Morb Mortal Wkly Rep 1997;46:603–6.

# ACOG Committee Opinion

Committee on Gynecologic Practice

Number 334, May 2006 (Replaces No. 186, September 1997)

# Role of the Obstetrician–Gynecologist in the Screening and Diagnosis of Breast Masses

*ABSTRACT: Obstetrician–gynecologists are in a favorable position to diagnose breast disease in their patients. Obstetrician–gynecologists are more likely to encounter a patient with breast cancer than a patient with any gynecologic cancer. The American College of Obstetricians and Gynecologists (ACOG) has adopted the goals of assisting in educating obstetrician–gynecologists in the diagnosis and treatment of breast cancer and in reducing mortality from breast cancer. To help meet these goals, ACOG has developed recommendations for the early diagnosis of breast disease.*

Obstetrician–gynecologists are in a favorable position to diagnose breast disease in their patients. Because more than 200,000 new cases of breast cancer are diagnosed each year, compared with fewer than 80,000 gynecologic cancers, obstetrician–gynecologists are more likely to encounter a patient with breast cancer than a patient with any gynecologic cancer. The American College of Obstetricians and Gynecologists (ACOG) has adopted the goals of assisting in educating obstetrician–gynecologists in the diagnosis and treatment of breast cancer and in reducing mortality from breast cancer. As an initial step toward these goals, ACOG has developed the following guidelines for the early diagnosis of breast disease:

1. There are factors that increase the risk for breast carcinoma in women. Information regarding risk factors for breast cancer should be elicited in the medical and family history.
2. Breast examination by visual inspection and palpation should be an integral part of initial obstetric and all complete gynecologic examinations. A clinical breast examination lacks the sensitivity to function as a comprehensive screening tool on its own; however, it may identify abnormalities that may go undetected by other techniques and can assist in directing further investigation.
3. Patients may be instructed in the technique of periodic self-examination of the breast. Although available randomized controlled trials do not confirm a reduction in overall breast cancer mortality in women per-

This document reflects emerging clinical and scientific advances as of the date issued and is subject to change. The information should not be construed as dictating an exclusive course of treatment or procedure to be followed.



ISSN 1074-861X

**The American College of Obstetricians and Gynecologists**
409 12th Street, SW
PO Box 96920
Washington, DC 20090-6920

12345/09876

Role of the obstetrician–gynecologist in the screening and diagnosis of breast masses. ACOG Committee Opinion 334. American College of Obstetricians and Gynecologists. Obstet Gynecol 2006;107:1213–4.

forming breast self-examination, awareness of normal breast findings and changes from these findings may lead to early detection for some women.

4. Patients should be encouraged to undergo screening by mammography in accordance with ACOG guidelines. Women who undergo mammography may be counseled that high false-positive rates (10% per screening in postmenopausal women and as high as 20% per screening in obese or premenopausal women) may result in further testing.
5. Obstetrician–gynecologists may perform diagnostic procedures when indicated or should make referrals to physicians who specialize in the diagnosis and treatment of breast disease. Institutions that grant physicians privileges to perform breast surgery should apply the same criteria for privileging to obstetrician–gynecologists as to other physicians.
6. A persistent palpable breast mass requires evaluation. A normal diagnostic mammography alone is not always sufficient to rule out malignant pathology in a patient with a palpable breast mass.
7. When a patient is referred to another physician for diagnostic testing or consultation, the obstetrician–gynecologist should ensure that the patient is provided with the following:

   - An explanation that she needs further care
   - The names of qualified physicians from whom the patient can receive care
   - An opportunity to have her questions answered
   - A summary of the history, physical examination, and diagnostic tests performed
   - Information for the consultant if diagnostic imaging is required for a reason of clinical concern and not just routine screening

Documentation of these steps and a description of the clinical findings should be included in the medical record.

## Bibliography

Breast cancer screening. ACOG Practice Bulletin No. 42. American College of Obstetricians and Gynecologists. Obstet Gynecol 2003;101:821–31.

Elmore JG, Carney PA, Abraham LA, Barlow WE, Egger JR, Fosse JS, et al. The association between obesity and screening mammography accuracy. Arch Intern Med 2004;164:1140–7.

Elmore JG, Barton MB, Moceri VM, Polk S, Arena PJ, Fletcher SW. Ten-year risk of false positive screening mammograms and clinical breast examinations. N Engl J Med 1998;338:1089–96.

Humphrey LL, Helfand M, Chan BK, Woolf SH. Breast cancer screening: a summary of the evidence for the U.S. Preventive Services Task Force. Ann Intern Med 2002;137:347–60.

Kosters JP, Gotzsche PC. Regular self-examination or clinical examination for early detection of breast cancer. The Cochrane Database of Systematic Reviews 2003, Issue 2. Art. No.: CD003373. DOI: 10.1002/14651858.CD003373.

Olsen O, Gotzsche PC. Screening for breast cancer with mammography. The Cochrane Database of Systematic Reviews 2001, Issue 4. Art. No.: CD001877. DOI: 10.1002/14651858.CD001877.

ACOG

Committee on Gynecologic Practice

# Committee Opinion

Number 336, June 2006 (Replaces No. 232, April 2000)

# Tamoxifen and Uterine Cancer

*ABSTRACT: Tamoxifen may be associated with endometrial proliferation, hyperplasia, polyp formation, invasive carcinoma, and uterine sarcoma. Any symptoms of endometrial hyperplasia or cancer reported by a postmenopausal woman taking tamoxifen should be evaluated. Premenopausal women treated with tamoxifen have no known increased risk of uterine cancer and as such require no additional monitoring beyond routine gynecologic care. If atypical endometrial hyperplasia develops, appropriate gynecologic management should be instituted, and the use of tamoxifen should be reassessed.*

Tamoxifen, a nonsteroidal antiestrogen agent, is used widely as adjunctive therapy for women with breast cancer. It has been approved by the U.S. Food and Drug Administration for the following indications:

- Adjuvant treatment of breast cancer
- Metastatic breast cancer
- Reduction in breast cancer incidence in high-risk women

Because obstetrician–gynecologists frequently treat women with breast cancer and women at risk for the disease, they may be consulted for advice on the proper follow-up of women receiving tamoxifen. The purpose of this Committee Opinion is to review the risk and to recommend care to prevent and detect uterine cancer in women receiving tamoxifen.

Tamoxifen is one of a class of agents known as selective estrogen receptor modulators (SERMs). Although the primary therapeutic effect of tamoxifen is derived from its antiestrogenic properties, this agent also has modest estrogenic activity. In standard dosages, tamoxifen may be associated with endometrial proliferation, hyperplasia, polyp formation, invasive carcinoma, and uterine sarcoma.

Most studies have found that the increased relative risk of developing endometrial cancer for women taking tamoxifen is two to three times higher than that of an age-matched population (1–3). The level of risk of endometrial cancer in women treated with tamoxifen is dose and time dependent. Studies suggest that the stage, grade, histology, and biology of tumors that develop in individuals treated with tamoxifen (20 mg/d) are no different from those that arise in the general population (3, 4). However, some reports have indicated that women treated with a higher dosage of tamoxifen

This document reflects emerging clinical and scientific advances as of the date issued and is subject to change. The information should not be construed as dictating an exclusive course of treatment or procedure to be followed.



ISSN 1074-861X

**The American College of Obstetricians and Gynecologists**
409 12th Street, SW
PO Box 96920
Washington, DC 20090-6920

12345/09876

Tamoxifen and uterine cancer. ACOG Committee Opinion No. 336. American College of Obstetricians and Gynecologists. Obstet Gynecol 2006;107:1475–8.

(40 mg/d) are more prone to develop more biologically aggressive tumors (5).

In one early study of the National Surgical Adjuvant Breast and Bowel Project (NSABP), the rate of endometrial cancer occurrence among tamoxifen users who were administered 20 mg/d was 1.6 per 1,000 patient years, compared with 0.2 per 1,000 patient years among control patients taking a placebo (3). In this study, the 5-year disease-free survival rate from breast cancer was 38% higher in the tamoxifen group than in the placebo group, suggesting that the small risk of developing endometrial cancer is outweighed by the significant survival benefit provided by tamoxifen therapy for women with breast cancer (3). The survival advantage with 5 years of tamoxifen therapy continued with long-term follow-up, but extending the duration of tamoxifen use to 10 years failed to improve the survival benefit gained from 5 years of tamoxifen use (6). In a more recent update of all NSABP trials of patients with breast cancer, the rate of endometrial cancer was 1.26 per 1,000 patient years in women treated with tamoxifen versus 0.58 per 1,000 patient years in the placebo group (7).

Uterine sarcomas consisting of malignant mixed müllerian tumors, leiomyosarcoma, and stroma cell sarcomas are a rare form of uterine malignancy occurring in 2–5% of all patients with uterine malignancies (8). In a review of all NSABP breast cancer treatment trials, the rate of sarcoma in women treated with tamoxifen was 17 per 100,000 patient years versus none in the placebo group (7). Similarly, in a separate trial of high-risk women without breast cancer taking tamoxifen as part of a breast cancer prevention trial with a median follow-up of 6.9 years, there were four sarcomas (17 per 100,000 patient years) in the tamoxifen group versus none in the placebo group (7). This is compared with the incidence of one to two per 100,000 patient years in the general population (9).

The NSABP prevention trial (P-1) data suggest that the risk for both invasive and noninvasive breast cancer is reduced markedly with tamoxifen prophylaxis. In this trial, however, the risk ratio for developing endometrial cancer was 2.53 in women using tamoxifen compared with women receiving a placebo (10). In addition, the ability of tamoxifen to induce endometrial malignancy as well as other histopathologic conditions appears to differ between premenopausal and postmenopausal women. In the prevention trial of high-risk women, there was no statistically significant difference in endometrial cancer rates between women treated with tamoxifen and those in the placebo group in the women aged 49 years and younger; however, in women aged 50 years and older, the risk ratio was 4.01 (95% confidence interval, 1.70–10.90) for those treated with tamoxifen versus those receiving placebo. The annual rate was 3.05 malignancies per 1,000 women treated with tamoxifen versus 0.76 malignancies per 1,000 women receiving placebo (10). Another study of women with breast cancer found that premenopausal women, treated or untreated, had no differences in endometrial thickness on ultrasound examination, uterine volume, or histopathologic findings, whereas postmenopausal women treated with tamoxifen had significantly more abnormalities (11).

Several approaches have been explored for screening asymptomatic women using tamoxifen for abnormal endometrial proliferation or endometrial cancer. Correlation is poor between ultrasonographic measurements of endometrial thickness and abnormal pathology in asymptomatic tamoxifen users because of tamoxifen-induced subepithelial stromal hypertrophy (12). In asymptomatic women using tamoxifen, screening for endometrial cancer with routine transvaginal ultrasonography, endometrial biopsy, or both has not been shown to be effective (13–15). Although asymptomatic postmenopausal tamoxifen-treated women should not have routine testing to diagnose endometrial pathology, sonohysterography has improved the accuracy of ultrasonography in excluding or detecting anatomical changes, when necessary (16).

Other data suggest that low- and high-risk groups of postmenopausal patients may be identified before the initiation of tamoxifen therapy for breast cancer (17–19). Pretreatment screening identified 85 asymptomatic patients with benign polyps in 510 postmenopausal patients with newly diagnosed breast cancer (16.7%). All polyps were removed. At the time of polypectomy, two patients had atypical hyperplasias and subsequently underwent hysterectomies. The rest were treated with tamoxifen, 20 mg/d, for up to 5 years. The incidence of atypical hyperplasia was 11.7% in the group with initial lesions versus 0.7% in the group without lesions ($P$ <.0001), an 18-fold increase in risk. In addition, polyps developed in 17.6% of the group with initial lesions versus 12.9% in the group without.

Although the concurrent use of progestin reduces the risk of endometrial hyperplasia and cancer in patients receiving unopposed estrogen, the effect of progestin on the course of breast cancer and on the endometrium of women receiving tamoxifen is not known. Therefore, such use cannot be advocated as a means of lowering risk in women taking tamoxifen.

On the basis of these data, the committee recommends the following:

- Postmenopausal women taking tamoxifen should be monitored closely for symptoms of endometrial hyperplasia or cancer.
- Premenopausal women treated with tamoxifen have no known increased risk of uterine cancer and as such require no additional monitoring beyond routine gynecologic care.
- Women taking tamoxifen should be informed about the risks of endometrial proliferation, endometrial hyperplasia, endometrial cancer, and uterine sarcomas. Women should be encouraged to promptly report any abnormal vaginal symptoms, including bloody discharge, spotting, staining, or leukorrhea.
- Any abnormal vaginal bleeding, bloody vaginal discharge, staining, or spotting should be investigated.
- Emerging evidence suggests the presence of high- and low-risk groups for development of atypical hyperplasias with tamoxifen treatment in postmenopausal women based on the presence or absence of benign endometrial polyps before therapy. Thus there may be a role for pretreatment screening of postmenopausal women with transvaginal ultrasonography, and sonohysterography when needed, or office hysteroscopy before initiation of tamoxifen therapy.
- Unless the patient has been identified to be at high risk for endometrial cancer, routine endometrial surveillance has not been effective in increasing the early detection of endometrial cancer in women using tamoxifen. Such surveillance may lead to more invasive and costly diagnostic procedures and, therefore, is not recommended.
- Tamoxifen use should be limited to 5 years' duration because a benefit beyond this time has not been documented.
- If atypical endometrial hyperplasia develops, appropriate gynecologic management should be instituted, and the use of tamoxifen should be reassessed. If tamoxifen therapy must be continued, hysterectomy should be considered in women with atypical endometrial hyperplasia. Tamoxifen use may be reinstituted following hysterectomy for endometrial carcinoma in consultation with the physician responsible for the woman's breast care.

## References


1. Sismondi P, Biglia N, Volpi E, Giai M, de Grandis T. Tamoxifen and endometrial cancer. Ann N Y Acad Sci 1994;734:310–21.
2. Bissett D, Davis JA, George WD. Gynaecological monitoring during tamoxifen therapy. Lancet 1994;344:1244.
3. Fisher B, Costantino JP, Redmond CK, Fisher ER, Wickerham DL, Cronin WM. Endometrial cancer in tamoxifen-treated breast cancer patients: findings from the National Surgical Adjuvant Breast and Bowel Project (NSABP) B-14. J Natl Cancer Inst 1994;86:527–37.
4. Barakat RR, Wong G, Curtin JP, Vlamis V, Hoskins WJ. Tamoxifen use in breast cancer patients who subsequently develop corpus cancer is not associated with a higher incidence of adverse histologic features. Gynecol Oncol 1994;55:164–8.
5. Magriples U, Naftolin F, Schwartz PE, Carcangiu ML. High-grade endometrial carcinoma in tamoxifen-treated breast cancer patients. J Clin Oncol 1993;11:485–90.
6. Fisher B, Dignam J, Bryant J, DeCillis A, Wickerham DL, Wolmark N, et al. Five versus more than five years of tamoxifen therapy for breast cancer patients with negative lymph nodes and estrogen receptor-positive tumors. J Natl Cancer Inst 1996;88:1529–42.
7. Wickerham DL, Fisher B, Wolmark N, Bryant J, Costantino J, Bernstein L, et al. Association of tamoxifen and uterine sarcoma. J Clin Oncol 2002;20:2758–60.
8. Averette HE, Nguyen H. Gynecologic cancer. In: Murphy GP, Lawrence W Jr, Lenhard RE Jr, editors. American Cancer Society textbook of clinical oncology. 2nd ed. Atlanta (GA): American Cancer Society; 1995. p. 552–79.
9. Mouridsen H, Palshof T, Patterson J, Battersby L. Tamoxifen in advanced breast cancer. Cancer Treat Rev 1978;5:131–41.
10. Fisher B, Costantino JP, Wickerham DL, Redmond CK, Kavanah M, Cronin WM, et al. Tamoxifen for prevention of breast cancer: report of the National Surgical Adjuvant Breast and Bowel Project P-1 Study. J Natl Cancer Inst 1998;90:1371–88.
11. Cheng WF, Lin HH, Torng PL, Huang SC. Comparison of endometrial changes among symptomatic tamoxifen-treated and nontreated premenopausal and postmenopausal breast cancer patients. Gynecol Oncol 1997;66:233–7.
12. Achiron R, Lipitz S, Sivan E, Goldenberg M, Horovitz A, Frenkel Y, et al. Changes mimicking endometrial neoplasia in postmenopausal, tamoxifen-treated women with breast cancer: a transvaginal Doppler study. Ultrasound Obstet Gynecol 1995;6:116–20.
13. Bertelli G, Venturini M, Del Mastro L, Garrone O, Cosso M, Gustavino C, et al. Tamoxifen and the endometrium:

findings of pelvic ultrasound examination and endometrial biopsy in asymptomatic breast cancer patients. Breast Cancer Res Treat 1998;47:41–6.
14. Fung MF, Reid A, Faught W, Le T, Chenier C, Verma S, et al. Prospective longitudinal study of ultrasound screening for endometrial abnormalities in women with breast cancer receiving tamoxifen. Gynecol Oncol 2003;91:154–9.
15. Love CD, Muir BB, Scrimgeour JB, Leonard RC, Dillon P, Dixon JM. Investigation of endometrial abnormalities in asymptomatic women treated with tamoxifen and an evaluation of the role of endometrial screening. J Clin Oncol 1999;17:2050–4.
16. Markovitch O, Tepper R, Aviram R, Fishman A, Shapira J, Cohen I. The value of sonohysterography in the prediction of endometrial pathologies in asymptomatic postmenopausal breast cancer tamoxifen-treated patients. Gynecol Oncol 2004;94:754–9.
17. Berliere M, Charles A, Galant C, Donnez J. Uterine side effects of tamoxifen: a need for systematic pretreatment screening. Obstet Gynecol 1998;91:40–4.
18. Berliere M, Radikov G, Galant C, Piette P, Marbaix E, Donnez J. Identification of women at high risk of developing endometrial cancer on tamoxifen. Eur J Cancer 2000;36(suppl 4):S35–6.
19. Vosse M, Renard F, Coibion M, Neven P, Nogaret JM, Hertens D. Endometrial disorders in 406 breast cancer patients on tamoxifen: the case for less intensive monitoring. Eur J Obstet Gynecol Reprod Biol 2002;101:58–63.

# ACOG Committee Opinion

Committee on Gynecologic Practice

Number 337, June 2006

This document reflects emerging clinical and scientific advances as of the date issued and is subject to change. The information should not be construed as dictating an exclusive course of treatment or procedure to be followed.



ISSN 1074-861X

**The American College of Obstetricians and Gynecologists**
409 12th Street, SW
PO Box 96920
Washington, DC 20090-6920

12345/09876

Noncontraceptive uses of the levonorgestrel intrauterine system. ACOG Committee Opinion No. 337. American College of Obstetricians and Gynecologists. Obstet Gynecol 2006;107:1479–82.

# Noncontraceptive Uses of the Levonorgestrel Intrauterine System

*ABSTRACT: The levonorgestrel intrauterine system, approved for contraceptive use for up to 5 years, also has noncontraceptive uses. It appears to reduce menstrual bleeding significantly in women with idiopathic menorrhagia. Current studies suggest that menopausal hormone therapy regimens combining the levonorgestrel intrauterine system with estradiol are effective in reducing climacteric symptoms and in inducing amenorrhea in most women after 1 year. Further studies are required before this device can be recommended as a treatment for endometriosis-associated pelvic pain, hyperplasia, or endometrial adenocarcinoma, or as adjuvant therapy with tamoxifen.*

In 2000, the U.S. Food and Drug Administration (FDA) approved the levonorgestrel-releasing intrauterine system for intrauterine contraception for up to 5 years. The purpose of this Committee Opinion is to address noncontraceptive uses of the levonorgestrel intrauterine system.

The system consists of a 32-mm T-shaped polyethylene frame with a steroid reservoir containing a mixture of 52 mg of levonorgestrel and silicone covered by a silicone membrane. After insertion, the initial release of levonorgestrel into the uterine cavity is 20 mcg/d. A stable plasma concentration of 150–200 pg/mL is achieved after the first few weeks (1). Although some degradation of concentration is seen over time—by 2 years of use, levels are closer to 100 pg/mL (2, 3)—the concentration is maintained for at least 5 years (1) and the typical histologic changes in the endometrium induced by the levonorgestrel intrauterine system have been observed for up to 7 years (4). The plasma concentration of levonorgestrel in patients using the levonorgestrel intrauterine system is less than 25% of that seen with 150 mcg of oral levonorgestrel (5).

## Menorrhagia

In women with idiopathic menorrhagia (generally defined as excessively heavy, regular menses in the absence of intracavitary pathology or coagulopathy), the levonorgestrel intrauterine system appears to reduce menstrual blood loss significantly. Reductions of up to 86% after 3 months and up to

97% after 12 months of use have been reported (6–9). At 12 months after insertion of the levonorgestrel intrauterine system, reported rates of amenorrhea vary between 20% and 80% (10–12).

Several randomized controlled trials have evaluated use of the levonorgestrel intrauterine system and other treatment modalities for menorrhagia (6, 11, 13–15). Most studies have been in Scandinavian populations. A Cochrane Collaboration review concluded that the levonorgestrel intrauterine system is significantly more effective than oral cyclical norethindrone as a treatment for heavy menstrual bleeding (16). Although the levonorgestrel intrauterine system results in a smaller mean reduction of menstrual blood loss at 1 year than does transcervical resection of the endometrium, the rates of patient satisfaction at 1 year are similar in both groups (6). Another trial reported a blood loss reduction of 79% in the group using the levonorgestrel intrauterine system versus 89% in the group undergoing transcervical resection of the endometrium (11). In terms of quality of life and cost-effectiveness, the levonorgestrel intrauterine system appears to be a cost-effective alternative to hysterectomy during the first 5 years of use (17, 18).

The most common side effects resulting in discontinuation of levonorgestrel intrauterine system therapy include irregular bleeding and hormonal side effects such as breast tenderness, mood changes, and acne (6). Other potential drawbacks include abdominal pain, infection, and difficult insertions requiring cervical dilation (6).

## Hormone Therapy

A number of trials have evaluated use of the levonorgestrel intrauterine system as an alternative delivery system for the progestin component of combined hormone therapy (HT) (5, 19–23). Current studies suggest that HT regimens combining the levonorgestrel intrauterine system with estradiol delivered by various methods (vaginal ring, gel, oral, transdermal) are effective in reducing climacteric symptoms and in inducing amenorrhea in 59–83% of women after 1 year (24, 25). The long-term health effects of the levonorgestrel intrauterine system as a means of hormone therapy during menopause are unknown. Although most studies suggest that the levonorgestrel intrauterine system often is associated with irregular bleeding in the first 1–3 months of use, amenorrhea may occur with long-term use (19). Women with persistent bleeding should be evaluated in the typical manner, regardless of the presence of the levonorgestrel intrauterine system. Endometrial biopsies after 1 and 5 years of levonorgestrel intrauterine system use as a component of HT have consistently shown atrophy, suggesting that the levonorgestrel intrauterine system protects the endometrium from hyperplasia (12, 22, 26). Furthermore, no cases of endometrial hyperplasia have been reported during treatment with a levonorgestrel intrauterine system combined with estrogen therapy (4, 12, 27, 28). The aforementioned studies used the FDA-approved levonorgestrel intrauterine system, which delivers 20 mcg/d; a smaller version of the product that may be more suitable for the postmenopausal uterus also has been studied (29, 30).

## Treatment of Endometrial Hyperplasia and Early Endometrial Cancer

The use of oral progestin therapy is a recognized treatment option in selected patients with atypical endometrial hyperplasia. Thus far, only one study of a series of 12 women with endometrial hyperplasia with or without atypia treated with a "frameless" levonorgestrel intrauterine system (releasing only 14 mcg/d of levonorgestrel) has been published, showing effective suppression of the endometrium (31). Two additional studies of small series (one of 12 women, one of four women) have assessed the feasibility of using a progestin-containing intrauterine system to treat grade 1, stage I endometrioid uterine adenocarcinoma in women who are poor operative candidates (32, 33). These preliminary results were consistent with other progestational agents.

## Adjuvant Therapy With Tamoxifen

Tamoxifen stimulates the endometrium and increases the risk of endometrial hyperplasia and malignancy (34). A randomized controlled trial of women with previous breast cancer using tamoxifen for more than 1 year suggested that the levonorgestrel intrauterine system may prevent tamoxifen-induced endometrial changes (35). However, this must be balanced against potential breakthrough bleeding associated with levonorgestrel intrauterine system use and the unproven safety of administering progestational agents to women with a history of breast cancer. Before the levonorgestrel intrauterine system can be recommended as an adjuvant therapy with tamoxifen in women with a history of breast cancer, long-term randomized trials are needed.

## Endometriosis and Pelvic Pain

Small pilot studies suggest that the levonorgestrel intrauterine system improves endometriosis-associated pelvic pain for up to 3 years (36–40). Although further studies are needed before the levonorgestrel intrauterine system can be recommended as a treatment for endometriosis-associated pelvic pain, it is reasonable to consider its use by women with endometriosis desiring effective, long-term contraception.

## Conclusion

There is sufficient evidence to support the use of the levonorgestrel intrauterine system as a treatment option for idiopathic menorrhagia. There also is sufficient evidence that the levonorgestrel intrauterine system protects against endometrial hyperplasia in women using menopausal estrogen therapy. Additional studies are required before this device can be recommended as a treatment for endometriosis-associated pelvic pain, hyperplasia, or endometrial adenocarcinoma, or as adjuvant therapy with tamoxifen.

## References


1. Mirena. In: Physicians' desk reference: PDR. 60th ed. Montvale (NJ): Thomson PDR; 2006. p. 810–5.
2. Nilsson CG, Lahteenmaki P, Luukkainen T. Levonorgestrel plasma concentrations and hormone profiles after insertion and after one year of treatment with a levonorgestrel-IUD. Contraception 1980;21:225–33.
3. Xiao BL, Zhou LY, Zhang XL, Jia MC, Luukainen T, Allonen H. Pharmacokinetic and pharmacodynamic studies of levonorgestrel-releasing intrauterine device. Contraception 1990;41:353–62.
4. Silverberg SG, Haukkamaa M, Arko H, Nilsson CG, Luukkainen T. Endometrial morphology during long-term use of levonorgestrel-releasing intrauterine devices. Int J Gynecol Pathol 1986;5:235–41.
5. Suhonen S, Allonen H, Lahteenmaki P. Sustained-release estradiol implants and a levonorgestrel-releasing intrauterine device in hormone replacement therapy. Am J Obstet Gynecol 1995;172:562–7.
6. Istre O, Trolle B. Treatment of menorrhagia with the levonorgestrel intrauterine system versus endometrial resection. Fertil Steril 2001;76:304–9.
7. Barrington JW, Bowen-Simpkins P. The levonorgestrel intrauterine system in the management of menorrhagia. Br J Obstet Gynaecol 1997;104:614–6.
8. Tang GW, Lo SS. Levonorgestrel intrauterine device in the treatment of menorrhagia in Chinese women: efficacy versus acceptability. Contraception 1995;51:231–5.
9. Andersson JK, Rybo G. Levonorgestrel-releasing intrauterine device in the treatment of menorrhagia. Br J Obstet Gynaecol 1990;97:690–4.
10. Ronnerdag M, Odlind V. Health effects of long-term use of the intrauterine levonorgestrel-releasing system. A follow-up study over 12 years of continuous use. Acta Obstet Gynecol Scand 1999;78:716–21.
11. Crosignani PG, Vercellini P, Mosconi P, Oldani S, Cortesi I, De Giorgi O. Levonorgestrel-releasing intrauterine device versus hysteroscopic endometrial resection in treatment of dysfunctional uterine bleeding. Obstet Gynecol 1997;90:257–63.
12. Varila E, Wahlstrom T, Rauramo I. A 5-year follow-up study on the use of a levonorgestrel intrauterine system in women receiving hormone replacement therapy. Fertil Steril 2001;76:969–73.
13. Lahteenmaki P, Haukkamaa M, Puolakka J, Riikonen U, Sainio S, Suvisaari J, et al. Open randomised study of use of levonorgestrel releasing intrauterine system as alternative to hysterectomy. BMJ 1998;316:1122–6.
14. Irvine GA, Campbell-Brown MB, Lumsden MA, Heikkila A, Walker JJ, Cameron IT. Randomized comparative trial of the levonorgestrel intrauterine system and norethisterone for treatment of idiopathic menorrhagia. Br J Obstet Gynaecol 1998;105:592–8.
15. Kittelsen N, Istre O. A randomized study comparing levonorgestrel intrauterine system (LNS IUS) and transcervical resection of the endometrium (TCRE) in the treatment of menorrhagia: preliminary results. Gynaecol Endosc 1998;7:61–5.
16. Lethaby AE, Cooke I, Rees M. Progesterone or progestogen-releasing intrauterine systems for heavy menstrual bleeding. The Cochrane Database of Systematic Reviews 2005, Issue 4. Art. No.: CD002126. DOI: 10.1002/14651858.CD002126.pub2.
17. Hurskainen R, Teperi J, Rissanen P, Aalto AM, Grenman S, Kivela A, et al. Quality of life and cost-effectiveness of levonorgestrel-releasing intrauterine system versus hysterectomy for treatment of menorrhagia: a randomised trial. Lancet 2001;357:273–7.
18. Hurskainen R, Teperi J, Rissanen P, Aalto AM, Grenman S, Kivela A, et al. Clinical outcomes and costs with the levonorgestrel-releasing intrauterine system or hysterectomy for treatment of menorrhagia: randomized trial 5-year follow up. JAMA 2004;291:1456–63.
19. Suvanto-Luukkonen E, Sundstrom H, Penttinen J, Laara E, Pramila S, Kauppila A. Percutaneous estradiol gel with an intrauterine levonorgestrel releasing device or natural progesterone in hormone replacement therapy. Maturitas 1997;26:211–7.
20. Andersson K, Mattsson LA, Rybo G, Stadberg E. Intrauterine release of levonorgestrel—a new way of adding progestogen in hormone replacement therapy. Obstet Gynecol 1992;79:963–7.
21. Raudaskoski TH, Lahti EI, Kauppila AJ, Apaja-Sarkkinen MA, Laatikainen TJ. Transdermal estrogen with a levonorgestrel-releasing intrauterine device for climacteric complaints: clinical and endometrial responses. Am J Obstet Gynecol 1995;172:114–9.

22. Kalogirou D, Antoniou G, Karakitsos P, Kalogirou O, Antoniou D, Giannikos L. A comparative study of the effects of an estradiol-releasing vaginal ring combined with an oral gestagen versus transdermal estrogen combined with a levonorgestrel-releasing IUD: clinical findings and endometrial response. Int J Fertil Menopausal Stud 1996;41:522–7.
23. Sturdee DW, Rantala ML, Colau JC, Zahradnik HP, Riphagen FE. The acceptability of a small intrauterine progestogen-releasing system for continuous combined hormone therapy in early postmenopausal women. Multicenter MLS Investigators. Climacteric 2004;7:404–11.
24. Riphagen FE. Intrauterine application of progestins in hormone replacement therapy: a review. Climacteric 2000;3:199–211.
25. Boon J, Scholten PC, Oldenhave A, Heintz PA. Continuous intrauterine compared with cyclic oral progestin administration in perimenopausal HRT. Maturitas 2003;46:69–77.
26. Suvanto-Luukkonen E, Kauppila A. The levonorgestrel intrauterine system in menopausal hormone replacement therapy: five-year experience. Fertil Steril 1999;72:161–3.
27. Suhonen S, Holmstrom T, Allonen H, Lahteenmaki P. Intrauterine and subdermal progestin administration in postmenopausal hormone replacement therapy. Fertil Steril 1995;63:336–42.
28. Suhonen S, Holmstrom T, Lahteenmaki P. Three-year follow-up of the use of a levonorgestrel-releasing intrauterine system in hormone replacement therapy. Acta Obstet Gynecol Scand 1997;76:145–50.
29. Raudaskoski T, Tapanainen J, Tomas E, Luotola H, Pekonen F, Ronni-Sivula H, et al. Intrauterine 10 microg and 20 microg levonorgestrel systems in postmenopausal women receiving oral oestrogen replacement therapy: clinical, endometrial and metabolic response. BJOG 2002;109:136–44.
30. Wildemeersch D, Schacht E, Wildemeersch P. Performance and acceptability of intrauterine release of levonorgestrel with a miniature delivery system for hormonal substitution therapy, contraception and treatment in peri and postmenopausal women. Maturitas 2003;44: 237–45.
31. Wildemeersch D, Dhont M. Treatment of nonatypical and atypical endometrial hyperplasia with a levonorgestrel-releasing intrauterine system. Am J Obstet Gynecol 2003;188:1297–8.
32. Dhar KK, NeedhiRajan T, Koslowski M, Woolas RP. Is levonorgestrel intrauterine system effective for treatment of early endometrial cancer? Report of four cases and review of the literature. Gynecol Oncol 2005;97:924–7.
33. Montz FJ, Bristow RE, Bovicelli A, Tomacruz R, Kurman RJ. Intrauterine progesterone treatment of early endometrial cancer. Am J Obstet Gynecol 2002;186:651–7.
34. Fisher B, Costantino JP, Wickerham DL, Redmond CK, Kavanah M, Cronin WM, et al. Tamoxifen for prevention of breast cancer: report of the National Surgical Adjuvant Breast and Bowel Project P-1 Study. J Natl Cancer Inst 1998;90:1371–88.
35. Gardner FJ, Konje JC, Abrams KR, Brown LJ, Khanna S, Al-Azzawi F, et al. Endometrial protection for tamoxifen-stimulated changes by a levonorgestrel-releasing intrauterine system: a randomised controlled trial. Lancet 2000;356:1711–7.
36. Vercellini P, Aimi G, Panazza S, De Giorgi O, Pesole A, Crosignani PG. A levonorgestrel-releasing intrauterine system for the treatment of dysmenorrhea associated with endometriosis: a pilot study. Fertil Steril 1999;72:505–8.
37. Fedele L, Bianchi S, Zanconato G, Portuese A, Raffaelli R. Use of a levonorgestrel-releasing intrauterine device in the treatment of rectovaginal endometriosis. Fertil Steril 2001;75:485–8.
38. Vercellini P, Frontino G, De Giorgi O, Aimi G, Zaina B, Crosignani PG. Comparison of a levonorgestrel-releasing intrauterine device versus expectant management after conservative surgery for symptomatic endometriosis: a pilot study. Fertil Steril 2003;80:305–9.
39. Lockhat FB, Emembolu JO, Konje JC. The efficacy, side-effects and continuation rates in women with symptomatic endometriosis undergoing treatment with an intra-uterine administered progestogen (levonorgestrel): a 3 year follow-up. Hum Reprod 2005;20:789–93.
40. Lockhat FB, Emembolu JO, Konje JC. Serum and peritoneal fluid levels of levonorgestrel in women with endometriosis who were treated with an intrauterine contraceptive device containing levonorgestrel. Fertil Steril 2005;83:398–404.

# ACOG Committee Opinion

Committee on Gynecologic Practice

American Society for Colposcopy and Cervical Pathology

This document reflects emerging clinical and scientific advances as of the date issued and is subject to change. The information should not be construed as dictating an exclusive course of treatment or procedure to be followed.

The Committee and Society wish to thank Hope K. Haefner, MD, and Mark Spitzer, MD, for their assistance in the development of this document.



ISSN 1074-861X

**The American College of Obstetricians and Gynecologists**
409 12th Street, SW
PO Box 96920
Washington, DC 20090-6920

12345/09876

Vulvodynia. ACOG Committee Opinion No. 345. American College of Obstetricians and Gynecologists. Obstet Gynecol 2006;108:1049–52.

Number 345, October 2006

## Vulvodynia

*ABSTRACT: Vulvodynia is a complex disorder that can be difficult to treat. It is described by most patients as burning, stinging, irritation, or rawness. Many treatment options have been used, including vulvar care measures, medication, biofeedback training, physical therapy, dietary modifications, sexual counseling, and surgery. A cotton swab test is used to distinguish generalized disease from localized disease. No one treatment is effective for all patients. A number of measures can be taken to prevent irritation, and several medications can be used to treat the condition.*

Vulvodynia is a complex disorder that can be difficult to treat. This Committee Opinion provides an introduction to the diagnosis and treatment of vulvodynia for the generalist obstetrician–gynecologist. It is adapted with permission from the 2005 American Society for Colposcopy and Cervical Pathology publication, "The Vulvodynia Guideline" (1).

### Terminology and Classification

Many women experience vulvar pain and discomfort that affects the quality of their lives. Vulvodynia is described by most patients as burning, stinging, irritation, or rawness. It is a condition in which pain is present although the vulva appears normal (other than erythema).

The most recent terminology and classification of vulvar pain by the International Society for the Study of Vulvovaginal Disease defines vulvodynia as "vulvar discomfort, most often described as burning pain, occurring in the absence of relevant visible findings or a specific, clinically identifiable, neurologic disorder" (2). It is not caused by commonly identified infection (eg, candidiasis, human papillomavirus, herpes), inflammation (eg, lichen planus, immunobullous disorder), neoplasia (eg, Paget's disease, squamous cell carcinoma), or a neurologic disorder (eg, herpes neuralgia, spinal nerve compression). The classification of vulvodynia is based on the site of the pain, whether it is generalized or localized, and whether it is provoked, unprovoked, or mixed. Although the term *vulvar dysesthesia* has been used in the past, there is now consensus to use the term *vulvodynia* and subcategorize it as localized or generalized.

Several causes have been proposed for vulvodynia, including embryologic abnormalities, increased urinary oxalates, genetic or immune factors, hormonal factors, inflammation, infection, and neuropathic changes. Most likely, there is not a single cause.

Because the etiology of vulvodynia is unknown, it is difficult to say whether localized vulvodynia (previously referred to as vestibulitis) and generalized vulvodynia are different manifestations of the same disease process. Distinguishing localized disease from generalized disease is fairly straightforward and is done with the cotton swab test as described in the following section. Early classification to localized or generalized vulvodynia can facilitate more timely and appropriate treatment.

## Diagnosis and Evaluation

Vulvodynia is a diagnosis of exclusion, a pain syndrome with no other identified cause. A thorough history should identify the patient's duration of pain, previous treatments, allergies, medical and surgical history, and sexual history.

Cotton swab testing (Fig. 1) is used to identify areas of localized pain and to classify the areas where there is mild, moderate, or severe pain. A diagram of pain locations may be helpful in assessing the pain over time. The vagina should be examined, and tests, including wet mount, vaginal pH, fungal culture, and Gram stain, should be performed as indicated. Fungal culture may identify resistant strains, but sensitivity testing usually is not required. Testing for human papillomavirus infection is unnecessary.

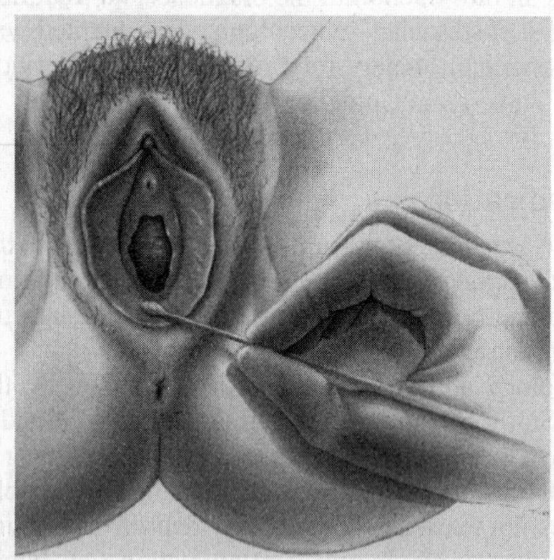

**Figure 1.** Cotton swab testing for vestibulodynia. The vestibule is tested at the 2-, 4-, 6-, 8-, and 10-o'clock positions. When pain is present, the patient is asked to quantify it as mild, moderate, or severe. (Haefner HK. Critique of new gynecologic surgical procedures: surgery for vulvar vestibulitis. Clin Obstet Gynecol 2000; 43:689–700.)

## Treatment

Most of the available evidence for treatment of vulvodynia is based on clinical experience, descriptive studies, or reports of expert committees. There are few randomized trials of vulvodynia treatments. Outlined here are treatments used by clinicians with an interest in vulvodynia. Multiple treatments have been used (Fig. 2), including vulvar care measures; topical, oral, and injectable medications; biofeedback training; physical therapy; dietary modifications; cognitive behavioral therapy; sexual counseling; and surgery. Newer treatments being used include acupuncture, hypnotherapy, nitroglycerin, and botulinum toxin.

Gentle care of the vulva is advised. The following vulvar care measures can minimize vulvar irritation:

- Wearing 100% cotton underwear (no underwear at night)
- Avoiding vulvar irritants (perfumes, dyes, shampoos, detergents) and douching
- Using mild soaps for bathing, with none applied to the vulva
- Cleaning the vulva with water only
- Avoiding the use of hair dryers on the vulvar area
- Patting the area dry after bathing, and applying a preservative-free emollient (such as vegetable oil or plain petrolatum) topically to hold moisture in the skin and improve the barrier function
- Switching to 100% cotton menstrual pads (if regular pads are irritating)
- Using adequate lubrication for intercourse
- Applying cool gel packs to the vulvar area
- Rinsing and patting dry the vulva after urination

Different medications have been tried as treatments for vulvar pain. These include topical, oral, and intralesional medications, as well as pudendal nerve blocks. Many of these medications are known to interact with other drugs, and many patients with vulvodynia may be taking multiple medications. Clinicians should check for any potential drug inter-

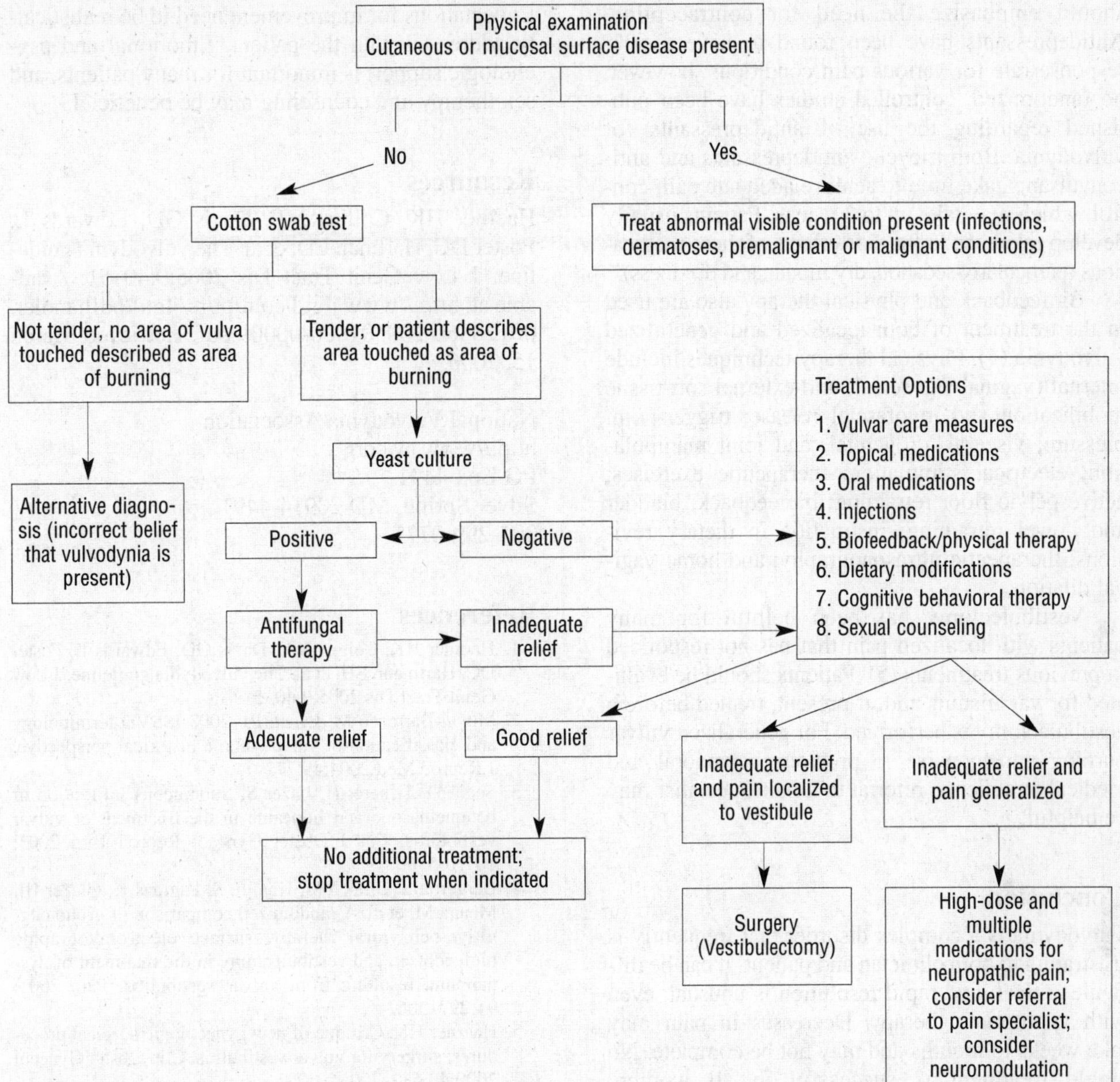


**Figure 2.** Vulvodynia treatment algorithm. (Adapted from Haefner HK, Collins ME, Davis GD, Edwards L, Foster DC, Hartmann EH, et al. The vulvodynia guideline. J Low Genit Tract Dis 2005;9:40–51.)

actions before prescribing a new medication. Before prescribing a new course of therapy, clinicians may stop use of all topical medication.

Commonly prescribed topical medications include a variety of local anesthetics (which can be applied immediately before intercourse or in extended use), estrogen cream, and tricyclic antidepressants compounded into topical form. Although topical steroids generally do not help patients with vulvodynia, trigger-point injections of a combination of steroid and bupivacaine have been successful for some patients with localized vulvodynia (3).

Tricyclic antidepressants and anticonvulsants can be used for vulvodynia pain control. When first prescribing drugs, clinicians should avoid polypharmacy. One drug should be prescribed at a time. Before prescribing antidepressants or anticonvulsants for a patient of reproductive age, the clinician should emphasize the need for contraception. Antidepressants have been found to have a 60% response rate for various pain conditions; however, no randomized, controlled studies have been published regarding the use of antidepressants for vulvodynia. Both tricyclic antidepressants and anticonvulsants take time to achieve adequate pain control, which may take up to 3 weeks. Patients usually develop tolerance to the side effects of these medications (particularly sedation, dry mouth, and dizziness).

Biofeedback and physical therapy also are used in the treatment of both localized and generalized vulvodynia (4). Physical therapy techniques include internal (vaginal and rectal) and external soft tissue mobilization and myofascial release; trigger-point pressure; visceral, urogenital, and joint manipulation; electrical stimulation; therapeutic exercises; active pelvic floor retraining; biofeedback; bladder and bowel retraining; instruction in dietary revisions; therapeutic ultrasonography; and home vaginal dilation.

Vestibulectomy has been helpful for many patients with localized pain that has not responded to previous treatments (5). Patients should be evaluated for vaginismus and, if present, treated before a vestibulectomy is performed. For generalized vulvar burning unresponsive to previous behavioral and medical treatments, referral to a pain specialist may be helpful.

## Conclusion

Vulvodynia is a complex disorder that frequently is frustrating to both clinician and patient. It can be difficult to treat, and rapid resolution is unusual, even with appropriate therapy. Decreases in pain may take weeks to months and may not be complete. No single treatment is successful in all women. Expectations for improvement need to be realistically addressed with the patient. Emotional and psychologic support is important for many patients, and sex therapy and counseling may be beneficial.

## Resources

Haefner HK, Collins ME, Davis GD, Edwards L, Foster DC, Hartman ED, et al. The vulvodynia guideline. J Low Genit Tract Dis 2005;9:40–51. Available at: http://www.jlgtd.com/pt/re/jlgtd/pdfhandler.00128360-200501000-00009.pdf. Retrieved March 15, 2006.

National Vulvodynia Association
http://www.nva.org
PO Box 4491
Silver Spring, MD 20914-4491
301-299-0775

## References


1. Haefner HK, Collins ME, Davis GD, Edwards L, Foster DC, Hartmann EH, et al. The vulvodynia guideline. J Low Genit Tract Dis 2005;9:40–51.
2. Moyal-Barracco M, Lynch PJ. 2003 ISSVD terminology and classification of vulvodynia: a historical perspective. J Reprod Med 2004;49:772–7.
3. Segal D, Tifheret H, Lazer S. Submucous infiltration of betamethasone and lidocaine in the treatment of vulvar vestibulitis. Eur J Obstet Gynecol Reprod Biol 2003; 107:105–6.
4. Bergeron S, Binik YM, Khalife S, Pagidas K, Glazer HI, Meana M, et al. A randomized comparison of group cognitive-behavioral therapy, surface electromyographic biofeedback, and vestibulectomy in the treatment of dyspareunia resulting from vulvar vestibulitis. Pain 2001; 91:297–306.
5. Haefner HK. Critique of new gynecologic surgical procedures: surgery for vulvar vestibulitis. Clin Obstet Gynecol 2000;43:689–700.

ACOG

Committee on Gynecologic Practice

# Committee Opinion

Number 356, December 2006

# Routine Cancer Screening

*ABSTRACT: Obstetrician–gynecologists serve as primary care physicians for many women. Because the obstetrician–gynecologist may be the only physician providing routine care, clinicians should be able to provide recommendations for routine cancer screenings, including those for nongynecologic cancers. This document summarizes recommendations of the American College of Obstetricians and Gynecologists for routine cancer screening for the average-risk American woman. The obstetrician–gynecologist should discuss both benefits and limitations of screening tests with the patient.*

Cancer is the second leading cause of death in women in the United States. The estimated number of women who will develop various types of cancer, the number of women estimated to die from these diseases, and the lifetime risks of developing and dying from these cancers are shown in Table 1. Many treatments are available, but early detection significantly improves treatment outcomes and reduces mortality. Routine cancer screening facilitates detection and treatment.

This document summarizes recommendations of the American College of Obstetricians and Gynecologists (ACOG) for routine cancer screening for the average-risk American woman. These recommendations address routine screening only. For example, this document does not provide follow-up screening recommendations for women with a history of cervical cytologic abnormalities or for those with a family history of breast or other cancers. Other ACOG publications providing screening recommendations for women at high risk are included in the bibliography. Resources for further information and screening updates are provided in the box.

Obstetrician–gynecologists serve as primary care physicians for many women. Because the obstetrician–gynecologist may be the only physician providing routine care, clinicians should be able to provide recommendations for routine cancer screenings, including those for nongynecologic cancers. The obstetrician–gynecologist should discuss both benefits and limitations of screening tests with the patient. Routine cancer screenings currently recommended by ACOG are summarized in Table 2.



ISSN 1074-861X

**The American College of Obstetricians and Gynecologists**
409 12th Street, SW
PO Box 96920
Washington, DC 20090-6920

12345/09876

Routine cancer screening. ACOG Committee Opinion No. 356. American College of Obstetricians and Gynecologists. Obstet Gynecol 2006;108:1611–13.

**Table 1.** Estimated Number and Lifetime Risk of Women Who Will Develop or Die From Various Types of Cancer in 2006

| Type of Cancer | Number of New Cases | Lifetime Risk of Developing, 1 in | Number of Deaths | Lifetime Risk of Dying From, 1 in |
|---|---|---|---|---|
| Breast | 212,920 | 8 | 40,970 | 34 |
| Lung | 81,770 | 17 | 72,130 | 20 |
| Colorectal | 75,810 | 18 | 27,300 | 45 |
| Endometrial | 41,200 | 38 | 7,350 | 196 |
| Skin | 30,420 | 77 | 3,720 | 500 |
| Ovarian | 20,180 | 68 | 15,310 | 95 |
| Cervical | 9,710 | 135 | 3,700 | 385 |

Data from Jemal A, Siegel R, Ward E, Murray T, Xu J, Smigal C, et al. Cancer statistics, 2006. CA Cancer J Clin 2006;56:106–30; and American Cancer Society. Lifetime probability of developing or dying from cancer. Atlanta (GA): ACS; 2006. Available at: http://www.cancer.org/docroot/CRI/content/CRI_2_6x_Lifetime_Probability_of_Developing_or_Dying_From_Cancer.asp. Retrieved August 18, 2006.

**Table 2.** Suggested Routine Cancer Screening Guidelines

| Topic | Guideline |
|---|---|
| General health counseling and cancer evaluation | All women should have a general health evaluation annually or as appropriate that should include evaluation for cancer and examination, as indicated, to detect signs of premalignant or malignant conditions. |
| Breast cancer | Mammography should be performed every 1–2 years beginning at age 40 years and yearly beginning at age 50 years. All women should have an annual clinical breast examination as part of the physical examination. Despite a lack of definitive data for or against breast self-examination, breast self-examination has the potential to detect palpable breast cancer and can be recommended. |
| Cervical cancer | Cervical cytology should be performed annually beginning at approximately 3 years after initiation of sexual intercourse but no later than age 21 years. Cervical cytology screening can be performed every 2–3 years after three consecutive negative test results if the patient is aged 30 years or older with no history of cervical intraepithelial neoplasia 2 or 3, immunosuppression, human immunodeficiency virus (HIV) infection, or diethylstilbestrol exposure in utero. Annual cervical cytology also is an option for women aged 30 years and older. The use of a combination of cervical cytology and HPV DNA screening is appropriate for women aged 30 years and older. If this combination is used, women who receive negative results on both tests should be rescreened no more frequently than every 3 years. |
| Colorectal cancer | Beginning at age 50 years, one of five screening options should be selected:<br>1) Yearly patient-collected fecal occult blood testing (FOBT) or fecal immunochemical testing (FIT)* *or*<br>2) Flexible sigmoidoscopy every 5 years *or*<br>3) Yearly patient-collected FOBT or FIT* plus flexible sigmoidoscopy every 5 years *or*<br>4) Double-contrast barium enema every 5 years *or*<br>5) Colonoscopy every 10 years |
| Endometrial cancer | Screening asymptomatic women for endometrial cancer and its precursors is not recommended at this time. |
| Lung cancer | Available screening techniques are not cost-effective and have not been shown to reduce mortality from lung cancer. Accordingly, routine lung cancer screening is not recommended. |
| Ovarian cancer | Currently, there are no effective techniques for the routine screening of asymptomatic, low-risk women for ovarian cancer. It appears that the best way to detect early ovarian cancer is for both the patient and her clinician to have a high index of suspicion of the diagnosis in the symptomatic woman, and both should be aware of the symptoms commonly associated with ovarian cancer. Persistent symptoms such as an increase in abdominal size, abdominal bloating, fatigue, abdominal pain, indigestion, inability to eat normally, urinary frequency, pelvic pain, constipation, back pain, urinary incontinence of recent onset, or unexplained weight loss should be evaluated with ovarian cancer being included in the differential diagnosis. |
| Skin cancer | Evaluate and counsel regarding exposure to ultraviolet rays. |

*Both FOBT and FIT require two or three samples of stool collected by the patient at home and returned for analysis. A single stool sample for FOBT or FIT obtained by digital rectal examination is not adequate for the detection of colorectal cancer.

**Resources for Updated Screening Recommendations and Further Information**

American College of Obstetricians and Gynecologists: www.acog.org

American Cancer Society: www.cancer.org

U.S. Preventive Services Task Force: www.ahrq.gov/clinic/uspstfix.htm

## Bibliography


### *General*

Primary and preventive care: periodic assessments. ACOG Committee Opinion No. 357. American College of Obstetricians and Gynecologists. Obstet Gynecol 2006;108:1615–21.

Jemal A, Siegel R, Ward E, Murray T, Xu J, Smigal C, et al. Cancer statistics, 2006. CA Cancer J Clin 2006;56:106–30.

Smith RA, Cokkinides V, Eyre HJ. American Cancer Society guidelines for the early detection of cancer, 2006. CA Cancer J Clin 2006;56:11–25; quiz 49–50.

### *Breast Cancer*

Breast cancer screening. ACOG Practice Bulletin No. 42. American College of Obstetricians and Gynecologists. Obstet Gynecol 2003;101:821–31.

Humphrey LL, Helfand M, Chan BK, Woolf SH. Breast cancer screening: a summary of the evidence for the U.S. Preventive Services Task Force. Ann Intern Med 2002;137:347–60.

### *Cervical Cancer*

Cervical cytology screening. ACOG Practice Bulletin No. 45. American College of Obstetricians and Gynecologists. Obstet Gynecol 2003;102:417–27.

U.S. Preventive Services Task Force. Screening for cervical cancer: recommendations and rationale. Rockville (MD): Agency for Healthcare Research and Quality; 2003. Available at: http://www.ahrq.gov/clinic/3rduspstf/cervcan/cercanrr.pdf. Retrieved August 21, 2006.

### *Ovarian Cancer*

The role of the generalist obstetrician–gynecologist in the early detection of ovarian cancer. ACOG Committee Opinion No. 280. American College of Obstetricians and Gynecologists. Obstet Gynecol 2002;100:1413–6.

Screening for ovarian cancer: recommendation statement. U.S. Preventive Services Task Force. Ann Fam Med 2004;2:260–2.

### *Colorectal Cancer*

Nolan TE, Schilder JM. Lower gastrointestinal tract disorders. Clin Updates Womens Health Care 2006;V(1):1–77.

Smith RA, von Eschenbach AC, Wender R, Levin B, Byers T, Rothenberger D, et al. American Cancer Society guidelines for the early detection of cancer: update of early detection guidelines for prostate, colorectal, and endometrial cancers. Also: update 2001—testing for early lung cancer detection [published erratum appears in CA Cancer J Clin 2001;51:150]. CA Cancer J Clin 2001;51:38–75; quiz 77–80.

U.S. Preventive Services Task Force. Screening for colorectal cancer: recommendations and rationale. Rockville (MD): Agency for Healthcare Research and Quality; 2002. Available at: http://www.ahrq.gov/clinic/3rduspstf/colorectal/colorr.pdf. Retrieved August 21, 2006.

Winawer SJ, Fletcher RH, Miller L, Godlee F, Stolar MH, Mulrow CD, et al. Colorectal cancer screening: clinical guidelines and rationale [published errata in Gastroenterology 1997;112:1060 and Gastroenterology 1998;114:625]. Gastroenterology 1997;112:594–642.

### *Lung Cancer*

American College of Obstetricians and Gynecologists. Smoking and women's health. In: Special issues in women's health. Washington, DC: ACOG; 2005. p. 151–67.

Humphrey LL, Teutsch S, Johnson M. Lung cancer screening with sputum cytologic examination, chest radiography, and computed tomography: an update for the U.S. Preventive Services Task Force. U.S. Preventive Services Task Force. Ann Intern Med 2004;140:740–53.

Lung cancer screening: recommendation statement. U.S. Preventive Services Task Force. Ann Intern Med 2004;140: 738–9.

### *Skin Cancer*

Screening for skin cancer: recommendations and rationale. U.S. Preventive Services Task Force. Am J Prev Med 2001; 20(suppl):44–6.

U.S. Preventive Services Task Force. Counseling to prevent skin cancer: recommendations and rationale. Rockville (MD): Agency for Healthcare Research and Quality; 2003. Available at: http://www.ahrq.gov/clinic/3rduspstf/skcancoun/skcounrr.pdf. Retrieved August 21, 2006.

ACOG Committee Opinion

Committee on Gynecologic Practice

THE AMERICAN COLLEGE OF OBSTETRICIANS AND GYNECOLOGISTS 1951 WOMEN'S HEALTH CARE PHYSICIANS

Number 357, December 2006 *(Replaces No. 292, November 2003)*

# Primary and Preventive Care: Periodic Assessments

*ABSTRACT: Periodic assessments offer an excellent opportunity for obstetricians and gynecologists to provide preventive screening, evaluation, and counseling. This Committee Opinion provides the recommendations of the American College of Obstetricians and Gynecologists' Committee on Gynecologic Practice for routine assessments in primary and preventive care for women based on age and risk factors.*

The following charts are updated versions of those previously published by the American College of Obstetricians and Gynecologists (ACOG) in Committee Opinion No. 292. This version replaces the previous version. The policies and recommendations of ACOG committees regarding specific aspects of the health care of women have been incorporated; they may differ from the recommendations of other groups. Although there will be differences of opinion regarding some specific recommendations, the major benefit to be derived should not be lost in debating those issues. The American College of Obstetricians and Gynecologists recommends that the first visit to the obstetrician–gynecologist for screening and the provision of preventive health care services and guidance take place between the ages of 13 and 15 years.

Periodic assessments provide an excellent opportunity to counsel patients about preventive care. These assessments, yearly or as appropriate, should include screening, evaluation, and counseling based on age and risk factors. Personal behavioral characteristics are important aspects of a woman's health. Positive behaviors, such as exercise, should be reinforced, and negative ones, such as smoking, should be discouraged. The following guidelines indicate routine assessments for nonpregnant women based on age groups and risk factors (see Table 1) and list leading causes of death and morbidity for each age group identified by various sources (see box). It is recognized that variations may be required to adjust to the needs of a specific individual. For example, certain risk factors may influence additional assessments and interventions. Physicians should be alert to high-risk factors (indicated by an asterisk and further elucidated in Table 1). During evaluation, the patient should be made aware of high-risk conditions that require targeted screening or treatment.



ISSN 1074-861X

**The American College of Obstetricians and Gynecologists**
409 12th Street, SW
PO Box 96920
Washington, DC 20090-6920

12345/09876

Primary and preventive care: periodic assessments. ACOG Committee Opinion No. 357. American College of Obstetricians and Gynecologists. Obstet Gynecol 2006;108:1615–22.

## Periodic Assessment
## Ages 13–18 Years

### Screening

*History*

- Reason for visit
- Health status: medical, menstrual, surgical, family
- Dietary/nutrition assessment
- Physical activity
- Use of complementary and alternative medicine
- Tobacco, alcohol, other drug use
- Abuse/neglect
- Sexual practices

*Physical Examination*

- Height
- Weight
- Body mass index (BMI)
- Blood pressure
- Secondary sexual characteristics (Tanner staging)
- Pelvic examination (when indicated by the medical history)
- Skin*

*Laboratory Testing*

*Periodic*

- Cervical cytology (annually beginning at approximately 3 years after initiation of sexual intercourse)
- Chlamydia and gonorrhea testing (if sexually active)

*High-Risk Groups**

- Hemoglobin level assessment
- Bacteriuria testing
- Sexually transmitted disease testing
- Human immunodeficiency virus (HIV) testing
- Genetic testing/counseling
- Rubella titer assessment
- Tuberculosis skin testing
- Lipid profile assessment
- Fasting glucose testing
- Hepatitis C virus testing
- Colorectal cancer screening†

### Evaluation and Counseling

*Sexuality*

- Development
- High-risk behaviors
- Preventing unwanted/unintended pregnancy
  - —Postponing sexual involvement
  - —Contraceptive options, including emergency contraception
- Sexually transmitted diseases
  - —Partner selection
  - —Barrier protection

*Fitness and Nutrition*

- Dietary/nutrition assessment (including eating disorders)
- Exercise: discussion of program
- Folic acid supplementation (0.4 mg/d)
- Calcium intake

*Psychosocial Evaluation*

- Suicide: depressive symptoms
- Interpersonal/family relationships
- Sexual identity
- Personal goal development
- Behavioral/learning disorders
- Abuse/neglect
- Satisfactory school experience
- Peer relationships
- Date rape prevention

*Cardiovascular Risk Factors*

- Family history
- Hypertension
- Dyslipidemia
- Obesity
- Diabetes mellitus

*Health/Risk Behaviors*

- Hygiene (including dental), fluoride supplementation*
- Injury prevention
  - —Safety belts and helmets
  - —Recreational hazards
  - —Firearms
  - —Hearing
  - —Occupational hazards
  - —School hazards
  - —Exercise and sports involvement
- Skin exposure to ultraviolet rays
- Tobacco, alcohol, other drug use

### Immunizations

*Periodic*

- Tetanus–diphtheria–pertussis booster (once between ages 11 years and 16 years)
- Hepatitis B vaccine (one series for those not previously immunized)
- Human papillomavirus vaccine (one series for those not previously immunized)
- Meningococcal conjugate vaccine (before entry into high school for those not previously immunized)

*High-Risk Groups**

- Influenza vaccine
- Hepatitis A vaccine
- Pneumococcal vaccine
- Measles–mumps–rubella vaccine
- Varicella vaccine

*Leading Causes of Death‡*

1. Accidents
2. Malignant neoplasms
3. Homicide
4. Suicide
5. Congenital anomalies
6. Diseases of the heart
7. Chronic lower respiratory diseases
8. Influenza and pneumonia
9. Septicemia
10. Pregnancy, childbirth, and puerperium

*Leading Causes of Morbidity‡*

- Acne
- Asthma
- Chlamydia
- Headache
- Mental disorders, including affective and neurotic disorders
- Nose, throat, ear, and upper respiratory infections
- Obesity
- Sexual assault
- Sexually transmitted diseases
- Urinary tract infections
- Vaginitis

*See Table 1.

†Only for those with a family history of familial adenomatous polyposis or 8 years after the start of pancolitis. For a more detailed discussion of colorectal cancer screening, see Smith RA, von Eschenbach AC, Wender R, Levin B, Byers T, Rothenberger D, et al. ACS American Cancer Society guidelines for the early detection of cancer: update of early detection guidelines for prostate, colorectal, and endometrial cancers. Also: update 2001—testing for early lung cancer detection. Prostate Cancer Advisory Committee, ACS Colorectal Cancer Advisory Committee, ACS Endometrial Cancer Advisory Committee [published erratum appears in CA Cancer J Clin 2001;51:150]. CA Cancer J Clin 2001;51:38–75; quiz 77–80.

‡See box.

## Periodic Assessment
## Ages 19–39 Years

### Screening

*History*

- Reason for visit
- Health status: medical, surgical, family
- Dietary/nutrition assessment
- Physical activity
- Use of complementary and alternative medicine
- Tobacco, alcohol, other drug use
- Abuse/neglect
- Sexual practices
- Urinary and fecal incontinence

*Physical Examination*

- Height
- Weight
- Body mass index (BMI)
- Blood pressure
- Neck: adenopathy, thyroid
- Breasts
- Abdomen
- Pelvic examination
- Skin*

*Laboratory Testing*

*Periodic*

- Cervical cytology (annually beginning no later than age 21 years; every 2–3 years after three consecutive negative test results if age 30 years or older with no history of cervical intraepithelial neoplasia 2 or 3, immunosuppression, human immunodeficiency virus [HIV] infection, or diethylstilbestrol exposure in utero)†
- Chlamydia testing (if aged 25 years or younger and sexually active)
- Human Immunodeficiency virus (HIV) testing‡

*High-Risk Groups**

- Hemoglobin level assessment
- Bacteriuria testing
- Mammography
- Fasting glucose testing
- Sexually transmitted disease testing
- Genetic testing/counseling
- Rubella titer assessment
- Tuberculosis skin testing
- Lipid profile assessment
- Thyroid-stimulating hormone testing
- Hepatitis C virus testing
- Colorectal cancer screening
- Bone density screening

### Evaluation and Counseling

*Sexuality and Reproductive Planning*

- High-risk behaviors
- Discussion of a reproductive health plan§
- Contraceptive options for prevention of unwanted pregnancy, including emergency contraception
- Preconception and genetic counseling
- Sexually transmitted diseases
  - —Partner selection
  - —Barrier protection
- Sexual function

*Fitness and Nutrition*

- Dietary/nutrition assessment
- Exercise: discussion of program
- Folic acid supplementation (0.4 mg/d)
- Calcium intake

*Psychosocial Evaluation*

- Interpersonal/family relationships
- Intimate partner violence
- Work satisfaction
- Lifestyle/stress
- Sleep disorders

*Cardiovascular Risk Factors*

- Family history
- Hypertension
- Dyslipidemia
- Obesity
- Diabetes mellitus
- Lifestyle

*Health/Risk Behaviors*

- Hygiene (including dental)
- Injury prevention
  - —Safety belts and helmets
  - —Occupational hazards
  - —Recreational hazards
  - —Firearms
  - —Hearing
  - —Exercise and sports involvement
- Breast self-examination||
- Chemoprophylaxis for breast cancer (for high-risk women aged 35 years or older)¶
- Skin exposure to ultraviolet rays
- Suicide: depressive symptoms
- Tobacco, alcohol, other drug use

### Immunizations

*Periodic*

- Human papillomavirus vaccine (one series for those aged 26 years or less and not previously immunized)
- Tetanus–diphtheria–pertussis booster (every 10 years)

*High-Risk Groups**

- Measles–mumps–rubella vaccine
- Hepatitis A vaccine
- Hepatitis B vaccine
- Influenza vaccine
- Meningococcal vaccine
- Pneumococcal vaccine
- Varicella vaccine

*Leading Causes of Death***

1. Malignant neoplasms
2. Accidents
3. Diseases of the heart
4. Suicide
5. Human immunodeficiency virus (HIV) disease
6. Homicide
7. Cerebrovascular diseases
8. Diabetes mellitus
9. Chronic liver diseases and cirrhosis
10. Chronic lower respiratory diseases

*Leading Causes of Morbidity***

- Acne
- Arthritis
- Asthma
- Back symptoms
- Cancer
- Chlamydia
- Depression
- Diabetes mellitus
- Gynecologic disorders
- Headache/migraine
- Hypertension
- Joint disorders
- Menstrual disorders
- Mental disorders, including affective and neurotic disorders
- Nose, throat, ear, and upper respiratory infections
- Obesity
- Sexual assault/domestic violence
- Sexually transmitted diseases
- Substance abuse
- Urinary tract infections

*See Table 1.

†For a more detailed discussion of cervical cytology screening, including the use of human papillomavirus DNA testing and screening after hysterectomy, see Cervical cytology screening. ACOG Practice Bulletin No. 45. American College of Obstetricians and Gynecologists. Obstet Gynecol 2003;102:417–27.

‡ Physicians should be aware of and follow their states' HIV screening requirements. For a more detailed discussion of HIV screening, see Branson BM, Handsfield HH, Lampe MA, Janssen RS, Taylor AW, Lyss SB, et al. Revised recommendations for HIV testing of adults, adolescents, and pregnant women in health care settings. Centers for Disease Control and Prevention. MMWR Recomm Rep 2006;55(RR-14):1–17; quiz CE1–4.

§For a more detailed discussion of the reproductive health plan, see The importance of preconception care in the continuum of women's health care. ACOG Committee Opinion No. 313. American College of Obstetricians and Gynecologists. Obstet Gynecol 2005;106:665-6.

||Despite a lack of definite data for or against breast self-examination, breast self-examination has the potential to detect palpable breast cancer and can be recommended.

¶For a more detailed discussion of risk assessment and chemoprevention therapy, see Selective estrogen receptor modulators. ACOG Practice Bulletin No. 39. American College of Obstetricians and Gynecologists. Obstet Gynecol 2002;100:835–43.

**See box.

## Periodic Assessment
## Ages 40–64 Years

**Screening**

*History*

- Reason for visit
- Health status: medical, surgical, family
- Dietary/nutrition assessment
- Physical activity
- Use of complementary and alternative medicine
- Tobacco, alcohol, other drug use
- Abuse/neglect
- Sexual practices
- Urinary and fecal incontinence

*Physical Examination*

- Height
- Weight
- Body mass index (BMI)
- Blood pressure
- Oral cavity
- Neck: adenopathy, thyroid
- Breasts, axillae
- Abdomen
- Pelvic examination
- Skin*

*Laboratory Testing*

*Periodic*

- Cervical cytology (every 2–3 years after three consecutive negative test results if no history of cervical intraepithelial neoplasia 2 or 3, immunosuppression, human immunodeficiency virus [HIV] infection, or diethylstilbestrol exposure in utero)†
- Mammography (every 1–2 years beginning at age 40 years, yearly beginning at age 50 years)
- Lipid profile assessment (every 5 years beginning at age 45 years)
- Colorectal cancer screening (beginning at age 50 years), using one of the following options:
  1. Yearly patient-collected fecal occult blood testing‡
  2. Flexible sigmoidoscopy every 5 years
  3. Yearly patient-collected fecal occult blood testing‡ plus flexible sigmoidoscopy every 5 years
  4. Double contrast barium enema every 5 years
  5. Colonoscopy every 10 years
- Fasting glucose testing (every 3 years after age 45 years)
- Thyroid-stimulating hormone screening (every 5 years beginning at age 50 years)
- Human immunodeficiency virus (HIV) testing§

*High-Risk Groups**

- Hemoglobin level assessment
- Bacteriuria testing
- Fasting glucose testing
- Sexually transmitted disease testing
- Tuberculosis skin testing
- Lipid profile assessment
- Thyroid-stimulating hormone testing
- Hepatitis C virus testing
- Colorectal cancer screening

**Evaluation and Counseling**

*Sexuality*‖

- High-risk behaviors
- Contraceptive options for prevention of unwanted pregnancy, including emergency contraception
- Sexually transmitted diseases
  - —Partner selection
  - —Barrier protection
- Sexual function

*Fitness and Nutrition*

- Dietary/nutrition assessment
- Exercise: discussion of program
- Folic acid supplementation (0.4 mg/d before age 50 years)
- Calcium intake

*Psychosocial Evaluation*

- Family relationships
- Intimate partner violence
- Work satisfaction
- Retirement planning
- Lifestyle/stress
- Sleep disorders

*Cardiovascular Risk Factors*

- Family history
- Hypertension
- Dyslipidemia
- Obesity
- Diabetes mellitus
- Lifestyle

*Health/Risk Behaviors*

- Hygiene (including dental)
- Hormone therapy
- Injury prevention
  - —Safety belts and helmets
  - —Occupational hazards
  - —Recreational hazards
  - —Exercise and sports involvement
  - —Firearms
  - —Hearing
- Breast self-examination¶
- Chemoprophylaxis for breast cancer (for high-risk women)**
- Skin exposure to ultraviolet rays
- Suicide: depressive symptoms
- Tobacco, alcohol, other drug use

**Immunizations**

*Periodic*

- Influenza vaccine (annually beginning at age 50 years)
- Tetanus-diphtheria-pertussis booster (every 10 years)

*High-Risk Groups**

- Measles–mumps–rubella vaccine
- Hepatitis A vaccine
- Hepatitis B vaccine
- Influenza vaccine
- Meningococcal vaccine
- Pneumococcal vaccine
- Varicella vaccine

*Leading Causes of Death*††

1. Malignant neoplasms
2. Diseases of the heart
3. Cerebrovascular diseases
4. Chronic lower respiratory diseases
5. Accidents
6. Diabetes mellitus
7. Chronic liver disease and cirrhosis
8. Septicemia
9. Suicide
10. Human immunodeficiency virus (HIV) disease

*Leading Causes of Morbidity*††

- Arthritis/osteoarthritis
- Asthma
- Cancer
- Cardiovascular disease
- Depression
- Diabetes mellitus
- Disorders of the urinary tract
- Headache/migraine
- Hypertension
- Menopause
- Mental disorders, including affective and neurotic disorders
- Musculoskeletal symptoms
- Nose, throat, ear, and upper respiratory infections
- Obesity
- Sexually transmitted diseases
- Ulcers
- Vision impairment

*See Table 1.

†For a more detailed discussion of cervical cytology screening, including the use of human papillomavirus DNA testing and screening after hysterectomy, see Cervical Cytology screening. ACOG Practice Bulletin No. 45. American College of Obstetricians and Gynecologists. Obstet Gynecol 2003;102:417–27.

‡Fecal occult blood testing (FOBT) requires two or three samples of stool collected by the patient at home and returned for analysis. A single stool sample for FOBT obtained by digital rectal examination is not adequate for the detection of colorectal cancer.

§ Physicians should be aware of and follow their states' HIV screening requirements. For a more detailed discussion of HIV screening, see Branson BM, Handsfield HH, Lampe MA, Janssen RS, Taylor AW, Lyss SB, et al. Revised recommendations for HIV testing of adults, adolescents, and pregnant women in health care settings. Centers for Disease Control and Prevention. MMWR Recomm Rep 2006;55(RR-14):1–17; quiz CE1–4.

‖Preconception and genetic counseling is appropriate for certain women in this age group.

¶Despite a lack of definitive data for or against breast self-examination, breast self-examination has the potential to detect palpable breast cancer and can be recommended.

**For a more detailed discussion of risk assessment and chemoprevention therapy, see Selective estrogen receptor modulators. ACOG Practice Bulletin No. 39. American College of Obstetricians and Gynecologists. Obstet Gynecol 2002;100:835–43.

††See box.

## Periodic Assessment
## Ages 65 Years and Older

### Screening

*History*

- Reason for visit
- Health status: medical, surgical, family
- Dietary/nutrition assessment
- Physical activity
- Use of complementary and alternative medicine
- Tobacco, alcohol, other drug use, and concurrent medication use
- Abuse/neglect
- Sexual practices
- Urinary and fecal incontinence

*Physical Examination*

- Height
- Weight
- Body mass index (BMI)
- Blood pressure
- Oral cavity
- Neck: adenopathy, thyroid
- Breasts, axillae
- Abdomen
- Pelvic examination
- Skin*

*Laboratory Testing*

*Periodic*

- Cervical cytology (every 2–3 years after three consecutive negative test results if no history of cervical intraepithelial neoplasia 2 or 3, immunosuppression, human immunodeficiency virus [HIV] infection, or diethylstilbestrol exposure in utero)†
- Urinalysis
- Mammography
- Lipid profile assessment (every 5 years)
- Colorectal cancer screening using one of the following methods:
  1. Yearly patient-collected fecal occult blood testing‡
  2. Flexible sigmoidoscopy every 5 years
  3. Yearly patient-collected fecal occult blood testing‡ plus flexible sigmoidoscopy every 5 years
  4. Double contrast barium enema every 5 years
  5. Colonoscopy every 10 years
- Fasting glucose testing (every 3 years)
- Bone density screening§
- Thyroid-stimulating hormone screening (every 5 years)

*High-Risk Groups**

- Hemoglobin level assessment
- Sexually transmitted disease testing
- Human immunodeficiency virus (HIV) testing
- Tuberculosis skin testing
- Thyroid-stimulating hormone screening
- Hepatitis C virus testing
- Colorectal cancer screening

### Evaluation and Counseling

*Sexuality*

- Sexual function
- Sexual behaviors
- Sexually transmitted diseases
  - —Partner selection
  - —Barrier protection

*Fitness and Nutrition*

- Dietary/nutrition assessment
- Exercise: discussion of program
- Calcium intake

*Psychosocial Evaluation*

- Neglect/abuse
- Lifestyle/stress
- Depression/sleep disorders
- Family relationships
- Work/retirement satisfaction

*Cardiovascular Risk Factors*

- Hypertension
- Dyslipidemia
- Obesity
- Diabetes mellitus
- Sedentary lifestyle

*Health/Risk Behaviors*

- Hygiene (including dental)
- Hormone therapy
- Injury prevention
  - —Safety belts and helmets
  - —Prevention of falls
  - —Occupational hazards
  - —Recreational hazards
  - —Exercise and sports involvement
  - —Firearms
- Visual acuity/glaucoma
- Hearing
- Breast self-examination‖
- Chemoprophylaxis for breast cancer (for high-risk women)¶
- Skin exposure to ultraviolet rays
- Suicide: depressive symptoms
- Tobacco, alcohol, other drug use

### Immunizations

*Periodic*

- Tetanus–diphtheria booster (every 10 years)
- Influenza vaccine (annually)
- Pneumococcal vaccine (once)

*High-Risk Groups**

- Hepatitis A vaccine
- Hepatitis B vaccine
- Meningococcal vaccine
- Varicella vaccine

*Leading Causes of Death***

1. Diseases of the heart
2. Malignant neoplasms
3. Cerebrovascular diseases
4. Chronic lower respiratory diseases
5. Alzheimer's disease
6. Influenza and pneumonia
7. Diabetes mellitus
8. Nephritis, nephrotic syndrome, and nephrosis
9. Accidents
10. Septicemia

*Leading Causes of Morbidity***

- Arthritis/osteoarthritis
- Asthma
- Cancer
- Cardiovascular disease
- Chronic obstructive pulmonary diseases
- Diabetes mellitus
- Diseases of the nervous system and sense organs
- Hearing and vision impairment
- Hypertension
- Mental disorders
- Musculoskeletal symptoms
- Nose, throat, ear, and upper respiratory infections
- Obesity
- Osteoporosis
- Pneumonia
- Ulcers
- Urinary incontinence
- Urinary tract infections
- Vertigo

*See Table 1.

†For a more detailed discussion of cervical cytology screening, including the use of human papillomavirus DNA testing and screening after hysterectomy, see Cervical Cytology screening. ACOG Practice Bulletin No. 45. American College of Obstetricians and Gynecologists. Obstet Gynecol 2003;102:417–27.

‡Fecal occult blood testing (FOBT) requires two or three samples of stool collected by the patient at home and returned for analysis. A single stool sample for FOBT obtained by digital rectal examination is not adequate for detection of colorectal cancer.

§In the absence of new risk factors, subsequent bone density screening should not be performed more frequently than every 2 years.

‖Despite a lack of definitive data for or against breast self-examination, breast self-examination has the potential to detect palpable breast cancer and can be recommended.

¶For a more detailed discussion of risk assessment and chemoprevention therapy, see Selective estrogen receptor modulators. ACOG Practice Bulletin No. 39. American College of Obstetricians and Gynecologists. Obstet Gynecol 2002;100:835–43.

**See box.

**Table 1.** High-Risk Factors

| Intervention | High-Risk Factor |
|---|---|
| Bacteriuria testing | Diabetes mellitus |
| Bone density screening* | Postmenopausal women younger than 65 years: history of prior fracture as an adult; family history of osteoporosis; Caucasian; dementia; poor nutrition; smoking; low weight and BMI; estrogen deficiency caused by early (age younger than 45 years) menopause, bilateral oophorectomy or prolonged (longer than 1 year) premenopausal amenorrhea; low lifelong calcium intake; alcoholism; impaired eyesight despite adequate correction; history of falls; inadequate physical activity<br>All women: certain diseases or medical conditions and those who take certain drugs associated with an increased risk of osteoporosis |
| Colorectal cancer screening† | Colorectal cancer or adenomatous polyps in first-degree relative younger than 60 years or in two or more first-degree relatives of any ages; family history of familial adenomatous polyposis or hereditary nonpolyposis colon cancer; history of colorectal cancer, adenomatous polyps, inflammatory bowel disease, chronic ulcerative colitis, or Crohn's disease |
| Fasting glucose testing | Overweight (BMI greater than or equal to 25); family history of diabetes mellitus; habitual physical inactivity; high-risk race/ethnicity (eg, African American, Hispanic, Native American, Asian, Pacific Islander); have given birth to a newborn weighing more than 9 lb or have a history of gestational diabetes mellitus; hypertension; high-density lipoprotein cholesterol level less than or equal to 35 mg/dL; triglyceride level greater than or equal to 250 mg/dL; history of impaired glucose tolerance or impaired fasting glucose; polycystic ovary syndrome; history of vascular disease |
| Fluoride supplementation | Live in area with inadequate water fluoridation (less than 0.7 ppm) |
| Genetic testing/counseling | Considering pregnancy and: patient, partner, or family member with history of genetic disorder or birth defect; exposure to teratogens; or African, Cajun, Caucasian, European, Eastern European (Ashkenazi) Jewish, French Canadian, Mediterranean, or Southeast Asian ancestry |
| Hemoglobin level assessment | Caribbean, Latin American, Asian, Mediterranean, or African ancestry; history of excessive menstrual flow |
| HAV vaccination | Chronic liver disease, clotting factor disorders, illegal drug users, individuals who work with HAV-infected nonhuman primates or with HAV in a research laboratory setting, individuals traveling to or working in countries that have high or intermediate endemicity of hepatitis A |
| HBV vaccination | Hemodialysis patients; patients who receive clotting factor concentrates; health care workers and public safety workers who have exposure to blood in the workplace; individuals in training in schools of medicine, dentistry, nursing, laboratory technology, and other allied health professions; injecting drug users; individuals with more than one sexual partner in the previous 6 months; individuals with a recently acquired STD; all clients in STD clinics; household contacts and sexual partners of individuals with chronic HBV infection; clients and staff of institutions for the developmentally disabled; international travelers who will be in countries with high or intermediate prevalence of chronic HBV infection for more than 6 months; inmates of correctional facilities |
| HCV testing | History of injecting illegal drugs; recipients of clotting factor concentrates before 1987; chronic (long-term) hemodialysis; persistently abnormal alanine aminotransferase levels; recipients of blood from donors who later tested positive for HCV infection; recipients of blood or blood-component transfusion or organ transplant before July 1992; occupational percutaneous or mucosal exposure to HCV-positive blood |
| HIV testing | More than one sexual partner since most recent HIV test or a sex partner with more than one sexual partner since most recent HIV test, seeking treatment for STDs, drug use by injection, history of prostitution, past or present sexual partner who is HIV positive or bisexual or injects drugs, long-term residence or birth in an area with high prevalence of HIV infection, history of transfusion from 1978 to 1985, invasive cervical cancer, adolescents who are or ever have been sexually active, adolescents entering detention facilities. Offer to women seeking preconception evaluation. |

*(continued)*

**Table 1.** High-Risk Factors *(continued)*

| Intervention | High-Risk Factor |
|---|---|
| Influenza vaccination | Anyone who wishes to reduce the chance of becoming ill with influenza; chronic cardiovascular or pulmonary disorders, including asthma; chronic metabolic diseases, including diabetes mellitus, renal dysfunction, hemoglobinopathies, and immunosuppression (including immunosuppression caused by medications or by HIV); residents and employees of nursing homes and other long-term care facilities; individuals likely to transmit influenza to high-risk individuals (eg, household members and caregivers of the elderly, children aged from birth to 59 months, and adults with high-risk conditions); those with any condition (eg, cognitive dysfunction, spinal cord injury, seizure or other neuromuscular disorder) that compromises respiratory function or the handling of respiratory secretions, or that increases the risk of aspiration; health care workers |
| Lipid profile assessment | Family history suggestive of familial hyperlipidemia; family history of premature (age younger than 50 years for men, age younger than 60 years for women) cardiovascular disease; diabetes mellitus; multiple coronary heart disease risk factors (eg, tobacco use, hypertension) |
| Mammography | Women who have had breast cancer or who have a first-degree relative (ie, mother, sister, or daughter) or multiple other relatives who have a history of premenopausal breast or breast and ovarian cancer |
| Meningococcal vaccination | Adults with anatomic or functional asplenia or terminal complement component deficiencies, first-year college students living in dormitories, microbiologists routinely exposed to *Neisseria meningitidis* isolates, military recruits, travel to hyperendemic or epidemic areas |
| MMR vaccination | Adults born in 1957 or later should be offered vaccination (one dose of MMR) if there is no proof of immunity or documentation of a dose given after first birthday; individuals vaccinated in 1963–1967 should be offered revaccination (two doses); health care workers, students entering college, international travelers, and rubella-negative postpartum patients should be offered a second dose. |
| Pneumococcal vaccination | Chronic illness, such as cardiovascular disease, pulmonary disease, diabetes mellitus, alcoholism, chronic liver disease, cerebrospinal fluid leaks, functional asplenia (eg, sickle cell disease) or splenectomy; exposure to an environment where pneumococcal outbreaks have occurred; immunocompromised patients (eg, HIV infection, hematologic or solid malignancies, chemotherapy, steroid therapy). Revaccination after 5 years may be appropriate for certain high-risk groups. |
| Rubella titer assessment | Childbearing age and no evidence of immunity |
| STD testing | History of multiple sexual partners or a sexual partner with multiple contacts, sexual contact with individuals with culture-proven STD, history of repeated episodes of STDs, attendance at clinics for STDs, women with developmental disabilities; routine screening for chlamydial infection for all sexually active women aged 25 years or younger and other asymptomatic women at high risk for infection; routine screening for gonorrheal infection for all sexually active adolescents and other asymptomatic women at high risk for infection; sexually active adolescents who exchange sex for drugs or money, use intravenous drugs, are entering a detention facility, or live in a high prevalence area should also be tested for syphilis. |
| Skin examination | Increased recreational or occupational exposure to sunlight; family or personal history of skin cancer; clinical evidence of precursor lesions |
| Thyroid-stimulating hormone testing | Strong family history of thyroid disease; autoimmune disease (evidence of subclinical hypothyroidism may be related to unfavorable lipid profiles) |
| Tuberculosis skin testing | HIV infection; close contact with individuals known or suspected to have tuberculosis; medical risk factors known to increase risk of disease if infected; born in country with high tuberculosis prevalence; medically underserved; low income; alcoholism; intravenous drug use; resident of long-term care facility (eg, correctional institutions, mental institutions, nursing homes and facilities); health professional working in high-risk health care facilities |
| Varicella vaccination | All susceptible adults and adolescents, including health care workers; household contacts of immunocompromised individuals; teachers; daycare workers; residents and staff of institutional settings, colleges, prisons, or military installations; adolescents and adults living in households with children; international travelers; nonpregnant women of childbearing age |

Abbreviations: BMI, body mass index; HAV, hepatitis A virus; HBV, hepatitis B virus; HCV, hepatitis C virus; HIV, human immunodeficiency virus; MMR, measles–mumps–rubella; STD, sexually transmitted disease.

*For a more detailed discussion of bone density screening, see Osteoporosis. ACOG Practice Bulletin 50. American College of Obstetricians and Gynecologists. Obstet Gynecol 2004;103:203–16.

†For a more detailed discussion of colorectal cancer screening, see Smith RA, von Eschenbach AC, Wender R, Levin B, Byers T, Rothenberger D, et al. American Cancer Society guidelines for the early detection of cancer: update of early detection guidelines for prostate, colorectal, and endometrial cancers. Also: update 2001—testing for early lung cancer detection. Prostate Cancer Advisory Committee, ACS Colorectal Cancer Advisory Committee, ACS Endometrial Cancer Advisory Committee [published erratum appears in CA Cancer J Clin 2001;51:150]. CA Cancer J Clin 2001;51:38–75; quiz 77–80.

**Sources of Leading Causes of Mortality and Morbidity**

Leading causes of mortality are provided by the Mortality Statistics Branch at the National Center for Health Statistics. Data are from 2002, the most recent year for which final data are available. The causes are ranked.

Leading causes of morbidity are unranked estimates based on information from the following sources:

- National Health Interview Survey, 2004
- National Ambulatory Medical Care Survey, 2004
- National Health and Nutrition Examination Survey, 2003–2004
- National Hospital Discharge Survey, 2004
- National Nursing Home Survey, 1999
- U.S. Department of Justice National Violence Against Women Survey, 2006
- U.S. Centers for Disease Control and Prevention Sexually Transmitted Disease Surveillance, 2004
- U.S. Centers for Disease Control and Prevention HIV/AIDS Surveillance Report, 2004

ACOG
TECHNOLOGY ASSESSMENT
IN OBSTETRICS AND GYNECOLOGY

NUMBER 3, SEPTEMBER 2003

This Technology Assessment was developed by the ACOG Committee on Gynecologic Practice with the assistance of Daniel Breitkopf, MD, Steven R. Goldstein, MD, and John W. Seeds, MD. This document reflects emerging clinical and scientific advances as of the date issued and is subject to change. The information should not be construed as dictating an exclusive course of treatment or procedure to be followed. Variations in practice may be warranted based on the needs of the individual patient, resources, and limitations unique to the institution or type of practice.

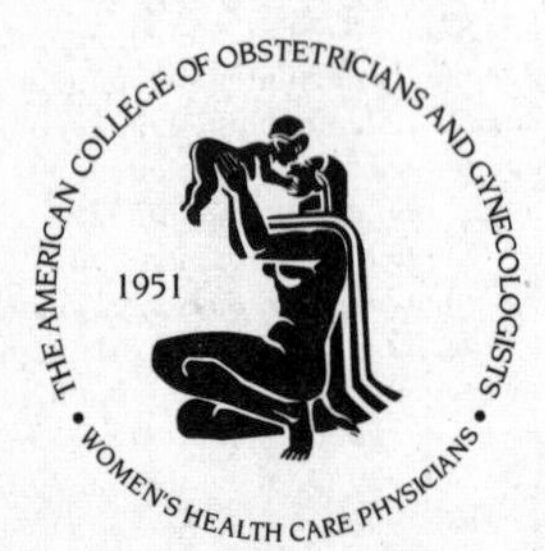


THE AMERICAN COLLEGE
OF OBSTETRICIANS
AND GYNECOLOGISTS
WOMEN'S HEALTH CARE PHYSICIANS

# Saline Infusion Sonohysterography

*ABSTRACT: Saline infusion sonohysterography consists of ultrasonographic imaging of the uterus and uterocervical cavity, using real-time ultrasonography during injection of sterile saline into the uterus. When properly performed, saline infusion sonohysterography can provide information about the uterus and endometrium. The most common indication for sonohysterography is abnormal uterine bleeding. Sonohysterography should not be performed in a woman who is pregnant or who could be pregnant or in a woman with a pelvic infection or unexplained pelvic tenderness. Physicians who perform or supervise diagnostic saline infusion sonohysterography should have training, experience, and demonstrated competence in gynecologic ultrasonography and saline infusion sonohysterography. Portions of this document were developed jointly with the American College of Radiology and the American Institute of Ultrasound in Medicine.*

This document has been developed to provide assistance to qualified physicians performing saline infusion sonohysterography. Properly performed sonohysterography can provide information about the uterus and endometrium. Additional studies may be necessary for a complete diagnosis. However, adherence to the following recommendations will maximize the diagnostic benefit of sonohysterography.

The clinical aspects of this document include sections addressing indications and contraindications, specifications of the examination, and equipment specifications that were developed collaboratively by the American College of Radiology, the American Institute of Ultrasound in Medicine, and the American College of Obstetricians and Gynecologists (ACOG). Sections of the document addressing physician qualifications and responsibilities, documentation, quality control, performance improvement, safety, infection control, and patient education are recommendations of the ACOG Committee on Gynecologic Practice.

Saline infusion sonohysterography consists of ultrasonographic imaging of the uterus and uterocervical cavity, using real-time ultrasonography during injection of sterile saline into the uterine cavity. The goal of sonohysterography is to detect abnormalities of the uterus and endometrium using real-time ultrasonography and static images with sufficient anatomic detail for diagnosis of normal and abnormal findings.

## INDICATIONS AND CONTRAINDICATIONS

The indications for sonohysterography include, but are not limited to, the following factors:

- Abnormal bleeding in premenopausal and postmenopausal women
- Infertility and habitual abortion
- Congenital abnormalities or anatomic variants of the uterine cavity or both
- Preoperative and postoperative evaluation of the uterine cavity, especially with regard to uterine myomata, polyps, and cysts
- Suspected uterine cavity synechiae
- Further evaluation of suspected abnormalities seen on endovaginal ultrasonography, including focal or diffuse endometrial thickening or debris
- Inadequate imaging of the endometrium by endovaginal ultrasonography

The most common indication for sonohysterography is abnormal uterine bleeding in both premenopausal and postmenopausal women.

Sonohysterography should not be performed in a woman who is pregnant or who could be pregnant. This usually is avoided by scheduling the examination in the follicular phase of the menstrual cycle, after the menstrual flow has essentially ceased, but before the patient has ovulated. In a patient with regular menstrual cycles, saline infusion sonohysterography should not, in most cases, be performed later than the 10th day of the menstrual cycle. Sonohysterography should not be performed in patients with a pelvic infection or unexplained pelvic tenderness, which may be caused by chronic pelvic inflammatory disease. Pelvic organ tenderness should be assessed during a preliminary endovaginal ultrasound examination. Active vaginal bleeding is not a contraindication to the procedure but may make the interpretation more challenging.

## PHYSICIAN QUALIFICATIONS AND RESPONSIBILITIES

Physicians who perform or supervise diagnostic saline infusion sonohysterography should be skilled in vaginal ultrasonography and transcervical placement of catheters. They should understand the indications, limitations, and possible complications of the procedure. Physicians should have training, experience, and demonstrated competence in gynecologic ultrasonography and saline infusion sonohysterography. Physicians are responsible for the documentation of the examination, quality control, and patient safety.

## SPECIFICATIONS OF THE EXAMINATION

### Patient Preparation

Referring physicians may elect to prescribe prophylactic antibiotics if patients routinely take them for other invasive procedures. If painful, dilated, or obstructed fallopian tubes (or a combination of these conditions) are found before saline infusion, and the patient is not taking prophylactic antibiotics, the examination should be delayed until treatment can be administered. In the presence of nontender hydrosalpinges, consideration may be given to administering antibiotics at the time of the examination. A pregnancy test is advised when clinically indicated. Patients should be asked if they have a latex allergy before latex sheaths are used.

### Procedure

Preliminary unenhanced endovaginal ultrasonography with measurements of the endometrium and evaluation of the uterus and ovaries should be performed before saline infusion sonohysterography. After the external os is cleansed, the cervical canal and/or uterine cavity should be catheterized using aseptic technique, and sterile saline should be administered under real-time ultrasonographic imaging. Imaging should include real-time scanning of the endometrium and cervical canal.

### Images

Appropriate images, in at least 2 planes, using a high-frequency endovaginal ultrasound probe should be produced and recorded to demonstrate normal and abnormal findings. Precatheterization images should be obtained, including the thickest bilayer endometrial measurement on a sagittal image.

The uterine cavity is filled with sterile saline, and representative images with a complete survey of the uterine cavity are obtained as necessary for diagnostic evaluation. If a balloon catheter is used for the examination, images should be obtained at the end of the procedure with the balloon deflated to fully evaluate the endometrial cavity, particularly the cervical canal and lower uterine segment.

## DOCUMENTATION

Appropriate documentation of a saline infusion sonohysterography examination is essential for clinical care and quality assessment and improvement. Documentation of biometry and anatomy is necessary to support clinical assessment and decision making as well as to establish that recommended guidelines were followed. An adequate written report should include patient identification, procedural technique, measurements, morphologic descriptions, and interpretation. Images of key findings and written reports from ultrasound examinations are considered part of the medical record and should be documented and stored appropriately. (In the *Current Procedural Terminology* [CPT], saline infusion sonohysterography is referred to as hysterosonography.)

## EQUIPMENT SPECIFICATIONS

Saline infusion sonohysterography must be conducted with an endovaginal transducer. If a patient has an enlarged uterus, additional transabdominal images may be required to fully evaluate the endometrium. The transducer should be adjusted to operate at the highest clinically appropriate frequency under the "as low as reasonably achievable" ALARA principle.

## QUALITY CONTROL, INFECTION CONTROL, AND PATIENT EDUCATION

Quality control is accomplished through careful record keeping, reliable archiving of reports and images, and clinical correlation with outcomes. Endovaginal transducers should always be covered with a single-use disposable latex or nonlatex cover. However, because no such disposable protective cover is without risk of rupture or defect, it is recommended that endovaginal transducers undergo appropriate antimicrobial and antiviral cleansing between patients.

The saline infusion sonohysterography procedure should be fully explained to the patient in advance. Because of the sensitive nature of the transvaginal examination, it may be advisable to have a chaperon present.

## BIBLIOGRAPHY

Bree RL, Bowerman RA, Bohm-Velez M, Benson CB, Doubilet PM, DeDreu S, et al. US evaluation of the uterus in patients with postmenopausal bleeding: A positive effect on diagnostic decision making. Radiology 2000;216:260–4.

Cohen JR, Luxman D, Sagi J, Yovel I, Wolman I, David MP. Sonohysterography for the diagnosis of endometrial thickening in postmenopausal bleeding—a preliminary report. J Am Assoc Gynecol Laparosc 1994;1:S7–8.

Doubilet PM. Society of Radiologists in Ultrasound Consensus Conference statement on postmenopausal bleeding. J Ultrasound Med 2001;20:1037–42.

Dubinsky TJ, Parvey HR, Gormaz G, Makland N. Transvaginal hysterosonography in the evaluation of small endoluminal masses. J Ultrasound Med 1995;14:1–6.

Dubinsky TJ, Stroehlein K, Abu-Ghazzeh Y, Parvey HR, Makland N. Prediction of benign and malignant endometrial disease: hysterosonographic-pathologic correlation. Radiology 1999;210:393–7.

Goldstein RB, Bree RL, Benson CB, Benacerraf BR, Bloss JD, Carlos R, et al. Evaluation of the woman with postmenopausal bleeding: Society of Radiologists in Ultrasound-Sponsored Consensus Conference statement. J Ultrasound Med 2001;20:1025–36.

Goldstein SR. Use of ultrasonohysterography for triage of perimenopausal patients with unexplained uterine bleeding. Am J Obstet Gynecol 1994;170:565–70.

Hann LE, Gretz EM, Bach AM, Francis SM. Sonohysterography for evaluation of the endometrium in women treated with tamoxifen. AJR Am J Roentgenol 2001;177:337–42.

Laifer-Narin S, Ragavendra N, Parmenter EK, Grant EG. False-normal appearance of the endometrium on conventional transvaginal sonography: comparison with saline hysterosonography. AJR Am J Roentgenol 2002;178:129–33.

Laifer-Narin SL, Ragavendra N, Lu DS, Sayre J, Perrella RR, Grant EG. Transvaginal saline hysterosonography: characteristics distinguishing malignant and various benign conditions. AJR Am J Roentgenol 1999;172:1513–20.

Lev-Toaff AS, Toaff ME, Liu JB, Merton DA, Goldberg BB. Value of sonohysterography in the diagnosis and management of abnormal uterine bleeding. Radiology 1996;201:179–84.

Merrill JA. Management of postmenopausal bleeding. Clin Obstet Gynecol 1981;24:285–99.

Parsons AK, Lense JJ. Sonohysterography for endometrial abnormalities: preliminary results. J Clin Ultrasound 1993;21:87–95.

Schwartz LB, Snyder J, Horan C, Porges RF, Nachtigall LE, Goldstein SR. The use of transvaginal ultrasound and saline infusion sonohysterography for the evaluation of asymptomatic postmenopausal breast cancer patients on tamoxifen. Ultrasound Obstet Gynecol 1998;11:48–53.

Sheth S, Hamper UM, Kurman RJ. Thickened endometrium in the postmenopausal woman: sonographic-pathologic correlation. Radiology 1993;187:135–9.

Syrop CH, Sahakian V. Transvaginal sonographic detection of endometrial polyps with fluid contrast augmentation. Obstet Gynecol 1992;79:1041–3.

**The American College of**
**Obstetricians and Gynecologists**
**409 12th Street, SW**
**PO Box 96920**
**Washington, DC 20090-6920**

12345/76543

Saline infusion sonohysterography. ACOG Technology Assessment in Obstetrics and Gynecology No. 3. American College of Obstetricians and Gynecologists. Obstet Gynecol 2003;102:659–62.

ACOG
TECHNOLOGY ASSESSMENT
IN OBSTETRICS AND GYNECOLOGY

NUMBER 4, AUGUST 2005

This Technology Assessment was developed by the ACOG Committee on Gynecologic Practice. This document reflects emerging clinical and scientific advances as of the date issued and is subject to change. The information should not be construed as dictating an exclusive course of treatment or procedure to be followed. Variations in practice may be warranted based on the needs of the individual patient, resources, and limitations unique to the institution or type of practice.

# Hysteroscopy

*ABSTRACT: Hysteroscopy is an effective, minimally invasive procedure for the diagnosis and treatment of intrauterine pathology. Selection of a distending medium requires consideration of the advantages, disadvantages, and risks associated with various media as well as their compatibility with electrosurgical or laser energy. Preoperative discussions with patients should address risks and benefits of the procedure, comorbidities, analgesia or anesthesia, and possible preoperative cervical dilation. Pregnancy, genital tract infection, and uterine carcinoma are contraindications to hysteroscopy. Possible complications include hemorrhage, fluid overload, perforation, visceral injury, infection, and embolization.*

Hysteroscopy is performed to view and treat pathology within the uterine cavity. Diagnostic hysteroscopy allows visualization of the endocervical canal, endometrial cavity, and fallopian tube ostia. Common abnormal findings include polyps, leiomyomata, intrauterine adhesions, and müllerian anomalies. Operative hysteroscopy incorporates the use of mechanical, electrosurgical, or laser instruments to treat intracavitary disease.

## INSTRUMENTATION

Hysteroscopes are available in both flexible and rigid models, all of which contain a telescope consisting of light bundles. Flexible hysteroscopes range in diameter from 2.7 mm to 5 mm and have a bendable tip that can be deflected in two directions ranging from 120 degrees to 160 degrees. Most also contain an operating channel for tubal catheterization or endometrial biopsy. Rigid hysteroscopes may consist of two or three pieces and range from 1 mm to 5 mm in diameter. Their tips have varying viewing angles (0, 12, 15, 30, and 70 degrees). An outer sheath fits over the telescope to allow inflow of a distending medium into the intrauterine cavity. This system allows fluid to return on the outside of the outer sheath passively from the intrauterine cavity through the cervix.

Continuous flow hysteroscopes consist of two channels to allow fluid to flow into the intrauterine cavity while debris and cloudy intrauterine fluid exit through perforations in the outer sheath to the outflow port. Fluid exiting the outflow port can be collected through tubing and returned to a device for the accurate measurement of fluid volume.

Operative hysteroscopes typically range from 8 mm to 10 mm in diameter and contain a working element. These hysteroscopes contain a retractable hand piece wherein electrosurgical tips (eg, roller-balls, loops, and vaporizing tips), lasers, or mechanical instruments (eg, scissors) can be attached.

## DISTENDING MEDIA

The uterine cavity requires distension for adequate visualization. Several distending media are available, and each has inherent advantages and disadvantages. It is critically important to understand which media are compatible with electrosurgical and laser energy. Furthermore, the risks associated with various media should be understood.

### Carbon Dioxide Gas

Carbon dioxide ($CO_2$), a colorless gas, is used in outpatient settings for diagnostic purposes. The advantages include the ease of cleaning and maintaining equipment and a clear view of the cavity in the absence of active bleeding or bubbles. To minimize the risk of gas embolization, the flow of $CO_2$ should be limited to 100 mL/min with intrauterine pressures less than 100 mm Hg. Insufflators designed for use in laparoscopy must not be used for hysteroscopy.

### Fluid Media

Fluid media have historically been divided into electrolyte and nonelectrolyte media, based on compatibility with electrosurgical procedures. However, it is now possible to use electrolyte media with bipolar electrosurgical systems. It also is important to understand which media are hypoosmolar. Media also are categorized by viscosity.

**Low-Viscosity, Electrolyte-Poor Fluid.** Low-viscosity, electrolyte-poor fluids include glycine, 1.5%, sorbitol, 3%, and mannitol, 5%. These fluids have been widely used for operative hysteroscopy. They are compatible with radiofrequency energy, which cuts, desiccates, and fulgurates intrauterine tissue. Monopolar devices require electrolyte-poor fluids. If electrolyte-containing fluid is used, the electrical current will dissipate away from the electrode, rendering it ineffective. Glycine, 1.5%, and sorbitol, 3%, are hypoosmolar. The use of these fluids can cause hyponatremia and decreased serum osmolality, with the potential for cerebral edema and death. Some clinicians have recommended mannitol, 5%, which is isoosmolar and acts as its own diuretic. It may cause hyponatremia but not decreased serum osmolality (1).

**Low-Viscosity Electrolyte Fluid.** Normal saline and lactated Ringer's solution are electrolyte fluids. The use of these fluids is advantageous because they are readily available and are isotonic. These solutions are the distending media of choice during diagnostic hysteroscopy and in operative cases where mechanical, laser, or bipolar energy is used. Although the risk of hyponatremia and decreased serum osmolality can be reduced by using these media, pulmonary edema can still occur, and careful attention should be paid to fluid input and output.

**High-Viscosity Fluid.** Dextran 70 is a colorless, viscous, polysaccharide liquid. The advantage of using this liquid is that it is immiscible with blood and, therefore, provides excellent visibility, especially in the presence of blood in the endometrial cavity. The major disadvantage of using dextran 70 is that it is sticky and, when dry, tends to harden and crystallize onto the equipment. It also can be a powerful plasma expander, and the volume usually is limited to 300 mL and must not exceed 500 mL. For every 100 mL absorbed, the plasma volume may expand by an additional 860 mL (2). Other concerns include anaphylaxis and disseminated intravascular coagulation. Beet sugar allergy is an absolute contraindication.

## PREOPERATIVE CONSIDERATIONS

A preoperative consultation allows the patient and physician to discuss the hysteroscopic procedure, weigh its inherent risks and benefits, and review the patient's medical history for any comorbid conditions. Appropriate analgesia or anesthesia should also be considered depending on the venue (ie, office versus operating room). Preoperative placement of laminar or osmotic dilators or pretreatment with misoprostol for cervical ripening may facilitate cervical dilation and decrease operative time (3).

## CONTRAINDICATIONS

Known viable pregnancy, known genital tract infections, and known uterine carcinomas are contraindications to hysteroscopy. Theoretically, hysteroscopy may cause reflux of neoplastic cells into the peritoneal cavity, although it is unclear if this adversely affects the prognosis (4, 5). However, hysteroscopy is acceptable as part of the evaluation of abnormal uterine bleeding.

## Prevention and Management of Complications

The most common perioperative complications associated with operative hysteroscopy are hemorrhage (2.4%), fluid overload (1.5%) (6), and cervical laceration (1–11%) (7). Other complications include uterine perforation, visceral injury, infection, $CO_2$ and air embolism, and, rarely, death. Late complications may include intrauterine adhesions and infertility.

### Hemorrhage

Hemorrhage may occur during hysteroscopic resection of the endometrium, myomata, uterine septa, or synechia. For cases in which there is continued bleeding, electrosurgical coagulation can be used (8). Alternative strategies such as injection of vasopressin at the bleeding site, Foley catheter balloon tamponade (9), or irrigation of the uterine cavity with epsilon aminocaproic acid can be attempted. In extreme cases, uterine artery embolization or hysterectomy may be necessary.

### Fluid Overload

Complications from fluid overload may best be avoided by limiting excess fluid absorption, recognizing and treating fluid overload promptly, and selecting a distending medium that minimizes risk.

The best way to limit excess fluid intravasation is to monitor the fluid deficit closely and frequently throughout the procedure. Newer methods of fluid monitoring based on measurement of fluid weight have made this more accurate; however, some of these systems can be expensive and may not be available in all settings. One difficulty in estimating fluid input and output is that commercially purchased 3-liter bags may be overfilled by up to 150–300 mL (10). Dilutional hyponatremia can be rapidly evaluated by serum sodium analysis.

Guidelines for fluid monitoring and the limits of fluid excess have been published (1) and adapted by the American College of Obstetricians and Gynecologists' Committee on Gynecologic Practice as follows:

- Hydration of patients undergoing hysteroscopy should be closely monitored preoperatively and intraoperatively.
- With low-viscosity, electrolyte-poor fluids, a deficit of 750 mL implies excessive intravasation, and the fluid deficit should be monitored at an extremely close interval. In elderly patients, patients with comorbid conditions, and patients with cardiovascular compromise, consideration should be given to terminating the procedure immediately.
- Depending on patient size and other factors, if fluid deficit reaches 1,000–1,500 mL of a nonelectrolyte solution or 2,500 mL of an electrolyte solution, further infusion should be stopped and the procedure should be promptly concluded. Electrolytes should be assessed, administration of diuretics considered, and further diagnostic and therapeutic intervention begun as indicated.
- In an outpatient setting with limited acute care and laboratory services, consideration should be given to discontinuing procedures at a lower fluid deficit threshold.
- An automated fluid monitoring system facilitates early recognition of excessive deficit in real-time totals.
- In the absence of automated monitoring, an individual should be designated to frequently measure intake and outflow and report the deficit to the operative team.

The treatment of fluid overload from hypotonic agents may require consultation and possibly transfer to an acute care facility. Whereas most women recover, seizures, permanent brain damage, and death have been reported with serum sodium levels of 116 ± 2 mmol/L (11). Although the rate at which severe hyponatremia should be corrected is controversial, most authors agree that if acute hyponatremia has existed for less than 24 hours, there are few long-term complications from rapid correction. Therapy is most often provided in the form of hypertonic saline in conjunction with loop-acting diuretics. Serum sodium levels should be increased by 1–2 mEq/L/h but by no more than 12 mEq/L in the first 24 hours (12). When patients present with hyponatremia of greater than 48 hours postoperatively, rapid correction should not be undertaken because it can lead to neurologic compromise, seizures, and death. Consultation is strongly encouraged in these situations and often requires slower correction in an intensive care setting.

### Perforation

Prior to performing hysteroscopy, a pelvic examination should be performed to determine uterine position. If resistance is encountered during insertion of the hysteroscope, the cervix may need further dilation. Midline uterine perforation rarely leads to significant morbidity unless a laser or electrosurgical device is used. Lateral uterine or cervical perforations can result in significant bleeding. Laparoscopy may be useful to determine the extent of damage, including the existence of bowel or bladder injury.

## Embolization

Air and $CO_2$ emboli are rare complications of hysteroscopy and may result in circulatory collapse. For such emboli to occur, there must be both vascular access and a pressure gradient between the site of access and the right side of the heart. In the conscious patient, chest pain and dyspnea may be noted. Other findings can include decreased oxygen saturation, the presence of a "mill wheel" heart murmur, hypotension, bradycardia, or tachycardia. In the anesthetized patient, cardiopulmonary status shows signs of collapse with sudden hypotension, decrease in oxygenation and/or in end-tidal $CO_2$, or cardiac dysrhythmias (13).

Management of this emergency consists of placing the patient in a left lateral decubitus position with the head tilted downward 5 degrees. This maneuver favors the movement of air in the right ventricle and right ventricular outflow tract toward the apex of the right ventricle (14). The air may be aspirated by passing a catheter down the jugular vein into the right ventricle, or possibly by performing cardiocentesis.

## SUMMARY

Hysteroscopy is an effective procedure for the diagnosis and treatment of intrauterine pathology. It is minimally invasive and can be used with a high degree of safety. Knowledge of potential dangers relating to distending media and intraoperative complications will enhance its safety.

## REFERENCES


1. Loffer FD, Bradley LD, Brill AI, Brooks PG, Cooper JM. Hysteroscopic fluid monitoring guidelines. The ad hoc committee on hysteroscopic training guidelines of the American Association of Gynecologic Laparoscopists. J Am Assoc Gyn Laparosc 2000;7:167–8.
2. Lukacsko P. Noncardiogenic pulmonary edema secondary to intrauterine instillation of 32% dextran 70. Fertil Steril 1985;44:560–1.
3. Thomas JA, Leyland N, Durand N, Windrim RC. The use of oral misoprostol as a cervical ripening agent in operative hysteroscopy: a double-blind, placebo-controlled trial. Am J Obstet Gynecol 2002;186:876–9.
4. Obermair A, Geramou M, Gucer F, Denison U, Graf AH, Kapshammer E, et al. Does hysteroscopy facilitate tumor cell dissemination? Incidence of peritoneal cytology from patients with early stage endometrial carcinoma following dilatation and curettage (D&C) versus hysteroscopy and D&C. Cancer 2000;88:139–43.
5. Arikan G, Reich O, Weiss U, Hahn T, Reinisch S, Tamussino K, et al. Are endometrial carcinoma cells disseminated at hysteroscopy functionally viable? Gynecol Oncol 2001;83:221–6.
6. Overton C, Hargreaves J, Maresh M. A national survey of the complications of endometrial destruction for menstrual disorders: the MISTLETOE study. Minimally Invasive Surgical Techniques—Laser, EndoThermal or Endoresection. Br J Obstet Gynaecol 1997;104:1351–9.
7. Preutthipan S, Herabutya Y. Vaginal misoprostol for cervical priming before operative hysteroscopy: a randomized control trial. Obstet Gynecol 2000;96:890–4.
8. Loffer FD. Complications of hysteroscopy—their cause, prevention, and correction. J Am Assoc Gynecol Laparosc 1995;3:11–26.
9. Goldrath MH. Uterine tamponade for the control of acute uterine bleeding. Am J Obstet Gynecol 1983;147:869–72.
10. Vulgaropulos SP, Haley LC, Hulka JF. Intrauterine pressure and fluid absorption during continuous flow hysteroscopy. Am J Obstet Gynecol 1992;167:386–390; discussion 390–1.
11. Arieff AI. Management of hyponatraemia. BMJ 1993; 307:305–8.
12. Witz CA, Silverberg CM, Burns WN, Schenken RS, Olive DL. Complications associated with the absorption of hysteroscopic fluid media. Fertil Steril 1993;60:745–56.
13. Stoloff DR, Isenberg RA, Brill AI. Venous air and gas emboli in operative hysteroscopy. J Am Assoc Gynecol Laparosc 2001;8:181–92.
14. deWet C, Harrison L, Jacobsohn E. Air embolism. In: Atlee JL, editor. Complications in anesthesia. Philadelphia (PA):WB Saunders;1999. p. 323–5.




**The American College of**
**Obstetricians and Gynecologists**
**409 12th Street, SW**
**PO Box 96920**
**Washington, DC 20090-6920**

12345/98765

Hysteroscopy. ACOG Technology Assessment in Obstetrics and Gynecology No. 4. American College of Obstetricians and Gynecologists. Obstet Gynecol 2005;106:439–42.

# COMMITTEE OPINIONS

## COMMITTEE ON HEALTH CARE FOR UNDERSERVED WOMEN



*Published in 2006

# COMMITTEE OPINIONS

ACOG **Committee Opinion**

Committee on
Health Care for
Underserved Women

Number 307, December 2004

The information should not be construed as dictating an exclusive course of treatment or procedure to be followed.

The Committee wishes to thank Kurt Barnhart, MD, MSCE; Jeffrey Ecker, MD; and Carol Tauer, PhD; for their assistance in the development of this document.



ISSN 1074-861X

**The American College of Obstetricians and Gynecologists**
409 12th Street, SW
PO Box 96920
Washington, DC 20090-6920

12345/87654

Partner consent for participation in women's reproductive health research. ACOG Committee Opinion No. 307. American College of Obstetricians and Gynecologists. Obstet Gynecol 2004; 104:1467–9.

# Partner Consent for Participation in Women's Reproductive Health Research

*ABSTRACT: Recent advances in reproductive medicine include treatment of subfertility as well as investigation of agents that may serve as both contraceptives and potential prophylaxis against sexually transmitted diseases, including potential protection from human immunodeficiency virus (HIV). Although there is no doubt regarding the need for informed consent by women participating in trials evaluating the safety and effectiveness of these novel agents and treatments, there has been some debate regarding the necessity and propriety of requiring consent from the partners of women involved in certain types of clinical trials involving reproductive health. Issues of partner consent are unique to research surrounding women's reproductive health as opposed to research pertaining to women's health, in general. This is due, in part, to a valid concern about a potential effect of the research on the partner. There are, therefore, legitimate reasons to obtain partner consent for a woman's participation in a clinical trial. In the absence of such reason, partner consent should not be mandated.*

## Background

A large number of clinical trials are currently being conducted in nearly every therapeutic area, including women's health. Women may be motivated to participate in clinical trials by altruism to further the care of women, by the ability to receive novel and state-of-the-art medical care, or by the benefits of highly supervised medical monitoring of treatment. Often women without health insurance choose to participate in these trials because such trials may provide enhanced access to care, the care provided is often rendered without cost, and there is reimbursement for time and travel. The American College of Obstetricians and Gynecologists supports the development of new devices and medications to advance women's health and reproductive options. The American College of Obstetricians and Gynecologists also endorses the highest ethical and moral conduct of clinical research. All women, regardless of socioeconomic status and race, should have access to enrollment in clinical trials. The decision to enter a clinical trial should be autonomous, without coercion, and after informed consent. Informed consent is the ability to understand the risks and benefits of one's participation in a research activity and to authorize one's participation in this activity freely (1).

A research subject is defined as "An individual who participates in a clinical trial, either as a recipient of the investigational product(s) or as a control." (2). In research on women's reproductive health, sometimes both the woman and her partner will be the subjects. For example, in a study designed to identify any risk or harm to a partner of a new contraceptive method, both the woman and her partner may be research subjects. If a partner is a subject in the research, informed consent for both participants is required. This Committee Opinion primarily addresses the need for partner consent in research for which the woman, and not a partner, is the research subject. The respect for the autonomy of research subjects to consent to participation is one of the pillars of The Belmont Report, promulgated by The National Commission for the Protection of Human Subjects of Biomedical and Behavioral Research in 1979 (3). The decision to reproduce or use contraceptives should remain autonomous for a woman even when enrolled in a clinical trial.

It also is important to note that the discussion and recommendations that follow do not pertain to research involving pregnant women. There are specific regulations that apply to federally funded research involving this population (4).

## Partner Consent Requirement Inconsistencies

Recent advances in reproductive medicine include treatment of subfertility as well as investigation of agents that may serve as both contraceptives and potential prophylaxis against sexually transmitted diseases, including potential protection from human immunodeficiency virus (HIV). Although there is no doubt regarding the need for informed consent by women participating in trials evaluating the safety and effectiveness of these novel agents and treatments, there has been some debate regarding the necessity and propriety of requiring consent from the partners of women involved in certain types of clinical trials involving reproductive health. Some local institutional review boards (IRB) have requested consent of a woman's partner and at other times a trial sponsor or an individual investigator has made the decision unilaterally. Because of the lack of guidance on this issue, there is great inconsistency regarding requirements for partner consent and the manner in which partner consent is obtained (see box "Methods of Obtaining Partner Consent").

## When Is Partner Consent Needed?

Issues of partner consent are unique to research surrounding women's reproductive health as opposed to research pertaining to women's health, in general. This is partly due to a valid concern about a potential impact of the research on the partner. Therefore, there are legitimate reasons to obtain partner consent for a woman's participation in a clinical trial. In the absence of such reason, partner consent should not be mandated. Partner consent should be obtained if:

- A sexual partner is a subject in the same clinical trial as the woman.
- A partner will be exposed to a novel agent and there is a potential for more than minimal risks* of exposure to the investigational agent.
- Data will be collected regarding a partner's acceptance of the investigational agent, or the impact of partner's acceptance of the agent on the female participant.
- Inclusion or exclusion criteria directly relate to a partner, for example, if testing of a partner is required for a woman to enroll in the trial (eg, semen analysis or testing for a sexually transmitted disease).

If, after careful consideration, it is determined that none of the previous conditions apply, partner consent is not warranted because it should not needlessly:

- Impose a barrier to participation for a woman
- Interfere with a woman's choice of reproductive options
- Interfere with a woman's right to make independent decisions about her reproductive health care due to an IRB's or regulatory agency's paternalistic reasons for partner consent

*According to applicable federal regulations, "*Minimal risk* means that the probability and magnitude of harm or discomfort anticipated in the research are not greater in and of themselves than those ordinarily encountered in daily life or during the performance of routine physical or psychological examinations or tests." (45 C.F.R §46.102[I]).

**Methods of Obtaining Partner Consent**

Several methods exist that may be used to obtain partner consent regarding a woman's participation in a clinical trial. The suitability of these methods depends on the particular research study. Some ways of obtaining partner consent include:

- Having a partner attend the screening visit and sign the consent at that time
- Giving a copy of the consent to the participant and having a partner come in for a separate visit to consent
- Mailing the consent and having it mailed back
- Performing the informed consent process over the telephone
- Obtaining a single informed consent that is signed by the woman and partner

## Recommendations

Recognizing the complexities of the conduct and consent requirements for trials in women's reproductive health, the following recommendations are made:

- The partner consent requirements of each clinical trial need to be individually evaluated and based on the best available scientific and medical evidence and ethical principles.
- When partner consent is required, efforts should be undertaken to decrease the likelihood that receipt of such consent will be a barrier for participation of a woman interested in enrolling in such a trial. The addition of consent adds complexity to all trials, often resulting in additional visits for the participant and partner. This can result in fewer women enrolling and a decrease in compliance.
- Whenever possible, the choice of a woman to enroll in a clinical trial regarding her reproductive function and health should be hers alone when it does not also include a partner as a research subject. In these instances, the woman, not the IRB or the researcher(s), considering the research study should determine the extent to which a partner is to be involved in the process of informed consent and the decision to participate. For example:

  —In the case of the study of a microbicide or barrier contraception efficacy, the risk to a partner is likely negligible (compared with the female partner) because of minimal contact time. If potential irritation to a male partner is suspected, it should be ruled out in the early stages of clinical investigation.

  —In contraceptive research where the participant may face an unintended pregnancy, a partner may be a potential father with the resultant legal and moral responsibilities for the child. However, the principle of autonomy, allowing a woman to make a choice to enter a trial regarding her reproductive rights, should take precedence (5). The American College of Obstetricians and Gynecologists does not support recognition of distinct paternal rights before the birth of a child (6).
- Regardless of the requirement for partner consent, communication with a partner about reproductive health and contraception use should be encouraged.

## References


1. American College of Obstetricians and Gynecologists. Informed consent. In: Ethics in obstetrics and gynecology. 2nd ed. Washington (DC): ACOG; 2004. p. 9–17.
2. International Conference On Harmonisation. Guideline for good clinical practice. ICH Harmonised Tripartite Guideline E6. London: ICH; 1997. Available at: http://www.proclinica.fr/GCPICH.pdf. Retrieved August 26, 2004.
3. The National Commission for the Protection of Human Subjects of Biomedical and Behavioral Research. The Belmont report: ethical principles and guidelines for the protection of human subjects of research. Washington, DC: U.S Department of Health and Human Services; 1979. Available at: http://www.hhs.gov/ohrp/humansubjects/guidance/belmont.htm. Retrieved August 26, 2004.
4. Protection of human subjects. 45 C.F.R §46 (2003). Available at: http://www.access.gpo.gov/nara/cfr/waisidx_03/45cfr46_03.html. Retrieved August 27, 2004.
5. Holder AR. Contraceptive research: do sex partners have rights? IRB 1982;4(2):6–7.
6. American College of Obstetricians and Gynecologists. Research involving women. In: Ethics in obstetrics and gynecology. 2nd ed. Washington (DC): ACOG; 2004. p. 86–91.

# ACOG Committee Opinion

Committee on Health Care for Underserved Women

Number 308, December 2004

This document does not define a standard of care nor should it be interpreted as legal advice.

The Committee wishes to thank Kurt Barnhart, MD, MSCE, for his assistance in the development of this document.



ISSN 1074-861X

**The American College of Obstetricians and Gynecologists**
409 12th Street, SW
PO Box 96920
Washington, DC 20090-6920

12345/87654

The uninsured. ACOG Committee Opinion No. 308. American College of Obstetricians and Gynecologists. Obstet Gynecol 2004;104:1471–4.

## The Uninsured

*ABSTRACT: The United States is one of the few industrialized nations in the world that does not guarantee access to health care for its population. Access to health care for all women is a paramount concern of obstetrician–gynecologists and the American College of Obstetricians and Gynecologists. Lack of health care coverage creates access issues that affect women, practitioners, and the health care system as a whole. The number of women in the United States without health care coverage grew 3 times faster than the number of men without such coverage during the late 1990s and early 2000s. A change in our currently fragmented health care system is warranted because the lack of coverage clearly matters to the millions of uninsured Americans. Pregnant women and infants are among the most vulnerable populations in the country and the American College of Obstetricians and Gynecologists believes that providing them with full insurance coverage must be a primary step in the process of providing coverage for all Americans. However, it is only the first step; it is critical to expand coverage for all Americans. Health professionals can play a pivotal role in improving access to needed health care by helping society understand the importance of broadening health insurance coverage.*

The United States is one of the few industrialized nations in the world that does not guarantee access to health care for its population. Of the 30 countries in the Organization of Economic Cooperation and Development, only Mexico and Turkey have a higher uninsured rate than the United States (1). Millions of women are caught in the gaps in the current health care system, leaving them in a vulnerable position regarding their health status. The number of women in the United States who are uninsured grew 3 times faster than the number of men without health insurance during the late 1990s and early 2000s (2). In 2003, it was estimated that of the 45 million Americans (15.6% of the total population) without health insurance for the entire year, 21.2 million were women (14.4% of all women) (3, 4). This represents an increase from 2002 when it was estimated that of the 43.6 million Americans (15.2% of the total population) without health insurance for the entire year, 20.2 million were women (13.9% of all women) (5). Approximately 13% of all pregnant women are uninsured (6).

Access to health care for all women is a paramount concern of obstetrician–gynecologists and the American College of Obstetricians and Gynecologists (ACOG). Lack of health care coverage creates access issues that affect women, practitioners, and the health care system as a whole. These issues have an effect on ACOG's core missions of education and service and are exacerbated by the ailing professional liability system.

## Effect on Women's Reproductive Health and Health Care

Having health insurance does not guarantee good health, but not having insurance is guaranteed to put Americans at higher risk for poorer health outcomes and economic disaster. The uninsured receive less preventive care, receive diagnoses at more advanced disease stages, and, once diseases are diagnosed, tend to receive less therapeutic care (drugs and surgical interventions) (7). Acquisition of health insurance reduces mortality rates for the uninsured by 10–15% (8). In terms of women's reproductive health and health care, the lack of health insurance may affect women in the following ways:

- Lack of insurance limits women's options for contraception (9).
- Uninsured women receive fewer prenatal care services than their insured counterparts (1).
- Eighteen percent of uninsured pregnant women reported that they did not receive some "needed" medical care versus 7.6% of privately insured and 8.1% of Medicaid-enrolled pregnant women (10).
- Uninsured pregnant women are more likely to experience an adverse maternal outcome (1).
- Uninsured newborns are more likely to experience adverse health outcomes than insured newborns. Infants of uninsured women are more likely to die than are those of insured women (1).
- Uninsured women with breast cancer have a 30–50% higher risk of dying than insured women (1). This is not surprising given that uninsured women aged 50–64 years are 3 times less likely to have had a mammogram or clinical breast examination in the past 2 years compared with insured women (11).
- Uninsured women aged 18–64 years are 3 times less likely to have had a needed Pap test in the past 3 years (11), contributing to a 60% greater risk of late-stage diagnosis of cervical cancer among uninsured women compared with insured women (12).

## The Capacity of the Health Care System to Serve the Uninsured

Uninsured patients receive health care via 3 primary sources—hospitals (including academic medical centers), office-based physicians, and clinics and direct care programs. The cost of uncompensated care is staggering; in 2004, it was estimated to be $40.7 billion. Despite the disincentives for providing such care, all of the aforementioned sources have taken on part of the burden. Most uncompensated care expenses are incurred by hospitals, where services are most costly. In 2001, hospitals accounted for $25.6 billion (63%) in uncompensated care. Office-based physicians and direct care programs or clinics accounted for $7.3 billion (18%) and $7.7 billion (19%) respectively, in uncompensated care (13). A 2001 Commonwealth Fund study found that the level of care provided by academic health centers to those who were unable to pay for their services increased as a percentage of gross patient revenues by more than 40% in the past decade (14). The number of patients treated at hospitals who are unable to pay is increasing as the number of uninsured grows. This is especially true for academic medical centers. All of the efforts to provide care to those unable to pay create adverse effects on profit margins, which in turn imperil the mission of institutions and facilities to provide health care for all patients, not just the uninsured.

The proportion of private physicians providing care to the uninsured is decreasing and those who provide such care are spending less time doing so (15). Specifically, the number of physicians providing any care to individuals unable to pay decreased from 76.3% in 1997 to 71.5% in 2001. In addition, the proportion of providers who spend more than 5% of their practice time treating patients who are unable to pay decreased between 1997 and 2001, while the proportion of providers who spend less than 5% of their practice time treating a low volume of such patients increased. In addition, the professional liability insurance crisis is threatening the availability of physicians and their capacity to provide care to the uninsured.

## Conclusions

Allowing health care to be driven by market forces has led to a lack of access for many of our citizens.

Provision of care to patients who are unable to pay by private physicians and the safety net of community clinics, public hospitals, and academic medical centers does not substitute for health insurance. A change in our currently fragmented health care system is, therefore, warranted because the lack of coverage clearly matters to the millions of uninsured Americans. This lack of coverage affects job decisions, financial security, access to care, and health status.

Health professionals can play a pivotal role in improving access to needed health care by helping society understand the importance of broadening health insurance coverage. Health care providers need to be advocates for the goal of securing quality, affordable coverage for every American with active support of proposed local, state, and national legislation. There are formidable obstacles to major progress in increasing the number of people who are insured. Among them are fiscal limitations, the political climate, and philosophical differences in approaches to resolving this problem.

In 1993, ACOG developed U.S. MaternaCare, which is a proposal designed to ensure that all women in the United States have access to a full range of pregnancy related services, including family planning and infant care. Pregnant women and infants are among the most vulnerable populations in the country, and ACOG believes that providing them with full insurance coverage must be a primary step in the process of providing coverage for all Americans. However, it is only the first step; it is critical to expand the basic benefits and coverage for all Americans. As a proposal for universal insurance coverage, U.S. MaternaCare was designed around a set of principles that ACOG continues to support. It uses and builds upon the existing strengths of the U.S. health care system, including multiple financing and delivery systems. It calls for coverage for all women regardless of their citizenship status, and includes a basic set of benefits that must be offered to all women. It asserts that any health care reform proposal must address issues of quality assurance, cost containment, and professional liability reform (16). Until these goals are achieved, continued support of the safety net system and provision of care in the community and office setting for the uninsured is essential. For a listing of resources on the topic of the uninsured, go to http://www.acog.org/goto/underserved.

## References


1. Institute of Medicine. Insuring America's health: principles and recommendations. Washington, DC: The Institute; 2004.
2. Labrew JM. Diagnosing disparities in health insurance for women: a prescription for change. New York (NY): The Commonwealth Fund; 2001. Available at: http://www.cmwf.org/programs/insurance/lambrew_disparities_493.pdf. Retrieved August 5, 2004.
3. DeNavas-Walt C, Proctor BD, Mills RJ. Income, poverty, and health insurance coverage in the United States: 2003. Current Population Reports. Washington, DC: U.S. Census Bureau; 2004. Available at: http://www.census.gov/prod/2004pubs/p60-226.pdf. Retrieved August 31, 2004.
4. U.S. Census Bureau. 2004 annual social and economic supplement. Current Population Survey. Washington, DC: Census Bureau; 2004. Available at: http://ferret.bls.census.gov/macro/032004/health/h01_001.htm. Retrieved August 31, 2004.
5. Mills RJ, Bhandari S. Health insurance coverage in the United States: 2002. Consumer income. Current Population Reports. Washington, DC: U.S. Census Bureau; 2003. Available at: http://www.census.gov/prod/2003pubs/p60 223.pdf. Retrieved August 5, 2004.
6. Thorpe KE, Flome J, Joski P. The distribution of health insurance coverage among pregnant women, 1999. New York (NY): March of Dimes; 2001. Available at: http://www.modimes.com/files/2001FinalThorpeReport.pdf. Retrieved August 5, 2004.
7. American College of Physicians - American Society of Internal Medicine. No health insurance? It's enough to make you sick. Philadelphia (PA): ACP-ASIM; 1999. Available at: http://www.acponline.org/uninsured/lack-consents.htm. Retrieved August 5, 2004.
8. Hadley J. Sicker and poorer: the consequences of being uninsured. A review of the research on the relationship between health insurance, health, work, income, and education. The Kaiser Commission on Medicaid and the Uninsured. Menlo Park (CA): The Henry J Kaiser Family Foundation; 2002. Available at: http://www.kff.org/uninsured/upload/13970_1.pdf. Retrieved September 2, 2004.
9. Sonfield A, Gold RB. New study documents major strides in drive for contraceptive coverage. Guttmacher Rep Pub Pol 2004;7(2):4–5, 14.
10. Bernstein AB. Insurance status and use of health services by pregnant women. Washington, DC: Alpha Center; 1999. Available at: http://www.marchofdimes.com/files/bernstein_paper.pdf. Retrieved September 2, 2004.
11. Ayanian JZ, Weissman JS, Schneider EC, Ginsburg JA, Zaslavsky AM. Unmet health needs of uninsured adults in the United States. JAMA 2000;284:2061–9.
12. Ferrante JM, Gonzalez EC, Roetzheim RG, Pal N, Woodard L. Clinical and demographic predictors of late-stage cervical cancer. Arch Fam Med 2000;9:439–45.
13. Hadley J, Holahan J. The cost of care for the uninsured: what do we spend, who pays, and what would full coverage add to medical spending? Issue update. The Kaiser Commission on Medicaid and the Uninsured. Menlo Park

(CA): The Henry J Kaiser Family Foundation; 2004. Available at: http://www.kff.org/uninsured/7084.cfm. Retrieved August 5, 2004.

14. The Commonwealth Fund. A shared responsibility: academic health centers and the provision of care to the poor and uninsured. A report of The Commonwealth Fund Task Force on Academic Health Centers. New York (NY): Commonwealth Fund; 2001. Available at: http://www.cmwf.org/programs/taskforc/AHC_indigentcare_443.pdf. Retrieved August 5, 2004.

15. Cunningham PJ. Mounting pressures: physicians serving Medicaid patients and the uninsured, 1997-2001. Track Rep 2002;(6):1–4.

16. American College of Obstetricians and Gynecologists. U.S. MaternaCare. A proposal for universal access to maternity care. Washington, DC: ACOG; 1993. Available at: http://www.acog.org/departments/dept_notice.cfm?recno=18&bulletin=2650. Retrieved August 5, 2004.

ACOG Committee Opinion

ACOG Committee on Health Care for Underserved Women

Number 312, August 2005

This information should not be construed as dictating an exclusive course of treatment or procedure to be followed.

The Committee wishes to thank Gene Burkett, MD; Ronald Chez, MD; and Eve Espey, MD, for their assistance in the development of this document.



ISSN 1074-861X

**The American College of Obstetricians and Gynecologists**
409 12th Street, SW
PO Box 96920
Washington, DC 20090-6920

12345/98765

Health Care for Homeless Women. ACOG Committee Opinion No. 312. American College of Obstetricians and Gynecologists. Obstet Gynecol 2005;106:429–34.

# Health Care for Homeless Women

*Abstract: Homelessness is a considerable social and health problem in the United States with far-reaching effects on the health of homeless women. Homeless women are at higher risk for injury and illness and are less likely to obtain needed health care than women who are not homeless. It is critical to undertake efforts to prevent homelessness. Until this can be accomplished, community-based services targeted specifically to this population that provide both health care and support services are essential. Health care providers can help address the needs of the homeless by identifying their own patients who may be homeless, treating their health problems, offering preventive care, and working with the community to improve the full range of resources available to these individuals.*

Approximately 3.5 million Americans are currently homeless (1), and as many as 14% of the U.S. population have been homeless at some time (2) (see box "Definition of Homelessness"). Women make up nearly one third of the homeless population and are one of the fastest growing groups (3). In the population of homeless individuals in families, 84% are women (4). Sixty percent of homeless women have children younger than 18 years, but many do not have custody of their children. There also are children who are homeless in their own right. This group includes runaways (5). Many homeless adolescents left home because of conflicts with parents over their sexual orientation (6). Most homeless adolescents are white and come from suburban and rural areas. They are more likely than other populations to experience depression and substance abuse, to have previously attempted suicide, and to have a history of sexual and physical abuse (7).

Extreme poverty is a universal characteristic of homeless individuals, but not all impoverished individuals become homeless. The shortage of low-income housing is a major precipitating factor to homelessness. It can render homeless even individuals who are not extremely poor. Unemployment or job loss, personal or family crisis, an increase in rent disproportionate to income, or reduction in public health benefits increase the likelihood of loss of a home among those at risk (4). For women, an additional risk factor is early motherhood (8).

Many homeless individuals lack education and money. Thirty-eight percent of homeless individuals did not graduate from high school and another 34% finished only high school. Slightly more than one quarter of homeless individuals have any education beyond high school. The average monthly

> **Definition of Homelessness**
>
> An individual is considered homeless if he or she lacks a fixed, regular, and adequate nighttime residence, or an individual who has a primary nighttime residence that is:
>
> a) a supervised publicly or privately operated shelter designed to provide temporary living accommodations (including welfare hotels, congregate shelters, and transitional housing for the mentally ill);
>
> b) a public or private place that provides a temporary residence for individuals intended to be institutionalized; or
>
> c) a public or private place not designed for, or ordinarily used as, regular sleeping accommodations for human beings.
>
> Interagency Council on the Homeless. Homelessness: programs and the people they serve. Findings of the National Survey of Homeless Assistance Providers and Clients. Washington, DC: U.S. Department of Housing and Urban Development, Office of Policy Development and Research; 1999.

income for a homeless family is $475 (46% of the federal poverty level for a family of three at the time of the study), and for a single homeless individual is $348 (51% of the federal poverty level for one person) (4). Other risk factors include lack of job skills, inadequate social support, problems with alcohol or illicit drugs, mental illness, experiences of violence and victimization, and previous incarceration.

## Impact of Homelessness on Women

Homelessness may be difficult to recognize. However, certain circumstances, many of which affect the individual's health, are seen more frequently in this population (see box "Common Characteristics of Homelessness"). Being homeless creates an increased risk for illness and injury resulting in high levels of morbidity and mortality (9). Homeless adolescent and adult women often participate in survival sex, which refers to the selling of sex to meet subsistence needs (10, 11). Approximately 26% of young homeless females reported having participated in survival sex (10). More than two thirds of homeless mothers have a diagnosis of mental illness. Cases of posttraumatic stress disorder, substance abuse disorders, and major depression are disproportionately higher among homeless women compared with other populations (12).

### *Violence*

Violence is common among homeless populations. Homeless individuals are at risk because they lack personal security when living outdoors or in a shelter. Twenty-two percent report having been physically assaulted or beaten up at least once while homeless (4). One study reported that 13% of homeless women, particularly those with mental illness, were sexually assaulted or raped in the past year, compared with 2.7% of the general population (13). Twenty-two percent of homeless adolescents report prior child abuse and 13% report sexual abuse (1, 4).

### *Gynecologic Health*

Among homeless women interviewed in Los Angeles, 66% used no method of contraception even though most had intercourse at least once per week. Fewer than 10% of homeless women report regular condom use although they are at high risk for sexually transmitted diseases (STDs) and human immunodeficiency virus (HIV) infection (14, 15), which are especially problematic in the homeless adolescent population (11). Pelvic inflammatory disease occurred in approximately 28% of homeless women, and 60% had a history of a least one STD (1).

### *Obstetric Health*

Pregnancy and recent birth are highly correlated with becoming homeless in the newly homeless population. At the time they requested emergency shelter, 35% of homeless women were pregnant and 26%

> **Common Characteristics of Homelessness**
>
> - Appearance: unkempt, disheveled, dirty, aggressive, hostile
> - Chronic recurrent diseases, including respiratory infections, hepatitis, asthma, arthritis, or tuberculosis
> - Multiple STDs or HIV
> - Substance abuse (alcohol and other substances)
> - Chronic mental illness with or without comorbidity, suicide attempts, posttraumatic stress disorders, stresses associated with sexual identity and orientation
> - Repetitive, nonspecific complaints for which a diagnosis cannot be found
> - Underweight with history of subnutrition or poor nutritional state
> - Domestic violence, including sexual abuse and victimization
> - No fixed address or multiple addresses in a short period
> - Lack of adherence with physician directives and orders

had given birth in the past year. Only 6% of women in the study who were not homeless were pregnant and only 11% had given birth in the past year (8). Homeless women often have little choice in the timing, the place, the partner, and the circumstances surrounding conception. Factors associated with unintended pregnancy were victimization, survival sex, lack of contraception, uncertain fertility status, desire for intimacy, and lack of hope for the future (16). Women younger than 21 years living on the streets are at much greater risk of having ever been pregnant than are young women living in households (5).

Adverse birth outcomes are substantially higher in homeless women than in the general population (17). In a study conducted in 1997, 17% of babies born to homeless women were low birth weight compared with 11% among those residing in low-income housing (17). The rate of low birth weight at the time of that study was 7.5% for all women (18). Similarly, 19% of births in the homeless population were preterm compared with 11% nationally (17, 18). Homeless women are less likely to receive prenatal care (19, 20). The more severe the homelessness (defined by whether or not the woman was homeless during the first trimester of her pregnancy, the number of times she had been homeless, and the percentage of her life during which she had been homeless), the less likely a woman is to receive prenatal care and the more likely an adverse pregnancy outcome will occur. Older homeless women and those who abuse drugs also are less likely to receive prenatal care. Other predictors of adverse pregnancy outcomes among homeless women include history of preterm birth, antenatal complications, and birth complications; STDs; low income; nulliparity; and being African American (17).

Adverse birth outcomes are higher in African-American homeless women than in homeless women of other races. In the homeless population, 22% of infants born to African-American women were low birth weight, whereas only 16% of Hispanic infants and 5% of non-Hispanic white infants were low birth weight. African-American homeless women are more likely to experience preterm birth. Homeless Native American women also appear to have a large proportion of preterm births and babies with low birth weight (17).

Homeless women may forgo meals in favor of alcohol and other drugs (20). Day-to-day survival stresses are superimposed on emotional distress, which may lead to new or increased substance abuse (20). Homeless pregnant women are prone to urinary tract infections and vaginal infections (20).

Children of homeless women are more likely to be separated from their mothers by social service providers. Forty-four percent of homeless mothers, compared with 8% of mothers receiving public assistance who are not homeless, were separated from their children. Homelessness was the major risk factor in such separation, although substance abuse, domestic violence, and maternal institutionalization also were risk factors. A substantial minority of these children are placed in foster care. (21). This separation from children may lead to emotional strain, anxiety, loss of control, instability, guilt, and insecurity among homeless mothers.

## Preventive Health

Homeless women receive breast examinations, mammograms, and Pap tests at lower rates than the general population (22–24). Although no studies have specifically examined cervical dysplasia and cancer in this population, homeless women have many risk factors for inadequate diagnosis, incomplete follow-up, and incomplete treatment because of the competing survival needs.

## Use of Health Care

Most homeless people seek care in hospital emergency rooms; only 27% go to an established ambulatory care provider. The younger homeless population is even more likely to receive care in the emergency room. Nearly three quarters of homeless individuals who are hospitalized have conditions that were preventable and could have been treated before admission compared with 41% of low-income individuals who are not homeless (25). Recurrent admission for the same diagnosis is common and occurs in approximately 40% of homeless adults, which imposes a financial burden on hospitals (1).

## Barriers to Health Care

Approximately 57% of homeless individuals lack a regular source of care compared with 24% of the poor and 19% of the general population (26). Nearly 25% of homeless individuals who reported a need for medical attention in the previous year were unable to obtain care. The following factors contribute to this situation (1, 4, 27, 28):

- Cost and lack of health insurance (55% of homeless individuals report that they have no medical insurance) and inability to purchase or acquire medications

- Lack of transportation to and from medical facilities
- Competing needs for survival (food, clothing, shelter)
- Mental illness and substance abuse
- Unstable lifestyle interfering with continuity of care and adherence with treatment
- Because an exhibition of toughness is necessary to survive on the streets, homeless individuals may at times deny that they have health problems. They also may have a fear of authority figures, including medical providers.
- Lack of availability of shelters and treatment facilities for the homeless
- Medical providers, including physicians, may prefer not to care for homeless individuals in their offices
- Inadequate inpatient discharge planning and follow-up care because of failure to recognize homelessness
- Lack of health care professionals' knowledge and information on services available within the community for homeless individuals

## Recommendations to Improve the Health of Homeless Women

Health care services for a homeless woman should be a part of a multifaceted approach tailored to her needs, perspectives, and values. Acceptance of the individual is critical to the provision of services. Accomplishing these goals is a major challenge to the obstetrician–gynecologist or any other health care provider. Often the resources required, including the necessary professionals and support services, are either not available in the community or difficult for the private provider to obtain. Even though individual obstetrician–gynecologists can and do provide services to homeless patients in their practices, it may be more beneficial for communities to develop organized services targeted specifically to this population that can better provide both health care and support services. Organized services can better implement both the preventive care and the obstetric and gynecologic care recommended in the guidelines of the American College of Obstetricians and Gynecologists (30). Prenatal care that coordinates with social services, rehabilitation programs, and housing programs to shelter homeless women during pregnancy should be the goal.

Health care professionals also can contribute to improved health care for homeless women by participating in the following activities:

- Care for homeless women in individual practices without bias.
- Volunteer or form volunteer groups to provide health care services at homeless shelters and soup kitchens. Adherence to treatment is enhanced when medical care is coupled with services to meet the survival needs of patients. Care should not be withheld because of concerns about lack of adherence.
- Seek donations of medications from pharmaceutical companies for use in homeless clinics and shelters.
- Implement health care programs for the homeless with local hospitals and clinics (see box "J.C. Lewis Health Center: An Example of Success").

### J.C. Lewis Health Center: An Example of Success

An example of a successful health care program for homeless women is the J.C. Lewis Health Center. This center is a 32-bed primary and respite care clinic in Savannah, Georgia, that has saved area hospitals $10.3 million in uncompensated care for the homeless. The center allows homeless individuals to gain access to primary care providers who manage acute and episodic health needs and diagnose, control, and monitor chronic health problems such as HIV, hypertension, and diabetes. The operation includes the staffing of four shelter-based primary care clinics across the city where health promotion and primary care divert homeless people from emergency rooms. Wellness care for the homeless includes physical examinations, screening for disease, and patient education. Respite care allows the hospital to release patients too sick to stay in shelters, but not sick enough to stay in the hospital. These individuals would otherwise have remained hospitalized. The health center also coordinates its services with housing and social services to help the individuals obtain permanent housing. Ninety-five percent of the respite care patients ended their homelessness after leaving the program.

Program funding is provided by hospitals (each contribute $250,000 to the program), public support through government grants ($244,000), philanthropic organizations ($164,000), and private citizens ($19,000). In addition, volunteers from the community, including doctors, nurses, and educators, donate their time to the health center, and the center receives in-kind contributions of pharmaceuticals and supplies.

The J.C. Lewis Health Center. Available at: http://www.unionmission.org. Retrieved June 6, 2005.

- Work with medical schools and residency programs to encourage modification of the educational curriculum to increase awareness of the problems associated with homelessness and to involve medical students and residents in care for homeless individuals as part of their training.
- Assess current community programs for homeless individuals and advocate for improved coordination of services between these programs and other special programs such as prenatal care, immunization, tuberculosis treatment, STD clinics, mental health care, and housing and legal aid.
- Advocate for professional liability protections for physicians who volunteer their services to the homeless.
- Encourage federal, state, and local governments to provide adequate funding for the provision of comprehensive health care services, including mental health treatment for all homeless individuals. (See box "Health Care for the Homeless Federal Program.")

**Health Care for the Homeless Federal Program**

The Health Care for the Homeless program is the only federal program with the sole responsibility of addressing the primary health care needs of homeless individuals. The Health Care for the Homeless program provides primary health care and substance abuse services at locations accessible to individuals who are homeless, emergency care with referrals to hospitals for inpatient care services or other needed services, outreach services to assist difficult-to-reach homeless individuals in gaining access to care, and assistance in establishing eligibility for entitlement programs and housing.

To increase access to services and resources for people who are homeless, the grantees of the Health Care for the Homeless program are encouraged to develop, or actively participate in, local coalitions of health care providers and social service agencies. These collaborations help ensure the adequate and appropriate delivery of services to the clients of the Health Care for the Homeless program. Each individual program determines which service delivery system or combination of systems is appropriate for the people it serves. Programs provide services in a variety of different settings, including traditional clinic sites, shelter-based clinics, and mobile units. In addition, they take health care services to locations where homeless individuals are found, such as streets, parks, and soup kitchens.

Bureau of Primary Health Care. Health Care for the Homeless Information Resource Center. 2004-2005 Health Care for the Homeless Grantee profiles. Available at: http://www.bphc.hrsa.gov/hchirc/directory/text_directory.htm. Retrieved June 6, 2005.

## The Prevention of Homelessness

Although it is critical to undertake efforts to improve the health of homeless women, it is even more important to undertake efforts to prevent homelessness. Increased federal, state, and local government support and provision of adequate funding for comprehensive programs for the prevention of homelessness, including increased availability of affordable, usually subsidized, housing are essential to this goal. Numerous studies indicate that affordable housing prevents homelessness more effectively than anything else. This applies to all groups of poor people, including those with persistent and severe mental illness or those with substance abuse problems (29). Additional research is needed to determine other efforts that would be effective at reducing this problem and thereby improve women's health and the overall health of society.

## References

1. Gelberg L, Arangua L. Homeless persons. In: Anderson RM, Rice TH, Kominski GF, editors. Changing the U.S. health care system: key issues in health services, policy, and management. San Francisco (CA): Jossey-Bass; 2001. p.332–86.
2. Link BG, Susser E, Stueve A, Phelan J, Moore RE, Struening E. Lifetime and five-year prevalence of homelessness in the United States. Am J Public Health 1994; 84:1907–12.
3. Hodnicki DR, Horner SD, Boyle JS. Women's perspectives on homelessness. Public Health Nurs 1992;9:257–62.
4. Interagency Council on the Homeless. Homelessness: programs and the people they serve. Findings of the National Survey of Homeless Assistance Providers and Clients. Washington, DC: U.S. Department of Housing and Urban Development, Office of Policy Development and Research; 1999.
5. Greene JM, Ringwalt CL. Pregnancy among three national samples of runaway and homeless youth. J Adolesc Health 1998;23:370–7.
6. Farrow JA, Deisher RW, Brown R, Kulig JW, Kipke MD. Health and health needs of homeless and runaway youth. A position paper of the Society for Adolescent Medicine. J Adolesc Health 1992;13:717–26.
7. Pennbridge J, Mackenzie RG, Swofford A. Risk profile of homeless pregnant adolescents and youth. J Adolesc Health 1991;12:534–8.
8. Weitzman BC. Pregnancy and childbirth: risk factors for homelessness? Fam Plann Perspect 1989;21:175–8.
9. Hwang SW. Is homelessness hazardous to your health? Obstacles to the demonstration of a causal relationship. Can J Public Health 2002;93:407–10.
10. Greene JM, Ennett ST, Ringwalt CL. Prevalence and correlates of survival sex among runaway and homeless youth. Am J Public Health 1999;89:1406–9.
11. Bailey SL, Camlin CS, Ennett ST. Substance use and risky sexual behavior among homeless and runaway youth. J Adolesc Health 1998;23:378–88.

12. Bassuk EL, Buckner JC, Perloff JN, Bassuk SS. Prevalence of mental health and substance use disorders among homeless and low-income housed mothers. Am J Psychiatry 1998;155:1561–4.
13. Wenzel SL, Leake BD, Gelberg L. Health of homeless women with recent experience of rape. J Gen Intern Med 2000;15:265–8.
14. Shuler PA, Gelberg L, Davis JE. Characteristics associated with the risk of unintended pregnancy among urban homeless women: use of the Shuler Nurse Practitioner Practice Model in research. J Am Acad Nurse Pract 1995;7:13–22.
15. Gelberg L, Leake BD, Lu MC, Andersen RM, Wenzel SL, Morgenstern H, et al. Use of contraceptive methods among homeless women for protection against unwanted pregnancies and sexually transmitted diseases: prior use and willingness to use in the future. Contraception 2001; 63:277–81.
16. Killion CM. Poverty and procreation among women. An anthropologic study with implications for health care providers. J Nurse Midwifery 1998;43:273–9.
17. Stein JA, Lu MC, Gelberg L. Severity of homelessness and adverse birth outcomes. Health Psychol 2000;19: 524–34.
18. Ventura SJ, Martin JA, Curtin SC, Mathews TJ. Births: final data for 1997. Natl Vital Stat Rep 1999;47(18):1–96.
19. Chavkin W, Kristal A, Seabron C, Guigli PE. The reproductive experience of women living in hotels for the homeless in New York City. NY State J Med 1987; 87: 10–3.
20. Killion CM. Special health care needs of homeless pregnant women. ANS Adv Nurs Sci 1995;18:44–56.
21. Cowal K, Shinn M, Weitzman BC, Stojanovic D, Labay L. Mother-child separations among homeless and housed families receiving public assistance in New York City. Am J Community Psychol 2002;30:711–30.
22. Chau S, Chin M, Chang J, Luecha A, Cheng E, Schlesinger J, et al. Cancer risk behaviors and screening rates among homeless adults in Los Angeles County. Cancer Epidemiol Biomarkers Prev 2002;11:431–8.
23. Long HL, Tulsky JP, Chambers DB, Alpers LS, Robertson MJ, Moss AR, et al. Cancer screening in homeless women: attitudes and behaviors. J Health Care Poor Underserved 1998;9:276–92.
24. Weinreb L, Goldberg R, Perloff J. Health characteristics and medical service use patterns of sheltered homeless and low-income housed mothers. J Gen Intern Med 1998; 13:389–97.
25. Salit SA, Kuhn EM, Hartz AJ, Vu JM, Mosso AL. Hospitalization costs associated with homelessness in New York City. N Engl J Med 1998;338:1734–40.
26. Gallagher TC, Andersen RM, Koegel P, Gelberg L. Determinants of regular source of care among homeless adults in Los Angeles. Med Care 1997;35:814–30.
27. Lim YW, Andersen R, Leake B, Cunningham W, Gelberg L. How accessible is medical care for homeless women? Med Care 2002;40:510–20.
28. Kushel MB, Vittinghoff E, Haas JS. Factors associated with the health care utilization of homeless persons. JAMA 2001;285:200–6.
29. U.S. Department of Housing and Urban Development, U.S. Department of Health and Human Services. Practical lessons: the 1998 National Symposium on Homelessness Research. Available at: http://aspe.hhs.gov/progsys/homeless/symposium/toc.htm. Retrieved April 12, 2005.
30. Primary and preventive care: periodic assessments. ACOG Committee Opinion No. 292. American College of Obstetricians and Gynecologists. Obstet Gynecol 2003; 102:1117–24.

ACOG Committee Opinion

Committee on Health Care for Underserved Women

Number 317, October 2005

This information should not be construed as dictating an exclusive course of treatment or procedure to be followed.

The Committee on Health Care for Underserved Women wishes to thank Raymond L. Cox, MD, MBA, for his invaluable assistance in the development of this document.



ISSN 1074-861X

**The American College of Obstetricians and Gynecologists**
409 12th Street, SW
PO Box 96920
Washington, DC 20090-6920

12345/98765

Racial and ethnic disparities in women's health. ACOG Committee Opinion No. 317. American College of Obstetricians and Gynecologists. Obstet Gynecol 2005;106:889–92

# Racial and Ethnic Disparities in Women's Health

*ABSTRACT: Significant racial and ethnic disparities exist in women's health. These health disparities largely result from differences in socioeconomic status and insurance status. Although many disparities diminish after taking these factors into account, some remain because of health care system-level, patient-level, and provider-level factors. The American College of Obstetricians and Gynecologists strongly supports the elimination of racial and ethnic disparities in the health and the health care of women. Health professionals are encouraged to engage in activities to help achieve this goal.*

Health disparities can be defined as "differences in the incidence, prevalence, mortality, and burden of diseases and other adverse health conditions that exist among specific population groups in the United States" (1). These differences can be assessed according to a variety of factors including gender, race or ethnicity, education, income, disability, geographic location, or sexual orientation (2). Although significant health disparities occur between men and women and among certain groups of women based on the factors mentioned previously, disparities are most likely to be experienced by women who are members of racial and ethnic minority groups. For example, disease and premature death occur disproportionately in minority women compared with non-Hispanic white women (3).

Approximately 44 million women in the United States, nearly one third of all women in this country, are members of racial and ethnic minority groups. African-American women and women of Hispanic origin together comprise roughly one quarter of the total population of U.S. women (4). The Hispanic population accounted for 22% of the 4 million births in the United States in 2003 (5). The largest segment of the immigrant population in the United States is from Latin America (6).

It is important to note that race and ethnicity are primarily social characteristics much more than they are biologic categories. However, race and ethnicity can provide useful information to women's health care providers about environmental, cultural, behavioral, and medical factors that may affect their patients' health. Also, the frequency of certain genetic variations may differ between racial or ethnic groups. For instance, there is an increased frequency of mutations for certain genetic diseases, such as Tay-Sachs disease, in individuals of Ashkenzic Jewish descent. These differences in the frequency of genetic variations generally are related to a common ancestral lineage (founder effect).

Genetic polymorphisms associated with increased susceptibility to disease also may vary in frequency in different racial and ethnic groups (7). Another consideration is the issue of gene-environment interaction. Genetic variations, even those that do not vary in frequency among racial or ethnic groups, may enhance susceptibility to an environmental exposure that occurs more frequently in a particular racial or ethnic group. Thus, although race and ethnicity are primarily social constructs, the impact of common ancestral lineage on the segregation and frequency of genetic variations in combination with the influence of cultural factors on environmental exposures cannot be ignored. All of these factors should be considered when trying to elucidate the multifactorial causes of health disparities.

## Examples of Racial and Ethnic Health Disparities Among Women

- During 1991–1995, heart disease death rates remained the highest for African-American women, followed by white, American Indian/Alaskan Native, and Asian/Pacific Islander women, with more than a twofold difference between the lowest and highest rates (8).
- Asian/Pacific Islander women, especially those who are Vietnamese; black women; and Hispanic white women have higher incidence rates of invasive cervical cancer than non-Hispanic white women (9, 10). Cervical cancer mortality rates are higher among American Indian/Alaskan Natives than among all racial and ethnic populations (3.7 per 100,000 population and 2.6 per 100,000 population, respectively) despite lower incidence (11).
- When compared with white women, black women have a higher mortality rate (34.7 per 100,000 compared with 25.9 per 100,000) for breast cancer despite a lower breast cancer incidence rate (10).
- Seventy-eight percent of the female population with acquired immunodeficiency syndrome (AIDS) is African American or Hispanic. Although American Indian/Alaskan Native women have a lower annual rate of new AIDS cases (4.8 per 100,000) than non-Hispanic black (50.2 per 100,000) and Hispanic (12.4 per 100,000) women, the rate is still more than twice the rate for non-Hispanic white women (2.0 per 100,000) (12).
- Non-Hispanic black and some Hispanic populations have preterm births at rates 60% and 27% higher, respectively, than the rate for non-Hispanic white women (13).
- African-American women have higher infant, fetal, and perinatal mortality rates than white women (14) (see Table 1).
- Although maternal mortality ratios for all ethnic groups have declined over the past half century, racial and ethnic disparities in maternal mortality have actually increased (15, 16). African-American women are three to six times more likely to have a pregnancy-related death than white women (16).

## Understanding the Causes of Health Disparities

Many health disparities are directly related to inequities in income, housing, safety, education, and job opportunities; they largely result from differences in socioeconomic status and insurance status. Although many disparities diminish after taking these factors into account, some remain because of health care system-level, patient-level, and provider-level factors (17).

The current U.S. health care financing paradigm inadvertently may contribute to disparities in health outcomes. The United States is the only developed country that does not extend health care as a right of citizenship. In the United States, health care is

**Table 1.** Infant, Fetal, and Perinatal Mortality by Race of Mother

| Race of Mother | Infant Mortality Rate | Fetal Mortality Rate | Perinatal Mortality Rate |
|---|---|---|---|
| White | 5.8 | 5.5 | 5.9 |
| Black or African American | 14.4 | 11.9 | 12.8 |

National Center for Health Statistics. Health, United States, 2004: with chartbook on trends in the health of Americans. Hyattsville (MD): NCHS; 2004. Available at: http://www.cdc.gov/nchs/data/hus/hus04.pdf. Retrieved June 23, 2005.

driven by market forces; the ultimate goal of the health care business is to maximize profit. For these reasons, this health care system contributes to a lack of access for citizens who are either uninsured or underinsured. The varying geographic availability of health care institutions also may contribute to racial and ethnic disparities in health care.

Access to health insurance coverage and care and utilization of care is significantly different for minority women. The following examples illustrate this point:

- Hispanic and African-American women are more likely to be uninsured than white women. In 2001, 16% of white women, 20% of African-American women, and 37% of Hispanic women 18–64 years of age were uninsured (18).
- Asian-American and Hispanic women are most likely to have not received preventive care in the past year. In 1998, 29% of Asian-American women and 21% of Hispanic women received no preventive services in the previous year compared with 16% of white women and 7% of African-American women. (19).
- The proportion of Asian-American women obtaining Pap tests was considerably lower than that for white women. Only approximately one half (49%) of Asian-American women reported receiving a Pap test in the previous year compared with 64% of white women (19).
- Non-Hispanic black, Hispanic, and American Indian women are more than twice as likely as non-Hispanic white women to begin prenatal care in the third trimester or not at all (5).

Evidence suggests that factors such as stereotyping and prejudice on the part of health care providers may contribute to racial and ethnic disparities in health (17). Additionally, cultural differences between the health care provider and patient can cause communication problems between the patient and the provider and can lead to an inaccurate understanding of the patient's symptoms. Ambiguities between health care providers' and patients' understanding and interpretation of information may contribute to disparities in care (17). For example, language and literacy barriers interfere with physician–patient communication and can contribute to culturally derived mistrust of the health care system and to reduced adherence to health care provider recommendations. Use of traditional or folk remedies can interfere with science-based treatments. There also are lifestyle risk factors, such as unhealthy diets, low levels of physical activity, and alcohol and tobacco use, which contribute to morbidity and mortality and are more prevalent among certain populations (3).

## ACOG Recommendations

The American College of Obstetricians and Gynecologists strongly supports the elimination of racial and ethnic disparities in women's health and health care as well as gender disparities in health and health care. The elimination of disparities in women's health and health care requires a comprehensive, multilevel strategy that involves all members of society. Our goal as health care providers and leaders must be to optimize individuals' health status and the quality of health care. We encourage health professionals to engage in the following activities:

1. Advocate for universal access to basic affordable health care (20).
2. Improve cultural competency in the physician–patient relationship and engage in cross-cultural educational activities to improve communication and language skills (21).
3. Use national best practice guidelines to reduce unintended variation in health care outcomes by gender, race, and ethnicity.
4. Provide high quality, compassionate, and ethically sound health care services to all. Engage in dialogue with patients to determine their care expectations, and counsel patients regarding the benefits of preventive health care and early screening, intervention, and treatment.
5. Advocate for increased public awareness of the benefits of preventive health care and early screening and intervention.
6. Encourage and become active in recruiting minorities to the health professions.
7. Advocate for improved access to programs that develop fluency in English among non-English speaking populations.
8. Acquire team-building skills to help attract and retain qualified nurses and other health professionals for provision of quality services to underserved women.

9. Conduct research to determine causes of health disparities and develop and evaluate interventions to address these causes.
10. Advocate for the continued collection of race-based data which is important in understanding disparities. Advocate for increased funding for this research.
11. Increase training of health care providers about racial, ethnic, and gender disparities in health and health care.
12. Support safety net providers, including public health systems, urban academic centers, and other health care delivery systems that are more likely to provide health care to minority populations.

## References


1. Fauci AS. Slideshow: The NIH Strategic Plan to Address Health Disparities. Bethesda (MD): National Institutes of Allergy and Infectious Diseases; 2000. Available at: http://www.niaid.nih.gov/director/healthdis.htm. Retrieved June 23, 2005.
2. U.S. Department of Health and Human Services. Healthy people 2010: understanding and improving health. 2nd ed. Washington, DC: U.S. Government Printing Office; 2000. Available at: http://www.healthypeople.gov/Document/pdf/uih/2010uih.pdf. Retrieved June 23, 2005.
3. Clark A, Fong C, Romans M. Health disparities among U.S. women of color: an overview. Washington, DC: The Jacobs Institute of Women's Health; 2002.
4. U.S. Bureau of the Census. Population by age, sex, race, and Hispanic or Latino origin for the United States: 2000(PHC-T-9). Washington, DC: The Bureau; 2001. Available at: http://www.census.gov/population/www/cen2000/phc-t9.html. Retrieved June 23, 2005.
5. Hamilton BE, Martin JA, Sutton PD. Births: preliminary data for 2003. Natl Vital Stat Rep 2004;53(9):1–17.
6. Larsen LJ. The foreign-born population in the United States: 2003: population characteristics. Current Population Reports, P20-539. Washington, DC: US Census Bureau; 2004. Available at: http://www.census.gov/prod/2004pubs/p20–551.pdf. Retrieved June 23, 2005.
7. Romero R, Kuivaniemi H, Tromp G, Olson J. The design, execution, and interpretation of genetic association studies to decipher complex diseases. Am J Obstet Gynecol 2002;187:1299–312.
8. Casper ML, Barnett E, Halverson JA, Elmes GA, Braham VE, Majeed ZA, et al. Racial and ethnic disparities in heart disease among women. In: Women and heart disease: an atlas of racial and ethnic disparities in mortality. 2nd ed. Atlanta (GA): Centers for Disease Control and Prevention; Morgantown (WV): West Virginia University, Office for Social Environment and Health Research; 2000. Available at: ftp://ftp.cdc.gov/pub/Publications/womens_atlas/00-atlas-all.pdf. Retrieved June 22, 2005. p. 19–24.
9. Satcher D. American women and health disparities [editorial]. J Am Med Womens Assoc 2001;56:131–2, 160.
10. Ries LA, Eisner MP, Kosary CL, Hankey BF, Miller BA, Clegg L, et al., editors. SEER cancer statistics review, 1975–2002. Bethesda (MD): National Cancer Institute; 2005. Available at: http://seer.cancer.gov/csr/1975_2002. Retrieved June 23, 2005.
11. Cancer mortality among American Indians and Alaska Natives—United States, 1994–1998. Centers for Disease Control and Prevention. MMWR Morb Mortal Wkly Rep 2003;52:704–7.
12. Centers for Disease Control and Prevention. HIV/AIDS Surveillance Report, 2003;15:1–46. Available at: http://www.cdc.gov/hiv/stats/2003SurveillanceReport.pdf. Retrieved June 22, 2005.
13. Martin JA, Hamilton BE, Sutton PD, Ventura SJ, Menacker F, Munson ML. Births: final data for 2002. Natl Vital Stat Rep 2003;52(10):1–113.
14. National Center for Health Statistics. Health, United States, 2004: with chartbook on trends in the health of Americans. Hyattsville (MD): NCHS; 2004. Available at: http://www.cdc.gov/nchs/data/hus/hus04.pdf. Retrieved June 23, 2005.
15. Differences in maternal mortality among black and white women—United States, 1990. MMWR Morb Mortal Wkly Rep 1995;44:6–7, 13–4.
16. State-specific maternal mortality among black and white women—United States, 1987–1996. MMWR Morb Mortal Wkly Rep 1999;48:492–6.
17. Institute of Medicine (US). Unequal treatment: confronting racial and ethnic disparities in healthcare. Washington, DC: The Institutes 2002.
18. Kaiser Family Foundation. Racial and ethnic disparities in women's health coverage and access to care: findings from the 2001 Kaiser Women's Health Survey. Menlo Park (CA): KFF; 2004. Available at: http://www.kff.org/womenshealth/loader.cfm?url=/commonspot/security/getfile.cfm&PageID=33087. Retrieved June 23, 2005.
19. Collins KS, Schoen C, Joseph S, Duchon L, Simantov E, Yellowitz M. Health concerns across a woman's lifespan: The Commonwealth Fund 1998 Survey of Women's Health. New York (NY): The Commonwealth Fund; 1999.
20. The uninsured. ACOG Committee Opinion No. 308. American College of Obstetricians and Gynecologists. Obstet Gynecol 2004;104:1471–4.
21. American College of Obstetricians and Gynecologists. Cultural competency, sensitivity and awareness in the delivery of health care. In: Special issues in women's health. Washington, DC: ACOG; 2005. p. 11–20.

ACOG

Committee on Health Care for Underserved Women

Committee on Obstetric Practice

# Committee Opinion

Number 316, October 2005

(Replaces Educational Bulletin 260, September 2000)

This document reflects emerging clinical and scientific advances as of the date issued and is subject to change. The information should not be construed as dictating an exclusive course of treatment or procedure to be followed.

The Committees would like to thank Kelli Mudd Miller, MD, and Kirsten Smith, MD, for their assistance in the development of this bulletin.



ISSN 1074-861X

**The American College of Obstetricians and Gynecologists**
409 12th Street, SW
PO Box 96920
Washington, DC 20090-6920

12345/98765

Smoking cessation during pregnancy. ACOG Committee Opinion No. 316. American College of Obstetricians and Gynecologists. Obstet Gynecol 2005;106:883–8.

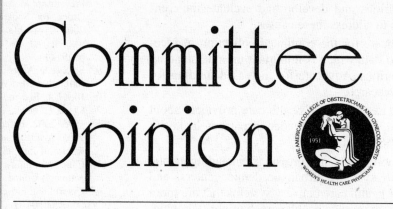

# Smoking Cessation During Pregnancy

*ABSTRACT: Smoking is one of the most important modifiable causes of poor pregnancy outcomes in the United States. An office-based protocol that systematically identifies pregnant women who smoke and offers treatment has been proved to increase quit rates. For pregnant women who are light to moderate smokers, a short counseling session with pregnancy-specific educational materials often is an effective intervention for smoking cessation. The 5 A's is an office-based intervention developed for use by trained practitioners. Techniques for smoking reduction, pharmacotherapy, and health care support systems can help smokers quit.*

## Epidemiology

Increased public education measures and public health campaigns in the United States have led to a decline in smoking during pregnancy (1). Pregnancy appears to motivate women to make lifestyle changes; approximately 46% of prepregnancy smokers quit during pregnancy (1). From 1990 to 2003, the rate of smoking reported by pregnant women decreased from 18.4% (2) to 11% (3). The smoking rate during pregnancy in 2002 for women ages 18 and 19 years was 18%, higher than that for pregnant women of any other age (4).

## Consequences of Maternal Smoking

The biologic evidence that maternal smoking has a detrimental effect on the fetus includes fetal hypoxia from increased carboxyhemoglobin; reduced blood flow to the uterus, placenta, and fetus; and direct effects of nicotine and other compounds in tobacco smoke on the placenta and fetus (5). Health risks associated with smoking during pregnancy include intrauterine growth restriction, placenta previa, and abruptio placentae (5). Adverse pregnancy outcomes include premature rupture of membranes (6, 7), low birth weight, and perinatal mortality (5). Evidence also suggests that smoking is associated with an increase in ectopic pregnancies (5). It is estimated that eliminating smoking during pregnancy would reduce infant deaths by 5% (8) and reduce the incidence of singleton low-birth-weight infants by 10.4% (9).

There is a strong association between smoking during pregnancy and sudden infant death syndrome (SIDS) (5). Children born to mothers who smoke during pregnancy are at increased risk for asthma (10), infantile colic (11), and childhood obesity (12). Successful smoking cessation before the third trimester eliminates much of the reduced birth weight caused by maternal smoking (5). Women who continue to smoke during pregnancy must achieve very low levels of tobacco use to see improvements in infant birth weight, and they must quit entirely if their infants are to have birth weights similar to those of women who do not smoke (13).

## Intervention

Both cessation of tobacco use and prevention of relapse to smoking are key clinical intervention strategies during pregnancy. Techniques for helping patients to stop smoking have included counseling, cognitive and behavioral therapy, hypnosis, acupuncture, and pharmacologic therapy. A 5–15-minute counseling session performed by appropriately trained health care providers is most effective with pregnant women who smoke fewer than 20 cigarettes per day (14). This intervention, known as the 5 A's, is appropriate for use during routine prenatal office visits and includes the following five steps: Ask, Advise, Assess, Assist, and Arrange. The intervention is adapted from the U.S. Public Health Service clinical practice guideline, "Treating Tobacco Use and Dependence" (14). Its effectiveness can be enhanced for those who smoke any amount by referring the patient to a pregnancy-specific smoker's "quitline." The approach described in the box and outlined as follows guides the provider through the interaction and in documentation of the treatment (14).

1. **Ask** about smoking status. Providers should ask the patient at the first prenatal visit to choose a statement that best describes her smoking status from a list of statements on smoking behavior (see the box). Using this multiple-choice method is more likely to elicit an accurate response than asking a question that elicits a simple "yes" or "no" answer. A smoking cessation chart, a tobacco use sticker, or a vital signs stamp that includes smoking status may be useful in the medical record to remind providers to ask patients about smoking status at follow-up visits (see resource box).
2. **Advise** patients who smoke to stop by providing clear, strong advice to quit with personalized messages about the benefits of quitting and the impact of continued smoking on the woman, fetus, and newborn. Congratulate patients who report having stopped smoking and affirm their efforts with a statement about the benefits of quitting.
3. **Assess** the patient's willingness to attempt to quit smoking within the next 30 days. One approach to this assessment is to say, "Quitting smoking is one of the most important things you can do for your health and your baby's health. If we can give you some help, are you willing to try?" If the patient is willing, the provider can move to the next step. If the patient is unwilling to try, providers may consider having a brief discussion with the patient to educate and reassure her about quitting (14). Quitting advice, assessment, and assistance should be offered at subsequent prenatal care visits.
4. **Assist** patients who are interested in quitting by providing pregnancy-specific, self-help smoking cessation materials (see resource box). Enhance the patient's problem-solving skills by asking when and where she typically smokes and suggesting how she might avoid these situations that trigger the desire to smoke. Offer support on the importance of 1) having a smoke-free space at home, 2) seeking out a "quitting buddy" such as a former smoker or nonsmoker both at work and at home, and 3) understanding nicotine withdrawal, such as irritability and cravings. Communicate caring and concern and encourage the patient to talk about the process of quitting.

   The provider also may refer the patient to a smoker's quitline. Telephone quitlines offer information, direct support, and ongoing counseling and have been very successful in helping pregnant smokers quit and remain smoke free (15). Great Start (1-866-66-START) is a national pregnancy-specific smoker's quitline operated by the American Legacy Foundation. Some states also have proactive direct fax referral capability for providers to connect pregnant smokers directly to their state quitline. By dialing the national quitline network (1-800-QUIT NOW), callers are routed immediately to their state smoker's quitline.

5. **Arrange** follow-up visits to track the progress of the patient's attempt to quit smoking. For current and former smokers, smoking status should be monitored throughout pregnancy, providing opportunities to congratulate and support success, reinforce steps taken toward quitting, and advise those still considering a cessation attempt.

Although counseling and pregnancy-specific materials are effective cessation aids for many pregnant women, some women continue to smoke. These women often are heavily addicted to nicotine and should be *Asked* and *Advised* and *Assessed* about smoking at follow-up visits. Women who continue to smoke may benefit from screening for alcohol use and other drug use (16). If the alcohol or drug use screen result is positive, information about the risks associated with alcohol and drug use during pregnancy should be added to the *Advise* step, and specific strategies for abstaining from alcohol and drugs should be discussed in the *Assist* step. Clinicians also may consider referring patients for additional psychosocial treatment (14).

Although quitting smoking early in pregnancy yields the greatest benefits for the pregnant woman and fetus, quitting at any point can be beneficial (14). The benefits of cutting down are difficult to measure or verify. The effort of women who cut down should be reinforced, but these women also should be reminded that quitting entirely brings the best results for their health, the health of the fetus, and that of their babies (17).

Approximately 60–80% of women who quit smoking during pregnancy return to smoking within a year postpartum (1). Former smokers should be counseled in the third trimester and at the postpartum visit and subsequent gynecology visits concerning relapse to smoking (18).

## Pharmacotherapy

The use of nicotine replacement products or other pharmaceuticals for smoking cessation aids during pregnancy and lactation have not been sufficiently evaluated to determine their efficacy or safety. Nicotine gum, lozenges, patches, inhalers, and special-dose antidepressants that reduce withdrawal symptoms, such as bupropion, should be considered for use during pregnancy and lactation only when nonpharmacologic treatments (eg, counseling) have failed. If the increased likelihood of

### Smoking Cessation Intervention for Pregnant Patients

**Ask**—1 minute

- Ask the patient to choose the statement that best describes her smoking status:
  A. I have NEVER smoked or have smoked FEWER THAN 100 cigarettes in my lifetime.
  B. I stopped smoking BEFORE I found out I was pregnant, and I am not smoking now.
  C. I stopped smoking AFTER I found out I was pregnant, and I am not smoking now.
  D. I smoke some now, but I have cut down on the number of cigarettes I smoke SINCE I found out I was pregnant.
  E. I smoke regularly now, about the same as BEFORE I found out I was pregnant.

If the patient stopped smoking before or after she found out she was pregnant (B or C), reinforce her decision to quit, congratulate her on success in quitting, and encourage her to stay smoke free throughout pregnancy and postpartum.

If the patient is still smoking (D or E), document smoking status in her medical record, and proceed to Advise, Assess, Assist, and Arrange.

**Advise**—1 minute

- Provide clear, strong advice to quit with personalized messages about the benefits of quitting and the impact of smoking and quitting on the woman, fetus, and newborn.

**Assess**—1 minute

- Assess the willingness of the patient to attempt to quit within 30 days.

If the patient is ready to quit, proceed to Assist.

If the patient is not ready, provide information to motivate the patient to quit and proceed to Arrange.

**Assist**—3 minutes

- Suggest and encourage the use of problem-solving methods and skills for smoking cessation (eg, identify situations that trigger the desire to smoke).
- Provide social support as part of the treatment (eg, "We can help you quit").
- Arrange social support in the smoker's environment (eg, identify a "quit buddy" and smoke-free space).
- Provide pregnancy-specific, self-help smoking cessation materials.

**Arrange**—1 minute or more

- Assess smoking status at subsequent prenatal visits and, if patient continues to smoke, encourage cessation.

Adapted from Melvin CL, Dolan-Mullen P, Windsor RA Jr, Whiteside HP, Goldenberg RL. Recommended cessation counselling for pregnant women who smoke: a review of the evidence. Tob Control 2000;9(suppl 3):III80–4. Reproduced with permission from the BMJ Publishing Group.

## Resources for Smoking Cessation

**The American College of Obstetricians and Gynecologists Resources for the Clinician**

American College of Obstetricians and Gynecologists. Smoking cessation during pregnancy: a clinician's guide to helping pregnant women quit smoking. Washington, DC: ACOG; 2002. Contains guidelines, a tool kit for the clinician, lecture guide, and CD-ROM. Request a copy by e-mail to: smoking@acog.org. Lecture guide is available online. Go to www.acog.org/goto/smoking.

Dartmouth Medical School. Smoking cessation for pregnancy and beyond: learn proven strategies to help your patients quit. Hanover (NH): Dartmouth Medical School; 2004. Available for purchase from the ACOG Distribution Center (800-762-2264, sales.acog.org): Item No. AA423; price: $25.

American College of Obstetricians and Gynecologists. Smoking and women's health. In: Special issues in women's health. Washington, DC: ACOG; 2005. p. 151–67. Available for purchase from the ACOG Distribution Center (800-762-2264, sales.acog.org): Item No. AA451; price: $59; ACOG members: $45. Available online to members. Go to www.acog.org/goto/underserved.

American College of Obstetricians and Gynecologists "Ask about tobacco use" chart stickers. Washington, DC: ACOG. Available for purchase from the ACOG Distribution Center (800-762-2264, sales.acog.org): Item No. AA268; price: $19/260 stickers; ACOG members: $15/260 stickers.

**Other Resources for the Clinician**

The following resources are for information purposes only. Referral to these sources and web sites does not imply the endorsement of ACOG. This list is not meant to be comprehensive. The exclusion of a source or web site does not reflect the quality of that source or web site. Please note that web sites are subject to change without notice.

Many states offer free or low-cost smoking cessation counseling services consisting of telephone quitlines, group or individual counseling programs, and materials to help the smoker quit and prevent relapse. Check with the state or local public health office or tobacco control program to access these resources.

Helping pregnant women quit smoking: progress and future directions. Nicotine Tob Res 2004; 6(suppl 2): S95–277.

National Partnership to Help Pregnant Smokers Quit: has tools on helping patients quit, assessing smokers' quitlines, and obtaining Medicaid reimbursement for smoking cessation services. Posters are also available.
Web: www.helppregnantsmokersquit.org.
E-mail: info@helppregnantsmokersquit.org.

British Medical Association. Smoking and reproductive life: the impact of smoking on sexual, reproductive and child health. London (UK): BMA; 2004. Available at: www.bma.org.uk/ap.nsf/Content/smokingreproductivelife/$file/smoking.pdf. Retrieved June 22, 2005.

Treating tobacco use and dependence: clinician's packet. A how-to guide for implementing the Public Health Service Clinical Practice Guidelines. Washington, DC: U.S. Public Health Service; 2003. Available at: www.surgeongeneral.gov/tobacco/clincpack.html. Retrieved June 22, 2005.

**Web Sites**

American Cancer Society
www.cancer.org

The American Heart Association
www.americanheart.org

The Centers for Disease Control and Prevention: Tobacco Information and Prevention Source (TIPS).
www.cdc.gov/tobacco
TIPS contains documents for health providers to implement tobacco control programs

The National Cancer Institute
www.cancer.gov

National Partnership to Help Pregnant Smokers Quit
www.helppregnantsmokersquit.org/quit/toll_free.asp
The partnership has a listing of states with pregnancy-specific quitlines.

Smoke-Free Families
www.smokefreefamilies.org

Smokefree.gov
www.smokefree.gov
Web site has multiple cessation strategies and information for smokers.

**Resources for Patients**

American College of Obstetricians and Gynecologists, Smoke-Free Families. Need help putting out that cigarette? Washington, DC: ACOG; Chapel Hill (NC): Smoke-Free Families; 2001. Available in English and Spanish for purchase from the ACOG Distribution Center (800-762-2264, sales.acog.org): Item Nos. AA424 and AA4245; price: $10/10 booklets.

You can quit smoking: support and advice from your prenatal care provider. Available at: www.surgeongeneral.gov/tobacco/prenatal.pdf. Retrieved June 22, 2005. Available for multiple orders from AHRQ (PO Box 8547, Silver Spring MD 20907-8547, 800-358-9295): Item No. AHRQ 00-0052.

Recomendaciones y apoyo de su médico de cuidados, Spanish language. Available at: www.surgeongeneral.gov/tobacco/prenatalsp.pdf. Retrieved June 22, 2005. Available for multiple orders from AHRQ (PO Box 8547, Silver Spring MD 20907-8547, 800-358-9295): Item No. AHRQ 00-0065.

American Legacy Foundation. Great start quitline. Available at: www.americanlegacy.org/greatstart/html/quitline.html. Retrieved: June 22, 2005. 866-66-START for toll free help Monday–Friday 8:00 AM–8:00 PM (Eastern Time) and Saturday 9:00 AM–4:00 PM. Counseling in English or Spanish.

smoking cessation, with its potential benefits, outweighs the unknown risk of nicotine replacement and potential concomitant smoking, nicotine replacement products or other pharmaceuticals may be considered (14). Because potential benefits seem to outweigh potential risks, research to determine the safety and efficacy of pharmacotherapy is underway. Some tobacco control experts have reported that if nicotine replacement therapy is used during pregnancy, products with intermittent dosages, such as the gum or inhaler, should be tried first (19). If the nicotine patch is used, it can be removed at night to reduce fetal nicotine exposure (20). Nicotine replacement therapy also may be considered during lactation. Optimally, smokers can be treated with these pharmacotherapies before conception.

## Support Systems

The Agency for Healthcare Research and Quality has recommended systems changes to help health care providers identify and treat tobacco users (14). These changes require the partnership of health care administrators and insurers, and include the following strategies: 1) provide education, resources, and feedback to promote provider involvement in smoking cessation; 2) promote hospital policies that support and provide smoking cessation services; 3) include effective smoking cessation treatments as paid or covered services in all health benefits packages; and 4) reimburse clinicians and specialists for delivery of effective tobacco dependence treatments and include these interventions among the defined duties of the clinicians (14).

## Coding

Office visits specifically addressing smoking cessation may be coded using International Classification of Diseases, Ninth Revision, Clinical Modification (ICD-9-CM) code 305.1 (tobacco use disorder, tobacco dependence from the Mental Health section) with Current Procedural Terminology* (CPT®) code 99401 or 99211:

* CPT code 99401 (preventive medicine counseling lasting approximately 15 minutes): If counseling is done by the physician at the time of a regular antepartum visit, use modifier 25 on code 99401. If counseling is done by the physician at another encounter, separate from the antepartum visit, no modifier is needed with code 99401.
* CPT code 99211: If a nurse counsels the patient, and if nurses are recognized by the insurance company as qualified providers of the service, code 99211 would be used instead of code 99401. If the nurse is not recognized as a caregiver, the services will not be covered unless provided by the physician.

Note that not all payers reimburse for counseling outside of the global package and some do not cover preventive services at all.

Many private and public insurers are changing policy to provide coverage for smoking cessation counseling for pregnant women. Although coverage for such counseling may have been denied previously, it may be prudent for the clinician to continue to submit for reimbursement for these services.

*Current Procedural Terminology (CPT) is copyright 2004 American Medical Association. All rights reserved. No fee schedules, basic units, relative values or related listings are included in CPT. The AMA assumes no liability for the data contained herein. CPT® is a trademark of the American Medical Association.

## References

1. Colman GJ, Joyce T. Trends in smoking before, during, and after pregnancy in ten states. Am J Prev Med 2003;24:29–35.
2. Smoking during pregnancy—United States—1990–2002. Centers for Disease Control and Prevention. MMWR Morb Mortal Wkly Rep 2004;53:911–5.
3. Hamilton BE, Martin JA, Sutton PD. Births: preliminary data for 2003. Centers for Disease Control and Prevention, National Center for Health Statistics. Natl Vital Stat Rep 2004;53(a):1–17.
4. National Center for Health Statistics. Health, United States, 2004: with chartbook on trends in the health of Americans. Hyattsville (MD): NCHS; 2004. Available at: http://www.cdc.gov/nchs/data/hus/hus04.pdf. Retrieved June 20, 2005.
5. U.S. Department of Health and Human Services. The health consequences of smoking: a report of the Surgeon General. Washington, DC: HHS; 2004. Available at: www.cdc.gov/tobacco/sgr/sgr_2004/chapters.htm. Retrieved June 20, 2005.
6. Castles A, Adams EK, Melvin CL, Kelsch C, Boulton ML. Effects of smoking during pregnancy. Five meta-analyses. Am J Prev Med 1999;16:208–15.
7. Spinillo A, Nicola S, Piazzi G, Ghazal K, Colonna L, Baltaro F. Epidemiological correlates of preterm premature rupture of membranes. Int J Gynaecol Obstet 1994; 47:7–15.

8. Salihu HM, Aliyu MH, Pierre-Louis BJ, Alexander GR. Levels of excess infant deaths attributable to maternal smoking during pregnancy in the United States. Matern Child Health J 2003;7:219–27.
9. Ventura SJ, Hamilton BE, Mathews TJ, Chandra A. Trends and variations in smoking during pregnancy and low birth weight: evidence from the birth certificate, 1990-2000. Pediatrics 2003;111:1176–80.
10. Li YF, Langholz B, Salam MT, Gilliland FD. Maternal and grandmaternal smoking patterns are associated with early childhood asthma. Chest 2005;127:1232–41.
11. Sondergaard C, Henriksen TB, Obel C, Wisborg K. Smoking during pregnancy and infantile colic. Pediatrics 2001;108:342–6.
12. von Kries R, Toschke AM, Koletzko B, Slikker W Jr. Maternal smoking during pregnancy and childhood obesity. Am J Epidemiol 2002;156:954–61.
13. England LJ, Kendrick JS, Wilson HG, Merritt RK, Gargiullo PM, Zahniser SC. Effects of smoking reduction during pregnancy on the birth weight of term infants. Am J Epidemiol 2001;154:694–701.
14. Fiore MC, Bailey WC, Cohen SJ, Dorfman SF, Goldstein MG, Gritz ER. Treating tobacco use and dependence. Clinical practice guideline. Rockville (MD): U.S. Department of Health and Human Services, Public Health Service; 2000.
15. Tomson T, Helgason AR, Gilljam H. Quitline in smoking cessation: a cost-effectiveness analysis. Int J Technol Assess Health Care 2004;20:469–74.
16. Ockene J, Ma Y, Zapka J, Pbert L, Valentine Goins K, Stoddard A. Spontaneous cessation to smoking and alcohol use among low-income pregnant women. Am J Prev Med 2002;23:150–9.
17. Melvin CL, Dolan-Mullen P, Windsor RA, Whiteside HP Jr, Goldenberg RL. Recommended cessation counselling for pregnant women who smoke: a review of the evidence. Tob Control 2000;9(suppl 3):III80–4.
18. Dolan Mullen P. How can more smoking suspension during pregnancy become lifelong abstinence? Lessons learned about predictors, interventions, and gaps in our accumulated knowledge. Nicotine Tob Res 2004;6(suppl 2):S217–38.
19. Benowitz N, Dempsey D. Pharmacotherapy for smoking cessation during pregnancy. Nicotine Tob Res 2004;6 (suppl 2):S189–202.
20. Windsor R, Oncken C, Henningfield J, Hartmann K, Edwards N. Behavioral and pharmacological treatment methods for pregnant smokers: issues for clinical practice. J Am Med Womens Assoc 2000;55:304–10.

# ACOG Committee Opinion

Committee on Health Care for Underserved Women

This information should not be construed as dictating an exclusive course of treatment or procedure to be followed.

The Committee on Health Care for Underserved Women wishes to thank Deborah Smith, MD, and Maureen Phipps, MD, for their assistance in the development of this document.



ISSN 1074-861X

**The American College of Obstetricians and Gynecologists**
409 12th Street, SW
PO Box 96920
Washington, DC 20090-6920

12345/09876

Psychosocial risk factors: perinatal screening and intervention. ACOG Committee Opinion No. 343. American College of Obstetricians and Gynecologists. Obstet Gynecol 2006;108:469–77.

Number 343, August 2006 *(Replaces Educational Bulletin 255, November 1999)*

# Psychosocial Risk Factors: Perinatal Screening and Intervention

*ABSTRACT: The American College of Obstetricians and Gynecologists advocates assessing for psychosocial risk factors and helping women manage psychosocial stressors as part of comprehensive care for women. Psychosocial screening of all women seeking pregnancy evaluation or prenatal care should be performed regardless of social status, educational level, or race and ethnicity. Because problems may arise during the pregnancy that were not present at the initial visit, it is best to perform psychosocial screening at least once each trimester to increase the likelihood of identifying important issues and reducing poor birth outcomes. When screening is completed, every effort should be made to identify areas of concern, validate major issues with the patient, provide information, and, if indicated, make suggestions for possible changes. When necessary, the health care provider should refer the patient for further evaluation or intervention. Psychosocial risk factors also should be considered in discharge planning after delivery. Many of the psychosocial issues that increase the risk for poor pregnancy outcome also can affect the health and welfare of the newborn. Screening should include assessment of barriers to care, unstable housing, unintended pregnancy, communication barriers, nutrition, tobacco use, substance use, depression, safety, intimate partner violence, and stress.*

The American College of Obstetricians and Gynecologists (ACOG) advocates addressing psychosocial issues faced by women and their families during the childbearing years. In general, psychosocial issues are nonbiomedical factors that affect mental and physical well-being. Screening for psychosocial risk factors may help predict a woman's attentiveness to personal health matters, her use of prenatal services, and the health status of her offspring (1).

Most women undergo psychologic adaptation to pregnancy and develop coping mechanisms to deal with the routine as well as unanticipated changes that pregnancy brings. This pregnancy-specific adaptation is greatly affected by a woman's beliefs, desires, and culture. Physicians should engage women in dialogue about these important influences. All women, including multiparous women, must receive help in the preparation for childbirth and parenting. Past obstetric events and infant outcomes, medical considerations in a current pregnancy, beliefs about and experience with breastfeeding, and family circumstances are some of the factors that influence the experience of labor, delivery, and early neonatal and postpartum adjustment. Additionally, some women experience social, economic, and personal difficulties in pregnancy. Some of these issues represent preexisting problems; others arise during the course of pregnancy and may be a result of the pregnancy itself. These are the challenges and issues commonly thought of as risk factors for adverse maternal, fetal, and infant outcomes.

An emerging body of evidence indicates that women place high value on attention to psychosocial issues and report greater satisfaction with physician visits when there is more "psychosocial talk" and less "biomedical talk" (2). Discussing and screening for psychosocial factors, including social support, intimate partner violence, lack of insurance coverage, unstable housing, adapting to parenting, and substance abuse, are beneficial.

## Addressing Psychosocial Factors in Pregnancy

Classically, prenatal protocols were intended to establish the diagnosis of pregnancy; monitor for the onset of complications, such as hypertensive disorders associated with pregnancy and preterm labor; identify feto-pelvic disproportion; and prevent sudden fetal death from certain conditions, such as maternal diabetes. During the two decades between 1970 and 1990, an appreciation of the significance of psychosocial issues during pregnancy emerged. Pivotal publications in the late 1980s formally recommended that preconception counseling and enhanced prenatal education and counseling be added to clinical practice (3, 4). One example is the explicit detection and management of behavioral risks, such as smoking, associated with low birth weight as an integral part of prenatal care.

Biomedical risks, such as complications of pregnancy, concomitant maternal disease, infection, nutritional deficiencies, and exposure to teratogens, are estimated to account for approximately one half of the incidence of low-birth-weight infants and of prematurity and their postnatal sequelae (5). An important portion of the remaining cases of these adverse pregnancy outcomes may be attributable to psychosocial stress even after controlling for the effects of recognized sociodemographic, obstetric, and behavioral risk factors (6, 7).

The analysis and commentary on the content of prenatal care also have begun to include assessment of quality of care, cultural appropriateness, and patient responsibility and satisfaction. The American College of Obstetricians and Gynecologists advocates assessing for psychosocial risk factors and helping women manage psychosocial stressors as part of comprehensive care for women (8, 9).

## Screening for Psychosocial Risk

Psychosocial screening of all women seeking pregnancy evaluation or prenatal care should be performed regardless of social status, educational level, or race and ethnicity. Given the sensitive nature of psychosocial assessment, every effort should be made to screen patients in private, especially when inquiring about intimate partner or domestic violence. Even then, patients may not be comfortable discussing problems with physicians until a trusting relationship has been formed.

During pregnancy, problems may arise that were not present at the initial visit; therefore, it is best to perform psychosocial screening at least once each trimester to increase the likelihood of identifying important issues and reducing poor birth outcomes. There is evidence that women who are screened for psychosocial issues once each trimester are half as likely as women who are not screened to have a low-birth-weight or preterm baby (10). Although psychosocial issues may be complex, there is a reasonable degree of specificity and sensitivity to single-item (one question per topic) screening instruments. The Healthy Start Program of the Florida Department of Health has designed a well-regarded screening system, which has been used widely and refined. The Healthy Start tool provides a concise and simple means of collecting psychosocial data that can be used for self-reporting or interview-style information retrieval (see the box). The questions from this tool are now included in the ACOG Obstetric Medical History form. Although many of the topics identified in this tool are discussed more fully in various ACOG documents (see "Resources"), consolidated information on these topics has been provided in this document for quick reference.

When screening is completed, every effort should be made to identify areas of concern, validate major issues with the patient, provide information, and, if indicated, make suggestions for possible

**Psychosocial Screening Tool**

1. Yes No Do you have any problems (job, transportation, etc.) that prevent you from keeping your health care appointments?
2. Yes No Do you feel unsafe where you live?
3. Yes No In the past 2 months, have you used any form of tobacco?
4. Yes No In the past 2 months, have you used drugs or alcohol (including beer, wine, or mixed drinks)?
5. Yes No In the past year, have you been threatened, hit, slapped, or kicked by anyone you know?
6. Yes No Has anyone forced you to perform any sexual act that you did not want to do?
7. On a 1-to-5 scale, how do you rate your current stress level?
   1 2 3 4 5
   Low High
8. How many times have you moved in the past 12 months?________
9. If you could change the timing of this pregnancy, would you want it
   - earlier
   - later
   - not at all
   - no change

Modified and reprinted with permission from Florida's Healthy Start Prenatal Risk Screening Instrument. Tallahassee (FL): Florida Department of Health; 1997. DH 3134.

changes. Screening positive for a condition often necessitates a referral to resources outside the practice for further evaluation or intervention (3). Therefore, having a well-developed referral network is important to provide care successfully for a broad range of medical and psychosocial issues. Constructing a resource list can help health care providers develop this network and is as straightforward as contacting local hospital social services departments and community centers. If additional assistance is needed with locating appropriate referral sites, local or state health officials may be helpful. Using previously collected information about community-based resources can help save time. Examples of commonly used resources include smoking cessation programs, weight loss programs, women's shelters, and medical assistance programs. Office practice staff can compile this information and be assigned to keeping it up-to-date. It is also important to obtain feedback from patients and staff on their experiences with the various resources.

Psychosocial risk factors also should be considered in discharge planning after delivery. Many of the psychosocial issues that increase the risk for poor pregnancy outcome also can affect the health and welfare of the newborn. In the absence of complications, a 48-hour hospital stay after a normal vaginal delivery or a 96-hour stay after a cesarean delivery is recommended (9). When outpatient follow-up may not be reliable, it is essential that women with significant psychosocial problems stay in the hospital after delivery as long as necessary to assess adequately the health of the mother and the newborn and educate the mother regarding postpartum issues and infant care. Documentation should include the nature of any problems identified, the chosen interventions, and plans for follow-up.

## Identification of Contributing Factors

***Barriers to Care***

Inadequate insurance coverage, inability to pay for health care services, and not knowing where to go for care are a few of the most common barriers to health care. Others include lack of transportation, family support, and child care (11). These barriers are especially problematic for adolescents. For individuals faced with these barriers, referral to an appropriate social service agency may be useful. These agencies can sometimes help women navigate the health care system. In particular, they can help women enroll in Medicaid, which covers the costs of medical care and transportation to and from medical and social service appointments and also subsidizes or provides free day care. They also can help women enroll in Early Head Start programs, which provide services to pregnant women and their families through a child's first 3 years of life. By flexible scheduling of appointments, inquiring about difficulties a patient may have with keeping appointments, and assisting with solutions, the health care provider increases the likelihood of adherence to prenatal care recommendations.

***Unstable Housing***

Frequent moves can indicate a variety of problems. For example, the patient may be having difficulty finding acceptable affordable housing. If this is the case, the patient can be referred to the appropriate social service agency for assistance. These local agencies also can provide information about other resources in the area, including health services, social support groups, and child care resources.

In addition, frequent moves may reflect violence in the home or may indicate legal problems. Inadequate housing also may be a source of environmental contamination and toxic exposure. Inquiring about the patient's feelings of isolation is important. If this is a problem, referral to any available neighborhood support groups or a counselor can be helpful.

***Unintended Pregnancy***

Approximately 49% of all pregnancies are unintended at the time of conception (12). This percentage is considerably higher among adolescents. An unintended pregnancy is defined as a pregnancy that was mistimed or unwanted at the time of conception. Research has shown that having an unintended pregnancy is a predictor of insufficient prenatal care, resulting in an increased risk of a poor birth outcome. Women with unintended pregnancies are more likely to smoke, drink alcohol, or abuse substances and have a greater likelihood of giving birth to a low-birth-weight infant. Their infants are more likely to die within the first year of life (13). In addition, the incidence of unintended pregnancy is higher among women who have been battered (14), and battering is more common during an unplanned pregnancy (15).

Unintended pregnancies often become accepted pregnancies that produce loved and wanted children. However, women with pregnancies that remain unwanted should be counseled about the full range of reproductive options, including abortion and adoption. Women must be allowed to make independent decisions about their own pregnancies. This choice remains a woman's right and must be respected.

It is important to reassess those factors that may have resulted in an unintended pregnancy during the pregnancy. Poor access to family planning services or lack of education and information should be addressed with discussion and counseling during the course of prenatal care or in the postpartum or postabortal period.

***Communication Barriers***

Barriers to care are magnified when the patient does not speak English. Federal and state laws mandate the provision of interpreter and translation services to patients with limited English proficiency. Innovative new technologies can make language access easier and more effective. One new method is the use of wireless headsets like those used during international meetings, which allow the physician to speak and hear in one language and the patient in another language. Another method is videoconferencing, linking a patient and physician at one location to an interpreter at another location through the use of computers with video cameras and microphones. If these services are not available, health care providers can ask the patient to identify a family member or friend who can act as a translator. This should be done as a last resort, however, because under these circumstances, information may be intentionally or unintentionally translated incorrectly. For example, in cases of intimate partner violence, if the abusive spouse is translating, he might omit a question about safety in the home, misrepresent the patient's response, or retaliate, and the patient may choose to conceal the abuse. Another partial solution is to provide written materials in appropriate languages for patients who do not speak English. If communication is not adequate, possibilities such as whether the patient should remain in the practice or be referred to a facility with better access to translators should be considered.

The Americans with Disabilities Act requires that health care providers have an adequate system of communication in place for interaction with women who are deaf or hard of hearing. This may include using a qualified interpreter for these women. For these women as well as those who are blind or have low vision, the appointment time length may be increased in order to obtain a complete medical history and physical database; conduct psychosocial screening; plan continued care; arrange communication systems, such as telephone relays; and obtain education resources, such as large-print materials.

***Nutrition***

Problems with nutrition can occur in women of any socioeconomic status. These problems range from an inability to acquire and prepare food to an eating disorder. If a woman cannot afford a sufficient supply of food, she should be referred to food pantries and other resources in her area. All low-income women should receive information about the Special Supplemental Nutrition Program for Women, Infants, and Children (WIC) and food stamp programs. Referrals to the appropriate social service agency or other available services can be helpful (9).

Women of low socioeconomic status often live in environments that do not allow for the adequate storage, refrigeration, or preparation of food. Many nutritionists are trained in alternative methods of food storage and preparation and would, therefore, be able to assist the patient upon referral. The nutritionist also could assess the patient's diet and suggest healthy foods that are inexpensive.

Questions should be asked, especially of adolescents and young women, about eating habits such as fasting or skipping meals, which may be indicative of anorexia and bulimia. If it is determined that the patient has an eating disorder, referrals to a mental health provider who specializes in this issue and a nutritionist for counseling about food management are essential (9). All WIC programs have nutritionists who are required to counsel patients on these matters. Hospitalization may be required for patients with eating disorders. Poor weight gain also may reflect substance abuse, intimate partner violence, or depression.

Women who are obese at the outset of pregnancy also may have altered body image and weight gain concerns. They may require specialized instruction regarding suggested weight gain during pregnancy to optimize nutritional status and reduce risk of future health problems (9, 16).

### *Tobacco Use*

Smoking tobacco is associated with increased perinatal mortality, ectopic pregnancy, and bleeding complications of pregnancy and a higher incidence of small-for-gestational-age babies, low-birth-weight babies, and preterm delivery. It is estimated that a 5% reduction in fetal and infant deaths and a 10.4% reduction in the incidence of singleton low-birth-weight infants (17) would be achieved if pregnant women stopped smoking (18). There is a strong association between smoking during pregnancy and sudden infant death syndrome (17). Children born to mothers who smoke during pregnancy are at increased risk for asthma (19), infantile colic (20), and childhood obesity (21). Therefore, it is essential that patients be screened for tobacco use and provided information on smoking cessation and why it is necessary to stop smoking during pregnancy (22, 23). Interventions by clinicians that are as brief as 5–15 minutes have been shown to be effective at improving smoking cessation rates (24).

### *Substance Use*

The use of mind-altering substances, including illegally obtained drugs, alcohol, or the recreational use of prescription or nonprescription drugs, puts the pregnant woman at an increased risk for preterm delivery and her fetus at increased risk for growth restriction, fetal alcohol syndrome, death, or long-term neurobehavioral effects. These pregnant women also are at increased risk for sexually transmitted diseases, including human immunodeficiency virus (HIV). Women who use or abuse these substances often obtain prenatal care late in the pregnancy, achieve poor weight gain, and frequently miss appointments, all of which can have negative effects on the health of the woman and her fetus. Substance abuse, by either the woman or her partner, also is associated with intimate partner violence. Asking patients about substances used at the time of the first prenatal visit is essential bearing in mind that often multiple substances are used; questions about a woman's partner's use of substances also may be helpful. If either inquiry indicates an area of concern, additional assessment is required (25).

### *Depression*

Mood disorders, especially depression, are among the leading causes of disease-related disability in women of childbearing age (26). Perinatal depression includes major and minor depression that occurs during pregnancy or within the 12-month period following birth (27). The prevalence of major depression is estimated to be as high as 11% at different times during pregnancy and is not appreciably different from rates among women who are not pregnant (27). However, depression has an impact on the development and management of pregnancy-related complications. Untreated depression has been associated with unfavorable health behaviors in pregnancy and subsequent fetal growth restriction, preterm delivery, placental abruption, or newborn irritability (28). Recent evidence-based reviews do not appear to distinguish between the different screening instruments for depression. Using the following two questions to screen for depression may be as effective as more lengthy tools. A positive response to both questions suggests the need for further evaluation.

1. Over the past 2 weeks, have you ever felt down, depressed, or hopeless?
2. Over the past 2 weeks, have you felt little interest or pleasure in doing things? (29)

Postpartum depression is defined as intense feelings of sadness, anxiety, or despair after childbirth that interfere with a mother's ability to function and that do not resolve. In such circumstances, there is an increased risk of serious harm to the mother or the infant. It is to be distinguished from "the baby blues," a period of mild depressive mood and lability that typically has its onset within 2–3 days postpartum and lasts up to 2 weeks. Women who lack psychosocial support, have a history of postpartum depression or other psychiatric illnesses, or have experienced a recent stressful life event are at greater risk for postpartum depression. Screening for these risk factors is, therefore, important. Other risk factors include child care stress, low self-esteem, and low socioeconomic status (30). Clinical practices that screen for depression should have systems in place to ensure that positive screening results are followed by accurate diagnosis, implementation of treatment, and follow-up either within the practice or through referral (31).

### *Safety*

Safety concerns can pertain to safety in the home or the immediate neighborhood. A patient may be unable to gain access to needed services and support because of fear. If there is immediate danger to the patient, alternative housing should be discussed. If there are children who are not safe in the household, a referral to the state's child protection agency may be required. The state agency can be contacted for specific reporting requirements. If the safety concern relates specifically to the house, such as structural defects, rat or insect infestation, or sanitation issues, further inquiry can determine the appropriate local health department referral or intervention. There also should be an inquiry about the presence of guns and other weapons in the home. If present, the patient should be counseled to remove the weapons or to carefully secure them and the ammunition separately (32).

### *Intimate Partner Violence*

The incidence of abuse during pregnancy ranges from 1% to 20% of all pregnant women (33). Many studies report that violence often begins in pregnancy; if already present, it may escalate (34). Research also suggests that violence may increase during the postpartum period (35). Given these findings, ACOG recommends screening every pregnant woman for intimate partner violence at the first prenatal visit, at least once in each trimester, and at the postpartum visit (36). There are characteristics that may serve as markers for abuse. Women who are abused are more likely to receive inadequate prenatal care. In particular, abused pregnant women seek prenatal care later in pregnancy (37), miss more appointments, and are more likely to cancel appointments on short notice than nonabused pregnant women (38).

If the woman believes that her safety is endangered if she returns to her home, shelter should be offered by contacting or referring her to social services, homeless shelters, or community services for battered women. If the patient is afraid for her safety and shelter space is not immediately available, sometimes special arrangements can be made to admit the patient into a hospital until other arrangements can be made. If the patient is not in need of immediate shelter, she should be provided with information on community resources and referred for continued assistance and support (36). Health care providers need to be aware that the patient is the best judge of her own safety. She, therefore, may choose to return home despite receiving advice to the contrary. Health care providers should honor such decisions.

### *Stress*

Not all women with high levels of psychosocial stress have adverse pregnancy outcomes. But there is a growing body of evidence indicating that individual psychosocial stress, strenuous physical activity, and fasting are independent risk factors for preterm birth and low-birth-weight neonates (39–43). Vulnerability to stress in pregnancy may vary according to the nature of the stressful experience, the timing with respect to gestational period, and the presence of other maternal risk factors combined with stress (39). Stress may be a factor that interacts with some of the other factors described previously. Community-level circumstances and conditions can affect health outcomes, and there is a well-established social class gradient in health and health care. Several clinical studies have found that women who are anxious during pregnancy tend to have smaller babies. Additionally, women with high levels of stress hormones such as corticotropin-releasing hormone are more likely to give birth preterm (44–46). A relationship also has been shown between stressful experiences, some forms of work stress, and depression and anxiety in pregnancy with preeclampsia, preterm birth and low birth weight, and reduced head circumference (6, 47).

Practitioners should identify patients under stress. The stress associated with pregnancy itself, concerns about labor and delivery, and projected fears about parenting often can be reduced by providing counseling, information, and social support during the course of prenatal care. Some patients may require evaluation and treatment by mental health practitioners to help identify and resolve distress. Lack of social support has been associated with morbidity and mortality (48, 49). Social support has been defined as resources and aid derived from one's social relationships. Social support may influence health by one of two mechanisms: a direct positive effect or a "buffering" effect. These effects are not mutually exclusive. A direct effect may be neuroendocrine or neuroimmune in origin. Buffering may be a result of either an increase in health-promoting behaviors or a decrease in risk behaviors or both. Intervention studies in evaluating direct effects in pregnant women have had mixed results but effects on behaviors have been demonstrated (49).

## Summary

Addressing the broad range of psychosocial issues with which pregnant women are confronted is an essential step toward improving women's health and birth outcomes. An effective system of referrals will be helpful in augmenting the screening and brief intervention that can be carried out in an office setting. To increase the likelihood of successful interventions, psychosocial screening should be performed on a regular basis and documented in the patient's prenatal record. Screening should include assessment of barriers to care, unstable housing, unintended pregnancy, communication barriers, nutrition, tobacco use, substance use, depression, safety, intimate partner violence, and stress.

## Resources

### *Resources for Practitioners*

American Academy of Pediatrics, American College of Obstetricians and Gynecologists. Guidelines for perinatal care. 5th ed. Elk Grove Village (IL): AAP; Washington, DC: ACOG; 2002.

American College of Obstetricians and Gynecologists. A clinician's guide to helping pregnant women quit smoking. A lecture guide. Washington, DC; ACOG; 2002. Available at: www.acog.org/from_home/departments/smoking/smoking slides.ppt. Retrieved March 24, 2006.

American College of Obstetricians and Gynecologists. "Ask about tobacco use" chart stickers. Washington, DC: ACOG. Available for purchase from the ACOG Distribution Center (800-762-2264, sales.acog.org): Item No. AA268; Price: $19/260 stickers; ACOG members: $15/260 stickers.

American College of Obstetricians and Gynecologists. Eating disorders. In: Health care for adolescents. Washington, DC: ACOG; 2003. p. 81–94.

American College of Obstetricians and Gynecologists. Intimate partner violence and domestic violence. In: Special issues in women's health. Washington, DC: ACOG; 2005. p. 169–88.

American College of Obstetricians and Gynecologists. Intimate partner violence and domestic violence. A slide lecture presentation. Washington, DC: ACOG; 2005.

American College of Obstetricians and Gynecologists. Obstetric medical history. Washington, DC: ACOG; 2002.

American College of Obstetricians and Gynecologists. Smoking and women's health. In: Special issues in women's health. Washington, DC: ACOG; 2005. p. 151–67.

American College of Obstetricians and Gynecologists. Smoking cessation during pregnancy: a clinician's guide to helping pregnant women quit smoking. Washington, DC: ACOG; 2002.

American College of Obstetricians and Gynecologists. Substance use: obstetric and gynecologic implications. In: Special issues in women's health. Washington, DC: ACOG; 2005. p. 105–50.

Dartmouth Medical School. Smoking cessation for pregnancy and beyond: learn proven strategies to help your patients quit. Hanover (NH): Trustees of Dartmouth College; 2004. Available for purchase through the ACOG Distribution Center (800-762-2264, sales.acog.org).

Obesity in pregnancy. ACOG Committee Opinion No. 315. American College of Obstetricians and Gynecologists. Obstet Gynecol 2005;106:671–5.

Smoking cessation during pregnancy. ACOG Committee Opinion No. 316. American College of Obstetricians and Gynecologists. Obstet Gynecol 2005;106:883–8.

### *Resources for Patients*

American College of Obstetricians and Gynecologists. Alcohol and women. ACOG Patient Education Pamphlet AP068. Washington, DC: ACOG; 2000.

American College of Obstetricians and Gynecologists. Depression. ACOG Patient Education Pamphlet AP106. Washington, DC: ACOG; 2005.

American College of Obstetricians and Gynecologists. Domestic violence. ACOG Patient Education Pamphlet AP083. Washington, DC: ACOG; 2002.

American College of Obstetricians and Gynecologists. It's time to quit smoking. ACOG Patient Education Pamphlet AP065. Washington, DC: ACOG; 2000.

American College of Obstetricians and Gynecologists, Smoke-free families. Need help putting out that cigarette? Washington, DC: ACOG; Chapel Hill (NC): Smoke-Free Families; 2001.

American College of Obstetricians and Gynecologists, Violencia domestica. ACOG Patient Education Pamphlet SP083. Washington, DC: ACOG; 2002.

## References


1. Goldenberg RL, Patterson ET, Freese MP. Maternal demographic, situational and psychosocial factors and their relationship to enrollment in prenatal care: a review of the literature. Women Health 1992;19:133–51.
2. Bertakis KD, Roter D, Putnam SM. The relationship of physician medical interview style to patient satisfaction. J Fam Pract 1991;32:175–81.
3. Institute of Medicine. Preventing low birthweight: summary. Washington, DC: The Institute; 1985.
4. Public Health Service, U.S. Department of Health and Human Services. Caring for our future: the content of prenatal care: a report of the Public Health Service Expert Panel on the Content of Prenatal Care. Washington, DC: PHS, USDHHS; 1989.
5. Enkin M, Keirse MJ, Neilson J, Crowther C, Duley L, Hodnett E, et al. Support for pregnant women. In: A guide to effective care in pregnancy and childbirth. Oxford (UK): Oxford University Press; 2000. p. 16–23.
6. Mulder EJ, Robles de Medina PG, Huizink AC, Van den Bergh BR, Buitelaar JK, Visser GH. Prenatal maternal stress: effects on pregnancy and the (unborn) child. Early Hum Dev 2002;70:3–14.
7. Federenko IS, Wadhwa PD. Women's mental health during pregnancy influences fetal and infant developmental and health outcomes. CNS Spectr 2004;9:198–206.
8. Primary and preventive care: periodic assessments. ACOG Committee Opinion No. 292. American College of Obstetricians and Gynecologists. Obstet Gynecol 2003;102:117–24.
9. American Academy of Pediatrics, American College of Obstetricians and Gynecologists. Guidelines for perinatal care. 5th ed. Elk Grove Village (IL): AAP; Washington, DC: ACOG; 2002.
10. Wilkinson DS, Korenbrot CC, Greene J. A performance indicator of psychosocial services in enhanced prenatal care of Medicaid-eligible women. Matern Child Health J 1998;2:131–43.
11. Brown SS. Drawing women into prenatal care. Fam Plann Perspect 1989;21:73–80.
12. National Center for Health Statistics. Healthy people 2000 review, 1998-99. Hyattsville (MD): NCHS; 1999.
13. Institute of Medicine. The best intentions: unintended pregnancy and the well-being of children and families. Committee on Unintended Pregnancy. Washington, DC: The Institute; 1995.
14. Stewart DE, Cecutti A. Physical abuse in pregnancy. CMAJ 1993;149:1257–63.
15. Fergusson DM, Horwood LJ, Kershaw KL, Shannon FT. Factors associated with reports of wife assault in New Zealand. J Marriage Fam 1986;48:407–12.
16. Obesity in pregnancy. ACOG Committee Opinion No. 315. American College of Obstetricians and Gynecologists. Obstet Gynecol 2005;106:671–5.
17. U.S. Department of Health and Human Services. The health consequences of smoking: a report of the Surgeon General. Washington, DC:USDHHS;2004. Available at: www.cdc.gov/tobacco/sgr/sgr_2004/chapters.htm. Retrieved March 24, 2006.
18. Salihu HM, Aliyu MH, Pierre-Louis BJ, Alexander GR. Levels of excess infant deaths attributable to maternal smoking during pregnancy in the United States. Matern Child Health J 2003;7:219–27.
19. Li YF, Langholz B, Salam MT, Gilliland FD. Maternal and grandmaternal smoking patterns are associated with early childhood asthma. Chest 2005;127:1232–41.
20. Sondergaard C, Henriksen TB, Obel C, Wisborg K. Smoking during pregnancy and infantile colic. Pediatrics 2001;108:342–6.
21. von Kries R, Toschke AM, Koletzko B, Slikker W Jr. Maternal smoking during pregnancy and childhood obesity. Am J Epidemiol 2002;156:954–61.
22. American College of Obstetricians and Gynecologists. Smoking and women's health. In: Special issues in women's health. Washington, DC: ACOG; 2005. p. 151–67.
23. Smoking cessation during pregnancy. ACOG Committee Opinion No. 316. American College of Obstetricians and Gynecologists. Obstet Gynecol 2005;106:883–8.
24. Dolan-Mullen P, Melvin CL, Windsor RA. A review of the evidence to recommend cessation counseling for pregnant women who smoke. Birmingham (AL): Smoke-Free Families Program, Department of Obstetrics and Gynecology, School of Medicine, University of Alabama at Birmingham; 1999.
25. American College of Obstetricians and Gynecologists. Substance use: obstetric and gynecologic implications. In: Special issues in women's health. Washington, DC: ACOG; 2005. p. 105–50.
26. Leibovci A, Chaudron L. Depression. In: Leppert PC, Peipert JF, editors. Primary care for women. 2nd ed. Philadelphia (PA): Lippincott Williams & Wilkins; 2004. p. 875–81.
27. Gaynes BN, Gavin N, Meltzer-Brody S, Lohr KN, Swinson T, Gartlehner G, et al. Perinatal depression: prevalence, screening accuracy, and screening outcomes. Evidence Report/Technology Assessment No. 119. (Prepared by the RTI–University of North Carolina Evidence-based Practice Center, under Contract No. 290-02-0016.) AHRQ Publication No. 05-E006-1. Rockville (MD): Agency for Healthcare Research and Quality; 2005.
28. Zuckerman B, Amaro H, Bauchner H, Cabral H. Depressive symptoms during pregnancy: relationship to poor health behaviors. Am J Obstet Gynecol 1989;160: 1107–11.
29. Pignone M, Gaynes BN, Rushton JL, Mulrow CD, Orleans CT, Whitener BL, et al. Screening for depression. (Prepared by the RTI–University of North Carolina Evidence-based Practice Center under Contract No. 290-97-0011.) Systematic Evidence Review No. 6. Rockville (MD): AHRQ; 2002. Available at: www.ahrq.gov/down

loads/pub/prevent/pdfser/depser.pdf. Retrieved March 24, 2006.

30. Beck CT. Revision of the postpartum depression predictors inventory. Obstet Gynecol Neonatal Nurs 2002;31: 394–402.
31. Screening for depression: recommendations and rationale. U.S. Preventive Services Task Force. Ann Intern Med 2002;136:760–4.
32. Firearm-related injuries affecting the pediatric population. Committee on Injury and Poison Prevention. American Academy of Pediatrics. Pediatrics 2000;105:888–95.
33. Gazmararian JA, Lazorick S, Spitz AM, Ballard TJ, Saltzman LE, Marks JS. Prevalence of violence against pregnant women [published erratum appears in JAMA 1997;277:1125]. JAMA 1996;275:1915–20.
34. Hillard PJ. Physical abuse in pregnancy. Obstet Gynecol 1985;66:185–90.
35. Stewart DE. Incidence of postpartum abuse in women with a history of abuse during pregnancy. CMAJ 1994; 151:1601–4.
36. American College of Obstetricians and Gynecologists. Intimate partner violence and domestic violence. In: Special issues in women's health. Washington, DC: ACOG; 2005. p. 169–88.
37. McFarlane J, Parker B, Soeken K, Bullock L. Assessing for abuse during pregnancy. Severity and frequency of injuries and associated entry into prenatal care. JAMA 1992;267:3176–8.
38. American Medical Association. Diagnostic and treatment guidelines on domestic violence. Chicago (IL): AMA; 1994.
39. Hobel C, Culhane J. Role of psychosocial and nutritional stress on poor pregnancy outcome. J Nutr 2003;133 (suppl 2):1709S–17S.
40. Hedegaard M, Henriksen TB, Sabroe S, Secher NJ. Psychological distress in pregnancy and preterm delivery. BMJ 1993;307:234–9.
41. Rini CK, Dunkel-Schetter C, Wadhwa PD, Sandman CA. Psychological adaptation and birth outcomes: the role of personal resources, stress, and sociocultural context in pregnancy. Health Psychol 1999;18:333–45.
42. Wadhwa PD, Sandman CA, Porto M, Dunkel-Schetter C, Garite TJ. The association between prenatal stress and infant birth weight and gestational age at birth: a prospective investigation. Am J Obstet Gynecol 1993;169:858–65.
43. Paarlberg KM, Vingerhoets AJ, Passchier J, Dekker GA, Van Geijn HP. Psychosocial factors and pregnancy outcome: a review with emphasis on methodological issues. J Psychosom Res 1995;39:563–95.
44. Teixeira JM, Fisk NM, Glover V. Association between maternal anxiety in pregnancy and increased uterine artery resistance index: cohort based study. BMJ 1999; 318:153–7.
45. Wadhwa PD, Porto M, Garite TJ, Chicz-DeMet A, Sandman CA. Maternal corticotropin-releasing hormone levels in the early third trimester predict length of gestation in human pregnancy. Am J Obstet Gynecol 1998; 179:1079–85.
46. Hobel CJ, Dunkel-Schetter C, Roesch SC, Castro LC, Arora CP. Maternal plasma corticotropin-releasing hormone associated with stress at 20 weeks' gestation in pregnancies ending in preterm delivery. Am J Obstet Gynecol 1999;180:S257–63.
47. Copper RL, Goldenberg RL, Das A, Elder N, Swain M, Norman G, et al. The preterm prediction study: maternal stress is associated with spontaneous preterm birth at less than thirty-five weeks' gestation. National Institute of Child Health and Human Development Maternal-Fetal Medicine Units Network. Am J Obstet Gynecol 1996; 175:1286–92.
48. Cohen S. Psychosocial models of the role of social support in the etiology of physical disease. Health Psychol 1988;7:269–97.
49. Orr ST. Social support and pregnancy outcome: a review of the literature. Clin Obstet Gynecol 2004;47:842–55; discussion 881–2.

# COMMITTEE OPINIONS

## COMMITTEE ON OBSTETRIC PRACTICE

# COMMITTEE OPINIONS

## COMMITTEE ON OBSTETRIC PRACTICE *(Continued)*



*Published in 2006

Committee on Obstetrics: Maternal and Fetal Medicine

Number 125—July 1993
*(Replaces #102, December 1991)*

# Placental Pathology

Recently, there has been heightened interest in clinical–pathologic correlation between placental abnormalities and adverse pregnancy outcome. When a skilled and systematic examination of the umbilical cord, membranes, and placenta is performed on properly prepared specimens, insight into antepartum pathophysiology may be gained under certain circumstances.

In most of these instances, such as chorioamnionitis, the diagnosis already will have been made on clinical grounds, with the placental examination providing confirmation. In other cases of poor outcome, a disorder that was not suspected clinically may be revealed by placental pathology. Examples of pathologic findings and the disorders they suggest include the microabscesses of listeriosis and amnion nodosum suggesting long-standing oligohydramnios. The underlying pathophysiology of these lesions has been confirmed by laboratory testing or consistent and specific clinical associations.

The significance of other findings, such as villous edema, hemorrhagic endovasculitis, and chronic villitis, has not been as well delineated. These lesions, among others, have been variously reported to correlate with poor short-term and long-term neonatal outcome. The paucity of properly designed studies of adequate size with appropriate outcome parameters has prevented universal agreement as to positive predictive values, underlying pathophysiology, or even the consistency of clinical correlations with these findings. Furthermore, the distribution of pathologists with the expertise to interpret more subtle placental findings is uneven from region to region. Although a protocol for obtaining routine placental pathologic examination under certain obstetric and neonatal conditions has been recommended (1), there are few data to support the clinical utility of this approach.

In addition to the issue of positive and negative predictive values of the spectrum of placental findings, there are practical concerns regarding examination of the placenta. In some instances, a neonatal problem may not be ascertained until days or weeks after birth, when the placenta is no longer available. Different approaches have been recommended to address this problem, including routinely examining all placentas, securing a small section from each placenta in a fixed state for an indefinite period, and saving all placentas unfixed at 4°C for 1 week before discarding. However, routine determinations of placental pathology are not feasible on either a cost or manpower basis, and a small portion of placenta obtained at random would be unlikely to provide useful information. The practice of saving all placentas for 1 week after delivery would permit ascertaining most neonatal problems in which pathologic examination of the placenta may be appropriate, but the effectiveness of this approach has not been proven.

In conclusion, an examination of the umbilical cord, membranes, and placenta may assist the obstetric care provider in clinical–pathologic correlation when there is an adverse perinatal outcome. However, the scientific basis for clinical correlation with placental pathology is still evolving, and the benefit of securing specimens on a routine basis is as yet unproven. Continued research and education in this field should be encouraged. Research should be designed with the goal of defining clinical indications for placental examination. In contrast, pathologic examination of the stillborn fetus and placenta is always potentially informative. Obstetric providers should be persistent in seeking consent from parents for autopsy examinations.

## REFERENCE

1. College of American Pathologists Conference XIX. The examination of the placenta: patient care and risk management. Arch Pathol Lab Med 1991;115: 641–732

The American College of Obstetricians and Gynecologists
409 12th Street, SW • Washington, DC 20024-2188

12345/76543

ACOG Committee Opinion

Committee on Obstetric Practice

Number 228, November 1999

# Induction of Labor with Misoprostol

Induction of labor is a common obstetric intervention in the United States, occurring in up to 15% of all pregnancies. The American College of Obstetricians and Gynecologists supports induction of labor as a worthwhile therapeutic option when the benefits of expeditious delivery outweigh the risks of continuing the pregnancy (1). Prostaglandin $E_2$ ($PGE_2$), applied locally to the cervix or vagina, has been widely studied as an induction agent, and has been found to be safe and effective (2, 3). Two such agents have been approved by the U.S. Food and Drug Administration for this purpose and are commercially available as dinoprostone preparations. Recent studies have explored the effectiveness and safety of misoprostol for induction of labor. This prostaglandin $E_1$ analogue is less expensive, more stable, and easier to store than dinoprostone preparations. However, misoprostol currently is approved by the U.S. Food and Drug Administration for the treatment of peptic ulcer disease and not for induction of labor. Moreover, the manufacturer does not plan to pursue approval for this indication (4).

At least 19 prospective, randomized clinical trials involving more than 1,900 patients receiving doses of misoprostol ranging from 25 mcg to 200 mcg in a variety of dosage schedules have been performed. Most researchers have administered misoprostol in tablet form into the posterior fornix of the vagina, but it also has been mixed into a hydroxymethylcellulose gel or applied intracervically.

In general, misoprostol has been found to be an effective agent for the induction of labor. When compared with placebo, misoprostol use decreased oxytocin requirements and achieved higher rates of vaginal delivery within 24 hours of induction. Misoprostol also compared favorably with intracervical and intravaginal $PGE_2$ preparations; many studies demonstrated shorter times to delivery and reduced oxytocin requirements after misoprostol administration (5). Some studies suggest that misoprostol may reduce the rate of cesarean delivery, but further randomized clinical trials using the 25 mcg dose are required to confirm this observation (5). There have been reports of uterine rupture following misoprostol use for cervical ripening in patients with prior uterine surgery. Thus, until reassuring studies are available, misoprostol is not recommended for cervical ripening in patients who have had prior cesarean delivery or major uterine surgery (6).

When given in doses of 50 mcg or more, misoprostol use has been associated with an increased rate of uterine tachysystole (six or more uterine con-

This document reflects emerging clinical and scientific advances as of the date issued and is subject to change. The information should not be construed as dictating an exclusive course of treatment or procedure to be followed.



ISSN 1074-861X

**The American College of Obstetricians and Gynecologists**
409 12th Street, SW
PO Box 96920
Washington, DC 20090-6920

12345/32109

tractions in 10 minutes in consecutive 10-minute intervals) compared with either placebo or $PGE_2$ preparations. In two studies in which 50 mcg of misoprostol was administered intravaginally every 4 hours, researchers found increased rates of meconium passage (7) and cesarean delivery due to uterine hyperstimulation syndrome (8) when compared with dinoprostone. However, an increase in neonatal morbidity after misoprostol administration has not been documented. In trials where 25 mcg of misoprostol was administered intravaginally as frequently as every 3 hours, there did not appear to be an increase in uterine tachysystole, hyperstimulation, or meconium passage when compared with $PGE_2$ (9, 10). Moreover, this dosing regimen appeared to be at least as effective in inducing labor as the $PGE_2$ preparations.

Currently, misoprostol is available in 100 mcg and 200 mcg tablets, and the 100 mcg tablet is not scored. If misoprostol is used for cervical ripening and induction, one quarter of a 100 mcg tablet (ie, approximately 25 mcg) should be considered for the initial dose.

Given the current evidence, intravaginal misoprostol tablets appear to be effective in inducing labor in pregnant women who have unfavorable cervices. The use of higher doses (50 mcg every 6 hours) may be appropriate in some situations, although increasing the dose appears to be associated most closely with uterine tachysystole and possibly with uterine hyperstimulation and meconium staining of amniotic fluid. Further prospective trials are required to define an optimal dosing regimen for misoprostol. However, misoprostol is not recommended for patients with prior uterine surgery (11). Patients undergoing such therapy should receive fetal heart rate and uterine activity monitoring in a hospital setting until further studies evaluate and confirm the safety of outpatient therapy.

## References


1. American College of Obstetricians and Gynecologists. Induction of labor. ACOG Practice Bulletin. Washington, DC: ACOG, 1999
2. Brindley BA, Sokol RJ. Induction and augmentation of labor: basis and methods for current practice. Obstet Gynecol Surv 1988;43:730–743
3. Rayburn WF. Prostaglandin $E_2$ gel for cervical ripening and induction of labor: a critical analysis. Am J Obstet Gynecol 1989;160:529–534
4. Bauer TA, Brown D, Chai LK. Vaginal misoprostol for term labor induction. Ann Pharmacother 1997;31: 1391–1393
5. Sanchez-Ramos L, Kaunitz AM, Wears RL, Delke I, Gaudier FL. Misoprostol for cervical ripening and labor induction: a meta-analysis. Obstet Gynecol 1997;89: 633–642
6. Hofmeyr GJ. Vaginal misoprostol for cervical ripening and labour induction in late pregnancy. The Cochrane Library 1999; Issue 2:1–18 (Meta-analysis)
7. Wing DA, Jones MM, Rahall A, Goodwin TM, Paul RH. A comparison of misoprostol and prostaglandin $E_2$ gel for preinduction cervical ripening and labor induction. Am J Obstet Gynecol 1995;172:1804–1810
8. Buser D, Mora G, Arias F. A randomized comparison between misoprostol and dinoprostone for cervical ripening and labor induction in patients with unfavorable cervices. Obstet Gynecol 1997;89:581–585
9. Wing DA, Paul RH. A comparison of different dosing regimens of vaginally administered misoprostol for preinduction cervical ripening and labor induction. Am J Obstet Gynecol 1996;175:158–164
10. Wing DA, Ortiz-Omphroy G, Paul RH. A comparison of intermittent vaginal administration of misoprostol with continuous dinoprostone for cervical ripening and labor induction. Am J Obstet Gynecol 1997;177:612–618
11. Wing DA, Lovett K, Paul RH. Disruption of prior uterine incision following misoprostol for labor induction in women with previous cesarean section. Obstet Gynecol 1998;91:828–830

ACOG Committee Opinion

Committee on Obstetric Practice

Number 234, May 2000 (*Replaces No. 219, August 1999*)

# Scheduled Cesarean Delivery and the Prevention of Vertical Transmission of HIV Infection



ISSN 1074-861X

**The American College of Obstetricians and Gynecologists**
409 12th Street, SW
PO Box 96920
Washington, DC 20090-6920

12345/43210

Prevention of transmission of the human immunodeficiency virus (HIV) from mother to fetus or newborn (vertical transmission) is a major goal in the care of pregnant women infected with HIV. An important advance in this regard was the demonstration that treatment of the mother with zidovudine (ZDV) during pregnancy and labor and of the neonate for the first 6 weeks after birth could reduce the transmission rate from 25% to 8% (1).

Continuing research into vertical transmission of HIV suggests that a substantial number of cases occur as the result of fetal exposure to the virus during labor and delivery; the precise mechanisms are not known. Transmission could occur by transplacental maternal–fetal microtransfusion of blood contaminated with the virus during uterine contractions or by exposure to the virus in maternal cervicovaginal secretions and blood at delivery. Data also indicate that the risk of vertical transmission is proportional to the concentration of virus in maternal plasma (viral load). At very low concentrations of virus in maternal plasma (viral load less than 1,000 copies per milliliter), the observed incidence of vertical transmission among 141 mother–infant pairs was 0 with a 95% upper confidence bound of about 2% (2, 3).

In theory, the risk of vertical transmission in mothers with high viral loads could be reduced by performing cesarean deliveries before the onset of labor and before rupture of membranes (termed *scheduled cesarean delivery* in this document). Early studies of the relationship between the mode of delivery and the risk of vertical transmission yielded inconsistent results. Data from two prospective cohort studies (4, 5), an international randomized trial (6), and a meta-analysis of individual patient data from 15 prospective cohort studies, including more than 7,800 mother–child pairs (7), indicate that there is a significant relationship between the mode of delivery and vertical transmission of HIV. This body of evidence, accumulated mostly before the use of highly active antiretroviral therapy (HAART) and without any data regarding maternal viral load, indicates that scheduled cesarean delivery reduces the likelihood of vertical transmission of HIV compared with either unscheduled cesarean delivery or vaginal delivery. This finding holds true whether or not the patient is receiving ZDV therapy. Whether cesarean delivery offers any benefit to women on HAART or to women with low or undetectable maternal viral loads is unknown. Data are insufficient to address the question of how long after the onset of labor or rupture of membranes the benefit is lost. It is clear that maternal morbidity is greater with cesarean delivery than with vaginal delivery, as is true for women not infected with HIV (8–10). Increases in postpartum morbidity seem to be greatest among women infected with HIV who have low CD4 cell counts (9).

Although many issues remain unresolved because of insufficient data, there is consensus that the following should be recommended:

- Patients should be counseled that in the absence of antiretroviral therapy, the risk of vertical transmission is approximately 25%. With ZDV therapy, the risk is reduced to 5–8%. When care includes both ZDV therapy and scheduled cesarean delivery, the risk is approximately 2%. A similar risk of 2% or less is seen among women with viral loads of less than 1,000 copies per milliliter, even without the systematic use of scheduled cesarean delivery. No combination of therapies can guarantee that a newborn will not become infected (a 0% transmission rate).
- Women infected with HIV, whose viral loads are greater than 1,000 copies per milliliter, should be counseled regarding the potential benefit of scheduled cesarean delivery to further reduce the risk of vertical transmission of HIV beyond that achievable with antiretroviral therapy alone.
- Neonates of women at highest risk for vertical transmission, with relatively high plasma viral loads, are most likely to benefit from scheduled cesarean delivery. Data are insufficient to demonstrate a benefit for neonates of women with plasma viral loads of less than 1,000 copies per milliliter. The available data indicate no reduction in the transmission rate if cesarean delivery is performed after the onset of labor or rupture of membranes. The decision regarding the route of delivery must be individualized in these circumstances.
- The patient's autonomy in making the decision regarding route of delivery must be respected. A patient's informed decision to undergo vaginal delivery must be honored, with cesarean delivery performed only for other accepted indications and with patient consent.
- Patients should receive antiretroviral chemotherapy during pregnancy according to currently accepted guidelines for adults (11). This should not be interrupted around the time of cesarean delivery. For those patients receiving ZDV, adequate levels of the drug in the blood should be achieved if the infusion is begun 3 hours preoperatively (1), according to the dosing schedule recommended by the Centers for Disease Control and Prevention (www.cdc.gov/hiv/treatment).
- Because morbidity is increased in HIV-infected women undergoing cesarean delivery, physicians should consider using prophylactic antibiotics during all such cesarean deliveries.
- The American College of Obstetricians and Gynecologists generally recommends that scheduled cesarean deliveries not be performed before 39 completed weeks of gestation. In women with HIV infection, however, delivery at 38 completed weeks of gestation is recommended to reduce the likelihood of onset of labor or rupture of membranes before delivery.
- Best clinical estimates of gestational age should be used for planning cesarean delivery. Amniocentesis to determine fetal lung maturity in pregnant women infected with HIV should be avoided whenever possible.
- Current recommendations for adults indicate that plasma viral load should be determined at baseline and then every 3 months or following changes in therapy (11). Plasma viral load should be monitored, according to these guidelines, during pregnancy as well. The patient's most recently determined viral load should be used to direct counseling regarding mode of delivery.
- Preoperative maternal health status affects the degree of risk of maternal morbidity associated with cesarean delivery. All women should be clearly informed of the risks associated with cesarean delivery. Ultimately, the decision to perform a cesarean delivery must be individualized in each case according to circumstances.

A skin-penetrating injury (eg, needlestick or scalpel laceration) is a risk to care providers during all deliveries, vaginal or cesarean. This risk is not greater during cesarean delivery, although there generally are more health care personnel present and, thus, at risk during a cesarean delivery than during a vaginal delivery (12). Appropriate care and precautions against such injuries always should be taken, but these concerns should not affect decisions regarding route of delivery (13).

In summary, cesarean delivery performed before the onset of labor and before rupture of membranes effectively reduces the risk of vertical transmission of HIV infection. Scheduled cesarean delivery should be discussed and recommended for women with viral loads greater than 1,000 copies per milliliter whether or not they are taking antiretroviral therapy. As with all complex clinical decisions, the choice of delivery must be individualized. Discussion of the option of scheduled cesarean delivery should begin as early as possible in pregnancy with every pregnant woman with HIV infection to give her an adequate opportunity to consider the choice and plan for the procedure. The risks, which are greater for the mother, must be balanced with the benefits expected for the neonate. The patient's autonomy must be respected when making the decision to perform a cesarean delivery, because the potential for maternal morbidity is significant.

## References

1. Connor EM, Sperling RS, Gelber R, Kiselev P, Scott G, O'Sullivan MJ, et al. Reduction of maternal-infant transmission of human immunodeficiency virus type 1 with zidovudine treatment. Pediatric AIDS Clinical Trials Group Protocol 076 Study Group. N Engl J Med 1994;331:1173–1180
2. Mofenson LM, Lambert JS, Stiehm ER, Bethel J, Meyer WA 3rd, Whitehouse J, et al. Risk factors for perinatal transmission of human immunodeficiency virus type 1 in women treated with zidovudine. Pediatric AIDS Clinical Trials Group Study 185 Team. N Engl J Med 1999;341:385–393
3. Garcia PM, Kalish LA, Pitt J, Minkoff H, Quinn T, Burchett SK, et al. Maternal levels of plasma human immunodeficiency virus type 1 RNA and the risk of perinatal transmission. Women and Infants Transmission Study Group. N Engl J Med 1999;341:394–402
4. Kind C, Rudin C, Siegrist CA, Wyler CA, Biedermann K, Lauper U, et al. Prevention of vertical HIV transmission: additive protective effect of elective cesarean section and zidovudine prophylaxis. AIDS 1998;12:205–210
5. Mandelbrot L, Le Chenadec J, Berrebi A, Bongain A, Benifla JL, Delfraissy JF, et al. Perinatal HIV-1 transmission: interaction between zidovudine prophylaxis and mode of delivery in the French Perinatal Cohort. JAMA 1998;280:55–60
6. The European Mode of Delivery Collaboration. Elective caesarean-section versus vaginal delivery in prevention of vertical HIV-1 transmission: a randomized clinical trial. Lancet 1999;353:1035–1039
7. The International Perinatal HIV Group. The mode of delivery and the risk of vertical transmission of human immunodeficiency virus type 1: a meta-analysis of 15 prospective cohort studies. N Engl J Med 1999;340:977–987
8. Nielsen TF, Hakegaard KH. Postoperative cesarean section morbidity: a prospective study. Am J Obstet Gynecol 1983; 146:911–915
9. Semprini AE, Castagna C, Ravizza M, Fiore S, Savasi V, Muggiasca ML, et al. The incidence of complications after cesarean section in 156 HIV-positive women. AIDS 1996; 9:913–917
10. Bulterys M, Chao A, Dushimimana A, Saah A. Fatal complications after cesarean section in HIV-infected women. AIDS 1996;10:923–924
11. Centers for Disease Control and Prevention. Report of the NIH Panel to define principles of therapy of HIV infection and guidelines for the use of antiretroviral agents in HIV-infected adults and adolescents. MMWR Morb Mortal Wkly Rep 1998;47(RR-5):1–82
12. Duff P, Robertson AW, Read JA. Single-dose cefazolin versus cefonicid for antibiotic prophylaxis in cesarean delivery. Obstet Gynecol 1987;70:718–721
13. Centers for Disease Control. Update: universal precautions for prevention of transmission of human immunodeficiency virus, hepatitis B virus, and other bloodborne pathogens in health-care settings. MMWR Morb Mortal Wkly Rep 1988;37:377–382;387–388

## Bibliography

Rodman JH, Robbins BL, Flynn PM, Fridland A. A systematic and cellular model for zidovudine plasma concentrations and intracellular phosphorylation in patients. J Infect Dis 1996;174: 490–499

# ACOG Committee Opinion

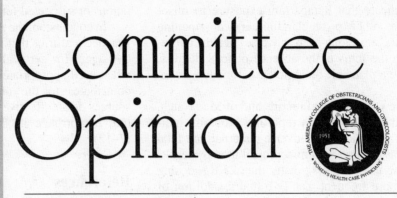

Committee on Obstetric Practice

Number 248, December 2000

## Response to Searle's Drug Warning on Misoprostol

On August 23, 2000, G.D. Searle & Co. issued a letter entitled "Important Drug Warning Concerning Unapproved Use of Intravaginal or Oral Misoprostol in Pregnant Women for Induction of Labor or Abortion." This letter cautions that Cytotec (misoprostol) is indicated for prevention of nonsteroidal-antiinflammatory-drug-induced gastric ulcers and states, *"...Cytotec administration by any route is contraindicated in women who are pregnant because it can cause abortion."* The letter further states that Searle has become aware of the drug's use for induction of labor or as a cervical ripening agent prior to termination of pregnancy. Moreover, the letter notes serious adverse events, including uterine hyperstimulation and uterine rupture, which have resulted in fetal and maternal death. Finally, the company cautions, *"In addition to the known and unknown acute risks to the mother and fetus, the effect of Cytotec on the later growth, development, and functional maturation of the child when Cytotec is used for induction of labor or cervical ripening has not been established."*

The American College of Obstetricians and Gynecologists (ACOG) is concerned about the content, timing, and tone of this letter. Given that misoprostol is commonly employed in conjunction with mifepristone (RU 486) to achieve nonsurgical early pregnancy terminations, the arrival of the Searle letter within weeks of the U.S. Food and Drug Administration's (FDA) approval of mifepristone could limit the use of this new option for reproductive choice. Also, although the letter correctly points out the potentially serious, but relatively rare, risks of misoprostol when employed for cervical ripening and labor induction, it fails to comment on the extensive clinical experience with this agent and the large body of published reports supporting its safety and efficacy when used appropriately. A recent review of the Cochrane Pregnancy and Childbirth group trials registry identified 26 clinical trials of misoprostol for cervical ripening or induction of labor or both (1). These studies indicate misoprostol is more effective than prostaglandin $E_2$ in achieving vaginal deliveries within 24 hours and reduces the need for and total amount of oxytocin augmentation. Although these studies do suggest misoprostol is associated with a higher incidence of uterine hyperstimulation and meconium-stained amniotic fluid, these complications were more common with higher doses (>25 μg) of misoprostol. Other recent reviews and

This document reflects emerging clinical and scientific advances as of the date issued and is subject to change. The information should not be construed as dictating an exclusive course of treatment or procedure to be followed.



ISSN 1074-861X

**The American College of Obstetricians and Gynecologists**
409 12th Street, SW
PO Box 96920
Washington, DC 20090-6920

12345/43210

clinical trials support these conclusions (2–4). No studies indicate that intrapartum exposure to misoprostol (or other prostaglandin cervical ripening agents) has any long-term adverse health consequences to the fetus in the absence of fetal distress, nor is there a plausible biologic basis for such a concern.

A review of published reports and of MedWatch, the FDA medical products reporting program, indicates the vast majority of adverse maternal and fetal outcomes associated with misoprostol therapy resulted from the use of doses greater than 25 μg, dosing intervals more frequent than 3–6 hours, addition of oxytocin less than 4 hours after the last misoprostol dose, or use of the drug in women with prior cesarean delivery or major uterine surgery. Grand multiparity also appears to be a relative risk factor for uterine rupture.

Thus, based on recently published series and a detailed review of adverse outcomes reported to the FDA, the ACOG Committee on Obstetric Practice strongly endorses its previous conclusion, published in Committee Opinion Number 228 (November 1999), *Induction of Labor with Misoprostol*, which states, *"Given the current evidence, intravaginal misoprostol tablets appear effective in inducing labor in pregnant women who have unfavorable cervices"* (5). Nonetheless, the committee would like to emphasize that the following clinical practices appear to minimize the risk of uterine hyperstimulation and rupture in patients undergoing cervical ripening or induction in the third trimester:

1. If misoprostol is to be used for cervical ripening or labor induction in the third trimester, one quarter of a 100-μg tablet (ie, approximately 25 μg) should be considered for the initial dose.
2. Doses should not be administered more frequently than every 3–6 hours.
3. Oxytocin should not be administered less than 4 hours after the last misoprostol dose.
4. Misoprostol should not be used in patients with a previous cesarean delivery or prior major uterine surgery.

The use of higher doses of misoprostol (eg, 50 μg every 6 hours) to induce labor may be appropriate in some situations, although there are reports that such doses increase the risk of complications, including uterine hyperstimulation and uterine rupture (6). There is insufficient clinical evidence to address the safety or efficacy of misoprostol in patients with multifetal gestations or suspected fetal macrosomia.

In conclusion, the ACOG Committee on Obstetric Practice reaffirms that misoprostol is a safe and effective agent for cervical ripening and labor induction when used appropriately. Moreover, misoprostol also contributes to the obstetrician–gynecologist's resources as an effective treatment for serious postpartum hemorrhage in the presence of uterine atony (7–12).

## References


1. Hofmeyr GJ, Gulmezoglu AM. Vaginal misoprostol for cervical ripening and labour induction in late pregnancy (Cochrane Review). In: The Cochrane Library, Issue 3, 2000. Oxford: Update Software
2. Wing DA. Labor induction with misoprostol. Am J Obstet Gynecol 1999;181:339–345
3. Nunes F, Rodrigues R, Meirinho M. Randomized comparison between intravaginal misoprostol and dinoprostone for cervical ripening and induction of labor. Am J Obstet Gynecol 1999;181:626–629
4. Blanchette HA, Nayak S, Erasmus S. Comparison of the safety and efficacy of intravaginal misoprostol (prostaglandin E1) with those of dinoprostone (prostaglandin E2) for cervical ripening and induction of labor in a community hospital. Am J Obstet Gynecol 1999;180:1551–1559
5. American College of Obstetricians and Gynecologists. Induction of labor with misoprostol. ACOG Committee Opinion 228. Washington, DC: ACOG, 1999
6. American College of Obstetricians and Gynecologists. Induction of labor. ACOG Practice Bulletin 10. Washington, DC: ACOG, 1999
7. El-Refaey H, O'Brien P, Morafa W, Walder J, Rodeck C. Use of oral misoprostol in the prevention of postpartum haemorrhage. Br J Obstet Gynaecol 1997;104:336–339
8. O'Brien P, El-Refaey H, Gordon A, Geary M, Rodeck CH. Rectally administered misoprostol for the treatment of postpartum hemorrhage unresponsive to oxytocin and ergometrine: a descriptive study. Obstet Gynecol 1998;92:212–214
9. Bamigboye AA, Hofmeyr GJ, Merrell DA. Rectal misoprostol in the prevention of postpartum hemorrhage: a placebo-controlled trial. Am J Obstet Gynecol 1998;179:1043–1046
10. Surbek DV, Fehr PM, Hosli I, Holzgreve W. Oral misoprostol for third stage of labor: a randomized placebo-controlled trial. Obstet Gynecol 1999;94:255–258
11. Hofmeyr GJ, Nikodem VC, de Jager M, Gelbart BR. A randomised placebo controlled trial of oral misoprostol in the third stage of labour. Br J Obstet Gynaecol 1998;105:971–975
12. Bamigboye AA, Merrell DA, Hofmeyr GJ, Mitchell R. Randomized comparison of rectal misoprostol with Syntometrine for management of third stage of labor. Acta Obstet Gynecol Scand 1998;77:178–181

ACOG Committee on Obstetric Practice

American Society of Anesthesiologists Committee on Obstetric Anesthesia

# Committee Opinion

Number 256, May 2001

## Optimal Goals for Anesthesia Care in Obstetrics

This joint statement from the American Society of Anesthesiologists (ASA) and the American College of Obstetricians and Gynecologists (ACOG) has been designed to address issues of concern to both specialties. Good obstetric care requires the availability of qualified personnel and equipment to administer general or regional anesthesia both electively and emergently. The extent and degree to which anesthesia services are available varies widely among hospitals. However, for any hospital providing obstetric care, certain optimal anesthesia goals should be sought. These include:

I. Availability of a licensed practitioner who is credentialed to administer an appropriate anesthetic whenever necessary
For many women, regional anesthesia (epidural, spinal, or combined spinal epidural) will be the most appropriate anesthetic.

II. Availability of a licensed practitioner who is credentialed to maintain support of vital functions in any obstetric emergency

III. Availability of anesthesia and surgical personnel to permit the start of a cesarean delivery within 30 minutes of the decision to perform the procedure; in cases of vaginal birth after cesarean delivery (VBAC), appropriate facilities and personnel, including obstetric anesthesia, nursing personnel, and a physician capable of monitoring labor and performing cesarean delivery, immediately available during active labor to perform an emergency cesarean delivery (1)
The definition of immediately available personnel and facilities remains a local decision based on each institution's available resources and geographic location.

IV. Appointment of a qualified anesthesiologist to be responsible for all anesthetics administered
There are many obstetric units where obstetricians or obstetrician-supervised nurse anesthetists administer anesthetics. The administration of general or regional anesthesia requires both medical judgment and technical skills. Thus, a physician with privileges in anesthesiology should be readily available.

This document reflects emerging clinical and scientific advances as of the date issued and is subject to change. The information should not be construed as dictating an exclusive course of treatment or procedure to be followed.



ISSN 1074-861X

**The American College of Obstetricians and Gynecologists**
409 12th Street, SW
PO Box 96920
Washington, DC 20090-6920

12345/54321

Persons administering or supervising obstetric anesthesia should be qualified to manage the infrequent but occasionally life-threatening complications of major regional anesthesia such as respiratory and cardiovascular failure, toxic local anesthetic convulsions, or vomiting and aspiration. Mastering and retaining the skills and knowledge necessary to manage these complications require adequate training and frequent application.

To ensure the safest and most effective anesthesia for obstetric patients, the director of anesthesia services, with the approval of the medical staff, should develop and enforce written policies regarding provision of obstetric anesthesia. These include:

I. Availability of a qualified physician with obstetric privileges to perform operative vaginal or cesarean delivery during administration of anesthesia

Regional and/or general anesthesia should not be administered until the patient has been examined and the fetal status and progress of labor evaluated by a qualified individual. A physician with obstetric privileges who has knowledge of the maternal and fetal status and the progress of labor, and who approves the initiation of labor anesthesia should be readily available to deal with any obstetric complications that may arise.

II. Availability of equipment, facilities, and support personnel equal to that provided in the surgical suite

This should include the availability of a properly equipped and staffed recovery room capable of receiving and caring for all patients recovering from major regional or general anesthesia. Birthing facilities, when used for analgesia or anesthesia, must be appropriately equipped to provide safe anesthetic care during labor and delivery or postanesthesia recovery care.

III. Personnel other than the surgical team should be immediately available to assume responsibility for resuscitation of the depressed newborn

The surgeon and anesthesiologist are responsible for the mother and may not be able to leave her to care for the newborn even when a regional anesthetic is functioning adequately. Individuals qualified to perform neonatal resuscitation should demonstrate:

A. Proficiency in rapid and accurate evaluation of the newborn condition, including Apgar scoring

B. Knowledge of the pathogenesis of a depressed newborn (acidosis, drugs, hypovolemia, trauma, anomalies, and infection), as well as specific indications for resuscitation

C. Proficiency in newborn airway management, laryngoscopy, endotracheal intubations, suctioning of airways, artificial ventilation, cardiac massage, and maintenance of thermal stability

In larger maternity units and those functioning as high-risk centers, 24-hour in-house anesthesia, obstetric and neonatal specialists are usually necessary. Preferably, the obstetric anesthesia services should be directed by an anesthesiologist with special training or experience in obstetric anesthesia. These units will also frequently require the availability of more sophisticated monitoring equipment and specially trained nursing personnel.

A survey jointly sponsored by the ASA and ACOG found that many hospitals in the United States have not yet achieved the goals mentioned previously. Deficiencies were most evident in smaller delivery units. Some small delivery units are necessary because of geographic considerations. Currently, approximately 50% of hospitals providing obstetric care have fewer than 500 deliveries per year. Providing comprehensive care for obstetric patients in these small units is extremely inefficient, not cost-effective and frequently impossible. Thus, the following recommendations are made:

1. Whenever possible, small units should consolidate.
2. When geographic factors require the existence of smaller units, these units should be part of a well-established regional perinatal system.

The availability of the appropriate personnel to assist in the management of a variety of obstetric problems is a necessary feature of good obstetric care. The presence of a pediatrician or other trained physician at a high-risk cesarean delivery to care for the newborn or the availability of an anesthesiologist during active labor and delivery when VBAC is attempted and at a breech or twin delivery are examples. Frequently, these professionals spend a considerable amount of time standing by for the possibility that their services may be needed emergently but may ultimately not be required to perform the tasks for which they are present. Reasonable compensation for these standby services is justifiable and necessary.

A variety of other mechanisms have been suggested to increase the availability and quality of anesthesia services in obstetrics. Improved hospital design, to place labor and delivery suites closer to the operating rooms, would allow for more efficient supervision of nurse anesthetists. Anesthesia equipment in the labor and delivery area must be comparable to that in the operating room.

Finally, good interpersonal relations between obstetricians and anesthesiologists are important. Joint meetings between the two departments should be encouraged. Anesthesiologists should recognize the special needs and concerns of the obstetrician and obstetricians should recognize the anesthesiologist as a consultant in the management of pain and life-support measures. Both should recognize the need to provide high quality care for all patients.

## Reference

1. American College of Obstetricians and Gynecologists. Vaginal birth after previous cesarean delivery. ACOG Practice Bulletin 5. Washington, DC: ACOG, 1999

## Bibliography

Committee on Perinatal Health. Toward improving the outcome of pregnancy: the 90s and beyond. White Plains, New York: March of Dimes Birth Defects Foundation, 1993

ACOG

Committee on Obstetric Practice

Committee Opinion

Number 258, September 2001

# Fetal Pulse Oximetry

*ABSTRACT: The U.S. Food and Drug Administration recently approved the marketing of the Nellcor N-400 Fetal Oxygen Saturation Monitoring System, a fetal pulse oximeter. The American College of Obstetricians and Gynecologists Committee on Obstetric Practice cannot endorse the adoption of this device in clinical practice at this time because of concerns that its introduction could further escalate the cost of medical care without necessarily improving clinical outcome. The committee recommends that prospective randomized clinical trials be conducted to evaluate the clinical use of this new technology in conjunction with fetal well-being assessment.*

Electronic fetal heart rate (FHR) monitoring is used routinely in labor to screen for fetal well-being. The diagnostic value of FHR monitoring is limited. When the FHR tracing is reassuring, it has a predictive value of 99% for fetal well-being, while an abnormal FHR tracing has a positive predictive value of only 50% for fetal compromise. Over the past three decades, the national cesarean delivery rate has increased significantly, in part, as a result of this technology intended to reduce perinatal morbidity and mortality and to prevent long-term neurologic damage. To further refine assessment of fetal well-being in labor, several diagnostic and intervention techniques have been introduced (eg, fetal scalp pH sampling, fetal scalp stimulation, and fetal acoustic stimulation). None of these methods have been universally or routinely adopted by clinicians.

The U.S. Food and Drug Administration (FDA) recently approved the marketing of the Nellcor N-400 Fetal Oxygen Saturation Monitoring System, a fetal pulse oximeter. The device's primary proposed use is as an adjunct to FHR monitoring to continuously monitor fetal intrapartum oxygen saturation in a singleton vertex fetus with a gestational age equal to or greater than 36 weeks in the presence of a nonreassuring heart rate pattern after fetal membranes have ruptured.

It is essential to recognize that the FDA primarily evaluates a device's safety and ability to accurately measure or quantify a certain physiologic function. It appears from the data supplied to the FDA by the company that this device, under certain conditions, can assess fetal oxygenation safely and effectively. The FDA had no additional outcome data available.

In a company-sponsored study, it has been reported that when the Nellcor N-400 Fetal Oxygen Saturation Monitoring System is used in conjunction



ISSN 1074-861X

**The American College of Obstetricians and Gynecologists**
409 12th Street, SW
PO Box 96920
Washington, DC 20090-6920

12345/54321

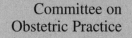

Fetal pulse oximetry. ACOG Committee Opinion No. 258. American College of Obstetricians and Gynecologists. Obstet Gynecol 2001;98:523-524

with FHR monitoring (under specific conditions), there was a reduction in cesarean delivery rates for nonreassuring FHR tracings, but there was no difference in the overall cesarean delivery rates as a result of an increase in cesarean delivery for dystocia (1). Several environmental factors and physiologic events (eg, fetal scalp congestion, color and thickness of fetal hair, skin thickness, vernix caseosa, site of application, fetal presentation, uterine activity, movement artifacts) can affect the accuracy of the fetal pulse oximetry readings. Reliable readings can be obtained approximately 60–70% of the time.

The American College of Obstetricians and Gynecologists Committee on Obstetric Practice currently cannot endorse the adoption of this device in clinical practice. The committee is particularly concerned that the introduction of this technology to clinical practice could further escalate the cost of medical care without necessarily improving clinical outcome. The committee recommends that prospective randomized clinical trials be conducted to evaluate the clinical use of this new technology in conjunction with fetal well-being assessment. Given that this technology is new, attention should be paid to any adverse outcomes, including falsely reassuring fetal pulse oximetry data. Moreover, such untoward events should be reported to FDA MedWatch, the FDA Medical Products Reporting Program.

## Reference

1. Garite TJ, Dildy GA, McNamara H, Nageotte MP, Boehm FH, Dellinger EH. A multicenter controlled trial of fetal pulse oximetry in the intrapartum management of nonreassuring fetal heart rate patterns. Am J Obstet Gynecol 2000;183:1049–1058

# ACOG Committee Opinion

Committee on Obstetric Practice

Number 260, October 2001

# Circumcision



ISSN 1074-861X

**The American College of Obstetricians and Gynecologists**
409 12th Street, SW
PO Box 96920
Washington, DC 20090-6920

12345/54321

Circumcision. ACOG Committee Opinion No. 260. American College of Obstetricians and Gynecologists. Obstet Gynecol 2001;98:707-708

*ABSTRACT: The American College of Obstetricians and Gynecologists supports the current position of the American Academy of Pediatrics that finds the existing evidence insufficient to recommend routine neonatal circumcision. Given this circumstance, parents should be given accurate and impartial information to help them make an informed decision. There is ample evidence that newborns circumcised without analgesia experience pain and stress. If circumcision is performed, analgesia should be provided.*

Some studies have shown potential medical benefits to newborn male circumcision; however, these benefits are modest. The exact incidence of complications after circumcision is not known, but data indicate that the rate is low, and the most common complications are local infection and bleeding. The current position of the American Academy of Pediatrics is that the existing evidence is insufficient to recommend routine neonatal circumcision. The American College of Obstetricians and Gynecologists Committee on Obstetric Practice supports this position. Given this circumstance, parents should be given accurate and impartial information to help them make an informed decision. It is reasonable for parents to take cultural, religious, and ethnic traditions, as well as medical factors, into consideration when making this decision. Circumcision of newborns should be performed only on healthy and stable infants.

There is ample evidence that newborns circumcised without analgesia experience pain and stress. Analgesia has been found to be safe and effective in reducing the pain associated with circumcision. Therefore, if circumcision is performed, analgesia should be provided. Swaddling, sucrose by mouth, and acetaminophen administration may reduce the stress response but are not sufficient for the operative pain and cannot be recommended as the sole method of analgesia. EMLA cream, dorsal penile nerve block, and subcutaneous ring block are all reasonable options, although the subcutaneous ring block may provide the most effective analgesia.

## References

1. Circumcision policy statement. Task Force on Circumcision. American Academy of Pediatrics. Pediatrics 1999;103:686–693
2. Prevention and management of pain and stress in the neonate. American Academy of Pediatrics. Committee on Fetus and Newborn. Committee on Drugs. Section on Anesthesiology. Section on Surgery. Canadian Paediatric Society. Fetus and Newborn Committee. Pediatrics 2000;105:454–461

ACOG

Committee on Obstetric Practice

# Committee Opinion

Number 264, December 2001

# Air Travel During Pregnancy

*ABSTRACT: In the absence of obstetric or medical complications, pregnant women can observe the same general precautions for air travel as the general population and can fly safely up to 36 weeks of gestation. In-craft environmental conditions such as low cabin humidity and changes in cabin pressure, coupled with the physiologic changes of pregnancy, do result in maternal adaptations, which could have transient effects on the fetus. Pregnant air travelers with medical problems that may be exacerbated by a hypoxic environment, but who must travel by air, should be prescribed supplemental oxygen during air travel. Pregnant women at significant risk for premature labor or with placental abnormalities should avoid air travel. Because air turbulence cannot be predicted and the risk for trauma is significant, pregnant women should be instructed to continuously use their seat belts while seated, as should all air travelers. Pregnant air travelers may take precautions to ease in-flight discomfort, and although no hard evidence exists, preventive measures can be employed to minimize risks.*

Air travel during pregnancy is safe for most women and most U.S. airlines allow pregnant women to fly up to 36 weeks of gestation. For specific airline requirements, the patient should check with the specific carrier because documentation of gestational age may be required. For international airlines the cutoff is 35 weeks of gestation.

In the absence of complications, pregnant women can observe the same general precautions while traveling as the general population. Travel is not recommended at any time during pregnancy for women who have either medical or obstetric complications for which likely emergencies cannot be predicted. Such complications may include increased risks for, or evidence of, preterm delivery, pregnancy induced hypertension, poorly controlled type 1 or type 2 diabetes, or sickle cell disease or trait, which may be exacerbated by high altitude. Pregnant women should be informed that the most common obstetric emergencies occur in the first and third trimesters.

Some unconfirmed reports indicate that flight attendants experience twice the incidence (relative risk=1.9) of first trimester spontaneous abortions as other women, but not other employed women. There is no evidence of an increased risk of spontaneous abortion among other air travelers (1). Most airlines restrict the working air travel of flight attendants after 20 weeks of gestation. Airlines also restrict commercial airline pilots from flying once pregnancy is diagnosed.



ISSN 1074-861X

**The American College of Obstetricians and Gynecologists**
409 12th Street, SW
PO Box 96920
Washington, DC 20090-6920

12345/54321

Air travel during pregnancy. ACOG Committee Opinion No. 264. American College of Obstetricians and Gynecologists. Obstet Gynecol 2001;98:1187–1188

In-craft environmental conditions such as changes in cabin pressure and low humidity, coupled with the physiologic changes of pregnancy, do result in maternal adaptations, which could have transient effects on the fetus. A significant environmental change is the reduction of cabin humidity to less than 25%, which causes hemoconcentration and increases the risk for venous thrombosis and potentially the risk for premature labor.

On long commercial flights traveling at 39,000–41,000 feet, cabin pressure is maintained at the equivalent of an altitude pressure of 8,000 feet. While at 32,000 feet the cabin pressure is set at the equivalent of 6,000 feet. The conditions at a cabin pressure of 8000 feet will create a more hypoxic environment than those at 6000 feet. Acute ascent to 6,000 feet does not elicit ominous fetal responses, but it does produce transient maternal cardiopulmonary adaptations. Among these adaptations are increased heart rate, increased blood pressure, and a significant decrease in aerobic capacity (2, 3). In pregnancy there is limited aerobic capacity. At 6,000 feet the oxygen consumption in pregnant women is 13% (L/min) lower than at sea level (3), in comparison with nonpregnant women for whom the decrease is only 3% lower (4). These changes are associated with a reduction in partial oxygen pressure, which should not affect normal pregnant women, but it could affect those with a compromised cardiovascular system. Therefore, pregnant air travelers with medical problems that may be exacerbated by a hypoxic environment, but who must travel by air, should be prescribed supplemental oxygen during air travel. Pregnant women at significant risk for premature labor or with placental abnormalities should avoid air travel.

Several precautions may ease discomfort for pregnant air travelers. For example, gas-producing foods or drinks should be avoided before scheduled flights since entrapped gases expand at altitude (5). Preventive antiemetic medication should be considered for women with increased nausea.

The risks associated with long hours of air travel immobilization and low cabin humidity, such as lower extremity edema and venous thrombotic events, have recently been the focus of attention for all air travelers. There are no published reports of such events in pregnancy; however, concerns regarding the relationship of venous stasis to in-flight thromboembolism have been raised. Despite the lack of tangible evidence, certain preventive measures can be employed to minimize these risks, ie, support stockings and periodic movement of the lower extremities. Because air turbulence cannot be predicted and the risk for trauma is significant, pregnant women should be instructed to continuously use their seatbelts while seated, as should all air travelers. The seatbelt should be belted low on the hipbones, between the protuberant abdomen and pelvis.

Available information suggests that noise vibration and cosmic radiation present a negligible risk for the pregnant air traveler (6, 7). In the absence of a reasonable expectation for obstetric or medical complications, air travel is safe for pregnant women up to 36 weeks of gestation.

## References


1. Daniell WE, Vaughan TL, Millies BA. Pregnancy outcomes among female flight attendants. Aviat Space Environ Med;1990;61:840–884
2. Huch R, Baumann H, Fallenstein F, Schneider KT, Holdener F, Huch A. Physiologic changes in pregnant women and their fetuses during jet air travel. Am J Obstet Gynecol 1986;154:996–1000
3. Artal R, Fortunato V, Welton A, Constantino N, Khodiguian N, Villalobos L, et al. A comparison of cardiopulmonary adaptations to exercise in pregnancy at sea level and altitude. Am J Obstet Gynecol 1995;172:1170–1178; discussion 1178–1180
4. Brooks GA, Fahey TD, White TP, Baldwin KM. Exercise, atmospheric pressure, air pollution, and travel. In: Exercise physiology: human bioenergetics and its applications. 3rd ed. Mountain View, California: Mayfield Publishing Company, 2000:504–436
5. Bia FJ. Medical considerations for the pregnant traveler. Infect Dis Clin N Am 1992;6:371–388
6. Morrell S, Taylor R, Lyle D. A review of health effects of aircraft noise. Aust N Z J Public Health 1997;21:221–236
7. Friedberg W, Faulkner DN, Snyder L, Darden EB Jr, O'Brien K. Galactic cosmic radiation exposure and associated health risks for air carrier crewmembers. Aviat Space Environ Med 1989;60:1104–1108

ACOG Committee Opinion

Committee on Obstetric Practice

Number 267, January 2002

# Exercise During Pregnancy and the Postpartum Period

*ABSTRACT: The physiologic and morphologic changes of pregnancy may interfere with the ability to engage safely in some forms of physical activity. A woman's overall health, including obstetric and medical risks, should be evaluated before prescribing an exercise program. Generally, participation in a wide range of recreational activities appears to be safe during pregnancy; however, each sport should be reviewed individually for its potential risk, and activities with a high risk of falling or those with a high risk of abdominal trauma should be avoided during pregnancy. Scuba diving also should be avoided throughout pregnancy because the fetus is at an increased risk for decompression sickness during this activity. In the absence of either medical or obstetric complications, 30 minutes or more of moderate exercise a day on most, if not all, days of the week is recommended for pregnant women.*

The current Centers for Disease Control and Prevention and American College of Sports Medicine recommendation for exercise, aimed at improving the health and well-being of nonpregnant individuals, suggests that an accumulation of 30 minutes or more of moderate exercise a day should occur on most, if not all, days of the week (1). In the absence of either medical or obstetric complications, pregnant women also can adopt this recommendation.

Given the potential risks, albeit rare, thorough clinical evaluation of each pregnant woman should be conducted before recommending an exercise program. In the absence of contraindications (see boxes), pregnant women should be encouraged to engage in regular, moderate intensity physical activity to continue to derive the same associated health benefits during their pregnancies as they did prior to pregnancy.

Epidemiologic data suggest that exercise may be beneficial in the primary prevention of gestational diabetes, particularly in morbidly obese women (BMI >33) (2). The American Diabetes Association has endorsed exercise as "a helpful adjunctive therapy" for gestational diabetes mellitus when euglycemia is not achieved by diet alone (3, 4).

The cardiovascular changes associated with pregnancy are an important consideration for pregnant women both at rest and during exercise. After the

This document reflects emerging clinical and scientific advances as of the date issued and is subject to change. The information should not be construed as dictating an exclusive course of treatment or procedure to be followed.



ISSN 1074-861X

**The American College of Obstetricians and Gynecologists**
409 12th Street, SW
PO Box 96920
Washington, DC 20090-6920

12345/65432

Exercise during pregnancy and the postpartum period. ACOG Committee Opinion No. 267. American College of Obstetricians and Gynecologists. Obstet Gynecol 2002;99:171–173

**Absolute Contraindications to Aerobic Exercise During Pregnancy**

- Hemodynamically significant heart disease
- Restrictive lung disease
- Incompetent cervix/cerclage
- Multiple gestation at risk for premature labor
- Persistent second- or third-trimester bleeding
- Placenta previa after 26 weeks of gestation
- Premature labor during the current pregnancy
- Ruptured membranes
- Preeclampsia/pregnancy-induced hypertension

**Relative Contraindications to Aerobic Exercise During Pregnancy**

- Severe anemia
- Unevaluated maternal cardiac arrhythmia
- Chronic bronchitis
- Poorly controlled type 1 diabetes
- Extreme morbid obesity
- Extreme underweight (BMI <12)
- History of extremely sedentary lifestyle
- Intrauterine growth restriction in current pregnancy
- Poorly controlled hypertension
- Orthopedic limitations
- Poorly controlled seizure disorder
- Poorly controlled hyperthyroidism
- Heavy smoker

first trimester, the supine position results in relative obstruction of venous return and, therefore, decreased cardiac output and orthostatic hypotension. For this reason, pregnant women should avoid supine positions during exercise as much as possible. Motionless standing also is associated with a significant decrease in cardiac output so this position should be avoided as much as possible (5).

Epidemiologic studies have long suggested that a link exists between strenuous physical activities, deficient diets, and the development of intrauterine growth restriction. This is particularly true for pregnant women engaged in physical work. It has been reported that pregnant women whose occupations require standing or repetitive, strenuous, physical work (eg, lifting) have a tendency to deliver earlier and have small-for-gestational-age infants (6). However, other reports have failed to confirm these associations suggesting that several factors or conditions have to be present for strenuous activities to affect fetal growth or outcome (7, 8).

In general, participation in a wide range of recreational activities appears to be safe. The safety of each sport is determined largely by the specific movements required by that sport. Participation in recreational sports with a high potential for contact, such as ice hockey, soccer, and basketball, could result in trauma to both the woman and fetus. Similarly, recreational activities with an increased risk of falling, such as gymnastics, horseback riding, downhill skiing, and vigorous racquet sports, have an inherently high risk for trauma in pregnant and nonpregnant women. Those activities with a high risk of falling or for abdominal trauma should be avoided during pregnancy (9). Scuba diving should be avoided throughout pregnancy because during this activity the fetus is at increased risk for decompression sickness secondary to the inability of the fetal pulmonary circulation to filter bubble formation (10).

Exertion at altitudes of up to 6,000 feet appears to be safe; however, engaging in physical activities at higher altitudes carries various risks (11). All women who are recreationally active should be made aware of signs of altitude sickness for which they should stop the exercise, descend from the altitude, and seek medical attention.

Data regarding the effects of exercise on core temperature during pregnancy are limited (12, 13, 14). There have been no reports that hyperthermia associated with exercise is teratogenic.

**Warning Signs to Terminate Exercise While Pregnant**

- Vaginal bleeding
- Dyspnea prior to exertion
- Dizziness
- Headache
- Chest pain
- Muscle weakness
- Calf pain or swelling (need to rule out thrombophlebitis)
- Preterm labor
- Decreased fetal movement
- Amniotic fluid leakage

Competitive athletes are likely to encounter the same physiologic limitations during pregnancy faced by recreational athletes during pregnancy. The competitors tend to maintain a more strenuous training schedule throughout pregnancy and resume high intensity postpartum training sooner. The concerns of the pregnant, competitive athlete fall into two general categories: 1) the effects of pregnancy on competitive ability, and 2) the effects of strenuous training and competition on pregnancy and the fetus. Such athletes may require close obstetric supervision.

Many of the physiologic and morphologic changes of pregnancy persist 4–6 weeks postpartum. Thus, prepregnancy exercise routines may be resumed gradually as soon as it is physically and medically safe. This will vary from one individual to another with some women able to resume an exercise routine within days of delivery. There are no published studies to indicate that, in the absence of medical complications, rapid resumption of activities will result in adverse effects. Having undergone detraining, resumption of activities should be gradual. No known maternal complications are associated with resumption of training (15). Moderate weight reduction while nursing is safe and does not compromise neonatal weight gain (16). Finally, a return to physical activity after pregnancy has been associated with decreased incidence of postpartum depression, but only if the exercise is stress relieving and not stress provoking (17).

## Conclusions and Recommendations

- Recreational and competitive athletes with uncomplicated pregnancies can remain active during pregnancy and should modify their usual exercise routines as medically indicated. The information on strenuous exercise is scarce; however, women who engage in such activities require close medical supervision.
- Previously inactive women and those with medical or obstetric complications should be evaluated before recommendations for physical activity during pregnancy are made. Exercise during pregnancy may provide additional health benefits to women with gestational diabetes.
- A physically active woman with a history of or risk for preterm labor or fetal growth restriction should be advised to reduce her activity in the second and third trimesters.

## References


1. American College of Sports Medicine. ACSM's guidelines for exercise testing and prescription. 6th ed. Philadelphia: Lippincott, Williams and Wilkins, 2000
2. Dye TD, Knox KL, Artal R, Aubry RH, Wojtowycz MA. Physical activity, obesity, and diabetes in pregnancy. Am J Epidemiol 1997;146:961–965
3. Jovanovic-Peterson L, Peterson CM. Exercise and the nutritional management of diabetes during pregnancy. Obstet Gynecol Clin North Am 1996;23:75–86
4. Bung P, Artal R. Gestational diabetes and exercise: a survey. Semin Perinatol 1996;20:328–333
5. Clark SL, Cotton DB, Pivarnik JM, Lee W, Hankins GD, Benedetti TJ, et al. Position change and central hemodynamic profile during normal third-trimester pregnancy and post partum. Am J Obstet Gynecol 1991;164:883–887 [erratum in Am J Obstet Gynecol 1991;165:241]
6. Launer LJ, Villar J, Kestler E, deOnis M. The effect of maternal work on fetal growth and duration of pregnancy: a prospective study. Br J Obstet Gynaecol 1990:97;62–70
7. Saurel-Cubizolles MJ, Kaminski M. Pregnant women's working conditions and their changes during pregnancy: a national study in France. Br J Ind Med 1987;44:236–243
8. Ahlborg G Jr, Bodin L, Hogstedt C. Heavy lifting during pregnancy—a hazard to the fetus? A prospective study. Int J Epidemiol 1990;19:90–97
9. Artal R, Sherman C. Exercise during pregnancy: safe and beneficial for most. Phys Sports Med 1999;27:51–52, 54, 57–58
10. Camporesi EM. Diving and pregnancy. Semin Perinatol 1996;20:292–302
11. Artal R, Fortunato V, Welton A, Constantino N, Khodiguian N, Villalobos L, et al. A comparison of cardiopulmonary adaptations to exercise in pregnancy at sea level and altitude. Am J Obstet Gynecol 1995;172: 1170–1180
12. Clapp JF 3rd, Capeless EL. Neonatal morphometrics after endurance exercise during pregnancy. Am J Obstet Gynecol 1990;163:1805–1811
13. Artal R, Wiswell RA, Drinkwater BL, eds. Exercise in Pregnancy. 2nd ed. Baltimore: Williams and Wilkins, 1991
14. Soultanakis HN, Artal R, Wiswell RA. Prolonged exercise in pregnancy: glucose homeostasis, ventilatory and cardiovascular responses. Semin Perinatol 1996;20:315–327
15. Hale RW, Milne L. The elite athlete and exercise in pregnancy. Semin Perinatol 1996;20:277–284
16. McCrory MA, Nommsen-Rivers LA, Mole PA, Lonnerdal B, Dewey KG. Randomized trial of the short-term effects of dieting compared with dieting plus aerobic exercise on lactation performance. Am J Clin Nutr 1999;69:959–967
17. Koltyn KF, Schultes SS. Psychological effects of an aerobic exercise session and a rest session following pregnancy. J Sports Med Phys Fitness 1997;37:287–291

ACOG Committee Opinion

Committee on Obstetric Practice

Number 268, February 2002

# Management of Asymptomatic Pregnant or Lactating Women Exposed to Anthrax

*ABSTRACT: Anthrax infections are diagnosed by isolating* Bacillus anthracis *from body fluids or by measuring specific antibodies in the blood of persons suspected to have the disease. It is recommended that asymptomatic pregnant and lactating women who have been exposed to a confirmed environmental contamination or a high-risk source as determined by the local Department of Health (not the women's health care provider) receive prophylactic treatment. A variety of antimicrobial regimens are available. Although some of these drugs may present risks to the developing fetus, these risks are clearly outweighed by the potential morbidity and mortality from anthrax. Guidelines for prophylactic treatment of anthrax and treatment of suspected active cases of anthrax are changing continually, and the Centers for Disease Control and Prevention web site should be consulted for the latest recommendations.*

Anthrax is an infection caused by *Bacillus anthracis*, an aerobic, gram-positive, spore-forming, nonmotile bacillus species. There are three primary clinical manifestations of the disease: 1) cutaneous, 2) inhalational, and 3) gastrointestinal.

*Cutaneous:* This is the most common presentation, accounting for 95% of naturally occurring infections. The organism's portal of entry is a cut or abrasion on the skin. The areas of greatest exposure are the hands, arms, face or neck. Potential sources of the organism include wool, hides, and leather and hair products of infected animals, particularly goats. Exposure also may result from a bioterrorist act (eg, a contaminated letter). Incubation periods may be as long as 12 days. Skin infection begins as a raised pruritic papule, resembling an insect bite. Within 1–2 days a vesicle develops, followed by a painless ulcer 1–3 cm in diameter with a characteristic black necrotic eschar in the center. Localized lymphangitis and painful lymphadenopathy may occur. Although antibiotic therapy does not appear to change the course of eschar formation and healing, it does decrease the risk of systemic disease. Mortality rates are 20% if untreated, but less than 1% with antibiotic therapy.

This document reflects emerging clinical and scientific advances as of the date issued and is subject to change. The information should not be construed as dictating an exclusive course of treatment or procedure to be followed.



ISSN 1074-861X

**The American College of Obstetricians and Gynecologists**
409 12th Street, SW
PO Box 96920
Washington, DC 20090-6920

12345/65432

Management of asymptomatic pregnant or lactating women exposed to anthrax. ACOG Committee Opinion No. 268. American College of Obstetricians and Gynecologists. Obstet Gynecol 2002;99:366–368

*Inhalational:* This is the most serious presentation, resulting from deposition of spore-bearing particles of 1–5 μm into the alveolar spaces. Macrophages ingest the spores that are then transported to the pulmonary lymphatics where they germinate. The asymptomatic incubation period usually is 1–7 days after exposure, but spores may germinate in the mediastinal lymphatics for up to 60 days. Once germination occurs, replicating bacteria release toxins leading to hemorrhage, edema, and necrosis. Initial symptoms resemble a flulike illness with fever, cough, and headache, but without rhinitis, followed by progressive dyspnea that rapidly progresses to respiratory failure and death within hours. Case-fatality estimates are extremely high, even with supportive care and appropriate antibiotics.

*Gastrointestinal:* The relatively rare intestinal form of anthrax follows ingestion, deposition, and subsequent germination of spores in the upper or lower gastrointestinal tract. The former leads to the oral-pharyngeal form of the disease marked by oral-esophageal ulcers and regional lymphadenopathy. The latter results in acute inflammation of the intestinal tract with symptoms that include anorexia, malaise, nausea, vomiting, and fever. Subsequently patients infected with gastrointestinal anthrax develop abdominal pain; hematemesis; severe, bloody diarrhea; and sepsis. Intestinal anthrax may be fatal in 25–60% of cases; the effect of early antibiotic therapy is unknown.

## Evaluation and Management of Possible Anthrax Exposure Caused by Bioterrorist Acts

The risk of anthrax exposure is remote for people not in direct contact with the contaminated object or site and is greatest for those present in the immediate vicinity of contamination. The disease is not spread by casual contact or by coughing and sneezing.

### *Active Infection*

Anthrax infections are diagnosed by isolating *B anthracis* from the blood, cerebrospinal fluid, skin lesions, or respiratory secretions or by measuring specific antibodies in the blood of persons suspected to have the disease. Rapid diagnostic immunoassays and polymerase chain reaction are available at national reference laboratories. Strategies of antimicrobial treatment of active anthrax infection are evolving. For the latest recommendations consult the Centers for Disease Control and Prevention (CDC) web site at www.cdc.gov/mmwr and www.bt.cdc.gov.

### *Exposure*

For asymptomatic individuals with low-risk exposure, antimicrobials are not warranted until there is an evident risk of actual exposure based on microbiologically documented anthrax as determined by law enforcement and public health authorities. The woman's health care provider is not the party to validate a threat.

In the current crisis, when screening for exposure is deemed necessary, it is conducted by nasal swab. The resultant secretions can be examined by Gram stain and culture. However, given the lack of reliability of nasal swab screening, postexposure prophylaxis is indicated only after confirmed or high-risk suspected exposure. In the latter cases, treatment can be stopped if anthrax is not documented.

For adult postexposure prophylaxis against anthrax infections, the CDC currently recommends 500 mg of ciprofloxacin orally every 12 hours for 60 days or 100 mg of doxycycline orally every 12 hours for 60 days.

## Management of Exposed Asymptomatic Pregnant or Lactating Women

At this time, the Committee on Obstetric Practice recommends that prophylaxis of asymptomatic pregnant and lactating women be limited to those women who have had exposure to a confirmed environmental contamination or who are exposed to a high-risk source as determined by the local Department of Health. Prophylaxis for asymptomatic pregnant or lactating women is 500 mg of ciprofloxacin orally every 12 hours for 60 days (6).

Ciprofloxacin and other fluoroquinolones generally are not used during pregnancy and lactation because of suggested irreversible drug-induced arthropathy associated with such treatment in a variety of species of adolescent animals (1–5). However, no clear evidence of teratogenicity has been demonstrated in humans (1–5). Despite these concerns, the potential morbidity and mortality from anthrax clearly outweighs these risks. Thus, if the bacteria are shown to be sensitive to penicillin, the treatment should be switched to 500 mg of amoxicillin orally three times a day for 60 days (6).

If a woman has been prescribed ciprofloxacin and is found to be pregnant, she should continue her course of antibiotics for the full 60 days (6) unless the bacteria are shown to be penicillin-sensitive. She should then be switched to amoxicillin. A 1999 expert review of published data on experiences with ciprofloxacin concluded that therapeutic doses during pregnancy are unlikely to pose substantial teratogenic risk, but the data are insufficient to state that there is no risk (1). In the case of penicillin- and ciprofloxacin-allergic patients, treatment should consist of doxycycline or penicillin desensitization should be considered if the organism is proved sensitive (6). In this situation, the risks of anthrax would far outweigh the risks of doxycycline to the fetus (ie, dental staining of the primary teeth and possible depressed bone growth and defective dental enamel).

The guidelines for prophylactic treatment of anthrax and treatment of suspected active cases of anthrax are continually evolving. Please refer to www.bt.cdc.gov and www.cdc.gov/mmwr for any updates in CDC treatment guidelines.

## References

1. Friedman JM, Polifka JE. Ciprofloxacin. In: Teratogenic effects of drugs: a resource for clinicians (TERIS). 2nd ed. Baltimore: The Johns Hopkins University Press, 2000: 149–150
2. Friedman JM, Polifka JE. Doxycyclicne. In: Teratogenic effects of drugs: a resource for clinicians (TERIS). 2nd ed. Baltimore: The Johns Hopkins University Press, 2000: 238–239
3. Center for Drug Evaluation and Research. U.S. Food and Drug Administration. CIPRO (Ciprofloxacin) use by pregnant and lactating women. Available at http://www.fda.gov/cder/drug/infopage/cipro/cipropreg.htm. Retrieved November 2, 2001
4. Center for Drug Evaluation and Research. U.S. Food and Drug Administration. Drug preparedness and response to bioterrorism. Available at http://www.fda.gov/cder/drugprepare/default.htm. Retrieved November 2, 2001
5. Center for Drug Evaluation and Research. U.S. Food and Drug Administration. Doxycycline (Vibramycin, Monodox, Doryx, Doxy, Atridox, Periodox, Vibra-Tabs) use by pregnant and lactating women. Available at http://www.fda.gov/cder/drug/infopage/penG_doxy/doxypreg.htm. Retrieved November 2, 2001
6. Updated recommendations for antimicrobial prophylaxis among asymptomatic pregnant women after exposure to bacillus anthracis. MMWR Morb Mortal Wkly Rep 2001; 50:960

## Resources

Inglesby TV, Henderson DA, Bartlett JG, Ascher MS, Eitzen E, Friedlander AM, et al. Anthrax as a biological weapon: medical and public health management. Working Group on Civilian Biodefense. JAMA 1999;281:1735–1745[erratum JAMA 2000;283:1963]

Update: investigation of anthrax associated with intentional exposure and interim public health guidelines, October 2001. MMWR Morb Mortal Wkly Rep 2001;50:889–893

Use of anthrax vaccine in the United States. MMWR Morb Mortal Wkly Rep 2000;49(RR-15):1–20

ACOG Committee Opinion

Committee on Obstetric Practice

Number 273, May 2002 (Replaces No. 210, October 1998)

# Antenatal Corticosteroid Therapy for Fetal Maturation

*ABSTRACT: The National Institute of Child Health and Human Development and the Office of Medical Applications of Research of the National Institutes of Health convened consensus conferences in 1994 and 2000 that recommended giving a single course of corticosteroids to all pregnant women between 24 and 34 weeks of gestation who are at risk of preterm delivery within 7 days. Because of insufficient scientific evidence, the consensus panel also recommended that repeat corticosteroid courses, including so-called "rescue therapy," should not be routinely used but should be reserved for women enrolled in clinical trials. Betamethasone and dexamethasone have been most widely studied and have generally been the preferred corticosteroids for antenatal treatment to accelerate fetal organ maturation. The American College of Obstetricians and Gynecologists' Committee on Obstetric Practice supports the conclusions of the consensus conferences.*

In August 2000, the National Institute of Child Health and Human Development and the Office of Medical Applications of Research of the National Institutes of Health reconvened a consensus conference on antenatal steroids, entitled "Consensus Development Conference on Antenatal Corticosteroids Revisited: Repeat Courses," to address the issue of repeated courses of corticosteroids for fetal maturation. The consensus panel from this conference reaffirmed the 1994 consensus panel's recommendation of giving a single course of corticosteroids to all pregnant women between 24 and 34 weeks of gestation who are at risk of preterm delivery within 7 days (1). Because of insufficient scientific evidence, the panel also recommended that repeat corticosteroid courses, including so-called "rescue therapy," should not be routinely used but should be reserved for women enrolled in clinical trials. Several of these randomized trials are in progress. The American College of Obstetricians and Gynecologists' Committee on Obstetric Practice supports the conclusions of the consensus conferences.

There is no convincing scientific evidence that antenatal corticosteroid therapy increases the risk of neonatal infection, although multiple courses have been associated with fetal adrenal suppression (2). Follow-up studies of children aged 12 years and younger exposed to at least one course of corticosteroid treatment indicate there is no apparent risk of adverse neurodevelopmental outcome associated with antenatal corticosteroids. There are

This document reflects emerging clinical and scientific advances as of the date issued and is subject to change. The information should not be construed as dictating an exclusive course of treatment or procedure to be followed.



ISSN 1074-861X

**The American College of Obstetricians and Gynecologists**
409 12th Street, SW
PO Box 96920
Washington, DC 20090-6920

12345/65432

Antenatal corticosteroid therapy for fetal maturation. ACOG Committee Opinion No. 273. American College of Obstetricians and Gynecologists. Obstet Gynecol 2002;99:871–873

inconclusive data that repeated courses of antenatal corticosteroids have been associated with a decrease in birth weight and neonatal head circumference (3, 4). The 2000 consensus panel concluded that studies regarding the possible benefits and risks of repeat courses of corticosteroids are limited because of their study design and "methodologic inconsistencies." The 2000 consensus panel noted that, although there is a suggestion of possible benefit from repeated doses (especially in the reduction and severity of respiratory distress), there also are animal and human data that suggest deleterious effects on the fetus regarding cerebral myelination, lung growth, and function of the hypothalamic–pituitary–adrenal axis. Maternal effects include increased infection and suppression of the hypothalamic–pituitary–adrenal axis (5, 6).

Betamethasone and dexamethasone are the most widely studied and have generally been the preferred corticosteroids used for antenatal treatment to accelerate fetal organ maturation. Both cross the placenta in their active form and have nearly identical biologic activity. Both lack mineralocorticoid activity and have relatively weak immunosuppressive activity with short-term use. Although betamethasone and dexamethasone differ only by a single methyl group, their pharmacokinetics differ. Betamethasone has a longer half-life because of its decreased clearance and larger volume of distribution (7). Meta-analyses of randomized trials have shown that, although both agents decrease the frequency of respiratory distress syndrome, only betamethasone decreases neonatal mortality (8). A recent large, uncontrolled retrospective study suggested that betamethasone also may have significant benefit in decreasing the rate of newborn cystic periventricular leukomalacia by approximately 50% compared with untreated and dexamethasone-treated women (9). The offspring of pregnant mice who were given betamethasone performed neurobehavioral developmental tasks better than the offspring of pregnant mice given dexamethasone (10). Furthermore, betamethasone requires fewer intramuscular injections. Betamethasone use, however, has been associated with a significant transient decrease in fetal movements and heart rate variability (11, 12).

The 2000 consensus panel reviewed all available reports on the safety and efficacy of betamethasone and dexamethasone. It did not find significant scientific evidence to support a recommendation that betamethasone should be used preferentially instead of dexamethasone. Thus, based on this information, the Committee on Obstetric Practice recommends either of the following corticosteroid regimens:

- Betamethasone (12 mg) given intramuscularly every 24 hours for two doses
- Dexamethasone (6 mg) given intramuscularly every 12 hours for four doses in patients at risk for preterm delivery between 24 and 34 weeks of gestation with intact membranes or between 24 and 32 weeks of gestation for patients with ruptured membranes

The use of corticosteroids after 34 weeks of gestation is not recommended unless there is evidence of fetal pulmonary immaturity.

## References


1. Antenatal corticosteroids revisited: repeat courses. NIH Consens Statement 2000;17(2):1–10
2. Kairalla AB. Hypothalamic-pituitary-adrenal axis function in premature neonates after extensive prenatal treatment with betamethasone: a case history. Am J Perinatol 1992;9:428–430
3. French NP, Hagan R, Evans SF, Godfrey RN, Newnham JP. Repeated antenatal corticosteroids: size at birth and subsequent development. Am J Obstet Gynecol 1999; 180:114–121
4. Guinn DA, Atkinson MW, Sullivan L, Lee M, MacGregor S, Parilla BV et al. Single vs weekly courses of antenatal corticosteroids for women at risk of preterm delivery: a randomized controlled trial. JAMA 2001;286:1581–1587
5. McKenna DS, Wittber GM, Nagaraja HN, Samuels P. The effects of repeat doses of antenatal corticosteroids on maternal adrenal function. Am J Obstet Gynecol 2000; 183:669–673
6. Abbasi S, Hirsch D, Davis J, Tolosa J, Stouffer N, Debbs R, et al. Effect of single versus multiple courses of antenatal corticosteroids on maternal and neonatal outcome. Am J Obstet Gynecol 2000;182:1243–1249
7. Fanaroff AA, Hack M. Periventricular leukomalacia—prospects for prevention [letter]. N Engl J Med 1999;341: 1229–1231
8. Ballard PL, Ballard RA. Scientific basis and therapeutic regimens for use of antenatal glucocorticoids. Am J Obstet Gynecol 1995;173:254–262
9. Baud O, Foix-L'Helias L, Kaminski M, Audiberet F, Jarreau PH, Papiernik E, et al. Antenatal glucocorticoid treatment and cystic periventricular leukomalacia in very premature infants. N Engl J Med 1999;341:1190–1196
10. Rayburn WF, Christensen HD, Gonzalez CL. A placebo-controlled comparison between betamethasone and dexamethasone for fetal maturation: differences in neurobehavioral development of mice offspring. Am J Obstet Gynecol 1997;176:842–850; discussion 850–851
11. Mulder EJ, Derks JB, Visser GH. Antenatal corticosteroid therapy and fetal behavior: a randomised study of the effects of betamethasone and dexamethasone. Br J Obstet Gynaecol 1997;104:1239–1247
12. Senat MV, Minoui S, Multon O, Fernandez H, Frydman R, Ville Y. Effect of dexamethasone and betamethasone on fetal heart rate variability in preterm labour: a randomised study. Br J Obstet Gynaecol 1998:105:749–755

ACOG Committee Opinion

Committee on Obstetric Practice

Number 275, September 2002 (Replaces No. 121, April 1993)



ISSN 1074-861X

**The American College of Obstetricians and Gynecologists**
409 12th Street, SW
PO Box 96920
Washington, DC 20090-6920

12345/65432

Obstetric management of patients with spinal cord injuries. ACOG Committee Opinion No. 275. American College of Obstetricians and Gynecologists. Obstet Gynecol 2002;100:625–7.

# Obstetric Management of Patients with Spinal Cord Injuries

*ABSTRACT: Effective rehabilitation and modern reproductive technology may increase the number of women considering pregnancy who have spinal cord injuries (SCIs). It is important that obstetricians caring for these patients are aware of the specific problems related to SCIs. Autonomic dysreflexia is the most significant medical complication seen in women with SCIs, and precautions should be taken to avoid stimuli that can lead to this potentially fatal syndrome. Women with SCIs may give birth vaginally, but when cesarean delivery is indicated, adequate anesthesia (spinal or epidural if possible) is needed.*

Approximately 11,000 new spinal cord injuries (SCIs) are reported per year in the United States. More than 50% occur in persons between the ages of 16 and 30 years, with women constituting approximately 18% of these cases. Effective rehabilitation and modern reproductive technology may increase the number of these patients considering pregnancy.

Ideally, women with SCIs who are considering pregnancy should have a preconceptional evaluation. Chronic medical conditions and the woman's adaptation to her disability must be evaluated. Baseline pulmonary function and renal studies may be appropriate. Also, it should be recognized that fertility in these patients usually is not affected, and family planning should be discussed.

It is important that obstetricians caring for such patients acquaint themselves with the problems related to SCIs that may occur throughout pregnancy. Common complications affecting women with SCIs include urinary tract infections, decubital ulcers, impaired pulmonary function, and autonomic dysreflexia. Additional potential complications include anemia, deep vein thrombosis, pulmonary emboli, and unattended delivery.

## Common Complications

### *Urinary Tract Infections*

Asymptomatic bacteruria occurs in a majority of patients with SCIs during pregnancy. The incidence of lower urinary tract infections and pyelonephritis also is increased. Incomplete bladder emptying, neurogenic bladder, urinary diversions, and indwelling catheters contribute to this risk. Frequent urine cultures or antibiotic suppression are indicated.

### *Decubital Ulcers*

Decubital ulcers are a frequently preventable complication in women with SCIs. During pregnancy, women with SCIs should have routine skin examinations, frequent position changes, adequate padding, and appropriately sized medical equipment (eg, wheelchairs). Weight gain and edema also may contribute to decubital ulceration.

### *Pulmonary Function*

Impaired pulmonary function may be present in women with high thoracic or cervical spine lesions. For patients with borderline function, ventilatory support and meticulous attention to pulmonary care is necessary during pregnancy and delivery. Supine positioning may further impair pulmonary function. Serial assessments of vital capacity will help assess the need for ventilatory assistance.

### *Autonomic Dysreflexia*

Autonomic dysreflexia is the most significant medical complication occurring in women with SCIs (85% of patients with lesions above T5 through T6 level). This condition is attributed to a loss of hypothalamic control of sympathetic spinal reflexes and occurs in patients with viable spinal cord segments distal to the level of injury. It can occur in patients with incomplete transections. In susceptible patients, afferent stimuli from a hollow viscus (eg, the bladder, bowel, or uterus) and from the skin below the level of the lesion or of the genital areas ascend in the spinothalamic tracts and posterior columns, which causes reflex sympathetic activation unmodified by the supraspinal centers. The resultant catecholamine release and vasoconstriction lead to hypertension associated with headache, bradycardia, tachycardia, cardiac arrhythmia, sweating, flushing, tingling, nasal congestion, piloerection, and, occasionally, respiratory distress. Uteroplacental vasoconstriction may result in fetal hypoxemia.

It is important to avoid stimuli that can lead to autonomic dysreflexia, such as distension or manipulation of the vagina, bladder, urethra, or bowel. During labor, the symptoms of autonomic dysreflexia are commonly synchronous with uterine contractions. The severity of the syndrome during labor ranges from unpleasant symptoms to hypertensive encephalopathy, cerebrovascular accidents, intraventricular and retinal hemorrhages, and death. Therefore, continual hemodynamic monitoring during labor is mandatory in all at-risk patients.

Although patients with SCIs may perceive no pain during labor, anesthesia should be used to prevent autonomic dysreflexia. Spinal or epidural anesthesia extending to the T10 level is the most reliable method of preventing autonomic dysreflexia by blocking stimuli that arise from pelvic organs. Therefore, antepartum consultation with an anesthesiologist and the establishment of a plan for induction of epidural or spinal anesthesia at the onset of labor is imperative. If autonomic dysreflexia occurs before a regional anesthetic is available or occurs despite regional anesthesia, hypertension may be treated with antihypertensive agents that have a rapid onset and short duration of action (eg, sodium nitroprusside or nitroglycerin), ganglionic blocking agents (eg, trimethaphan), adrenergic blocking agents (eg, guanethidine), or a direct vasodilator (eg, hydralazine).

If there is evidence of autonomic dysreflexia during the second stage of labor, delivery can be expedited by forceps or vacuum assisted delivery with adequate anesthesia. If autonomic dysreflexia during labor cannot be controlled by any means, cesarean delivery may be necessary. Adequate anesthesia, spinal or epidural if possible, is needed for cesarean deliveries in all patients with SCIs.

## Ascertainment of Labor

Women with SCIs may give birth vaginally. Women with spinal cord transection above the T10 segment may have painless labor. In a patient with total transection at a lower thoracic level, labor pain may be so reduced that the patient is unaware of uterine contractions, especially during sleep. However, symptoms under the control of the sympathetic nervous system (eg, abdominal or leg spasms, shortness of breath, increased spasticity) concurrent with uterine contractions may make patients aware of labor. Patients should be instructed in uterine palpation techniques to detect contractions at home.

## General Support

Excess weight gain may increase the difficulty of moving and transporting pregnant women with SCIs. Muscle-strengthening exercises may be recommended for the upper extremities of nonquadriplegic patients. For all patients, elevation of the legs and range-of-motion exercises may be implemented as pregnancy advances. The possibility of an increased need for social support services also should be addressed.

## Bibliography

American Society of Anesthesiologists. Standards for basic anesthetic monitoring. In: ASA standards, guidelines and statements. Park Ridge (IL): ASA; 2000. p. 5–6.

Atterbury JL, Groome LJ. Pregnancy in women with spinal cord injuries. Nurs Clin North Am 1998;33:603–13.

Baker EB, Cardenas DD. Pregnancy in spinal cord injured women. Arch Phys Med Rehabil 1996;77:501–7.

Baker EB, Cardena DD, Benedetti TJ. Risks associated with pregnancy in spinal cord-injured women. Obstet Gynecol 1992;80:425–8.

Hambly PR, Martin B. Anaesthesia for chronic spinal cord lesions. Anaesthesia 1998;53:273–89.

Nobunaga AI, Go BK, Karunas RB. Recent demographic and injury trends in people served by the Model Spinal Cord Injury Care Systems. Arch Phys Med Rehabil 1999;80:1372–82.

Paonessa K, Fernand R. Spinal cord injury and pregnancy. Spine 1991;16:596–8.

Verduyn WH. Spinal cord injured women, pregnancy and delivery. Paraplegia 1986;24:231–40.

ACOG Committee Opinion

Committee on Obstetric Practice

Number 276, October 2002

This document reflects emerging clinical and scientific advances as of the date issued and is subject to change. The information should not be construed as dictating an exclusive course of treatment or procedure to be followed.



ISSN 1074-861X

**The American College of Obstetricians and Gynecologists**
409 12th Street, SW
PO Box 96920
Washington, DC 20090-6920

12345/65432

Safety of Lovenox in pregnancy. Committee Opinion No. 276. American College of Obstetricians and Gynecologists. Obstet Gynecol 2002;100:845–6.

# Safety of Lovenox in Pregnancy

*ABSTRACT: Lovenox (enoxaparin sodium) therapy appears to be safe and efficacious for pregnant women who are candidates for either prophylactic or therapeutic heparin. However, the use of enoxaparin and other low-molecular-weight heparins for therapeutic anticoagulation is not recommended for pregnant women with prosthetic heart valves. Additionally, enoxaparin should be used with caution or discontinued before administration of epidural for pain relief during labor.*

Aventis Pharmaceuticals has issued a letter to health professionals describing the addition of warnings and precautions to their Lovenox Injection (enoxaparin sodium) prescribing information. The "Warnings" section notes that Lovenox Injection is not recommended for thromboprophylaxis in patients with prosthetic heart valves because of reports of valvular thrombosis in patients who were apparently adequately anticoagulated. The cases reported by the manufacturer and in the literature suggest a relatively frequent occurrence of valvular thromboses in pregnant women treated with low-molecular-weight heparin, possibly caused by the hypercoagulability of pregnancy (1, 2). The American College of Obstetricians and Gynecologists' (ACOG) Committee on Obstetric Practice concurs that low-molecular-weight heparins should not be used for anticoagulation in pregnant women with prosthetic heart valves.

The "Precautions" section now includes a paragraph in the "Pregnancy" subsection that reports the occurrence of congenital anomalies in infants of women treated with Lovenox Injection during pregnancy, but it notes that a "cause and effect relationship has not been established nor has the incidence been shown to be higher than in the general population." The Committee on Obstetric Practice does not believe that Lovenox Injection presents a teratogenic risk for the following three reasons: 1) the agent does not cross the placenta, providing no biologic plausibility for such a risk (3); 2) a large study by Lepercq and associates described pregnancy outcomes in 604 women treated with enoxaparin during 624 pregnancies and observed a congenital anomaly rate of 2.5%, which is consistent with the rate in the general population (4); and 3) the variety of anomalies reported by Aventis Pharmaceuticals, and their rare occurrence, suggests no specific pathogenic pattern or increased frequency.

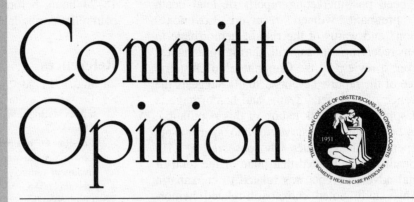

Aventis Pharmaceuticals also states that there "have been post-marketing reports of fetal death when pregnant women received Lovenox® Injection" and warns of the risk of hemorrhage in women receiving enoxaparin during pregnancy. However, a review by the Committee on Obstetric Practice of the reported events actually suggests the occurrence of both fetal deaths and hemorrhage is rare despite the high-risk nature of this population. This is borne out in the survey of enoxaparin users by Lepercq and associates who observed a 1.1% fetal death rate and noted that none of the fetal or neonatal adverse events was related to enoxaparin (4). This study noted enoxaparin-related hemorrhage occurred in 1 of 624 pregnancies, and the occurrence of recurrent maternal venous thrombotic events in this high-risk population was 1.3%.

Enoxaparin therapy appears to be safe and efficacious when used in pregnant women. The Committee on Obstetric Practice reiterates the recommendations made by ACOG that "Patients who are candidates for either prophylactic or therapeutic heparin may be given enoxaparin or dalteparin during pregnancy" (5). In addition, the Committee on Obstetric Practice recommends against the use of enoxaparin and other low-molecular-weight heparins for therapeutic anticoagulation in pregnant women with prosthetic heart valves. Enoxaparin should not be used 18–24 hours before administration of epidural for pain relief during labor (6).

## References

1. Rowan JA, McCowan LM, Raudkivi PJ, North RA. Enoxaparin treatment in women with mechanical heart valves during pregnancy. Am J Obstet Gynecol 2001; 185:633–7.
2. Lev-Ran O, Kramer A, Gurevitch J, Shapira I, Mohr R. Low-molecular-weight heparin for prosthetic heart valves: treatment failure. Ann Thorac Surg 2000;69:264–5; discussion 265–6.
3. Dimitrakakis C, Papageorgiou P, Papageorgiou I, Antzaklis A, Sakarelou N, Michalas S. Absence of transplacental passage of the low molecular weight heparin enoxaparin. Haemostasis 2000;30:243–8.
4. Lepercq J, Conard J, Borel-Derlon A, Damon JY, Boudignat O, Francoual C, et al. Venous thromboembolism during pregnancy: a retrospective study of enoxaparin safety in 624 pregnancies. BJOG 2001;108:1134–40.
5. American College of Obstetricians and Gynecologists. Thromboembolism in pregnancy. ACOG Practice Bulletin 19. Washington DC: ACOG; 2000.
6. Horlocker TT, Wedel DJ. Neuraxial block and low-molecular-weight heparin: balancing perioperative analgesia and thromboprophylaxis. Reg Anesth Pain Med 1998;23(suppl 2):164–77.

ACOG Committee Opinion

Committee on Obstetric Practice

Number 279, December 2002 (Replaces No. 173, June 1996)

# Prevention of Early-Onset Group B Streptococcal Disease in Newborns

*ABSTRACT: During the past two decades, group B streptococci (GBS), or* Streptococcus agalactiae, *has emerged as an important cause of perinatal morbidity and mortality. Intrapartum administration of antibiotics to the woman (during labor or after rupture of membranes, but before delivery) has been demonstrated to reduce early-onset neonatal GBS disease. In 1996, the federal Centers for Disease Control and Prevention (CDC), the American College of Obstetricians and Gynecologists, and the American Academy of Pediatrics recommended that obstetric providers adopt either a culture-based or a risk-based approach for the prevention of early-onset GBS. A recent multistate retrospective cohort study of live births in 1998 and 1999 of residents from eight areas of the Active Bacterial Core Surveillance/Emerging Infections Program network suggests that the culture-based approach is superior to the risk-based approach. The Committee on Obstetric Practice supports the new CDC recommendations that obstetric providers adopt a culture-based strategy for the prevention of early-onset GBS disease in the newborn. It is important to acknowledge that complete implementation of this complex strategy will not eliminate all cases of early-onset GBS.*

During the past two decades, group B streptococci (GBS), or *Streptococcus agalactiae*, has emerged as an important cause of perinatal morbidity and mortality (1, 2). The gram-positive organism can colonize the lower gastrointestinal tract, and secondary spread to the genitourinary tract is common. Between 10% and 30% of pregnant women are colonized with GBS in the vagina or rectum (3–6). The organism may cause urinary tract infection, amnionitis, endometritis, sepsis, or, rarely, meningitis (7–12).

Vertical transmission of GBS during labor or delivery may result in invasive infection in the newborn during the first week of life. This is known as early-onset GBS infection, resulting in approximately 1,600 cases and 80 deaths annually (13). Late-onset GBS disease in the newborn may be the result of vertical transmission or of nosocomial or community-acquired infection. Invasive GBS disease in the newborn is characterized primarily by sepsis, pneumonia, or meningitis. The incidence of invasive GBS infections among pregnant women in the United States decreased by 21% from 1993 to 1998 to an incidence of 0.23 per 1,000 live births (1). Morbidity caused by

This document reflects emerging clinical and scientific advances as of the date issued and is subject to change. The information should not be construed as dictating an exclusive course of treatment or procedure to be followed.



ISSN 1074-861X

**The American College of Obstetricians and Gynecologists**
409 12th Street, SW
PO Box 96920
Washington, DC 20090-6920

12345/65432

Prevention of early-onset group B streptococcal disease in newborns. ACOG Committee Opinion No. 279. American College of Obstetricians and Gynecologists. Obstet Gynecol 2002;100:1405–12.

overwhelming sepsis and neurologic sequelae of meningitis also is clinically important but more difficult to estimate.

## Factors Associated with Early-Onset Disease

A number of obstetric factors have been associated with an increased likelihood of early-onset GBS disease in the newborn (14). These include maternal colonization of the vagina and rectum with GBS, premature births, prolonged rupture of membranes, or intrapartum fever. The incidence of GBS disease also is higher among infants born to African-American women (15, 16), to Hispanic women, and to women younger than 20 years (16, 17). Neonates born to women with a prior GBS-infected infant (18–20) or women with heavy colonization such as that seen with GBS bacteriuria equal to or greater than $10^4$ colony-forming units (CFU) (21–25) or low levels of anti-GBS capsular antibody, also are more likely to be infected (26).

Intrapartum administration of antibiotics to the women (during labor or after rupture of membranes, but before delivery) has been demonstrated to reduce early-onset neonatal GBS disease. Coinciding with active prevention efforts in the 1990s, the incidence of early-onset disease decreased by 70% to 0.5 cases per 1,000 live births in 1999. Projections derived from 1999 active surveillance data from the Active Bacterial Core Surveillance/Emerging Infections Program Network (27) estimate that intrapartum antibiotics prevented nearly 4,500 early-onset cases and 225 deaths that year (1, 2). Other countries that have adopted perinatal GBS prevention guidelines similar to the United States' guidelines have seen comparable decreases in early-onset disease incidence (28–30). Recent estimates of early-onset disease incidence in the United States suggest a slight increase in incidence from 1999 to 2000, consistent with a plateau in the impact of prevention efforts.

## Strategies for Intrapartum Antibiotic Prophylaxis

In 1996, the federal Centers for Disease Control and Prevention (CDC) (31), the American College of Obstetricians and Gynecologists (ACOG), and the American Academy of Pediatrics (AAP) recommended that obstetric providers adopt either a culture-based or a risk-based approach for the prevention of early-onset GBS. Using the risk-based approach, women with preterm labor (<37 weeks of gestation), preterm premature rupture of membranes (preterm PROM) (<37 weeks of gestation), rupture of membranes greater than or equal to 18 hours, or maternal fever during labor (≥38°C or 100.4°F) receive intrapartum antibiotic prophylaxis. With both culture-based and risk-based approaches, women with GBS bacteriuria during their current pregnancy or women who previously gave birth to an infant with early-onset GBS disease were candidates for intrapartum antibiotic prophylaxis. The culture-based approach requires obtaining a single swab from the lower vagina (introitus) and perianal area, placing the swab in transport media, and using selective broth media. Use of prenatal cultures remote from term to identify women who are colonized with GBS at delivery may not be accurate, and since 1996, the CDC, ACOG, and AAP have recommended obtaining rectovaginal cultures at 35–37 weeks of gestation with the culture-based approach. All women who are GBS culture positive should be treated with intrapartum antibiotic prophylaxis in labor. Still, intrapartum antibiotic prophylaxis should be administered to women with preterm labor or preterm PROM who are in labor.

A recent multistate retrospective cohort study of live births in 1998 and 1999 of residents from eight areas of the Active Bacterial Core Surveillance/Emerging Infections Program network suggests that the culture-based approach is superior to the risk-based approach (32). All cases of early-onset GBS identified by population-based surveillance in these areas were identified. The provider's intended strategy was unknown; thus, women without documented prenatal GBS screening were considered to have been managed by the risk-based approach. The study used data abstracted from records of 5,144 births, including 312 early-onset GBS cases. Univariate analysis showed that intrapartum fever equal to or greater than 38°C or a previous infant with GBS disease was associated with the highest risks of early-onset GBS disease with a relative risk (RR) of 5.99 (95% confidence interval [CI], 4.28–8.38) and RR of 3.79 (95% CI, 1.3–11.11), respectively. In addition, all risk factors (ie, preterm delivery, prolonged rupture of membranes ≤18 hours, inadequate prenatal care, black race, Hispanic ethnicity, and maternal age <20 years) except GBS bacteriuria were significantly associated with early-onset GBS. The risk of having an infant with early-onset GBS was significantly lower in the culture cohort relative to the risk cohort with an adjusted RR of 0.46 (95% CI, 0.37–0.60). Moreover, of the 312 infants with early-onset GBS, 63% of the mothers had no risk factors. Even when the women who had no strategy applied were excluded (n=207, including 30 early-onset GBS cases), the culture approach remained protective with an adjusted RR of 0.48 (95% CI, 0.37–0.63).

In addition, a number of small studies have evaluated compliance of hospitals with GBS guideline recommendations and found that a greater proportion of GBS-positive women receive intrapartum prophylaxis under the culture-based approach than with the risk-based approach (28, 32–39). Data from a large cohort of term infants with early-onset GBS infections found that more than one half of the term infants with culture-proven infection were born to women with no obstetric risk factors (40). Based on CDC surveillance data, the risk-based approach fails to identify approximately 50% of infants with GBS sepsis (41).

## Commentary

The Committee on Obstetric Practice recognizes that some of these recent studies have methodologic flaws. Still, they represent the best available comparison of the risk-based and culture-based strategies to date. Larger studies or randomized studies are not likely to be conducted; therefore, the Committee supports the new CDC recommendation that obstetric providers adopt a culture-based strategy for the prevention of early-onset GBS disease in the newborn (see Fig. 1). The Committee agrees with the CDC that the risk-based approach is no longer an acceptable alternative except for circumstances where culture results are not available before delivery. Laboratories must process GBS cultures correctly using the recommended selective broth media for results to be accurate. Culture specimens should be collected by swabbing the lower vagina and rectum (ie, through the anal sphincter), not by speculum examination, to maximize the likelihood of GBS recovery (see box). Laboratories also must

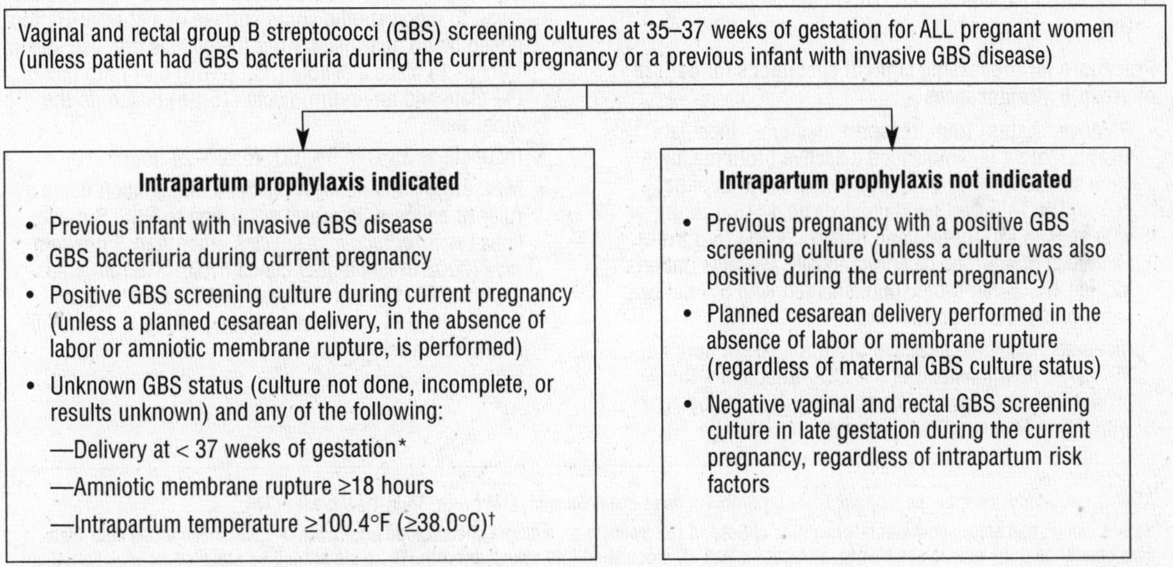

Vaginal and rectal group B streptococci (GBS) screening cultures at 35–37 weeks of gestation for ALL pregnant women (unless patient had GBS bacteriuria during the current pregnancy or a previous infant with invasive GBS disease)

**Intrapartum prophylaxis indicated**

- Previous infant with invasive GBS disease
- GBS bacteriuria during current pregnancy
- Positive GBS screening culture during current pregnancy (unless a planned cesarean delivery, in the absence of labor or amniotic membrane rupture, is performed)
- Unknown GBS status (culture not done, incomplete, or results unknown) and any of the following:
  —Delivery at < 37 weeks of gestation*
  —Amniotic membrane rupture ≥18 hours
  —Intrapartum temperature ≥100.4°F (≥38.0°C)†

**Intrapartum prophylaxis not indicated**

- Previous pregnancy with a positive GBS screening culture (unless a culture was also positive during the current pregnancy)
- Planned cesarean delivery performed in the absence of labor or membrane rupture (regardless of maternal GBS culture status)
- Negative vaginal and rectal GBS screening culture in late gestation during the current pregnancy, regardless of intrapartum risk factors

*If onset of labor or rupture of amniotic membranes occurs at <37 weeks of gestation and there is a significant risk for preterm delivery (as assessed by the clinician), follow the suggested algorithm for GBS prophylaxis as indicated by the CDC.

† If amnionitis is suspected, broad-spectrum antibiotic therapy that includes an agent known to be active against GBS should replace GBS prophylaxis.

Schrag S, Gorwitz R, Fultz-Butts K, Schuchat A. Prevention of perinatal group B streptococcal disease. Revised guidelines from CDC. MMWR Recomm Rep 2002;51(RR-11):1–22.

**Fig. 1.** Indications for intrapartum antibiotic prophylaxis to prevent perinatal group B streptococcal disease under a universal prenatal screening strategy based on combined vaginal and rectal cultures collected at 35–37 weeks of gestation from all pregnant women.

## Procedures for collecting and processing clinical specimens for group B streptococcal culture and performing susceptibility testing to clindamycin and erythromycin

**Procedure for collecting clinical specimens for culture of group B streptococcus at 35–37 weeks of gestation**

- Swab the lower vagina (vaginal introitus), followed by the rectum (ie, insert swab through the anal sphincter) using the same swab or two different swabs. Cultures should be collected in the outpatient setting by the health care provider or the patient herself, with appropriate instruction. Cervical cultures are not recommended and a speculum should not be used for culture collection.
- Place the swab(s) into a nonnutritive transport medium. Appropriate transport systems (eg, Amies or Stuart without charcoal) are commercially available. If vaginal and rectal swabs were collected separately, both swabs can be placed into the same container of medium. Transport media will maintain GBS viability for up to 4 days at room temperature or under refrigeration.
- Specimen labels should clearly identify that specimens are for group B streptococcal culture. If susceptibility testing is ordered for penicillin-allergic women, specimen labels should also identify the patient as penicillin allergic and should specify that susceptibility testing for clindamycin and erythromycin should be performed if GBS is isolated.

**Procedure for processing clinical specimens for culture of group B streptococcus**

- Remove swab(s) from transport medium.* Inoculate swab(s) into a recommended selective broth medium, such as Todd-Hewitt broth supplemented with either gentamicin (8 μg/mL) and nalidixic acid (15 μg/mL), or with colistin (10 μg/mL) and nalidixic acid (15 μg/mL). Examples of appropriate commercially available options include Trans-Vag broth supplemented with 5% defibrinated sheep blood or LIM broth.†
- Incubate inoculated selective broth for 18–24 hours at 35°–37°C in ambient air of 5% $CO_2$. Subculture the broth to a sheep blood agar plate (eg, tryptic soy agar with 5% defibrinated sheep blood).
- Inspect and identify organisms suggestive of GBS (ie, narrow zone of beta hemolysis, gram-positive cocci, catalase negative). Note that hemolysis may be difficult to observe, so typical colonies without hemolysis should also be further tested. If GBS is not identified after incubation for 18–24 hours, reincubate and inspect at 48 hours to identify suspected organisms.
- Various streptococcus grouping latex agglutination tests or other tests for GBS antigen detection (eg, genetic probe) may be used for specific identification, or the cAMP test may be employed for presumptive identification.

**Procedure for clindamycin and erythromycin disk susceptibility testing of isolates, when ordered for penicillin-allergic patients‡**

- Use a cotton swab to make a suspension from an 18–24-hour growth of the organism in saline or Mueller-Hinton broth to match a 0.5 McFarland turbidity standard.
- Within 15 minutes of adjusting the turbidity, dip a sterile cotton swab into the adjusted suspension. The swab should be rotated several times and pressed firmly on the inside wall of the tube above the fluid level. Use the swab to inoculate the entire surface of a Mueller-Hinton sheep blood agar plate. After the plate is dry, use sterile forceps to place a clindamycin (2-μg) disk onto half of the plate and an erythromycin (15-μg) disk onto the other half.
- Incubate at 35°C in 5% $CO_2$ for 20–24 hours.
- Measure the diameter of the zone of inhibition using a ruler or calipers. Interpret according to NCCLS guidelines for *Streptococcus* species other than *S pneumoniae* (2002 breakpoints:‡ clindamycin: ≥19 mm = susceptible, 16–18 = intermediate, ≤15 = resistant; erythromycin: ≥21 mm = susceptible, 16–20 = intermediate, ≤ 15 = resistant).

---

cAMP, cyclic adenosine monophosphate; CNA, Columbia colistin–nalidixic acid; LIM broth, Todd-Hewitt with CNA.

*Before inoculation step, some laboratories may choose to roll swab(s) on a single sheep blood agar plate or CNA sheep blood agar plate. This should be done only in addition to, and not instead of, inoculation into selective broth. The plate should be streaked for isolation, incubated at 35–37°C in ambient air or 5% $CO_2$ for 18–24 hours and inspected for organisms suggestive of GBS as described above. If suspected colonies are confirmed as GBS, the broth can be discarded, thus shortening the time to obtain culture results.

† Source: Fenton, LJ, Harper MH. Evaluation of colistin and nalidixic acid in Todd-Hewitt broth for selective isolation of group B streptococci. J Clin Microbiol 1979;9:167–9. Although Trans-Vag medium is often available without sheep blood, direct comparison of medium with and without sheep blood has shown higher yield when blood is added. LIM broth also may benefit from the addition of sheep blood, although the improvement in yield is smaller and sufficient data are not yet available to support a recommendation.

‡ Source: NCCLS. Performance standard for antimicrobial susceptibility testing. M100-S12, Table 2H, Wayne Pa.: NCCLS, 2002. NCCLS recommends disk diffusion (M-2) or broth microdilution testing (M-7) for susceptibility testing of GBS. Commercial systems that have been cleared or approved for testing of streptococci other than *S pneumoniae* may also be used. Penicillin susceptibility testing is not routinely recommended for GBS because penicillin-resistant isolates have not been confirmed to date.

Schrag S, Gorwitz R, Fultz-Butts K, Schuchat A. Prevention of perinatal group B streptococcal disease. Revised guidelines from CDC. MMWR Recomm Rep 2002;51(RR-11):1–22.

communicate culture results to the obstetric provider, the anticipated site of delivery if possible, and the patient so that intrapartum antibiotic prophylaxis can be given to all GBS-positive women. For women who have GBS bacteriuria in any concentration during the current pregnancy or who have previously given birth to an infant with early-onset GBS disease, GBS cultures are not required. Those women should automatically receive intrapartum prophylaxis. Urine specimens should be labeled to indicate they were obtained from a pregnant woman so laboratories can report any presence of GBS bacteriuria in specimens obtained from pregnant women. If, at anytime during pregnancy, GBS is present in urine in concentrations equal to or greater than $10^5$, antibiotics for asymptomatic bacteriuria or a symptomatic urinary tract infection should be administered, as it would be for any other organism in significant concentration (42, 43). Women who had GBS colonization during a previous pregnancy may no longer be colonized during subsequent pregnancies and require GBS culture evaluation with each pregnancy.

Penicillin remains the agent of choice for intrapartum prophylaxis. Ampicillin is an acceptable alternative, but penicillin is preferred. However, data also show that GBS isolates are increasingly resistant to second-line therapies. Up to 15% of GBS isolates are resistant to clindamycin and 7–25% of isolates are resistant to erythromycin (44). This pattern of resistance has led to a change in the recommendations for second-line therapies (see Table 1). Intravenous administration is the only route recommended for intrapartum GBS prophylaxis because of the higher intraamniotic concentrations achieved with this route. Of note, erythromycin does not cross the placenta.

The benefit of GBS prevention must be weighed against the risk to the woman and her fetus of maternal allergic reactions to antibiotics during labor. Although the risk of fatal anaphylaxis has been estimated at 1 per 100,000 (45, 46), the risk of less severe anaphylactic or allergic reactions is important. In the recent CDC surveillance project of more than 5,000 live births, there was a single, nonfatal anaphylactic reaction (13, 47). The Committee agrees with the CDC that local health agencies should establish surveillance systems to monitor the incidence of early-onset neonatal GBS disease, the emergence of infection in women and their newborns that is caused by resistant organisms, and other complications of widespread maternal antibiotic administration such as severe allergic reactions.

The Committee believes that when culture results are not available, intrapartum prophylaxis should be offered only on the basis of the presence

**Table 1.** Recommended Regimens for Intrapartum Antimicrobial Prophylaxis for Perinatal Group B Streptococcal Disease Prevention*

| Regimens | Antimicrobial |
|---|---|
| Recommended | Penicillin G, 5 million units IV initial dose, then 2.5 million units IV every 4 hours until delivery |
| Alternative | Ampicillin, 2 g IV initial dose, then 1 g IV every 4 hours until delivery |
| If penicillin allergic† | |
| • Patients not at high risk for anaphylaxis | Cefazolin, 2 g IV initial dose, then 1 g IV every 8 hours until delivery |
| • Patients at high risk for anaphylaxis‡ | |
| —GBS susceptible to clindamycin and erythromycin§ | Clindamycin, 900 mg IV every 8 hours until delivery<br>OR<br>Erythromycin, 500 mg IV every 6 hours until delivery |
| —GBS resistant to clindamycin or erythromycin or susceptibility unknown | Vancomycin,‖ 1 g IV every 12 hours until delivery |

GBS, group B streptococci; IV, intravenously.

*Broader-spectrum agents, including an agent active against GBS, may be necessary for treatment of chorioamnionitis.

† History of penicillin allergy should be assessed to determine whether a high risk for anaphylaxis is present. Penicillin-allergic patients at high risk for anaphylaxis are those who have experienced immediate hypersensitivity to penicillin including a history of penicillin-related anaphylaxis; other high-risk patients are those with asthma or other diseases that would make anaphylaxis more dangerous or difficult to treat, such as persons being treated with beta-adrenergic–blocking agents.

‡ If laboratory facilities are adequate, clindamycin and erythromycin susceptibility testing should be performed on prenatal GBS isolates from penicillin-allergic women at high risk for anaphylaxis.

§ Resistance to erythromycin often but not always is associated with clindamycin resistance. If a strain is resistant to erythromycin but appears susceptible to clindamycin, it may still have inducible resistance to clindamycin.

‖ Cefazolin is preferred over vancomycin for women with a history of penicillin allergy other than immediate hypersensitivity reactions, and pharmacologic data suggest it achieves effective intraamniotic concentrations. Vancomycin should be reserved for penicillin-allergic women at high risk for anaphylaxis.

Schrag S, Gorwitz R, Fultz-Butts K, Schuchat A. Prevention of perinatal group B streptococcal disease. Revised guidelines from CDC. MMWR Recomm Rep 2002;51(RR-11):1–22.

of intrapartum risk factors for early-onset GBS disease (see previous description and Fig. 1). The Committee strongly discourages using a hybrid of both strategies (eg, administering intrapartum antibiotics to a woman with rupture of membranes ≥18 hours despite a negative GBS culture at 35–37 weeks of gestation).

The Committee has insufficient data to suggest a specific course of management for women with threatened preterm labor or preterm PROM when delivery is postponed successfully. Determining the timing of intrapartum prophylaxis in these women is challenging. Management of preterm PROM and threatened preterm labor should be guided by clinical considerations. The Committee supports CDC's potential management scheme (see Fig. 2).

The Committee concurs with the CDC that intrapartum prophylaxis is not recommended for women undergoing a planned cesarean delivery in the absence of labor or rupture of membranes, regardless of the GBS colonization status. A retrospective study at a single institution (48) and a review of CDC surveillance data showed that the risk of transmission of GBS from a colonized woman to her infant during a prelabor cesarean delivery with intact membranes is low. Patients expected to undergo planned cesarean deliveries should nonetheless undergo culture screening at 35–37 weeks of gestation because onset of labor or rupture of membranes may occur before the planned cesarean delivery. If intrapartum prophylaxis is administered before a planned cesarean delivery,

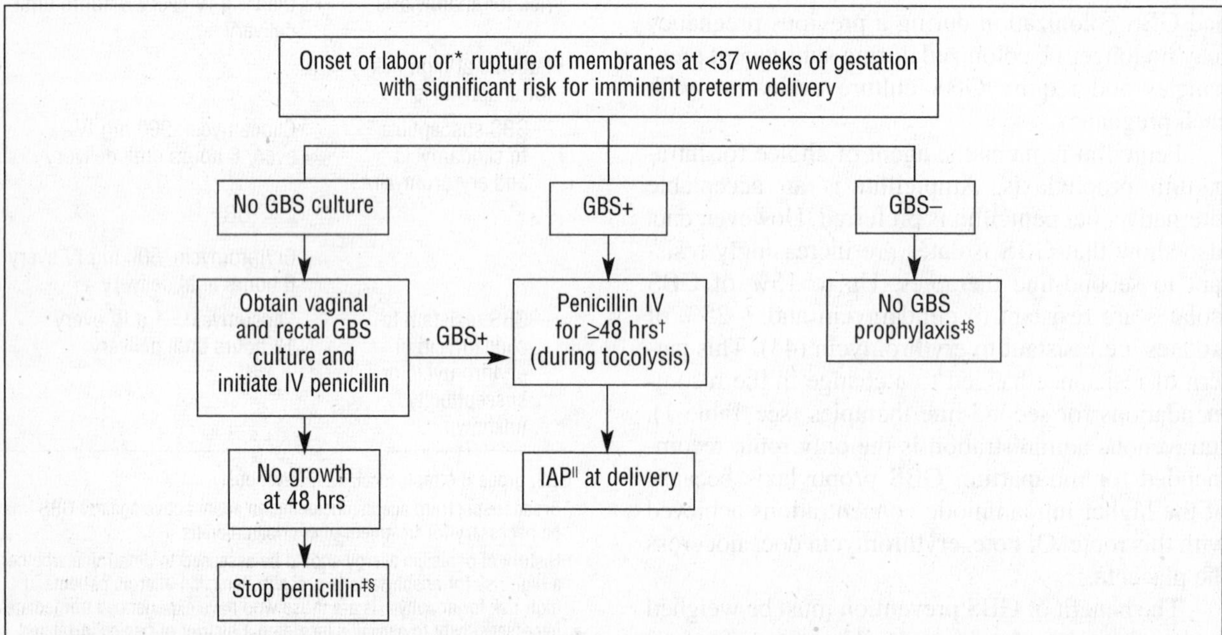

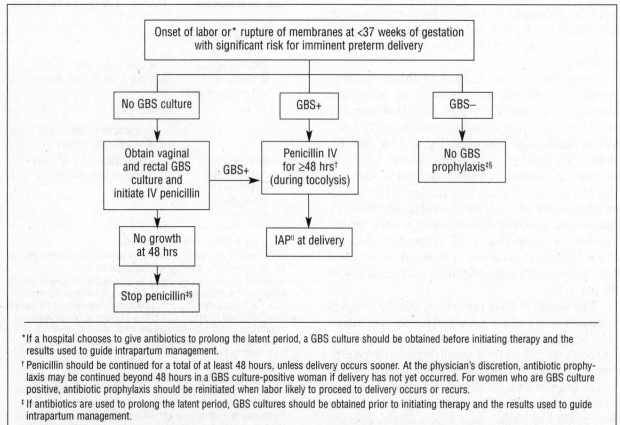

*If a hospital chooses to give antibiotics to prolong the latent period, a GBS culture should be obtained before initiating therapy and the results used to guide intrapartum management.

† Penicillin should be continued for a total of at least 48 hours, unless delivery occurs sooner. At the physician's discretion, antibiotic prophylaxis may be continued beyond 48 hours in a GBS culture-positive woman if delivery has not yet occurred. For women who are GBS culture positive, antibiotic prophylaxis should be reinitiated when labor likely to proceed to delivery occurs or recurs.

‡ If antibiotics are used to prolong the latent period, GBS cultures should be obtained prior to initiating therapy and the results used to guide intrapartum management.

§ If delivery has not occurred within 4 weeks, a vaginal and rectal GBS screening culture should be repeated and the patient should be managed as described, based on the result of the repeat culture.

‖ Intrapartum antibiotic prophylaxis.

Adapted from Schrag S, Gorwitz R, Fultz-Butts K, Schuchat A. Prevention of perinatal group B streptococcal disease. Revised guidelines from CDC. MMWR Recomm Rep 2002;51(RR-11):1–22.

**Fig. 2**. Sample algorithm for group B streptococci (GBS) prophylaxis for women with threatened preterm delivery. This algorithm is not an exclusive course of management. Variations that incorporate individual circumstances or institutional preferences may be appropriate.

the timing of administration of antibiotics and the timing of incision should be individualized (49).

The Committee has insufficient data to support or discourage the use of scalp electrodes or fetal scalp/blood pH determinations in women known to be GBS colonized. Furthermore, the risks of membrane stripping in GBS-colonized women have not been investigated in well-designed prospective studies. Therefore, data are insufficient to encourage or discourage this practice in women known to be GBS colonized.

Current rapid tests for the detection of GBS colonization at the time of labor or rupture of membranes do not have sufficient sensitivity and specificity to eliminate the need for culture-based prenatal screening (50, 51).

The Committee on Obstetric Practice recognizes that compliance with the culture-based approach will require the implementation of several steps. Patient and professional materials are available from ACOG (sales.acog.org and www.acog.org) and the CDC (www.cdc.gov.ncidod/dbmd/gbs). Success of the culture-based approach will require the following:

- Obtaining accurate culture data
- Appropriate processing of the culture by laboratories
- Timely reporting of results to obstetric providers
- Administering intrapartum prophylaxis to culture-positive women

It is important to acknowledge that complete implementation of this complex strategy still will not eliminate all cases of early-onset GBS.

## References

1. Schrag SJ, Zywicki S, Farley MM, Reingold AL, Harrison LH, Lefkowitz LB, et al. Group B streptococcal disease in the era of intrapartum antibiotic prophylaxis. N Engl J Med 2000;342:15–20.
2. Early-onset group B streptococcal disease—United States, 1998-1999. Centers for Disease Control and Prevention. MMWR Morb Mortal Wkly Rep 2000;49: 793–6.
3. Anthony BF, Okada DM, Hobel CJ. Epidemiology of group B Streptococcus: longitudinal observations during pregnancy. J Infect Dis 1978;137:524–30.
4. Regan JA, Klebanoff MA, Nugent RP. The epidemiology of group B streptococcal colonization in pregnancy. Vaginal Infections and Prematurity Study Group. Obstet Gynecol 1991;77:604–10.
5. Dillon HC Jr, Gray E, Pass MA, Gray BM. Anorectal and vaginal carriage of group B streptococci during pregnancy. J Infect Dis 1982;145:794–9.
6. Boyer KM, Gadzala CA, Kelly PD, Burd LI, Gotoff SP. Selective intrapartum chemoprophylaxis of neonatal group B streptococcal early-onset disease. II. Predictive value of prenatal cultures. J Infect Dis 1983;148:802–9.
7. Pass MA, Gray BM, Dillon HC Jr. Puerperal and perinatal infections with group B streptococci. Am J Obstet Gynecol 1982;143:147–52.
8. Bobitt JR, Ledger WJ. Amniotic fluid analysis. Its role in maternal neonatal infection. Obstet Gynecol 1978;51:56–62.
9. Braun TI, Pinover W, Sih P. Group B streptococcal meningitis in a pregnant woman before the onset of labor. Clin Infect Dis 1995;21:1042–3.
10. Yancey MK, Duff P, Clark P, Kurtzer T, Frentzen BH, Kubilis P. Peripartum infection associated with vaginal group B streptococcal colonization. Obstet Gynecol 1994;84:816–9.
11. Fox BC. Delayed-onset postpartum meningitis due to group B streptococcus. Clin Infect Dis 1994;19:350.
12. Aharoni A, Potasman I, Levitan Z, Golan D, Sharf M. Postpartum maternal group B streptococcal meningitis. Rev Infect Dis 1990;12:273–6.
13. Schrag S, Gorwitz R, Fultz-Butts K, Schuchat A. Prevention of perinatal group B streptococcal disease. Revised guidelines from CDC. MMWR Recomm Rep 2002;51(RR-11):1–22.
14. Boyer KM, Gotoff SP. Strategies for chemoprophylaxis of GBS early-onset infections. Antibiot Chemother 1985; 35:267–80.
15. Zangwill KM, Schuchat A, Wenger JD. Group B streptococcal disease in the United States, 1990: report from a multistate active surveillance system. Mor Mortal Wkly Rep CDC Surveill Summ 1992;41(6):25–32.
16. Schuchat A, Oxtoby M, Cochi S, Sikes RK, Hightower A, Plikaytis B, et al. Population-based risk factors for neonatal group B streptococcal disease: results of a cohort study in metropolitan Atlanta. J Infect Dis 1990;162:672–7.
17. Schuchat A, Deaver-Robinson K, Plikaytis BD, Zangwill KM, Mohle-Boetani J, Wenger JD. Multistate case-control study of maternal risk factors for neonatal group B streptococcal disease. The Active Surveillance Study Group. Pediatr Infect Dis J 1994;13:623–9.
18. Carstensen H, Christensen KK, Grennert L, Persson K, Polberger S. Early-onset neonatal group B streptococcal septicaemia in siblings. J Infect 1988;17:201–4.
19. Faxelius G, Bremme K, Kvist-Christensen K, Christensen P, Ringertz S. Neonatal septicemia due to group B streptococci-perinatal risk factors and outcome of subsequent pregnancies. J Perinat Med 1988;16:423–30.
20. Christensen KK, Dahlander K, Linden V, Svenningsen N, Christensen P. Obstetrical care in future pregnancies after fetal loss in group B streptococcal septicemia. A prevention program based on bacteriological and immunological follow-up. Eur J Obstet Gynecol Reprod Biol 1981;12: 143–50.
21. Pass MA, Gray BM, Khare S, Dillon HC Jr. Prospective studies of group B streptococcal infections in infants. J Pediatr 1979;95:437–43.
22. Wood EG, Dillon HC Jr. A prospective study of group B streptococcal bacteriuria in pregnancy. Am J Obstet Gynecol 1981;140:515–20.
23. Moller M, Thomsen AC, Borch K, Dinesen K, Zdravkovic M. Rupture of fetal membranes and premature delivery

associated with group B streptococci in urine of pregnant women. Lancet 1984;2(8394):69–70.
24. Liston TE, Harris RE, Foshee S, Null DM Jr. Relationship of neonatal pneumonia to maternal urinary and neonatal isolates of group B streptococci. South Med J 1979;72: 1410–2.
25. Persson K, Christensen KK, Christensen P, Forsgren A, Jorgensen C, Persson PH. Asymptomatic bacteriuria during pregnancy with special reference to group B streptococci. Scand J Infect Dis 1985;17:195–9.
26. Baker CJ, Kasper DL. Correlation of maternal antibody deficiency with susceptibility to neonatal group B streptococcal infection. N Engl J Med 1976;294:753–6.
27. Schuchat A, Hilger T, Zell E, Farley M, Reingold A, Harrison L, et al. Active bacterial core surveillance of the emerging infections program network. Emerging Infect Dis 2001;7:92–9.
28. Jeffery HE, Moses Lahra M. Eight-year outcome of universal screening and intrapartum antibiotics for maternal group B streptococcal carriers. Pediatrics 1998;101:E2.
29. Isaacs D, Royle JA. Intrapartum antibiotics and early onset neonatal sepsis caused by group B streptococcus and by other organisms in Australia. Australasian Study Group for Neonatal Infections. Pediatr Infect Dis J 1999;18:524–8.
30. Davies HD, Adair CE, Schuchat A, Low DE, Sauve RS, McGeer A. Physicians' prevention practices and incidence of neonatal group B streptococcal disease in 2 Canadian regions. CMAJ 2001;164:479–85.
31. Prevention of perinatal group B streptococcal disease: a public health perspective. Centers for Disease Control and Prevention. MMWR Recomm Rep1996;45:1–24.
32. Schrag SJ, Zell ER, Lynfield R, Roome A, Arnold KE, Craig AS, et al. A population-based comparison of strategies to prevent early-onset group B streptococcal disease in neonates. N Engl J Med 2002;347:233–9.
33. Hafner E, Sterniste W, Rosen A, Schuchter K, Plattner M, Asboth F, et al. Group B streptococci during pregnancy: a comparison of two screening and treatment protocols. Am J Obstet Gynecol 1998;179:677–81.
34. Lieu TA, Mohle-Boetani JC, Ray GT, Ackerson LM, Walton DL. Neonatal group B streptococcal infection in a managed care population. Perinatal Group B Streptococcal Infection Study Group. Obstet Gynecol 1998;92: 21–7.
35. Factor SH, Levine OS, Nasser A, Potter J, Fajardo A, O'Sullivan MJ, et al. Impact of a risk-based prevention policy on neonatal group B streptococcal disease. Am J Obstet Gynecol 1998;179:1568–71.
36. Cheon-Lee E, Amstey MS. Compliance with the Centers for Disease Control and Prevention antenatal culture protocol for preventing group B streptococcal neonatal sepsis. Am J Obstet Gynecol 1998;179:77–9.
37. Katz VL, Moos MK, Cefalo RC, Thorp JM Jr, Bowes WA Jr, Wells SD. Group B streptococci: results of a protocol of antepartum screening and intrapartum treatment. Am J Obstet Gynecol 1994;170:521–6.
38. Gilson GJ, Christensen F, Romero H, Bekes K, Silva L, Qualls CR. Prevention of group B streptococcus early-onset neonatal sepsis: comparison of the Center for Disease Control and Prevention screening-based protocol to a risk-based protocol in infants at greater than 37 weeks' gestation. J Perinatol 2000;20:491–5.
39. Brozanski BS, Jones JG, Krohn MA, Sweet RL. Effect of a screening-based prevention policy on prevalence of early-onset group B streptococcal sepsis. Obstet Gynecol 2000;95:496–501.
40. Bromberger P, Lawrence JM, Braun D, Saunders B, Contreras R, Petitti DB. The influence of intrapartum antibiotics on the clinical spectrum of early-onset group B streptococcal infection in term infants. Pediatrics 2000; 106:244–50.
41. Rosenstein NE, Schuchat A. Opportunities for prevention of perinatal group B streptococcal disease: a multistate surveillance analysis. The Neonatal Group B Streptococcal Disease Study Group. Obstet Gynecol 1997;90: 901–6.
42. Persson K, Bjerre B, Elfstrom L, Polberger S, Forsgren A. Group B streptococci at delivery: high count in urine increases risk for neonatal colonization. Scand J Infect Dis 1986;18:525–31.
43. Persson K, Bjerre B, Elfstrom L, Forsgren A. Longitudinal study of group B streptococcal carriage during late pregnancy. Scand J Infect Dis 1987;19:325–9.
44. Pearlman MD, Pierson CL, Faix RG. Frequent resistance of clinical group B streptococci isolates to clindamycin and erythromycin. Obstet Gynecol 1998;92:258–61.
45. Schwartz B, Schuchat A, Oxtoby MJ, Cochi SL, Hightower A, Broome CV. Invasive group B streptococcal disease in adults. A population-based study in metropolitan Atlanta. JAMA 1991;266:1112–4.
46. Hardman JG, Limbird LE, Molinoff PB, Ruddon RW, Gilman AG, editors. Goodman and Gilman's the pharmacological basis of therapeutics. 9th ed. New York: McGraw-Hill; 1996.
47. Dunn AB, Blomquist J, Khouzami V. Anaphylaxis in labor secondary to prophylaxis against group B Streptococcus: a case report. J Reprod Med 1999;44:381–4.
48. Ramus RM, McIntire DD, Wendel GD Jr. Antibiotic chemoprophylaxis for group B strep is not necessary with elective cesarean section at term [abstract]. Am J Obstet Gynecol 1999;180:S85.
49. Hager WD, Schuchat A, Gibbs R, Sweet R, Mead P, Larsen JW. Prevention of perinatal group B streptococcal infection: current controversies. Obstet Gynecol 2000;96: 141–5.
50. Yancey MK, Armer T, Clark P, Duff P. Assessment of rapid identification tests for genital carriage of group B streptococci. Obstet Gynecol 1992;80:1038–47.
51. Walker CK, Crombleholme WR, Ohm-Smith MJ, Sweet RL. Comparison of rapid tests for detection of group B streptococcal colonization. Am J Perinatol 1992;9: 304–8.

ACOG Committee Opinion

Committee on Obstetric Practice

Number 281, December 2002

# Rubella Vaccination

*ABSTRACT: The incidence of rubella decreased from 0.45 per 100,000 in 1990 to 0.1 per 100,000 in 1999. Although there is a nationwide shortage of rubella vaccine, women who are rubella susceptible during pregnancy should receive MMR (measles–mumps–rubella) vaccination postpartum. In October 2001, the federal Centers for Disease Control and Prevention changed the recommendations concerning the pregnancy interval after receiving rubella vaccine. This interval has been reduced from 3 months to 1 month.*

The incidence of rubella decreased from 0.45 per 100,000 in 1990 to 0.1 per 100,000 in 1999 (1). There have been cluster outbreaks, especially among persons born outside of the United States. Although there is a nationwide shortage of rubella vaccine, women who are rubella susceptible during pregnancy should receive MMR (measles–mumps–rubella) vaccination postpartum. The appropriate test for assessing rubella immunity is the immunoglobulin G serology. There is no contraindication to giving MMR vaccination while breastfeeding. Receipt of rubella vaccination in a new mother does not pose a risk of transmission of the virus to the newborn or to other children in her household. Receipt of rubella vaccination during pregnancy is not an indication for interruption of that pregnancy.

In October 2001, the federal Centers for Disease Control and Prevention changed the recommendations concerning the pregnancy interval after receiving rubella vaccine. This interval has been reduced from 3 months to 1 month (2). The safe interval for measles and mumps vaccination was already 1 month.

## References

1. Reef SE, Frey TK, Theall K, Abernathy E, Burnett CL, Icenogle J, et al. The changing epidemiology of rubella in the 1990s: on the verge of elimination and new challenges for control and prevention. JAMA 2002;287:464-72.
2. Revised ACIP recommendation for avoiding pregnancy after receiving a rubella-containing vaccine. MMWR Morb Mortal Wkly Rep 2001;50:1117.

This document reflects emerging clinical and scientific advances as of the date issued and is subject to change. The information should not be construed as dictating an exclusive course of treatment or procedure to be followed.



ISSN 1074-861X

**The American College of Obstetricians and Gynecologists**
409 12th Street, SW
PO Box 96920
Washington, DC 20090-6920

12345/65432

Rubella vaccination. ACOG Committee Opinion No. 281. American College of Obstetricians and Gynecologists. Obstet Gynecol 2002;100:1417.

ACOG Committee Opinion

Committee on Obstetric Practice

Number 282, January 2003



ISSN 1074-861X

**The American College of Obstetricians and Gynecologists**
409 12th Street, SW
PO Box 96920
Washington, DC 20090-6920

12345/76543

Immunization during pregnancy. ACOG Committee Opinion No. 282. American College of Obstetricians and Gynecologists. Obstet Gynecol 2003; 101:207–12.

# Immunization During Pregnancy

*ABSTRACT: Preconceptional immunization of pregnant women to prevent disease in the offspring, when practical, is preferred to vaccination of pregnant women. The benefits of immunization to the pregnant woman and her neonate usually outweigh the theoretic risks of adverse effects. Current information on the safety of vaccines given during pregnancy is subject to change and can be verified from the Centers for Disease Control and Prevention web site at www.cdc.gov/nip.*

The benefits of immunization to the pregnant woman and her neonate usually outweigh the theoretic risks of adverse effects. The theoretic risks of the vaccination of pregnant women with killed virus vaccines have not been identified.

Current recommendations for immunization of pregnant women are presented in Table 1. Although new information continues to confirm the safety of vaccines intentionally or inadvertently given during pregnancy, current information is subject to change because the effects of many diseases and vaccines on the pregnant woman or the fetus may be rare and infrequently reported. (For further information and updates refer to www.cdc.gov/nip.)

In the decision of whether to immunize a pregnant woman with other vaccines not listed in Table 1, the risk for exposure to disease and its deleterious effects on the pregnant woman and the fetus must be balanced against the efficacy of the vaccine and any beneficial effects resulting from it. Preconceptional immunization of women to prevent disease in the offspring, when practical, is preferred to vaccination of pregnant women with certain vaccines. Vaccination of women during the postpartum period, especially for rubella and varicella, should be encouraged. Women susceptible to rubella should be vaccinated with measles–mumps–rubella on postpartum discharge from the hospital.

**Table 1.** Immunization During Pregnancy

| Immunobiologic Agent | Risk from Disease to Pregnant Woman | Risk from Disease to Fetus or Neonate | Type of Immunizing Agent | Risk from Immunizing Agent to Fetus | Indications for Immunization During Pregnancy | Dose Schedule* | Comments |
|---|---|---|---|---|---|---|---|
| | | | *LIVE VIRUS VACCINES* | | | | |
| Measles | Significant morbidity, low mortality; not altered by pregnancy | Significant increase in abortion rate; may cause malformations | Live attenuated virus vaccine | None confirmed | Contraindicated (see immune globulins) | Single dose SC, preferably as measles–mumps–rubella† | Vaccination of susceptible women should be part of postpartum care. Breastfeeding is not a contraindication. |
| Mumps | Low morbidity and mortality; not altered by pregnancy | Possible increased rate of abortion in first trimester | Live attenuated virus vaccine | None confirmed | Contraindicated | Single dose SC, preferably as measles–mumps–rubella | Vaccination of susceptible women should be part of postpartum care |
| Poliomyelitis | No increased incidence in pregnancy, but may be more severe if it does occur | Anoxic fetal damage reported; 50% mortality in neonatal disease | Live attenuated virus (oral polio vaccine) and enhanced-potency inactivated virus vaccine‡ | None confirmed | Not routinely recommended for women in the United States, except women at increased risk of exposure | *Primary:* Two doses of enhanced-potency inactivated virus SC at 4–8 week intervals and a third dose 6–12 months after the second dose<br>*Immediate protection:* One dose oral polio vaccine (in outbreak setting) | Vaccine indicated for susceptible pregnant women traveling in endemic areas or in other high-risk situations |
| Rubella | Low morbidity and mortality; not altered by pregnancy | High rate of abortion and congenital rubella syndrome | Live attenuated virus vaccine | None confirmed | Contraindicated, but congenital rubella syndrome has never been described after vaccine | Single dose SC, preferably as measles–mumps–rubella | Teratogenicity of vaccine is theoretic, not confirmed to date; vaccination of susceptible women should be part of postpartum care |
| Yellow fever | Significant morbidity and mortality; not altered by pregnancy | Unknown | Live attenuated virus vaccine | Unknown | Contraindicated except if exposure is unavoidable | Single dose SC | Postponement of travel preferable to vaccination, if possible |

| | | | | | | | |
|---|---|---|---|---|---|---|---|
| Varicella | Possible increase in severe pneumonia | Can cause congenital varicella in 2% of fetuses infected during the second trimester | Live attenuated virus vaccine | None confirmed | Contraindicated, but no adverse outcomes reported if given in pregnancy | Two doses needed with second dose given 4–8 weeks after first dose. Should be strongly encouraged | Teratogenicity of vaccine is theoretic, outcomes reported weeks 4–8 not confirmed to date. Vaccination of susceptible women should be considered postpartum |
| | | | | *OTHER* | | | |
| Influenza | Increase in morbidity and mortality during epidemic of new antigenic strain | Possible increased abortion rate; no malformations confirmed | Inactivated virus vaccine | None confirmed | All women who are pregnant in the second and third trimester during the flu season (October–March); women at high risk for pulmonary complications regardless of trimester | One dose IM every year | — |
| Rabies | Near 100% fatality; not altered by pregnancy | Determined by maternal disease | Killed virus vaccine | Unknown | Indications for prophylaxis not altered by pregnancy; each case considered individually | Public health authorities to be consulted for indications, dosage, and route of administration | — |
| Hepatitis B | Possible increased severity during third trimester | Possible increase in abortion rate and preterm birth; neonatal hepatitis can occur; high risk of newborn carrier state | Purified surface antigen produced by recombinant technology | None reported | Pre-exposure and postexposure for women at risk of infection | Three-dose series IM at 0, 1, and 6 months | Used with hepatitis B immune globulin for some exposures; exposed newborn needs birth dose vaccination and immune globulin as soon as possible. All infants should receive birth dose of vaccine. |
| Hepatitis A | No increased risk during pregnancy | — | Inactivated virus | None reported | Pre-exposure and postexposure for women at risk of infection; international travelers | Two-dose schedule 6 months apart | — |

| | | | | | | | |
|---|---|---|---|---|---|---|---|
| | | | *INACTIVATED BACTERIAL VACCINES* | | | | |
| Pneumococcus | No increased risk during pregnancy; no increase in severity of disease | Unknown, but depends on maternal illness | Polyvalent polysaccharide vaccine | None reported | Recommended for women with asplenia; metabolic, renal, cardiac, pulmonary diseases; smokers; immuno-suppressed. Indica-tions not altered by pregnancy. | In adults, one SC or IM dose only; consider repeat dose in 6 years for high-risk women | — |
| Meningococcus | Significant morbidity and mortality; not altered by pregnancy | Unknown, but depends on maternal illness | Quadrivalent polysaccharide vaccine | None reported | Indications not altered by pregnancy; vaccination recommended in unusual outbreak situations | One SC dose; public health authorities consulted | — |
| Typhoid | Significant morbidity and mortality; not altered by pregnancy | Unknown | Killed or live attenuated oral bacterial vaccine | None confirmed | Not recommended routinely except for close, continued exposure or travel to endemic areas | Killed *Primary:* Two injections SC at least 4 weeks apart. *Booster:* Single dose SC or ID (depending on type of product) *Booster:* Schedule not yet determined | Oral vaccine preferred |
| Anthrax | Significant morbidity and mortality; not altered by pregnancy | Unknown, but depends on maternal illness | Preparation from cell-free filtrate of *B anthracis*; no dead or live bacteria | None confirmed | Not routinely recommended unless pregnant women work directly with *B anthracis*, imported animal hides, potentially infected animals in high incidence areas (not United States) or military personnel deployed to high-risk exposure areas | Six-dose primary vaccination SC, then annual booster vaccination | Teratogenicity of vaccine theoretical |

*(continued)*

**Table 1.** Immunization During Pregnancy *(continued)*

| Immunobiologic Agent | Risk from Disease to Pregnant Woman | Risk from Disease to Fetus or Neonate | Type of Immunizing Agent | Risk from Immunizing Agent to Fetus | Indications for Immunization During Pregnancy | Dose Schedule* | Comments |
|---|---|---|---|---|---|---|---|
| | | | | *TOXOIDS* | | | |
| Tetanus–diphtheria | Severe morbidity; tetanus mortality 30%; diphtheria mortality 10%; unaltered by pregnancy | Neonatal tetanus mortality 60% | Combined tetanus–diphtheria toxoids preferred: adult tetanus–diphtheria formulation | None confirmed | Lack of primary series, or no booster within past 10 years | *Primary:* Two doses IM at 1–2-month interval with a third dose 6–12 months after the second. *Booster:* Single dose IM every 10 years after completion of primary series | Updating of immune status should be part of antepartum care |
| | | | | *SPECIFIC IMMUNE GLOBULINS* | | | |
| Hepatitis B | Possible increased severity during third trimester | Possible increase in abortion rate and preterm birth; neonatal hepatitis can occur; high risk of carriage in newborn | Hepatitis B immune globulin | None reported | Postexposure prophylaxis | Depends on exposure; consult Immunization Practices Advisory committee recommendations (IM) | Usually given with hepatitis B virus vaccine; exposed newborn needs immediate postexposure prophylaxis |
| Rabies | Near 100% fatality; not altered by pregnancy | Determined by maternal disease | Rabies immune globulin | None reported | Postexposure prophylaxis | Half dose at injury site, half dose in deltoid | Used in conjunction with rabies killed virus vaccine |
| Tetanus | Severe morbidity; mortality 60% | Neonatal tetanus mortality 60% | Tetanus immune globulin | None reported | Postexposure prophylaxis | One dose IM | Used in conjunction with tetanus toxoid |

| | | | | | | | |
|---|---|---|---|---|---|---|---|
| Varicella | Possible increase in severe varicella pneumonia | Can cause congenital varicella with increased mortality in neonatal period; very rarely causes congenital defects | Varicella–zoster immune globulin (obtained from the American Red Cross) | None reported | Should be considered for healthy pregnant women exposed to varicella to protect against maternal, not congenital, infection | One dose IM within 96 hours of exposure | Indicated also for newborns of women who developed varicella within 4 days before delivery or 2 days following delivery; approximately 90–95% of adults are immune to varicella; not indicated for prevention of congenital varicella |
| *STANDARD IMMUNE GLOBULINS* | | | | | | | |
| Hepatitis A | Possible increased severity during third trimester | Probable increase in abortion rate and preterm birth; possible transmission to neonate at delivery if woman is incubating the virus or is acutely ill at that time | Standard immune globulin | None reported | Postexposure prophylaxis, but hepatitis A virus vaccine should be used with hepatitis A immune globulin | 0.02 mL/kg IM in one dose of immune globulin | Immune globulin should be given as soon as possible and within 2 weeks of exposure; infants born to women who are incubating the virus or are acutely ill at delivery should receive one dose of 0.5 mL as soon as possible after birth |

*Abbreviations: ID, intradermally; IM, intramuscularly; PO, orally; and SC, subcutaneously.

†Two doses necessary for adequate vaccination of students entering institutions of higher education, newly hired medical personnel, and international travelers.

‡Inactivated polio vaccine recommended for nonimmunized adults at increased risk.

Data from General recommendations on immunization. Recommendations of the Advisory Committee on Immunization Practices (ACIP) and the American Academy of Family Physicians (AAFP). Centers for Disease Control. MMWR Recomm Rep;51(RR-2):1–35. Available at http://www.cdc.gov/mmwr/preview/mmwrhtml/rr5102a1.htm. Retrieved October 11, 2002.

ACOG

Committee on Obstetric Practice

Committee Opinion

Number 283, May 2003

# New U.S. Food and Drug Administration Labeling on Cytotec (Misoprostol) Use and Pregnancy

*ABSTRACT: On April 17, 2002, the U.S. Food and Drug Administration approved a new label for the use of Cytotec (misoprostol) during pregnancy. The new labeling does not contain claims regarding the efficacy and/or safety of Cytotec when it is used for cervical ripening for the induction of labor nor does it stipulate doses or dosing intervals. Therefore, the Committee on Obstetric Practice reminds Fellows that this agent should be used as previously recommended.*

On April 17, 2002, the U.S. Food and Drug Administration (FDA) approved a new label for the use of Cytotec (misoprostol) during pregnancy. The FDA describes the major labeling changes and their rationale as follows (see also the FDA's web site at www.fda.gov/medwatch/safety/2002/safety02.htm#cytote). The new labeling:

- Revises the contraindication and precaution that Cytotec should not be used in women who are pregnant by stating that the contraindication is for pregnant women who are using Cytotec to reduce the risk of nonsteroidal antiinflammatory drug (NSAID)-induced stomach ulcers.
  - *Rationale*—The drug has a recognized use by ob-gyns to induce labor, delivery, and is part of the FDA-approved regimen for use with mifepristone to induce abortion in pregnancies of 49 days or less. The contraindication now refers to the drug's approved indication, for reducing the risk of NSAID-induced gastric ulcers.
- Creates a new labor and delivery section of the labeling and provides safety information related to those uses.
  - *Rationale*—21 CFR 201.57(f)(7) requires labeling to include drug-effect information if a drug has a recognized use during labor or delivery, whether or not the use is stated in the indications section of the labeling.
- Provides new information that uterine rupture, an adverse event reported with Cytotec, is associated with risk factors such as later trimester pregnancies, higher doses of the drug, including the manufactured 100-mcg

This document reflects emerging clinical and scientific advances as of the date issued and is subject to change. The information should not be construed as dictating an exclusive course of treatment or procedure to be followed.



ISSN 1074-861X

**The American College of Obstetricians and Gynecologists**
409 12th Street, SW
PO Box 96920
Washington, DC 20090-6920

12345/76543

New U.S. Food and Drug Administration labeling on Cytotec (misoprostol) use and pregnancy. ACOG Committee Opinion No. 283. American College of Obstetricians and Gynecologists. Obstet Gynecol 2003;101:1049–50.

tablets, prior cesarean delivery or uterine surgery, and having had five or more previous pregnancies.

— *Rationale*—Risk factors allow physicians to identify patients who may be at greater risk for these adverse events. This information may guide safer use of the drug.

The new labeling does not contain claims regarding the efficacy and/or safety of Cytotec when it is used for cervical ripening for the induction of labor nor does it stipulate doses or dosing intervals. Therefore, the Committee on Obstetric Practice reminds Fellows that this agent should be used as previously recommended (see box) (1–3).

**Recommended Uses of Cytotec**

- If misoprostol is to be used for cervical ripening or labor induction in the third trimester, one quarter of a 100-μg tablet (ie, approximately 25 μg) should be considered for the initial dose. The use of higher doses (50 μg every 6 hours) may be appropriate in some situations, although increasing the dose appears to be associated with uterine tachysystole and possibly with uterine hyperstimulation and meconium staining of amniotic fluid.
- Doses should not be administered more frequently than every 3–6 hours.
- Oxytocin should not be administered less than 4 hours after the last misoprostol dose.
- Patients undergoing cervical ripening or labor induction with misoprostol for labor induction should undergo fetal heart rate and uterine activity monitoring in a hospital setting.
- Misoprostol should not be used for cervical ripening for the induction of labor in patients with a previous cesarean delivery or prior major uterine surgery.

## References


1. American College of Obstetricians and Gynecologists. Induction of labor with misoprostol. ACOG Committee Opinion 228. Washington, DC: ACOG; 1999.
2. American College of Obstetricians and Gynecologists. Response to Searle's drug warning on misoprostol. ACOG Committee Opinion 248. Washington, DC: ACOG; 2000.
3. American College of Obstetricians and Gynecologists. Induction of labor. ACOG Practice Bulletin 10. Washington, DC: ACOG; 1999.

ACOG

Committee on Obstetric Practice

# Committee Opinion

Number 284, August 2003

# Nonobstetric Surgery in Pregnancy

*ABSTRACT: Although there are no data to support specific recommendations regarding nonobstetric surgery and anesthesia in pregnancy, it is important for nonobstetric physicians to obtain obstetric consultation before performing nonobstetric surgery. The decision to use fetal monitoring should be individualized, and each case warrants a team approach for optimal safety of the woman and her baby.*

The American College of Obstetricians and Gynecologists' Committee on Obstetric Practice acknowledges that the issue of nonobstetric surgery and anesthesia in pregnancy is an important concern for physicians who care for women; however, there are no data to allow us to make specific recommendations. It is important for physicians to obtain obstetric consultation before performing nonobstetric surgery because obstetricians are uniquely qualified to discuss aspects of maternal physiology and anatomy that may affect intraoperative maternal–fetal well-being. The decision to use fetal monitoring should be individualized, and, if used, may be based on gestational age, type of surgery, and facilities available. Ultimately, each case warrants a team approach (anesthesia, obstetrics, surgery) for optimal safety of the woman and her baby.



ISSN 1074-861X

**The American College of Obstetricians and Gynecologists**
409 12th Street, SW
PO Box 96920
Washington, DC 20090-6920

12345/76543

Nonobstetric surgery in pregnancy. ACOG Committee Opinion No. 284. American College of Obstetricians and Gynecologists. Obstet Gynecol 2003;102:431.

ACOG Committee Opinion

Committee on Obstetric Practice

Number 291, November 2003

# Use of Progesterone to Reduce Preterm Birth

*ABSTRACT: Preterm birth affects 12% of all births in the United States. Recent studies support the hypothesis that progesterone supplementation reduces preterm birth in a select group of women (ie, those with a prior spontaneous birth at <37 weeks of gestation). Despite the apparent benefits of progesterone in this high-risk population, the ideal progesterone formulation is unknown. The American College of Obstetricians and Gynecologists Committee on Obstetric Practice believes that further studies are needed to evaluate the use of progesterone in patients with other high-risk obstetric factors, such as multiple gestations, short cervical length, or positive test results for cervicovaginal fetal fibronectin. When progesterone is used, it is important to restrict its use to only women with a documented history of a previous spontaneous birth at less than 37 weeks of gestation because unresolved issues remain, such as optimal route of drug delivery and long-term safety of the drug.*

Preterm birth affects 12% of all births in the United States. This statistic has led multiple investigators to identify those women at greatest risk (eg, those with prior preterm delivery, maternal weight <50 kg, African-American race, bleeding, and concurrent sexually transmitted diseases). Despite identification of these risk factors, no interventions to date have been associated with a decrease in preterm delivery rates.

A recent large randomized placebo-controlled trial comparing 17α hydroxyprogesterone caproate "17P" therapy to prevent preterm birth in a select, high-risk group of women (documented history of a previous spontaneous preterm birth <37 weeks of gestation) was conducted for the National Institute of Child Health and Human Development (NICHD) Maternal-Fetal Medicine Units Network (1). A total of 459 women with a history of previous spontaneous births at less than 37 weeks of gestation were enrolled between 16 weeks and 20 weeks of gestation. Of note, the mean gestational age of their previous preterm deliveries was 30.7 weeks. They were randomly assigned to receive weekly intramuscular injections of 17P (n = 306) or placebo (n = 153). The study was stopped early when results showed a significant protection against recurrent preterm birth for all races of women who received 17P (Table 1).

A recent small randomized placebo-controlled trial of supplemental vaginal progesterone (100 mg daily) in 142 women at high risk for preterm birth

This document reflects emerging clinical and scientific advances as of the date issued and is subject to change. The information should not be construed as dictating an exclusive course of treatment or procedure to be followed.



ISSN 1074-861X

**The American College of Obstetricians and Gynecologists**
409 12th Street, SW
PO Box 96920
Washington, DC 20090-6920

12345/76543

Use of progesterone to reduce preterm birth. ACOG Committee Opinion No. 291. American College of Obstetricians and Gynecologists. Obstet Gynecol 2003;102:1115–6.

**Table 1.** Rates of Preterm Labor with Progesterone Therapy or Placebo

| Gestation | Placebo Group (n = 153) | Progesterone Group (n = 306) | Relative Risk | Confidence Interval | *P* |
|---|---|---|---|---|---|
| <37 wk | 54.9% | 36.3% | 0.66 | 0.54–0.81 | .0001 |
| <35 wk | 30.7% | 20.6% | 0.67 | 0.48–0.93 | .0165 |
| <32 wk | 19.6% | 11.4% | 0.58 | 0.37–0.91 | .0180 |

Data from Meis PJ, Klebanoff M, Thom E, Dombrowski MP, Sibai B, Moawad AH, et al. Prevention of recurrent preterm delivery by 17 alpha-hydroxyprogesterone caproate. N Engl J Med 2003;348:2379–85.

(women with at least 1 previous spontaneous preterm birth, prophylactic cervical cerclage, and uterine malformation) revealed that for delivery at less than 34 weeks of gestation, the preterm birth rate was significantly lower among women receiving progesterone than among those receiving placebo (2.7% versus 18.6%) (2). The results of this study and the NICHD trial support the hypothesis that progesterone supplementation reduces preterm birth in a select very high-risk group of women.

Despite the apparent benefits of progesterone in a high-risk population, the ideal progesterone formulation is unknown. The 17P used in the NICHD trial was specially formulated for research and is not currently commercially available on a wide scale. Progesterone has been studied only as a prophylactic measure in asymptomatic women, not as a tocolytic agent. Whether vaginal progesterone is equally efficacious remains to be proved in a larger population. The American College of Obstetricians and Gynecologists Committee on Obstetric Practice believes that further studies are needed to evaluate the use of progesterone in patients with other high-risk obstetric factors, such as multiple gestations, short cervical length, or positive test results for cervicovaginal fetal fibronectin. When progesterone is used, it is important to restrict its use to only women with a documented history of a previous spontaneous birth at less than 37 weeks of gestation because unresolved issues remain, such as optimal route of drug delivery and long-term safety of the drug.

## References


1. Meis PJ, Klebanoff M, Thom E, Dombrowski MP, Sibai B, Moawad AH, et al. Prevention of recurrent preterm delivery by 17 alpha-hydroxyprogesterone caproate. N Engl J Med 2003;348:2379–85.
2. da Fonseca EB, Bittar RE, Carvalho MH, Zugaib M. Prophylactic administration of progesterone by vaginal suppository to reduce the incidence of spontaneous preterm birth in women at increased risk: a randomized placebo-controlled double-blind study. Am J Obstet Gynecol 2003;188:419–24.

ACOG

Committee on Obstetric Practice

American Society of Anesthesiologists

# Committee Opinion

Number 295, July 2004 (Replaces No. 231, February 2000)

## Pain Relief During Labor

*ABSTRACT: Pain management should be provided whenever medically indicated. The American Society of Anesthesiologists (ASA) and the American College of Obstetricians and Gynecologists (ACOG) believe that women requesting epidural analgesia during labor should not be deprived of this service based on their insurance or inadequate nursing participation in the management of regional analgesic modalities. Furthermore, in an effort to allow the maximum number of patients to benefit from neuraxial analgesia, ASA and ACOG believe that labor nurses should not be restricted from participating in the management of pain relief during labor.*

Labor causes severe pain for many women. There is no other circumstance where it is considered acceptable for an individual to experience untreated severe pain, amenable to safe intervention, while under a physician's care. In the absence of a medical contraindication, maternal request is a sufficient medical indication for pain relief during labor. Pain management should be provided whenever medically indicated.

Of the various pharmacologic methods used for pain relief during labor and delivery, neuraxial analgesia techniques (epidural, spinal, and combined spinal–epidural) are the most flexible, effective, and least depressing to the central nervous system, allowing for an alert participating woman and an alert neonate. The American Society of Anesthesiologists (ASA) and the American College of Obstetricians and Gynecologists (ACOG) believe that women requesting epidural analgesia during labor should not be deprived of this service based on their insurance or inadequate nursing participation in the management of regional analgesic modalities. In addition, third-party payers who provide reimbursement for obstetric services should not deny reimbursement for labor analgesia because of an absence of "other medical indications." Although the availability of various methods of labor analgesia will vary from hospital to hospital, within an institution the methods available should not be based on a patient's ability to pay. Furthermore, in an effort to allow the maximum number of patients to benefit from neuraxial analgesia, ASA and ACOG believe that labor nurses should not be restricted from participating in the management of pain relief during labor. Under appropriate physician supervision, labor and delivery nursing personnel who have been properly educated and have demonstrated current competence should be able to participate in the management of epidural infusions, including adjusting dosage and discontinuing infusions.



ISSN 1074-861X

**The American College of Obstetricians and Gynecologists**
409 12th Street, SW
PO Box 96920
Washington, DC 20090-6920

12345/87654

Pain relief during labor. ACOG Committee Opinion No. 295. American College of Obstetricians and Gynecologists. Obstet Gynecol 2004;104:213.

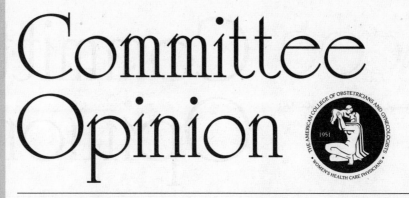

ACOG Committee Opinion

Committee on Obstetric Practice

Number 299, September 2004 (*Replaces No. 158, September 1995*)

# Guidelines for Diagnostic Imaging During Pregnancy

*ABSTRACT: Undergoing a single diagnostic X-ray procedure does not result in radiation exposure adequate to threaten the well-being of the developing preembryo, embryo, or fetus and is not an indication for therapeutic abortion. When multiple diagnostic X-rays are anticipated during pregnancy, imaging procedures not associated with ionizing radiation, such as ultrasonography and magnetic resonance imaging, should be considered. Additionally, it may be helpful to consult an expert in dosimetry calculation to determine estimated fetal dose. The use of radioactive isotopes of iodine is contraindicated for therapeutic use during pregnancy. Other radiopaque and paramagnetic contrast agents have not been studied in humans, but animal studies suggest that these agents are unlikely to cause harm to the developing human fetus. Although imaging techniques requiring these agents may be diagnostically beneficial, these techniques should be used during pregnancy only if potential benefits justify potential risks to the fetus.*

Various imaging modalities are available for diagnostic use during pregnancy. These include X-ray, ultrasonography, magnetic resonance imaging (MRI), and nuclear medicine studies. Of these, diagnostic X-ray is the most frequent cause of anxiety for obstetricians and patients. Much of this anxiety is secondary to a general belief that any radiation exposure is harmful and will result in an anomalous fetus. This anxiety could lead to inappropriate therapeutic abortion and litigation. Actually, most diagnostic radiologic procedures are associated with little, if any, known significant fetal risks. Moreover, according to the American College of Radiology, no single diagnostic X-ray procedure results in radiation exposure to a degree that would threaten the well-being of the developing preembryo, embryo, or fetus (1). Thus, exposure to a single X-ray during pregnancy is not an indication for therapeutic abortion (2, 3).

Some women are exposed to X-rays before the diagnosis of pregnancy. Occasionally, X-ray procedures will be indicated during pregnancy for significant medical problems or trauma. To enable physicians to counsel patients appropriately, the following information is provided about the potential risks and measures that can reduce diagnostic X-ray exposure.



ISSN 1074-861X

**The American College of Obstetricians and Gynecologists**
409 12th Street, SW
PO Box 96920
Washington, DC 20090-6920

12345/87654

Guidelines for diagnostic imaging during pregnancy. ACOG Committee Opinion No. 299. American College of Obstetricians and Gynecologists. Obstet Gynecol 2004;104:647–51.

## X-Ray Exposure

Ionizing radiation can result in the following 3 harmful effects: 1) cell death and teratogenic effects, 2) carcinogenesis, and 3) genetic effects or mutations in germ cells (2, 3). There is little or no information to estimate either the frequency or magnitude of adverse genetic effects on future generations.

Units traditionally used to measure the effects of X-ray include the rad and roentgen equivalents man (rem). Modern units include the gray (Gy) and sievert (Sv). The definitions of these units of measure are summarized in Table 1.

The estimated fetal exposure from some common radiologic procedures is summarized in Table 2. A plain X-ray generally exposes the fetus to very small amounts of radiation. Commonly during pregnancy, the uterus is shielded for nonpelvic procedures. With the exception of barium enema or small bowel series, most fluoroscopic examinations result in fetal exposure of millirads. Radiation exposure from computed tomography (CT) varies depending on the number and spacing of adjacent image sections. Although CT pelvimetry can result in fetal exposures as high as 1.5 rad, exposure can be reduced to approximately 250 mrad (including fetal gonad exposure) by using a low-exposure technique (4).

Spiral (or helical) CT allows continuous scanning of the patient as the couch is moved through the scanner, providing superior speed and image quality. Radiation exposure is affected by slice thickness, the number of cuts obtained, and the "pitch," a ratio defined as the distance the couch travels during one 360-degree rotation divided by the section thickness. The patient dose is proportional to 1 per pitch. Under typical use with a pitch of 1 or greater, the radiation exposure to the fetus from spiral CT is comparable to conventional CT (5).

### *Cell Death and Teratogenic Effects*

Data from an animal study suggest that exposure to high-dose ionizing radiation (ie, much greater than that used in diagnostic procedures) before implantation will most likely be lethal to the embryo (2). In other words, cell death is most likely an "all or none" phenomenon in early embryonic development.

Myriad teratogenic effects have developed in animals exposed to large doses of radiation (ie, 100–200 rad). However, in humans, growth restriction, microcephaly, and mental retardation are the most common adverse effects from high-dose radiation (3, 6, 7). Based on data from atomic bomb survivors, it appears that the risk of central nervous system effects is greatest with exposure at 8–15 weeks of gestation, with no proven risk at less than 8 weeks of gestation or at greater than 25 weeks of gestation (3, 8). Thus, at 8–15 weeks of gestation, the fetus is at greatest risk for radiation-induced mental retardation, and the risk appears to be a "non-threshold linear function of dose" at doses of at least 20 rad (3, 6, 8, 9). For example, the risk of severe mental retardation in fetuses exposed to ionizing radiation is approximately 40% at 100 rad of exposure and as high as 60% at 150 rad of exposure (3, 8). It has been suggested that a threshold for this adverse effect may exist in the range of 20–40 rad (7, 8). Even multiple diagnostic X-ray procedures rarely result in ionizing radiation exposure to this degree. Fetal risks of anomalies, growth restriction, or abortions are not increased with radiation exposure of less than 5 rad, a level above the range of exposure for diagnostic procedures (2).

### *Carcinogenesis*

The risk of carcinogenesis as a result of in utero exposure to ionizing radiation is unclear but is prob-

**Table 1.** Some Measures of Ionizing Radiation

| Measure | Definition | Unit | Unit |
|---|---|---|---|
| Exposure | Number of ions produced by X-rays per kilogram of air | Roentgen (R) | Roentgen (R) |
| Dose | Amount of energy deposited per kilogram of tissue | Rad (rad)* | Gray (Gy)<br>1 Gy = 100 rad |
| Relative effective dose | Amount of energy deposited per kilogram of tissue normalized for biological effectiveness | Roentgen equivalents man (rem)* | Sievert (Sv)<br>1 Sv = 100 rem |

*For diagnostic X-rays, 1 rad = 1 rem

Cunningham FG, Gant NF, Leveno KJ, Gilstrap LC 3rd, Hauth JC, Wenstrom KD. General considerations and maternal evaluation. In: Williams obstetrics. 21st ed. New York (NY): McGraw-Hill; 2001. p. 1143–58. Reproduced with permission of The McGraw-Hill Companies.

**Table 2.** Estimated Fetal Exposure From Some Common Radiologic Procedures

| Procedure | Fetal Exposure |
|---|---|
| Chest X-ray (2 views) | 0.02–0.07 mrad |
| Abdominal film (single view) | 100 mrad |
| Intravenous pyelography | ≥1 rad* |
| Hip film (single view) | 200 mrad |
| Mammography | 7–20 mrad |
| Barium enema or small bowel series | 2–4 rad |
| CT† scan of head or chest | <1 rad |
| CT scan of abdomen and lumbar spine | 3.5 rad |
| CT pelvimetry | 250 mrad |

*Exposure depends on the number of films

†Abbreviation: CT, computed tomography

Data from Cunningham FG, Gant NF, Leveno KJ, Gilstrap LC 3rd, Hauth JC, Wenstrom KD. General considerations and maternal evaluation. In: Williams obstetrics. 21st ed. New York (NY): McGraw-Hill; 2001. p. 1143–58.

ably very small. It is estimated that a 1–2 rad fetal exposure may increase the risk of leukemia by a factor of 1.5–2.0 over natural incidence and that an estimated 1 in 2,000 children exposed to ionizing radiation in utero will develop childhood leukemia. This is increased from a background rate of approximately 1 in 3,000 (2, 10). If elective abortion were chosen in every instance of fetal exposure to radiation, 1,999 exposed, normal fetuses would be aborted for each case of leukemia prevented (2, 11). It has been estimated that the risk of radiation-induced carcinogenesis may indeed be higher in children compared with adults, but such risks are not likely to exceed 1 in 1,000 children per rad (12). Thus, abortion should not be recommended solely on the basis of exposure to diagnostic radiation.

## Ultrasonography

Ultrasonography involves the use of sound waves and is not a form of ionizing radiation. There have been no reports of documented adverse fetal effects for diagnostic ultrasound procedures, including duplex Doppler imaging. Energy exposure from ultrasonography has been arbitrarily limited to 94 mW/cm$^2$ by the U.S. Food and Drug Administration. There are no contraindications to ultrasound procedures during pregnancy, and this modality has largely replaced X-ray as the primary method of fetal imaging during pregnancy.

## Magnetic Resonance Imaging

With MRI, magnets that alter the energy state of hydrogen protons are used instead of ionizing radiation (13). This technique could prove especially useful for diagnosis and evaluation of fetal central nervous system anomalies and placental abnormalities (eg, accreta, previa).

## Nuclear Medicine

Nuclear studies such as pulmonary ventilation–perfusion, thyroid, bone, and renal scans are performed by "tagging" a chemical agent with a radioisotope. The fetal exposure depends on the physical and biochemical properties of the radioisotope (6).

Technetium Tc 99m is one of the most commonly used isotopes and is used for brain, bone, renal, and cardiovascular scans. In general, these latter procedures result in a uterus, embryo, or fetal exposure of less than 0.5 rad (6, 12).

One of the more common nuclear medicine studies performed during pregnancy is the ventilation–perfusion scan for suspected pulmonary embolism. Macroaggregated albumin labeled with Technetium Tc 99m is used for the perfusion portion, and inhaled xenon gas ($^{127}$Xe or $^{133}$Xe) is used for the ventilation portion. The amount of radiation to which the fetus is exposed is extremely small (approximately 50 mrad) (14).

In a 2002 study, investigators calculated the mean fetal radiation exposure resulting from helical (spiral) CT in healthy pregnant women and compared it with reported fetal radiation doses for ventilation–perfusion lung scanning (approximately 100–370 μGy) (15). Although the exposure from ventilation–perfusion is relatively low, the study found that the mean fetal doses associated with helical CT were lower. Although exposure varied with gestational age (3.3–20.2 μGy for the first trimester, 7.9–76.7 μGy for the second trimester, and 51.3–130.8 μGy for the third trimester), 20 of 23 study patients exhibited a mean fetal dose of less than 60 μGy for all 3 trimesters.

Radioactive iodine readily crosses the placenta and can adversely affect the fetal thyroid, especially if used after 10–12 weeks of gestation. Radioactive isotopes of iodine used for treatment of hyperthyroidism are contraindicated during pregnancy, and such therapy should be delayed until after delivery. If a diagnostic scan of the thyroid is essential,

$^{123}$I or Technetium Tc 99m should be used in place of $^{131}$I (14).

## Contrast Agents

A variety of oral and intravascular contrast agents are used with X-ray and magnetic imaging procedures. Most radiopaque agents used with CT and conventional radiography contain derivatives of iodine and have not been studied in humans; however iohexol, iopamidol, iothalamate, ioversol, ioxaglate, and metrizamide have been studied in animals and do not appear to be teratogenic (16). Neonatal hypothyroidism has been associated with some iodinated agents taken during pregnancy (17). For this reason, these compounds generally are avoided unless essential for correct diagnosis. Studies requiring views before and after the administration of contrast agents will necessarily have greater radiation exposure. Although some radiopaque agents pass into the breast milk, they have not been associated with problems in nursing babies (16).

Paramagnetic contrast agents used during MRI have not been studied in pregnant women. Animal studies have demonstrated increased rates of spontaneous abortion, skeletal abnormalities, and visceral abnormalities when given at 2–7 times the recommended human dose (18, 19). It is not known if these compounds are excreted into human milk. Generally, these agents should be used during pregnancy only if the potential benefit justifies the potential risk to the fetus as demonstrated in animal studies.

## Guidelines

The following guidelines for X-ray examination or exposure during pregnancy are suggested:

1. Women should be counseled that X-ray exposure from a single diagnostic procedure does not result in harmful fetal effects. Specifically, exposure to less than 5 rad has not been associated with an increase in fetal anomalies or pregnancy loss.
2. Concern about possible effects of high-dose ionizing radiation exposure should not prevent medically indicated diagnostic X-ray procedures from being performed on a pregnant woman. During pregnancy, other imaging procedures not associated with ionizing radiation (eg, ultrasonography, MRI) should be considered instead of X-rays when appropriate.
3. Ultrasonography and MRI are not associated with known adverse fetal effects.
4. Consultation with an expert in dosimetry calculation may be helpful in calculating estimated fetal dose when multiple diagnostic X-rays are performed on a pregnant patient.
5. The use of radioactive isotopes of iodine is contraindicated for therapeutic use during pregnancy.
6. Radiopaque and paramagnetic contrast agents are unlikely to cause harm and may be of diagnostic benefit, but these agents should be used during pregnancy only if the potential benefit justifies the potential risk to the fetus.

## References


1. Gray JE. Safety (risk) of diagnostic radiology exposures. In: American College of Radiology. Radiation risk: a primer. Reston (VA): ACR; 1996. p. 15–7.
2. Brent RL. The effect of embryonic and fetal exposure to x-ray, microwaves, and ultrasound: counseling the pregnant and nonpregnant patient about these risks. Semin Oncol 1989;16:347–68.
3. Hall EJ. Scientific view of low-level radiation risks. Radiographics 1991;11:509–18.
4. Moore MM, Shearer DR. Fetal dose estimates for CT pelvimetry. Radiology 1989;171:265–7.
5. Parry RA, Glaze SA, Archer BR. The AAPM/RSNA physics tutorial for residents. Typical patient radiation doses in diagnostic radiology. Radiographics 1999;19: 1289–302.
6. Cunningham FG, Gant NF, Leveno KJ, Gilstrap LC 3rd, Hauth JC, Wenstrom KD. General considerations and maternal evaluation. In: Williams obstetrics. 21st ed. New York (NY): McGraw-Hill; 2001. p. 1143–58.
7. Otake M, Yoshimaru H, Schull WJ. Severe mental retardation among prenatally exposed survivors of the atomic bombing of Hiroshima and Nagasaki: a comparison of the T65DR and DS86 dosimetry systems. Technical report; RERF TR 87-16. Hiroshima: Radiation Effects Research Foundation; 1988.
8. National Research Council. Other somatic and fetal effects. In: Health effects of exposure to low levels of ionizing radiation: BEIR V. Washington, DC: National Academy Press; 1990:352–70.
9. Schull WJ, Otake M. Neurological deficit among survivors exposed to the atomic bombing of Hiroshima and Nagasaki: a reassessment and new directions. In: Kriegel H, Schmahl W, Gerber GB, Stieve FE, editors. Radiation risks to the developing nervous system. Neuherberg, June 18-29, 1985, Munich. Stuttgart: G Fischer Verlag; 1986. p. 399–419.

10. Miller RW. Epidemiological conclusions from radiation toxicity studies. In: Fry RJ, Grahn D, Griem ML, Rust JH, editors. Late effects of radiation: proceedings of the colloquium held at the Center for Continuing Education, the University of Chicago, Illinois, May 1969. New York (NY): Van Nostrand Reinhold; 1970. p. 245–56.
11. Early diagnosis of pregnancy: a symposium. J Reprod Med 1981;26(suppl 4):149–78.
12. Mettler FA Jr, Guiberteau MJ. Essentials of nuclear medicine imaging. 4th ed. Philadelphia (PA): WB Saunders; 1998.
13. Curry TS 3rd, Dowdey JE, Murry RC Jr, editors. Christensen's physics of diagnostic radiology. 4th ed. Philadelphia (PA): Lea & Febiger; 1990.
14. Ginsberg JS, Hirsh J, Rainbow AJ, Coates G. Risks to the fetus of radiologic procedures used in the diagnosis of maternal venous thromboembolic disease. Thromb Haemost 1989;61:189–96.
15. Winer-Muram HT, Boone JM, Brown HL, Jennings SG, Mabie WC, Lombardo GT. Pulmonary embolism in pregnant patients: fetal radiation dose with helical CT. Radiology 2002;224:487–92.
16. Radiopaque agents (diagnostic). MedlinePlus drug information. Available at: http://www.nlm.nih.gov/medlineplus/druginfo/uspdi/202997.html. Retrieved June 17, 2004.
17. Mehta PS, Metha SJ, Vorherr H. Congenital iodide goiter and hypothyroidism: a review. Obstet Gynecol Surv 1983;38:237–47.
18. Gadodiamide (systemic). In: USP DI: drug information for the health care professional. 24th ed. Greenwood Village (CO): Microdemex; 2004. Available at http://uspdi.micromedex.com/v1/excluded/Gadodiamide(Systemic).pdf. Retrieved June 17, 2004.
19. Gadoteridol (systemic). In: USP DI: drug information for the health care professional. 24th ed. Greenwood Village (CO): Microdemex; 2004. Available at: http://uspdi.micromedex.com/v1/excluded/Gadoteridol(Systemic).pdf. Retrieved June 17, 2004.

# ACOG Committee Opinion

Committee on Obstetric Practice

Number 304, November 2004

This document reflects emerging clinical and scientific advances as of the date issued and is subject to change. The information should not be construed as dictating an exclusive course of treatment or procedure to be followed.



ISSN 1074-861X

**The American College of Obstetricians and Gynecologists**
409 12th Street, SW
PO Box 96920
Washington, DC 20090-6920

12345/87654

Prenatal and perinatal human immunodeficiency virus testing: expanded recommendations. ACOG Committee Opinion No. 304. American College of Obstetricians and Gynecologists. Obstet Gynecol 2004;104:1119–24.

## Prenatal and Perinatal Human Immunodeficiency Virus Testing: Expanded Recommendations

*ABSTRACT: Early identification and treatment of all pregnant women with human immunodeficiency virus (HIV) is the best way to prevent neonatal disease. Pregnant women universally should be tested for HIV infection with patient notification as part of the routine battery of prenatal blood tests unless they decline the test (ie, opt-out approach). Repeat testing in the third trimester and rapid HIV testing at labor and delivery are additional strategies to further reduce the rate of perinatal HIV transmission. The Committee on Obstetric Practice makes the following recommendations: follow an opt-out prenatal HIV testing approach where legally possible; repeat offer of HIV testing in the third trimester to women in areas with high HIV prevalence, women known to be at high risk for HIV infection, and women who declined testing earlier in pregnancy, as allowed by state laws and regulations; use conventional HIV testing for women who are candidates for third-trimester testing; use rapid HIV testing in labor for women with undocumented HIV status; and if a rapid HIV test result is positive, initiate antiretroviral prophylaxis (with consent) without waiting for the results of the confirmatory test.*

The Centers for Disease Control and Prevention (CDC) estimates that 40,000 new human immunodeficiency virus (HIV) infections still occur in the United States each year (1). This figure includes approximately 300 infants infected via mother to child (vertical) transmission (2). Antiretroviral medications given to women with HIV perinatally and to their newborns in the first weeks of life reduce the vertical transmission rate from 25% to 2% or less (3–6). Even instituting maternal prophylaxis during labor and delivery or neonatal prophylaxis within 24–48 hours of delivery can substantially decrease rates of infection in infants (4). A retrospective review of HIV-exposed infants in New York State showed a transmission rate of approximately 10% when zidovudine prophylaxis was begun intrapartum and for newborns up to 48 hours of life (4). However, when neonatal prophylaxis was begun on day 3 of life or later, the transmission rate was 18.4% compared with 26.6% in the absence of any prophylaxis. Early identification and treatment of pregnant women and treatment of newborns in the first hours of life are essential to prevent neonatal disease.

## Prenatal Approaches to Offering Human Immunodeficiency Virus Testing: Opt-In Versus Opt-Out

Variations of 2 prenatal HIV testing strategies are being practiced by obstetric providers in the United States. The opt-in approach is the strategy that requires specific informed consent, usually in writing, and is the foundation for most state laws and regulations in effect today.

The opt-out approach is the strategy in which universal HIV testing with patient notification is a routine component of prenatal care. A pregnant woman is notified that she will be tested for HIV as part of the routine battery of prenatal blood tests unless she declines. If a patient declines HIV testing, this should be noted in the medical record. The use of patient notification provides women the opportunity to decline testing but eliminates the requirement to obtain specific informed consent. Although no states currently have adopted an opt-out approach as defined previously, some states have adopted variations of this approach and others are reviewing the opt-out approach.

The opt-out approach is associated with greater testing rates than the opt-in approach. Medical record surveys, laboratory data, and population-based surveys (1998–2001) report 85% to 98% HIV testing rates in surveyed areas using the opt-out approach, compared with testing rates ranging from 25% to 83% in surveyed areas using the opt-in approach (7). Based on these data, in 2003 the CDC revised its guidelines to recommend the opt-out approach (8). Additionally, the CDC recommends that jurisdictions with statutory barriers to such routine prenatal screening consider revising them.* The American College of Obstetricians and Gynecologists, the American Academy of Pediatrics (9), and the CDC recommend the opt-out approach (8, 9).

Physicians should be aware of and follow their states' prenatal HIV screening requirements. Specific prenatal HIV screening requirements may be verified by contacting state or local public health departments.

*Gerberding JL, Jaffe HW. Dear colleague letter from CDC and NCHSTP directors on HIV testing. Atlanta (GA): Centers for Disease Control and Prevention; 2003. Available at: http://www.cdc.gov/hiv/rapid_testing/rt-appendix_a.htm. Retrieved June 30, 2004.

## Conventional Prenatal Human Immunodeficiency Virus Testing

The conventional HIV testing algorithm, which generally takes up to 2 weeks to process, begins with a screening test, the enzyme-linked immunosorbent assay (ELISA), that detects antibodies to HIV; if the results are positive, it is followed by a confirmatory test, either a Western blot or an immunofluorescence assay (IFA). A positive ELISA test result is not diagnostic of HIV infection unless confirmed by the Western blot or IFA. The sensitivity and specificity of ELISA with a confirmatory Western blot test are greater than 99%. The false-positive rate for ELISA with a confirmatory Western blot test is 1 in 59,000 tests. If the ELISA test result is positive and the Western blot or IFA test result is negative, the patient is not infected and repeat testing is not indicated.

If the ELISA test result is repeatedly positive and the Western blot result contains some but not all of the viral bands required to make a definitive diagnosis, the test result is labeled indeterminate. Most patients with indeterminate test results are not infected with HIV. However, consultation with a provider well versed in HIV infection is recommended. This specialist may suggest viral load testing or repeat testing later in pregnancy to rule out the possibility of recent infection.

If the screening (eg, ELISA) and confirmatory (eg, Western blot or IFA) test results are both positive, the patient should be given her results in person. The implications of HIV infection and vertical transmission should be discussed with the patient. Additional laboratory evaluation, including CD4 count, HIV viral load, hepatitis C virus antibody, complete blood count with platelet count, and baseline chemistries with liver function tests, will be useful before prescribing antiretroviral prophylaxis. Consultation with a provider well versed in HIV infection is recommended.

## Repeat Human Immunodeficiency Virus Testing in the Third Trimester

Routine universal repeat testing in the third trimester may be considered in health care facilities in areas with high HIV prevalence among women of childbearing age (ie, 5 per 1,000 or 0.5% or greater). Additionally, although physicians need to be aware of and follow their states' perinatal HIV screening guidelines, repeat testing in the third trimester, preferably before 36 weeks of gestation, is recommended for pregnant women at high risk for acquiring HIV (10). Criteria for repeat testing can include:

- A history of a sexually transmitted disease
- Illicit drug use or the exchange of sex for money or drugs
- Multiple sex partners during pregnancy or a sex partner(s) known to be HIV-positive or at high risk
- Signs or symptoms suggestive of acute HIV infection at any time during pregnancy

Women who are candidates for third-trimester testing, including those who previously declined testing earlier in pregnancy, should be given a conventional HIV test rather than waiting to receive a rapid test at labor and delivery as allowed by state laws and regulations.

## Rapid Human Immunodeficiency Virus Testing

Rapid HIV testing can be used to identify HIV infection in women who arrive at labor and delivery with undocumented HIV status and to provide an opportunity to begin prophylaxis of previously undiagnosed infection before delivery. A negative rapid HIV test result is definitive. A positive HIV test result is not definitive and must be confirmed with a supplemental test, such as a Western blot or IFA (11); however, antiretroviral prophylaxis should be initiated (with consent) without waiting for the results of the confirmatory test to further reduce possible transmission to the infant.

A rapid HIV test is an HIV screening test with results available within hours. Data from several studies indicate that 40–85% (11–14) of infants infected with HIV are born to women whose HIV infection is unknown to their obstetric provider before delivery. Some of these women have had no opportunity to learn their HIV status before labor, and recent data suggest that knowledge of HIV status, even if only obtained in labor, will allow the use of therapies that may reduce rates of vertical transmission. If a rapid test is used in labor and HIV antibodies are detected, the pregnant woman should be encouraged to start antiretroviral prophylaxis. Recommendations for the use of antiretroviral medications in pregnant women infected with HIV-1 are available at http://www.aidsinfo.nih.gov/guidelines/perinatal/PER_062304.html and are updated frequently (15). In some cases, cesarean delivery may provide additional protection against vertical HIV transmission; however, once labor has begun or rupture of membranes has occurred, the utility of cesarean delivery is unknown.

When selecting a rapid HIV test for use during labor and delivery, it is important to consider the accuracy of the test and the site where testing will be performed. Tests that require serum or plasma (eg, Reveal) are more suitable for use in the laboratory, whereas tests that can be performed with whole blood (eg, OraQuick, Uni-Gold) without specimen processing can be performed more easily in the labor and delivery unit (11). Performance evaluations on 3 U.S. Food and Drug Administration (FDA)-approved rapid HIV tests (OraQuick, Reveal, and Uni-Gold) indicate a sensitivity of 100%, 99.8%, and 100% (95% confidence interval), respectively, and a specificity of 99.9%, 99.1% (serum), and 99.7% (95% confidence interval), respectively (11, 16) (Table 1).

The CDC-sponsored Mother-Infant Rapid Intervention at Delivery (MIRIAD) Study Group examined the use of rapid testing using OraQuick or enzyme immunoassay (EIA) in 4,849 prenatal patients with unknown HIV status in a multistate hospital study (16). Human immunodeficiency virus-1 test results were positive for 34 women (HIV prevalence 7/1,000). Data from that study showed a sensitivity for OraQuick of 100% and a specificity of 99.9% with a positive predictive value of 90% compared with 76% for EIA. Offering rapid HIV testing during labor is feasible in obstetric settings, and the OraQuick Rapid HIV-1 Antibody Test, used on whole blood specimens, delivers accurate and timely (20–40 minutes) test results (11).

As with all screening tests before confirmation, the likelihood of a false-positive result is higher in populations with low HIV prevalence when compared with populations with high HIV prevalence. Additionally, at present it is not known how the false-positive rate for rapid testing will compare with the false-positive rate for conventional testing. Available calculated comparisons of the positive predictive values of 3 FDA-approved rapid HIV-1 antibody tests (OraQuick, Reveal, and Uni-Gold) and for the HIV-1 EIA in populations with differing HIV prevalence rates are shown in Table 1.

If the rapid HIV test result is positive, the obstetric provider should take the following steps:

1. Tell the woman she may have HIV infection and that her neonate also may be exposed
2. Explain that the rapid test result is preliminary and that false-positive results are possible
3. Assure the woman that a second test is being done right away to confirm the positive rapid test result
4. Initiate (with consent) antiretroviral prophylaxis without waiting for the results of the confirmatory test to reduce the risk of transmission to the infant
5. Tell the woman that she should postpone breastfeeding until the confirmatory result is available because she should not breastfeed if she is infected with HIV
6. Inform pediatric colleagues of positive maternal test results, as allowed by federal and state privacy laws, so that they may institute the appropriate neonatal prophylaxis

If the results of the rapid test and the confirmatory test are discrepant, both tests should be repeated and consultation with an infectious disease specialist is recommended. Additionally, all antiretroviral prophylaxis should be stopped if the confirmatory test result is negative (11).

Oral fluid based rapid HIV testing (OraQuick Rapid HIV-1/2 Antibody Test) is now available. This may be another option for perinatal testing in the future (see http://www.cdc.gov/hiv and http://www.fda.gov/cber/pma/p01004710.htm).

## Recommendations

Given the enormous advances in HIV prophylaxis for pregnant women and newborns, it is clear that early identification and treatment of all pregnant women with HIV is the best way to prevent neona-

**Table 1.** Estimated Positive Predictive Value of a Single Screening Test for Human Immunodeficiency Virus in Populations With Differing Human Immunodeficiency Virus Prevalence*

| | Estimated Positive Predictive Value (%) | | | |
|---|---|---|---|---|
| **Human Immunodeficiency Virus Prevalence (%)** | **OraQuick† (blood) (CLIA-waived)** | **Reveal† (serum) (CLIA-moderate complexity)** | **Uni-Gold† (blood) (CLIA-moderate complexity)** | **Single Enzyme Immunoassay (EIA) (CLIA-high complexity)** |
| 10 | 99 | 92 | 97 | 98 |
| 5 | 98 | 85 | 95 | 96 |
| 2 | 95 | 69 | 87 | 91 |
| 1 | 91 | 53 | 77 | 83 |
| 0.5 | 83 | 36 | 63 | 71 |
| 0.3 | 75 | 25 | 50 | 60 |
| 0.1 | 50 | 10 | 25 | 33 |
| Test sensitivity (95% CI) | 100 | 99.8 | 100 | — |
| Test specificity (95% CI) | 99.9 | 99.1 | 99.7 | 99.8 |

Abbreviation: CI, confidence interval; CLIA, Clinical Laboratory Improvement Act.

*Based on point estimate for specificity from the Mother-Infant Rapid Intervention at Delivery study for OraQuick and enzyme immunoassay (Bulterys M, Jamieson DJ, O'Sullivan MJ, Cohen MH, Maupin R, Nesheim S, et al. Rapid HIV-1 testing during labor: a multicenter study. Mother-Infant Rapid Intervention at Delivery (MIRIAD) Study Group. JAMA 2004;292:219–23.) and from the U.S. Food and Drug Administration summary basis of approval for the other tests (Rapid HIV antibody testing during labor and delivery for women of unknown HIV status: a practical guide and model protocol. Centers for Disease Control and Prevention. Atlanta (GA): CDC; 2004. Available at: http://www.cdc.gov/hiv/rapid/testing/materials/Labor&DeliveryRapidTesting.pdf.). In practice, the specificity and actual positive predictive value may differ from these estimates.

†Trade names are for identification purposes only and do not imply endorsement by the U.S. Department of Health and Human Services, the Centers for Disease Control and Prevention, or the American College of Obstetricians and Gynecologists.

Modified from Rapid HIV antibody testing during labor and delivery for women of unknown HIV status: a practical guide and model protocol. Centers for Disease Control and Prevention. Atlanta (GA): CDC; 2004.

tal disease. Pregnant women universally should be tested for HIV infection with patient notification as part of the routine battery of prenatal blood tests unless they decline the test (opt-out approach). The American College of Obstetricians and Gynecologists, the American Academy of Pediatrics, and the CDC[†] recommend the opt-out approach (8, 9). There are encouraging results from the MIRIAD Study Group (16) and other evidence (3–6, 11) to suggest that antiretroviral prophylaxis started in labor and delivery and for the infant in the first hours of life also can substantially reduce vertical transmission of the HIV virus. Therefore, the Committee on Obstetric Practice makes the following recommendations:

- Follow an opt-out prenatal HIV testing approach where legally possible
- Repeat offer of HIV testing in the third trimester to women in areas with high HIV prevalence, women known to be at high risk for HIV infection, and women who declined testing earlier in pregnancy, as allowed by state laws and regulations
- Use conventional HIV testing for women who are candidates for third-trimester testing
- Use rapid HIV testing in labor for women with undocumented HIV status
- If a rapid HIV test result is positive, initiate antiretroviral prophylaxis (with consent) without waiting for the results of the confirmatory test

## References


1. HIV/AIDS update: a glance at the HIV epidemic. Atlanta (GA): Centers for Disease Control and Prevention. Available at: http://www.cdc.gov/nchstp/od/news/At-a-Glance.pdf. Retrieved June 22, 2004.
2. Centers for Disease Control and Prevention. HIV/AIDS Surveillance Report 2002;14:1–40. Available at: http://www.cdc.gov/hiv/stats/hasr1402/2002surveillanceReport.pdf. Retrieved June 24, 2004.
3. Recommendations of the U.S. Public Health Service Task Force on the use of zidovudine to reduce perinatal transmission of human immunodeficiency virus. MMWR Recomm Rep 1994;43(RR-11):1–20.


[†]Gerberding JL, Jaffe HW. Dear colleague letter from CDC and NCHSTP directors on HIV testing. Atlanta (GA): Centers for Disease Control and Prevention; 2003. Available at: http://www.cdc.gov/hiv/rapid_testing/rt-appendix_a.htm. Retrieved June 30, 2004.


4. Wade NA, Birkhead GS, Warren BL, Charbonneau TT, French PT, Wang L, et al. Abbreviated regimens of zidovudine prophylaxis and perinatal transmission of human immunodeficiency virus. N Engl J Med 1998;339:1409–14.
5. Mofenson LM, Lambert JS, Stiehm ER, Bethel J, Meyer WA 3rd, Whitehouse J, et al. Risk factors for perinatal transmission of human immunodeficiency virus type 1 in women treated with zidovudine. Pediatric AIDS Clinical Trials Group Study 185 Team. N Engl J Med 1999;341:385–93.
6. Garcia PM, Kalish LA, Pitt J, Minkoff H, Quinn TC, Burchett SK, et al. Maternal levels of plasma human immunodeficiency virus type 1 RNA and the risk of perinatal transmission. Women and Infants Transmission Study Group. N Engl J Med 1999;341:394–402.
7. HIV testing among pregnant women—United States and Canada, 1998–2001. MMWR Morb Mortal Wkly Rep 2002;51:1013–6.
8. Advancing HIV prevention: new strategies for a changing epidemic—United States, 2003. MMWR Morb Mortal Wkly Rep 2003;52:329–32.
9. American Academy of Pediatrics, American College of Obstetricians and Gynecologists. Joint statement on human immunodeficiency virus screening. ACOG Policy Statement 75. Elk Grove Village (IL): AAP; Washington, DC: ACOG; 1999.
10. Revised recommendations for HIV screening of pregnant women. Centers for Disease Control and Prevention. MMWR Recomm Rep 2001;50(RR-19):63–85; quiz CE1-19a2–CE6-19a2.
11. Rapid HIV antibody testing during labor and delivery for women of unknown HIV status: a practical guide and model protocol. Centers for Disease Control and Prevention. Atlanta (GA): CDC; 2004. Available at: http://www.cdc.gov/hiv/rapid/testing/materials/Labor&DeliveryRapidTesting.pdf.
12. Peters V, Liu KL, Dominguez K, Frederick T, Melville S, Hsu H, et al. Missed opportunities for perinatal HIV prevention among HIV-exposed infants born 1996–2000, pediatric spectrum of HIV disease cohort. Pediatrics 2003;111:1186–91.
13. Gross E, Burr CK. HIV counseling and testing in pregnancy. N J Med 2003;100 (suppl):21–6; quiz 67–8.
14. Paul SM, Grimes-Dennis J, Burr CK, DiFerdinando GT. Rapid diagnostic testing for HIV. Clinical indications. N J Med 2002;99:20–4; quiz 24–6.
15. Recommendations for use of antiretroviral drugs in pregnant HIV-infected women for maternal health and interventions to reduce perinatal HIV-1 transmission in the United States. Public Health Service Task Force. Rockville (MD): U.S. Department of Health and Human Services. Available at: http://www.aidsinfo.nih.gov/guidelines/perinatal/PER_062304.html. Retrieved July 16, 2004.
16. Bulterys M, Jamieson DJ, O'Sullivan MJ, Cohen MH, Maupin R, Nesheim S, et al. Rapid HIV-1 testing during labor: a multicenter study. Mother-Infant Rapid Intervention at Delivery (MIRIAD) Study Group. JAMA 2004;292:219–23.

## Resources

### *Publications*

American College of Obstetricians and Gynecologists. Scheduled cesarean delivery and the prevention of vertical transmission of HIV infection. ACOG Committee Opinion 234. Washington, DC: ACOG; 2000.

Institute of Medicine (US). Reducing the odds: preventing perinatal transmission of HIV in the United States. Washington, DC: The Institute; 1999.

### *Organizations*

American College of Obstetricians and Gynecologists (http://www.acog.org; http://sales.acog.org)

CDC Division of HIV/AIDS Prevention: (404) 639-0900

Centers for Disease Control and Prevention (http://www.cdc.gov/hiv)

National AIDS Hotline: 800-342-AIDS (2437) (English); 800-344-7432 (Spanish); 800-243-7889 (TTY)

National HIV Telephone Consultation Service (for physician consultation only): 800-933-3413

State public health departments

ACOG Committee Opinion

Committee on Obstetric Practice

Number 305, November 2004

# Influenza Vaccination and Treatment During Pregnancy

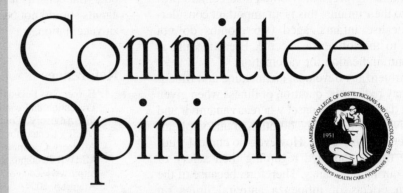

*ABSTRACT: Influenza vaccination is an essential element of prenatal care. The American College of Obstetricians and Gynecologists' Committee on Obstetric Practice supports the Centers for Disease Control and Prevention's expanded recommendation that women who will be pregnant during the influenza season (October through mid May) should be vaccinated. The ideal time to administer the vaccine is October and November; however, it is appropriate to vaccinate patients throughout the influenza season as long as the vaccine supply lasts. This intramuscular, inactivated vaccine may be used in all 3 trimesters. Because of the unknown effects of influenza antiviral drugs on pregnant women and their fetuses, the Committee on Obstetric Practice recommends that these antiviral agents should be used during pregnancy only if the potential benefits justify the potential risks.*

Influenza vaccination is an essential element of prenatal care. The risks of serious illness associated with influenza are increased in young children and pregnant women. The influenza epidemic in 2003 resulted in numerous hospitalizations for cardiopulmonary complications among pregnant women and some deaths among young children (1).

The American College of Obstetricians and Gynecologists' Committee on Obstetric Practice supports the Centers for Disease Control and Prevention's expanded recommendation that women who will be pregnant during the influenza season (October through mid May) should be vaccinated (1). The ideal time to administer the vaccine is October and November; however, it is appropriate to vaccinate patients throughout the influenza season as long as the vaccine supply lasts. This intramuscular, inactivated vaccine may be used in all 3 trimesters. One study of influenza vaccination of more than 2,000 pregnant women demonstrated no adverse fetal effects associated with influenza vaccination (2). Any theoretical risk of the vaccination is outweighed by its benefits. Likewise, the benefits of the vaccine outweigh any unproven potential concerns about traces of thimerosal preservative, which exist only in the multidose vials (see http://www.cdc.gov/mmwr/preview/mmwrhtml/rr53e430a1.htm). It should be noted that the intranasal vaccine spray contains a live, attenuated virus and should not be used during pregnancy.



ISSN 1074-861X

**The American College of Obstetricians and Gynecologists**
409 12th Street, SW
PO Box 96920
Washington, DC 20090-6920

12345/87654

Influenza vaccination and treatment during pregnancy. ACOG Committee Opinion No. 305. American College of Obstetricians and Gynecologists. Obstet Gynecol 2004;104:1125–6.

Immunizing pregnant women also confers protection to their infants; this is an important consideration because infants' aged 0–6 months do not respond to the influenza vaccine. Breastfeeding is not a contraindication for vaccination.

If influenza A develops, amantadine and rimantadine may reduce the duration of illness when given within 2 days of illness onset whereas zanamivir and oseltamivir may reduce the duration of uncomplicated influenza A and B (1). However, no clinical studies have been conducted regarding their safety or efficacy during pregnancy. Therefore, because of the unknown effects of influenza antiviral drugs on pregnant women and their fetuses, the Committee on Obstetric Practice recommends that these antiviral agents should be used during pregnancy only if the potential benefits justify the potential risks. Antiviral agents should not be used as a substitute for influenza vaccination.

## References

1. Harper SA, Fukuda K, Uyeki TM, Cox NJ, Bridges CB. Prevention and control of influenza: recommendations of the Advisory Committee on Immunization Practices (ACIP). Centers for Disease Control and Prevention (CDC) Advisory Committee on Immunization Practices (ACIP). MMWR Recomm Rep 2004;53(RR-6):1–40. Available at: http://www.cdc.gov/mmwr/PDF/rr/rr5306.pdf. Retrieved August 6, 2004.
2. Heinonen OP, Shapiro S, Monson RR, Hartz SC, Rosenberg L, Slone D. Immunization during pregnancy against poliomyelitis and influenza in relation to childhood malignancy. Int J Epidemiol 1973;2:229–35.

ACOG Committee Opinion

Committee on Obstetric Practice

Number 315, September 2005

# Obesity in Pregnancy

*ABSTRACT: One third of adult women in the United States are obese. During pregnancy, obese women are at increased risk for several adverse perinatal outcomes, including anesthetic, perioperative, and other maternal and fetal complications. Obstetricians should provide preconception counseling and education about the possible complications and should encourage obese patients to undertake a weight reduction program before attempting pregnancy. Obstetricians also should address prenatal and peripartum care considerations that may be especially relevant for obese patients, including those who have undergone bariatric surgery.*

The prevalence of obesity in the United States has increased dramatically over the past 20 years. The World Health Organization and the National Institutes of Health define *normal weight* as a body mass index (BMI) of 18.5–24.9, *overweight* as a BMI of 25–29.9, and *obesity* as a BMI of 30 or greater. Obesity is further categorized by BMI into Class I (30–34.9), Class II (35–39.9), and Class III or extreme obesity (≥40) (1, 2). (For online BMI calculator, see www.nhlbisupport.com/bmi.) The most recent National Health and Nutrition Examination Survey (NHANES) for 1999–2002 found that approximately one third of adult women are obese (3). This problem is greatest among non-Hispanic black women (49%) compared with Mexican-American women (38%) and non-Hispanic white women (31%) (3).

Obese women are at increased risk for several pregnancy complications; therefore, preconception assessment and counseling are strongly encouraged. Obstetricians should provide education about the possible complications and should encourage obese patients to undertake a weight reduction program, including diet, exercise, and behavior modification, before attempting pregnancy. Specific medical clearance may be indicated for some patients.

At least three cohort studies suggest that obesity is an independent risk factor for spontaneous abortion among women who undergo infertility treatment (4–6). Given this association, obese women should be encouraged to lose weight before beginning infertility therapy. Data also link obesity with spontaneous abortion among women after natural conception (7).

In a prospective multicenter study of more than 16,000 patients, Class I (BMI 30–34.9) and Class II (BMI 35–39.9) obesity was associated with an increased risk of gestational hypertension (odds ratio [OR] = 2.5 and 3.2, respectively), preeclampsia (OR = 1.6 and 3.3), gestational diabetes (OR = 2.6 and 4.0), and fetal macrosomia (OR = 1.7 and 1.9), when compared with

This document reflects emerging clinical and scientific advances as of the date issued and is subject to change. The information should not be construed as dictating an exclusive course of treatment or procedure to be followed.



ISSN 1074-861X

**The American College of Obstetricians and Gynecologists**
409 12th Street, SW
PO Box 96920
Washington, DC 20090-6920

12345/98765

Obesity in pregnancy. ACOG Committee Opinion No. 315. American College of Obstetricians and Gynecologists. Obstet Gynecol 2005;106:671–5.

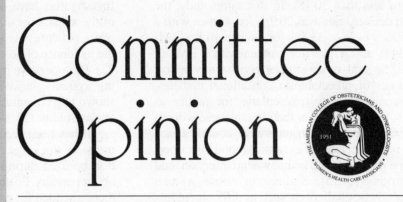

a BMI of less than 30 (8). In this same study, the cesarean delivery rate was 20.7% for women with a BMI of 29.9 or less, 33.8% for women with a BMI of 30–34.9, and 47.4% for women with a BMI of 35–39.9. Several other studies consistently report higher rates of preeclampsia, gestational diabetes, and cesarean delivery, particularly for failure to progress, in obese women than in nonobese women (9–12). Operative and postoperative complications include increased rates of excessive blood loss, operative time greater than 2 hours, wound infection, and endometritis (13–15). Surgery in obese women poses anesthetic challenges, such as difficult epidural and spinal placement requiring multiple attempts and intraoperative respiratory events from failed or difficult intubation (16). Sleep apnea occurring in this group of women may further complicate anesthetic management and postoperative care (17).

Height and weight should be recorded for all women at the initial prenatal visit to allow calculation of the BMI. Recommendations for prenatal weight gain should be made based on the Institute of Medicine (IOM) guidelines, which suggest a gain of 25–35 lb for women of normal weight, 15–25 lb for overweight women, and 15 lb for obese women (18). Nutrition consultation should be offered to all obese women, and they should be encouraged to follow an exercise program. This consultation should continue postpartum and before attempting another pregnancy. Consideration should be given to screening for gestational diabetes upon presentation or during the first trimester and repeating it later in pregnancy if the initial screening result is negative. Because these patients are at increased risk for emergent cesarean delivery and anesthetic complications, anesthesiology consultation before delivery is encouraged (19).

It is important to discuss potential intrapartum complications, such as difficulty estimating fetal weight (even with ultrasonography), inability to obtain interpretable external fetal heart rate and uterine contraction patterns, and difficulty performing an emergent cesarean delivery. If an anesthesiology consultation was not obtained antepartum, it should be conducted early in labor to allow adequate time for development of an anesthetic plan.

If obese patients require cesarean delivery, they should receive antibiotic prophylaxis even if surgery is elective (14). Obese women who require cesarean delivery are more likely to have an increased incidence of wound breakdowns and infections (20). Attempts to decrease these postoperative complications have included closure of the subcutaneous layers and the placement of subcutaneous drains. Investigators have demonstrated that suture closure of the subcutaneous layer after cesarean delivery in obese patients may lead to a significant reduction in the incidence of postoperative wound disruption (21, 22). Postoperative placement of subcutaneous draining systems, however, have not consistently been shown to be of value in reducing postcesarean delivery morbidity (23, 24).

It has been recommended that graduated compression stockings, hydration, and early mobilization be used during and after cesarean delivery in obese patients. Postpartum heparin therapy has been recommended for patients thought to be at high risk for venous thromboembolism (25, 26); however, data are insufficient to determine whether the benefits of heparin prophylaxis in this group of patients outweigh the risks (27, 28).

Women with a BMI of 35 or greater who have preexisting medical conditions, such as hypertension or diabetes, may benefit from a cardiac evaluation (29). Because of the increased likelihood of complicated and emergent cesarean delivery, extremely obese women may require specific resources such as additional blood products, a large operating table, and extra personnel in the delivery room. Particular attention to the type and placement of the surgical incision is needed (ie, placing the incision above the panniculus adiposus) (20, 30). The success rate of attempted vaginal birth after cesarean delivery is very low in extremely obese women (31). There are additional logistical challenges to monitoring labor and performing an emergent cesarean delivery in the extremely obese patient. Therefore, these patients should be counseled about these possible complications of an emergent cesarean delivery.

The number of obese women of childbearing age considering bariatric surgery is increasing, resulting in questions about pregnancy after these types of surgeries. Early case reports and series described various pregnancy complications after bariatric surgery such as gastrointestinal bleeding (32), anemia (33), intrauterine growth restriction (34), and neural tube defects (35, 36). However, recent studies suggest that previous bariatric surgery is not associated with adverse perinatal outcomes (37, 38). Researchers have determined that pregnancies after bariatric surgery are less likely to be complicated by gestational diabetes, hypertension, macrosomia, and cesarean delivery than are pregnancies of obese women who have not had the surgery (38–40).

Bariatric surgical procedures are categorized into two main types: malabsorptive procedures (jejunoileal bypass and biliopancreatic diversion) and restrictive procedures (gastric banding and vertical banded gastroplasty). Both types of procedures can result in deficiencies in iron, vitamin $B_{12}$, folate, and calcium. Women who have undergone bariatric surgery require the following counseling before and during pregnancy:

- Patients with adjustable gastric banding should be advised that they are at risk of becoming pregnant unexpectedly after weight loss following surgery (39).
- All patients are advised to delay pregnancy for 12–18 months after surgery to avoid pregnancy during the rapid weight loss phase (39).
- Women with a gastric band should be monitored by their general surgeons during pregnancy because adjustment of the band may be necessary (41).
- Patients should be evaluated for nutritional deficiencies and vitamin supplementation where indicated.

In counseling all obese women about potential pregnancy complications, it is important to inform them of the fetal risks (eg, prematurity, stillbirth, neural tube defect, and macrosomia). Some studies have reported a greater rate of premature delivery for obese women than for women of normal weight (9, 42). However, in a study of more than 2,900 obese women, prepregnancy obesity was associated with a lower rate of spontaneous preterm birth (43). A large Swedish cohort study reported a greater risk of antepartum stillbirth among obese patients than among women who had a BMI of less than 20 (42). Data establish that the risk of neural tube defects among obese women is double that among women of normal weight, after correcting for diabetes as a potential confounding factor (44–46). The benefit of folic acid doses higher than 400 μg has not been studied in nondiabetic obese women. Multiple studies have shown that maternal obesity and excessive weight gain during pregnancy are associated with macrosomic and large-for-gestational-age infants (10, 19, 47, 48). Furthermore, these large-for-gestational-age infants are at increased risk for childhood obesity (11, 49). The decision to perform a primary cesarean delivery for these obese women is based on the previously recommended maternal and fetal indications. A cesarean delivery should be considered for those patients who have a fetus with a fetal weight estimated to be greater than 5,000 g if the patient does not have diabetes (50) or greater than 4,500 g if the patient has diabetes (51).

Recommendations for obese women who are pregnant or planning a pregnancy include the following:

- Preconception counseling
- Provision of specific information concerning the maternal and fetal risks of obesity in pregnancy
- Consideration of screening for gestational diabetes upon presentation or in the first trimester, and repeated screening later in pregnancy if results are initially negative
- Assessment and possible supplementation of vitamin $B_{12}$, folate, iron, and calcium for women who have undergone bariatric surgery
- Possible use of graduated compression stockings, hydration, and early mobilization during and after cesarean delivery
- Anesthesiology consultation
- Continuation of nutrition counseling and exercise program after delivery, and consultation with weight loss specialists before attempting another pregnancy

## References


1. World Health Organization. Obesity: preventing and managing the global epidemic. Geneva, Switzerland: World Health Organization; 2000. WHO technical report series 894.
2. National Heart, Lung, and Blood Institute (NHLBI) and National Institute for Diabetes and Digestive and Kidney Diseases (NIDDK). Clinical guidelines on the identification, evaluation and treatment of overweight and obesity in adults. The evidence report. Obes Res 1998;6(suppl 2):51S–210S.
3. Hedley AA, Ogden CL, Johnson CL, Carroll MD, Curtin LR, Flegal KM. Prevalence of overweight and obesity among US children, adolescents, and adults, 1999-2002. JAMA 2004;291:2847–50.
4. Bellver J, Rossal LP, Bosch E, Zuniga A, Corona JT, Melendez F, et al. Obesity and the risk of spontaneous abortion after oocyte donation. Fertil Steril 2003;79:1136–40.
5. Fedorcsak P, Storeng R, Dale PO, Tanbo T, Abyholm T. Obesity is a risk factor for early pregnancy loss after IVF or ICSI. Acta Obstet Gynecol Scand 2000;79:43–8.
6. Wang JX, Davies MJ, Norman RJ. Obesity increases the risk of spontaneous abortion during infertility treatment. Obes Res 2002;10:551–4.
7. Lashen H, Fear K, Sturdee DW. Obesity is associated with increased risk of first trimester and recurrent miscarriage: matched case-control study. Hum Reprod 2004;19:1644–6.
8. Weiss JL, Malone FD, Emig D, Ball RH, Nyberg DA, Comstock CH, et al. Obesity, obstetric complications and cesarean delivery rate—a population-based screening

study. FASTER Research Consortium. Am J Obstet Gynecol 2004;190:1091–7.
9. Baeten JM, Bukusi EA, Lambe M. Pregnancy complications and outcomes among overweight and obese nulliparous women. Am J Public Health 2001:91:436–40.
10. Cedergren MI. Maternal morbid obesity and the risk of adverse pregnancy outcome. Obstet Gynecol 2004;103: 219–24.
11. Sebire NJ, Jolly M, Harris JP, Wadsworth J, Joffe M, Beard RW, et al. Maternal obesity and pregnancy outcome: a study of 287,213 pregnancies in London. Int J Obes Relat Metab Disord 2001;25:1175–82.
12. Young TK, Woodmansee B. Factors that are associated with cesarean delivery in a large private practice: the importance of prepregnancy body mass index and weight gain. Am J Obstet Gynecol 2002;187:312–8; discussion 318–20.
13. Kabiru W, Raynor BD. Obstetric outcomes associated with increase in BMI category during pregnancy. Am J Obstet Gynecol 2004:191:928–32.
14. Myles TD, Gooch J, Santolaya J. Obesity as an independent risk factor for infectious morbidity in patients who undergo cesarean delivery. Obstet Gynecol 2002;100: 959–64.
15. Perlow JH, Morgan MA. Massive maternal obesity and perioperative cesarean morbidity. Am J Obstet Gynecol 1994;170:560–5.
16. Hood DD, Dewan DM. Anesthetic and obstetric outcome in morbidly obese parturients. Anesthesiology 1993;79: 1210–8.
17. Maasilta P, Bachour A, Teramo K, Polo O, Laitinen LA. Sleep-related disordered breathing during pregnancy in obese women. Chest 2001;120:1448–54.
18. Institute of Medicine (US). Nutritional status and weight gain. In: Nutrition during pregnancy. Washington, DC: National Academy Press; 1990. p. 27–233.
19. Rode L, Nilas L, Wojdemann K, Tabor A. Obesity-related complications in Danish single cephalic term pregnancies. Obstet Gynecol 2005;105:537–42.
20. Wall PD, Deucy EE, Glantz JC, Pressman EK. Vertical skin incisions and wound complications in the obese parturient. Obstet Gynecol 2003;102(5 pt):952–6.
21. Cetin A, Cetin M. Superficial wound disruption after cesarean section: effect of the depth and closure of subcutaneous tissue. Int J Gynaecol Obstet 1997;57:17–21.
22. Chelmow D, Rodriguez EJ, Sabatini MM. Suture closure of subcutaneous fat and wound disruption after cesarean section: a meta-analysis. Obstet Gynecol 2004;103: 974–80.
23. Al-Inany H, Youssef G, Abd ElMaguid A, Abdel Hamid M, Naguib A. Value of subcutaneous drainage system in obese females undergoing cesarean section using Pfannenstiel incision. Gynecol Obstet Invest 2002;53: 75–8.
24. Magann EF, Chauhan SP, Rodts-Palenik S, Bufkin L, Martin JN Jr, Morrison JC. Subcutaneous stitch closure versus subcutaneous drain to prevent wound disruption after cesarean delivery: a randomized clinical trial. Am J Obstet Gynecol 2002;186:1119–23.
25. Bates SM, Greer IA, Hirsh J, Ginsberg JS. Use of antithrombotic agents during pregnancy: the Seventh ACCP Conference on Antithrombotic and Thrombolytic Therapy. Chest 2004;126:627S–44S.
26. Royal College of Obstetricians and Gynaecologists. Report of the RCOG working party on prophylaxis against thromboembolism in gynaecology and obstetrics. London: RCOG; 1995.
27. Gates S, Brocklehurst P, Davis LJ. Prophylaxis for venous thromboembolic disease in pregnancy and the early postnatal period. The Cochrane Database of Systematic Reviews 2002, Issue 2. Art. No.: CD001689. DOI: 10. 1002/14651858.CD001689.
28. Hague WM, North RA, Gallus AS, Walters BN, Orlikowski C, Burrows RF, et al. Anticoagulation in pregnancy and the puerperium. Working Group on behalf of the Obstetric Medicine Group of Australasia. Med J Aust 2001;175:258–63.
29. Tomoda S, Tamura T, Sudo Y, Ogita S. Effects of obesity on pregnant women: maternal hemodynamic change. Am J Perinatol 1996;13:73–8.
30. Houston MC, Raynor BD. Postoperative morbidity in the morbidly obese parturient woman: supraumbilical and low transverse abdominal approaches. Am J Obstet Gynecol 2000;182:1033–5.
31. Chauhan SP, Magann EF, Carroll CS, Barrilleaux PS, Scardo JA, Martin JN Jr. Mode of delivery for the morbidly obese with prior cesarean delivery: vaginal versus repeat cesarean section. Am J Obstet Gynecol 2001; 185:349–54.
32. Ramirez MM, Turrentine MA. Gastrointestinal hemorrhage during pregnancy in a patient with a history of vertical-banded gastroplasty. Am J Obstet Gynecol 1995; 173:1630–1.
33. Gurewitsch ED, Smith-Levitin M, Mack J. Pregnancy following gastric bypass surgery for morbid obesity. Obstet Gynecol 1996;88:658–61.
34. Granstrom L, Granstrom L, Backman L. Fetal growth retardation after gastric banding. Acta Obstet Gynecol Scand 1990;69:533–6.
35. Haddow JE, Hill LE, Kloza EM, Thanhauser D. Neural tube defects after gastric bypass. Lancet 1986;1:1330.
36. Martin L, Chavez GF, Adams MJ Jr, Mason EE, Hanson JW, Haddow JE, et al. Gastric bypass surgery as maternal risk factor for neural tube defects. Lancet 1988;1:640–1.
37. Marceau P, Kaufman D, Biron S, Hould FS, Lebel S, Marceau S, et al. Outcome of pregnancies after biliopancreatic diversion. Obes Surg 2004;14:318–24.
38. Sheiner E, Levy A, Silverberg D, Menes TS, Levy I, Katz M, et al. Pregnancy after bariatric surgery is not associated with adverse perinatal outcome. Am J Obstet Gynecol 2004;190:1335–40.
39. Martin LF, Finigan KM, Nolan TE. Pregnancy after adjustable gastric banding. Obstet Gynecol 2000;95: 927–30.
40. Wittgrove AC, Jester L, Wittgrove P, Clark GW. Pregnancy following gastric bypass for morbid obesity. Obes Surg 1998;8:461–4; discussion 465–6.
41. Weiss HG, Nehoda H, Labeck B, Hourmont K, Marth C, Aigner F. Pregnancies after adjustable gastric banding. Obes Surg 2001;11:303–6.
42. Cnattingius S, Bergstrom R, Lipworth L, Kramer MS. Prepregnancy weight and the risk of adverse pregnancy outcomes. N Engl J Med 1998;338:147–52.
43. Hendler I, Blackwell SC, Treadwell MC, Bujold E, Sokol RJ, Sorokin Y. Does advanced ultrasound equipment improve the adequacy of ultrasound visualization of fetal

cardiac structures in the obese gravid woman? Am J Obstet Gynecol 2004;190;1616–9; discussion 1619–20.

44. Shaw GM, Velie EM, Schaffer D. Risk of neural tube defect-affected pregnancies among obese women. JAMA 1996;275:1093–6.
45. Waller DK, Mills JL, Simpson JL, Cunningham GC, Conley MR, Lassman MR, et al. Are obese women at higher risk for producing malformed offspring? Am J Obstet Gynecol 1994;170:541–8.
46. Werler MM, Louick C, Shapiro S, Mitchell AA. Prepregnancy weight in relation to risk of neural tube defects. JAMA 1996;275:1089–92.
47. Stephansson O, Dickman PW, Johansson A, Cnattingius S. Maternal weight, pregnancy weight gain, and the risk of antepartum stillbirth. Am J Obstet Gynecol 2001; 184:463–9.
48. Watkins ML, Rasmussen SA, Honein MA, Botto LD, Moore CA. Maternal obesity and risk for birth defects. Pediatrics 2003;111:1152–8.
49. Hediger ML, Overpeck MD, McGlynn A, Kuczmarski RJ, Maurer KR, Davis WW. Growth and fatness at three to six years of age of children born small- or large-for-gestational age. Pediatrics 1999;104:e33.
50. Spellacy WN, Miller S, Winegar A, Peterson PQ. Macrosomia—maternal characteristics and infant complications. Obstet Gynecol 1985;66:158–61.
51. Lipscomb KR, Gregory K, Shaw K. The outcome of macrosomic infants weighing at least 4500 grams: Los Angeles County + University of Southern California experience. Obstet Gynecol 1995;85:558–64.

# ACOG Committee Opinion

Committee on Obstetric Practice

Number 326, December 2005

This document reflects emerging clinical and scientific advances as of the date issued and is subject to change. The information should not be construed as dictating an exclusive course of treatment or procedure to be followed.



ISSN 1074-861X

**The American College of Obstetricians and Gynecologists**
409 12th Street, SW
PO Box 96920
Washington, DC 20090-6920

12345/98765

Inappropriate use of the terms fetal distress and birth asphyxia. ACOG Committee Opinion No. 326. American College of Obstetricians and Gynecologists. Obstet Gynecol 2005;106:1469–70.

# Inappropriate Use of the Terms Fetal Distress and Birth Asphyxia

*ABSTRACT: The Committee on Obstetric Practice is concerned about the continued use of the term "fetal distress" as an antepartum or intrapartum diagnosis and the term "birth asphyxia" as a neonatal diagnosis. The Committee reaffirms that the term fetal distress is imprecise and nonspecific. The communication between clinicians caring for the woman and those caring for her neonate is best served by replacing the term fetal distress with "nonreassuring fetal status," followed by a further description of findings (eg, repetitive variable decelerations, fetal tachycardia or bradycardia, late decelerations, or low biophysical profile). Also, the term birth asphyxia is a nonspecific diagnosis and should not be used.*

The Committee on Obstetric Practice is concerned about the continued use of the term "fetal distress" as an antepartum or intrapartum diagnosis and the term "birth asphyxia" as a neonatal diagnosis. The Committee reaffirms that the term fetal distress is imprecise and nonspecific. The term has a low positive predictive value even in high-risk populations and often is associated with an infant who is in good condition at birth as determined by the Apgar score or umbilical cord blood gas analysis or both. The communication between clinicians caring for the woman and those caring for her neonate is best served by replacing the term fetal distress with "nonreassuring fetal status," followed by a further description of findings (eg, repetitive variable decelerations, fetal tachycardia or bradycardia, late decelerations, or low biophysical profile). Whereas in the past, the term fetal distress generally referred to an ill fetus, nonreassuring fetal status describes the clinician's interpretation of data regarding fetal status (ie, the clinician is not reassured by the findings). This term acknowledges the imprecision inherent in the interpretation of the data. Therefore, the diagnosis of nonreassuring fetal status can be consistent with the delivery of a vigorous neonate.

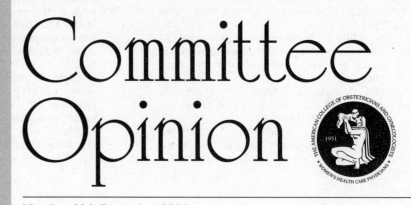

Because of the implications of the term fetal distress, its use may result in inappropriate actions, such as an unnecessarily urgent delivery under general anesthesia. Fetal heart rate patterns or auscultatory findings should be considered when the degree of urgency, mode of delivery, and type of anesthesia to be given are determined. Performing a cesarean delivery for a nonreassuring fetal heart rate pattern does not necessarily preclude the use of regional anesthesia.

Since October 1, 1998, all inclusion terms except "metabolic acidemia" have been removed from the International Classification of Diseases code for fetal distress. The Committee believes that there should be uniformity in wording. *The International Classification of Diseases, Ninth Revision, Clinical Modification* code for fetal distress is based on fetal metabolic acidemia and excludes abnormal fetal acid–base balance, abnormality in fetal heart rate or rhythm, fetal bradycardia, fetal tachycardia, and meconium in liquor.

The term birth asphyxia is a nonspecific diagnosis and should not be used. The Committee strongly supports the criteria required to define an acute intrapartum hypoxic event sufficient to cause cerebral palsy, as modified by the ACOG Task Force on Neonatal Encephalopathy and Cerebral Palsy from the template provided by the International Cerebral Palsy Task Force (1) (Box 1).

**Criteria to Define an Acute Intrapartum Hypoxic Event as Sufficient to Cause Cerebral Palsy**

**1.1**: Essential criteria (must meet all four)

1. Evidence of a metabolic acidosis in fetal umbilical cord arterial blood obtained at delivery (pH <7 and base deficit ≥12 mmol/L)
2. Early onset of severe or moderate neonatal encephalopathy in infants born at 34 or more weeks of gestation
3. Cerebral palsy of the spastic quadriplegic or dyskinetic type*
4. Exclusion of other identifiable etiologies, such as trauma, coagulation disorders, infectious conditions, or genetic disorders

**1.2**: Criteria that collectively suggest an intrapartum timing (within close proximity to labor and delivery, eg, 0–48 hours) but are nonspecific to asphyxial insults

1. A sentinel (signal) hypoxic event occurring immediately before or during labor
2. A sudden and sustained fetal bradycardia or the absence of fetal heart rate variability in the presence of persistent, late, or variable decelerations, usually after a hypoxic sentinel event when the pattern was previously normal
3. Apgar scores of 0–3 beyond 5 minutes
4. Onset of multisystem involvement within 72 hours of birth
5. Early imaging study showing evidence of acute nonfocal cerebral abnormality

*Spastic quadriplegia and, less commonly, dyskinetic cerebral palsy are the only types of cerebral palsy associated with acute hypoxic intrapartum events. Spastic quadriplegia is not specific to intrapartum hypoxia. Hemiparetic cerebral palsy, hemiplegic cerebral palsy, spastic diplegia, and ataxia are unlikely to result from acute intrapartum hypoxia (Nelson KB, Grether JK. Potentially asphyxiating conditions and spastic cerebral palsy in infants of normal birth weight. Am J Obstet Gynecol 1998;179:507–13.).

Modified from MacLennan A. A template for defining a causal relation between acute intrapartum events and cerebral palsy: international consensus statement. BMJ 1999;319:1054–9.

## References

1. American College of Obstetricians and Gynecologists and American Academy of Pediatrics. Neonatal encephalopathy and cerebral palsy: defining the pathogenesis and pathophysiology. Washington, DC: American College of Obstetricians and Gynecologists; 2003.

ACOG Committee Opinion

Committee on Obstetric Practice

American Academy of Pediatrics

DEDICATED TO THE HEALTH OF ALL CHILDREN™

Committee on Fetus and Newborn

Number 333, May 2006 (Replaces No. 174, July 1996)

This document reflects clinical and scientific advances as of the date issued and is subject to change. The information should not be construed as dictating an exclusive course of treatment or procedure to be followed.



ISSN 1074-861X

**The American College of Obstetricians and Gynecologists**
409 12th Street, SW
PO Box 96920
Washington, DC 20090-6920

12345/09876

The Apgar score. ACOG Committee Opinion No. 333. American Academy of Pediatrics; American College of Obstetricians and Gynecologists. Obstet Gynecol 2006;107:1209–12.

# The Apgar Score

*ABSTRACT. The Apgar score provides a convenient shorthand for reporting the status of the newborn infant and the response to resuscitation. The Apgar score has been used inappropriately to predict specific neurologic outcome in the term infant. There are no consistent data on the significance of the Apgar score in preterm infants. The Apgar score has limitations, and it is inappropriate to use it alone to establish the diagnosis of asphyxia. An Apgar score assigned during resuscitation is not equivalent to a score assigned to a spontaneously breathing infant. An expanded Apgar score reporting form will account for concurrent resuscitative interventions and provide information to improve systems of perinatal and neonatal care.*

## Introduction

In 1952, Dr. Virginia Apgar devised a scoring system that was a rapid method of assessing the clinical status of the newborn infant at 1 minute of age and the need for prompt intervention to establish breathing (1). A second report evaluating a larger number of patients was published in 1958 (2). This scoring system provided a standardized assessment for infants after delivery. The Apgar score comprises 5 components: heart rate, respiratory effort, muscle tone, reflex irritability, and color, each of which is given a score of 0, 1, or 2. The score is now reported at 1 and 5 minutes after birth. The Apgar score continues to provide a convenient shorthand for reporting the status of the newborn infant and the response to resuscitation. The Apgar score has been used inappropriately in term infants to predict specific neurologic outcome. Because there are no consistent data on the significance of the Apgar score in preterm infants, in this population the score should not be used for any purpose other than ongoing assessment in the delivery room. The purpose of this statement is to place the Apgar score in its proper perspective.

The neonatal resuscitation program (NRP) guidelines state that "Apgar scores should not be used to dictate appropriate resuscitative actions, nor should interventions for depressed infants be delayed until the 1-minute assessment" (3). However, an Apgar score that remains 0 beyond 10 minutes of age may be useful in determining whether additional resuscitative efforts are indicated (4). The current NRP guidelines state that "if there is no heart rate after 10 minutes of complete and adequate resuscitation efforts, and there is no evidence of other causes of newborn compromise, discontinuation of resuscitation efforts may be appropriate. Current data indicate that, after 10 minutes of asystole, newborns are very unlikely to survive, or the rare survivor is likely to survive with severe disability" (3).

Previously, an Apgar score of 3 or less at 5 minutes was considered an essential requirement for the diagnosis of perinatal asphyxia. *Neonatal Encephalopathy and Cerebral Palsy: Defining the Pathogenesis and Pathophysiology*, produced in 2003 by the American College of Obstetricians and Gynecologists in collaboration with the American Academy of Pediatrics, lists an Apgar score of 0 to 3 beyond 5 minutes as one suggestive criterion for an intrapartum asphyxial insult (5). However, a persistently low Apgar score alone is not a specific indicator for intrapartum compromise. Further, although the score is used widely in outcome studies, its inappropriate use has led to an erroneous definition of asphyxia. Intrapartum asphyxia implies fetal hypercarbia and hypoxemia, which, if prolonged, will result in metabolic acidemia. Because the intrapartum disruption of uterine or fetal blood flow is rarely, if ever, absolute, asphyxia is an imprecise, general term. Descriptions such as hypercarbia, hypoxia, and metabolic, respiratory, or lactic acidemia are more precise for immediate assessment of the newborn infant and retrospective assessment of intrapartum management.

## Limitations of the Apgar Score

It is important to recognize the limitations of the Apgar score. The Apgar score is an expression of the infant's physiologic condition, has a limited time frame, and includes subjective components. In addition, the biochemical disturbance must be significant before the score is affected. Elements of the score such as tone, color, and reflex irritability partially depend on the physiologic maturity of the infant. The healthy preterm infant with no evidence of asphyxia may receive a low score only because of immaturity (6). A number of factors may influence an Apgar score, including but not limited to drugs, trauma, congenital anomalies, infections, hypoxia, hypovolemia, and preterm birth (7). The incidence of low Apgar scores is inversely related to birth weight, and a low score is limited in predicting morbidity or mortality (8). Accordingly, it is inappropriate to use an Apgar score alone to establish the diagnosis of asphyxia.

## Apgar Score and Resuscitation

The 5-minute Apgar score, and particularly a change in the score between 1 and 5 minutes, is a useful index of the response to resuscitation. If the Apgar score is less than 7 at 5 minutes, the NRP guidelines state that the assessment should be repeated every 5 minutes up to 20 minutes (3). However, an Apgar score assigned during a resuscitation is not equivalent to a score assigned to a spontaneously breathing infant (9). There is no accepted standard for reporting an Apgar score in infants undergoing resuscitation after birth, because many of the elements contributing to the score are altered by resuscitation. The concept of an "assisted" score that accounts for resuscitative interventions has been suggested, but the predictive reliability has not been studied. To describe such infants correctly and provide accurate documentation and data collection, an expanded Apgar score report form is proposed (Fig. 1).

## Prediction of Outcome

A low 1-minute Apgar score alone does not correlate with the infant's future outcome. A retrospective analysis concluded that the 5-minute Apgar score remained a valid predictor of neonatal mortality, but using it to predict long-term outcome was inappropriate (10). On the other hand, another study stated that low Apgar scores at 5 minutes are associated with death or cerebral palsy, and this association increased if both 1- and 5-minute scores were low (11).

An Apgar score at 5 minutes in term infants correlates poorly with future neurologic outcomes. For example, a score of 0 to 3 at 5 minutes was associated with a slightly increased risk of cerebral palsy compared with higher scores (12). Conversely, 75% of children with cerebral palsy had normal scores at 5 minutes (12). In addition, a low 5-minute score in combination with other markers of asphyxia may identify infants at risk of developing seizures (odds ratio: 39; 95% confidence interval: 3.9–392.5) (13). The risk of poor neurologic outcomes increases when the Apgar score is 3 or less at 10, 15, and 20 minutes (7).

A 5-minute Apgar score of 7 to 10 is considered normal. Scores of 4, 5, and 6 are intermediate and

Apgar Score

Gestational age____________weeks

| Sign | 0 | 1 | 2 | 1 minute | 5 minute | 10 minute | 15 minute | 20 minute |
|---|---|---|---|---|---|---|---|---|
| Color | Blue or Pale | Acrocyanotic | Completely Pink | | | | | |
| Heart rate | Absent | <100 minute | >100 minute | | | | | |
| Reflex irritability | No Response | Grimace | Cry or Active Withdrawal | | | | | |
| Muscle tone | Limp | Some Flexion | Active Motion | | | | | |
| Respiration | Absent | Weak Cry; Hypoventilation | Good, Crying | | | | | |
| | | | Total | | | | | |

Comments:

| | Resuscitation | | | | |
|---|---|---|---|---|---|
| Minutes | 1 | 5 | 10 | 15 | 20 |
| Oxygen | | | | | |
| PPV/NCPAP | | | | | |
| ETT | | | | | |
| Chest Compressions | | | | | |
| Epinephrine | | | | | |

**Fig. 1.** Expanded Apgar score form. Record the score in the appropriate place at specific time intervals. The additional resuscitative measures (if appropriate) are recorded at the same time that the score is reported using a check mark in the appropriate box. Use the comment box to list other factors including maternal medications and/or the response to resuscitation between the recorded times of scoring. PPV/NCPAP indicates positive-pressure ventilation/nasal continuous positive airway pressure; ETT, endotracheal tube.

are not markers of increased risk of neurologic dysfunction. Such scores may be the result of physiologic immaturity, maternal medications, the presence of congenital malformations, and other factors. Because of these other conditions, the Apgar score alone cannot be considered evidence of or a consequence of asphyxia. Other factors including nonreassuring fetal heart rate monitoring patterns and abnormalities in umbilical arterial blood gases, clinical cerebral function, neuroimaging studies, neonatal electroencephalography, placental pathology, hematologic studies, and multisystem organ dysfunction need to be considered when defining an intrapartum hypoxic–ischemic event as a cause of cerebral palsy (5).

## Other Applications

Monitoring of low Apgar scores from a delivery service can be useful. Individual case reviews can identify needs for focused educational programs and improvement in systems of perinatal care. Analyzing trends allows assessment of the impact of quality improvement interventions.

## Conclusion

The Apgar score describes the condition of the newborn infant immediately after birth (14), and when properly applied, is a tool for standardized assessment. It also provides a mechanism to record fetal-to-neonatal transition. An Apgar score of 0 to 3 at 5 minutes may correlate with neonatal mortality but alone does not predict later neurologic dysfunction. The Apgar score is affected by gestational age, maternal medications, resuscitation, and cardiorespiratory and neurologic conditions. Low 1- and 5-minute Apgar scores alone are not conclusive markers of an acute intrapartum hypoxic event. Resuscitative interventions modify the components of the Apgar score. There is a need for perinatal health care professionals to be consistent in assigning an Apgar score during a resuscitation. The American Academy of Pediatrics and the American

College of Obstetricians and Gynecologists propose use of an expanded Apgar score reporting form that accounts for concurrent resuscitative interventions.

## References


1. Apgar V. A proposal for a new method of evaluation of the newborn infant. Curr Res Anesth Analg 1953;32:260–7.
2. Apgar V, Holaday DA, James LS, Weisbrot IM, Berrien C. Evaluation of the newborn infant; second report. JAMA 1958;168:1985–8.
3. American Academy of Pediatrics, American Heart Association. Textbook of neonatal resuscitation. 4th ed. Elk Grove Village (IL): American Academy of Pediatrics; Dallas (TX): American Heart Association; 2000.
4. Jain L, Ferre C, Vidyasagar D, Nath S, Sheftel D. Cardiopulmonary resuscitation of apparently stillborn infants: survival and long-term outcome. J Pediatr 1991;118:778–82.
5. American Academy of Pediatrics, American College of Obstetricians and Gynecologists. Neonatal encephalopathy and cerebral palsy: defining the pathogenesis and pathophysiology. Elk Grove Village (IL): AAP; Washington, DC: ACOG; 2003.
6. Catlin EA, Carpenter MW, Brann BS 4th, Mayfield SR, Shaul PW, Goldstein M, et al. The Apgar score revisited: influence of gestational age. J Pediatr 1986;109:865–8.
7. Freeman JM, Nelson KB. Intrapartum asphyxia and cerebral palsy. Pediatrics 1988;82:240–9.
8. Hegyi T, Carbone T, Anwar M, Ostfeld B, Hiatt M, Koons A, et al. The Apgar score and its components in the preterm infant. Pediatrics 1998;101:77–81.
9. Lopriore E, van Burk GF, Walther FJ, de Beaufort AJ. Correct use of the Apgar score for resuscitated and intubated newborn babies: questionnaire study. BMJ 2004; 329:143–4.
10. Casey BM, McIntire DD, Leveno KJ. The continuing value of the Apgar score for the assessment of newborn infants. N Engl J Med 2001;344:467–71.
11. Moster D, Lie RT, Irgens LM, Bjerkedal T, Markestad T. The association of Apgar score with subsequent death and cerebral palsy: a population-based study in term infants. J Pediatr 2001;138:798–803.
12. Nelson KB, Ellenberg JH. Apgar scores as predictors of chronic neurologic disability. Pediatrics 1981;68:36–44.
13. Perlman JM, Risser R. Can asphyxiated infants at risk for neonatal seizures be rapidly identified by current high-risk markers? Pediatrics 1996;97:456–62.
14. Papile LA. The Apgar score in the 21st century. N Engl J Med 2001;344:519–20.

ACOG Committee Opinion

Committee on Obstetric Practice

Number 339, June 2006 (Replaces No. 269, February 2002)

# Analgesia and Cesarean Delivery Rates

*ABSTRACT: Neuraxial analgesia techniques are the most effective and least depressant treatments for labor pain. The American College of Obstetricians and Gynecologists previously recommended that practitioners delay initiating epidural analgesia in nulliparous women until the cervical dilatation reached 4–5 cm. However, more recent studies have shown that epidural analgesia does not increase the risks of cesarean delivery. The choice of analgesic technique, agent, and dosage is based on many factors, including patient preference, medical status, and contraindications. The fear of unnecessary cesarean delivery should not influence the method of pain relief that women can choose during labor.*

Neuraxial analgesia techniques (epidural, spinal, and combined spinal–epidural) are the most effective and least depressant treatments for labor pain (1, 2). Early studies generated concern that the benefits of neuraxial analgesia may be offset by an associated increase in the risk of cesarean delivery (3, 4). Recent studies, however, have determined that when compared with intravenous systemic opioid analgesia, the initiation of early neuraxial analgesia does not increase the risk of cesarean delivery (5–7).

In 2000, the American College of Obstetricians and Gynecologists (ACOG) Task Force on Cesarean Delivery recommended that "when feasible, obstetric practitioners should delay the administration of epidural anesthesia in nulliparous women until the cervical dilatation reaches at least 4–5 cm" (8). This recommendation was based on earlier studies, which suggested that epidural analgesia increased the risk of cesarean delivery by as much as 12-fold (3, 4, 9, 10). Furthermore, certain studies demonstrated an even greater association between epidural analgesia and cesarean delivery in women who received their epidurals before reaching cervical dilatation of 5 cm (3, 9). In 2002, an evaluation of cesarean delivery sponsored by ACOG concluded, "there is considerable evidence suggesting that there is in fact an association between the use of epidural analgesia for pain relief during labor and the risk of cesarean delivery (8).

Since the last Committee Opinion on analgesia and cesarean delivery, additional studies have addressed the issue of neuraxial analgesia and its association with cesarean delivery. Three recent meta-analyses systematical-

This document reflects emerging clinical and scientific advances as of the date issued and is subject to change. The information should not be construed as dictating an exclusive course of treatment or procedure to be followed.



ISSN 1074-861X

**The American College of Obstetricians and Gynecologists**
409 12th Street, SW
PO Box 96920
Washington, DC 20090-6920

12345/09876

Analgesia and cesarean delivery rates. ACOG Committee Opinion No. 339. American College of Obstetricians and Gynecologists. Obstet Gynecol 2006;107:1487–8.

ly and independently reviewed the previous literature, and all concluded that epidural analgesia does not increase the rates of cesarean delivery (odds ratio 1.00–1.04; 95% confidence interval, 0.71–1.48) (11–13). In addition, three recent randomized controlled trials clearly demonstrated no difference in rate of cesarean deliveries between women who had received epidurals and women who had received only intravenous analgesia (5–7). Furthermore, a randomized trial comparing epidurals done early in labor versus epidurals done later in labor demonstrated no difference in the incidence of cesarean delivery (17.8% versus 20.7%) (5). The use of intrathecal analgesia and the concentration of the local anesthetic used in an epidural also have no impact on the rate of cesarean delivery (5, 13–15).

Therefore, ACOG reaffirms the opinion it published jointly with the American Society of Anesthesiologists, in which the following statement was articulated: "Labor causes severe pain for many women. There is no other circumstance where it is considered acceptable for an individual to experience untreated severe pain, amenable to safe intervention, while under a physician's care. In the absence of a medical contraindication, maternal request is a sufficient medical indication for pain relief during labor" (16). The fear of unnecessary cesarean delivery should not influence the method of pain relief that women can choose during labor.

The American College of Obstetricians and Gynecologists recognizes that many techniques are available for analgesia in laboring patients. None of the techniques appears to be associated with an increased risk of cesarean delivery. The choice of technique, agent, and dosage is based on many factors, including patient preference, medical status, and contraindications. Decisions regarding analgesia should be closely coordinated among the obstetrician, the anesthesiologist, the patient, and skilled support personnel.

## References


1. Gibbs CP, Krischer J, Peckham BM, Sharp H, Kirschbaum TH. Obstetric anesthesia: a national survey. Anesthesiology 1986;65:298–306.
2. Hawkins JL, Gibbs CP, Orleans M, Martin-Salvaj G, Beaty B. Obstetric anesthesia work force survey, 1981 versus 1992. Anesthesiology 1997;87:135–43.
3. Thorp JA, Hu DH, Albin RM, McNitt J, Meyer BA, Cohen GR, et al. The effect of intrapartum epidural analgesia on nulliparous labor: a randomized, controlled, prospective trial. Am J Obstet Gynecol 1993;169:851–8.
4. Ramin SM, Gambling DR, Lucas MJ, Sharma SK, Sidawi JE, Leveno KJ. Randomized trial of epidural versus intravenous analgesia during labor. Obstet Gynecol 1995; 86:783–9.
5. Wong CA, Scavone BM, Peaceman AM, McCarthy RJ, Sullivan JT, Diaz NT, et al. The risk of cesarean delivery with neuraxial analgesia given early versus late in labor. N Engl J Med. 2005;352:655–65.
6. Sharma SK, Alexander JM, Messick G, Bloom SL, McIntire DD, Wiley J, et al. Cesarean delivery: a randomized trial of epidural analgesia versus intravenous meperidine analgesia during labor in nulliparous women. Anesthesiology 2002;96:546–51.
7. Halpern SH, Muir H, Breen TW, Campbell DC, Barrett J, Liston R, et al. A multicenter randomized controlled trial comparing patient-controlled epidural with intravenous analgesia for pain relief in labor. Anesth Analg 2004; 99:1532–8.
8. American College of Obstetricians and Gynecologists. Evaluation of cesarean delivery. Washington, DC: ACOG; 2000.
9. Lieberman E, Lang JM, Cohen A, D'Agostino R Jr, Datta S, Frigoletto FD Jr. Association of epidural analgesia with cesarean delivery in nulliparas. Obstet Gynecol 1996; 88:993–1000.
10. Howell C, Chalmers I. A review of prospectively controlled comparisons of epidural with non-epidural forms of pain relief during labour. Int J Obstet Anesth 1992;1:93–110.
11. Leighton BL, Halpern SH. The effects of epidural analgesia on labor, maternal, and neonatal outcomes: a systemic review. Am J Obstet Gynecol 2002;186:S69–77.
12. Liu EH, Sia AT. Rates of caesarean section and instrumental vaginal delivery in nulliparous women after low concentration epidural infusion or opiod analgesia: systemic review. BMJ 2004;328:1410.
13. Sharma SK, McIntire DD, Wiley J, Leveno KJ. Labor analgesia and cesarean delivery: an individual patient meta-analysis of nulliparous women. Anesthesiology 2004;100:142–8.
14. Effect of low-dose mobile versus traditional epidural techniques on mode of delivery: a randomised controlled trial. Comparative Obstetric Mobile Epidural Trial (COMET) Study Group UK. Lancet 2001;358:19–23.
15. Chestnut DH, McGrath JM, Vincent RD Jr, Penning DH, Choi WW, Bates JN, et al. Does early administration of epidural analgesia affect obstetric outcome in nulliparous women who are in spontaneous labor? Anesthesiology 1994;80:1201–8.
16. Pain relief during labor. ACOG Committee Opinion No. 295. American College of Obstetricians and Gynecologists. Obstet Gynecol 2004;104:213.

ACOG Committee Opinion

Committee on Obstetric Practice

Number 340, July 2006 (Replaces No. 265, December 2001)

This document reflects emerging clinical and scientific advances as of the date issued and is subject to change. The information should not be construed as dictating an exclusive course of treatment or procedure to be followed.



ISSN 1074-861X

**The American College of Obstetricians and Gynecologists**
409 12th Street, SW
PO Box 96920
Washington, DC 20090-6920

12345/09876

Mode of term singleton breech delivery. ACOG Committee Opinion No. 340. American College of Obstetricians and Gynecologists. Obstet Gynecol 2006;108:235–7.

# Mode of Term Singleton Breech Delivery

*ABSTRACT: In light of recent studies that further clarify the long-term risks of vaginal breech delivery, the American College of Obstetricians and Gynecologists recommends that the decision regarding mode of delivery should depend on the experience of the health care provider. Cesarean delivery will be the preferred mode for most physicians because of the diminishing expertise in vaginal breech delivery. Planned vaginal delivery of a term singleton breech fetus may be reasonable under hospital-specific protocol guidelines for both eligibility and labor management. Before a vaginal breech delivery is planned, women should be informed that the risk of perinatal or neonatal mortality or short-term serious neonatal morbidity may be higher than if a cesarean delivery is planned, and the patient's informed consent should be documented.*

During the past decade, there has been an increasing trend in the United States to perform cesarean delivery for term singleton fetuses in a breech presentation. In 2002, the rate of cesarean deliveries for women in labor with breech presentation was 86.9% (1). The number of practitioners with the skills and experience to perform vaginal breech delivery has decreased. Even in academic medical centers where faculty support for teaching vaginal breech delivery to residents remains high, there may be insufficient volume of vaginal breech deliveries to adequately teach this procedure (2).

In 2000, researchers conducted a large, international multicenter randomized clinical trial comparing a policy of planned cesarean delivery with planned vaginal delivery (Term Breech Trial) (3). These investigators noted that perinatal mortality, neonatal mortality, and serious neonatal morbidity were significantly lower among the planned cesarean delivery group compared with the planned vaginal delivery group (17/1,039 [1.6%] versus 52/1,039 [5%]), although there was no difference in maternal morbidity or mortality observed between the groups (3). The benefits of planned cesarean delivery remained for all subgroups identified by the baseline variables (eg, older and younger women, nulliparous and multiparous women, frank and complete type of breech presentation). They found that the reduction in risk attributable to planned cesarean delivery was greatest among centers in industrialized nations with low overall perinatal mortality rates (0.4% versus

5.7%). In countries with low perinatal mortality rates, the reduction in risk was driven primarily by the pooled rates of perinatal or neonatal mortality and serious neonatal morbidity, rather than by the rates of mortality alone (0% versus 0.6%). Given the results of this exceptionally large and well-controlled clinical trial, the American College of Obstetricians and Gynecologists' Committee on Obstetric Practice in 2001 recommended that planned vaginal delivery of a term singleton breech was no longer appropriate.

Since that time, there have been additional publications that modify the original conclusions of the 2000 Term Breech Trial. The same researchers have published three follow-up studies examining maternal outcomes at 3 months postpartum, as well as outcomes for mothers and children 2 years after the births (4–6). At 3 months postpartum, the risk of urinary incontinence was lower for women in the planned cesarean delivery group; however, there was no difference at 2 years. At 2 years postpartum, maternal morbidity, which was assessed via questionnaire in 917 of 1,159 (79.1%), was not different for most maternal parameters, including breastfeeding, pain, depression, menstrual problems, fatigue, and distressing memories of the birth experience (5).

The follow-up study to address outcomes of the children at 2 years involved 85 centers (with both high and low perinatal mortality rates) that were chosen at the start of the original trial. Most children, 923 of 1,159 (79.6%), were assessed first by a screening questionnaire (Ages and Stages) that was completed by their parents (4). All abnormal results were further evaluated with a clinical neurodevelopment assessment. The risk of death or neurodevelopmental delay was no different in the planned cesarean delivery group compared with the planned vaginal delivery group (14 children [3.1%] versus 13 children [2.8%]; relative risk, 1.09; 95% CI, 0.52–2.30; $P = 0.85$). There are several explanations for this seemingly contradictory finding. The follow-up study was underpowered to show a clinically important benefit from cesarean delivery if this were true. Only 6 of the 16 infants who died in the neonatal period were from centers participating in the follow-up to 2 years (one in the planned cesarean delivery group, five in the planned vaginal delivery group), and most of the children with serious neonatal morbidity after birth survived and developed normally. In this cohort, 17 out of 18 children with serious morbidity in the original study were normal at this 24-month follow-up. Another explanation is that the use of pooled mortality and morbidity data at the time of birth overstated the true long-term risks of vaginal delivery (7).

A recent retrospective observational report reviewed neonatal outcome in the Netherlands before and after the publication of the Term Breech Trial (8). Between 1998 and 2002, 35,453 term infants were delivered. The cesarean delivery rate for breech presentation increased from 50% to 80% within 2 months of the trial's publication and remained elevated. The combined neonatal mortality rate decreased from 0.35% to 0.18%, and the incidence of reported birth trauma decreased from 0.29% to 0.08%. Of interest, a decrease in mortality also was seen in the emergency cesarean delivery group and the vaginal delivery group, a finding that the authors attribute to better selection of candidates for vaginal breech delivery.

There are many retrospective reports of vaginal breech delivery that follow very specific protocols and note excellent neonatal outcomes. One report noted 298 women in a vaginal breech trial with no perinatal morbidity and mortality (9). Another report noted similar outcomes in 481 women with planned vaginal delivery (10). Although they are not randomized trials, these reports detail the outcomes of specific management protocols and document the potential safety of a vaginal delivery in the properly selected patient. The initial criteria used in these reports were similar: gestational age greater than 37 weeks, frank or complete breech presentation, no fetal anomalies on ultrasound examination, adequate maternal pelvis, and estimated fetal weight between 2,500 g and 4,000 g. In addition, the protocol presented by one report required documentation of fetal head flexion and adequate amniotic fluid volume, defined as a 3-cm vertical pocket (9). Oxytocin induction or augmentation was not offered, and strict criteria were established for normal labor progress.

In light of the recent publications that further clarify the long-term risks of vaginal breech delivery, the American College of Obstetricians and Gynecologists' Committee on Obstetric Practice issues the following recommendations:

- The decision regarding the mode of delivery should depend on the experience of the health care provider. Cesarean delivery will be the preferred mode of delivery for most physicians because of the diminishing expertise in vaginal breech delivery.

- Obstetricians should offer and perform external cephalic version whenever possible.
- Planned vaginal delivery of a term singleton breech fetus may be reasonable under hospital-specific protocol guidelines for both eligibility and labor management.
- In those instances in which breech vaginal deliveries are pursued, great caution should be exercised, and detailed patient informed consent should be documented.
- Before embarking on a plan for a vaginal breech delivery, women should be informed that the risk of perinatal or neonatal mortality or short-term serious neonatal morbidity may be higher than if a cesarean delivery is planned.
- There are no recent data to support the recommendation of cesarean delivery to patients whose second twin is in a nonvertex presentation, although a large multicenter randomized controlled trial is in progress (www.utoronto.ca/miru/tbs).

## References


1. Martin JA, Hamilton BE, Sutton PD, Ventura SJ, Menacker F, Munson ML. Births: final data for 2002. Natl Vital Stat Rep 2003;52(10):1–113.
2. Lavin JP Jr, Eaton J, Hopkins M. Teaching vaginal breech delivery and external cephalic version. A survey of faculty attitudes. J Reprod Med 2000;45:808–12.
3. Hannah ME, Hannah WJ, Hewson SA, Hodnett ED, Saigal S, Willan AR. Planned caesarean section versus planned vaginal birth for breech presentation at term: a randomised multicentre trial. Term Breech Trial Collaborative Group. Lancet 2000;356:1375–83.
4. Whyte H, Hannah ME, Saigal S, Hannah WJ, Hewson S, Amankwah K, et al. Outcomes of children at 2 years after planned cesarean birth versus planned vaginal birth for breech presentation at term: the International Randomized Term Breech Trial. Term Breech Trial Collaborative Group. Am J Obstet Gynecol 2004;191:864–71.
5. Hannah ME, Whyte H, Hannah WJ, Hewson S, Amankwah K, Cheng M, et al. Maternal outcomes at 2 years after planned cesarean section versus planned vaginal birth for breech presentation at term: the international randomized Term Breech Trial. Term Breech Trial Collaborative Group. Am J Obstet Gynecol 2004;191:917–27.
6. Su M, Hannah WJ, Willan A, Ross S, Hannah ME. Planned caesarean section decreases the risk of adverse perinatal outcome due to both labour and delivery complications in the Term Breech Trial. Term Breech Trial Collaborative Group. BJOG 2004;111:1065–74.
7. Kotaska A. Inappropiate use of randomised trials to evaluate complex phenomena: case study of vaginal breech delivery [published erratum appears in BMJ 2004;329:1385]. BMJ 2004;329:1039–42.
8. Rietberg CC, Elferink-Stinkens PM, Visser GH. The effect of the Term Breech Trial on medical intervention behaviour and neonatal outcome in The Netherlands: an analysis of 35,453 term breech infants. BJOG 2005;112:205–9.
9. Alarab M, Regan C, O'Connell MP, Keane DP, O'Herlihy C, Foley ME. Singleton vaginal breech delivery at term: still a safe option. Obstet Gynecol 2004;103:407–12.
10. Guiliani A, Scholl WM, Basver A, Tamussino KF. Mode of delivery and outcome of 699 term singleton breech deliveries at a single center. Am J Obstet Gynecol 2002;187:1694–8.

ACOG Committee Opinion

Committee on Obstetric Practice

Number 342, August 2006 (Replaces No. 271, April 2002)

This document reflects emerging clinical and scientific advances as of the date issued and is subject to change. The information should not be construed as dictating an exclusive course of treatment or procedure to be followed.



ISSN 1074-861X

**The American College of Obstetricians and Gynecologists**
409 12th Street, SW
PO Box 96920
Washington, DC 20090-6920

12345/09876

Induction of labor for vaginal birth after cesarean delivery. ACOG Committee Opinion No. 342. American College of Obstetricians and Gynecologists. Obstet Gynecol 2006;108:465–67.

# Induction of Labor for Vaginal Birth After Cesarean Delivery

*ABSTRACT: Induction of labor in women who have had cesarean deliveries may be necessary because of fetal or maternal indications. The potentially increased risk of uterine rupture should be discussed with the patient and documented in the medical record. Selecting women most likely to give birth vaginally and avoiding the sequential use of prostaglandins and oxytocin appear to offer the lowest risks. Misoprostol should not be used in patients who have had cesarean deliveries or major uterine surgery.*

An ongoing controversy surrounds whether induction of labor with or without prostaglandins (specifically, the prostaglandin $E_2$ series) significantly increases the baseline risk of uterine rupture during labor. Induction with misoprostol (prostaglandin $E_1$) in women who have had cesarean deliveries has been shown, in a randomized trial, to be associated with a significant risk of uterine rupture, with two cases of uterine rupture out of 17 women treated with 25-mcg doses of misoprostol (1). This trial was stopped because of the increased rupture rate, and the Committee on Obstetric Practice continues to recommend that misoprostol not be used for induction of labor in women who have had cesarean deliveries or major uterine surgery (2–4). Since the last Committee on Obstetric Practice Opinion on induction of labor for vaginal birth after cesarean delivery was published, additional studies have addressed the issue of induction of labor with or without prostaglandins in women who have had cesarean deliveries.

Several studies noted an increased risk of uterine rupture from induction of labor in women who have had cesarean deliveries (5–7). A population-based, retrospective cohort study of the relationship of uterine rupture to vaginal birth after cesarean delivery using vital records and abstracted hospital discharge International Classification of Diseases, 9th Revision, Clinical Modification (ICD-9-CM) code diagnoses reviewed 20,095 women with histories of cesarean deliveries for their first delivery (5). The risk of uterine rupture was compared between patients who had repeat cesarean deliveries, patients giving birth after spontaneous onset of labor, and patients who had labor induced with or without the use of prostaglandins. There were 91 cases of uterine rupture with rates of 1.6 per 1,000 (0.16%) for repeat cesarean delivery, 5.2 per 1,000 (0.52%) for spontaneous labor, 7.7 per 1,000 (0.77%) for labor induced without prostaglandins, and 24.5 per 1,000 (2.4%) for prostaglandin-induced labor. Compared with women who gave birth by elective repeat cesarean delivery, the relative risk (RR) of uterine rupture was significantly higher among women who had spontaneous labor (RR, 3.3; 95% confidence interval [CI], 1.8–6), induction of labor without prostaglandins (RR, 4.9; 95% CI, 2.4–9.7), and induction of labor with prostaglandins (RR, 15.6; 95% CI, 8.1–30). There was no difference in the risks of uterine rupture between spontaneous labor and labor induced without prostaglandins. The authors acknowledged that they did not confirm the diagnoses of uterine rupture by examining medical records. Furthermore, their use of ICD-9-CM codes may have resulted in an overstatement of the actual incidence of uterine rupture because a single code is used for both uterine incision extension and uterine rupture (5). In another study, only 40% of ICD-9-CM-coded uterine ruptures were actually found to be uterine ruptures when the charts were reviewed, which raises a concern about the reliability of these findings (8).

In a larger, more recent, prospective, multicenter study, 33,699 women who had cesarean deliveries (17,898 and 15,801 with trial of labor or elective repeat cesarean deliveries, respectively) were studied (9). Charts were reviewed to document uterine rupture. There was no difference in the incidence of hysterectomy, thromboembolic disease, or maternal death between these two groups. Augmentation or induction of labor was associated with an increased risk of uterine rupture compared with spontaneous labor. There were 124 cases of uterine rupture, and the rate of uterine rupture in the trial of labor group was 0.4% for spontaneous labor, 0.9% for augmentation of labor, and 1% for induction of labor. In the group of women in whom labor was induced, the rate of uterine rupture was 1.1% when only oxytocin was used and 1.4% when any prostaglandins were used in combination with oxytocin; this result was not significantly different. There were no cases of uterine rupture in the group of women in whom labor was induced who received only prostaglandins. The prostaglandins used in this group included misoprostol, dinoprostone, and prostaglandin $E_2$ gel. This absence of uterine rupture likely represents women who went into labor "easily," requiring no oxytocin after prostaglandin administration. In another large study evaluating 25,005 women, induction or augmentation of labor was associated with an increased risk of uterine rupture (10). There was no significantly increased association between oxytocin or prostaglandins not used in combination with uterine rupture compared with women who went into spontaneous labor (10). The risk of uterine rupture was significantly increased with sequential use of prostaglandins and oxytocin (odds ratio, 4.54; 95% CI, 1.66–12.42) (10). Uterine rupture was confirmed with chart reviews in this study.

The rate of uterine rupture was significantly higher in women who had failed trials of labor (2.3%) compared with successful trials of labor (0.1%) (9). These results are similar to a study that reported nearly identical rates of uterine rupture (2% versus 0.1% in failed versus successful trials of labor) (11). Together, these studies (5, 9–11) suggest that rates of uterine rupture are likely increased by induction of labor more than by spontaneous labor, but the magnitude of risk is still low (1–2.4%). Additionally, sequential use of prostaglandins and oxytocin may further increase risk. Consistently, the highest rates of uterine rupture are associated with failed trials of labor (2–2.3% versus 0.1% for successful trials of labor). These more recent data do not confirm a specific increase in uterine rupture with the use of prostaglandins alone. The three largest studies vary in the quality of data, and data quality should be incorporated into any decision to use these data. Two of the three studies were prospective and confirmed uterine rupture with chart reviews (9–10). These two studies reported lower rates of uterine rupture with induction and prostaglandin induction of labor (1–1.4%). The third study was smaller, retrospective, and did not confirm uterine rupture with chart reviews, and it reported the highest rate of uterine rupture with the use of prostaglandins (2.4%) (5).

Induction of labor may be necessary for women who have had cesarean deliveries, for a maternal or fetal indication. Induction of labor remains a reasonable option, but the potentially increased risk of uterine rupture associated with any induction should be discussed with the patient and documented in the medical record. Selecting women most likely to give birth vaginally and avoiding sequential use of prostaglandins and oxytocin appear to offer the lowest risks of uterine rupture. Misoprostol should not be used in patients who have had cesarean deliveries or major uterine surgery.

## References


1. Wing DA, Lovett K, Paul RH. Disruption of prior uterine incision following misoprostol for labor induction in women with previous cesarean delivery. Obstet Gynecol 1998;91:828–30.
2. American College of Obstetricians and Gynecologists. Response to Searle's drug warning on misoprostol. ACOG Committee Opinion 248. Washington, DC: ACOG; 2000.
3. American College of Obstetricians and Gynecologists. Induction of labor with misoprostol. ACOG Committee Opinion 228. Washington, DC: ACOG; 1999.
4. American College of Obstetricians and Gynecologists. Induction of labor. ACOG Practice Bulletin 10. Washington, DC: ACOG; 1999.
5. Lydon-Rochelle M, Holt VL, Easterling TR, Martin DP. Risk of uterine rupture during labor among women with a prior cesarean delivery. N Engl J Med 2001;345:3–8.
6. Ravasia DJ, Wood SL, Pollard JK. Uterine rupture during induced trial of labor among women with previous cesarean delivery. Am J Obstet Gynecol 2000;183:1176–9.
7. Zelop CM, Shipp TD, Repke JT, Cohen A, Caughey AB, Lieberman E. Uterine rupture during induced or augmented labor in gravid women with one prior cesarean delivery. Am J Obstet Gynecol 1999;181:882–6.
8. Use of hospital discharge data to monitor uterine rupture—Massachusetts, 1990–1997. Centers for Disease Control and Prevention (CDC). MMWR Morb Mortal Wkly Rep 2000;49:245–8.
9. Landon MB, Hauth JC, Leveno KJ, Spong CY, Leindecker S, Varner MW, et al. Maternal and perinatal outcomes associated with a trial of labor after prior cesarean delivery. National Institute of Child Health and Human Development Maternal–Fetal Medicine Units Network. N Engl J Med 2004;351:2581–9.
10. Macones GA, Peipert J, Nelson DB, Odibo A, Stevens EJ, Stamilio DM, et al. Maternal complications with vaginal birth after cesarean delivery: a multicenter study. Am J Obstet Gynecol 2005;193:1656–62.
11. Wen SW, Rusen ID, Walker M, Liston R, Kramer MS, Baskett T, et al. Comparison of maternal mortality and morbidity between trial of labor and elective cesarean section among women with previous cesarean delivery. Maternal Health Study Group, Canadian Perinatal Surveillance System. Am J Obstet Gynecol 2004;191:1263–9.

ACOG Committee Opinion

Committee on Obstetric Practice

Number 346, October 2006

This document reflects emerging clinical and scientific advances as of the date issued and is subject to change. The information should not be construed as dictating an exclusive course of treatment or procedure to be followed.



ISSN 1074-861X

**The American College of Obstetricians and Gynecologists**
409 12th Street, SW
PO Box 96920
Washington, DC 20090-6920

12345/09876

Amnioinfusion does not prevent meconium aspiration syndrome. ACOG Committee Opinion No. 346. American College of Obstetricians and Gynecologists. Obstet Gynecol 2006;108:1053–5.

# Amnioinfusion Does Not Prevent Meconium Aspiration Syndrome

*ABSTRACT: Amnioinfusion has been advocated as a technique to reduce the incidence of meconium aspiration and to improve neonatal outcome. However, a large proportion of women with meconium-stained amniotic fluid have infants who have taken in meconium within the trachea or bronchioles before meconium passage has been noted and before amnioinfusion can be performed by the obstetrician; meconium passage may predate labor. Based on current literature, routine prophylactic amnioinfusion for the dilution of meconium-stained amniotic fluid is not recommended. Prophylactic use of amnioinfusion for meconium-stained amniotic fluid should be done only in the setting of additional clinical trials. However, amnioinfusion remains a reasonable approach in the treatment of repetitive variable decelerations, regardless of amniotic fluid meconium status.*

Meconium-stained amniotic fluid is a common obstetric situation, occurring in 12–22% of women in labor (1, 2). Meconium aspiration syndrome is a major complication in the neonate. This syndrome occurs in up to 10% of infants who have been exposed to meconium-stained amniotic fluid, with significant morbidity and mortality.

Amnioinfusion has been advocated as a technique to reduce the incidence of meconium aspiration and to improve neonatal outcome. Although generally considered safe, reported complications associated with amnioinfusion include uterine hypertonus, uterine rupture, placental abruption, chorioamnionitis, nonreassuring fetal heart rate tracing, maternal pulmonary embolus, and maternal death (3). The purported benefit of amnioinfusion for the dilution of meconium-stained amniotic fluid is dilution of thick clumps of meconium. However, a large proportion of women with meconium-stained amniotic fluid have infants who have taken in meconium within the trachea or bronchioles before meconium passage has been noted and before amnioinfusion can be performed by the obstetrician. Furthermore, meconium aspiration syndrome is hypothesized to predate labor in many cases (4). Studies were performed to evaluate whether prophylactic amnioinfusion for meconium-stained amniotic fluid would be beneficial and if it would decrease the incidence of meconium aspiration syndrome (5–18).

The initial trials of amnioinfusion generally consisted of small studies that randomized women with moderate to thick meconium-stained amniotic fluid to receive prophylactic amnioinfusion or no amnioinfusion. These studies suggested that women receiving amnioinfusion had fewer operative deliveries and fetuses with significantly less distress and less meconium below the vocal cords (5–11). Two meta-analyses also found that amnioinfusion significantly reduced the frequency of meconium aspiration syndrome and the incidence of meconium below the vocal cords in fetuses of pregnant women with meconium-stained amniotic fluid treated with amnioinfusion (12, 13).

A randomized trial in women with meconium-stained amniotic fluid evaluated prophylactic amnioinfusion versus therapeutic amnioinfusion for variable decelerations occurring after enrollment (14). The authors found no differences in operative deliveries, fetal distress, Apgar scores, the incidence of meconium below the fetal vocal cords, or umbilical artery blood pH values between the groups. There were four cases of meconium aspiration syndrome; three occurred in the prophylactic amnioinfusion group. Of the women receiving standard care, only 16% required therapeutic amnioinfusion for repetitive severe variable decelerations. These findings are consistent with studies evaluating institutional protocols of routine prophylactic amnioinfusion for thick meconium that found that meconium aspiration syndrome continued to occur at the same rate, with no improvement in neonatal outcome (15–17).

A large, international, multicenter trial randomized 1,998 women in labor at 36 weeks of gestation or later with thick meconium-stained amniotic fluid to amnioinfusion or no amnioinfusion, after stratification according to the presence or absence of variable decelerations (18). The number of women enrolled in this well-conducted study was greater than in all other prior studies combined. The authors found that amnioinfusion did not reduce perinatal death (0.5 % in both groups) or moderate or severe meconium aspiration (4.4 % versus 3.1 % in controls), nor was there a significant reduction in cesarean delivery (31.8 % versus 29.0 % in controls). Although the absence of benefit from amnioinfusion occurred whether or not there were variable decelerations, the study did not have adequate power to definitively determine if amnioinfusion was efficacious in the subgroup of women with decelerations.

Based on current literature, routine prophylactic amnioinfusion for meconium-stained amniotic fluid is not recommended. Prophylactic use of amnioinfusion for meconium-stained amniotic fluid should be done only in the setting of additional clinical trials. Data are not available on whether amnioinfusion for fetal heart rate decelerations in the presence of meconium-stained amniotic fluid decreases meconium aspiration syndrome or other meconium-related morbidities. However, amnioinfusion remains a reasonable approach in the treatment of repetitive variable decelerations, regardless of amniotic fluid meconium status (19).

## References


1. Katz VL, Bowes WA Jr. Meconium aspiration syndrome: reflections on a murky subject. Am J Obstet Gynecol 1992;166:171–83.
2. Nathan L, Leveno KJ, Carmody TJ 3rd, Kelly AM, Sherman ML. Meconium: a 1990s perspective on an old obstetric hazard. Obstet Gynecol 1994;83:329–32.
3. Wenstrom K, Andrews WW, Maher JE. Amnioinfusion survey: prevalence, protocols, and complications. Obstet Gynecol 1995;86:572–6.
4. Ghidini A, Spong CY. Severe meconium aspiration syndrome is not caused by aspiration of meconium. Am J Obstet Gynecol 2001;185:931–8.
5. Wenstrom KD, Parsons MT. The prevention of meconium aspiration in labor using amnioinfusion. Obstet Gynecol 1989;73:647–51.
6. Sadovsky Y, Amon E, Bade ME, Petrie RH. Prophylactic amnioinfusion during labor complicated by meconium: a preliminary report. Am J Obstet Gynecol 1989;161: 613–7.
7. Macri CJ, Schrimmer DB, Leung A, Greenspoon JS, Paul RH. Prophylactic amnioinfusion improves outcome of pregnancy complicated by thick meconium and oligohydramnios. Am J Obstet Gynecol 1992;167:117–21.
8. Cialone PR, Sherer DM, Ryan RM, Sinkin RA, Abramowicz JS. Amnioinfusion during labor complicated by particulate meconium-stained amniotic fluid decreases neonatal morbidity. Am J Obstet Gynecol 1994;170: 842–9.
9. Eriksen NL, Hostetter M, Parisi VM. Prophylactic amnioinfusion in pregnancies complicated by thick meconium. Am J Obstet Gynecol 1994;171:1026–30.
10. Puertas A, Paz Carrillo MP, Molto L, Alvarez M, Sedeno S, Miranda JA. Meconium-stained amniotic fluid in labor: a randomized trial of prophylactic amnioinfusion. Eur J Obstet Gynecol Reprod Biol 2001;99:33–7.
11. Rathor AM, Singh R, Ramji S, Tripathi R. Randomised trial of amnioinfusion during labour with meconium stained amniotic fluid. BJOG 2002;109:17–20.
12. Pierce J, Gaudier FL, Sanchez-Ramos L. Intrapartum amnioinfusion for meconium-stained fluid: meta-analysis of prospective clinical trials. Obstet Gynecol 2000;95: 1051–6.

13. Hofmeyr GJ. Amnioinfusion for meconium-stained liquor in labour. The Cochrane Database of Systematic Reviews 2002, Issue 1. Art. No.: CD000014. DOI: 10.1002/14651858.CD000014.
14. Spong CY, Ogundipe OA, Ross MG. Prophylactic amnioinfusion for meconium-stained amniotic fluid. Am J Obstet Gynecol 1994;171:931–5.
15. De Meeus JB, D'Halluin G, Bascou V, Ellia F, Magnin G. Prophylactic intrapartum amnioinfusion: a controlled retrospective study of 135 cases. Eur J Obstet Gynecol Reprod Biol 1997;72:141–8.
16. Rogers MS, Lau TK, Wang CC, Yu KM. Amnioinfusion for the prevention of meconium aspiration during labour. Aust N Z J Obstet Gynaecol 1996;36:407–10.
17. Usta IM, Mercer BM, Aswad NK, Sibai BM. The impact of a policy of amnioinfusion for meconium-stained amniotic fluid. Obstet Gynecol 1995;85:237–41.
18. Fraser WD, Hofmeyr J, Lede R, Faron G, Alexander S, Goffinet F, et al. Amnioinfusion for the prevention of the meconium aspiration syndrome. Amnioinfusion Trial Group. N Engl J Med 2005;353:909–17.
19. Miyazaki FS, Nevarez F. Saline amnioinfusion for relief of repetitive variable decelerations: a prospective randomized study. Am J Obstet Gynecol 1985;153:301–6.

ACOG Committee Opinion

Committee on Obstetric Practice

Number 348, November 2006

# Umbilical Cord Blood Gas and Acid-Base Analysis



ISSN 1074-861X

**The American College of Obstetricians and Gynecologists**
409 12th Street, SW
PO Box 96920
Washington, DC 20090-6920

12345/09876

Umbilical cord blood gas and acid-base analysis. ACOG Committee Opinion No. 348. American College of Obstetricians and Gynecologists. Obstet Gynecol 2006;108:1319–22.

*ABSTRACT: Umbilical cord blood gas and acid-base assessment are the most objective determinations of the fetal metabolic condition at the moment of birth. Moderate and severe newborn encephalopathy, respiratory complications, and composite complication scores increase with an umbilical arterial base deficit of 12–16 mmol/L. Moderate or severe newborn complications occur in 10% of neonates who have this level of acidemia and the rate increases to 40% in neonates who have an umbilical arterial base deficit greater than 16 mmol/L at birth. Immediately after the delivery of the neonate, a segment of umbilical cord should be double-clamped, divided, and placed on the delivery table. Physicians should attempt to obtain venous and arterial cord blood samples in circumstances of cesarean delivery for fetal compromise, low 5-minute Apgar score, severe growth restriction, abnormal fetal heart rate tracing, maternal thyroid disease, intrapartum fever, or multifetal gestation.*

Laboratory research demonstrates a complex relationship between fetal (antepartum and intrapartum) asphyxia, newborn asphyxia, and possible resulting brain damage. The degree, duration, and nature of the asphyxic insult are modulated by the quality of the cardiovascular compensatory response. A task force set up by the World Federation of Neurology Group defined asphyxia as a condition of impaired blood gas exchange, leading, if it persists, to progressive hypoxemia and hypercapnia (1). This is a precise definition of asphyxia as it may affect the fetus and neonate. In the American College of Obstetricians and Gynecologists' Task Force on Neonatal Encephalopathy and Cerebral Palsy report, asphyxia is defined as:

> . . . [a] clinical situation of damaging acidemia, hypoxia, and metabolic acidosis. This definition, although traditional, is not specific to cause. A more complete definition of birth asphyxia includes a requirement for a recognizable sentinel event capable of interrupting oxygen supply to the fetus or infant. This definition fails to include conditions that are not readily recognized clinically, such as occult abruption, but is probably correct in a majority of cases. (2)

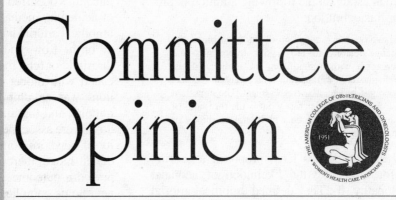

Asphyxia may occur in a transient fashion that, although of physiologic interest, has no pathologic sequelae. Significant fetal exposure to asphyxia leads to tissue oxygen debt, accumulation of fixed acids, and a metabolic acidosis. Thus, for intrapartum fetal asphyxia the following addition is proposed for this definition:

> Fetal asphyxia is a condition of impaired blood gas exchange leading to progressive hypoxemia and hypercapnia with a significant metabolic acidosis. The diagnosis of intrapartum fetal asphyxia requires a blood gas and acid-base assessment. The important question for the clinician is what is the threshold of metabolic acidosis beyond which fetal morbidity or mortality may occur?

Low and associates have proposed a scoring system for predicting the likelihood of neonatal encephalopathy (3). They defined umbilical arterial base deficits at birth as mild at 4–8 mmol/L, moderate at 8–12 mmol/L, and severe at greater than 12 mmol/L. Newborn complications in the central nervous system, respiratory system, cardiovascular system, and kidney during the 5 days after delivery were documented. Assessment of the central nervous system included clinical evidence of newborn encephalopathy defined as minor with irritability or jitteriness, moderate with profound lethargy or abnormal tone, and severe with coma or abnormal tone and seizures. Cardiovascular complications were classified as minor with bradycardia (100 beats per minute or less) or tachycardia (170 beats per minute or more), moderate with hypotension or hypertension (defined by the 95% confidence limits for blood pressure in term neonates), and severe with abnormal electrocardiographic or echocardiographic findings. Respiratory complications were classified as minor if requiring supplementary oxygen, moderate if requiring continuous positive airway pressure or ventilation less than 24 hours, and severe if requiring mechanical ventilation more than 24 hours. Abnormalities of renal function were classified as minor if hematuria was observed, moderate with an elevation of serum creatinine level (greater than 100 mmol/L)*, and severe with anuria or oliguria (less than 1 mL/kg/h). A scoring system expressed the magnitude of the complications in each neonate. The score for each complication was "1" for minor, "2" for moderate, and "4" for severe. The maximum complication score was "16". Moderate and severe newborn encephalopathy, respiratory complications, and composite complication scores were increased with an umbilical arterial base deficit of 12–16 mmol/L. Moderate or severe newborn complications occurred in 10% of neonates with this level of acidemia, increasing to 40% in neonates with an umbilical arterial base deficit greater than 16 mmol/L at birth. Low and associates concluded that the threshold of fetal metabolic acidosis at delivery associated with moderate or severe newborn complications was an umbilical arterial base deficit of 12 mmol/L and that increasing levels of metabolic acidosis were associated with a progression of the severity of newborn complications (3). At the mild base deficit range, there is no association with abnormal newborn outcome. A similar threshold for neonatal neurologic complications has been reported by other investigators (4, 5). Importantly, and in contrast to moderate or severe levels of acidemia, term neonates exposed to mild antepartum fetal asphyxia were not at an increased risk of minor motor or cognitive defects at the age of 4–8 years compared with controls with no evidence of asphyxia (6).

## Term Infants

The prevalence of fetal asphyxia, ranging from mild to severe at delivery, in the term infant is reported at 25 per 1,000 live births; of these, 15% are either moderate or severe (3.75 per 1,000) (7). Even at these levels of acidemia, it must be appreciated that most fetuses will not be injured, yielding a final overall incidence of neonatal encephalopathy attributable to intrapartum hypoxia, in the absence of any other preconception or antepartum abnormalities, of approximately 1.6 per 10,000 (8, 9). Similar observations have been reported from Japan, where among a series of 10,030 infants there were nine cases of cerebral palsy at age 1 year or older diagnosed by pediatric neurologists. Analysis of these cases reveals that preexisting asphyxia existed before the initiation of fetal monitoring in six cases; two of the cases involved cytomegalovirus infections and one case involved a maternal amniotic fluid embolism (10). These investigators concluded that in low-risk pregnancies, cerebral palsy caused by intrapartum asphyxia was restricted to unavoidable intrapartum accidents.

## Preterm Infants

Low and colleagues reported that the prevalence of asphyxia in preterm infants was 73 per 1,000 live

*In the United States, creatinine level is expressed in mg/dL. To convert creatinine in mmol/L to mg/dL, the value should be divided by 88.4. In this case, 100 mmol/L is 1.14. mg/dL.

births (7). Of these, 50% were at the moderate to severe level of asphyxia. The authors caution that it remains to be determined how often the asphyxia recognized at delivery may have been present before the onset of labor. This point is particularly germane in the preterm infant, inasmuch as medical or obstetric complications or both often are the preceding event necessitating the preterm delivery. Examples include significant degrees of intrauterine growth restriction, placental abruption, chorioamnionitis with funisitis, and severe preeclampsia, each of which has been shown to be a significant independent risk factor for moderate or severe neonatal encephalopathy (8, 9).

## Acidemia and Cerebral Palsy

Both the International Cerebral Palsy Task Force and the American College of Obstetricians and Gynecologists' Task Force on Neonatal Encephalopathy and Cerebral Palsy have published criteria to define an acute intrapartum event as sufficient to cause cerebral palsy (2, 11). Among the essential criteria cited by both task forces is evidence of metabolic acidosis in fetal umbilical cord arterial blood obtained at delivery (pH less than 7 and base deficit greater than or equal to 12 mmol/L) (see box). Additionally, the National Collaborating Center for Women's and Children's Health, commissioned by the National Institute for Clinical Excellence, has recommended that umbilical artery pH be performed after all cesarean deliveries for suspected fetal compromise, to allow review of fetal well-being and to guide ongoing care of the infant (12).

## Technique for Obtaining Cord Blood Samples

Immediately after the delivery of the neonate, a segment of umbilical cord should be double-clamped, divided, and placed on the delivery table pending assignment of the 5-minute Apgar score. Values from the umbilical cord artery provide the most accurate information regarding fetal and newborn acid-base status. A clamped segment of cord is stable for pH and blood gas assessment for at least 60 minutes, and a cord blood sample in a syringe flushed with heparin is stable for up to 60 minutes (13, 14). If the 5-minute Apgar score is satisfactory and the infant appears stable and vigorous, the segment of umbilical cord can be discarded. If a serious abnormality that arose in the delivery process or a problem with the neonate's condition or both persist at or beyond the first 5 minutes, blood can be drawn from the cord segment and sent to the laboratory for blood gas analysis. Analysis of paired arterial and venous specimens should prevent debate over whether a true arterial specimen was obtained. Therefore, the Committee on Obstetric Practice recommends obtaining an arterial umbilical cord blood sample, but, where possible, obtaining both venous and arterial samples (paired specimen). It is important to label the sample as either venous or arterial. Similarly, in known high-risk circumstances, such as severe growth restriction, an abnormal fetal heart rate tracing, maternal thyroid disease, intrapartum fever, or multifetal gestations, it is prudent to obtain blood gas and acid-base assessments (2). It should be noted that it occasionally may be difficult to obtain an adequate cord arterial blood sample. If the practitioner encounters difficulty in obtaining arterial blood from the umbilical cord (ie, in a very preterm infant), a sample obtained from an artery on

**Criteria to Define an Acute Intrapartum Hypoxic Event as Sufficient to Cause Cerebral Palsy**

Essential criteria (must meet all four):

1. Evidence of a metabolic acidosis in fetal umbilical cord arterial blood obtained at delivery (pH <7 and base deficit ≥12 mmol/L)
2. Early onset of severe or moderate neonatal encephalopathy in infants born at 34 or more weeks of gestation
3. Cerebral palsy of the spastic quadriplegic or dyskinetic type*
4. Exclusion of other identifiable etiologies, such as trauma, coagulation disorders, infectious conditions, or genetic disorders

*Spastic quadriplegia and, less commonly, dyskinetic cerebral palsy are the only types of cerebral palsy associated with acute hypoxic intrapartum events. Spastic quadriplegia is not specific to intrapartum hypoxia. Hemiparetic cerebral palsy, hemiplegic cerebral palsy, spastic diplegia, and ataxia are unlikely to result from acute intrapartum hypoxia (Nelson KB, Grether JK. Potentially asphyxiating conditions and spastic cerebral palsy in infants of normal birth weight. Am J Obstet Gynecol 1998;179: 507–13.).

Excerpted from American Academy of Pediatrics, American College of Obstetricians and Gynecologists. Neonatal encephalopathy and cerebral palsy: defining the pathogenesis and pathophysiology. Elk Grove Village (IL): AAP; Washington, DC: ACOG; 2003. Modified from MacLennan A. A template for defining a causal relation between acute intrapartum events and cerebral palsy: international consensus statement. BMJ 1999;319:1054–9.

the chorionic surface of the placenta will provide accurate results (15). These arteries are relatively easy to identify because they cross over the veins.

## Conclusion

Umbilical cord arterial blood acid-base and gas assessment remains the most objective determination of the fetal metabolic condition at the moment of birth. Thresholds have been established below which it is unlikely that an intrapartum asphyxial insult will have resulted in neurologic injury to the infant. Additionally, most infants born with umbilical arterial metabolic acidemia at a level consistent with causing a neurologic injury will, in fact, develop normally.

Physicians should attempt to obtain venous and arterial cord blood samples in the following situations:

- Cesarean delivery for fetal compromise
- Low 5-minute Apgar score
- Severe growth restriction
- Abnormal fetal heart rate tracing
- Maternal thyroid disease
- Intrapartum fever
- Multifetal gestations

## References


1. Bax M, Nelson KB. Birth asphyxia: a statement. World Federation of Neurology Group. Dev Med Child Neurol 1993;35:1022–4.
2. American Academy of Pediatrics, American College of Obstetricians and Gynecologists. Neonatal encephalopathy and cerebral palsy: defining the pathogenesis and pathophysiology. Elk Grove Village (IL): AAP; Washington, DC: ACOG; 2003.
3. Low JA, Lindsay BG, Derrick EJ. Threshold of metabolic acidosis associated with newborn complications. Am J Obstet Gynecol 1997;177:1391–4.
4. Winkler CL, Hauth JC, Tucker JM, Owen J, Brumfield CG. Neonatal complications at term as related to the degree of umbilical artery acidemia. Am J Obstet Gynecol 1991;164:637–41.
5. Goldaber KG, Gilstrap LC, 3rd, Leveno KJ, Dax JS, McIntire DD. Pathologic fetal acidemia. Obstet Gynecol 1991;78:1103–7.
6. Handley-Derry M, Low JA, Burke SO, Waurick M, Killen H, Derrick EJ. Intrapartum fetal asphyxia and the occurrence of minor deficits in 4- to 8-year-old children. Dev Med Child Neurol 1997;39:508–14.
7. Low JA. Determining the contribution of asphyxia to brain damage in the neonate. J Obstet Gynaecol Res 2004;30:276–86.
8. Badawi N, Kurinczuk JJ, Keogh JM, Alessandri LM, O'Sullivan F, Burton PR, et al. Antepartum risk factors for newborn encephalopathy: the Western Australian case-control study. BMJ 1998;317:1549–53.
9. Badawi N, Kurinczuk JJ, Keogh JM, Alessandri LM, O'Sullivan F, Burton PR, et al. Intrapartum risk factors for newborn encephalopathy: the Western Australian case-control study. BMJ 1998;317:1554–8.
10. Sameshima H, Ikenoue T, Ikeda T, Kamitomo M, Ibara S. Unselected low-risk pregnancies and the effect of continuous intrapartum fetal heart rate monitoring on umbilical blood gases and cerebral palsy. Am J Obstet Gynecol 2004;190:118–23.
11. MacLennan A. A template for defining a causal relation between acute intrapartum events and cerebral palsy: international consensus statement. BMJ 1999;319: 1054–9.
12. National Collaborating Centre for Women's and Children's Health. Caesarean section. London (UK): RCOG Press; 2004.
13. Duerbeck NB, Chaffin DG, Seeds JW. A practical approach to umbilical artery pH and blood gas determinations. Obstet Gynecol 1992;79:959–62.
14. Strickland DM, Gilstrap LC 3rd, Hauth JC, Widmer K. Umbilical cord pH and PCO2: effect of interval from delivery to determination. Am J Obstet Gynecol 1984; 148:191–4.
15. Riley RJ, Johnson JW. Collecting and analyzing cord blood gases. Clin Obstet Gynecol 1993;36:13–23.

ACOG Committee Opinion

Committee on Obstetric Practice

Number 354, December 2006

# Treatment With Selective Serotonin Reuptake Inhibitors During Pregnancy



ISSN 1074-861X

**The American College of Obstetricians and Gynecologists**
409 12th Street, SW
PO Box 96920
Washington, DC 20090-6920

12345/09876

Treatment with selective serotonin reuptake inhibitors during pregnancy. ACOG Committee Opinion No. 354. American College of Obstetricians and Gynecologists. Obstet Gynecol 2006;108:1601–3.

*ABSTRACT: Depression is a common condition among women of reproductive age, and selective serotonin reuptake inhibitors (SSRIs) are frequently used for the treatment of depression. However, recent reports regarding SSRI use during pregnancy have raised concerns about fetal cardiac defects, newborn persistent pulmonary hypertension, and other negative effects. The potential risks associated with SSRI use throughout pregnancy must be considered in the context of the risk of relapse of depression if maintenance treatment is discontinued. The American College of Obstetricians and Gynecologists' Committee on Obstetric Practice recommends that treatment with all SSRIs or selective norepinephrine reuptake inhibitors or both during pregnancy be individualized and paroxetine use among pregnant women or women planning to become pregnant be avoided, if possible.*

Women of reproductive age experience the peak prevalence of major depressive disorders (1). A recent systematic review suggests that approximately 1 in 10 women will have depression (major or minor) at any given point during pregnancy and the postpartum period (2). Selective serotonin reuptake inhibitors (SSRIs) are commonly used to treat depression, and their use during pregnancy has been well documented (1–8). There is a paucity of data regarding the prevalence of SSRI use during pregnancy, although a recent report suggests a prevalence of 2–3% (9).

Although numerous investigators have not found an increased risk of major congenital malformations associated with the use of SSRIs during pregnancy (6, 7, 10), GlaxoSmithKline has reported two recent unpublished reports from a Swedish national registry and a U.S. insurance claims database that have raised concerns about an increased risk of congenital cardiac malformations (atrial and ventricular septal defects) associated with first trimester exposure to the SSRI paroxetine (Paxil) (www.gskus.com/news/paroxetine/paxil_letter_e3.pdf). The U.S. Food and Drug Administration subsequently issued a public health advisory regarding the use of paroxetine during pregnancy, and the manufacturer changed paroxetine's pregnancy category from C to D (www.fda.gov/cder/drug/advisory/paroxetine200512.htm). Category C is reserved for drugs that have teratogenic effects in animal studies but have not been adequately studied in humans. Category C drugs should be used only if the potential benefit justifies the potential risk to the fetus. A Category D drug has been found to have a harmful effect on human fetuses. As such, the current label for paroxetine suggests that adequate well-controlled or observational studies in pregnant women have demonstrated a risk to the fetus. However, the benefits of paroxetine therapy may outweigh the potential risk. These two registry-based studies suggested a 1.5–2-fold increased risk for an infant to have a cardiac defect; the results were specific to paroxetine and no inferences were made regarding other SSRIs.

In addition to concerns about congenital malformations, exposure to SSRIs late in pregnancy has been associated with transient neonatal complications, including jitteriness, mild respiratory distress, transient tachypnea of the newborn, weak cry, poor tone, and admission to a neonatal intensive care unit (4, 11–14). A more recent U.S. Food and Drug Administration public health advisory highlighted concerns about the risk of depression relapse and newborn persistent pulmonary hypertension with SSRI use (www.fda.gov/cder/drug/advisory/SSRI_PPHN200607.htm). The first study referenced found that women who discontinued antidepressants during pregnancy had five times the risk of depression relapse than those who continued to take the medications (3). In the second study, a large case–control study found a sixfold increase in the risk of persistent pulmonary hypertension for newborns whose mothers used SSRIs after 20 weeks of gestation, which suggests that this rare (approximately 6–12 per 1,000 exposed women) but severe complication may occur in addition to milder forms of poor neonatal adaptation (15). When a formal scoring system was systematically used to assess newborns in exposed and unexposed cohorts, 30% of neonates exposed to SSRIs during late pregnancy developed neonatal abstinence syndrome (16).

The potential risk of SSRI use throughout pregnancy must be considered in the context of the risk of relapse of depression if maintenance treatment is discontinued. Untreated depression may increase the risk of low weight gain, sexually transmitted diseases, and alcohol and substance abuse, all of which have maternal and fetal health implications. A multicenter prospective study monitored 201 women with a history of major depression who were not clinically depressed at the time of conception but were taking antidepressant medication. Approximately two thirds of women who discontinued antidepressants relapsed during their pregnancies compared with 26% of women who relapsed among the women who maintained their therapy. Most women were treated with SSRIs or dual-action SSRIs and selective norepinephrine reuptake inhibitors. A long history of depressive illness and a history of recurrent relapses were associated with relapse during pregnancy, regardless of whether women made a change in their use of antidepressants (3).

The American College of Obstetricians and Gynecologists' Committee on Obstetric Practice recommends that treatment with all SSRIs or selective norepinephrine reuptake inhibitors or both during pregnancy be individualized. Decisions about treatment of depression should incorporate the clinical expertise of the mental health clinician and obstetrician, and the process should actively engage the patient's values and perceptions when framing the discussion of the risks and benefits of treatment.

At this time, paroxetine use among pregnant women and women planning pregnancy should be avoided, if possible. Fetal echocardiography should be considered for women who were exposed to paroxetine in early pregnancy. Because abrupt discontinuation of paroxetine has been associated with withdrawal symptoms, discontinuation of this agent should occur according to the product's prescribing information. Optimally, shared decision making among obstetric and mental health clinicians and women should occur before pregnancy. However, given that approximately 50% of pregnancies are not planned, preconception planning for women with depression will not always happen, and decisions regarding treatment with SSRIs will undoubtedly occur during gestation.

## References


1. Kessler RC, McGonagle KA, Swartz M, Blazer DG, Nelson CB. Sex and depression in the National Comorbidity Survey. I: lifetime prevalence, chronicity and recurrence. J Affect Disord 1993;29:85–96.
2. Gavin NI, Gaynes BN, Lohr KN, Meltzer-Brody S, Gartlehner G, Swinson T. Perinatal depression: a systematic review of prevalence and incidence. Obstet Gynecol 2005;106:1071–83.

3. Cohen LS, Altshuler LL, Harlow BL, Nonacs R, Newport DJ, Viguera AC, et al. Relapse of major depression during pregnancy in women who maintain or discontinue antidepressant treatment [published erratum appears in JAMA 2006;296:170]. JAMA 2006;295:499–507.
4. Moses-Kolko EL, Bogen D, Perel J, Bregar A, Uhl K, Levin B, et al. Neonatal signs after late in utero exposure to serotonin reuptake inhibitors: literature review and implications for clinical applications. JAMA 2005;293:2372–83.
5. Wisner KL, Zarin DA, Holmboe ES, Appelbaum PS, Gelenberg AJ, Leonard HL, et al. Risk-benefit decision making for treatment of depression during pregnancy. Am J Psychiatry 2000;157:1933–40.
6. Wen SW, Yang Q, Garner P, Fraser W, Olatunbosun O, Nimrod C, et al. Selective serotonin reuptake inhibitors and adverse pregnancy outcomes. Am J Obstet Gynecol 2006;194:961–6.
7. Malm H, Klaukka T, Neuvonen PJ. Risks associated with selective serotonin reuptake inhibitors in pregnancy. Obstet Gynecol 2005;106:1289–96.
8. Lamberg L. Risks and benefits key to psychotropic use during pregnancy and postpartum period. JAMA 2005; 294:1604–8.
9. Reefhuis J, Rasmussen SA, Friedman JM. Selective serotonin-reuptake inhibitors and persistent pulmonary hypertension of the newborn [letter]. N Eng J Med 2006; 354:2188–9.
10. Einarson TR, Einarson A. Newer antidepressants in pregnancy and rates of major malformations: a meta-analysis of prospective comparative studies. Pharmacoepidemiol Drug Saf 2005;14:823–7.
11. Chambers CD, Johnson KA, Dick LM, Felix RJ, Jones KL. Birth outcomes in pregnant women taking fluoxetine. N Eng J Med 1996;335:1010–15.
12. Costei AM, Kozer E, Ho T, Ito S, Koren G. Perinatal outcome following third trimester exposure to paroxetine. Arch Pediatr Adolesc Med 2002;156:1129–32.
13. Kallen B. Neonate characteristics after maternal use of antidepressants late in pregnancy. Arch Pediatr Adolesc Med 2004;158:312–6.
14. Zeskind PS, Stephens LE. Maternal selective serotonin reuptake inhibitor use during pregnancy and newborn neurobehavior. Pediatrics 2004;113:368–75.
15. Chambers CD, Hernandez-Diaz S, Van Marter LJ, Werler MM, Louik C, Jones KL, et al. Selective serotonin-reuptake inhibitors and risk of persistent pulmonary hypertension of the newborn. N Eng J Med 2006;354:579–87.
16. Levinson-Castiel R, Merlob P, Linder N, Sirota L, Klinger G. Neonatal abstinence syndrome after in utero exposure to selective serotonin reuptake inhibitors in term infants. Arch Pediatr Adolesc Med 2006;160:173–6.

# COMMITTEE OPINIONS

## COMMITTEE ON PRIMARY CARE

# COMMITTEE OPINIONS

ACOG Committee Opinion

Committee on Primary Care

Number 227, November 1999

# Complementary and Alternative Medicine

The Committee wishes to thank Ronald A. Chez, MD, for his assistance in the development of this opinion. This document reflects emerging clinical and scientific advances as of the date issued and is subject to change. The information should not be construed as dictating an exclusive course of treatment or procedure to be followed.



**The American College of Obstetricians and Gynecologists**
409 12th Street, SW
PO Box 96920
Washington, DC 20090-6920

12345/32109

In 1990, 34% of adults in the United States used complementary and alternative medicine (CAM). In 1997, 42% of adults in the United States and Canada used CAM, and the use by women was 49%. This trend of increased CAM use will continue as it is reinforced and supported by continuing media attention; intense commercial efforts by providers of CAM products and services, including proprietary pharmaceutical companies; third-party reimbursement for some CAM practices and products; and the increasing over-the-counter access to CAM products in drugstores and supermarkets. The purpose of this Committee Opinion is to provide an overview of CAM, to recommend that physicians ask patients about their use of CAM, and to provide sources of additional information about the subject.

The physician, in the role of patient advocate, has an ethical responsibility to promote and protect the patient's well-being. This function includes the ability to engage in a dialogue that honors the patient's values and promotes shared decision making. Inquiring about the patient's motivation for and use of CAM and providing information on safety and effectiveness can be integral to this role.

Complementary and alternative medicine can be defined as those systems, practices, interventions, modalities, professions, therapies, applications, theories, or claims that are currently not an integral part of the dominant or conventional medical system (known as allopathy in North America). Importantly, over time some of the individual modalities do overlap with or become integrated into Western medicine. The spectrum of CAM encompasses over 350 different techniques and treatments. These can be classified into at least seven major categories:

1. *Mind–body interventions* include yoga, relaxation response techniques, meditation, t'ai chi, hypnotherapy, spirituality, support groups, and biofeedback.
2. *Alternative systems of medical practice* are exemplified by Traditional Chinese Medicine. Other systems in this category include homeopathy, ayurveda, naturopathy, chiropractic, Native-American medicine, and the various forms of acupuncture.

3. *Pharmacologic and biologic* treatments, a diverse and large category, includes folk medicine, medicinal plants, processed blood products, and autogenous vaccines.
4. *Herbal medicine,* another large category, is the use of botanicals with pharmacologic activity. A number of these substances have formed the basis of the Western pharmacopeia. Currently, the public's attention is focused on St. John's wort for depressive disorders, echinacea for upper respiratory infections, valerian for sleep disorders, garlic for hypercholesterolemia, and ginkgo biloba for circulatory disorders.
5. *Diet and nutrition* encompass the use of vitamins, minerals, and nutritional supplements in general, and cancer and cardiovascular disease diets in particular. Treatments include megadosing, elimination of or excessive intake of certain foods, vegetarian and macrobiotic diets, and diets associated with various physicians.
6. *Manual healing methods* include massage, chiropractic and osteopathic manipulation, and biofield therapeutics (eg, Reiki, polarity, reflexology, and therapeutic touch).
7. *Bioelectromagnetic applications* include the use of magnets for musculoskeletal and neurologic pain; low-frequency thermal waves in diathermy; nonionizing, nonthermal applications such as pulsed electromagnetic waves as now used in the treatment of bone fractures; and transcutaneous electrical nerve stimulation for pain relief.

Most patients who use CAM are self-referred and do not tell their physicians they are doing so. Thus, their medical record is incomplete, and the possibility of medical risk cannot be addressed. Patients can be asked questions similar to "Have you used or have you been considering other kinds of treatment or medications for relief of your symptoms or to maintain wellness?" Follow-up questions to a positive answer can include asking when she decided to use CAM, what results she was expecting, how she chose the method, and how it has worked for her. This information can then be documented in the patient's medical record.

Safety is the critical issue when a patient asks about the merit of using a CAM product or intervention. The potential can exist for both direct and indirect risks. These risks can include patient delay in or avoidance of seeking appropriate conventional treatment, a misdiagnosis, toxic reactions from ingested substances, and interference with the mechanism of action of a prescribed drug or treatment.

Over-the-counter herbal preparations and dietary supplements, such as those marketed to relieve menopausal symptoms, may be of particular concern to the obstetrician–gynecologist. As defined in the 1994 Dietary Supplement and Health Education Act passed by Congress and as opposed to prescription items, these products are not subject to standardized manufacture, supporting clinical data, or approval or supervision by the U.S. Food and Drug Administration. Thus, there can be uncertainty as to the identity of the active ingredient and the amount of its dose. Also, the chemical composition may vary from manufacturer to manufacturer and by lot number, and there may be adulteration without this being identified on the label. Some of these problems will be addressed with the new federal regulation requiring that dietary supplement ingredients are labeled in a manner analogous to food labels, increased legislated U.S. Food and Drug Administration authority for these products, and increased attention by the Federal Trade Commission to advertised claims.

Concerns about safety can be tempered for some CAM modalities. For instance, it is unlikely that homeopathic preparations, acupuncture, biofeedback, or prayer will be associated with direct adverse side effects. In contrast, intravenous hydrogen peroxide, chelation therapy, and megadosing of supplements can be toxic and dangerous. Accordingly, when informed that the patient is using CAM, her clinician can advise if there is supporting published research, warn about real or potential dangers, ascertain if it can be continued in conjunction with conventional treatment, and monitor for positive and negative effects over time.

Some patients will request a referral to a local alternative care provider. Any such referral should be made only to a state-licensed provider and at an arm's length relationship. All states license chiropractors, but not all license other CAM providers, such as naturopaths, acupuncturists, or massage therapists. Physicians should be aware of possible liability consequences of such referrals. If the referral itself is negligent because it is inconsistent with reasonable practice, the referring physician may be exposed to liability if the patient is injured by the subsequent treatment. Also, liability may arise if the referring physician supervises the CAM care, jointly treats the patient, or knows or should have known that the CAM provider is incompetent.

It can be anticipated that patients will continue to use CAM with or without physician referral. Accompanying this use is the public's expectation that health insurance plans will reimburse for CAM treatment. A growing number of third-party payers have responded by doing so under a variety of clinical guidelines. This willingness can result in conflict between physicians and CAM providers if important operational issues are not addressed. These issues include the creation of protocols and plans of care for specific diagnoses, procedures for monitoring and follow-up with finite clinical endpoints, evidence for safety and effectiveness, and identified criteria for referral to conventional care.

Each physician can determine to what extent he or she wishes to learn more about various aspects of CAM. There are a number of ways to obtain information. Clinical studies in peer-reviewed, conventional medical journals now appear on a regular basis. In addition to continuing medical education courses, there are peer-reviewed medical journals, textbooks, and newsletters devoted to the subject. Computer databases and webpages specifically oriented to CAM now are accessible by both physicians and patients.

In the coming years, it is probable that there will be a blending of conventional medicine with various CAM therapies as evidence-based research data support clinical decision making in patient care. This comprehensive approach may become known as integrated medical care.

## Bibliography

Blumenthal M, ed. The complete German Commission E Monographs. Therapeutic guide to herbal medicines. Austin, TX: American Botanical Council, 1998

Chez RA, Jonas WB, Eisenberg D. The physician and complementary and alternative medicine. In: Jonas WB, Levin JS, eds. Essentials of Complementary and Alternative Medicine. Philadelphia: Lippincott Williams & Wilkins, 1999:31–45

Jonas WB, Levin JS, eds. Essentials of complementary and alternative medicine. Philadelphia: Lippincott Williams and Wilkins, 1999

National Institutes of Health. Alternative medicine: expanding medical horizons: a report to the National Institutes of Health on alternative medical systems and practices in the United States. National Institutes of Health, Workshop on Alternative Medicine, 1995; NIH publication no. 94-066

Newall CA, Anderson LA, Phillipson JD. Herbal medicines, a guide for health-care professionals. London: Pharmaceutical Press, 1996

PDR for Herbal Medicines. Montvale, NJ: Medical Economics Co., 1998

Segen JC. Dictionary of alternative medicine. Stamford, Connecticut: Appleton & Lange, 1998

## Resources

### *Newsletters*

Complementary Medicine for the Physician, W.B. Saunders Periodicals Customer Service, 6277 Sea Harbor Drive, Orlando, FL 32887-4800, (800) 654-2452

Alternative Therapies in Women's Health, American Health Consultants, PO Box 740056, Atlanta, GA 30374, (800) 688-2421

Alternative Medicine Alert, American Health Consultants, PO Box 740056, Atlanta, GA 30374, (800) 688-2421

HerbalGram, American Botanical Council, PO Box 144345, Austin, TX 78714-4345, (800) 373-7105

### *Web Sites*

The National Library of Medicine (http://www.ncbi.nlm.nih.gov/PubMed/)

The National Center for Complementary and Alternative Medicine (http://nccam.nih.gov/)

The NIH Office of Dietary Supplements (http://odp.od.nih.gov/ods/)

The Richard and Hinda Rosenthal Center for Complementary & Alternative Medicine (http://cpmcnet.columbia.edu/dept/rosenthal/)

The American Botanical Council (http://www.herbalgram.org/)

HealthWorld Online (http://www.healthy.net/)

Quackwatch (www.quackwatch.com)

# COMMITTEE OPINIONS

## COMMITTEE ON PROFESSIONAL LIABILITY

# COMMITTEE OPINIONS

ACOG Committee Opinion

Committee on Professional Liability

Number 309, February 2005 (Replaces No. 236, June 2000)

This document provides risk management information that is current as of the date issued and is subject to change. This document does not define a standard of care nor should it be interpreted as legal advice.



ISSN 1074-861X

**The American College of Obstetricians and Gynecologists**
409 12th Street, SW
PO Box 96920
Washington, DC 20090-6920

12345/98765

Coping with the stress of medical professional liability litigation. ACOG Committee Opinion No. 309. American College of Obstetricians and Gynecologists. Obstet Gynecol 2005;105:453–4.

# Coping With the Stress of Medical Professional Liability Litigation

*ABSTRACT: Obstetrician–gynecologists should recognize that being a defendant in a medical professional liability lawsuit can be one of life's most stressful experiences. Coping with the stress of medical professional liability litigation is an ongoing, complex process in which physicians often must struggle to regain a sense of professional mastery and control of their practices. Open communication with family members will assist in reducing emotional isolation and self-blame; however, legal and clinical aspects of a case must be kept confidential. Peer support and individual professional counseling can be of great benefit. Rapid intervention facilitates healthier coping strategies and can restore a sense of equilibrium and self-esteem during an unpredictable time.*

The American College of Obstetricians and Gynecologists (ACOG) has long been concerned about the psychologic and emotional impact of medical professional liability litigation on physicians, especially because 76.3% of ACOG Fellows have been sued at least once in their careers (1). Defendant physicians may experience a wide range of distressing emotions and increased stress, which can disrupt their personal lives and the lives of their families, their relationships with patients, and their medical practices. Because a medical professional liability case in obstetrics and gynecology takes an average of 4 years to resolve (1), this stressful period can seem interminable for all involved.

Common responses to medical liability litigation include feelings of shock, outrage, denial, anxiety, guilt, shame, and despair. Coping with medical professional liability litigation is an ongoing, complex process in which physicians often must struggle to regain a sense of professional mastery and control of their practices.

Claims managers and defense attorneys often advise physicians not to speak to anyone regarding any aspect of the medical liability case. Nevertheless, physicians often need to express emotional responses to being sued. Literal adherence to the advice to "speak to no one" can result in isolation, increased stress, and dysfunctional behavior. Guidance on interventions for impaired or dysfunctional physician behavior is addressed elsewhere (2).

Such behavior may jeopardize family relationships and also may affect the physician's ability to function professionally and to represent himself or herself appropriately and effectively during a trial. Therefore, the physician is encouraged to inform family members of the lawsuit, the allegations, the potential for publicity, and any expected testimony while maintaining confidentiality. Children should be told about the lawsuit and their questions honestly answered, commensurate with their age and ability to process the information. Open communication with family members will assist in reducing emotional isolation and self-blame.

Certainly, legal and clinical aspects of a case must be kept confidential. An exception to this rule, however, might be made in the context of professional counseling. Any clinical aspects of a medical professional liability case that are discussed in counseling should be disclosed within the confines of a formal counselor–patient relationship to ensure the confidentiality privilege. Confidentiality may be lost if third parties are present.

Obstetrician–gynecologists should recognize that being a defendant in a medical professional liability lawsuit can be one of life's most stressful experiences. Although negative emotions in response to a lawsuit are normal, physicians may need help from professionals or peers to cope with this stress. Residents, as young physicians in training, may be particularly vulnerable to the psychologic and emotional upheaval that often occurs when named in a medical liability claim. State or local medical societies and medical liability insurance carriers often sponsor support groups for defendant physicians and their families. Support mechanisms for residents also may be available through residency program directors, departmental chairs, departments of risk management, or mentors. In the absence of such services, individual professional counseling can be of great benefit. Rapid intervention facilitates healthier coping strategies and can restore a sense of equilibrium and self-esteem during an unpredictable time.

## References

1. American College of Obstetricians and Gynecologists. Overview of the 2003 ACOG Survey on Professional Liability. ACOG Clin Rev 2004;9(6):1, 13–6.
2. American College of Obstetricians and Gynecologists. Guidelines for women's health care. 2nd ed. Washington, DC: ACOG; 2002. p. 21–24.

## Bibliography

American Academy of Pediatrics. Coping with malpractice litigation stress. In: Medical liability for pediatricians. 6th ed. Elk Grove Village (IL): AAP; 2004. p. 187–92.

Brazeau CM. Coping with the stress of being sued. Fam Pract Manag 2001;8(5):41–4.

Charles SC. The stress of litigation: do we still have something to fear? Prim Care Update Ob/Gyns 2003;10:60–5.

Charles SC. Coping with a medical malpractice suit. West J Med 2001;174:55–8.

Charles SC. How to handle the stress of litigation. Clin Plast Surg 1999;26:69–77, vii.

Hutchison JR, Hutchison S. The toughest part of being sued. Med Econ 1995;72(23):36–7, 41–4, 48, passim.

Sett KM. The impact of malpractice litigation on physicians. Forum 1998;19(4):13–5.

# COMMITTEE OPINIONS

## COMMITTEE ON PATIENT SAFETY AND QUALITY IMPROVEMENT



*Published in 2006

# COMMITTEE OPINIONS

# ACOG Committee Opinion

Committee on Quality Improvement and Patient Safety

Number 286, October 2003

# Patient Safety in Obstetrics and Gynecology

*ABSTRACT: Emphasis on patient safety has increased in the past few years mostly in response to the Institute of Medicine report* To Err Is Human: Building a Safer Health System. *Obstetrician–gynecologists should incorporate elements of patient safety into their practices and also encourage others to use these practices.*

The American College of Obstetricians and Gynecologists (ACOG) is committed to improving quality and safety in women's health care. The Institute of Medicine report, *To Err Is Human: Building a Safer Health System*, notes that errors in health care are a significant cause of death and injury (1). Despite disagreements over the actual numbers cited, all health care professionals agree that patient safety is extremely important and should be addressed by the overall health care system. The American College of Obstetricians and Gynecologists continues to emphasize its long-standing commitment to quality and patient safety by codifying a set of objectives that should be adopted by obstetrician–gynecologists in their practices. Obstetrician–gynecologists are encouraged to promulgate these principles in the hospitals and other settings where they practice.

## Objectives

I. Develop a commitment to encourage a culture of patient safety

Safety should be viewed as an essential component of a broader commitment to the provision of optimal health care for women. Promoting safety requires that all those in the health care environment recognize that the potential for errors exists and that teamwork and communication are the basis for fostering change and preventing errors. A culture of safety should be the framework for any effort to reduce medical errors. Women's health care should be delivered in a learning environment that encourages disclosure and exchange of information in the event of errors, near misses, and adverse outcomes.

A systems view of clinical processes also is a key element in supporting this culture. Consequently, all health care systems should be designed with the objective to minimize errors.

This document reflects emerging concepts on patient safety and is subject to change. The information should not be construed as dictating an exclusive course of treatment or procedure to be followed.



ISSN 1074-861X

**The American College of Obstetricians and Gynecologists**
409 12th Street, SW
PO Box 96920
Washington, DC 20090-6920

12345/76543

Patient safety in obstetrics and gynecology. ACOG Committee Opinion No. 286. American College of Obstetricians and Gynecologists. Obstet Gynecol 2003;102:883–5.

The first step in the delivery of safe health care should be to identify and study the patterns and causes of error occurrence within delivery systems. Obstetrician–gynecologists should adopt and develop those safe practices that reduce the likelihood of system failures that can cause adverse outcomes.

The role of leadership, whether in the inpatient or outpatient setting, is essential in facilitating an effective patient safety program. Strong leadership within obstetrics and gynecology is necessary to advocate for the provision of both financial and human resources to achieve patient safety goals. Efforts devoted to optimizing communication and collaboration among the various members of the health care team are equally important in promoting these principles of patient safety.

II. Implement recommended safe medication practices

Most medical errors are caused by problems associated with the use of medications; therefore, efforts to reduce the occurrence of these errors should be ongoing. Although computerized physician order entry systems can be effective in reducing prescribing errors, they are costly and their use is not widespread. In the absence of computerized physician order entry systems, the following steps should be adopted to reduce errors in prescribing and administering medications (2):

- Improve legibility of handwriting
- Avoid use of nonstandard abbreviations
- Check for drug allergies and sensitivities
- Always use a leading 0 for doses of less than 1 unit (eg, 0.1 mg, not .1 mg), and never use a trailing 0 after a decimal (eg, 1 mg, not 1.0 mg): "always lead, never follow"
- All verbal orders should be written down by the individual receiving the order and read back to the prescriber verbatim to ensure accuracy

III. Reduce the likelihood of surgical errors

Surgical errors may involve the performance of the incorrect operation or a procedure on the wrong site or wrong patient. Although these errors occur much less frequently than medication errors, the consequences of these errors are always significant. The attending obstetrician–gynecologist who is ultimately responsible for the patient's care should work with other operating room personnel, such as nurses and anesthesiologists, to be certain that systems are in place to ensure proper patient and procedure identification. The obstetrician–gynecologist also should use a preoperative verification process to confirm, with the patient, the intended procedure to be performed.

IV. Improve communication

According to the *Code of Professional Ethics of the American College of Obstetricians and Gynecologists*, "the patient–physician relationship has an ethical basis and is built on confidentiality, trust, and honesty" (3). It also states "the obstetrician–gynecologist should deal honestly with patients and colleagues.... This includes not misrepresenting himself or herself through any form of communication in an untruthful, misleading, or deceptive manner." The American College of Obstetricians and Gynecologists encourages the development and use of a disclosure policy to communicate an unexpected outcome, as defined by the institution, when it occurs; to take immediate necessary steps to neutralize or limit any harm to the patient; to engage in the critical analysis of the incident; and to learn from the error and, by system redesign, to decrease the likelihood of recurrence. The American College of Obstetricians and Gynecologists believes that it is the moral obligation of every physician to communicate honestly with patients, particularly those who experience an adverse outcome. Open communication and transparency in health care will increase trust, improve patient satisfaction, and may decrease liability exposure (4).

V. Identify and resolve system problems

Generally, most medical errors should be handled in a nonpunitive environment to improve reporting and to gain an understanding of the breadth of problems in health care systems. However, willful violation of rules, repetitive errors despite attempts at corrective action, and criminal or egregious activity in the health care environment may require punitive actions or other interventions to protect patients or staff from harm. To improve patient safety, physicians should openly disclose errors and near misses and encourage their colleagues to do the same. This will promote and increase error reporting and identify potentially hidden problems, as well as motivate providers to find system problems and collaborate to resolve system failures.

VI. Establish a partnership with patients to improve safety

Patients who are involved in making their health care decisions have better outcomes than those who are not (5). According to ACOG's *Ethics in Obstetrics and Gynecology*, the "involvement of patients in [decisions about their own medical care] is good for their health—not only because it is a protection against treatment that patients might consider harmful, but because it contributes positively to their well-being" (6). Patients should be encouraged to ask questions about medical procedures, the medications they are taking, and any other aspect of their care. Patient education materials developed by ACOG and other organizations are available.

VII. Make safety a priority in every aspect of practice

The discipline of obstetrics and gynecology has a long tradition of leadership in quality assessment activities, which have been associated with an increase in patient safety. The quest for patient safety is an ongoing, continuously refined process incorporating information sharing and collaboration into daily practice. Emphasizing compassion, communication, and patient-focused care will aid in creating a culture of excellence. Opportunities to improve patient safety should be used whenever identified.

## References


1. Institute of Medicine. To err is human: building a safer health system. Washington, DC: National Academy Press; 2000.
2. Pearlman MD, Erickson TB. Patient safety series: safe medication prescribing. ACOG Clin Rev 2002;7(7):1–2, 11–4.
3. American College of Obstetricians and Gynecologists. Code of professional ethics of the American College of Obstetricians and Gynecologists. Ethics in obstetrics and gynecology. Washington, DC: ACOG; 2002. p. 97–101.
4. Kraman SS, Hamm G. Risk management: extreme honesty may be the best policy. Ann Intern Med 1999;131: 963–7.
5. Kaplan SH, Gandek B, Greenfield S, Rogers W, Ware JE. Patient and visit characteristics related to physicians' participatory decision-making style. Results from the Medical Outcomes Study. Med Care 1995;33:1176–87.
6. American College of Obstetricians and Gynecologists. Ethics in obstetrics and gynecology. Washington, DC: ACOG; 2002.


## Resources

Agency for Healthcare Research and Quality
www.ahrq.gov/qual/errorsix.htm

Department of Veterans Affairs (VA) National Center for Patient Safety
www.patientsafety.gov

Joint Commission on Accreditation of Healthcare Organizations
www.jcaho.org/accredited+organizations/patient+safety

National Patient Safety Foundation
www.npsf.org

# ACOG Committee Opinion

Committee on Quality Improvement and Patient Safety

Number 320, November 2005

# Partnering With Patients to Improve Safety

*ABSTRACT: Actively involving patients in their care will lead to increased patient satisfaction, increased diagnostic accuracy, enhanced adherence to therapeutic recommendations, and ultimately, improved health quality. Partnering with patients in the office setting by sharing information and enhancing communication can lead to improved patient health care and satisfaction.*

The foundation for a positive physician–patient interaction is formed by establishing a partnership and creating a meaningful dialogue. Accomplishing this in a brief office visit may be challenging, but with adequate planning these encounters can be structured in a positive way. Improving communication with patients, listening to their concerns, and facilitating active partnerships should be central to any patient safety strategy (1). Involving patients in planning and delivering health services also is recommended as a means of improving the quality of services (2). Additionally, several studies indicate that physician–patient communication problems may account for an increase in medical professional liability actions (3, 4).

## Information Sharing

Patients are responsible for providing their physicians with the information that is necessary to reach an accurate diagnosis or treatment plan. To facilitate this process, patients should be encouraged to discuss the reasons for their visits and ask questions such as, "What is my primary problem?" "What do I need to do?" and "Why is it important for me to do this?"(5). In response, physicians should actively listen to engage their patients. Physicians also can solicit the patient's concerns and opinions by asking open-ended questions and asking patients to share key information such as their medical history (including illnesses, immunizations, and hospitalizations), medication history (including over-the-counter [OTC] medications, and dietary supplements), and any allergies, reactions, or sensitivities experienced after taking medication.

This document reflects emerging concepts on patient safety and is subject to change. The information should not be construed as dictating an exclusive course of treatment or procedure to be followed.



**The American College of Obstetricians and Gynecologists**
409 12th Street, SW
PO Box 96920
Washington, DC 20090-6920

12345/98765

Partnering with patients to improve safety. ACOG Committee Opinion No. 320. American College of Obstetricians and Gynecologists. Obstet Gynecol 2005;106:1123–5.

## Health Literacy

According to an Institute of Medicine report,"nearly half of all American adults—90 million people—have difficulty understanding and acting upon health information" (6). The Institute of Medicine defines health literacy as "the degree to which individuals have the capacity to obtain, process, and understand basic health information and services needed to make appropriate health decisions" (6). Cultural barriers also can impede physician–patient communication. Consequently, it is important for clinicians to use proven strategies to facilitate communication with patients. Listed as follows are examples of useful methods:

- Speaking slowly and using plain, nonmedical language
- Limiting the amount of information provided and repeating the information
- Using teach-back or show-me techniques (asking the patient to repeat any instructions given) to confirm that the patient understands
- Making patients feel comfortable to ask questions (7)
- Providing written materials to reinforce oral explanations

## Informed Consent

Informed consent is a process, not a form. At the end of this process, the patient should understand her diagnosis, recommended treatment, potential complications, and treatment options. This discussion should be documented in the medical record. It often is helpful to invite the patient to bring a relative or a close friend to this discussion. There are many commercially available videotapes and printed materials, including those produced by ACOG, that can reinforce—but not replace—this process.

## Medications

Medication errors are the largest source of preventable adverse events. It is important for patients to provide their physicians with a list of the prescription and nonprescription medications they take. Whenever new prescriptions are given, patients should be told why the medication is being prescribed and given instructions for taking the medication. For example, if a medication is to be taken three times per day, the patient should be told what time of day the medication should be taken, whether it should be taken with food or without food, how much should be taken at one time, how long the medication should be continued, possible interactions with other medications the patient is taking, and whether any medications (including OTC medications), foods, or alcohol are contraindicated while taking this medication. Physicians should encourage their patients to maintain a list of all the medications, including herbal supplements and OTC medications, they are taking and share the list with any other physicians they may be seeing. Medication forms to facilitate this process have been developed by some groups (see Resources).

## Follow-up

Physicians should develop a system to track test results and communicate those results to patients. Tracking strategies in the office may include log books or computer prompts. Clinicians should inform their patients that no news is not necessarily good news. Patients should be given a reasonable time frame within which they should expect to hear about their test results, and they should be encouraged to call if they have not heard from the office at the end of that period.

## Conclusion

Partnering with patients to improve communication results in increased patient satisfaction, increased diagnostic accuracy, enhanced adherence to therapeutic recommendations, and improved health quality. In addition to the physician, other staff, such as nurses and physician assistants, may play an important role in ensuring appropriate communication. More time may be required during the patient encounter, but overall, these measures will save time, improve patient safety and satisfaction, and will be worth the additional effort.

## References

1. Vincent CA, Coulter A. Patient safety: what about the patient? Qual Saf Health Care 2002;11:76–80.
2. Crawford MJ, Rutter D, Manley C, Weaver T, Bhui K, Fulop N, et al. Systematic review of involving patients in the planning and development of health care. BMJ 2002; 325:1263.

3. Hickson GB, Clayton EW, Githens PB, Sloan FA. Factors that prompted families to file medical malpractice claims following perinatal injuries. JAMA 1992;267:1359–63.
4. Hickson GB, Clayton EW, Entman SS, Miller CS, Githens PB, Whetten-Goldstein K, et al. Obstetricians' prior malpractice experience and patients' satisfaction with care. JAMA 1994;272:1583–7.
5. Partnership for Clear Health Communication. Ask me 3: good questions for your good health. Available at: http://www.askme3.org/pdfs/Patient_Eng.pdf. Retrieved July 29, 2005.
6. Institute of Medicine (US). Health literacy. A prescription to end confusion. Washington, DC: National Academies Press; 2004.
7. Weiss BD. Health literacy: a manual for clinicians. Chicago (IL): American Medical Association; 2003.

## Resources

National Patient Safety Foundation
www.npsf.org

Institute for Safe Medical Practice
www.ismp.org

ACOG Committee Opinion

Committee on Quality Improvement and Patient Safety

Number 327, January 2006

# "Do Not Use" Abbreviations

*ABSTRACT: There are numerous abbreviations used in health care that have several different meanings. Some of these abbreviations may be mistaken for other abbreviations, numbers, or symbols, and these mistakes can have serious consequences. Therefore, the Joint Commission on Accreditation of Healthcare Organizations has established an "Official 'Do Not Use' List" of abbreviations as part of its accreditation standards. It is important for obstetrician–gynecologists to consider this list when using these and other abbreviations in their practice settings.*

In 2004, as part of its National Patient Safety Goals, the Joint Commission on Accreditation of Healthcare Organizations (Joint Commission) added a list of "do not use" abbreviations as part of Goal 2B, "standardize a list of abbreviations, acronyms and symbols that are not to be used throughout the organization." This list has subsequently been reaffirmed by the Joint Commission (Table 1).

The list is used for accreditation purposes in all clinical settings. The scope of this list should apply to all orders, not just medication orders, and all medication documentation, either handwritten or preprinted. The use of abbreviations on this list remains one of the most frequent noncompliance findings of Joint Commission surveys.

There are several other items that may possibly be added to the list, although they are currently not considered for accreditation purposes:

- The symbols ">" and "<"
- All abbreviations for drug names
- Apothecary units (eg, drams or grains)
- The symbol "@"
- The abbreviation "cc"
- The abbreviation "µg"

Because of the potential for ambiguity that might result in a medication error and subsequent patient harm, using fewer or perhaps no abbreviations is suggested.

This document reflects emerging concepts on patient safety and is subject to change. The information should not be construed as dictating an exclusive course of treatment or procedure to be followed.



ISSN 1074-861X

**The American College of Obstetricians and Gynecologists**
409 12th Street, SW
PO Box 96920
Washington, DC 20090-6920

12345/09876

"Do not use" abbreviations. ACOG Committee Opinion No. 327. American College of Obstetricians and Gynecologists. Obstet Gynecol 2006;107:213–4

**Table 1.** Official "Do Not Use" List*

| Do Not Use | Potential Problem | Use Instead |
|---|---|---|
| U (unit) | Mistaken for "0" (zero), the number "4" (four), or "cc" | Write "unit" |
| IU (International Unit) | Mistaken for IV (intravenous) or the number 10 (ten) | Write "International Unit" |
| Q.D., QD, q.d., qd (daily) | Mistaken for each other | Write "daily" |
| Q.O.D., QOD, q.o.d., qod (every other day) | Period after the Q mistaken for "I" and the "O" mistaken for "I" | Write "every other day" |
| Trailing zero (X.0 mg)† | Decimal point is missed | Write X mg |
| Lack of leading zero (.X mg) | | Write 0.X mg |
| MS | Can mean morphine sulfate or magnesium sulfate | Write "morphine sulfate" |
| $MSO_4$ and $MgSO_4$ | Confused for one another | Write "magnesium sulfate" |

*Applies to all orders and all medication-related documentation that is handwritten (including free-text computer entry) or on preprinted forms.

†A "trailing zero" may be used only where required to demonstrate the level of precision of the value being reported, such as for laboratory results, imaging studies that report size of lesions, or catheter/tube sizes. It may not be used in medication orders or other medication-related documentation.

Joint Commission on Accreditation of Healthcare Organizations. Official "do not use" list. Available at: http://www.jcaho.org/accredited+organizations/laboratory+services/npsg/06_dnu_list.pdf. Retrieved September 8, 2005.

## Bibliography

Joint Commission on Accreditation of Healthcare Organizations. Facts about the official "do not use" list. Available at: http://www.jcaho.org/accredited+organizations/patient+safety/dnu_facts.htm. Retrieved September 8, 2005.

ACOG Committee Opinion

Committee on Quality Improvement and Patient Safety

Number 328, February 2006

This document reflects emerging concepts on patient safety and is subject to change. The information should not be construed as dictating an exclusive course of treatment or procedure to be followed.



ISSN 1074-861X

**The American College of Obstetricians and Gynecologists**
409 12th Street, SW
PO Box 96920
Washington, DC 20090-6920

12345/09876

Patient safety in the surgical environment. ACOG Committee Opinion No. 328. American College of Obstetricians and Gynecologists. Obstet Gynecol 2006;107:429–33.

# Patient Safety in the Surgical Environment

*ABSTRACT: Ensuring patient safety in the operating room begins before the patient enters the operative suite and includes attention to all applicable types of preventable medical errors (including, for example, medication errors), but surgical errors are unique to this environment. Steps to prevent wrong-site, wrong-person, or wrong-procedure errors have been recommended. Prevention of surgical errors requires the attention of all personnel involved in the patient's care.*

Potentially preventable surgical errors have received increasing attention in recent years, although they appear to occur relatively infrequently compared with other classes of medical errors. The Joint Commission on Accreditation of Healthcare Organizations (JCAHO) has published two Sentinel Event Alerts addressing wrong-site surgery, the latest in 2001. Sentinel Event Alert 24 reported 150 cases of wrong-site, wrong-person, or wrong-procedure surgery, of which 126 had root cause analysis information (1). Wrong-site surgery was most common during orthopedic or podiatric procedures (41%). Although no obstetric or gynecologic cases were reported in the JCAHO series, no surgical specialty is immune from surgical errors.

## Terminology

The term *wrong-site surgery* often is used to refer to any surgical procedure performed on the wrong patient, wrong body part, wrong side of the body, or at the wrong level of the correctly identified anatomic site. The following terms can be used to describe the various specific errors:

- *Wrong-side surgery* indicates a surgical procedure performed on the wrong extremity or side of the patient's body (eg, the left ovary rather than the right ovary).
- *Wrong-patient surgery* describes a surgical procedure performed on a different person than the one intended to receive the operation.
- *Wrong-level surgery* and *wrong-part surgery* are used to indicate surgical procedures that are performed at the correct operative site, but at the wrong level or part of the operative field or patient's anatomy.

## Systems Approach

Particularly because of the potential for serious harm from surgical errors, vigorous efforts are required to eliminate or reduce their frequency. Preventing this type of error appears to be amenable to a systems approach involving a team effort by all individuals participating in the surgical process. Although all members of the surgical team share in this responsibility, the primary surgeon should oversee these efforts. The Joint Commission on Accreditation of Healthcare Organizations has identified the following factors that may contribute to an increased risk of wrong-site surgery:

- Multiple surgeons involved in the case
- Multiple procedures during a single surgical visit
- Unusual time pressures to start or complete the procedure
- Unusual physical characteristics, including morbid obesity or physical deformity

A common theme in cases of wrong-site surgery involves failed communication between the surgeon or surgeons, the other members of the health care team, and the patient. Communication is crucial throughout the surgical process, particularly during the preoperative assessment of the patient and the procedures used to verify the operative site. Effective preoperative patient assessment includes a review of the medical record or imaging studies immediately before starting surgery. To facilitate this step, all relevant information sources, verified by a predetermined checklist, should be available in the operating room and rechecked by the entire surgical team before the operation begins. Whenever possible, the patient (or the patient's designee) should be involved in the process of identifying the correct surgical site, both during the informed consent process and in the physical act of marking the intended surgical site in the preoperative area. A formal procedure for final confirmation of the correct patient and surgical site (a "time out") that requires the participation of all members of the surgical team may be helpful. It is inappropriate to place total reliance on the surgeon to identify the correct surgical site or to assume that the surgeon should never be questioned. The risk of error may be reduced by involving the entire surgical team in the site verification process and encouraging any member of that team to point out a possible error without fear of ridicule or reprimand.

## The Universal Protocol

In 2003, JCAHO published "Universal Protocol for Preventing Wrong Site, Wrong Procedure, and Wrong Person Surgery" (2). The universal protocol is based on three levels of activity before initiation of any surgical procedure:

1. *Preoperative verification process*

   The health care team ensures that all relevant documents and studies are available before the procedure starts and that the documents have been reviewed and are consistent with each other, with the patient's expectations, and with the team's understanding of the intended patient, procedure, site, and, as applicable, any implants. The team must address missing information or discrepancies before starting the procedure.

2. *Marking of the operative site*

   The health care team, including the patient (if possible), identifies unambiguously the intended site of incision or insertion by marking all operative sites involving laterality, multiple structures, or multiple levels.

3. *"Time out" before starting the procedure*

   The operative team conducts a final verification of the correct patient, procedure, site, and, as applicable, implants.

A relatively new but essential element of this overall process is the formal enlistment of active involvement by the patient to avert errors in the operative arena. Involving the patient in this manner requires personal effort by the surgeon to educate the patient during the preoperative evaluation process. The patient, who has the greatest stake in avoiding errors, thus becomes integrally involved in helping ensure that errors are avoided.

## Granting Privileges for New Procedures

New techniques and new equipment are important components for developing and delivering the best quality care in the operating room, but they also represent sources of potential surgical error. Prudence demands that, whenever possible, a surgeon who is incorporating a new surgical technique should be assisted or supervised by a colleague more experienced in the technique until competency has been satisfactorily demonstrated. In some circumstances, however, a technique may be so innovative that no other surgeon at that locale has more experience. In such situations, it may be wise to arrange for extra support staff or surgical backup to be available should difficulties arise. The surgeon involved should have already documented skills and experience in the related surgical arena and should have solicited and received the advice and support of other experienced surgeons.

When new equipment is introduced, all members of the surgical team must be trained on and practice with the new equipment as appropriate for the extent of their involvement, and all personnel involved must be aware of all safety features, warnings, and alarms of the device. Whenever possible, the institution's medical engineering department should inspect the equipment and verify that it is functioning properly before the equipment is put into clinical use. Any informational material (eg, user's manuals, operating instructions) provided by the manufacturer of the equipment should be carefully reviewed by the principal users and should be familiar to anyone using the equipment. Stickers attached to the device or plastic cards summarizing instructions for proper use may be helpful until everyone involved is comfortable with the new equipment. All necessary adaptors, attachments, and supplies should be in the room or readily available before beginning surgery using the new equipment. Any recommended protective devices, such as eye shields or special draping material, should be used for the safety of all concerned. The lead surgeon using the new equipment should have demonstrated competency using the device, resulting in the granting of privileges. Leaders of each surgically oriented department will determine the specific requirements for granting privileges to their members for the use of new techniques or equipment. It is never appropriate for nonmedical, noncredentialed individuals, such as industry representatives, to perform the actual surgery. Such individuals should be excluded from the operating room if their presence would present a distraction or discomfort for any member of the essential operating room team.

## Stress and Fatigue

A well-recognized source of human error is unusual stress and fatigue. According to the Health and Safety Laboratory, Britain's leading industrial health and safety facility and an agency of the British Health and Safety Executive, "Disrupted sleep patterns and inadequate sleep can result in fatigue and reduced levels of cognitive performance thus increasing the risk of an accident.... [H]uman error arising from fatigue may have catastrophic results in safety critical environments" (3). Sleep deprivation can cause errors in performing even the most familiar tasks; for example, the National Traffic Safety Administration reports that sleepy drivers cause at least 100,000 automobile accidents annually in the United States, resulting in approximately 40,000 injuries and 1,500 deaths (4). For this reason, many industries have already imposed strict limitations on working hours for individuals in vulnerable occupations, such as truck drivers, airline pilots and crew members, air traffic controllers, and power plant personnel. The Accreditation Council on Graduate Medical Education (ACGME) has enacted restrictions on resident work hours to prevent sleep deprivation, stress, and fatigue that might increase the risk of error (5, 6). Although no legal restrictions have yet been imposed on the work hours of practicing physicians, common sense dictates that the surgeon and the surgical team should be alert and well rested when initiating major surgical procedures. Emergency situations may be particularly hazardous as an environment for error, especially if the surgical team is stressed and fatigued already. Adequate backup personnel should be available to relieve individuals who detect diminished performance in themselves or others due to fatigue, so that the risk of errors is not increased.

## Medication Errors

The surgical environment deserves heightened vigilance to prevent medication errors because medication orders often are given verbally rather than in writing, making such orders particularly vulnerable to misinterpretation or misapplication. Increased stress or confusion during urgent situations in the operating room may increase the possibility of error in prescribing, administering, or monitoring medications. For these reasons, medication error in the surgical arena may not be addressed by the safety measures (eg, electronic order entry) proved effective in other environments. It may be wise for the surgical team to agree on protocols for administering commonly used medications or treatments and to practice their implementation. Timely and effective communication between the surgical and anesthesia teams during the entire procedure may help avoid errors that could result from misunderstanding.

## Teaching

Trainees, such as obstetric–gynecologic residents, surgical residents, anesthesiology residents, medical students, nursing students, and operating room technician students, may be part of the surgical environment in the operating room or labor and delivery suite. The education process in these environments presents special challenges in protecting patient safety. It is a fundamental principle that all trainees must be meticulously supervised and assisted when participating in surgery. Both the trainee and the supervisor should be alert, well rested, and well prepared in advance for the surgical procedure being performed. Because patient safety depends on effective communication among all members of the health care team, trainees should be conversant in the pertinent terminology before starting the procedure. The presence of noninvolved individuals as observers in the operating room or delivery suite may be a distraction to the surgical team and, therefore, should receive careful consideration before they are admitted. The current development of virtual surgery training techniques may become useful for students to learn and practice surgical skills before attempting procedures in the operating room.

## Obstetric Surgery

Operating on pregnant patients creates unique responsibilities in ensuring patient safety because two or more patients are involved simultaneously—the woman and the fetus(es)—each with different needs. Adequate personnel who will ensure proper attention to the condition of each patient must be present. Particular attention is needed to address administration of the different medications appropriate for the pregnant patient and her fetus and the newborn patient or patients, such as dosage and timing of antibiotics or analgesics for mother or newborn or both. The obstetric surgeon also is challenged to communicate with a pediatrics team in a timely and effective manner to reduce the possibility of error in care of the neonate. The occasional use of blood transfusion opens another potential avenue for introduction of error because calling for the administration of blood products may take place under especially stressful and hectic conditions. Much obstetric surgery is by nature unplanned as the course of the delivery unfolds, and obstetric emergencies can progress rapidly, increasing the possibility of error if protocols and standardized procedures are skipped or abbreviated.

## Freestanding Surgical Units

In recent years, many surgical procedures traditionally performed only in hospitals or similar institutions have increasingly been performed in physicians' offices, freestanding surgical facilities, or "surgi-centers." This trend has produced cost savings and convenience for patients as well as providers and will likely continue. However, because these facilities may not be subject to the same level of scrutiny or administrative oversight as hospitals, surgeons who use these facilities must be particularly vigilant against inadequate training of personnel, inappropriate or poorly maintained equipment and instruments, and ineffective protocols or practices, all of which may increase the likelihood of medical error and jeopardy to patient safety.

## Distractions

Beepers, radios, telephone calls, and other potential distractions in the surgical environment should be kept to a minimum, if allowed at all, especially during critical stages of the operation. Nonessential conversation should be postponed until surgery is finished. Similarly, it may be preferable to ask nonessential personnel to remain outside the operating room while surgery is being performed.

## Conclusion

Although medical errors can occur in any aspect of medicine, the surgical environment presents additional, special challenges to safeguarding patient safety. Because these injuries can be serious, particular care is appropriate in creating systems and routines that reduce the likelihood of wrong-patient, wrong-side, and wrong-part surgical errors. The wide variety of techniques, instruments, and technology used for surgical procedures makes granting privileges of surgeons critically important. Freestanding surgical units may need to be particularly vigilant in ensuring that personnel and equipment are in good condition for surgery. Protocols and procedures to identify and manage stress and fatigue in surgical personnel may help to avoid surgical errors and patient injuries. The operating room is an appropriate educational environment, but the presence of observers at any level must not be allowed to compromise patient safety. Patient safety in surgery demands the full attention of skilled individuals using well-functioning equipment under adequate supervision.

## References


1. A follow-up review of wrong site surgery. Joint Commission on Accreditation of Healthcare Organizations. Sentinel Event Alert 2001;24. Available at: http://www.jcaho.org/about+us/news+letters/sentinel+event+alert/sea_24.htm. Retrieved September 15, 2005.
2. Joint Commission on Accreditation of Healthcare Organizations. Universal protocol for preventing wrong site, wrong procedure, and wrong person surgery. Available at http://www.jcaho.org/accredited+organizations/patient+safety/universal+protocol/wss_universal+protocol.htm. Retrieved September 15, 2005.
3. Health and Safety Laboratory (UK). Case studies—fatigue and shiftwork in safety critical industries. Available at: http://www.hsl.gov.uk/case-studies/fatigue.htm. Retrieved September 15, 2005.
4. National Highway Traffic Safety Administration. The dangers of drowsy driving—some startling statistics. Available at: http://www.nhtsa.dot.gov/people/injury/drowsy_driving1/human/drows_driving. Retrieved September 15, 2005.
5. Accreditation Council for Graduate Medical Education. Statement of justification/impact for the final approval of common standards related to resident duty hours. Available at: http://www.acgme.org/acwebsite/dutyhours/dh_impactstatement.pdf. Retrieved September 15, 2005.
6. Buysse D, Barzansky B, Dinges D, Hogan E, Hunt CE, Owens J, et al. Sleep, fatigue, and medical training: setting an agenda for optimal learning and patient care. Sleep 2003;26:218–25.

ACOG Committee Opinion

Committee on Quality Improvement and Patient Safety

Number 329, March 2006

# Tracking and Reminder Systems

*ABSTRACT: An accurate and effective tracking or reminder system is useful for the modern practice of obstetrics and gynecology. It is not adequate to rely solely on the patient to complete all ordered studies and to follow up on physician recommendations. Obstetrician–gynecologists have an obligation to their patients to encourage them to complete studies believed essential for patient care within an acceptable time frame. Each office should establish a simple, reliable tracking and reminder system to improve patient safety and quality of care and to minimize missed diagnoses.*

The accurate and timely flow of information between patients and clinicians is important for safe and effective care. Patient visits often require some form of follow-up involving further testing, referrals, communication of test results, or consultations. Physicians' offices should have procedures in place to track these events effectively and to enhance quality of care and patient safety. An effective and reliable reminder system need not be complex or expensive but is a necessity for obstetric and gynecologic care in all practice settings. Failure to follow up may cause delayed or missed diagnoses, which may result in an adverse patient outcome and potential liability for the physician. Although it is recognized that patients have responsibility for following through on their physicians' recommendations, courts have held that the health care professional is responsible for contacting patients about laboratory, imaging, or consultation results. An adequate tracking system can help in reducing risks and providing safe, high-quality patient care. Clinicians should recognize the potential to improve patient safety by adopting tracking and reminder systems.

The process for good patient follow-up begins with the practitioner explaining to the patient at the initial visit any needed test, referral, or follow-up and documenting this discussion in the chart. Clear information and instructions will help the patient participate in her care and understand why a test or appointment is important. The next step is logging these open items into a tracking or reminder system promptly and reviewing them frequently and regularly according to the office's established procedures.

An appropriate tracking system can be manual or electronic. A successful system may be in the form of a log book, card files, file folders, computer system, or any system accessible for ongoing updating and monitoring.

This document reflects emerging concepts on patient safety and is subject to change. The information should not be construed as dictating an exclusive course of treatment or procedure to be followed.



ISSN 1074-861X

**The American College of Obstetricians and Gynecologists**
409 12th Street, SW
PO Box 96920
Washington, DC 20090-6920

12345/09876

Tracking and reminder systems. ACOG Committee Opinion No. 329. American College of Obstetricians and Gynecologists. Obstet Gynecol 2006;107:745-7.

Computerized systems can be helpful, but they also may be expensive and time-consuming to establish and are not necessary. In most clinical situations, a simple paper-based "tickler system" can be developed. No matter what system is used, correct and prompt data entry is a necessity.

Once information is entered into the system, it should be retrieved and reviewed regularly with accompanying documentation of any actions taken or discussions with the patient. Information on each patient should be reviewed throughout the entire process from data input through resolution. Allowing all personnel who participate in tracking to provide input into the system design and implementation should encourage its use. To decrease risk of system failure, the number of steps should be minimized and the number of responsible people limited. However, if possible, the responsibility should not rest with only one person.

## Trackable Events

Each office should prioritize items according to their importance for tracking. As the system is tested and improved, additional elements can be added. The following list reflects common tracking needs for many obstetric and gynecologic practices.

- Pap test results and follow-up, need for colposcopy
- Mammography results and necessary follow-up
- All laboratory tests and radiologic studies
- Pathology reports
- Routine as well as special obstetric testing, such as multiple marker studies
- After-hours and on-call emergencies, including follow-up on laboratory and radiologic studies from the hospital and emergency department

Follow-up appointments should be scheduled. Patients should be reminded about the importance of keeping their postoperative visits and other follow-up appointments. Whenever a patient does not appear for a scheduled appointment, that fact should be recorded in her medical record. Although patients cannot be forced to keep their appointments, an attempt should be made to contact them when an appointment is missed and to assist them in rescheduling. Each office should develop a procedure for dealing with patients who do not appear for an appointment after several appointments have been made. Because different state laws apply, the procedure should be appropriate to the state.

Referrals to consultants should be tracked, noting whether the patient has visited with the consultant and whether the consultant's report has been filed in the chart. Referrals of patients from other clinicians also should be tracked, with notification to the referring physician once the patient has been seen.

## Suggested Characteristics of the Reminder System

The following characteristics are important for any reminder system, whether electronic or paper-based.

- Policies and procedures. An office policy and procedure on tracking should be developed with input from the staff. All office members should agree to follow the same protocols. The office policy should address how to contact the patient and how to document the follow-up in the patient's chart. Usual time frames for when to expect various types of results should be defined, and a protocol should be established for dealing with delayed or missing reports.
- HIPAA compliance. When contacting patients, physicians and their staff must follow Health Insurance Portability and Accountability Act (HIPAA) regulations. For example, postcard reminders are not compliant. In addition, e-mail is not HIPAA compliant unless both the office and the patient's systems are secure. Most personal e-mail services are not secure.
- Specificity. The reminder system should contain specific data and dates, including the dates for receipt of information and timelines for notifying the patient.
- Central location. The reminder system should be centrally located in the office and should not be kept in individual patient charts. Reminders should be accessible to the entire staff.
- Reliability. The tracking system should not be the responsibility of a single individual. It should be updated and monitored regularly. Office staff should be cross-trained so that the system is reliable and efficient.

## Sample Tracking Form

A tracking form can pinpoint key follow-up areas. Listed as follows are the important elements to be tracked:

- Date ordered
- Patient name
- Identifying number
- Test, procedure, consult, or referral
- Date of results
- Follow-up required
- Evaluation completed and patient notified

All printed results, including Pap tests, mammograms, consults, and pathology reports, should be reviewed, initialed, and dated by a clinician who has been designated to perform this function. Results should then be filed permanently in the patient chart, including a notation of what follow-up testing or procedures are recommended.

The "no news is good news" approach is not recommended as a standard practice for follow-up. Patients should be made aware of the office practice for notification of results and should be encouraged to call back for results if they are not received in a timely fashion. However, the office should not rely solely on the patient to call back for results but should have a more effective system. Computerized tracking and reminder systems are available with custom alerts, telephone reminders, and telephone numbers to call for automated test results using individual identifying numbers. Such systems are not required for appropriate follow-up and patient notification and can be difficult, time-consuming, and expensive to implement. Any tracking and reminder system may seem initially to require extra time and cost; however, use of tracking systems rapidly becomes routine for the practice and will enhance the quality of care, patient outcomes, and patient satisfaction while helping to enhance patient safety.

Designing and implementing a tracking and reminder system also provide an opportunity to develop further a culture of safety in the office. A system that is standardized, simple, and accessible to all potential users will reduce the likelihood of error. When problems or mistakes occur, staff should be encouraged to report them. Errors are a valuable way to learn why and how systems fail, and exploring the causes of errors provides an opportunity to improve those systems. Ultimately, an informed and involved patient, a well-designed tracking system, and clinicians and staff who feel safe to discuss system failures will render safer patient care and improve outcomes.

## Resources

National Patient Safety Foundation
1120 MASS MoCA Way
North Adams, MA 01247
(413) 663-8900
http://www.npsf.org

Joint Commission on Accreditation of Healthcare Organizations
One Renaissance Boulevard
Oakbrook Terrace, IL 60181
(630) 792-5000
http://www.jcaho.org/accredited+organization/patient+safety

Institute for Healthcare Improvement
20 University Road, 7th Floor
Cambridge, MA 02138
(617) 301-4800
http://www.ihi.org/ihi

Copic Companies
7351 Lowry Boulevard
Denver, CO 80230
(800) 421-1834
http://www.callcopic.com

Norcal Mutual Insurance Company
560 Davis Street
San Francisco, CA 94111
(800) 652-1051
www.norcalmutual.com

# ACOG Committee Opinion

Committee on Quality Improvement and Patient Safety

Number 331, April 2006

# Safe Use of Medication

*ABSTRACT: Medication use errors are the largest single source of preventable adverse events. To minimize the risk of medication use errors, obstetrician–gynecologists should focus on several elements of medication order writing, such as the appropriate use of decimals and zeros, standard abbreviations, and assuring legibility. Additionally, it is important to assist the patient in understanding the medical condition for which a medication is prescribed. Focusing on elements that may prevent prescription errors and helping patients understand how to use prescribed medication properly may help lower the occurrence of medication use errors.*

Safe use of medication is a systems issue, encompassing more than written prescriptions. Physicians have an obligation to seek improvement in medication use safety, which entails the entire process of integrating medications into the patient's clinical setting. The following definition of a medication error demonstrates the broad areas that the clinician should consider:

> A medication error is any preventable event that may cause or lead to inappropriate medication use or patient harm while the medication is in the control of the health care professional, patient, or consumer. Such events may be related to professional practice, health care products, procedures, and systems, including prescribing; order communication; product labeling, packaging, and nomenclature; compounding; dispensing; distribution; administration; education; monitoring; and use. (1)

Some events listed in this definition are outside the purview of the physician, such as product labeling, color of medication, and nomenclature assigned when a drug is introduced to the public. However, errors in the prescription, formulation, and administration of pharmaceutical agents are common and, in many cases, preventable causes of patient harm.

## Medication Use

As part of their daily practice of medicine, clinicians should become familiar with the medications that are available to treat their patients, and there are several steps they can take to accomplish this:

- Maintaining up-to-date references of current medications
- Understanding the indications of the medication considered, including all alternative therapies

This document reflects emerging concepts on patient safety and is subject to change. The information should not be construed as dictating an exclusive course of treatment or procedure to be followed.



ISSN 1074-861X

**The American College of Obstetricians and Gynecologists**
409 12th Street, SW
PO Box 96920
Washington, DC 20090-6920

12345/09876

Safe use of medication. ACOG Committee Opinion No. 331. American College of Obstetricians and Gynecologists. Obstet Gynecol 2006;107:969–72.

- Considering conditions that may affect the efficacy of the medication, such as dosing schedules, route of administration, patient weight, and renal and hepatic functioning
- Understanding the interactions of considered agents with other medications used by the patient as well as therapies being considered (including surgical treatments)
- Ensuring that a patient's current medication is continued, if appropriate, when admitting that patient to the hospital and that additional medication used during the hospital stay is compatible with the patient's current therapeutic regimen.

Medication ordering errors are the leading cause of medical errors (2). Much of the published literature regarding medical errors has focused on the types and causes of these errors, centering on clinical problems such as allergy-related contraindications that go undetected, inappropriate dosage forms, and excessive dosing (3–4). Medication ordering errors also arise from more technical causes, such as poorly written or misinterpreted handwritten medication orders.

The complexity of prescribing drugs is attributed, in part, to the number of agents, which has increased at a staggering rate. Prescription problems such as illegible words, missing components, and the inappropriate use of abbreviations have been anecdotally reported for many years. The problem has been compounded in recent years because of the influx of new drugs with "look-alike" and "sound-alike" names, making prescription interpretation more difficult (5).

## Medication Order Writing

Medication order writing is one aspect of medical care that is within the control of every prescriber. The essentials of safely writing medication orders include focusing on certain elements of the order as follows:

- Medication order legibility
- Missing medication order components
- Decimals and zeros
- Abbreviations
- "As needed" (pro re nata) medication orders
- Similarity of trade names
- Sound-alike drugs
- Verbal medication orders

### *Order Legibility*

Computerized physician order entry systems virtually eliminate prescription legibility concerns. However, they are expensive and lack widespread implementation. Until computerized physician order entry systems become more widely available, prescribers should be particularly diligent about the legibility of their prescription orders (6).

### *Missing Medication Order Components*

To prepare a complete, legible medication order, the following components must be clearly written on the medication order form:

- Name of the drug
- Dose to be given
- Route of administration
- Frequency of administration (or rate)
- Reason or conditions under which the drug should be administered (if prescribing pro re nata)
- Patient's weight and age (if relevant to dosing)

If any of these components are missing, the medication order is incomplete. Filling an incomplete medication order substantially increases the risk of a medication error. The prescriber's signature and identification number also should be written or printed on the prescription.

### *Decimals and Use of Leading and Trailing Zeroes*

One area that contributes to medication errors is the misuse of leading and trailing zeroes with decimal points. The decimal point often is not seen when the medication order is read (especially when a copy of the order is used to fill the prescription rather than the original medication order), potentially causing a 10-fold overdose. A leading zero should always be used when prescribing doses of less than 1 (Fig. 1). Similarly, a whole number should never be followed by a decimal point and a zero (Fig. 2). A mnemonic for these constructions is, "always lead, never follow."

### *Inappropriate Abbreviations*

In medication orders, the use of nonstandardized abbreviations creates confusion and can contribute to medication errors if the abbreviations are not interpreted as they are intended by the prescriber. Most health care institutions have standardized lists of acceptable abbreviations. National organizations

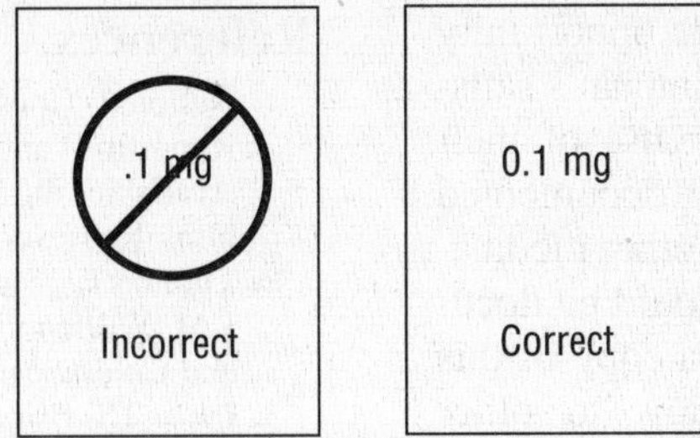


**Fig. 1**

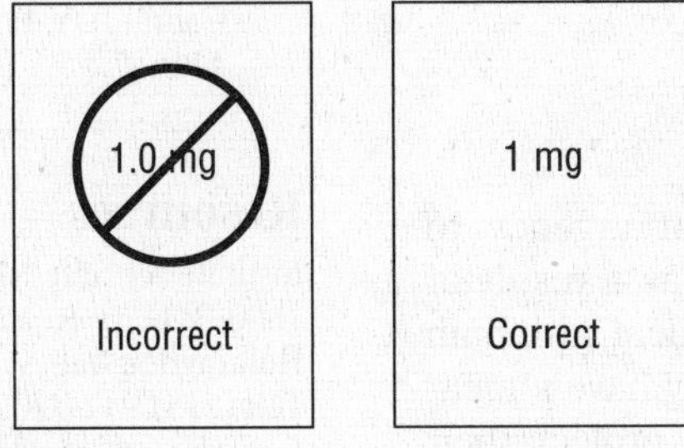


**Fig. 2**

also have made recommendations about acceptable abbreviations. Some organizations provide alerts about dangerous abbreviations and other medication safety related recommendations on their web sites (see Resources). The following general guidelines should be followed when using abbreviations:

- Drug names should not be abbreviated.
- Q.D. should not be used to abbreviate "once daily." Sometimes the dot that follows the "Q" looks like an "I" and the abbreviation appears to be QID. There is no safe abbreviation for "once daily"; it should always be written out.
- O.D. should not be used to abbreviate "once daily." O.D. is properly interpreted as "right eye." Use of this abbreviation to represent "once daily" has resulted in prescription administration errors with liquid medications such as saturated solution of potassium. There is no safe abbreviation for "once daily"; it should always be spelled out.
- The metric system should be used.
- The word "unit" should not be abbreviated. The handwritten "U" or "u" may often look like a "0" (zero) and may cause a 10-fold overdose.

### *Pro Re Nata Medication Orders*

When prescribing a medication, it is helpful to provide the reasons for giving the medication or parameters for giving a pro re nata dose. This is particularly helpful in preventing errors with sound-alike and look-alike medications or for medications that are to be given on an as-needed basis.

### *Verbal Medication Orders*

Verbal medication orders should be limited to urgent situations in which written (or electronic) medication orders are not feasible. To assure accuracy, verbal medication orders (whether in person or by telephone) should be followed by a request that the person receiving the order repeats the order to the prescriber. Because many drugs have sound-alike names, it may be helpful to include the indication for the drug in verbal medication orders.

## Patient Education

Clinicians should assist the patient in understanding the medical condition for which a medication has been prescribed. Engaging the patient in her own care improves compliance, outcome, and patient satisfaction and reduces error. This requires the concerted effort of all members of the medical team, both in and out of the hospital. Such education may take the form of oral communication or handouts that explain the use, dosage, expected benefits, and possible side effects of the medication that is prescribed. Patients should be given ample opportunity to ask questions and reiterate, to the clinician's satisfaction, their understanding of proper use of their medications. Allergies should be well documented and reviewed with the patient. A list of other medications currently in use by the patient should be documented, and the patient should retain a copy of this list for personal benefit and to show to other providers in the future. Including family members who will assist the patient in medication use in such education will help assure accurate use of the prescribed medication.

## Conclusion

All physicians feel a strong sense of urgency to reduce the medical errors that occur as a result of their care. Because obstetricians often deal with both the pregnant woman and her fetus, they have a measurably increased need to vigilantly protect their patients. Following these suggestions will not only reduce errors but, more importantly, will create the awareness necessary to provide care more safely. The Committee on Quality Improvement and Patient Safety encourages physicians to begin examining all aspects of patient safety, both in the hospital setting as well as within their offices.

## References


1. National Coordinating Council for Medication Error Reporting and Prevention. About medication errors. Available at: http://www.nccmerp.org/aboutMedErrors.html. Retrieved January 28, 2005.
2. Thomas EJ, Studdert DM, Newhouse JP, Zbar BI, Howard KM, Williams EJ, et al. Cost of medical injuries in Utah and Colorado. Injury 1999;36:255–64.
3. Lesar TS, Briceland L, Stein DS. Factors related to errors in medication prescribing. JAMA 1997;277:312–7.
4. Davis NM, Cohen MR, Teplitsky B. Look-alike and sound-alike drug names: the problem and the solution. Hosp Pharm 1992;27:95–110.
5. Cabral JDY. Poor physician penmanship. JAMA 1997;278:1116–7.


## Resources

Institute for Safe Medication Practices
1800 Byberry Road, Suite 810
Huntingdon Valley, PA 19006
Tel: (215) 947-7707
E-mail: ismpinfo@ismp.org
Web: www.ismp.org

National Coordinating Council for Medication Error Reporting and Prevention
Web: www.nccmerp.org

# ACOG Committee Opinion

Committee on Quality Improvement and Patient Safety

Number 353, December 2006

## Medical Emergency Preparedness

*ABSTRACT: Patient care emergencies may occur at any time in a hospital or an outpatient setting. To respond to these emergencies, it is important that obstetrician–gynecologists prepare themselves by assessing potential emergencies that might occur, creating plans that include establishing early warning systems, designating specialized first responders, conducting emergency drills, and debriefing staff after actual events to identify what went well and what are opportunities for improvement. Having such systems in place may reduce or prevent the severity of medical emergencies.*

A practicing obstetrician–gynecologist may be faced with a sudden patient emergency at any time. Whether it is severe shoulder dystocia, catastrophic surgical hemorrhage, or an anaphylactic reaction to an injection in the office, it will require prompt corrective action. Preparing for potential emergency events requires planning for potential events, advance provisioning of resources, establishing an early warning system, designating specialized first responders, and holding drills to ensure that everyone knows what to do in an emergency. Beyond these basics, certain principles of communication and teamwork will enhance the effectiveness of the emergency response.

### Planning

Planning for potential emergency events may be simple or complex. At a minimum, it should involve an assessment of the potential or actual risks related to the practice setting or the patient population. For instance, in the outpatient setting, are medications given or procedures performed that may result in anaphylaxis, airway embarrassment, or hemorrhage? In the inpatient setting, unit data or risk management data may reflect common and uncommon emergency situations that have occurred.

### Advance Provision of Resources

A common practice for health-care-related emergencies is the availability of the "crash cart." All physicians should be familiar with the crash cart. By placing all necessary items in one place, one ensures that time is not lost gathering supplies in an emergency. Appropriate changes should be made to

This document reflects emerging concepts on patient safety and is subject to change. The information should not be construed as dictating an exclusive course of treatment or procedure to be followed.



ISSN 1074-861X

**The American College of Obstetricians and Gynecologists**
409 12th Street, SW
PO Box 96920
Washington, DC 20090-6920

12345/09876

Medical emergency preparedness. ACOG Committee Opinion No. 353. American College of Obstetricians and Gynecologists. Obstet Gynecol 2006;108:1597–9.

the cart as evidence-based changes are made to the Advanced Cardiac Life Support protocol. Advance provision of resources also may be extended to the management of eclampsia and malignant hyperthermia. Physicians in outpatient settings may wish to create a small kit for handling allergic reactions if they are not able to maintain a full crash cart. As with a crash cart, the kit must be maintained regularly to ensure supplies are not expired. All providers need to know how to access the kit.

## Early Warning Systems

Some emergencies are truly sudden and catastrophic, such as a ruptured aneurysm, massive pulmonary embolus, or complete abruptio placentae in the setting of trauma. However, many physiologic emergencies are preceded by a period of instability during which timely intervention may head off ensuing disaster. The medical emergency team (discussed later) is set up to handle such emergencies. Even without the use of a medical emergency team, however, nurses and other bedside caregivers need to realize that certain changes in a patient's condition can indicate an emergency that requires immediate intervention and correction. These changes include some events not usually understood as emergencies, such as agitation or new onset difficulty with movement. Ideally, each service will examine its own historical call data to determine which events require activation of the early warning system. It is imperative that bedside personnel be able to request immediate help, without recrimination, when such changes occur. For example, the nurse who calls the medical emergency team regarding the anxious postoperative patient with newly onset shortness of breath must not be dismissed as failing to recognize a panic attack but instead thanked for following protocol. The protocol should provide for a full evaluation of the problem. Some organizations have formalized the emergency communication process with the development of a communication tool, such as "SBAR" (Situation, Background, Assessment, and Recommendation); all providers are encouraged to follow it to clearly communicate the patient care issue. Standardized responses will increase the efficiency of care and allow a continuous quality improvement process to assess the effectiveness of the interventions.

## Specialized First Responders

Medical emergency teams are designated emergency response teams. Activation of the team to the bedside occurs when predefined criteria are met, although the team also may be activated for other reasons. Activation should be a no-fault process. The team is available at all times with authority to summon further help as needed. By designating criteria that define an emergency, it becomes clear when to call for help. For example, if a maternal or postoperative heart rate of more than 140 beats per minute is the criterion, the nurse who notes such heart rate must immediately call the medical emergency team. This contrasts with the common practice of calling an attending physician and awaiting a call back for orders before intervention. Activation of the emergency response system before a full arrest may lead to improved survival of hospitalized patients and decreased admissions to an intensive care unit. It is important to emphasize that if there is a teaching service, calling the house officer does not substitute triggering the medical emergency team. Similarly, calling the in-house physician in a nonteaching setting does not substitute activating the medical emergency team. Medical emergency teams usually have advanced practice nurses and respiratory therapists as first responders and are expected to respond to the problem in a standardized fashion. The goal of standardized response and rapid effective recognition and correction of problems is better met with a small stable group. Creation of medical emergency teams is one of the patient safety initiatives currently being promoted by the Institute for Healthcare Improvement and the American Medical Association. Blueprints for setting up such a team, as well as other resources, may be found at the web sites of these organizations (see Resources for contact information).

## Emergency Drills

The principle that standardized care can result in safer care applies to emergencies as well as to routine care. Thus, each service should consider a protocol for management of common emergencies, such as emergency cesarean deliveries. The fields of aviation and anesthesia both have invested heavily in the concept of simulation training or the emergency drill. This training may use a sophisticated simulated environment but it also may use the everyday work space in a mock event. Protocols also can be reinforced by prominently displayed posters, pocket cards, or other aids.

Using drills to train physicians to respond to emergencies has several theoretical advantages. Adult learning theory supports the importance of experiential learning. Emergencies do not occur on paper; they occur in a specific physical setting and may involve a group of nurses, physicians, and other health care providers attempting to respond. By conducting a drill in a realistic simulator or in the actual patient care setting, issues related to the physical environment become obvious. Are the necessary drugs readily available? Can the personnel in the patient room easily obtain blood products or does someone need to be designated to coordinate obtaining products with the nursing station? How much time does it actually take to get from the farthest corner of the labor suite to the delivery room?

Emergency drills also allow physicians and others to practice principles of effective communication in a crisis. Many aspects of the medical environment work against effective communication, including the often hierarchical nature of the training and work setting and the different educational backgrounds and levels of understanding of the care giving team. Many physicians are accustomed to talking "to" nurses. Effective teamwork requires talking "with" each other. It requires that there be a team leader coordinating the response, but it should also empower all members of the team to share information. By practicing together, barriers hindering communication and teamwork can be overcome. Effective drills may lead to improved standardization of response, provider satisfaction, and patient outcomes.

## Conclusion

The obstetrician–gynecologist practices in an environment where true emergencies will eventually occur. Preparation for these situations requires that supplies and an educated team be in place before the event. The exact nature of the preparation will depend on the work environment and the resources available.

## Bibliography

Hamman WR. The complexity of team training: what we have learned from aviation and its application to medicine. Qual Saf Health Care 2004; 13(suppl):i72–9.

## Resources

Institute for Healthcare Improvement
Establish a Rapid Response Team
20 University Road, 7th Floor
Cambridge, MA 02138
Tel: 866-787-0831
Web: http://www.ihi.org/IHI/Topics/CriticalCare/IntensiveCare/Changes/EstablishaRapidResponseTeam.htm

American Medical Association
Advancing Quality Improvement in Patient Care
515 N. State Street
Chicago, IL 60610
Tel: 800-621-8335
Web: http://www.ama-assn.org/go/quality

MORE$^{OB}$
Managing Obstetrical Risk Efficiently
The Society of Obstetricians and Gynecologists of Canada
780 Echo Drive
Ottawa, ON K1S 5R7
Tel: 800-561-2416
Web: www.moreob.com

# POLICY STATEMENTS

# POLICY STATEMENTS

# ACOG *Statement of Policy*

As issued by the ACOG Executive Board

***This document was developed by a joint task force of the American Academy of Family Physicians and the American College of Obstetricians and Gynecologists.***

## AAFP--ACOG JOINT STATEMENT ON COOPERATIVE PRACTICE AND HOSPITAL PRIVILEGES

Access to maternity care is an important public health concern in the United States. Providing comprehensive perinatal services to a diverse population requires a cooperative relationship among a variety of health professionals, including social workers, health educators, nurses and physicians. Prenatal care, labor and delivery, and postpartum care have historically been provided by midwives, family physicians and obstetricians. All three remain the major caregivers today. A cooperative and collaborative relationship among obstetricians, family physicians and nurse midwives is essential for provision of consistent, high-quality care to pregnant women.

Regardless of specialty, there should be shared common standards of perinatal care. This requires a cooperative working environment and shared decision making. Clear guidelines for consultation and referral for complications should be developed jointly. When appropriate, early and ongoing consultation regarding a woman's care is necessary for the best possible outcome and is an important part of risk management and prevention of professional liability problems. All family physicians and obstetricians on the medical staff of the obstetric unit should agree to such guidelines and be willing to work together for the best care of patients. This includes a willingness on the part of obstetricians to provide consultation and back-up for family physicians who provide maternity care. The family physician should have knowledge, skills and judgment to determine when timely consultation and/or referral may be appropriate.

The most important objective of the physician must be the provision of the highest standards of care, regardless of specialty. Quality patient care requires that all providers should practice within their degree of ability as determined by training, experience and current competence. A joint practice committee with obstetricians and family physicians should be established in health care organizations to determine and monitor standards of care and to determine proctoring guidelines. A collegial working relationship between family physicians and obstetricians is essential if we are to provide access to quality care for pregnant women in this country.

The American College of Obstetricians and Gynecologists
409 12th Street, SW, PO Box 96920 • Washington, DC 20090-6920 Telephone 202-638-5577

A. Practice privileges

The assignment of hospital privileges is a local responsibility and privileges should be granted on the basis of training, experience and demonstrated current competence. All physicians should be held to thesame standards for granting of privileges, regardless of specialty, in order to assure the provision of high-quality patient care. Prearranged, collaborative relationships should be established to ensure ongoing consultations, as well as consultations needed for emergencies.

The standard of training should allow any physician who receives training in a cognitive or surgical skill to meet the criteria for privileges in that area of practice. Provisional privileges in primary care, obstetric care and cesarean delivery should be granted regardless of specialty as long as training criteria and experience are documented. All physicians should be subject to a proctorship period to allow demonstration of ability and current competence. These principles should apply to all health care systems.

B. Interdepartmental relationships

Privileges recommended by the department of family practice shall be the responsibility of the department of family practice. Similarly, privileges recommended by the department of obstetrics-gynecology shall be the responsibility of the department of obstetrics-gynecology. When privileges are recommended jointly by the departments of family practice and obstetrics-gynecology, they shall be the joint responsibility of the two departments.

Published July 1980
Reformatted July 1988
Revised and Retitled March 1998

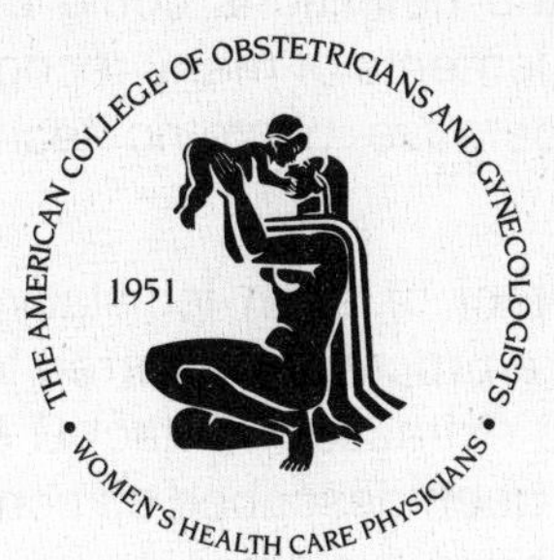


# ACOG *Statement of Policy*

As issued by the ACOG Executive Board

## ABORTION POLICY

The following statement is the American College of Obstetricians and Gynecologists' (ACOG) general policy related to abortion, with specific reference to the procedure referred to as "intact dilatation and extraction" (intact D & X).

1. The abortion debate in this country is marked by serious moral pluralism. Different positions in the debate represent different but important values. The diversity of beliefs should be respected.

2. ACOG recognizes that the issue of support of or opposition to abortion is a matter of profound moral conviction to its members. ACOG, therefore, respects the need and responsibility of its members to determine their individual positions based on personal values or beliefs.

3. Termination of pregnancy before viability is a medical matter between the patient and physician, subject to the physician's clinical judgment, the patient's informed consent and the availability of appropriate facilities.

4. The need for abortions, other than those indicated by serious fetal anomalies or conditions which threaten maternal welfare, represents failures in the social environment and the educational system.

   The most effective way to reduce the number of abortions is to prevent unwanted and unintended pregnancies. This can be accomplished by open and honest education, beginning in the home, religious institutions and the primary schools. This education should stress the biology of reproduction and the responsibilities involved by boys, girls, men and women in creating life and the desirability of delaying pregnancies until circumstances are appropriate and pregnancies are planned.

   In addition, everyone should be made aware of the dangers of sexually transmitted diseases and the means of protecting each other from their transmission. To accomplish these aims, support of the community and the school system is essential.

   The medical curriculum should be expanded to include a focus on the components of reproductive biology which pertain to conception control. Physicians should be encouraged to apply these principles in their own practices and to support them at the community level.

   Society also has a responsibility to support research leading to improved methods of contraception for men and women.

5. Informed consent is an expression of respect for the patient as a person; it particularly respects a patient's moral right to bodily integrity, to self-determination regarding sexuality and reproductive capacities, and to

The American College of Obstetricians and Gynecologists
409 12th Street, SW, PO Box 96920 • Washington, DC 20090-6920 Telephone 202-638-5577

the support of the patient's freedom within caring relationships.

A pregnant woman should be fully informed in a balanced manner about all options, including raising the child herself, placing the child for adoption, and abortion. The information conveyed should be appropriate to the duration of the pregnancy. The professional should make every effort to avoid introducing personal bias.

6. ACOG supports access to care for all individuals, irrespective of financial status, and supports the availability of all reproductive options. ACOG opposes unnecessary regulations that limit or delay access to care.
7. If abortion is to be performed, it should be performed safely and as early as possible.
8. ACOG opposes the harassment of abortion providers and patients.
9. ACOG strongly supports those activities which prevent unintended pregnancy.

The College continues to affirm the legal right of a woman to obtain an abortion prior to fetal viability. ACOG is opposed to abortion of the healthy fetus that has attained viability in a healthy woman. Viability is the capacity of the fetus to survive outside the mother's uterus. Whether or not this capacity exists is a medical determination, may vary with each pregnancy and is a matter for the judgment of the responsible attending physician.

**Intact Dilatation and Extraction**

The debate regarding legislation to prohibit a method of abortion, such as the legislation banning "partial birth abortion," and "brain sucking abortions," has prompted questions regarding these procedures. It is difficult to respond to these questions because the descriptions are vague and do not delineate a specific procedure recognized in the medical literature. Moreover, the definitions could be interpreted to include elements of many recognized abortion and operative obstetric techniques.

ACOG believes the intent of such legislative proposals is to prohibit a procedure referred to as "intact dilatation and extraction" (Intact D & X). This procedure has been described as containing all of the following four elements:

1. deliberate dilatation of the cervix, usually over a sequence of days;
2. instrumental conversion of the fetus to a footling breech;
3. breech extraction of the body excepting the head; **and**
4. partial evacuation of the intracranial contents of a living fetus to effect vaginal delivery of a dead but otherwise intact fetus.

Because these elements are part of established obstetric techniques, it must be emphasized that unless all four elements are present in sequence, the procedure is not an intact D & X. Abortion intends to terminate a pregnancy while preserving the life and health of the mother. When abortion is performed after 16 weeks, intact D & X is one method of terminating a pregnancy.

The physician, in consultation with the patient, must choose the most appropriate method based upon the patient's individual circumstances.

According to the Centers for Disease Control and Prevention (CDC), only 5.3% of abortions performed in the United States in 1993, the most recent data available, were performed after the 16th week of pregnancy. A preliminary figure published by the CDC for 1994 is 5.6%. The CDC does not collect data on the specific method of abortion, so it is unknown how many of these were performed using intact D & X. Other data show that second trimester transvaginal instrumental abortion is a safe procedure.

Terminating a pregnancy is performed in some circumstances to save the life or preserve the health of the mother.

Intact D & X is one of the methods available in some of these situations. A select panel convened by ACOG could identify no circumstances under which this procedure, as defined above, would be the only option to save the life or preserve the health of the woman. An intact D & X, however, may be the best or most appropriate procedure in a particular circumstance to save the life or preserve the health of a woman, and only the doctor, in consultation with the patient, based upon the woman's particular circumstances can make this decision. The potential exists that legislation prohibiting specific medical practices, such as intact D & X, may outlaw techniques that are critical to the lives and health of American women. **The intervention of legislative bodies into medical decision making is inappropriate, ill advised, and dangerous.**

Approval by the Executive Board
General policy: January 1993
Reaffirmed and revised: July 1997
Intact D & X statement: January 1997
Combined and reaffirmed: September 2000
Reaffirmed: July 2004

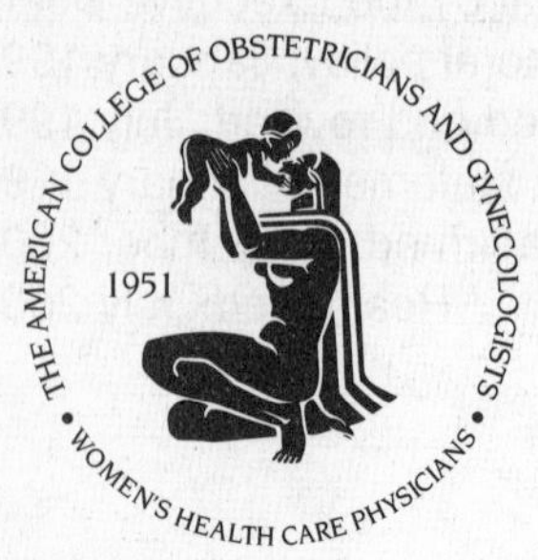


# ACOG *Statement of Policy*

As issued by the ACOG Executive Board

## ACCESS TO WOMEN'S HEALTH CARE

Excellence in women's health care is an essential element of the long-term physical, intellectual, social and economic well-being of any society. It is a basic determinant of the health of future generations.

The American College of Obstetricians and Gynecologists is the representative organization of physicians who are qualified specialists in providing health services unique to women. ACOG calls for quality health care appropriate to every woman's needs throughout her life and for assuring that a full array of clinical services be available to women without costly delays or the imposition of geographic, financial, attitudinal or legal barriers.

The College and its membership are committed to facilitating both access to and quality of women's health care. Fellows should exercise their responsibility to improve the health status of women and their offspring both in the traditional patient-physician relationships and by working within their community and at the state and national levels to assure access to high-quality programs meeting the health needs of all women. Fellows must not discriminate against patients based on race, color, national origin, religion, sexual orientation, or any other basis that would constitute illegal discrimination.

In addition, it is critical that all Americans be provided with adequate and affordable health coverage. There remains a considerable and increasing portion of the American population that does not have health insurance coverage. As a result, those individuals often defer obtaining preventive and medical services, jeopardizing the health and well being of themselves and their families. The College supports universal coverage that is designed to improve the individual and collective health of society. Expanding health coverage to all Americans must become a high priority.

Approved by the Executive Board July 1988
Amended September 1999
Amended and Reaffirmed July 2003
Amended and Reaffirmed July 2006

The American College of Obstetricians and Gynecologists
409 12th Street, SW, PO Box 96920 • Washington, DC 20090-6920 Telephone 202-638-5577

# ACOG *Statement of Policy*

As issued by the ACOG Executive Board

***A joint policy statement from the American College of Obstetricians and Gynecologists, the Society of Obstetricians and Gynaecologists of Canada, the Central American Federation of Associations and Societies of Obstetrics and Gynecology, the Gynaecologic Oncologists of Canada, the Society of Canadian Colposcopists, the Society of Gynecologic Oncologists, and the Royal College of Obstetricians and Gynaecologists.***

## CERVICAL CANCER PREVENTION IN LOW-RESOURCE SETTINGS

Cervical cancer is the third most common cancer in the world and the leading cause of cancer death among women in developing countries (1). Worldwide, an estimated 470,000 new cases occur and 233,000 women die annually from cervical cancer (2, 3). Eighty percent of these deaths occur where resources are the most limited (4).

Where organized comprehensive detection, treatment, and referral programs have been implemented, the incidence and mortality of this cancer have decreased dramatically (5). However, implementing programs characteristic of industrialized countries—including testing, treatment, quality assurance, follow-up, and information system components on a widespread basis—requires considerable resources and a high level of program coordination. These programs are impractical and unaffordable in low-resource settings. Yet, women deserve access to services that can safely, effectively, and affordably prevent cervical cancer.

Given the recognized obstacles to implementing cytology-based screening and the limited range of treatment methods available in low-resource settings, other program options are needed. Such options must be feasible and sustainable, and the optimal strategy for a particular setting will necessarily vary given local resource constraints; disease prevalence; and capacity for training, supervision, and infrastructure.

One evidence-based approach designed to prevent cervical cancer in low-resource settings is the “single-visit approach.” This approach links a detection method with an immediate management option, such as an offer of treatment or referral, provided by appropriately trained and supervised personnel. There is growing evidence that a single-visit approach, incorporating visual inspection of the cervix with acetic acid wash (VIA), followed by an immediate offer of treatment with cryotherapy for eligible lesions, is a safe, acceptable, and cost-effective approach to cervical cancer prevention (6–9).

The American College of Obstetricians and Gynecologists
409 12th Street, SW, PO Box 96920 • Washington, DC 20090-6920 Telephone 202 638 5577

The American College of Obstetricians and Gynecologists, the Society of Obstetricians and Gynaecologists of Canada, the Central American Federation of Associations and Societies of Obstetrics and Gynecology, the Gynaecologic Oncologists of Canada, the Society of Canadian Colposcopists, the Society of Gynecologic Oncologists, and the Royal College of Obstetricians and Gynaecologists recognize the value of VIA linked to immediate cryotherapy (or referral). It is a viable option for reducing over time the incidence of cervical cancer in settings where services are limited and where other approaches are considered impractical or too expensive.

The obstetric–gynecologic organizations supporting this statement have an important role to play in increasing the capacity of obstetric–gynecologic associations worldwide to include feasible and sustainable cervical cancer prevention programs as part of their national women's health strategies. In turn, national societies of obstetrics and gynecology have an important responsibility to educate both policy makers and the public about the importance of programs aimed at preventing cervical cancer in their countries.

Recognizing both the worldwide burden of this disease and the increasingly important role that women play in socioeconomic development, funding agencies should be aware of the public health importance of cervical cancer. They should be prepared to help underwrite cost-effective, resource-appropriate interventions to prevent unnecessary deaths caused by this disease.

**References**

1. World Health Organization. State of the art new vaccines: research and development. Initiative for Vaccine Research. Geneva: WHO; 2003. Available at: http://www.who.int/vaccine_research/documents/en/stateofart_excler.pdf. Retrieved November 21, 2003.
2. Program for Appropriate Technology in Health. Cervical cancer prevention. Reproductive Health Outlook. Seattle (WA): PATH; 2003. Available at: http://www.rho.org/assets/RHO_cxca_10-9-03.pdf. Retrieved November 21, 2003.
3. International Agency for Research on Cancer. GLOBOCAN 2000 database: cancer incidence, mortality, and prevalence worldwide. Lyons (FR): IARC; 2001.
4. Parkin DM, Pisani P, Ferlay J. Estimates of the worldwide incidence of eighteen major cancers in 1985. Int J Cancer 1993;54:594–606.
5. Sankaranarayanan R, Budukh AM, Rajkumar R. Effective screening programmes for cervical cancer in low- and middle-income developing countries. Bull World Health Organ 2001;79:954–62.
6. Gaffikin L, Blumenthal PD, Emerson M, Limpaphayom K; Royal Thai College of Obstetricians and Gynaecologists (RTCOG)/JHPIEGO Corporation Cervical Cancer Prevention Group [corrected]. Safety, acceptability, and feasibility of a single visit approach to cervical cancer prevention in rural Thailand: a demonstration project. Lancet 2003;361:814-20.

7. Mandelblatt J, Lawrence W, Gaffikin L, Limpaphayom KK, Lumbiganon P, Warakamin S, et al. Costs and benefits of different strategies to screen for cervical cancer in less-developed countries. J Natl Cancer Inst 2002;94:1469–83.
8. Goldie SJ, Kuhn L, Denny L, Pollack A, Wright TC. Policy analysis of cervical cancer screening strategies in low-resource settings: clinical benefits and cost effectiveness [published erratum appears in JAMA 2001;286:1026]. JAMA 2001;285:3107–15.
9. Martin-Hirsch PL, Paraskevaidis E, Kitchener H. Surgery for cervical intraepithelial neoplasia (Cochrane Review). In: The Cochrane Library, Issue 4, 2003. Chichester, UK: John Wiley & Sons, Ltd.

# ACOG *Statement of Policy*

As issued by the ACOG Executive Board

This document was developed jointly by the American Academy of Pediatrics and the American College of Obstetricians and Gynecologists.

## JOINT STATEMENT OF ACOG/AAP ON HUMAN IMMUNODEFICIENCY VIRUS SCREENING

The problem of perinatal transmission of HIV infection was first appreciated in 1982. In 1991, the Institute of Medicine (IOM) recommended a policy of routine counseling and offering testing (with specific informed consent) for HIV infection to all pregnant women. Since 1991, there have been major advances in the treatment of HIV infection, including demonstration in 1994 of the efficacy of zidovudine to reduce perinatal transmission. The U.S. Public Health Service subsequently issued guidelines for use of zidovudine to reduce perinatal transmission and for counseling and voluntary testing for pregnant women. Dramatic declines in reported pediatric AIDS cases have been observed as a consequence of implementation of these guidelines. However, for a variety of reasons, screening pregnant women in the United States has been far from universal and infected babies continue to be born to undiagnosed infected women. Further reduction in the rate of perinatal HIV infection will require wider application of both screening to identify infected women, and treatments, which have demonstrated efficacy in reducing vertical transmission.

The IOM recently completed a study of interventions that would be helpful to further reduce the rate of perinatal HIV infection in the United States (Reducing the Odds). They have recommended that “the United States should adopt a national policy of universal HIV testing, with patient notification, as a routine component of prenatal care”. Early diagnosis of HIV infection in pregnant women allows them to institute effective antiretroviral therapy for their own health and to reduce the risk of HIV transmission to their infants. The use of “patient notification” provides women the opportunity to decline to be tested but eliminates the obligation to provide extensive pretest counseling, which has been a barrier to testing in many settings. Care providers would be charged with responsibility for the details of how the notification would take place. The IOM has recommended universal testing for two reasons. First, attempts to identify those "at risk" for infection inevitably fail to identify some infected individuals. Second, universal testing of all pregnant women avoids stereotyping and stigmatizing any social or ethnic group. The IOM recognizes in its report that many states now have laws requiring a formal, and in many cases written informed consent process prior to testing. They recommend that the Federal government adopt policies that will encourage these states to change their laws.

The AAP and the ACOG strongly support efforts to further reduce the rate of perinatal transmission of HIV in the United States. We therefore support the recommendation of the IOM for universal HIV testing with patient notification as a routine component of prenatal care. If a patient declines testing, this should be noted in the medical record. We recognize that current laws in some states may prevent implementation of this recommendation at this time. We encourage our members and Fellows to include counseling as a routine part of care, but not as a prerequisite for, and barrier to, prenatal HIV testing.

Approved by the ACOG Executive Board, May 1999
Approved by the AAP Executive Board, May 1999
Reaffirmed by the AAP Executive Board, September 2005
Reaffirmed by the ACOG Executive Board, July 2006

# ACOG *Statement of Policy*

As issued by the ACOG Executive Board

## JOINT STATEMENT OF PRACTICE RELATIONSHIPS BETWEEN OBSTETRICIAN-GYNECOLOGISTS AND CERTIFIED NURSE-MIDWIVES/CERTIFIED MIDWIVES*

The American College of Obstetricians and Gynecologists (ACOG) and the American College of Nurse-Midwives (ACNM) recognize that in those circumstances in which obstetrician-gynecologists and certified nurse-midwives/certified midwives collaborate in the care of women, the quality of those practices is enhanced by a working relationship characterized by mutual respect and trust as well as professional responsibility and accountability. When obstetrician-gynecologists and certified nurse-midwives/certified midwives collaborate, they should concur on a clear mechanism for consultation, collaboration and referral based on the individual needs of each patient.

Recognizing the high level of responsibility that obstetrician-gynecologists and certified nurse-midwives/certified midwives assume when providing care to women, ACOG and ACNM affirm their commitment to promote appropriate standards for education and certification of their respective members, to support appropriate practice guidelines, and to facilitate communication and collegial relationships between obstetrician-gynecologists and certified nurse-midwives/certified midwives.

*Certified nurse-midwives are registered nurses who have graduated from a midwifery education program accredited by the ACNM Division of Accreditation and have passed a national certification examination administered by the ACNM Certification Council, Inc. Certified midwives are graduates of a Division of Accreditation accredited, university-affiliated midwifery education program, have successfully completed the same science requirements and ACNM Certification Council, Inc., national certification examination as certified nurse-midwives and adhere to the same professional standards as certified nurse-midwives.

American College of Nurse-Midwives
American College of Obstetricians and Gynecologists
October 1, 2002

The American College of Obstetricians and Gynecologists
409 12th Street, SW, PO Box 96920 • Washington, DC 20090-6920 Telephone 202 638 5577

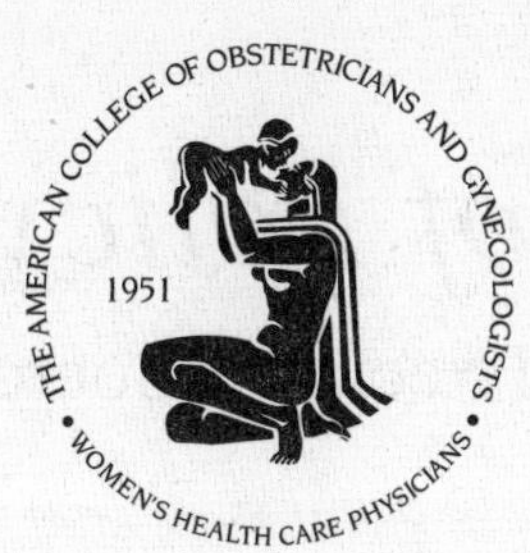


# ACOG *Statement of Policy*

As issued by the ACOG Executive Board

## LAY MIDWIFERY

The American College of Obstetricians and Gynecologists (ACOG) is the representative organization of physicians who are qualified specialists in providing health services to women. ACOG is committed to facilitating access to women's health care that is both safe and high quality. One method of attaining this goal is to assure that providers of care meet educational and professional standards of a certification process. ACOG recognizes the educational and professional standards currently used by the American Midwifery Certification Board (AMCB)* to evaluate and certify midwives. While ACOG supports women having a choice in determining their providers of care, ACOG does not support the provision of care by lay midwives or other midwives who are not certified by the AMCB.

*The American Midwifery Certification Board (AMCB), formerly known as the ACNM Certification Council (ACC), was incorporated in 1991. The AMCB develops and administers the national certification examination for Certified Nurse-Midwives (CNMs) and Certified Midwives (CMs). CNMs are registered nurses who have graduated from a midwifery education program accredited by the American College of Nurse Midwives Division of Accreditation and have passed a national certification examination administered by AMCB. Certified midwives have also graduated from a midwifery education program accredited by the American College of Nurse Midwives Division of Accreditation, have successfully completed the same requirements, have passed the same AMCB national certification examination as certified nurse-midwives and adhere to the same professional standards as certified nurse-midwives.

Approved by the Executive Board
February 2006

The American College of Obstetricians and Gynecologists
409 12th Street, SW, PO Box 96920 • Washington, DC 20090-6920 Telephone 202 638 5577

# ACOG *Statement of Policy*

As issued by the ACOG Executive Board

## TOBACCO ADVERTISING AIMED AT WOMEN AND ADOLESCENTS

The American College of Obstetricians and Gynecologists opposes the unconscionable targeting of women of all ages by the tobacco industry.

The health risks of tobacco use to women are well documented. It also is well known that smoking by a pregnant woman may be harmful to her fetus. It is unnecessary to catalogue all of these risks here. Because of these well-known dangers, it is irresponsible for tobacco companies to single out women, especially those who are young, educationally or otherwise disadvantaged women, and encourage them to smoke.

Specifically, tobacco companies must stop targeting their advertising to encourage adolescent women to smoke cigarettes. The health of all women and future generations demands that consideration.

Approved by the Executive Board July 1990
Reaffirmed July 2000
Revised and approved July 2004

The American College of Obstetricians and Gynecologists
409 12th Street, SW, PO Box 96920 • Washington, DC 20090-6920 Telephone 202-638-5577

# APPENDIX

## CONTENTS FROM OTHER ACOG RESOURCES*

### ETHICS IN OBSTETRICS AND GYNECOLOGY, SECOND EDITION



### GUIDELINES FOR PERINATAL CARE, FIFTH EDITION



*Page numbers refer to those in the original publication. ACOG members can view full text at www.acog.org.

## GUIDELINES FOR WOMEN'S HEALTH CARE, SECOND EDITION

## HEALTH CARE FOR ADOLESCENTS



## SPECIAL ISSUES IN WOMEN'S HEALTH

THE AMERICAN COLLEGE OF OBSTETRICIANS AND GYNECOLOGISTS
1951
WOMEN'S HEALTH CARE PHYSICIANS
ACOG Committee Opinions


# List of Titles

**December 2006**

Committee Opinions are intended to provide timely information on controversial issues, ethical concerns, and emerging approaches to clinical management. They represent the considered views of the sponsoring committee based on interpretation of published data in peer-reviewed journals. Committee Opinions are reviewed periodically for continued relevance or needed update. *Note:* Because individual Committee Opinions are withdrawn from and added to the series on a continuing basis, the titles listed in this index may not be identical to those contained in complete sets. Also listed are Technology Assessments, which provide an overview of technology in obstetrics and gynecology.

*The following titles have been withdrawn from circulation:*

*Committee Opinions*

191 Length of Hospital Stay for Gynecologic Procedures
265 Mode of Term Singleton Breech Delivery (Replaced by Committee Opinion No. 340)
266 Placenta Accreta (Replaced by Practice Bulletin No. 76)
271 Induction of Labor for Vaginal Birth After Cesarean Delivery (Replaced by Committee Opinion No. 342)
274 Nonsurgical Diagnosis and Management of Vaginal Agenesis (Replaced by Committee Opinion No. 355)
292 Primary and Preventive Care: Periodic Assessments (Replaced by Committee Opinion No. 357)
306 Informed Refusal

| Number | Title | Publication Date | Reaffirmed Date |
|---|---|---|---|
| *Committee on Adolescent Health Care* | | | |
| 300 | Cervical Cancer Screening in Adolescents (Obstet Gynecol 2004;104:885–9) | October 2004 | |
| 301 | Sexually Transmitted Diseases in Adolescents (Obstet Gynecol 2004;104:891–8) | October 2004 | |
| 302 | Guidelines for Adolescent Health Research (Obstet Gynecol 2004;104:899–902) | October 2004 | |
| 310 | Endometriosis in Adolescents (Obstet Gynecol 2005;105:921–7) | April 2005 | |
| 314 | Meningococcal Vaccination for Adolescents (Obstet Gynecol 2005;106:667–9) | September 2005 | |
| 330 | Evaluation and Management of Abnormal Cervical Cytology and Histology in the Adolescent (Obstet Gynecol 2006;107:963–8) | April 2006 | |
| 335 | The Initial Reproductive Health Visit (Obstet Gynecol 2006;107:1215–9) | May 2006 | |
| *344 | Human Papillomavirus Vaccination *(Joint with the ACOG Working Group on Immunization)* (Obstet Gynecol 2006;108:699–705) | September 2006 | |
| *349 | Menstruation in Girls and Adolescents: Using the Menstrual Cycle as a Vital Sign *(Joint with American Academy of Pediatrics)* (Obstet Gynecol 2006;108:1323–8) | November 2006 | |
| *350 | Breast Concerns in the Adolescent (Obstet Gynecol 2006;108:1329–36) | November 2006 | |
| *351 | The Overweight Adolescent: Prevention, Treatment, and Obstetric–Gynecologic Implications (Obstet Gynecol 2006;108:1337–48) | November 2006 | |
| *355 | Vaginal Agenesis: Diagnosis, Management, and Routine Care (Obstet Gynecol 2006;108:1605–9) | December 2006 | |
| *Committee on Coding and Nomenclature* | | | |
| 205 | Tubal Ligation with Cesarean Delivery (Obstet Gynecol Vol. 92, No. 2) | August 1998 | |
| 249 | Coding Responsibility (Obstet Gynecol Vol. 97, No. 1) | January 2001 | 2005 |
| 250 | Inappropriate Reimbursement Practices by Third-Party Payers (Obstet Gynecol Vol. 97, No. 1) | January 2001 | |
| *Committee on Ethics* (see also *Ethics in Obstetrics and Gynecology)* | | | |
| †294 | At-Risk Drinking and Illicit Drug Use: Ethical Issues in Obstetric and Gynecologic Practice (Obstet Gynecol 2004;103:1021–31) | May 2004 | |
| †297 | Nonmedical Use of Obstetric Ultrasonography (Obstet Gynecol 2004;104:423–4) | August 2004 | |

| Number | Title | Publication Date | Reaffirmed Date |
|---|---|---|---|
| *Committee on Ethics* (continued) | | | |
| †321 | Maternal Decision Making, Ethics, and the Law (Obstet Gynecol 2005;106:1127–37) | November 2005 | |
| *†341 | Ethical Ways for Physicians to Market a Practice (Obstet Gynecol 2006;108:239–42) | July 2006 | |
| *†347 | Using Preimplantation Embryos for Research (Obstet Gynecol 2006;108:1305–17) | November 2006 | |
| *†352 | Innovative Practice: Ethical Guidelines (Obstet Gynecol 2006;108:1589–95) | December 2006 | |
| *Committee on Genetics* | | | |
| 183 | Routine Storage of Umbilical Cord Blood for Potential Future Transplantation *(Joint with Committee on Obstetric Practice)* | April 1997 | 2004 |
| 189 | Advanced Paternal Age: Risks to the Fetus | October 1997 | 2006 |
| 212 | Screening for Canavan Disease (Obstet Gynecol Vol. 92, No. 5) | November 1998 | 2004 |
| 230 | Maternal Phenylketonuria (Obstet Gynecol Vol. 95, No. 1) | January 2000 | 2004 |
| 257 | Genetic Evaluation of Stillbirths and Neonatal Deaths (Obstet Gynecol Vol. 97, No. 5) | May 2001 | |
| 287 | Newborn Screening (Obstet Gynecol 2003;102:887–9) | October 2003 | |
| 296 | First-Trimester Screening for Fetal Aneuploidy *(Joint with Committee on Obstetric Practice)* (Obstet Gynecol 2004;104:215–7) | July 2004 | |
| 298 | Prenatal and Preconceptional Carrier Screening for Genetic Diseases in Individuals of Eastern European Jewish Descent (Obstet Gynecol 2004;104:425–8) | August 2004 | 2006 |
| 318 | Screening for Tay–Sachs Disease (Obstet Gynecol 2005;106:893–4) | October 2005 | |
| 324 | Perinatal Risks Associated With Assisted Reproductive Technology *(Joint with Committees on Obstetric Practice and Gynecologic Practice)* (Obstet Gynecol 2005;106:1143–6) | November 2005 | |
| 325 | Update on Carrier Screening for Cystic Fibrosis (Obstet Gynecol 2005;106:1465–8) | December 2005 | |
| 338 | Screening for Fragile X Syndrome (Obstet Gynecol 2006;107:1483–5) | June 2006 | |
| ■ 1 | Genetics and Molecular Diagnostic Testing (Obstet Gynecol 2002;100:193–211) | July 2002 | 2006 |
| *Committee on Gynecologic Practice* | | | |
| 240 | Statement on Surgical Assistants (Obstet Gynecol Vol. 96, No. 2) *(Joint with Committee on Obstetric Practice)* | August 2000 | 2006 |
| 243 | Performance and Interpretation of Imaging Studies by Obstetrician–Gynecologists (Obstet Gynecol Vol. 96, No. 5) | November 2000 | 2005 |
| 253 | Nongynecologic Procedures (Obstet Gynecol Vol. 97, No. 3) | March 2001 | 2006 |
| 272 | Follow-up of Abnormal Screening Mammography (Obstet Gynecol 2002;99:869) | May 2002 | 2005 |
| 278 | Avoiding Inappropriate Clinical Decisions Based on False-Positive Human Chorionic Gonadotropin Test Results (Obstet Gynecol 2002;100:1057–9) | November 2002 | 2005 |
| 280 | The Role of the Generalist Obstetrician–Gynecologist in the Early Detection of Ovarian Cancer *(Joint with Society of Gynecologic Oncologists)* (Obstet Gynecol 2002;100:1413–6) | December 2002 | 2005 |
| 285 | Induced Abortion and Breast Cancer Risk (Obstet Gynecol 2003;102:433–5) | August 2003 | 2005 |
| 288 | Professional Liability and Gynecology-Only Practice *(Joint with Committees on Obstetric Practice and Professional Liability)* (Obstet Gynecol 2003;102:891) | October 2003 | 2006 |
| 293 | Uterine Artery Embolization (Obstet Gynecol 2004;103:403–4) | February 2004 | 2006 |
| 311 | Appropriate Use of Laparoscopically Assisted Vaginal Hysterectomy (Obstet Gynecol 2005;105:929–30) | April 2005 | |
| 313 | The Importance of Preconception Care in the Continuum of Women's Health Care (Obstet Gynecol 2005;106:665–6) | September 2005 | |
| 319 | The Role of the Obstetrician–Gynecologist in the Assessment and Management of Obesity (Obstet Gynecol 2005;106:895–9) | October 2005 | |
| 322 | Compounded Bioidentical Hormones (Obstet Gynecol 2005;106:1139–40) | November 2005 | |
| 323 | Elective Coincidental Appendectomy (Obstet Gynecol 2005;106:1141–2) | November 2005 | |
| 324 | Perinatal Risks Associated With Assisted Reproductive Technology *(Joint with Committees on Obstetric Practice and Genetics)* (Obstet Gynecol 2005;106:1143–6) | November 2005 | |
| 332 | Hepatitis B and Hepatitis C Virus Infections in Obstetrician–Gynecologists (Obstet Gynecol 2006;107:1207–8) | May 2006 | |
| 334 | Role of the Obstetrician–Gynecologists in the Screening and Diagnosis of Breast Masses (Obstet Gynecol 2006;107:1213–4) | May 2006 | |

| Number | Title | Publication Date | Reaffirmed Date |
|---|---|---|---|
| | *Committee on Gynecologic Practice* (continued) | | |
| 336 | Tamoxifen and Uterine Cancer (Obstet Gynecol 2006;107:1475–8) | June 2006 | |
| 337 | Noncontraceptive Uses of the Levonorgestrel Intrauterine System (Obstet Gynecol 2006;107:1479–82) | June 2006 | |
| *345 | Vulvodynia *(Joint with the American Society for Colposcopy and Cervical Pathology)* (Obstet Gynecol 2006;108:1049–52) | October 2006 | |
| *356 | Routine Cancer Screening (Obstet Gynecol 2006;108:1611–13) | December 2006 | |
| *357 | Primary and Preventive Care: Periodic Assessments (Obstet Gynecol 2006;108:1615–22) | December 2006 | |
| ■ 3 | Saline Infusion Sonohysterography (Obstet Gynecol 2003;102:659–62) | September 2003 | 2005 |
| ■ 4 | Hysteroscopy (Obstet Gynecol 2005;106:439–42) | August 2005 | |
| | *Committee on Health Care for Underserved Women* | | |
| 307 | Partner Consent for Participation in Women's Reproductive Health Research (Obstet Gynecol 2004;104:1467–9) | December 2004 | |
| 308 | The Uninsured (Obstet Gynecol 2004;104:1471–4) | December 2004 | |
| 312 | Health Care for Homeless Women (Obstet Gynecol 2005;106:429–34) | August 2005 | |
| 317 | Racial and Ethnic Disparities in Women's Health (Obstet Gynecol 2005;106:889–92) | October 2005 | |
| 316 | Smoking Cessation During Pregnancy *(Joint with Committee on Obstetric Practice)* (Obstet Gynecol 2005;106:883–8) | October 2005 | |
| *343 | Psychosocial Risk Factors: Perinatal Screening and Intervention (Obstet Gynecol 2006;108:469–77) | August 2006 | |
| | *Committee on Obstetric Practice* | | |
| 125 | Placental Pathology | July 1993 | 2006 |
| 183 | Routine Storage of Umbilical Cord Blood for Potential Future Transplantation *(Joint with Committee on Genetics)* | April 1997 | 2004 |
| 228 | Induction of Labor with Misoprostol (Obstet Gynecol Vol. 94, No. 5) | November 1999 | 2006 |
| 234 | Scheduled Cesarean Delivery and the Prevention of Vertical Transmission of HIV Infection (Obstet Gynecol Vol. 95, No. 5) | May 2000 | 2006 |
| 240 | Statement on Surgical Assistants *(Joint with Committee on Gynecologic Practice)* (Obstet Gynecol Vol. 96, No. 2) | August 2000 | 2006 |
| 248 | Response to Searle's Drug Warning on Misoprostol (Obstet Gynecol Vol. 96, No. 6) | December 2000 | 2006 |
| 256 | Optimal Goals for Anesthesia Care in Obstetrics *(Joint with American Society of Anesthesiologists)* (Obstet Gynecol Vol. 97, No. 5) | May 2001 | 2006 |
| 258 | Fetal Pulse Oximetry (Obstet Gynecol 2001;98:523–524) | September 2001 | 2004 |
| 260 | Circumcision (Obstet Gynecol 2001;98:707–708) | October 2001 | 2004 |
| 264 | Air Travel During Pregnancy (Obstet Gynecol 2001;98:1187–1188) | December 2001 | 2006 |
| 267 | Exercise During Pregnancy and the Postpartum Period (Obstet Gynecol 2002;99:171–173) | January 2002 | 2005 |
| 268 | Management of Asymptomatic Pregnant or Lactating Women Exposed to Anthrax (Obstet Gynecol 2002;99:366–368) | February 2002 | 2005 |
| 273 | Antenatal Corticosteroid Therapy for Fetal Maturation (Obstet Gynecol 2002;99:871–873) | May 2002 | 2005 |
| 275 | Obstetric Management of Patients with Spinal Cord Injuries (Obstet Gynecol 2002;100:625–7) | September 2002 | 2005 |
| 276 | Safety of Lovenox in Pregnancy (Obstet Gynecol 2002;100:845–6) | October 2002 | 2005 |
| 279 | Prevention of Early-Onset Group B Streptococcal Disease in Newborns (Obstet Gynecol 2002;100:1405–12) | December 2002 | 2005 |
| 281 | Rubella Vaccination (Obstet Gynecol 2002;100:1417) | December 2002 | 2005 |
| 282 | Immunization During Pregnancy (Obstet Gynecol 2003;101:207–12) | January 2003 | 2005 |
| 283 | New U.S. Food and Drug Administration Labeling on Cytotec (Misoprostol) Use and Pregnancy (Obstet Gynecol 2003;101:1049–50) | May 2003 | 2006 |
| 284 | Nonobstetric Surgery in Pregnancy (Obstet Gynecol 2003;102:431) | August 2003 | 2006 |
| 288 | Professional Liability and Gynecology-Only Practice *(Joint with Committees on Gynecologic Practice and Professional Liability)* (Obstet Gynecol 2003;102:891) | October 2003 | 2006 |
| 291 | Use of Progesterone to Reduce Preterm Birth (Obstet Gynecol 2003;102:1115–6) | November 2003 | 2006 |
| 295 | Pain Relief During Labor *(Joint with American Society of Anesthesiologists)* (Obstet Gynecol 2004;104:213) | July 2004 | 2006 |
| 296 | First-Trimester Screening for Fetal Aneuploidy *(Joint with Committee on Genetics)* (Obstet Gynecol 2004;104:215–7) | July 2004 | |

| Number | Title | Publication Date | Reaffirmed Date |
|---|---|---|---|
| *Committee on Obstetric Practice* (continued) | | | |
| 299 | Guidelines for Diagnostic Imaging During Pregnancy (Obstet Gynecol 2004;104:647–51) | September 2004 | |
| 304 | Prenatal and Perinatal Human Immunodeficiency Virus Testing: Expanded Recommendations (Obstet Gynecol 2004;104:1119–24) | November 2004 | |
| 305 | Influenza Vaccination and Treatment During Pregnancy (Obstet Gynecol 2004;104:1125–6) | November 2004 | |
| 315 | Obesity in Pregnancy (Obstet Gynecol 2005;106:671–5) | September 2005 | |
| 316 | Smoking Cessation During Pregnancy *(Joint with Committee on Health Care for Underserved Women)* (Obstet Gynecol 2005;106:883–8) | October 2005 | |
| 324 | Perinatal Risks Associated With Assisted Reproductive Technology *(Joint with Committees on Genetics and Gynecologic Practice)* (Obstet Gynecol 2005;106:1143–6) | November 2005 | |
| 326 | Inappropriate Use of the Terms Fetal Distress and Birth Asphyxia (Obstet Gynecol 2005;106:1469–70) | December 2005 | |
| 333 | The Apgar Score *(Joint with American Academy of Pediatrics)* (Obstet Gynecol 2006;107:1209–12) | May 2006 | |
| 339 | Analgesia and Cesarean Delivery Rates (Obstet Gynecol 2006;107:1487–8) | June 2006 | |
| *340 | Mode of Term Singleton Breech Delivery (Obstet Gynecol 2006;108:235–7) | July 2006 | |
| *342 | Induction of Labor for Vaginal Birth After Cesarean Delivery (Obstet Gynecol 2006;108:465–7) | August 2006 | |
| *346 | Amnioinfusion Does Not Prevent Meconium Aspiration Syndrome (Obstet Gynecol 2006;108:1053–5) | October 2006 | |
| *348 | Umbilical Cord Blood Gas and Acid Base Analysis (Obstet Gynecol 2006;108:1319–22) | November 2006 | |
| *354 | Treatment With Selective Serotonin Reuptake Inhibitors During Pregnancy (Obstet Gynecol 2006;108:1601–3) | December 2006 | |
| *Committee on Primary Care* | | | |
| 227 | Complementary and Alternative Medicine (Obstet Gynecol Vol. 94, No. 5) | November 1999 | 2004 |
| *Committee on Professional Liability* | | | |
| 288 | Professional Liability and Gynecology-Only Practice *(Joint with Committees on Obstetric Practice and Gynecologic Practice)* (Obstet Gynecol 2003;102:891) | October 2003 | 2006 |
| 309 | Coping With the Stress of Medical Professional Liability Litigation (Obstet Gynecol 2005;105:453–4) | February 2005 | |
| *Committee on Patient Safety and Quality Improvement* | | | |
| 286 | Patient Safety in Obstetrics and Gynecology (Obstet Gynecol 2003;102:883–5) | October 2003 | 2006 |
| 320 | Partnering With Patients to Improve Safety (Obstet Gynecol 2005;106:1123–5) | November 2005 | |
| 327 | "Do Not Use" Abbreviations (Obstet Gynecol 2006;107:213–4) | January 2006 | |
| 328 | Patient Safety in the Surgical Environment (Obstet Gynecol 2006;107:429–33) | February 2006 | |
| 329 | Tracking and Reminder Systems (Obstet Gynecol 2006;107:745–7) | March 2006 | |
| 331 | Safe Use of Medication (Obstet Gynecol 2006;107:969–72) | April 2006 | |
| *353 | Medical Emergency Preparedness (Obstet Gynecol 2006;108:1597–9) | December 2006 | |

**Current Committee Opinions and Technology Assessments**

■1 ■3 ■4 125 183 189 205 212 227 228 230 234 240 243 248 249 250 253 256 257 258 260
264 267 268 272 273 275 276 278 279 280 281 282 283 284 285 286 287 288 291 293 294 295
296 297 298 299 300 301 302 304 305 307 308 309 310 311 312 313 314 315 316 317 318 319
320 321 322 323 324 325 326 327 328 329 330 331 332 333 334 335 336 337 338 339 340 341
342 343 344 345 346 347 348 349 350 351 352 353 354 355 356 357

Committee Opinions are available on a subscription basis, and complete sets may be purchased. For ordering information, contact the ACOG Distribution Center at 800-762-2264, or order online at sales.acog.org.

*Title issued since publication of last index

†Title issued since publication of *Ethics in Obstetrics and Gynecology*, Second Edition

AC002

■ Technology Assessment

# ACOG EDUCATIONAL and PRACTICE BULLETINS

## LIST OF TITLES — DECEMBER 2006

Educational and Practice Bulletins provide obstetricians and gynecologists with current information on established techniques and clinical management guidelines. ACOG continuously surveys the field for advances to be incorporated in these series and monitors existing bulletins to ensure they are current. Individual bulletins are withdrawn from and added to the series on a continuing basis and reaffirmed periodically (reaffirmed dates appear parenthetically after the respecitve titles).

***The following titles have been withdrawn from circulation:***

***Educational Bulletins***

227 Management of Isoimmunization in Pregnancy *(Replaced by Practice Bulletin No. 75)*

255 Psychosocial Risk Factors: Perinatal Screening and Intervention *(Replaced by Committee Opinion No. 343)*

258 Breastfeeding: Maternal and Infant Aspects

***Practice Bulletin***

23 Antibiotic Prophylaxis for Gynecologic Procedures *(Replaced by Practice Bulletin No. 74)*

***Current Bulletins***

| | | | | | | |
|---|---|---|---|---|---|---|
| ▸ 1 | ▸ 3 | ▸ 4 | ▸ 6 | ▸ 7 | ▸ 8 | ▸ 9 |
| ▸10 | ▸11 | ▸12 | ▸13 | ▸14 | ▸15 | ▸16 |
| ▸17 | ▸19 | ▸20 | ▸21 | ▸22 | ▸24 | ▸27 |
| ▸28 | ▸29 | ▸30 | ▸31 | ▸33 | ▸34 | ▸35 |
| ▸36 | ▸37 | ▸38 | ▸39 | ▸40 | ▸41 | ▸42 |
| ▸43 | ▸44 | ▸45 | ▸46 | ▸47 | ▸48 | ▸49 |
| ▸50 | ▸51 | ▸52 | ▸53 | ▸54 | ▸55 | ▸56 |
| ▸57 | ▸58 | ▸59 | ▸60 | ▸61 | ▸63 | ▸64 |
| ▸65 | ▸66 | ▸67 | ▸68 | ▸69 | ▸70 | ▸71 |
| ▸72 | ▸73 | ▸74 | ▸75 | ▸76 | 230 | 236 |
| 248 | 251 | | | | | |

## Obstetrics

- ▶ 1 Premature Rupture of Membranes (June 1998, Obstet Gynecol Vol. 91, No. 6) (4/05)
- ▶ 4 Prevention of Rh D Alloimmunization (May 1999, Obstet Gynecol Vol. 93, No. 5) (4/05)
- ▶ 6 Thrombocytopenia in Pregnancy (September 1999, Obstet Gynecol Vol. 94, No. 3) (4/05)
- ▶ 8 Management of Herpes in Pregnancy (October 1999, Obstet Gynecol Vol. 94, No. 4) (4/05)
- ▶ 9 Antepartum Fetal Surveillance (October 1999, Obstet Gynecol Vol. 94, No. 4) (9/01)
- ▶ 10 Induction of Labor (November 1999, Obstet Gynecol Vol. 94, No. 5) (10/05)
- ▶ 12 Intrauterine Growth Restriction (January 2000, Obstet Gynecol Vol. 95, No. 1) (4/05)
- ▶ 13 External Cephalic Version (February 2000, Obstet Gynecol Vol. 95, No. 2) (10/05)
- ▶ 17 Operative Vaginal Delivery (June 2000, Obstet Gynecol Vol. 95, No. 6) (10/05)
- ▶ 19 Thromboembolism in Pregnancy (August 2000, Obstet Gynecol Vol. 96, No. 2) (10/05)
- ▶ 20 Perinatal Viral and Parasitic Infections (September 2000, Obstet Gynecol Vol. 96, No. 3) (10/05)
- ▶ 22 Fetal Macrosomia (November 2000, Obstet Gynecol Vol. 96, No. 5) (10/05)
- ▶ 24 Management of Recurrent Early Pregnancy Loss (February 2001, Obstet Gynecol Vol. 97, No. 2) (10/05)
- ▶ 27 Prenatal Diagnosis of Fetal Chromosomal Abnormalities (May 2001, Obstet Gynecol Vol. 97, No. 5) (10/05)
- ▶ 29 Chronic Hypertension in Pregnancy (Obstet Gynecol 2001;98:177–185) (2/06)
- ▶ 30 Gestational Diabetes (Obstet Gynecol 2001;98:525–538) (2/06)
- ▶ 31 Assessment of Risk Factors for Preterm Birth (Obstet Gynecol 2001;98:709–716) (4/03)
- ▶ 33 Diagnosis and Management of Preeclampsia and Eclampsia (Obstet Gynecol 2002;99:159–167) (4/04)
- ▶ 36 Obstetric Analgesia and Anesthesia (Obstet Gynecol 2002;100:177–191) (4/04)
- ▶ 37 Thyroid Disease in Pregnancy (Obstet Gynecol 2002;100:387–396) (4/04)

## Obstetrics *(continued)*

- ▶ 38 Perinatal Care at the Threshold of Viability (Obstet Gynecol 2002;100:617–24) (4/04)
- ▶ 40 Shoulder Dystocia (Obstet Gynecol 2002;100:1045–50) (4/04)
- ▶ 43 Management of Preterm Labor (Obstet Gynecol 2003;101:1039–47) (9/06)
- ▶ 44 Neural Tube Defects (Obstet Gynecol 2003;102:203–13) (9/06)
- ▶ 47 Prophylactic Antibiotics in Labor and Delivery (Obstet Gynecol 2003;102:875–82) (9/06)
- ▶ 48 Cervical Insufficiency (Obstet Gynecol 2003;102:1091–9) (9/06)
- ▶ 49 Dystocia and Augmentation of Labor (Obstet Gynecol 2003;102:1445–54) (9/06)
- ▶ 52 Nausea and Vomiting of Pregnancy (Obstet Gynecol 2004;103:803–15)
- ▶ 54 Vaginal Birth After Previous Cesarean Delivery (Obstet Gynecol 2004;104:203–12)
- ▶ 55 Management of Postterm Pregnancy (Obstet Gynecol 2004;104:639–46)
- ▶ 56 Multiple Gestation: Complicated Twin, Triplet, and High-Order Multifetal Pregnancy (Obstet Gynecol 2004;104:869–83)
- ▶ 58 Ultrasonography in Pregnancy (Obstet Gynecol 2004;104:1449–58)
- ▶ 60 Pregestational Diabetes Mellitus (Obstet Gynecol 2005;105:675–85)
- ▶ 64 Hemoglobinopathies in Pregnancy (Obstet Gynecol 2005;106:203–11)
- ▶ 68 Antiphospholipid Syndrome (Obstet Gynecol 2005;106:1113–21)
- ▶ 70 Intrapartum Fetal Heart Rate Monitoring (Obstet Gynecol 2005;106:1453–61)
- ▶ 71 Episiotomy (Obstet Gynecol 2006;107:957–62)
- ▶ *75 Management of Alloimmunization During Pregnancy (Obstet Gynecol 2006;108:457–64)
- ▶ *76 Postpartum Hemorrhage (Obstet Gynecol 2006;108:1039–47)
- 230 Assessment of Fetal Lung Maturity (November 1996) (9/01)
- 236 Teratology (April 1997) (2/06)
- 248 Viral Hepatitis in Pregnancy (July 1998, Obstet Gynecol Vol. 92, No. 1) (2/06)
- 251 Obstetric Aspects of Trauma Management (September 1998, Obstet Gynecol Vol. 92, No. 3) (2/06)

## Gynecology

- ▶ 3 Medical Management of Tubal Pregnancy (December 1998, Obstet Gynecol Vol. 92, No. 6) (4/05)
- ▶ 7 Prophylactic Oophorectomy (September 1999, Obstet Gynecol Vol. 94, No. 3) (10/05)
- ▶ 11 Medical Management of Endometriosis (December 1999, Obstet Gynecol Vol. 94, No. 6) (10/05)
- ▶ 14 Management of Anovulatory Bleeding (March 2000, Obstet Gynecol Vol. 95, No. 3) (3/02)
- ▶ 15 Premenstrual Syndrome (April 2000, Obstet Gynecol Vol. 95, No. 4) (10/05)
- ▶ 16 Surgical Alternatives to Hysterectomy in the Management of Leiomyomas (May 2000, Obstet Gynecol Vol. 95, No. 5) (10/05)
- ▶ 21 Prevention of Deep Vein Thrombosis and Pulmonary Embolism (October 2000, Obstet Gynecol Vol. 96, No. 4) (10/05)
- ▶ 28 Use of Botanicals for Management of Menopausal Symptoms (June 2001, Obstet Gynecol Vol. 97, No. 6) (10/04)
- ▶ 34 Management of Infertility Caused by Ovulatory Dysfunction (Obstet Gynecol 2002;99:347–358) (10/06)
- ▶ 35 Diagnosis and Treatment of Cervical Carcinomas (Obstet Gynecol 2002;99:855–867) (10/06)
- ▶ 39 Selective Estrogen Receptor Modulators (Obstet Gynecol 2002;100:835–44) (10/06)
- ▶ 41 Polycystic Ovary Syndrome (Obstet Gynecol 2002;100:1389–402) (10/06)
- ▶ 42 Breast Cancer Screening (Obstet Gynecol 2003;101:821–32) (10/06)
- ▶ 45 Cervical Cytology Screening (Obstet Gynecol 2003;102:417–27) (4/05)
- ▶ 46 Benefits and Risks of Sterilization (Obstet Gynecol 2003;102:647–58) (4/05)
- ▶ 50 Osteoporosis (Obstet Gynecol 2004;103:203–16) (2/06)
- ▶ 51 Chronic Pelvic Pain (Obstet Gynecol 2004;103:589–605) (2/06)
- ▶ 53 Diagnosis and Treatment of Gestational Trophoblastic Disease (Obstet Gynecol 2004;103:1365–77) (2/06)
- ▶ 57 Gynecologic Herpes Simplex Virus Infections (Obstet Gynecol 2004;104:1111–7) (2/06)
- ▶ 59 Intrauterine Device (Obstet Gynecol 2005;105:223–32)
- ▶ 61 Human Papillomavirus (Obstet Gynecol 2005;105:905–18)
- ▶ 63 Urinary Incontinence in Women (Obstet Gynecol 2005;105:1533–45)
- ▶ 65 Management of Endometrial Cancer (Obstet Gynecol 2005;106:413–25)
- ▶ 66 Management of Abnormal Cervical Cytology and Histology (Obstet Gynecol 2005;106:645–64)
- ▶ 67 Medical Management of Abortion (Obstet Gynecol 2005;106:871–82)
- ▶ 69 Emergency Contraception (Obstet Gynecol 2005;106:1443–52)
- ▶ 72 Vaginitis (Obstet Gynecol 2006;107:1195–1206)
- ▶ 73 Use of Hormonal Contraception in Women With Coexisting Medical Conditions (Obstet Gynecol 2006;107:1453–72)
- ▶ *74 Antibiotic Prophylaxis for Gynecologic Procedures (Obstet Gynecol 2006;108:225–34)

Practice and Educational Bulletins are available on a subscription basis, and complete sets may be purchased. For ordering information, contact the ACOG Distribution Center at 800-762-2264, or order online at sales.acog.org.

*Title issued since publication of last listing
▶ Practice Bulletin

AT005

# Subjec

# t Index

# Index

Volume I includes pages 1–453; Volume II includes pages 455–1237

*Note:* Page numbers followed by *b*, *f*, or *t* indicate boxes, figures, or tables, respectively.

## A

## C

## E

## G

## H

## I

## J



## K



## L

## M

## S

## T

## W